P9-ELH-847

LIFT

TAKE YOUR STUDYING
TO THE NEXT LEVEL.

This book comes with 1-year digital access to the
Examples & Explanations for this course.

Step 1: Go to **www.CasebookConnect.com/LIFT** and redeem your access code to get started.

Step 2: Go to your BOOKSHELF and select your online *Examples & Explanations* to start reading, highlighting, and taking notes in the margins of your e-book.

Step 3: Select the STUDY tab in your toolbar to access the questions from your book in interactive format, designed to give you extra practice and help you master the course material.

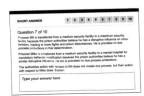

Is this a used casebook? Access code already scratched off?

You can purchase the online *Examples & Explanations* and still access all of the powerful tools listed above. Please visit CasebookConnect.com/Catalog to learn more about Connected Study Aids.

REAL ESTATE TRANSACTIONS

ASPEN CASEBOOK SERIES

Real Estate Transactions

Problems, Cases, and Materials

Fifth Edition

ROBIN PAUL MALLOY

E. I. White Chair and Distinguished Professor of Law
Kauffman Professor of Entrepreneurship and Innovation
Director, Center on Property, Citizenship,
and Social Entrepreneurism
College of Law, Syracuse University

JAMES CHARLES SMITH

John Byrd Martin Professor of Law
University of Georgia School of Law

Wolters Kluwer

Published by Wolters Kluwer in New York.

Wolters Kluwer Legal & Regulatory U.S. serves customers worldwide with
CCH, Aspen Publishers, and Kluwer Law International products.
(www.WKLegaledu.com)

To contact Customer Service, e-mail customer.service@wolterskluwer.com,
call 1-800-234-1660, fax 1-800-901-9075, or mail correspondence to:

Wolters Kluwer
Attn: Order Department
PO Box 990
Frederick, MD 21705

Printed in the United States of America.

1 2 3 4 5 6 7 8 9 0

ISBN 978-1-4548-7106-4

Library of Congress Cataloging-in-Publication Data

Names: Malloy, Robin Paul, 1956- author. | Smith, James Charles, 1952- author.
Title: Real estate transactions problems, cases, and materials / Robin Paul Malloy,
    E. I. White Chair and Distinguished Professor of Law, Kauffman Professor of
    Entrepreneurship and Innovation Director, Center on Property, Citizenship,
    and Social Entrepreneurism College of Law, Syracuse University, James Charles
    Smith, John Byrd Martin Professor of Law, University of Georgia School of Law.
Description: Fifth edition. | New York : Wolters Kluwer, [2016] | Series: Aspen
    casebook series
Identifiers: LCCN 2016049349 | ISBN 9781454871064
Subjects: LCSH: Vendors and purchasers — United States. | Real estate business —
    Law and legislation — United States. | Real property — United States. | LCGFT:
    Casebooks
Classification: LCC KF665.A4 M35 2016 | DDC 346.7304/37 — dc23
LC record available at https://lccn.loc.gov/2016049349

About Wolters Kluwer Legal & Regulatory U.S.

Wolters Kluwer Legal & Regulatory U.S. delivers expert content and solutions in the areas of law, corporate compliance, health compliance, reimbursement, and legal education. Its practical solutions help customers successfully navigate the demands of a changing environment to drive their daily activities, enhance decision quality and inspire confident outcomes.

Serving customers worldwide, its legal and regulatory portfolio includes products under the Aspen Publishers, CCH Incorporated, Kluwer Law International, ftwilliam.com and MediRegs names. They are regarded as exceptional and trusted resources for general legal and practice-specific knowledge, compliance and risk management, dynamic workflow solutions, and expert commentary.

Summary of Contents

Contents

Preface

In this book we focus on three goals.

First, we place transactions in their market context, carefully explaining how various sales and finance markets work. Once students understand how markets operate — how banks, developers, and investors make money — they can then understand what drives transactions: the motivations of the parties, the risks involved, and the ways that parties use the law to advance their interests.

Second, we integrate issues of professional responsibility into our materials, illustrating the stresses of legal practice and the areas in which real estate attorneys most often encounter trouble. Because we want students to see that professional responsibility is not merely an abstraction, we weave discussions of ethical problems into the study of actual cases.

Third, we include problem sets throughout the book to enhance the learning of legal analysis and lawyering skills. Our goal is to balance theory and practice by emphasizing what successful transaction lawyers do on a daily basis. Mindful of recent American Bar Association requirements for developing outcome guidelines and assessments for students, we recommend assigning some of the problems to students to prepare written answers for submission and assessment. The assessment scores earned on each problem assigned might constitute part of the student's grade for the course. In addition to providing an opportunity, beyond the final examination, for a student to demonstrate mastery of the material, writing up the problems can provide a faculty member with important information about student learning. Among the outcomes that can be assessed are a student's ability to: (1) identify the important legal issues in a fact pattern; (2) identify and apply controlling law to the relevant facts; (3) develop a logical and persuasive resolution to the problem; and (4) write in an organized and clear manner to effectively communicate useful knowledge to the reader.

Our overarching goal is to make the materials comprehensible yet challenging. We assume the student knows nothing beyond the rudiments of property and contract law. Each chapter includes text that highlights the pertinent general rules and transactional considerations. In addition to the text, we present cases and problems that illustrate how the key rules play out in practice. Our selection of cases is designed to highlight the transactional nature of underlying legal problems and the economic dimensions of the parties' exchange. The problems reinforce and test the scope of principles addressed in text and in the cases. We've also found that the problems provide a rich starting point for the discussion of lawyering strategies and transactional tactics.

Our materials also emphasize the way that modern real estate transactions cross a wide range of subject matters within the standard law school curriculum. The student will encounter problems that might have arisen in many other courses, among them contracts, commercial law, torts, corporations or business organizations, constitutional law, land use, and environmental law. As is true throughout the book, our goal is to help students understand how real estate transactions fit into a "big picture" so that they can begin to appreciate the rich multidimensional context in which they will practice.

This fifth edition of the book retains the streamlined coverage made popular in our third edition, making it possible to use the entire book in one three-credit hour course. In this edition, we've included new cases and the latest information on law, markets, and ethics in every chapter. The result is a better and more complete casebook that professors and students will find comprehensive, understandable, and easy to use.

As with each of our earlier editions, we could not have prepared this book without the help and support of many people. First and foremost, we thank our family members and friends. In addition, we wish to acknowledge those people who have made special contributions to the success of our project. In particular, we appreciate the continuing support of the management and staff at Wolters-Kluwer (Aspen), with special thanks to Darren Kelly, and grateful appreciation to Carol McGeehan, who had the wisdom to originally commission the first edition of our book. We likewise thank Dennis W. Polio, and Shannon M. Crane for research assistance. And finally, we thank the many people who have used our book over the years and who have taken the time to contact us to offer suggestions and comments. Their input helped us to continuously improve the book with each new edition.

We welcome your input.

Robin Paul Malloy
rpmalloy@law.syr.edu

James Charles Smith
jim@uga.edu

Robin   **Jim**

The successful practice of law, like marathon running, requires a commitment to preparation, hard work, and the relentless pursuit of excellence.

Acknowledgments

The authors gratefully acknowledge the permissions granted to reproduce the following materials.

Books and articles

Simes, L. M., & C. B. Taylor, Model Title Standards 14, 16-17, 36-38 (1960). Reprinted by permission of the University of Michigan.

Williams, M. G., & H. J. Onsrud, What Every Lawyer Should Know About Title Surveys, in Land Surveys: A Guide for Lawyers 3-13 (3d ed. 2012). Copyright American Bar Association. All rights reserved. Reprinted by permission of the authors and the publisher.

Illustrations

Bala Plaza photograph, by Cathy Seidler-Coenen.

Smith, James Charles, photograph by Action Sports International, Tucker, GA.

Survey for Rupard by McLeroy, B (Aug. 16, 1995). Reprinted by permission.

Trump World Tower photograph, reprinted by permission of the Trump Organization.

REAL ESTATE TRANSACTIONS

1

Market Context for Real Estate Transactions

A good legal education develops a lawyer's critical thinking skills; but a transactional law practice involves more than critical thinking. In transactional practices and all other law practices clients do not pay for thinking. They pay for the results you achieve on their behalf. What you know and how you think are key ingredients in determining those results, but from the client's perspective they are not the main point. Focusing on results means a transactional lawyer must clearly understand the client's objectives, appreciate the client's market assumptions and expectations, and strategically employ the law to manage the transaction and achieve the desired outcome.

In developing an understanding of transactional lawyering, our starting point is the simple concept of *value*. Parties engage in private market transactions hoping to create, capture, and control value. This makes a transactional law practice very different from a litigation practice, in which one spends a great deal of time reconstructing the past and establishing the facts of a prior event. In a real estate transactions practice, the primary actors look to the future. They see a farm field and imagine a new housing community; they see an underutilized city block and imagine a new high-rise office building; they live in a rental apartment and imagine home ownership. Real estate transactions are about creating the future, shaping the built environment, and obtaining a piece of the "American Dream" via property ownership. The real estate transactions lawyer plays a central role in the realization of these dreams. To do this, transactional lawyers must know much more than the bodies of law that govern their areas of practice. The law provides the basic tools of lawyering, but the lawyer is an expert who needs to understand how the law fits into the larger process of social exchange. This larger process encompasses human factors, as the lawyer constantly interacts and deals with clients and other people. The practice of real estate law is people-oriented.

A lawyer adds value to a real estate transaction in <u>three important ways</u>.·
① First, the real estate transactions lawyer *strategically structures and documents the transaction.* The lawyer must know what documents are needed to accomplish the goal of a client or the parties. For example, this means knowing the difference between the language of a general warranty deed and a special warranty deed. It also means knowing when to use simple standardized forms and when to draft unique and complex provisions and documents. Drafting appropriate documents requires knowledge of the meaning of every sentence and word in the document, and it means being able to explain the way in which each contributes to the successful structure and completion of the transaction. Frequently there are multiple ways of achieving a client's transactional objective. The lawyer must *identify alternative strategies for achieving the goal.* For example, if a client seeks to acquire an office building that is for sale, the lawyer should use her knowledge and judgment to assist the client in selecting among strategic choices that may include a cash transaction, a credit transaction with financing provided by the seller, a credit transaction with mortgage financing provided by an institutional lender, a contract for deed, a purchase of the building coupled with a ground lease of the land, or an acquisition of the corporate entity that owns the property instead of a direct purchase of the property. Each alternative way of structuring the deal accomplishes the client's goal of gaining use and control of the building. At the same time, each approach presents different risks and opportunities, including different remedies for a party's breach and different consequences for tax planning. Structuring the transaction also includes working to *coordinate third parties* involved in the transaction. The lawyer must arrange the legal obligations and relationships with persons such as brokers, lenders, home inspectors, title companies, and surveyors.

② Second, the lawyer *manages and organizes time.* The timeline of a transaction proceeds from initial negotiation to executing the contract to closing on the exchange. A simple transaction may take several months; a complex one may take several years. The transactional lawyer must organize the *order of events* and *time for performance* by clearly defining the times and dates for parties to undertake and complete various aspects of the transaction. In addition to establishing the chronological order of performance, matters of *priority of interests* arise when organizing activity across an extended period of time. Priority rules govern the legal relationship between competing interest and claims to property. Chronological time can be adjusted in terms of legal priority as a result of recording acts and concepts such as subrogation, marshaling of assets, and the relation-back doctrine. Thus, time and priority are two different concepts. Time is also relevant in terms of the *time value of money.* A lawyer must manage and account for the present discounted value of a property, including such things as knowing how to identify an appropriate discount rate; and a lawyer must also be familiar with concepts such as a "quick sale" price for property relative to a "fair market value" price.

③   Third, the lawyer *manages risk.* To a large extent the lawyer is hired to identify and manage the wide assortment of risks that can and should be anticipated in a particular transaction. The lawyer must use her knowledge of the law to structure a managed approach to the variety of risks that may arise and to protect, as much as possible, the client's value expectations from the transaction. As a manager of risk, the lawyer must use the law to clearly and fully define the relationship and expectations of the parties. The lawyer's role in risk management consists of three elements, which we remember using the mnemonic *IRS* (**i**dentify, **r**educe, and **s**hift). The first task is to *Identify potential risks.* The lawyer must be skilled at identifying areas of risk and concern that might frustrate achievement of the client's goals. The more transactions one does and the more problems one experiences, the more one understands the nature and scope of the various risks that can disrupt a transaction. Next, the lawyer should *Reduce the probability of loss from identifiable risks.* Frequently identified risks may be reduced by taking preventive steps. For example, the risk of a title problem is reduced by doing a survey and a title examination. Likewise, the risk of a structural defect or an environmental problem is decreased by having a building inspector review the property. Similarly, a lender can reduce credit risk by ordering a credit report of the borrower. Last, the lawyer tries to *Shift the cost of risks that are not otherwise eliminated.* Not all identified risks can be eliminated. For example, we can reduce the risk of fire but not eliminate it, so building owners are often required to obtain fire insurance. Likewise, we can reduce the risk of a title defect, but in our property system we cannot entirely eliminate the risk of a defect; thus, we have title insurance. There are ways to shift the risk to a least-cost avoider. When there is no appropriately priced insurance, the parties can shift risk by adjusting contract terms and price to allocate the risk to the party best able and most willing to accept it.

A. TYPES OF REAL ESTATE TRANSACTIONAL PRACTICE

There are many types of real estate practice, but most transactional lawyers tend to think of the field as divided into two major market segments: residential and commercial. The legal work encountered in these two market segments is generally similar in nature but different in scope. There are also regional variations in what work is typically handled by lawyers in law firm settings rather than by other professionals. Each type of real estate practice must be sensitive to its own market context. In the past, there was not as drastic a split between residential and commercial real estate practices, and the knowledge needed for a real estate practice was often thought to be finite and circumscribed. Real estate practitioners could fare quite well if they could do title work and draft, with reasonable proficiency, standard types of instruments used in the jurisdiction where they practiced — deeds, leases, promissory notes, mortgages, oil and gas leases, and conveyances of other property interests. Their basic title work consisted of reviewing title to properties in accordance with local procedures and solving title defects and other title problems. In rural and small urban areas, lawyers often combined real estate with probate and trust work.

The practice of real estate law has changed during the past few decades, because the real estate business has changed. Now there is a significant difference between the scope of a residential and a commercial real estate practice. A residential real estate practice involves home sales (including single-family homes, condominiums, and cooperatives) and purchase financing. Occasionally the residential practitioner handles other matters as well, such as refinancing home loans, leasing, subdivision covenants, home-owners' associations, and nuisance disputes. In residential transactions, the lawyer is likely to represent one of three parties: buyer, seller, or lender. In some cases, the lawyer will represent more than one party, but this raises ethical problems concerning dual representation (this is discussed in detail in future chapters). A lawyer in a residential practice may be employed prior to or after a contract of purchase and sale has been entered into by the parties. Obviously, it is better to educate your clients to engage you to represent them before any contracts are signed. The contract is the main blueprint for the entire transaction, and the lawyer has the best opportunity for successful risk management when she is involved at the outset. If a client sees a lawyer after the contract has been entered into, there is much less that can be done for the client, because many risks and obligations have already been expressly or implicitly covered (or omitted) by the agreement. If both parties (buyer and seller) have attorneys prior to contracting, there is ample opportunity for negotiation.

Although residential transactions sometimes involve substantial precontract negotiation between the buyer and the seller, usually very little is negotiated beyond the terms stated in a series of printed forms. This is also true with residential financing. Most residential mortgage financing is done on standardized forms with little or no room for negotiation with the lender. The lender will typically carry several types of mortgages that are structured to appeal to different market and risk motivations, but other than selecting the type of standard financing form offered, there is generally no negotiation concerning the terms of any given choice. For example, a lender may offer a choice between a 30-year or 15-year fixed rate mortgage and several differently priced adjustable rate mortgages, but the specific legal terms of all of these choices will be fixed by a standardized form. Lenders typically view residential transactions as low-profit activities with high administrative costs, so they seek efficiency and profit by using standard forms and concentrating on volume.

In most parts of the country, lawyers share the field of residential practice with nonlawyers. Real estate brokers, title companies, and escrow-closing agencies are among the types of nonlawyers who generally compete for a significant portion of the work. In many parts of the country, these nonlaw-yers can fill in simple contract forms, assist buyers in the selection of a mort-gage, and often prepare most or all of the closing documents. As a consequence, the residential market has become very competitive for law-yers; unless a lawyer has a niche with very wealthy clients, the key to success has become high volume and a standardized practice (just as for lenders). Many such lawyers employ paralegals to do most of the transactional work in an effort to keep costs down. Similarly, in today's computerized world, costs can be reduced by using one or more of the many highly effective software packages that generate the standard forms and documents used in a residen-tial closing. Even title information, in the more populated parts of the coun-try, is fully available online, thus reducing the cost of a simple residential title search. As a consequence of the intrusion of nonlawyers, the standardization of the practice, and the slim profit margins, there are generally fewer real estate lawyers involved in residential transactions today than in the past.

A commercial real estate practice builds on the basic contract, property, and mortgage law foundations of a residential transaction. It is much more interdisciplinary in nature than a residential practice, and it requires a greater understanding of financial and market information. Commercial real estate activities are national and international in scope and involve complex financial and development vehicles. The underlying object of these transactions is property, but commercial transactions are fully inte-grated commercial undertakings. They require the real estate lawyer to be competent in areas that transcend the traditional principles of contract, property, and mortgage law. Now, the commercial real estate lawyer must deal with law related to a number of other subjects, including taxation; corporations; business associations; securities; bankruptcy; the environ-ment; land use and zoning; takings; torts; administrative law; the full range of the Uniform Commercial Code (UCC), with special concern for Articles 2 Sales, 2A Leases, 3 Negotiable Instruments, 4A Fund Transfers, and 9 Secured Transactions; antitrust; and antidiscrimination regulations, including the Americans with Disabilities Act. She must also have an under-standing of market forces, including the basic principles of finance, econom-ics, and accounting. The commercial real estate lawyer prepares many contracts and documents that are not strictly real estate in nature. Some non–real-estate contracts might include partnership agreements, building management contracts, utility service agreements, cable television contracts, construction contracts, and mortgage securitization agreements, among others. Although some commercial real estate lawyers specialize in particular aspects of the practice, all must have an understanding of the connection between their specialty and the bigger picture that makes up the client's overall objective.

Given the changing nature of real estate law, driven by the tremendous financial market integration that has occurred in the past few years, it is safe to say that today even a residential practitioner must fully understand the workings of the commercial real estate market. This is because commercial real estate projects (subdivisions, condominiums, etc.) end up being the subject of residential sales, and residential mortgage markets are affected by activities in commercial lending markets. It is impossible to be a knowledgeable residential practitioner if you do not understand the bigger context in which a residential transaction is situated. At the same time, the commercial real estate lawyer must first encounter and learn the basics of a residential transaction if she is eventually to understand the scope and complexity of commercial real estate development and financing. The basic residential transaction contains all the essential elements necessary for understanding commercial real estate development. In the commercial setting, however, the basic problems become more complex, because the number of parties, legal interests, and market factors increases.

B. MARKET CHOICES AND PROFITS

All real estate transactions involve the process of capturing or creating value. The parties are typically looking for profits, equity appreciation, or cash flow from their involvement in a real estate transaction. Sometimes, however, the economic benefits of a transaction are indirect motivators for an exchange. For instance, the benefits or values may relate to gaining control or autonomy, as in moving out of an apartment and into a single-family home; or a buyer may not expect a great deal of equity appreciation from buying a particular piece of real estate but may instead seek the tax benefits of the deal. This is often a motivating factor for high-income people to purchase expensive homes so that they can get tax benefits for such things as interest paid on the home mortgage. Whatever the particular circumstances are for a given transaction, it is clear that most real estate transactions are pursued for basic economic considerations of self-interest. This concept is simple and straightforward. To illustrate this, just ask yourself why you, as a lawyer, will facilitate the real estate transaction for the client. Generally, the lawyer is there for the same reason as everyone else — to earn a fee and to benefit from the business. The important thing to remember is that everyone else in the transaction is there for a similar reason.

A person who seeks value by entering into a real estate transaction is making a *market choice*. Like most other market transactions, a real estate transaction is undertaken or completed by choice because it makes sense for a number of reasons, including ones that are purely economic. Market factors are what motivate people to engage in real estate transactions. Developers, landlords, lenders, and other parties engage in transactions as a market choice because they hope to capture or create value. Consequently, if the potential for gain is eliminated from real estate activities, people won't be interested in them.

Market choices relate closely to the idea of profit. A desirable market choice is one that will be *profitable*, but the meaning of this term can vary with different circumstances. Not all motivations for doing a transaction are easily quantifiable, so it may be difficult to do a cost–benefit analysis of an anticipated exchange.

Profit from an exchange is typically considered in two different ways. These include *accounting profits* and *economic profits*. Accounting profits are based on covering the cost of a transaction. Economic profits measure the amount of accounting profit against the comparative return that could have been earned from undertaking an alternative transaction of comparable risk. Generally, a client will expect a transaction to cover the accounting costs and return an accounting profit. In the long run, a client's commitment to a particular type of business activity will also be influenced, in part, by the potential for economic profits.

C. RISK AND RETURN

For every market choice, there is a relationship between risk and return. The return may be described as value that is created and captured or as accounting profit or economic profit, with the latter term implying that there are alternative market choices bearing similar risk. The crucial relationship between risk and return is understood easily by thinking about something as simple as a savings account at the bank. As savers of money, we all want the best return on our investment. If one bank is paying us 1 percent to deposit our money and another is paying us 5 percent, we are likely to move our money to the location where we capture the most value. This is simple and straightforward, but what if the risks are different? How might one respond if the bank offering a 1 percent return on savings accounts was 100 percent insured by the federal government and therefore, the saver knew she couldn't lose her money, if the other bank paying 5 percent was not insured and was rumored to have some financial problems? In confronting this market choice, one has to consider the relationship between the risk and the rate of return offered by each bank. The riskier investment choice must provide a higher rate of return to attract investment. The potential investor is forced to weigh her aversion to risk against her desire for higher potential returns.

D. VALUE, UTILITY, AND COMPARATIVE ADVANTAGE

Discussions of market choice often include the terms *value, utility*, and *comparative advantage*, and therefore it is useful to examine these related ideas. First, let's look more closely at the concept of value. We have said that one helpful way to understand a real estate transaction is to think of it in terms of various parties attempting to capture or create value from their efforts. To appreciate this, we need to have some useful concept of what we mean by the term *value*. In simple economic terms, value is related to a concept called utility. *Utility* is a measure of how much an individual values a particular good, service, or activity. One can measure utility by observing the trade-offs that people make in the assorted choices of daily living. Some people work long hours to increase their income, whereas others forgo added income from work by pursuing more leisure time. In observing the tradeoff between work and leisure, one sees the relative utility that different people get from alternative ways to use their time (time being a scarce commodity and therefore valuable). Utility analysis tries to measure how much value or enjoyment a person gets from a particular thing or activity. In most cases it is easiest to rely on some tangible or outward proxy or device for measuring the degree of utility represented by any given set of tradeoffs between competing opportunities. Generally, money is used as a proxy, with a person's willingness to pay equated to the utility she derives from the activity or transaction. For instance, if John will pay $200,000 for a particular property and Morgan will only pay $180,000 for the same property, we can say that John values the property more than Morgan, or that John has a higher utility for the property.

When considering John's and Morgan's utility for the property, we must keep in mind that there is a problem with using price as a proxy for utility, because it assumes that all people have a meaningful way of registering their preferences in the marketplace. The difficulty stems from the fact that resources and bargaining power in our society are not equally distributed. Therefore, it may be true that John will pay $200,000 for a property for which Morgan will offer only $180,000, but it may also be true that Morgan would be willing to pay as much as $250,000 for that property if she had access to better credit. Limited by credit constraints and buying power, Morgan is unable to register, in dollar terms, her full level of personal preference for this particular property. Thus, the price proxy on which our market system operates is not a perfect measure of utility in terms of willingness to pay, but rather serves as a proxy for the combined notion of willingness and ability to pay. Consequently, we should always consider accessibility to credit and the distribution of resources before jumping to any significant conclusions about the actual preferences and values of particular market actors.

Likewise, social policy concerning real estate matters must be understood against a market backdrop that produces exchanges motivated not only by the desires of the actors, but also by the resources they already control. As a result, prior accumulated wealth has a major influence on market activities. The distribution of wealth has an important impact on the types of products offered in the real estate market; moreover, there is evidence that it affects access to credit and housing markets based on race and gender.

As real estate lawyers, we are often called on to determine the legal reliability and completeness of essential information underlying the client's judgments and expectations. We are also engaged to structure transactions so as to protect the value of the client's plans. To do this we must truly understand the market choices and preferences that shape the client's market outlook and transactional motivation. In this context, the *value* of the lawyer rests in her ability to facilitate the client's investment expectations. The lawyer is selling expertise, or *comparative market advantage*, in understanding the legal rules and infrastructure necessary to protect the client's expectations and to complete the desired transaction. The client is treating law and the legal system as a commodity. The law is a product that forms a necessary part of a successful real estate transaction, and the lawyer is hired to provide a level of **skill and confidence** in the delivery of this product that exceeds the performance of nonlawyers. This added level of skill is the lawyer's comparative advantage in facilitating the transaction, and it is generally thought that these skills increase with time and experience. Thus, more senior lawyers and lawyers with a specialized practice gain more expertise and advantage over others, and consequently command higher fees for their services.

Although the lawyer has a comparative advantage or expertise in the delivery of legal services, clients involved in commercial real estate generally perceive themselves as having a comparative advantage in their sector of business. Part of the lawyer's job is to protect that advantage and adequately constrain the client's liabilities with respect to matters outside the client's area of perceived advantage.

Market activities and functions are broken down along lines of comparative advantage based on an individual's or an entity's expertise in doing specific tasks more efficiently and cost-effectively than others. The real estate lawyer, quite frequently, is hired to facilitate the demarcation of these lines or functions, and she is expected to do so in a way that gives maximum advantage to the client while ensuring minimal exposure for loss. In other words, the lawyer is called on not only to facilitate the client's market transactions, but also to define both the client's role and the particular aspects of the market structure in which the transaction will take place.

Problem 1A

Consider two different situations. First, consider Ann, a developer seeking to acquire a parcel of land in the urban center of a mid-size city for purposes of constructing a hotel that she plans to operate under a major hotel brand name, such as Hilton or Hyatt. This would be a multimillion-dollar deal requiring land acquisition plus financing, construction, franchising, marketing, and regulatory compliance. Second, consider Jamar and Hannah, a couple who have lived together for the past five years but are not formally married. Jamar and

Hannah want to buy a home together. They have identified a three-bedroom loft in a newly renovated building in the urban center of the same city.

(a) In both situations, what questions might you ask the client in order to elicit the kind of information you will need to understand their goals and objectives? What goals and objectives can you imagine in each situation?

(b) Is it easy to determine who the client is in each situation? In Ann's project, is the client Ann; Ann's development corporation; Ann's potential investors; others? In the case of Jamar and Hannah, are they both your client or is just one of them your client? How will you clearly define the client, the objective, and your undertaking?

(c) How do you determine, in each situation, the client's market assumptions and expectations?

(d) In each case, how will you assess the reasonableness of the client's assumptions and expectations? Is it your job to question and advise the client on market factors that are not per se legal matters?

(e) In each case, to what extent does the client's ability to pay your fee impact the advice you give and the actions you are willing to undertake on their behalf?

E. CATEGORIES OF COSTS

In pursuing real estate transactions, parties incur four specific types of costs: *transaction, out-of-pocket, opportunity,* and *sunk costs.* These categories of cost affect market choice, and they also directly or indirectly influence the calculation of damages in the event that a transaction runs into difficulty.

Transaction costs are the costs associated with undertaking a particular exchange. They are the costs of collecting information, negotiating, cooperating, and regulatory compliance. It is important to keep in mind that as a lawyer engaged to assist the client in legal matters related to an exchange, you, too, are a transaction cost from the client's perspective. One goal of a person confronted with transaction cost, as well a goal of a legal system concerned with facilitating market exchanges, is to reduce the costs of transactions.

Out-of-pocket costs are actual expenses incurred in doing a project, whereas *opportunity costs* are associated with the market choices one gives up to pursue the selected choice. In every transaction, each party has both an out-of-pocket cost and an opportunity cost. When a person gives value in exchange for another item, the value surrendered is the out-of-pocket cost, which might be cash, land, legal rights, or something else. In simple terms, consider John's payment of $200,000 to purchase a property. The $200,000 is his out-of-pocket cost. John's opportunity cost, however, includes all the other things he might have done with that $200,000 but which he must now forgo, such as buying a boat or investing in the stock of a new venture capital group. Having made a choice to purchase a particular real property, John will measure his accounting profits or losses by the return he gets from the property, and he will measure his economic profits or losses with reference to the return he might have earned from other investments. Although accounting profits will likely keep John out of bankruptcy and in the market for the short run, competitive economic profits are necessary for the long-term viability of real estate markets relative to other investments and alternative capital market choices.

Sunk costs are a special type or category of out-of-pocket costs. They are costs that cannot be recovered when a party abandons a course of action. The problem with sunk costs is deciding at what point, and under what conditions, one should stay in or exit from a transaction. To answer this question, one needs to evaluate the potential costs and consequences of both staying in and getting out of a deal. The decision involves legal consequences, such as damages or penalties, as well as business considerations, such as the ability to pursue other transactions in the future. Staying in an exchange that has gone sour means that one will continue to invest resources in a transaction that is no longer expected to generate the returns that initially made it seem attractive. New information about the marketplace or the project may have changed the expectations for profit, but the disappointed investor also knows that she has already committed a lot of money and resources to the undertaking. This confronts the investor with the difficult choice of whether it makes more sense to invest additional time and resources in an effort to turn a project around, or simply to abandon the undertaking in a way that best limits the losses, including legal exposure.

Problem 1B

Your client, Rick, is interested in buying a home in south Florida. He has identified a property listed for sale at $725,000. It is located along a canal in a nice area not too far from Miami. Rick knows that this is an area of Florida that had a serious problem with defective Chinese-manufactured drywall used in the construction of many homes. The homes in his area estimated to have the defective drywall are 10 percent. The defective drywall was made with waste material from scrubbers on coal-fired power plants, also called "fly ash." These materials can leak into the air and emit one of several sulfur compounds, including sulfur dioxide and hydrogen sulfide. When combined with moisture in the air, these sulfur compounds create sulfuric acid which can corrode heating and air conditioning units, refrigeration units, electrical wiring, and plumbing. Health concerns include allergic reactions, coughing, sinus and throat infections, eye irritation, and respiratory problems. To rip out and replace a house's defective drywall may cost as much as $150,000.

(a) What steps might you recommend to reduce the risk of loss from potential contamination, and what legal consequences should arise in the event that the house is in fact contaminated? Recognizing that once a contract is executed legal obligations are undertaken, what might you do prior to executing a contract to reduce Rick's risk? Assuming Rick wants to be sure to get this property and wants to execute a contract to obligate the seller, how might you draft the contract of purchase and still protect Rick from the risk of loss? Would contract tools such as warranties and conditions aid to shift and manage risk; and if so, how?

(b) Assume that the seller and Rick are able to reach an agreement about price, and that Rick plans to finance his purchase by getting a mortgage loan. What further issues does Rick need to address in the contract given his financing plans?

(c) Assume that Rick hired you as his attorney after he had worked with a real estate broker who introduced him to the property, arranged for him to sign a purchase contract at $725,000, and collected a $100,000 earnest money deposit. The broker agreement he signed indicated that the broker would get a 7 percent commission on the contract price. Rick knew nothing about the local defective drywall problems before signing the purchase contract. You tell him about the drywall situation, and he decides not to close on the contract. Do you think he still owes a commission to the broker if the sale is never completed? What should happen to his deposit?

(d) What transaction costs, out-of-pocket costs, opportunity costs, and sunk costs has Rick incurred in the above scenarios? If he goes forward, what additional costs is he likely to incur?

F. TRANSACTIONAL MISBEHAVIOR

As clients try to get out of contractual commitments, seek to renegotiate terms, or just plain attempt to get more than they bargained for, we uncover the problem of *transactional misbehavior*. Transactional misbehavior occurs when a party to a transaction tries to change the dynamics of the deal after the deal has been struck. To understand transactional misbehavior, we must recall that there is a direct relationship between risk and price. In market terms, the greater the risk assumed by a given party, the higher rate of return that party will expect as a reward for engaging in the activity. Recall our example of putting money in a no-risk government-insured savings account for a guaranteed 1 percent rate of return. Compare this situation to an offer by a real estate developer that promises a 30 percent return on money invested but admits that there is only a 60 percent chance of success. If asked to consider these two choices, an investor has to think carefully about the potential returns as well as her own aversion to risk.

In a given transaction, if an investor can have a beneficial (self-serving) after-the-fact effect on the expected rates of return or associated risks, then she has an incentive to misbehave. This means that parties can have an incentive to act differently after entering an agreement than before the undertaking. In short, the underlying premise of transactional misbehavior is that each party to a transaction has an economic incentive to modify the initial allocation of risks so as to enhance her own rate of return. This premise hinges on an understanding that the parties entered into a legally enforceable agreement that locks in a specific set of risk assumptions and market expectations. Once locked into a negotiated price and risk relationship, each party can, in effect, improve her position or rate of return by acting in a way that shifts the calculus in her favor.

A goal of good transactional lawyering is to recognize the potential for transactional misbehavior, and to structure the transaction to reduce the risk of such behavior. By reducing the opportunities for transactional misbehavior, the lawyer enhances the opportunity to protect the client's transactional expectations.

Rent-seeking behavior is often a species of transactional misbehavior. Real estate transactions are only partially concerned with property per se as tangible, physical matter. Much transactional value comes from the legal and financial markets that make them possible. The basic proposition is that law and legal regulations are a primary source of the economic value of real property, and this law is not frozen or static. Parties sometimes try to capture or create value by discovering or manipulating legal opportunities. In so doing, they treat law as a commodity in which, like other commodities, they invest. For instance, the market value of a vacant piece of real estate may depend more on the zoning laws that define its permitted uses than on any other factor. Consequently, much value can be created for a particular property by effecting a favorable zoning use classification. Thus, it makes economic sense to invest money to effect a change in the property's zoning status. Generally, excluding other cost considerations, a person should be willing to spend almost as much money on changing an unfavorable zoning rule as she estimates that a favorable rule will add to the value of the property.

G. CATEGORIES OF MARKET RISK

Throughout our discussion up to now, we have referred to the concept of risk as an important factor to consider in planning every real estate transaction. Risk is one component of cost in evaluating a transaction. At this point we'll develop a more specific understanding of the nature of risk and its major forms by elaborating two significant categories of market risk: *temporal risk* and *transactional risk*.

1. Temporal Risk

Temporal risk concerns a variety of risk factors related to time. These risks can relate to past, present, or future information about a property or a transaction. Very few activities in a complex society can be done simultaneously, and consequently almost all real estate transactions are carried out over a period of time. There will be time for negotiating before entering into any specific agreements, there will be time involved in carrying out the terms of an agreement, and there will be time after the closing of a transaction when legal obligations may still be outstanding. Time as a factor in a transaction affects both value and risk. The effect of time on monetary value, often referred to by the phrase "the time value of money," is very important. Stated simply, this means that a dollar today is worth more than a dollar tomorrow.

There are a number of reasons for this, but the easiest explanation is the effect of inflation. We know that in periods of inflation, as time passes, the purchasing power of a dollar falls. It still is a dollar, but it takes more dollars to acquire or control the same goods and resources. If, for example, we assume an inflation rate of 15 percent per year, a dollar today would be worth only 85 cents one year from now; stated differently, what one could buy for a dollar today would cost $1.15 one year from now. One can easily see that inflation has opposite effects on borrowers and lenders. A borrower enjoys the advantages of inflation by getting money today and paying back in the future with dollars that are worth less. At the same time, a lender naturally has quite the opposite view of this situation.

Another important element of time-value risk relates to the old adage "a bird in the hand is worth two in the bush." This simply means that having one's money or performance now is better than merely having an expectation that it will be available at some date in the future. This is true for a number of reasons; but consider one simple point: the promise to pay or to perform in the future always involves a risk of nonperformance, therefore it is often best to have the other party perform first. In this way one enhances her opportunity to receive actual performance rather than a mere right to sue for nonperformance at a later date.

Having considered the relationship between time and value, it is important to look more closely at temporal risk related to past, present, and future informational concerns. *Past* or *historical risk* refers to an inability to be certain about historical information upon which particular business judgments rely in calculating the desirability of a current transaction. For instance, in approving a borrower for a loan, a bank would consider the credit history of the borrower. In making a decision about the borrower's credit risk, the bank would invest in historical information. The bank would hope that the past information would shed some light on the borrower's likely conduct in the future. The bank would probably include a credit check among the reports it commissioned in its effort to evaluate the risk of a loan. The credit report provides a great deal of information about the borrower and her payment history to a wide variety of creditors over a period of years. Although such a report can be useful, it might contain an error. Errors could be of a type favorable to the borrower (not picking up past credit problems) or harmful to her (reporting on credit problems that do not in fact exist). Errors against the borrower can cost her a good rate on a loan, and errors in her favor can cost the bank money by causing it to underprice the risk of its loan. In each case, there is a risk of inaccuracy concerning information about the past. This is historical risk.

The second category of temporal risk concerns *present risk*. Present risk centers on information relied on for purposes of establishing the presence or absence of specific conditions that would affect the property or the transaction. We may, for instance, want an inspection of the improvements on the property to make sure that the improvements comply with all current building and zoning codes and regulations. Here, we have at least two initial areas where error can arise. First, we may make a mistake in our reading of the codes and regulations and thereby fail to apply the appropriate standard in measuring compliance. Second, even if we properly determine the code rules and regulations, we may misapply the standard by not measuring or calculating accurately. For instance, a zoning code that requires a certain number of parking spaces for a building may use a formula based on the building's net square footage of useable space. First, we would need to find this regulation and figure out what was meant by *net square footage*; second, we would need to apply that formula to the property and then check the actual spaces for compliance with the number from the formula. As one can imagine, actual codes can be very confusing about the way square footage is to be measured, and about what types of areas count as parking spaces. Consequently, errors can be made about the present status of the property. Finally, we have the problem of *future risk* — the risk of not being able to predict the future. We can make educated guesses, but there is always a risk that our expectations about the future will be inaccurate; just look at how often government budget projections are wrong because of failed assumptions about future inflation rates, interest rates, and employment rates. Future risk also presents problems in the form of revisions to prior information. The future may reveal new information about historical conclusions, thereby revealing their inaccuracy. Likewise, the future may reveal that determinations about the present status of the property were incorrect. Such is the case when the presence of termites is revealed after closing on a property despite the pre-closing inspection report to the contrary. Future risk, therefore, not only concerns the inability to correctly predict the future, but also encompasses the problem of new information that changes the calculus of prior decisions.

2. *Transactional Risk*

In addition to temporal risk, there are also transactional risks, which include *investor or ownership risk*, *marketplace risk*, *credit risk*, and *transfer risk*. Each category of risk should be understood and appreciated if one is to analyze a real estate transaction properly. Sometimes these areas of risk analysis will overlap or be difficult to separate. The important point is that the lawyer must have a general understanding of the nature of transactional risk so that she can properly approach and manage an exchange.

Investor or *ownership risk*, which is sometimes called *entrepreneurial risk*, defines the position of a person who is an equity stakeholder in property. Simple elements of ownership risk involve liability for environmental problems that affect the property and tort liability for injuries that occur to certain categories of visitors to the property. Ownership risk also includes contract liability of an owner contracting for goods and services or the construction of improvements that will benefit the property. The owner as entrepreneur also takes on the risk of depreciating value of property and the risk that a construction project may be unsuccessful. If a project is unsuccessful or if an owner becomes liable as a result of her activity, there will be a cost or a loss.

The other side of this coin, however, is the potential for profit and gain if the real estate appreciates in value. The owner of real property is the one who benefits when property values rise. If the value of a home or commercial property appreciates, the owner wins the reward. The owner will also receive the benefit if any valuable minerals are discovered on the property.

A second key category of transactional risk involves the marketplace. *Marketplace risks* are those associated with general market forces that can affect the profitability of any given transaction. This type of risk is different from investor or ownership risk, because it affects all market participants and is generally not property-specific. The parties' structure of a transaction is often governed by their expectations concerning market forces. Changes in those expectations during the life of a transaction may dramatically alter the value of the exchange to each party. All the parties have to make some guesses — one hopes educated and informed guesses — about the future state of the market and plan their transaction around specified parameters. (In some respects, because market risk involves problems of future information, it is also properly considered a form of temporal risk, as discussed earlier.) Examples of marketplace risk are the risk of inflation or a general downturn in the economy.

In addition to affecting value, market factors can also affect liquidity. *Liquidity* is the measure of how quickly a person can exchange her investments for cash or other assets. Cash is very liquid, because it is easy to exchange for other things. Likewise, most publicly traded stocks are considered liquid, because there is a large and ready market for them. In contrast, liquidity for real estate can vary widely and can change over time. When it takes six months to a year to sell a piece of real estate, it would not be considered a very liquid investment. As market conditions fluctuate, a risk is imposed on real estate transactions, because market changes will affect the liquidity of a particular holding.

Credit risk is another element of transactional risk. The most obvious area of credit risk involves financing transactions, but it arises in other transactions whenever payment and performance are not simultaneous. A lender who extends credit should be concerned about two primary risk areas: the borrower's *ability* to pay, and *willingness* to pay. Assessing ability to pay requires an investigation into the income, credit history, and net worth of the borrower, as well as an investigation into the stability of the borrower's income flow and employment. Additionally, in a commercial undertaking, the borrower's past record or experience with similar types of activities is important. Although assessing the ability to pay might be thought of as a purely historical inquiry, it also has a forward-looking element. Often the ability to pay is related to market risk, because changes in the market may affect a person's income or employment. During an economic downturn, people on commission income or in particular industries may experience a decline in money resources or outright lose their jobs. Even in times of economic growth, some sectors of the economy do worse than others.

Credit risk involves more than just the risk of *inability* to pay or perform; it also involves a party's *willingness* to pay and perform. Everyone who extends credit knows that some people have the means or ability to pay and yet do not pay. Nonsimultaneous performance by all parties to a transaction, therefore, means that credit is extended with the possibility of future unwillingness to perform.

Transactional risk also includes a variety of potential problems that can arise from the actual mechanics of transfer — *transfer risk*. Whether it is the purchase and sale agreement between seller and buyer or the loan agreement between borrower and lender, the concept is the same. Risk arises from the process of transfer because of the possibility that any particular promise, warranty, or representation made by one party to another party may prove to be untrue or unenforceable, or at least not live up to the expectation of the party meant to be benefited. It can also arise from mistakes in document preparation, from errors in recording, or as a consequence of lost documentation. The more complex the transaction and the longer the period of time over which the transaction is to be conducted, the higher the level of risk.

Problem 1C

Your client, First National Bank and Trust (FNBT), is making a $10 million loan to Back Bay Partners (BBP) for the redevelopment of an old and unused factory building into a small apartment building as part of an urban revitalization program. The factory project is expected to take 20 months to complete. BBP's three partners, Joe, Frank, and Sharon, have extensive experience in successfully converting old factory buildings to contemporary loft apartments. They have previously financed a number of similar projects with FNBT. Because these redevelopment loans are always more risky than standard new construction projects, FNBT wants to make certain that Joe, Frank, and

Sharon will stay with the project until its completion. Given that the loan documents and the actual title to the property will be in the name of BBP, how might you draft the mortgage and related documents to reduce the risk of individual partners exiting the transaction early?

H. LAWYERS' PROFESSIONAL RESPONSIBILITIES

Understanding real estate transactions in a market context raises certain questions about the professional responsibility of a lawyer. First and foremost is the question of the lawyer's role in the transaction. Should the lawyer in a real estate transaction be merely an instrument for the client's will and manipulation for a favorable market position? Or are there ethical limitations that make it inappropriate for her to act in a way that maximizes the client's return no matter what? The lawyer cannot function as a mere economic actor seeking to maximize profit, because the lawyer is subject to a code of professional conduct, which incorporates values and obligations that may not always be consistent with the client's market objectives. Still, there are issues of just how far a lawyer should or can go in promoting a client's business objectives. The idea of the lawyer as zealous advocate incorporates the marketplace image of an unrelenting fighter or tool of the client's desires. In contrast is the view of the lawyer as an officer of the court with public duties. Existing within this tension is a further question: Does the lawyer's role change with the context of the setting in which she is engaged? In other words, does a lawyer have as much support for zealous advocacy in the pursuit of a client's market interests as our society tends to allow in the defense of a client accused of a serious crime? Stated differently, should zealous advocacy mean different things in a market context than it does in a criminal law context — and, if so, why? These are difficult questions for which there are no easy answers. Keep these questions in mind while thinking about the different types of real estate practice.

fees

A discussion of the market context for real estate transactions would be incomplete if we did not say a few words about the manner in which lawyers expect to get paid for the legal services they provide. Legal fees are a subject covered by the American Bar Association *Model Rules of Professional Conduct.* Under these rules, lawyers are expected to charge clients reasonable fees based on such factors as the complexity of the work, the amount of effort and expertise required, the likelihood that other employment opportunities will be forgone by taking on the matter, the significance of or the amount involved in the matter, the time limitation imposed, and any special reputational skills or talents possessed by the attorney. In all cases, it is best to think of work done for a client as a professional employment contract, thus indicating the desirability of reducing the arrangement to writing, as would be prudent in other contractual contexts.

This written agreement generally takes the form of a fee agreement letter addressed to the client that explains the legal services to be provided in exchange for compensation. Although this agreement is often drafted in the form of a letter, it is advisable to have the client sign off on the letter, indicating that she understands and agrees to the terms. The fee agreement letter should be prepared early in the relationship, and the manner of earning compensation should be clearly defined, such as by a set rate per hour, a percentage based on the value of the transaction, a flat fee, or some other basis. The letter should also indicate when compensation is expected to be paid: at the completion of the transaction, every 30 days, or in some other manner. It is important to identify the manner in which late fees and overdue payment will be handled. The taking of a retainer should also be spelled out, and provisions for costs (copies, express mail charges, travel, filing fees, title searches, etc.) should also be addressed if costs are to be treated as separate from the professional fee. If the fee will include added or bonus payment for a successful outcome, then this, too, should be specifically stated; indeed, under Model Rule 1.5(c), contingency fee and bonus fee agreements *must* be written. In short, one of the first obligations owed to a client is a clear explanation of the professional services that you are competent to provide, and a clear statement of the manner in which you expect to be paid. Having this understanding in writing will avoid many problems later on.

MARSH v. WALLACE
United States District Court, Southern District of Mississippi, 2009
666 F. Supp. 2d 651

Tom S. Lee, District Judge. In 2006, plaintiffs Kirk David Marsh, Kirk Russel Marsh and Marsh Investment Group, LLP entered into a $4.9 million transaction with defendant Alden "Bubber" Wallace for the purchase of approximately 150 residential rental properties which Wallace owned in Meridian and Quitman, Mississippi. After their purchase, plaintiffs came to believe they had been duped into purchasing the properties based on misrepresentations by Bubber Wallace, his wife Priscilla "Missy" Wallace, and by defendant Richard O'Dom, as to the historical monthly income of the properties. They filed this lawsuit seeking to recover damages against these three defendants for fraud, negligent misrepresentation and conspiracy. In addition, . . . they have sued John Howell, the "closing attorney" for the transaction, alleging claims for breach of fiduciary duty and negligence. The case was tried to the bench over a period of eight days in January and March 2009, and the court, based on the evidence adduced at trial, makes the following findings and conclusions.

Alden Wallace first became involved in the residential rental business in Meridian, Mississippi in the mid-1980s. Over time, he acquired around 150 rental properties [which] were held in a number of limited liability companies (LLCs) owned by Wallace and his wife, Missy. . . .

After forming Marsh Investment Group, Russel began looking for investment opportunities. In December 2005, he came across a listing on the internet by a Phil Coggins for some rental properties owned by Alden "Bubber" Wallace in Meridian, Mississippi. Russel contacted Wallace by phone in January 2006 to get financial information on the properties, and was told to contact . . . Richard O'Dom. O'Dom, the evidence showed, had been a banker (including bank president and owner) for more than thirty years, was a long-time close friend of Bubber Wallace and for some two years had been helping Wallace to try to refinance the debt on Wallace's rental properties. . . .

[O'Dom provided Russel with documents setting forth income and expenses for the properties for the preceding twelve months, and after a few weeks of regular communication the Marshes] decided to go forward with the purchase at Mr. Wallace's asking price of $4.9 million.

On May 6, 2006, the Marshes signed a purchase agreement for the properties that had been prepared by Bubber Wallace's attorney, Bill Ready. Wallace recommended to the Marshes that attorney John Howell do the title work on the properties, and possibly close the transaction, because he had previously done title work on the properties, and in a visit to Meridian in early June, Russel Marsh was taken to Howell's office and introduced to him by O'Dom. Russel met with Howell briefly and discussed with Howell his doing the title work for the transaction.

. . . O'Dom introduced Russel to [a] local banker, Charles Young with Citizens Bank in Meridian, as a potential lender for their purchase.

In the discussions with Young, it became apparent to Russel and O'Dom that the Marshes would not be able to acquire financing for the purchase from Citizens Bank. O'Dom conveyed to Wallace that the Marshes were having difficulty securing financing, and in response, Wallace suggested that the Marshes assume the existing debts on the properties and give Wallace a note on the remainder of the $4.9 million purchase price, to which the Marshes agreed. Around this time, Russel Marsh became concerned that if they were to purchase the properties outright, there could be a problem with due-on-sale clauses in the existing mortgages on the properties, and decided that instead of buying the properties directly, they should purchase the LLCs in which the properties were held. So, by mid-June, the parties' transaction had changed from a direct purchase of the properties with lender financing for the entire purchase, to a purchase of the LLCs, with assumption of existing debt and seller financing of the remainder of the purchase price. . . .

Following the closing, the Marshes experienced significantly less rental income from the properties than they had anticipated based on the historical income figures represented in the [information provided to them by O'Dom]. . . .

[The court held that the evidence did not support the plaintiffs' claims of intentional or negligent misrepresentation or fraud against the Wallaces or O'Dom.]

Plaintiffs have advanced claims for legal malpractice against attorney John Howell, both for breach of fiduciary duty and for negligence. As the Mississippi Supreme Court has explained, legal malpractice covers any professional misconduct by an attorney, whether attributable to negligence, i.e., breach of the standard of care, or to breach of the fiduciary obligations, i.e., breach of the standard of conduct. Lane v. Oustalet, 873 So. 2d 92, 98-99 (Miss. 2004). . . .

The Marshes have alleged that Howell breached his fiduciary duty of loyalty to them by undertaking to represent them in their transaction with Bubber Wallace while burdened with conflicts of interest arising from the fact that he had a personal interest in recovering $36,000 in overdue legal fees which he hoped to recover out of the proceeds of the Marsh/Wallace closing, and also because, as to the subject transaction, in addition to representing the Marshes, he was representing his long-time client, Wallace, whose interests were adverse to the Marshes'.

Addressing a lawyer's duties to his client, the Mississippi Supreme Court has recognized that, in addition to a duty of care, "[e]ach lawyer owes each client a . . . duty, not wholly separable from the duty of care but sufficiently distinct that we afford it its own label, viz. the duty of loyalty, or, sometimes, fidelity. We speak here of the fiduciary nature of the lawyer's duties to his client, of confidentiality and of candor and disclosure." Waggoner v. Williamson, 8 So. 3d 147, 154 (Miss. 2009). This duty of loyalty includes "a duty to inform his client of all matters of reasonable importance related to the representation or arising therefrom," including that he must in all cases inform the client of any conflict of interest. Id. A conflict of interest arises where "there is a substantial risk that the lawyer's representation of the client would be materially and adversely affected by the lawyer's own interests or by the lawyer's duties to another current client, a former client, or a third person." Restatement (Third) of the Law Governing Lawyers §121. In such situations, the lawyer's duty of loyalty includes a duty to "avoid conflicting interests that might impair the representation." Waggoner, 8 So. 3d at 154.[8]

---

8. On the subject of conflicts of interest, Rule 1.7 of the Code of Professional Responsibility of the Mississippi State Bar, states:

    (a) A lawyer shall not represent a client if the representation of that client will be directly adverse to another client, unless the lawyer reasonably believes:

        (1) the representation will not adversely affect the relationship with the other client; and

        (2) each client has given knowing and informed consent after consultation. The consultation shall include explanation of the implications of the adverse representation and the advantages and risks involved.

It is undisputed that at the time of the subject transaction, Bubber Wallace owed Howell $36,000 in attorney's fees, most of which ($28,000) was for title work Howell had previously done on Wallace's properties (in connection with a prior deal that never closed) and some of which was, as described by Howell, "just an accumulation of fees owed from [his] representing Wallace in the past." After the Marshes signed a contract in May 2006 to purchase Wallace's rental properties, Wallace suggested to the Marshes that they get Howell to do the title work since he had previously done title work on the properties and could give them a good price for doing the work. At Wallace's suggestion, Russel Marsh met with John Howell in early June, and agreed to have Howell do the title work. After Russel and Wallace agreed that the Marshes should purchase the LLCs rather than buying the properties directly, this was communicated to Howell, likely by Wallace. Subsequently, Kirk Marsh contacted Howell about closing the purchase of the LLCs, and toward that end, drafting agreements transferring ownership of the LLCs to Marsh Investment Group. Howell drafted transfer agreements based on a form he acquired from William Ready, and he then forwarded the draft agreements to Kirk Marsh. The two worked together toward finalizing the transfer agreements, which were executed by Wallace and the Marshes at the "dry" (pre)closing in June. In addition to the transfer agreements, Howell also prepared for the June closing a HUD-1 statement,[*] which listed Wallace's $36,000 debt to Howell among the debts Wallace would pay from funds he would receive from the Marshes. Howell also prepared a promissory note from the Marshes to Wallace, along with promissory notes in favor of Missy Wallace, Nell Wallace and Harold Wright.

Following the June closing, Howell prepared additional documents, including a revised HUD-1, which, again, reflected Wallace's $36,000 debt to him; a continuing guaranty agreement for the Marshes to sign, which Wallace had required of them; certificates of title for Commercial Bank; and a general pledge agreement by which the Marshes agreed to assume Wallace's existing debts on the properties.

(b) A lawyer shall not represent a client if the representation of that client may be materially limited by the lawyer's responsibilities to another client or to a third person, or by the lawyer's own interests, unless the lawyer reasonably believes:
   (1) the representation will not be adversely affected; and
   (2) the client has given knowing and informed consent after consultation. The consultation shall include explanation of the implications of the representation and the advantages and risks involved.

The Rules of Professional Conduct do not provide a basis for civil liability but rather are intended for a lawyer's self-governance and disciplinary purposes. They can, however, provide guidance as to a lawyer's standard of conduct. *See* Singleton v. Stegall, 580 So. 2d 1242, 1244 n.4 (Miss. 1991).

* [A HUD-1 Settlement Statement is a standardized disclosure form developed by the federal Department of Housing and Urban Development (HUD) to itemize all closing charges–Eds.]

Owing to the fact of his prior representation of Wallace and the fact that he was owed $36,000 in legal fees by Wallace, plaintiffs charge that Howell had a conflict of interest based on his personal financial interest in Wallace's transaction with them is hardly controversial. Indeed, Howell acknowledges that in light of these circumstances, the best course of action would have been for him to have obtained a written consent and waiver from Russel Marsh at their first meeting in early June. However, he points out that no statute or law required such written consent or waiver. And, he insists both that he reasonably believed that these circumstances would not adversely affect his representation of any party in the transaction and that he did expressly inform Russel both of his prior representation of Wallace and of the existing debt owed to him by Wallace. Howell maintains that Russel, fully aware of these facts, consented, initially, to Howell's doing the title work on the properties, and then, to Howell's handling the closing, even after the transaction changed from a direct purchase of the properties to the Marshes' purchase of Wallace's LLCs. In short, he contends the Marshes were aware of his potential conflict of interest and consented to his handling the transaction. The Marshes, on the other hand, contend they were unaware of Wallace's indebtedness to Howell for prior legal work, and that since this was never disclosed to them, they never had the opportunity to decide whether to consent to Howell's representation; and they contend that, had they known this fact, they probably would not have agreed to Howell's involvement in the transaction.

While Howell's personal financial interest in the transaction indisputably created a conflict of interest, the court finds that, contrary to the Marshes' urging, his interest was disclosed and that the Marshes knew of Howell's interest from the outset. In his testimony at trial, Russel Marsh could not recall precisely what Howell told him in their initial meeting in early June. He did recall having been told at some point that Howell had previously done title work; but he did not recall Howell's saying that he had previously done title work for Wallace's rental properties. Moreover, Russel did not recall Howell telling him he was owed $36,000 for legal work Howell had previously done for Wallace. Howell, on the other hand, was clear in his recollection that he specifically and clearly informed Russel that he had previously done legal work for Wallace, including title searches on his rental properties, and that Wallace owed him $36,000 in legal fees for this past work. In fact, Howell produced contemporaneous notes of his meeting with Russel which reflect that he informed Russel of these matters. Thus, when they were provided at the June closing (and later at the July closing) with the list of Wallace's debts, neither Marsh questioned or objected to the inclusion of a $36,000 debt to Howell because they had already been made aware of it.

Having considered the evidence, the court finds that Russel Marsh was apprised of Howell's prior representation of Wallace and of Wallace's debt to Howell. . . .

Plaintiffs also contend that Howell had a conflict of interest in the subject transaction arising from his dual representation of the Marshes, as buyers, and Wallace, as the seller/lender, whom he had regularly represented for a number of years, including in matters directly related to Wallace's rental business. From the court's perspective, it seems that Howell's role in the transaction was never well-defined, particularly as the transaction evolved, and as a consequence is now subject to conflicting assertions by the parties.

At the time Howell first became involved, the transaction, as negotiated and agreed between Wallace and the Marshes, was one in which the Marshes would directly purchase Wallace's rental properties. The Marshes had signed a contract for the purchases a month before Howell became involved, and they had already paid their $50,000 in earnest money. The Marshes did not hire an attorney — Howell or anyone else — to assist them in negotiating their agreement with Wallace or to draft the contract for purchase; rather, they had signed a contract that was prepared by Wallace's attorney, William Ready, which agreement included a $4.9 million purchase price and identified the properties being purchased. That contract gave them a thirty-day contingency period in which to investigate the transaction and any representations relating thereto, which period expired before Russel Marsh ever met or spoke with John Howell. Only after entering this agreement did the Marshes, at Wallace's suggestion, engage Howell to do the necessary title work for the transaction. At that point, Wallace had already gone to Howell with the Marsh contract and discussed with him the prospect of Howell's doing the title work; and by that time, Howell had already suggested to Wallace that he do the closing, as well.

Initially, Russel Marsh met with Howell for around fifteen minutes and hired him to do the title work — or, according to the Marshes, agreed to allow him do the title work — for a discounted fee that Wallace had already negotiated with Howell. At that time, there was no discussion between Russel and Howell of Howell's doing the closing. Later, after the Marshes decided to buy Wallace's LLCs in which the properties were held instead of buying the properties outright, the Marshes contacted Howell and asked him to draft agreements transferring ownership of the LLCs from Wallace to the Marshes, and to do the closing. There was no discussion at that time, or at any other, with the Marshes or with Wallace, of whom Howell was representing in the transaction, and specifically, of whether he was representing the Marshes or both the Marshes and Wallace. He simply proceeded forward, initially drafting the transfer agreements in consultation with Kirk Marsh, continuing with the title work and preparing documents the parties required and/or requested for the closing.

When asked at trial whom he thought he represented in the transaction, Howell asserted that the Marshes were his only clients in the transaction; he did not represent Wallace. Wallace, likewise, maintained that he had no attorney in the transaction (other than Ready, who only prepared the original contract for sale). On the other hand, Kirk Marsh testified that he never thought Howell represented only him and Russel; rather, he saw Howell as "the closing attorney," who represented everyone in the transaction. Mr. Marsh explained that initially he and Russel had simply agreed with Wallace's suggestion that Howell do the title work (though he would not say that he and Russel "hired" Howell). He explained that when the transaction changed in June, he and Russel "wanted somebody, a lawyer — or we wanted to make sure that this thing was done correctly. So we agreed to use Mr. Howell to prepare documents for the transfer of the LLCs." . . .

As courts have often acknowledged, "[r]eal estate closings present a particularly thorny dilemma for the bar because a closing attorney often undertakes responsibilities to various parties to the transaction, in contrast to the typical situation in which each party is zealously represented by counsel." Credit Union Cent. Falls v. Groff, 966 A.2d 1262, 1267 (R.I. 2009). Thus, as plaintiffs note, in the context of a real estate closing, where several parties might reasonably rely on the closing attorney's work, the duty of loyalty requires an attorney to be particularly vigilant in delineating whom the attorney represents. . . .

Notwithstanding Howell's current assertion that he always considered the Marshes to be his only clients, to the exclusion of Wallace, it seems more likely he never had a clear understanding of whom he was representing. What is even more likely, in the court's view, is that, whether or not he viewed himself as doing so, Howell undertook to represent both sides to get the transaction closed; and by doing so without disclosing to the Marshes the manifest potential for conflict of interest and hence without obtaining their informed consent to his representation, he violated his fiduciary duty to them. *See* Hartford Acc. & Indem. Co. v. Foster, 528 So. 2d 255, 268 (Miss. 1988) (holding that "even if the lawyer reasonably believes (and from an objective point of view) believes he can faithfully represent dual parties with adverse interests, he must still fully explain all implications of the advantages as well as the risks of his representation to both parties, and assure himself that they both have given knowing and informed consent"). . . . It was Howell's affirmative duty to secure their informed consent, which was not done. Thus, to the extent they may have agreed to his dual representation, the court concludes they did not do so knowingly. . . .

The Marshes have contended that in light of Howell's representation of them under a conflict of interest, they did not receive the representation for which they paid, and as a matter of equity, should recover the fees they paid Howell for his representation of them, totaling $19,425. The court agrees, and concludes that they should recover this amount from Howell. . . .

Problem 1D

For several years you have represented a developer who builds large communities of single-family homes. The developer has asked you to provide closing services for all of the homes that it will sell in its new $85 million community, Happy Town. It plans to compensate you by paying you $1,200 for each sale that closes. For any scheduled closings in which the sale does not close for any reason, you will receive nothing — not even reimbursement for out-of-pocket expenses. Consistent with the usual practice in the community, almost none of the homebuyers will retain their own legal counsel.

(a) What obligations, if any, do you have to the homebuyers? Is it necessary that you disclose anything about your compensation arrangement to the buyers? How can you reduce the risk that a buyer becomes disappointed with some aspect of the transaction and claims that you have not behaved properly?

(b) Suppose that you do title work for the closings, and that pursuant to the contracts of sale signed by the buyers, they are responsible for paying for the title work. The HUD-1 statements, to be given to and signed by the buyers, will reflect the buyer's payment of $700 for the value of your title examination work. Should you have to point this out to the buyers, or is it sufficient to expect that they will read the HUD-1? The HUD-1 statement does not reflect your client's payment to you of $1,200 for closing the deal. Is this a problem?

(c) The economy is in a downspin, and so are the finances of your client. Promotional materials for Happy Town depicted amenities including an Olympic-size swimming pool and tennis courts, surrounded by a large green area, with a statement that these improvements would be open at the end of the "Phase I development." Your client had planned to begin construction of these amenities next month, but the client has just told you that it's putting these plans on hold — on "indefinite hold." You have four closings scheduled over the next two weeks. Your client does not plan to disclose this change of plans to buyers who are under contract. What should you do? Do you have any obligation to the buyers?

2
Real Estate Brokers

Real estate brokers perform the critical task of finding the parties for the deal. Usually the parties have never met and do not know each other until the broker brings them together. The broker thus plays the role of transactional intermediary in the market for property sale and exchange, but the broker does not simply disappear once the parties are found. Instead, the broker continues to facilitate the transaction by assisting the parties with matters such as contract negotiation, inspections of the property, and financing arrangements.

Brokers are information specialists; the primary service they offer is market information, which has great value because of brokers' training and experience and the systems they have created to share market data. They have access to information that the parties need about properties and the terms at which prospective participants are willing to deal. Brokers also have information about other market transactions that can provide guidance in determining the market value for a particular deal.

All 50 states regulate the business of real estate brokerage in order to create and maintain professional standards and to protect members of the public who interact with brokers. A state administrative agency, often called the *real estate commission* or the *department of real estate*, is responsible for enforcing the laws pertaining to brokers. There are two levels of licenses. A *broker* has a "full" license, and although he may work as an employee of a brokerage firm, he is qualified, just like an attorney, to "hang out his own shingle." In contrast, a real estate *salesperson* has a license that permits him to act as a broker only under the supervision of a licensed broker. Many states require that a broker first work as a salesperson before obtaining a broker's license.

Slightly more than half of the active brokers and salespersons in the United States are members of the National Association of Realtors (NAR), a trade association founded in 1908. The term *realtor*, which NAR has trademarked, means an NAR member, although in popular parlance it is often used as a synonym for *broker*. All the state associations of real estate brokers and most local real estate boards are members of NAR.

Brokers earn their living by collecting commissions. For a sale transaction, the commission is a percentage of the sales price. Other methods of compensating brokers are possible, such as a flat fee or payment on an hourly basis for time spent, but these are rarely used.

In residential real estate sales, commissions paid to brokers who provide a full range of services (as opposed to "discount brokers," who are a small part of the market in most communities) typically range from 5 to 7 percent of the sales price. Sellers sometimes think such commissions are too high. After all, a 6 percent commission on a house sold for $200,000 is the tidy sum of $12,000. For this reason, a good number of homeowners try to sell without using a broker, a practice sometimes identified by the acronym FSBO (pronounced *fizzbo*) — for sale by owner. Many times FSBO attempts fail, either because the seller fails to attract a buyer or because the seller finds a buyer but agrees to less advantageous terms than a professional broker would have obtained.

In sale transactions, the broker's client is usually the seller. When a property owner hires a broker to sell his property, their contract is known as a *listing*. Typically, it is a written contract; usually it is better for both parties that they put the terms of the brokerage in writing. Indeed, some states have passed a special statute of frauds that requires a written broker's contract and bars a broker from recovering on an oral brokerage arrangement. In other states, an oral listing contract, if proven, is enforceable.

Four types of listing agreements for selling property are presently in common use. Under an *open listing* (nonexclusive listing), the broker earns his commission if he procures a ready, willing, and able buyer for the property. Other brokers can be engaged by the seller, in which event the first one to procure a buyer earns the commission. In addition, the seller can sell his property by himself, without a broker's help, in which event no commission is payable.

The *exclusive agency* agreement contains a promise by the seller not to engage another broker during the term of the agreement. The broker is the exclusive agent with respect to the listed property. If the owner sells using another agent, the exclusive agent is still entitled to his commission. As with the open listing, however, the owner may sell by his own efforts and thereby avoid a commission.

The *exclusive right to sell agreement* (or exclusive listing) is the most protective of the broker's expectation of earning the commission. The seller is obligated to pay the commission if any buyer purchases the property during the term of the agreement. It does not matter whether the broker procures the buyer, whether another broker finds the buyer, or whether the buyer and seller meet without the assistance of any broker.

The fourth type of agreement, the *net listing*, is less common than the other three types. The commission is not specified as a percentage, and the seller agrees to pay the broker all amounts received in excess of a set price established by the broker and the seller. The word *net* means that the seller is guaranteed a net amount of sales proceeds — but that is also the limit of what the seller can get from the sale. The broker typically has discretion with respect to setting the listing price and will seek to sell at a higher price and pocket the difference. For example, the agreement might say that the seller is to receive a net price of $300,000, and the broker might set an initial asking price of $330,000.

Many brokers are members of a *Multiple Listing Service* (MLS), which facilitates the sharing of listings among the MLS members. Real estate markets are by definition geographically local, and so are MLSs, which typically are citywide, countywide, or metropolitan. Each member broker submits new listings to the MLS, which compiles a directory or database with information pertaining to all current listings. The MLS broadens the market exposure for listed properties, which may benefit the seller. A potential buyer who contacts any member broker has the opportunity to see and consider any of the MLS properties. Almost all listings turned in to MLSs are exclusive right to sell listings. MLSs concentrate on residential properties, but most services also accept listings for vacant land and commercial properties.

The seller does not pay a higher commission by virtue of the listing going into a MLS. The broker who enters into the listing agreement with the seller is known as the *listing broker*. If a customer of another member broker buys the property, that broker is known as the *selling broker* or *cooperating broker*. The MLS agreements require a division of the standard commission between the listing broker and the selling broker. Often the division is 50 percent to each broker, but this can vary according to the local MLS regulations.

The internet and modern information technology are changing real estate brokerage, just as they are changing virtually all occupations, including the practice of law. One contemporary online service (Redfin) employs agents on an annual salary basis with potential bonuses being based on customer reviews. The practice has not yet had a major impact on the market. Other popular online discount services are provided through such entities as Zillow and Trulia. These providers offer information online but then send potential customers to actual brokers. Current evidence indicates that even though over 40 percent of homebuyers now use internet sources to gather information and start a home search, 90 percent still use a broker to purchase a property. The reasons that internet applications have not dramatically reduced the use of actual brokers using a traditional commission-based business model are not clear. It is suggested, however, that people want a lot of help, advice, and "hand-holding" when making a home purchase, which is likely to be the biggest single investment a person makes in his lifetime. Another explanation is that there are usually two brokers involved in a transaction. Because of this, it is easier for established and traditional brokers to put pressure on participants in the market to direct business away from sellers and buyers who have not engaged a traditional broker.

Problem 2A

Steven and Sarah have owned a two-bedroom suburban home outside of Denver for the past three years. Having recently completed their college education, they are relocating to Cedar City on the east coast where they have lined up new jobs, which will start in six months. They want to buy a larger home with a spacious lot in Cedar City. Given the paperwork involved in selling and buying a home, Steven and Sarah decide to hire a broker in Denver to sell their current home and will look for a broker in Cedar City to facilitate their new home search and purchase. To afford a new home in Cedar City they will first need to sell their Denver home. They have learned that there are several different types of broker agreements, with different payment terms and other implications. They ask for your advice with respect to brokerage arrangements. What should they seek and expect? They also ask your opinion regarding the possibility of simply trying to sell the home on their own without a broker. What questions might you want to ask Steven and Sarah?

A. BROKERS' DUTIES TO CLIENTS

When a person hires a broker, their relationship is governed chiefly by the law of contracts and the law of agency. With respect to his client, the broker, just like the lawyer, is a fiduciary. Though there are many other aspects of fiduciary relationships that may bear on the broker-client relationship, three primary duties often come into play: the broker's *duty of loyalty*, the broker's *duty of disclosure*, and the broker's *duty of confidentiality*.

Loyalty encompasses traits such as honesty and fidelity. The broker should do his utmost to protect the client and advance the client's interest. The client wants to engage in a real estate transaction to create value, and it is the broker's role to assist in creating value by using his time, experience, and knowledge. In selling property, one aspect of loyalty concerns property value and price. The seller wants to sell at the highest price possible, and the broker is charged with the duty of obtaining a sufficient sales price.

Closely related to loyalty is the broker's duty of disclosure. When a broker learns facts or other information that are material to the client's position or interests, the broker should promptly tell the client. The broker must keep the client informed.

The duty of confidentiality is the flip side of the disclosure duty. In the course of representing a client, the broker gains information about the client's objectives and the property that, absent the client's consent, should not be disclosed to third parties. Sometimes the client's interest is simply privacy, but often the information has economic value.

To whom does the broker owe the duties of loyalty, disclosure, and confidentiality? Usually the identity of the broker's principal or client is plain and clear, but this is not always the case. Most of the time, the broker represents the seller. The broker met the seller prior to the buyer's coming on the scene, and usually the broker and the seller have signed a listing agreement that details their agency relationship, the commission arrangements, and other matters related to the undertaking.

There are several reasons why the identification of agency relationships sometimes gets complicated or obscured. First, *dual agency* is permissible in most states. This means a broker may lawfully represent both the seller and the buyer in the same transaction, provided that the broker discloses the dual agency to both parties who consent to the arrangement. Dual agency poses obvious problems, such as the potential for conflicting duties of loyalty, disclosure, and confidentiality. Nevertheless, the practice is allowed; because of its risks, however, many brokers have adopted the policy of not engaging in dual agency relationships.

Second, brokers do many things to facilitate transactions, and the context of any dispute that arises may affect the issue of who represents whom. A broker who is clearly the seller's agent for the primary duty of selling the property may act as the buyer's agent with respect to a collateral task. For example, if a broker helps the buyer obtain financing, with respect to this work the broker may be the buyer's agent. With respect to some chores, such as preparing documents required for the closing, the broker may be a dual agent of both parties. ∕buyer's

Third, agent relationships tend to get confused when two brokers, a listing broker and a selling broker, are involved with the same transaction. This happens in a large percentage of residential sales within the MLS system. The listing broker is clearly the seller's agent. It is the position of the selling broker, or cooperating broker, that clouds matters. The selling broker is the agent who deals directly with the prospective buyer, typically showing the buyer a number of properties that may suit his needs. This broker tries hard to find just the right house for the buyer, who often gets the justifiable impression that the broker is on his side, working for him. Yet the traditional rule is that the selling broker, just like the listing broker, is the seller's agent, even though the seller and the selling broker may meet for the first time at closing or may never meet. The selling broker is considered the listing broker's *subagent*, who is engaged by the listing broker to help perform his task. This view is reinforced by the scheme for compensating the selling broker. The buyer does not pay the selling broker; instead, the listing broker shares part of his commission with the selling broker.

The traditional subagency rule has been widely criticized on two grounds: first, that buyers are misled into thinking that the selling broker is *their* agent; and second, that buyers deserve representation at the critical stage of selecting a property and negotiating the terms of a purchase contract. Presently, more than 40 states mandate a written disclosure, either by statute or by broker's regulation. The disclosure forms vary widely from state to state. Most states expressly permit not only seller's agents but also buyer's agents (discussed later) and, with consent of both parties, dual agency.

Over the years, the percentage of homebuyers who hire buyer's brokers has risen steadily, as the obvious advantages have become better known. This is partially due to market specialization, with many brokers choosing to concentrate on buyer representation and advertise their services as such. Moreover, statutorily required disclosures of agency relationships have raised awareness among homebuyers that they have a choice in the matter.

A number of states offer an alternative to the formation of agency relationships with seller and buyer, and the alternative is known as *transaction brokerage* or *nonagency brokerage*. Under this arrangement, the broker sells services but has no formal agency relationship with either party. The broker's role is described as facilitator, intermediary, or middleman. Transaction brokerage avoids the creation of fiduciary duties, thereby implying that the broker should not become an advocate for, or give advice to, either party. The primary advantage of transaction brokerage from the broker's perspective is risk reduction. Beginning in the 1990s, many states passed statutes defining transaction or nonagency brokerage and authorize brokers, upon proper disclosure, to enter into such relationships. Some states have a statutory presumption that a broker acts as a transaction broker, which is overcome only if a writing expressly establishes an agency relationship. *E.g.*, Colo. Rev. Stat. §12-61-803(2); Fla. Stat. §475.278(1)(b).

Problem 2B

Sarah bought a condominium four years ago for $260,000, and she now wants to sell it. She contacts Brandi, a local broker, and enters into a written brokerage agreement authorizing her to list the property for sale at a price of $275,000. Kevin contacts Brandi, saying he would like to buy a condominium. Brandi shows Sarah's condominium to Kevin. He appears to like the property, but says that the most he is willing to offer is $240,000. How should Brandi react? Should her strategy differ if she and Sarah previously had a conversation in which Sarah said, "I think my listing price is reasonable and should be attractive to lots of buyers. I expect to get my asking price, or very close to it." Alternatively, how should Brandi respond to Kevin if Sarah previously said, "I'm desperate to sell my house. The loan balance is $238,500, and I just can't afford to live here any longer. I want to move immediately." Does it make a difference if the brokerage agreement is an open listing, an exclusive agency, or an exclusive listing? Is it fair to Sarah if Brandi offers to show Kevin other condominiums that have asking prices in the range of $240,000 to $260,000?

RANGEL v. DENNY
Court of Appeal of Louisiana, Second Circuit, 2012
104 So. 3d 68

GASKINS, Judge. The plaintiffs, Anthony Bryan Rangel and Bridgette Rangel, appeal from a trial court judgment sustaining an exception of no cause of action in favor of J. Wesley Dowling and Associates, Inc. ("Dowling"). For the following reasons, we reverse and remand for further proceedings.

FACTS

The plaintiffs entered into a contract in February 2010, with Dowling to sell their house situated on 40 acres of land in DeSoto Parish. According to the allegations in the plaintiffs' pleadings, the sale was to include mineral rights to 20 acres, the plaintiffs were to retain the mineral rights to 20 acres, and the contract provided that the plaintiffs were to inform Dowling if a prospective buyer contacted them directly. The plaintiffs alleged that, in July 2010, they were contacted by Marlon and Cynthia Curtis about buying the house, and that they notified Dowling and requested that it provide a prospective buyer's contract. The plaintiffs claimed that Dowling refused to do so because the company did not represent the Curtises. According to the plaintiffs, Mr. Rangel then personally drafted an agreement for the Curtises to buy the house, land and 20 acres of mineral rights, for approximately $396,000.

The plaintiffs pled that, before the Curtises received approval for their loan, the plaintiffs moved out of the house and signed a six-month apartment lease, as well as a lease for a business space for Mrs. Rangel to carry on her business as a barber. The plaintiffs claimed that the Curtises were not able to obtain financing and backed out of the agreement to purchase the house. They contended that the Curtises could not get financing for the house because their lending institution would not accept the appraisal of the house.

In June 2011, the plaintiffs filed a petition for damages against Dowling and the Curtises for negligence and for breach of contract.[1] The plaintiffs alleged that the Curtises breached their contract forcing the plaintiffs to sell

---

1. The plaintiffs originally hired Bryce Denny as their lawyer to represent them in this matter, but later hired new counsel. The plaintiffs included Mr. Denny as a defendant in this suit. However, no claims regarding him are at issue in the present matter and are not discussed herein.

mineral rights to cover the cost of their mortgage, apartment rent, and expenses.

Regarding Dowling, the plaintiffs alleged that the company was obligated or owed a duty to provide professional services, negotiate the sale, provide a legal and binding contract to the Curtises, and follow through to successfully close the deal. The plaintiffs contended that Dowling committed errors and omissions and breached its duty to them. The plaintiffs speculated that the Curtises knew or should have known that Dowling was obligated to provide them with an agreement to buy or sell and that they may have thought that the agreement drafted by Mr. Rangel was not binding. . . .

. . . The plaintiffs filed an amended petition for damages, alleging that Dowling failed to represent them in a manner that was consistent with the customs and practices of the real estate profession and caused or contributed to the plaintiffs' damages and injuries. The plaintiffs claimed that it is customary for real estate agents/brokers to assist the purchaser and seller with alternative means of financing when prospective buyers are turned down for loans.

The plaintiffs contended that their agreement with Dowling required the company to review the purchase offer, discuss financing alternatives, work to successfully close the sale, and assist in reappraising the property or supplementing the appraisal. They claimed that Dowling did not do those things.

The plaintiffs claimed that it is customary for a real estate agent to assist and represent an unrepresented buyer or a buyer who does not have his/her own real estate agent. The plaintiffs contended that Dowling had a duty when representing a buyer or seller to complete the purchase agreement form prescribed by the Louisiana Real Estate Commission in making an offer to purchase or sell residential property under La. R.S. 37:1449.1.[2] According to the plaintiffs, Dowling breached this duty.

The plaintiffs asserted that it is customary for real estate agents or brokers to inform or advise sellers not to move out of their house or rely on buy/sell agreements to their detriment until a loan has been made and the money has been paid. They urged that, had Dowling so advised them, they would not have moved out of their house and would not have incurred many of the damages they suffered such as apartment expenses, moving costs, business lease expenses, storage costs, additional insurance, and loss of mineral rights.

On October 26, 2011, Dowling filed [an] exception of no cause of action to the plaintiffs' amended petition. Dowling claimed that it had no duty to perform the acts complained of by the plaintiffs. Dowling stated that,

---

2. La. R.S. 37:1449.1 provides in pertinent part:

    A. A licensee representing either the buyer or seller of residential real property shall complete the purchase agreement form prescribed by the Louisiana Real Estate Commission in making an offer to purchase or sell residential real property. No person shall alter the purchase agreement form; however, addendums or amendments to the purchase agreement form may be utilized.

if it did have such a duty, the plaintiffs' damages were not caused by Dowling's failure to perform any duties. Rather, their damages were caused by the Curtises in breaching their contract with the plaintiffs. . . .

Dowling claimed that the plaintiffs did not allege any facts under which they would have avoided being damaged if Dowling had reviewed the contract between the plaintiffs and the Curtises or provided a purchase agreement form. Dowling asserted that it had no duty to reappraise the property and did not have a duty to advise the plaintiffs not to move out of their house prior to finalizing the sale.

On November 30, 2011, the trial court entered a judgment sustaining Dowling's exception of no cause of action. Dowling was dismissed from the suit with prejudice. . . .

. . . The court found that the plaintiffs failed to allege sufficient facts to satisfy the causation element of their claims against Dowling. According to the trial court, the allegations against Dowling are based upon pure speculation that had Dowling assisted with the sale and financing, the buyers, who had no contractual relationship with Dowling, would not have breached their contract. . . .

DISCUSSION

. . . .

An exception of no cause of action is sustained only when it appears beyond doubt that the plaintiff can prove no set of facts in support of any claim which would entitle him to relief. If the petition states a cause of action on any ground or portion of the demand, the exception should be overruled. . . .

A real estate broker is a professional who holds himself out as trained and experienced to render a specialized service in real estate transactions. The broker stands in a fiduciary relationship to his client and is bound to exercise reasonable care, skill, and diligence in the performance of his duties. Trés Chic in a Week L.L.C. v. Home Realty Store, 993 So. 2d 228 (La. Ct. App. 1st Cir. 2008). The duties of a real estate licensee representing clients are set forth in La. R.S. 9:3893, which specifies in pertinent part:

A. A licensee representing a client shall:
   (1) Perform the terms of the brokerage agreement between a broker and the client.
   (2) Promote the best interests of the client by:
       (a) Seeking a transaction at the price and terms stated in the brokerage agreement or at a price and upon terms otherwise acceptable to the client.
       (b) Timely presenting all offers to and from the client, unless the client has waived this duty.

(c) Timely accounting for all money and property received in which the client has, may have, or should have had an interest.

(3) Exercise reasonable skill and care in the performance of brokerage services.

B. A licensee representing a client does not breach a duty or obligation to the client by showing alternative properties to prospective buyers or tenants or by showing properties in which the client is interested to other prospective buyers or tenants.

C. A licensee representing a buyer or tenant client does not breach a duty or obligation to that client by working on the basis that the licensee shall receive a higher fee or compensation based on a higher selling price.

D. A licensee shall not be liable to a client for providing false information to the client if the false information was provided to the licensee by a customer unless the licensee knew or should have known the information was false.

E. Nothing in this Section shall be construed as changing a licensee's legal duty as to negligent or fraudulent misrepresentation of material information. . . .

Ultimately, the precise duties of a real estate broker must be determined by an examination of the nature of the task the real estate broker undertakes to perform and by the agreements the broker makes with the involved parties. . . .

Under La. R.S. 9:3893, a real estate licensee has a duty to exercise reasonable skill and care in the performance of brokerage services. As set forth above, La. 37:1449.1 provides that a licensee representing either the buyer or the seller of residential property shall complete the purchase agreement form prescribed by the Louisiana Real Estate Commission in making an offer to purchase or sell residential real property. The plaintiffs have pled that Dowling breached its duty to the plaintiffs in several ways. They claim that Dowling breached its duty to professionally represent the plaintiffs, failed to negotiate the sale, failed to produce a contract that was approved by the Louisiana Real Estate Commission, failed to review all purchase offers, failed to follow up on remaining details of the sale, failed to discuss financing alternatives appropriate for the property, and failed to work to successfully close the sale. The plaintiffs maintain that they alleged that it is customary for a real estate broker to represent an unrepresented buyer. According to the plaintiffs, the main breaches occurred when Dowling failed to complete a purchase agreement form between the Rangels and the Curtises and in failing to tell the Rangels not to move out of the house before the Curtises were approved for their loan. The plaintiffs claim that they would not have moved if Dowling had told them this.

In this matter, accepting the facts in the petition and annexed documents as true, making all reasonable inferences in favor of the plaintiffs, and not examining any evidence to support or controvert the exception, we find that the plaintiffs did state a cause of action against Dowling and the trial court erred in ruling otherwise. While we find that the plaintiffs have articulated a cause of action, we also note that, on a motion for summary judgment or at trial, either party may present expert testimony concerning the duty, or lack thereof, of a real estate agent or broker to his contracted seller, as well as developing the facts, communications, and circumstances to show the breach of any duty owed to the plaintiffs and whether damages resulted from the breach. Accordingly, we find that the trial court erred in sustaining the exception of no cause of action in this case.

CONCLUSION

We reverse the trial court decision sustaining the exception of no cause of action filed by the defendant, J. Wesley Dowling and Associates, Inc. The exception of no cause of action is overruled and the matter is remanded to the trial court for further proceedings. Costs in this court are assessed to Dowling.

Problem 2C

Now that you have completed your legal studies and have passed the bar examination, your cousin Vinnie calls you for some free legal advice. It seems that cousin Vinnie has won $400,000 in the lottery and is in the market for a new home. In the absence of this good luck, Vinnie would not be buying a home. In fact, Vinnie, age 38, has lived at home with his parents all his life. This will be his first adventure into home ownership. In order to get started Vinnie wants your advice on the advisability of using a buyer's broker. Vinnie wants to know what it means to be a buyer's broker, as he has friends who have purchased homes and just contacted a broker who showed them a lot of homes until they found what they liked. Wouldn't any broker engaged by Vinnie be a buyer's broker? In explaining the concept of a buyer's broker, please inform Vinnie about alternative arrangements that he should consider. Explain the broker's obligations to Vinnie in each of the different potential arrangements.

B. BROKERS' DUTIES TO NONCLIENTS

HOLMES v. SUMMER
Court of Appeal, Fourth District, California, 2010
116 Cal. Rptr. 3d 419

MOORE, Justice. Particularly in these days of rampant foreclosures and short sales, "[t]he manner in which California's licensed real estate brokers and salesmen conduct business is a matter of public interest and concern." Wilson v. Lewis, 165 Cal. Rptr. 396, 398 (Ct. App. 1980). When the real estate professionals involved in the purchase and sale of a residential property do not disclose to the buyer that the property is so greatly overencumbered that it is almost certain clear title cannot be conveyed for the agreed[-]upon price, the transaction is doomed to fail. Not only is the buyer stung, but the marketplace is disrupted and the stream of commerce is impeded. When properties made unsellable by their debt load are listed for sale without appropriate disclosures and sales fall through, purchasers become leery of the marketplace and lenders preparing to extend credit to those purchasers waste valuable time in processing useless loans. In the presently downtrodden economy, it behooves us all for business transactions to come to fruition and for the members of the public to have confidence in real estate agents and brokers.

The case before us presents the interesting question of whether the real estate brokers representing a seller of residential real property are under an obligation to the buyers of that property to disclose that it is overencumbered and cannot in fact be sold to them at the agreed[-]upon purchase price unless either the lenders agree to short sales or the seller deposits a whopping $392,000 in cash into escrow to cover the shortfall. Here, the buyers and the seller agreed to the purchase and sale of a residential real property for the price of $749,000. Unbeknownst to the buyers, the property was subject to a first deed of trust in the amount of $695,000, a second deed of trust in the amount of $196,000 and a third deed of trust in the amount of $250,000, for a total debt of $1,141,000, and the lenders had not agreed to accept less than the amounts due under the loans in order to release their deeds of trust. According to the buyers, after they signed the deal with the seller, they sold their existing home in order to enable them to complete the purchase of the seller's property. Only then did they learn that the seller could not convey clear title because the property was overencumbered.

In a lawsuit against the seller's brokers, the trial court sustained a demurrer without leave to amend, holding that the brokers owed no duty of disclosure to the buyers. The buyers appeal. We reverse, holding that, under the facts of this case, the brokers were obligated to disclose to the buyers that there was a substantial risk that the seller could not transfer title free and clear of monetary liens and encumbrances.

FACTS

Phil and Jenille Holmes (buyers) made the following allegations in their first amended complaint against Sieglinde Summer and Beneficial Services, Inc. (collectively brokers). Summer is a licensed real estate broker who represented the seller of certain residential real property located in Huntington Beach, California. Summer was employed by Beneficial Services, Inc., which operated a Re/Max office in Huntington Beach.

The brokers listed the property for sale on a multiple listing service, advertising a price of $749,000 to $799,000. The listing noted that the seller was motivated and that Summer would receive a 3 percent commission for the sale. The buyers saw the listing on the multiple listing service Web site and became interested in the property. Summer showed them the property, and made no mention of any encumbrances on the property that might affect the ability of the seller to sell at the advertised price.

The buyers offered to purchase the property for $700,000, free and clear of all monetary liens and encumbrances other than a new loan in the amount of $460,000, escrow to close in 60 days. The brokers prepared a counter offer on the seller's behalf, with a sales price of $749,000 and a 30-day escrow. The buyers accepted the counter offer. The counter offer did not disclose that the property was subject to three deeds of trust totaling $1,141,000. Unbeknownst to the buyers at the time they signed the purchase documents, the property could not be transferred to them free and clear of all monetary liens and encumbrances, other than their own purchase money deed of trust, because the existing debt on the property far exceeded the purchase price. The buyers suffered damage in an amount to be proven at trial.

The first amended complaint asserted causes of action for negligence, for negligent misrepresentation, and for deceit — based on both misrepresentation and the failure to disclose. The brokers filed a demurrer. They argued that the lawsuit was a disguised effort to require the brokers to guarantee the seller's performance. They also asserted that if the seller decided to sell the property at a loss, such that it would have to come up with cash to close the transaction, but then changed its mind, that was a business decision for which the brokers could not be held liable.

In their opposition to the demurrer, the buyers stated that Summer had admitted both that she knew about the excess debt when she listed the property on the multiple listing service and that she did not disclose the excess debt to the buyers. The buyers also alleged that Summer was actually attempting to arrange a "short sale," which would have required the lenders to accept less money than was owing to them in order to retire the debt against the property. In addition, the buyers asserted that, during escrow, the lenders refused to discount the loans and demanded full payment before they would release their liens against the property.

The court sustained the demurrer without leave to amend and ordered the dismissal of the first amended complaint. Judgment was entered accordingly.

Discussion

. . . .

According to the allegations, the brokers represented that the property could be purchased for $749,000, and indeed negotiated a sale for that price, even though they knew that the property was encumbered with $1,141,000 in debt. In other words, the brokers knew that the property could not in fact be sold, for the price of $749,000, free and clear of monetary liens and encumbrances, unless either two or more lenders agreed to discount the debt on the property by a total amount of $392,000 or the seller put at least $392,000 in cash into the escrow in order to pay off the lenders. $392,000 is not exactly "chump change." This is a substantial amount of money either for lenders to [forgo] collecting or for a seller to "cough up," so to speak. Furthermore, the seller had to gain the cooperation of not just one, but two or more lenders to obtain the necessary debt relief. Considering the magnitude of the discrepancy between the sales price and the total debt on the property, the buyers argue the brokers were obligated to disclose the excess debt because it indicated a substantial risk, over and above that inherent in the routine residential sales transaction, that the escrow would not close.

The brokers, on the other hand, argue that they were precluded from disclosing the financial issues affecting the transaction. They say that for them to have made the disclosure in question would have required them to disclose the seller's confidential financial information or its strategy in determining the price at which it would be willing to sell. The brokers also assert that it would have required them to disclose that the seller might lose money on the property. . . .

As the buyers point out, "It is now settled in California that where the seller knows of facts materially affecting the value or desirability of the property which are known or accessible only to him and also knows that such facts are not known to, or within the reach of the diligent attention and observation of the buyer, the seller is under a duty to disclose them to the buyer." *Lingsch v. Savage*, 29 Cal. Rptr. 201, 204 (Ct. App. 1963). When the seller's real estate agent or broker is also aware of such facts, "he [or she] is under the same duty of disclosure." *Id.* at 205. A real estate agent or broker may be liable "for mere nondisclosure since his [or her] conduct in the transaction *amounts to a representation of the nonexistence of the facts which he has failed to disclose.*" *Id.* (emphasis in original).

According to the buyers, the monetary liens and encumbrances on the property affected both the value and the desirability of the property. Because the brokers were aware of the magnitude of the debt, and should have known that the buyers were not aware of the same, the brokers had a duty to disclose the problem. By their silence, the brokers represented the nonexistence of any impediments to the transfer of title free and clear of monetary liens and encumbrances. The brokers, on the other hand, contend there is no connection between the amount of debt on the property and the value or desirability of the property, at least where, as here, the seller agrees to sell the property free and clear of monetary liens and encumbrances. In other words, the physical characteristics and intrinsic desirability of the property are distinct from the financing.

The latter viewpoint misses the big picture. While a buyer may be harmed by acquiring title to a property with undisclosed defects, such as hazardous waste or soils subsidence problems, a buyer may also be harmed by entering into an escrow to purchase property when it is highly likely that, unbeknownst to the buyer, the escrow will never close. . . .

Although the duty to disclose a physical property defect is not at issue, we observe that real estate agents or brokers have been held to have a duty to disclose matters that do not pertain to physical defects, but otherwise affect the desirability of the purchase. *See, e.g.,* Alexander v. McKnight, 9 Cal. Rptr. 2d 453 (Ct. App. 1992) (duty to disclose neighborhood nuisance); Reed v. King, 193 Cal. Rptr. 130 (Ct. App. 1983) (duty to disclose murders on the property); Lingsch v. Savage, *supra* (duty to disclose that improvements were constructed in violation of building codes or zoning regulations). . . .

We observe that the *Code of Ethics and Standards of Practice of the National Association of Realtors* (2010), in the introductory words preceding the preamble, states: "While the Code of Ethics establishes obligations that may be higher than those mandated by law, in any instance where the Code of Ethics and the law conflict, the obligations of the law must take precedence." The solution to the conflict between the duty to disclose and the duty to maintain client confidentiality is clear. When the duty of fairness to all parties requires the disclosure to the buyer of confidential information reflecting a substantial risk that the escrow will not close, then the seller's real estate agent or broker must obtain the seller's permission to disclose such confidential information to the buyer, before the buyer enters into a contract to purchase the property. In a case such as the one before us, where the seller's financial situation is so precarious, if the seller is unwilling to consent to the disclosure of confidential information, and the real estate agent or broker nonetheless chooses to undertake representation of the seller, he or she does so at the peril of liability in the event the transaction goes awry due to the undisclosed risks involved. Of course, in this case, the brokers could have disclosed the existence of the deeds of trust of record without disclosing any confidential information. . . .

. . . [W]e conclude that the brokers in the matter before us had a duty to disclose to the buyers the existence of the deeds of trust of record, of which the brokers allegedly were aware. When a seller's real estate agent or broker is aware that the existing amount of debt on the residential real property being sold far exceeds the sales price of the property, such that either the lender's consent to a substantial discount of the debt will be required or the seller will need to put a considerable amount of cash into the escrow in order to be able to clear the debt and convey title free and clear, there is a duty on that agent or broker to disclose the state of affairs to the buyer, so the buyer can make an informed choice whether or not to enter into a transaction that has a considerable risk of failure. . . .

. . . The seller's agents, here the brokers, had a duty to disclose that third[-]party approvals were required before the sale could be consummated, unless of course the brokers had reason to believe that the seller had at least $392,000 in cash available to close escrow.

By so holding, we do not convert the seller's fiduciary into the buyer's fiduciary. The seller's agent under a listing agreement owes the seller "[a] fiduciary duty of utmost care, integrity, honesty, and loyalty. . . ." Civ. Code

§2079.16. Although the seller's agent does not generally owe a fiduciary duty to the buyer, he or she nonetheless owes the buyer the affirmative duties of care, honesty, good faith, fair dealing and disclosure. . . .

The judgment is reversed. The buyers, appellants Phil and Jenille Holmes, shall recover their costs on appeal.

C. BROKER'S RIGHT TO A COMMISSION

In most sales transactions, the broker is paid his commission at closing, with the seller using part of the price paid by the buyer for this purpose. When the broker is paid this way, the legal question of when the broker earned the commission does not arise. The issue becomes important only if, for some reason, after the broker finds a potential buyer, the sale does not go forward to close.

In this type of situation, the general rule followed by a majority of American jurisdictions is favorable to the broker. The broker earns his commission when he produces a customer who is ready, willing, and able to purchase upon terms acceptable to the owner. This is interpreted to mean that the broker finishes his undertaking prior to closing, when he presents his client, the owner, with an acceptable written offer to purchase.

In spite of the general rule, sellers frequently defeat brokers' claims for commissions on sales that fail to close. One well-recognized exception to the general rule involves conditions set forth in the contract of sale. Most contracts have express conditions that, if not satisfied, give one or both parties the right to terminate the contract. If the sale fails to close due to an unsatisfied condition, the broker is generally not entitled to a commission.

Sellers have also won many cases based on express contract. The basic rule that the commission is earned when a buyer is found is subject to modification by the parties. The broker and the seller are free to replace the implied rule with an express provision of their own. A savvy seller would negotiate for a term making closing an express condition to payment of the commission. Sellers, however, infrequently do this. For residential sales, they almost never are represented by a lawyer in connection with the listing agreement, and for commercial sales, they also often forgo legal representation at this stage. As a result, brokers generally control the terms of the listing agreement, using standardized agreements prepared by local or state brokers' associations or in-house forms prepared by or for the broker's office.

Beginning with New Jersey in Ellsworth Dobbs, Inc. v. Johnson, 236 A.2d 843 (N.J. 1967), a number of courts have protected sellers simply by overruling the traditional doctrine. Under the new minority rule, for the broker to earn the commission, not only must he find a ready, willing, and able buyer, but also the sale must close. If the buyer defaults, no commission is payable. There is one exception to the new rule. If the failure to complete the sale is caused by the seller's wrongful default or interference, then a commission is payable. The reasoning is that the seller should not be able to deprive the broker of his commission by refusing to go forward. This rule is an emerging trend, although most states still follow the traditional rule. In states following the trend, it is sometimes not clear whether the parties retain freedom of contract to replace the new implied rule with a pro-broker term. For example, can the broker expressly contract for the traditional rule, with the seller thus waiving the benefit of the new rule? One judicial view disallows such a contract on public policy grounds, reasoning that such a contract is unconscionable due to an inequality of bargaining position and knowledge between broker and customer. The *Ellsworth Dobbs* court took this position.

When considering a commission dispute, the presence of earnest money or a down payment paid by the buyer is an additional consideration to bear in mind. If a buyer defaults after signing a contract, the earnest money is often forfeited to the seller. Many brokers' listing contracts expressly give the broker the right to take all or part of the commission out of the forfeited earnest money. This approach helps the seller, in that the seller does not have to come up with funds out-of-pocket to pay the commission. However, it may surprise a seller who did not pay close attention to the clause, which typically appears as boilerplate in the listing contract, the sales contract, or both.

Occasionally, the seller's agent or subagent has sought damages against a buyer who defaulted after signing a contract with the agent's principal. The theory is that the buyer's wrongful conduct has deprived the broker of the commission that he would have collected. Traditionally, the lack of an express contract barred such claims, based on the notion that liability should be predicated on privity. In addition, the broker had the alternative remedy of collecting the commission from the seller, even though the transaction had not closed. In turn, the seller who coughed up the commission generally had an action against the defaulting buyer for consequential damages.

Under the modern trend that insulates the seller from liability for the commission when the buyer defaults, it is much harder for the broker to collect a commission from the seller for a sale that does not close. Thus, there is greater incentive for brokers to pursue defaulting buyers. With the demise of the doctrine of privity in much of our law, some states have permitted brokers to recover based on contract and tort theories. Under contract analysis, an implied contract is found if the broker performs some services for the buyer. In exchange, the buyer has impliedly promised the broker that he will complete the transaction. Alternatively, recovery is justified by calling the broker a third-party beneficiary of the purchase agreement between the buyer and the seller. Under tort analysis, the defaulting buyer has engaged in tortious interference with contract. This is especially likely to succeed when the broker, such as a subagent who serves as a cooperating broker, has a working relationship with the buyer. The reasoning is that the buyer who defaults has tortiously interfered with the listing contract, pursuant to which the broker was to earn a commission. This deprives the broker of his prospective economic advantage.

HILLIS v. LAKE
Supreme Judicial Court of Massachusetts, 1995
658 N.E.2d 687

GREANEY, Justice. The plaintiffs [Duane Hillis and John Brady], partners in a real estate brokerage firm, brought this action in the Superior Court to recover a commission on a sale of real estate. The complaint asserted claims of breach of contract, quantum meruit, and a violation of G.L. c.93A, §11 (1994 ed.). The case was tried before a judge sitting without a jury. The judge concluded that the plaintiffs were entitled to a commission with interest and, on her finding of a violation of G.L. c.93A, an award of attorney's fees. The Appeals Court reversed the judgment. . . . We also conclude, in substantial agreement with the reasoning of the Appeals Court, that the plaintiffs were not entitled to a commission. . . . We also take the opportunity to state that Bennett v. McCabe, 808 F.2d 178 (1st Cir. 1987), on which the plaintiffs rely, and which supports their position, is not a correct statement of Massachusetts law on the point with which we are concerned.

. . . Donald Lake, and his wife, Joanna, in their capacity as trustees of Lakeland Park Trust (defendants), were the owners of a parcel of real estate in Peabody which they had purchased in 1984, with the intent of developing the land as an industrial park. Before purchasing the property, Lake had it examined for the presence of hazardous materials as defined by G.L. c.21E. Hazardous materials were not found. Lake also owned a construction company, and his intention in developing the park was to build to suit for prospective tenants. John Brady, a partner in a commercial real estate firm, met Lake in 1986, while Brady was seeking a suitable site for a building for his client, Federal Express. An agreement was concluded between Lake and Federal Express, which became one of the first tenants of the industrial park.

After this successful collaboration, at Lake's request, Brady became the exclusive broker for the industrial park. The agreement between Lake and Brady was oral. It was understood that Lake was only interested in tenants for whom he would construct a building, and who, after construction was completed, might lease or purchase outright the resulting structure. Brady's commissions were to be five percent of the gross sale price.

FIRST AGREEMENT

Around April, 1988, Brady received an inquiry from the vice-president of Patriot Properties, Inc. (Patriot), who indicated that the company wanted to construct an office building. Brady showed the property in Peabody to principals of the company, and he arranged a meeting between Lake and

Patriot's principals. On June 14, 1988, a purchase and sale agreement was executed between Patriot and the defendants for the purchase of land and a building constructed to Patriot's specifications. The purchase price was set at $1,810,000. The agreement provided for a broker's commission of $54,300, payable "if and provided the Closing occurs as herein described."[4] With a $400,000 construction mortgage from the Bank of New England in hand, Lake's construction company commenced construction of the building. At all times, Patriot's principals intended to seek additional investors in the project. It was anticipated that Patriot's principals would own a thirty-seven and one-half percent interest in the project and two other investors would own the remainder.

The purchase and sale agreement obligated Patriot to provide a mortgage commitment letter to the defendants. By a letter dated September 28, 1988, First American Bank issued a financing commitment in the amount of $1,410,000. A condition of the commitment was a requirement that, at the option of the bank, it would be provided with evidence that the property did not contain any hazardous materials. In response to this requirement, the defendants and Patriot executed an addendum to the purchase and sale agreement, in which the defendants warranted that the property was free of hazardous materials.[5] The bank, nonetheless, insisted on an inspection, which disclosed the presence of contamination in the ground water.[6] The bank withdrew its financing commitment, and the investors other than Patriot also withdrew from participation in the project. Patriot, however, which had been occupying the already completed building rent free for several months, remained interested in completing the purchase.

SECOND AGREEMENT

By June, 1989, Patriot had located another investor, Ro-Jo Realty Trust, whose principals agreed to acquire a twenty-five percent interest in the project. As had been the case under the first agreement, Patriot's principals would acquire a thirty-seven and one-half percent interest in the project. To conclude the transaction, Lake himself agreed to acquire the remaining thirty-seven and one-half percent interest in the project. A joint venture was formed, known as the Five Lakeland Park Partners, which became the sole beneficiary of a newly organized trust, the Five Lakeland Park Trust.

4. Brady had agreed to reduce his commission to three percent of the purchase price. The plaintiffs did not sign the purchase and sale agreement.

5. In signing the addendum, Patriot acknowledged receipt of a copy of the report on the G.L. c.21E inspection that had been conducted in 1984, in conjunction with the defendants' purchase of the property. Patriot also agreed to assume the cost of further inspections for hazardous materials.

6. It was subsequently determined that gasoline had leaked from an underground tank installed by Federal Express in connection with its business operation in the industrial park. The judge made no finding that the defendants knew about the leak or about contamination from any other source, and no such finding would have been warranted.

Each of the three partners contributed a share in the initial capitalization ($500,000) of the project in proportion to his, or its, interest in the project. On June 13, 1989, the building and land were sold by the defendants to Five Lakeland Park Trust for $1,810,000. The parties did not obtain financing for the deal from a third party. Lake himself financed the transaction. The buyer paid $400,000 in cash, and executed a mortgage note to the defendant in the amount of $1,410,000, secured by a purchase money mortgage on the property. An agreement concluded simultaneously with the sale provided that:

> [i]f, on or before [June 12, 1991] the Seller delivers to the Buyer a report of a qualified environmental scientist or engineer . . . stating that there is no evidence of hazardous waste or oil . . . present on the Property . . . the Buyer shall exercise its best efforts to pay the unpaid principal balance and accrued interest due on the [mortgage note] as soon as is reasonably practical. . . . If the Seller has not delivered the Report . . . to the Buyer on or before [June 12, 1991], the Buyer, at its option, may elect to require the Seller to repurchase the Property from the Buyer for the sum of [$1,810,000].

The defendants used the $400,000 in cash received at the time of the sale to pay off the construction mortgage held by the Bank of New England. From June 13, 1989, through approximately October 3, 1991, monthly payments were made by Five Lakeland Park Trust on the mortgage notes. Lake contributed his pro rata share to these payments. At the end of two years, the defendants were not able to produce certification that the contamination on the property had been cleaned up. In keeping with the June 13, 1989, agreement, the defendants repurchased the property and discharged the mortgage. The $400,000 cash contribution was refunded to the investors in proportion to their shares in the project. The plaintiffs received no commission on the June 13, 1989, sale of the property.

Based on these facts, the judge concluded that the sale contemplated in the first agreement "did not close in accordance with the parties' contract only because of the seller's inability to back up its promise that the land was free of toxic materials such as gasoline." This lapse on the defendants' part was sufficient, in the judge's view, to require payment of a broker's commission to the plaintiffs. We do not agree that the conditions for payment of a broker's commission were met.

> When a broker is engaged by an owner of property to find a purchaser for it, the broker earns his commission when (a) he produces a purchaser ready, willing and able to buy on the terms fixed by the owner, (b) the purchaser enters into a binding contract with the owner to do so, and (c) the purchaser completes the transaction by closing the title in accordance with the provisions of the contract.

Tristram's Landing, Inc. v. Wait, 327 N.E.2d 727, 731 (Mass. 1975), *quoting* Ellsworth Dobbs, Inc. v. Johnson, 236 A.2d 843, 855 (N.J. 1967). The third requirement was not met here because no closing occurred under the first agreement.

The requirement that the sale actually be consummated, however, is subject to an exception. We have said that a broker has an enforceable claim when the first two requirements are met but "the failure of completion of the contract results from the wrongful act or interference of the seller." *Id.* . . .

The exception does not apply to this case. The defendants had not agreed to remove hazardous materials from the property. As the Appeals Court observed:

> The Addendum provided that the failure of the defendants' representation was an occasion only for Patriot's right to terminate the agreement, not for a claim to damages for a wilful default in the obligations of the defendants. Any failure of the defendants' representation was to be regarded as the same as the failure of Patriot, for example, to obtain a mortgage commitment letter: each event was an occasion to terminate the transaction without fault by or liability to either party.

646 N.E.2d at 1085. We agree with this analysis. The judge did not find, and no such finding would have been warranted on the evidence, that the failure of the sale was the product of any bad faith or wrongful interference by the defendants. We conclude that the failure of the first agreement was not caused by any wrongful conduct on the defendants' part.

As the Appeals Court correctly recognized, the plaintiffs would still be entitled to a commission "if the second agreement was merely different from the first agreement in form, not substance, and if there was a closing on that agreement, or a wilful default by the defendants." *Id.* at 1085-86. *See* Bonin v. Chestnut Hill Towers Realty Corp., 466 N.E.2d 90, 95 (Mass. 1984) (commission due when transaction, "while different in form, conformed in substance to the terms of the agreement"). Here, the second agreement differed substantially from the first agreement, and the difference rendered the second agreement substantially less favorable to the defendants than the first agreement had been.

Under the first agreement, the defendants would have been guaranteed a return of $1,810,000 minus the cost of their investment in the project. That investment would have consisted only of some portion of the original purchase price of the property and the approximately $400,000 cost of constructing the building to Patriot's specifications. Any risk of default by the purchaser would have rested with the bank which loaned the funds to Patriot and its fellow investors to make the purchase. In contrast, the second agreement required that the defendants assume virtually all of the financial risk associated with the project. The financial risk to the defendants under the second agreement was twofold. Because the defendants were the holders of the mortgage on the property, the risk of default by the purchaser fell wholly on the defendants. In addition, the sale under the second agreement was contingent: if the defendants were unable to provide assurance, within two years, that contamination on the property had been eliminated, the sale would be rescinded. That these financial risks to the defendants were significant is proved by the fact that the sale was rescinded in 1991. Moreover, under the second agreement, instead of an outright conveyance of the entire property, Lake was required to retain a thirty-seven and one-half percent interest in the project, which might or might not have proved profitable, but which created additional financial risks and apparently was not an investment envisioned during the discussions between Brady and Lake.[7] Clearly, the second agreement, which would appear attributable to some desperation on the defendants' part, differed in substance from the first agreement. Thus, we agree with the Appeals Court that the plaintiffs were not entitled to a commission on the basis of the sale under the second agreement.[8]

We comment briefly on Bennett v. McCabe, 808 F.2d 178 (1st Cir. 1987). In that case, the parties executed a purchase and sale agreement for the purchase of a motel. The real estate broker received a ten percent deposit from the buyer which was held in escrow pending the closing. Prior to the closing, the parties discovered a defect in title which no one knew of previously. When the seller was unable to correct the defect in a timely manner, the seller asked the broker to return the deposit to the prospective purchaser. The broker declined and brought an action in the United States District Court for the District of Massachusetts seeking to recover a broker's commission. The District Court granted summary judgment for the defendants on the basis of Tristram's Landing v. Wait, *supra*. The United States Court of Appeals for the First Circuit reversed. The Court of Appeals detected a "gray area" in the *Tristram's Landing* decision concerning a default by a seller that did not amount to wrongful acts or interference. *Id.* at 181. The Court of Appeals held that the seller would be liable for a broker's commission even if the seller's default was innocent, concluding that this court would adopt this conclusion if it were faced with facts like those in the *Bennett* case. *Id.* at 182. In so doing, the Court of Appeals assumed that this court would prefer a "bright line rule" which would award a broker the commission when the

7. Under the agreement between Brady and Lake, the defendants would have been required to pay a commission in the absence of an outright sale if a tenant was found who was willing (like Federal Express) to enter into a long-term lease on a building constructed to the prospective lessor's specifications. The second agreement was not analogous to a long-term lease.

8. The plaintiffs place weight on a June 2, 1989, letter written by Lake to Brady that terminated the parties' brokerage agreement. In the letter, Lake also indicated that he intended to pay any commissions due to the plaintiffs and noted: "We have already discussed Patriot Properties and that commission will be paid as soon as possible." There was conflicting testimony on the content of the discussion between Lake and Brady to which the letter referred. As the Appeals Court noted, "[i]n particular, it is unclear whether, or the extent to which, the restructured deal of June 12th was fully formed on June 2d, and, if so, what impact the new structure was to have on the plaintiffs' right to a commission."646 N.E.2d at 1084 n.9. In view of our conclusion that, as a matter of law, the plaintiffs were not entitled to a commission in the circumstances present here, we give no significance to Lake's ambiguous promise to pay.

seller defaults on a binding purchase and sale agreement whether the default is innocent or motivated by bad faith. *Id.* at 183-84.

The *Bennett* decision does not state Massachusetts law correctly. . . . In circumstances like those present in this case and in the *Bennett* case, the broker is not entitled to a commission unless it appears that the closing is prevented by wrongful conduct on the seller's part. . . .

The judgment is reversed, and a new judgment is to enter in favor of all defendants on the counts in the plaintiffs' complaint.

Problem 2D

Ted and Karen Troop list their four-bedroom colonial home for sale with Brandy, a local broker. On January 10 they sign an exclusive listing agreement, with a term of four months, a selling price of $380,000, and a commission of 5 percent. On February 23, Brandy presents a contract from Sam for $358,000, along with a check for $5,000 of earnest money made payable to a local title company. The Troops accept the contract and sign it, but the transaction never closes. In which of the following situations has Brandy earned a commission? If Brandy has earned a commission, when is it payable?

(a) The reason the transaction never closes is that Sam changes his mind and defaults.

(b) The reason the transaction never closes is that Sam has a poor credit history, and even though he has a high-paying job, he is turned down for a mortgage loan.

(c) The reason the transaction never closes is that the Troops change their mind about selling their house. They negotiate a rescission with Sam, which provides for the return of his earnest money plus the Troops' payment to Sam of an additional $2,000.

(d) The reason the transaction never closes is that the title search discloses an easement on the property, to which Sam objects.

D. BROKERS AND LAWYERS

1. Unauthorized Practice of Law

The core of a broker's work in helping a client to sell or buy real estate consists of marketing and negotiation, but it often goes beyond these measures. Many of the steps required to complete a sale have legal aspects. To be licensed, one of the subjects brokers must study and pass an examination on is real estate law. The line between a broker's expertise as a market intermediary and as an advisor on matters that may have legal consequence is sometimes difficult to define. If a broker is not to engage in the practice of law, a line must be drawn somehow and somewhere. This gives rise to several questions. What are a broker's proper activities, and when has he engaged in the unauthorized practice of law? May the broker draft the contract of sale? Help the buyer obtain financing? Perform title clearing work? Prepare deeds and other closing documents?

Over the years, many state and local bar associations have challenged broker practices as constituting the unauthorized practice of law. Consequently, courts have struggled with the problem of defining the limits on the broker's role. Earlier courts often prohibited brokers from completing any instruments affecting the legal rights of sellers and buyers, whether standard forms or not. Most states now permit brokers to prepare standard-form contracts of sale for customers, at least in some circumstances. In many states, the standard contracts must be approved by a bar association or a licensed attorney. The following three tests are widely used today to define the scope of brokers' services with respect to document preparation:

Contracts Versus Conveyances Test. The broker may prepare the contract of sale or earnest money contract between the parties and other ancillary documents, such as a loan application or escrow instructions, but may not prepare closing instruments that convey interests in land.

Simple-Complex Test. If the transaction is simple and straightforward, a broker is permitted to select standard-form instruments and assist the parties in filling in blanks. The broker cannot furnish documents for a complex transaction or an unusual feature of a simple transaction, such as creation of an easement.

Incidental Test. Broker drafting of instruments is authorized if it is incidental to the broker's business and the party pays no separate charge for this service.

Problem 2E

Stan is selling his house to Patricia. The closing, conducted by a title company officer, is attended by both parties, the listing broker, and the selling broker. Neither party is represented by an attorney. Patricia says, "I want to know whether there are covenants and restrictions on the property." The listing broker says, "Yes, haven't you seen them?" and hands her a copy of the recorded neighborhood covenants (eight pages in length). Patricia asks whether she can put a swimming pool in the backyard. How should the brokers respond?

Does it make a difference whether the selling agent is a subagent, representing Stan, or a buyer's broker, representing Patricia? Would it make a difference if, instead of a question related to recorded covenants, Patricia asks the brokers, "I've recently heard about a lot of homes having mold problems, and that can be a huge problem. I haven't had a mold inspection. Is it too late? What do you think I should do?"

2. *Lawyers Acting as Brokers*

Statutes that provide for the regulation of brokers typically provide exemptions for certain persons — for instance, persons representing themselves, fiduciaries, auctioneers, and newspapers. Attorneys are exempt in almost all states, but the scope of the exemption varies. Some states confer on attorneys a total exemption from the licensing requirements, allowing them to collect commissions for finding buyers or arranging other transactions. In most states, the exemption is limited to brokerage services that are incidental to the attorney's law practice. Thus, an attorney can sell or rent property only for clients for whom his primary work is the provision of legal services.

In re *ROTH*
Supreme Court of New Jersey, 1990
577 A.2d 490

PER CURIAM. This is an attorney-disciplinary matter. Respondent, Lee B. Roth, was found to have violated our ethics rules by attempting to obtain a real estate commission in a transaction in which he also served as the attorney for a prospective buyer of residential real estate. The case impels us to determine the appropriate ethics standards governing an attorney who undertakes to represent a client as both attorney and real estate broker in the same transaction.

The charges in this case were brought before the District XIII Ethics Committee (DEC), which found that respondent's conduct in representing a client as both an attorney and real estate broker reflected adversely on his fitness to practice law in violation of Disciplinary Rule (DR) 1-102(A)(6), which provided that "[a] lawyer shall not . . . [e]ngage in any other conduct that adversely reflects on his fitness to practice law". . . .

I

Respondent has been a member of the New Jersey bar since 1962 and is a well-respected authority on real estate law. Although at the time this matter arose respondent had taken the course to become a real estate broker and had passed the examination administered to real estate salespeople, he was not a licensed real estate broker. In January 1984, a paralegal employed in respondent's law firm became interested in purchasing a house she had seen for sale located in Flemington, New Jersey. The listing price for the house was $123,900. The paralegal asked respondent to assist her in purchasing the house and in finding a way of lowering the purchase price.

Respondent told her that he would act as both her lawyer and broker in the transaction, and that as the selling real estate broker, he would be entitled to a fifty-percent share of the commission, which he would apply to a reduction in the purchase price. Respondent's client subsequently communicated with the real estate agency owned by Carl D. Bayuk, who was the listing broker. She expressed interest in the property and stated that respondent would act both as her attorney and as the selling real estate broker. Because he was confused about respondent's dual role as attorney and broker, Bayuk called respondent directly, and respondent explained to Bayuk that, as an attorney, he, respondent, was authorized to sell real estate without a broker's license and that he would be entitled to half of the six-percent commission.

offers

On January 20, 1984, respondent's client made a written offer of $114,000 to the sellers expressly conditioned on "the assumption that you have agreed to pay your real estate broker six percent (in this case $6,840) and that your real estate broker will divide the commission with our lawyer, who agrees that that commission be credited against the purchase price." That offer was rejected, as was a second offer, conditioned on the identical terms, for $118,500. Shortly thereafter, the property was sold to another buyer for the full listing price.

The listing real estate broker, Bayuk, subsequently filed an ethics complaint against respondent. At the hearing before the DEC, respondent stated that he had advised both his client and Bayuk that he would act as the attorney and the selling real estate broker. He testified that he did not intend to benefit personally from the arrangement and that his share of the real estate commission was to have been applied on behalf of his client to reduce the purchase price of the property.

The DEC found that respondent had not performed any brokerage services and therefore was not entitled to any brokerage commission. . . . [On appeal the Disciplinary Review Board] also concluded that respondent had violated [DR 1-102(A)(6)] and recommended that respondent be publicly reprimanded.

II

It is not unlawful or unethical per se for an attorney to engage in the business of a real estate broker. The Advisory Committee on Professional Ethics has concluded that an attorney who is also licensed as a broker may conduct business in both fields, so long as he or she separates the two. *See, e.g.*, Opinion 124, 91 N.J.L.J. 108 (1968). As the DEC noted below, "There would appear to be no impediment to respondent engaging in the real estate brokerage business upon obtaining a proper license and upon taking appropriate steps to separate such a brokerage business from his practice of law." An attorney who is not so licensed may also perform brokerage activities. Although the law governing the licensing of real estate brokers, N.J.S.A. 45:15-1 to -42, provides in pertinent part that "no person shall engage either directly or indirectly in the business of a real estate broker or salesman . . . without being licensed," it exempts certain classes of people, including attorneys, from that requirement. N.J.S.A. 45:15-4. Thus attorneys are authorized to engage in the business of a real estate broker or salesperson without being licensed as such. The primary question posed in this matter, however, is not whether respondent could lawfully undertake to perform brokerage activities, but whether in this transaction he compromised his professional responsibilities as an attorney by engaging in such dual activities and seeking dual compensation. . . .

Our courts have had few occasions to examine the statutory "attorney" exemption of N.J.S.A. 45:15-4. In Spirito v. New Jersey Real Estate Commission, 434 A.2d 623 (N.J. Super. Ct. 1981), the Appellate Division rejected the notion that the statutory exemption makes an attorney's license the equivalent of a real estate broker's license. The court declined to grant a real estate broker's license to an attorney who claimed a right to the license by virtue of the statutory exemption. It held that an attorney is not entitled to a broker's license without meeting the apprenticeship and licensing requirements of the real estate licensing law, N.J.S.A. 45:15-1 to -42. . . .

. . . [A]n attorney who does not hold a license under Title 45 but seeks to act as both a broker and a lawyer for the same client in the same transaction, must confine any broker's services to those that are obviously minor, incidental, ancillary, and subordinate to the legal services entailed in the client's representation. An unlicensed attorney who acts in a substantial capacity as a broker acts beyond the authority conferred by law under Title 45, and to that extent acts improperly as an attorney and in a manner that reflects adversely on the legal profession. DR 1-102(A)(6). . . .

In determining whether brokerage services may fairly be characterized as incidental to legal services, the compensability of such brokerage services is highly relevant. Common sense and ordinary experience tell us that an attorney who performs sufficient work as a broker to be entitled to a commission for those services would not be acting as broker in a manner only incidental to the normal practice of law. Conversely, an attorney performing brokerage services that are really only incidental to his or her work as a lawyer would not be entitled to a commission because . . . those incidental services would be substantially less significant than the "activities normally associated with a real estate broker." We therefore hold that an attorney whose actions as a broker are undertaken pursuant to the "attorney" exemption to the licensing law, N.J.S.A. 45:15-4, may perform brokerage services that are only incidental to the normal practice of law, which cannot be the basis for a claim of compensation as a broker. . . .

We acknowledge that it may be difficult to assess the professional mix of attorney and brokerage services in a given transaction to determine with any degree of confidence whether the latter is really only incidental to the former. Nevertheless, attorneys are expected and required to make that evaluation. Attorneys are held to a higher standard of ethical propriety than are members of the general public. . . . Accordingly, we conclude that an attorney is ethically obligated to perform only those brokerage services that are incidental or ancillary to the performance of legal services in a given transaction on behalf of the same client. It follows that in such situations, an attorney may not be independently and separately compensated for brokerage services.

III

. . . In addressing the areas of overlap between real estate brokers and attorneys, we have sought to draw a fairly bright line of separation. New Jersey State Bar Association v. New Jersey Association of Realtor Boards, 461 A.2d 1112 (N.J. 1983), exemplifies that concern. Just as we there guarded against brokers engaging in the unauthorized practice of law, here we concern ourselves with attorneys who engage in inappropriate or improper brokerage activities. Regardless of whether he or she is licensed as a broker, when an attorney seeks a real estate commission for his or her efforts on behalf of a client, the danger of conflict, actual, potential, or perceived, is great. . . .

As noted, respondent was not a licensed broker at the time he sought to obtain a portion of the broker's commission. Had he been licensed, however, his actions would have been prohibited by N.J.S.A. 45:15-17(i). That statutory provision proscribes "[c]ollecting a commission as a real estate broker in a transaction, when at the same time representing either party in a transaction in a different capacity for consideration." In Mortgage Bankers Association of New Jersey v. New Jersey Real Estate Commission, 491 A.2d 1317 (N.J. Super. Ct. 1985), *rev'd and remanded*, 506 A.2d 733 (N.J. 1986), the Appellate Division concluded that N.J.S.A. 45:15-17(i) prohibits a broker who receives a commission from the seller in a real estate transaction from also earning consideration for assisting the buyer in obtaining mortgage financing. In *Mortgage Bankers,* the court was concerned by the potential for a conflict of interest in situations involving dual compensation for dual representation. "We are thus persuaded that . . . the legislature's intent was to permit dual representation by consent but only if there was no dual compensation therefor." 491 A.2d at 1325. We see no lessened obligation when the dual representation and dual compensation involves that of broker and lawyer.

Although respondent testified that he did not intend to profit from the commission, the application of his commission on behalf of his client in this fashion might nevertheless have constituted an indirect benefit to respondent. Had the sale occurred, respondent's actions would arguably have been tantamount to his actually receiving a commission, notwithstanding his gift over to his client.

In sum, we conclude that an unacceptable conflict of interest is created if an attorney who is not licensed as a real estate broker claims or accepts a commission for participating as a broker in the purchase or sale of real estate if the attorney also represents one of the parties in the transaction. That conflict, however, may be overcome if the brokerage activities are incidental to the legal services rendered and do not generate any entitlement to compensation. We agree with amicus New Jersey Real Estate Commission that an attorney's real estate activities "must be limited to only those necessary to fulfill his legal representations of a client, but in no sense is he an actual real estate broker, nor should he be compensated as such."

IV

We are satisfied that an attorney who seeks to obtain a commission for brokerage services in connection with legal services rendered in the same transaction for the same client will have violated our ethics rules. In this case, respondent's conduct violated DR 1-102(A)(6); his conduct "reflects adversely on his fitness to practice law." Under our more recent Rules of Professional Conduct, we conclude that activities similar to respondent's would violate our Rules of Professional Conduct, prohibiting attorneys from representing clients in cases "involving conflict or apparent conflict," RPC 1.7(c), and in cases in which representation will result in a violation of "other law," RPC 1.16(a)(1).

An attorney who in the future violates the ethics standards as explained herein will assuredly be subject to professional discipline. We note that in the present case, however, respondent did not act nefariously or with venality. His dual role as attorney and broker was fully disclosed to all interested parties at the outset of respondent's involvement. He expressly informed complainant that he intended to apply his share of the commission to reduce the purchase price for his client. . . . Moreover, as amicus New Jersey State Bar Association emphasizes, there was no clear precedent governing or proscribing respondent's actions. That amicus also points out that other states, contrary to our own approach, *see, e.g.*, N.J.S.A. 45:15-17(i), permit attorneys to share commissions.

Both the dearth of relevant opinions and the lack of clear legislative or regulatory mandate support the perception that there was no "clear prohibition" of respondent's actions. We therefore conclude that respondent acted in the good-faith belief that his conduct did not violate disciplinary standards. Under these circumstances, this opinion is efficacious both to explain the nature of the underlying ethical misconduct and to discourage its repetition. Accordingly, we see no reason grounded in the public's confidence in the legal profession to impose formal discipline.

Problem 2F

Nathan and Paula own a two-story 4,000-square-foot home located on a ½ acre lot in the city. The home has five bedrooms and three bathrooms. It was ideal for raising their children. Now the children have all moved out and have their own lives and homes. While most of their children now live in different states, the middle child, Claire, lives about 20 miles away in a community with a mixed variety of housing options. Nathan and Paula have located a small one-level ranch style home that is about 800 square feet sitting on a ⅛ acre lot in the same community where Claire resides. They figure that they can sell the family home for about $600,000 and that the new house will cost them $125,000. They talked to a broker who says she will be happy to list the family home and work with them in buying the new home. The standard commission on selling a home is 6 percent and the broker will require Nathan and Paula to pay this amount on the sale of the family home. Even though Nathan and Paula will not be directly responsible for the broker commission on the new home they will purchase, they know that their broker will split a 6 percent commission that will be charged to the seller of that home by the seller's listing agent. Their broker has a form contract ready to go for the sale of the family home and another for the purchase of the new home. Nathan and Paula wonder if they should have a lawyer involved in the transaction and ask you if they should engage an attorney to review the contracts and advise on the deal. They tell you that their broker informed them that residential home sales are all done on standard forms approved by the local board of realtors and the county bar association. Thus, they wonder whether an attorney will add any value to their transactions or simply add to the cost of the sale and purchase. What advice will you give them? Can you explain the lawyer's duty to them as clients? They also want to know, if they consider hiring a lawyer, what a reasonable fee is for the lawyer's services: $250, $500, or something else?

Problem 2G

Gracie recently graduated from law school and is practicing real estate law. Though admitted to the state bar, she is not a licensed broker. The state Real Estate License Act has an attorney exemption, which provides: "nor shall this Act be construed to include in any way services rendered by an attorney at law."

Through a newspaper ad, Gracie finds a two-bedroom house at an asking price of $300,000. She calls the advertised phone number, reaching Steve, the listing broker. The property is listed with the local multiple listing service, with a total commission of 6 percent to be split equally between the listing broker and selling broker. Gracie sees the house and loves it. She drafts a contract of sale, offering $300,000, but with a provision stating: "Purchaser declares that she is representing herself as broker. Accordingly, Purchaser hereby claims a right to the 3 percent commission customarily paid to selling brokers." The contract of sale, as is typical in the community, has a signature blank for the brokers to sign. Gracie fully signs the contract and submits it to Steve. He not only refuses to sign the contract but also refuses to forward it to the owner,

Carl. Gracie therefore contacts Carl directly. Carl wants to accept the offer, but Steve insists that the offer is improper and unethical. One week later, Carl terminates his listing agreement with Steve, alleging that Steve violated his duties of loyalty. Carl promptly sells the house to Gracie for $287,000, and the parties close the transaction without using the services of any broker. Steve sues both Carl and Gracie, claiming they are jointly and severally liable for a 6 percent commission. What result?

3

Preparing to Contract

Contract law is an important cornerstone in the foundation of any real estate transaction. Real property law is a second cornerstone, interfacing with contract law in every transaction. The parties must come to some understanding concerning what will be exchanged and how and when the exchange will proceed. They must agree on the subject of their contract, which is often much more complicated than it might seem at first. Precise identification of the property under consideration involves issues of physical quantity and the legal quality of the estate. For example, as to quantity there may be questions of exactly how many acres or square feet the buyer should get; what fixtures and personal property stay with the property; and whether air, water, and mineral rights are included or excluded. As to quality of the estate, matters of fee simple versus life estates or long-term tenancy arrangements may come into play. Besides identifying the subject of the exchange, the parties must address many other issues in their negotiations, such as financing, title protection, and environmental and zoning compliance. There will be need for definitions, representations, warranties, conditions, inspections, investigations, and consequences in the event of any variety of planned or unplanned happenings.

In Chapter 1 we discuss a variety of risk factors that can have an effect on the potential value of a real estate transaction. We also discuss the relationship between risk and price. At this point, we must take a moment to recall these concepts as we consider the dynamics of contract preparation. The relationship between price and risk is such that the more risk a party has, the less valuable the transaction is to it. Risk, in this sense, is like a cost. When the contract terms allocate more risk to the buyer, the purchase price must be lowered. When more risk is allocated to the seller, the seller will desire an upward adjustment in the sales price. Thus, the buyer and the seller have inverse relationships in the tradeoff between risk and price.

This tradeoff is illustrated in Figure 3-1. In this diagram, price is on the horizontal axis and risk is on the vertical axis. The intersection of the horizontal and vertical axis is marked as point zero, reflecting a point of zero risk and zero price impact. Moving out along the price axis shows a rise in price from 0 to 20. Moving out along the risk axis shows a rise in risk factors from 0 to 20. The downward-sloping line for the buyer illustrates the idea that a buyer will be willing to pay a higher price for a property when the seller takes on more and more of the risk associated with the transaction. At the same time, it illustrates that the buyer will pay a lower price if she has to take on a lot of risk. A buyer would have a high degree of risk, for example, in the case of an "as is" sale. Similarly, the upward-sloping seller's line depicts the relationship between risk and price for the seller. The greater the risk to a seller, the higher the selling price; the lower the risk, the lower the selling price. The parties can negotiate tradeoffs anywhere along these lines. Moreover, different people might have different tolerances to risk or different abilities to effectively manage or lower risk or its consequences. In such situations, the parties may find it mutually beneficial to allocate risk to the least risk-averse party or the best risk avoider and have the least impact on cost and price. These kinds of tradeoffs will be an important part of the contract preparation period. This is especially true in transactions in which the parties do not already know each other well, because they will need to invest time through the negotiation process to learn about each other's risk/price tradeoff schedules.

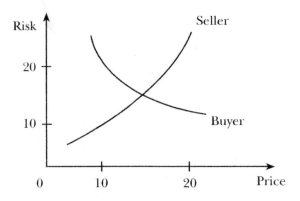

Figure 3-1
Relationship Between Risk and Price

A. REAL ESTATE TRANSACTIONS TIMELINE*

In preparing to enter into a contract for a real estate transaction, the parties and the lawyers must have a sense of what should or might happen after the contract is signed. They need to know where they are going. Thus, an overview of the entire contract process will help us develop a feel for the different stages involved. The diagram that follows depicts a timeline of contracting activities, broken down into four functional stages.

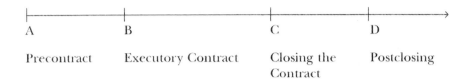

Figure 3-2
Contracting Activities Timeline

Understanding the "big picture" shown by this timeline will lead to effective lawyering. The good lawyer must negotiate and assess a transaction in the precontract stage with an understanding of all that might possibly follow. To best advise a client and to draft a complete and advantageous contract, the lawyer must contemplate and address all that might go wrong or become problematic at a later time during the covered relationship. To do this, one must first get a firm grasp of the issues, rules, and concerns that arise in each individual stage and then appreciate how they relate to the other stages. Ultimately, everything that is learned must be brought back to the precontract stage as a basis for informing the lawyer about the matters that must be discussed and clarified, so that the transaction will proceed smoothly and without any unfavorable surprises for the client. We will now briefly discuss the dynamics that generally characterize each of the four stages.

Time Period "A → B"

The precontract stage is characterized by information gathering and negotiation. The parties engage in activities designed to get information on a possible transaction. They explore market possibilities and the viability of alternative market choices.

Precontract negotiation begins when the potential parties have identified each other. During the course of negotiation, temporal risk concerning information continually challenges both parties. One must gather good information in order to assess the value of the transaction, and both the buyer and the seller are trying to maximize the informational advantage while hoping that the other side is not withholding important material to the contrary. Each side must seek to discover as much as possible on her own and also confront the issue of when it may be advantageous or obligatory to disclose particular information to the other party. The law may or may not be clear as to what has to be disclosed, when disclosure is required, and who must do the disclosing.

Time Period "B → C"

After completing the precontract negotiation stage, either the parties have aborted their plans to go forward or they have struck a deal, thereby entering the "executory contract" period. This period runs from the moment of entering into the contract until the moment of "closing" the contract. In a standard residential home sale, the gap in time between contracting and closing typically is anywhere from one to three months. In a commercial situation, the period might be much longer, perhaps as much as 6 to 18 months, or longer. The parties' contract is usually evidenced by some formal writing or writings that set out and establish their relationship to each other and to the property, and during the executory contract period the parties undertake to accomplish the tasks and fulfill the promises identified in their contract. The doctrine of *equitable conversion* applies at the time of fully executing the contract document. Under the doctrine of equitable conversion, title is split, with the legal title remaining in the seller and the equitable title in the buyer.

Time Period "C → D"

The parties complete their contractual undertakings by means of an activity known as *closing* or *settlement*, which puts an end to the executory contract stage. It is a time when the title that was split by the doctrine of equitable conversion is brought back together and is vested in the buyer as owner of the full interest conveyed by the seller. The closing is typically a meeting scheduled at the office of the lender, one of the attorneys, or the title company.

The actual process of closing can vary with the state or community where the property is located or the particular circumstances of the transaction. In many parts of the country, most closings are conducted as ceremonies where everybody gathers at a prearranged meeting time. In other areas, however, an alternative arrangement called an *escrow closing* is commonly used, which dispenses with the need for everyone to be physically present at once. With an escrow, each party can show up separately to deposit papers and money in escrow, with the closing officer having the responsibility of finishing the closing when everything is complete.

All the activity at closing centers around the formal acts of the buyer delivering the purchase price to the seller and the seller delivering the instrument of conveyance to the buyer. At closing, the *doctrine of merger* applies. The doctrine of merger provides that all promises prior to the closing are merged into the final documents taken at closing. Thus, warranties in the instrument of conveyance replace the warranties that were in the contract.

Time Period "D →"

The last stage in the real estate transaction is the postclosing period. This is the stage that reminds us that "the job isn't over until the paperwork is done." At the end of the closing meeting there will be many executed documents. Some of these documents, such as the warranty deed and any mortgage, will have to be recorded in the public records. In addition, certain things, like issuance of the final title insurance policy, cannot be completed until the necessary closing documents are officially available from the public records. All of this means that there are still parts of the deal to be completed after the formal closing. During this period, things can go wrong. Documents may get lost before being properly recorded, or documents may get misfiled or filed with the wrong attachments. These problems will delay the preparation of final title work and can seriously impair the completion of the transaction.

B. UNDERSTANDING THE CONSEQUENCES OF SIMPLE RULES

In preparing to contract, the lawyer must think carefully about the practical implications of simple legal rules. It is not enough to simply know the rules that govern real estate transfers; one must be able to respond to the implications behind the rules and take appropriate steps in contracting for any exchange. As an example of this process, consider one of the most basic rules of real property conveyancing. To have a valid conveyance of real property, the law requires that there be both a grantor and a grantee. The grantor is the party transferring the property, and the grantee is the party receiving the transfer or grant. A second simple rule of contract law states that a party to a contract ordinarily may assign her contractual rights to a third person. The assignee becomes the owner of the assignor's rights, but nothing more. Generally a person cannot transfer greater rights than she holds. Both the grantor-grantee rule and the assignment rule are straightforward and easy to memorize, but what are their implications for real estate contracting?

Problem 3A

(a) Your client Margaret seeks to purchase a property from ABC, Inc., for $3 million, which ABC will convey by warranty deed. How will you make sure that Margaret gets a proper conveyance? What documents will you need to see to assess the existence and authority of ABC to function as a proper grantor of the property?

[handwritten margin note: · proof of auth · good record title]

(b) Suppose the closing documents including the warranty deed are signed only by the vice president of ABC. Will that be sufficient for a proper conveyance? *depends on if auth*

(c) What, if anything, should the contract say about the nature of the deed of conveyance? Draft some provisions to put into a contract to make certain that you and your client have a right to see and approve any and all documents you believe are necessary to support the conveyance, and to clarify the mechanics of who will execute and transfer the property. *√ + to convey*

(d) Assume that your client Margaret enters into the contract to purchase ABC's property, with closing set for six months after contract execution. Two months after signing the contract Margaret agrees to assign the contract to Giovanni for a $250,000 profit. ABC objects to the assignment of the contract at a higher price to Giovanni and asserts that Margaret cannot do so without its permission. Do you understand the nature of ABC's objection? Do you believe that ABC, Inc. should have the right to prevent Margaret from assigning the contract or does Margaret have a right to assign the contract without any need for ABC's approval? What is the legal basis for your answer? If ABC cannot prevent this assignment, what should it do to enhance the likelihood that it can prevent such attempted assignments in future contracts?

(e) Now assume that you represent Giovanni in connection with the proposed assignment of the ABC contract from Margaret. First, what rights does Giovanni get when he takes an assignment from Margaret? Second, when Giovanni takes an assignment from Margaret, can ABC, Inc. legally refuse to close and avoid a transfer of the property to him? What risks do you perceive for Giovanni in taking an assignment and relying solely on reading a copy of the contract that Margaret provides him? What steps might you take in advising Giovanni about the risk of taking over a contract that has been in the executory stage for a stated period of time? In taking the assignment should Giovanni enter into an assignment agreement with Margaret; and if so, what provisions might you want in the contract of assignment to manage the identified risks?

(f) Suppose that you represented Margaret in connection with the negotiation and drafting of the ABC contract. After the contract is signed, Margaret and Giovanni begin to discuss the proposed assignment, and they decide that they could save a lot of money if they used one lawyer to do their transaction rather than each paying for a lawyer. Consequently, they ask you to represent both of them in connection with the assignment. How do you respond?

C. LETTERS OF INTENT, OPTIONS, AND CONTRACT ENFORCEABILITY

Sometimes people negotiate about a transaction and exchange written information without intending to enter into a binding agreement. There will be many occasions when people exchange various offers and counteroffers or when they submit in writing some, but not all, terms of a proposed offer. The more complex the transaction, the more likely that various written pieces of information will be exchanged so that the parties can make progress toward reaching an overall basis for agreement. The exchanges of such information raise some common legal problems. The first problem is identifying the point in time when mere negotiations become a binding contract. Another is to determine whether the writing is a contract for a real estate transfer or merely an option to purchase at a later date, on specific terms, when and if the option is exercised. Finally, problems arise concerning the *statute of frauds* and the *parol evidence rule*.

The parol evidence rule prohibits the admission of prior written or prior or contemporaneous oral evidence that adds to or is inconsistent with the final written agreement between the parties. This assumes that the parties intended the final written agreement to be fully integrated. Such a presumption is usually implied unless there is clear evidence to the contrary. Many standard written contracts include a term stating that the document is the full and complete agreement between the parties. Such a provision is an *integration clause* and is meant to raise the parol evidence bar.

The statute of frauds prohibits the enforcement of oral agreements unless there is a writing signed by the party to be charged. The writing must generally set out essential terms, such as the identification of the property to be exchanged, the price, and the names of the parties. These two legal doctrines are often related. A contract for the sale of real estate must be in writing, but the nature, extent, and scope of the required writing are often in dispute. Similarly, the writing may not state all the terms of the exchange, and the parties may be in disagreement about many of its details. Sometimes the parties will disagree about the very purpose of a writing. One party may assert that it forms the basis of an enforceable contract, while the other believes that it merely embraces some preliminary points of negotiation.

In a fundamental way, the key objectives of the letter of intent and the option contract are similar. Both arrangements seek a result that temporarily takes a property off the market while giving the buyer more time to consider the merits and demerits of a possible purchase. With a letter of intent, the parties generally proceed with an expectation that a very limited time will pass between the expression of intent to do a deal and the actual formulation of a binding contract to proceed with such an undertaking. In addition, the letter of intent is usually given without financial consideration. In contrast, an option is usually granted on the basis of money paid in exchange for taking the property off the market while the buyer contemplates the desirability of going forward. Options, therefore, generally express by their terms uncertainty as to the ultimate sale and purchase of the property. Letters of intent, in contrast, do not generally express such contingency, which heightens the risk that they will serve as evidence of an actual contract of sale and purchase.

Given the risk associated with letters of intent, it is often wise to avoid using them, but one may find that particular commercial clients like the idea of being able to do "handshake" deals, to be papered in detail by lawyers at a later time. Some clients also like the idea of getting a seller to hold a property off the market without paying an option fee. Consequently, a lawyer may have to use the letter-of-intent approach simply because her clients demand it. This is fine as long as the client is made aware of the potential risks associated with the use of a letter of intent.

GMH ASSOCIATES, INC. v. PRUDENTIAL REALTY GROUP
Superior Court of Pennsylvania, 2000
752 A.2d 889, appeal denied, 795 A.2d 976 (Pa. Sup. Ct. 2000)

CAVANAUGH, Judge. [O]n May 13, 1996, appellant, Prudential Realty Group (hereinafter "Prudential" and/or "Seller"), entered into a Letter of Interest (LOI) with appellee, GMH Associates (hereinafter "GMH" or "Buyer"), for the sale of commercial real estate in Montgomery County known as Bala Plaza (the Property).[2] The LOI contained certain terms and conditions previously discussed between the parties regarding the contemplated sale of the Property, including the following: the Property would be sold "AS IS" for a purchase price of $109.25 million; Buyer had begun "due diligence" and would complete same by 5 p.m. on July 3, 1996; the parties would endeavor to execute a formal, written contract of sale by that date; and the transaction would close on July 19, 1996.[3] The LOI contained the following clause in large, bold print:

NOTWITHSTANDING THAT EITHER OR BOTH PARTIES MAY EXPEND SUBSTANTIAL EFFORTS AND SUMS IN ANTICIPATION OF ENTERING A CONTRACT, THE PARTIES ACKNOWLEDGE THAT IN NO EVENT WILL THIS LETTER BE CONSTRUED AS AN ENFORCEABLE CONTRACT TO SELL OR PURCHASE THE PROPERTY AND EACH PARTY ACCEPTS THE RISK THAT NO SUCH CONTRACT WILL BE EXECUTED.

2. Prudential held title to the Property. Prudential's agent charged with handling the details of the transaction was Devon Glenn. Appellant, CB Commercial Real Estate Group was the entity Prudential used to market the Property. Appellant Douglas Joseph is CB Commercial's agent. Gary Holloway is the CEO and sole shareholder of appellee Buyer, GMH. Bruce Robinson is GMH's Chief Financial Officer.
3. The record shows that in the weeks preceding the execution of the LOI, Buyer had inspected the Property and had begun conducting its "due diligence," i.e., its review of matters relating to, *inter alia*, title, land use, applicable zoning laws, profitability of existing and prospective leases and physical condition of the Property.

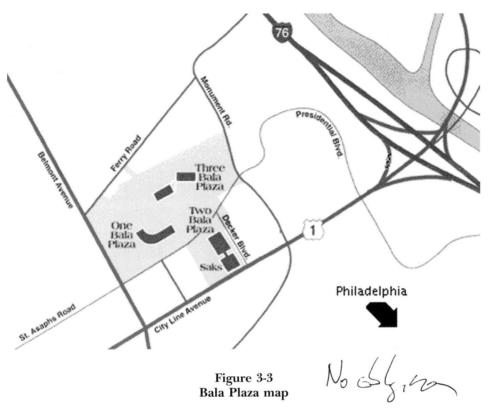

Figure 3-3
Bala Plaza map

No bbj, m

Immediately below the bold print the LOI stated that "each party shall be free to terminate negotiations with the other for any reason whatsoever, at any time prior to the execution of the Contract without incurring liability to the other." The LOI further stated:

> Any Contract which may be negotiated shall not be binding on Seller until it has been approved by the senior corporate officers and the Law Department of Seller and by the Finance Committee of Seller's Board of Directors. Such approvals are conditions precedent to the Seller's obligation to perform under the terms of the Contract, and may be withheld for any reason or for no reason.

At trial, it was established that Seller told Buyer that in exchange for Buyer's execution of the LOI, Seller would take the property "off the market." The record is also clear that both parties were aware, prior to executing the LOI, that Buyer was negotiating a master lease/purchase option agreement with a prospective tenant, the Allegheny Health and Education Research Foundation (hereinafter "Allegheny" or "AHERF"). Under this prospective agreement, on the same day Seller would convey the Property to Buyer, Allegheny would purchase the ground beneath a portion of Bala

Figure 3-4
Saks store and Two Bala Plaza office building

Plaza from Buyer for $6.2 million and would enter into a long-term lease with Buyer for office space in one of the Bala Plaza buildings.[4]

In late May or early June of 1996, Allegheny informed Buyer that it would be unable to negotiate the lease/purchase transaction for 90 days. . . . At the same time, Buyer notified Seller that its due diligence had uncovered some $3 million in capital improvements the Property required. Thus, Buyer sought to obtain a $3 million credit toward, or reduction below, the stated LOI purchase price.

On July 1st, Seller verbally agreed to Buyer's request to extend the closing date to July 31st. At the same time, Buyer suggested an "earn-out" proposal to Seller. Under the terms of this proposal, Buyer would forward to Seller, sometime after closing, a portion of the proceeds Buyer expected to receive as the result of executing the lease/purchase option with Allegheny. In early July, Buyer's verbal offer for the property was $103 million in cash at closing plus a post-closing "earn out" payment of $3.25 million after Buyer concluded its lease/purchase agreement with Allegheny. The remaining $3 million of the LOI purchase price would be deemed a capital improvements credit. Thus, the unconditional LOI purchase price of $109.25 million

4. The court found that Seller knew that Buyer "was in a 'Catch-22' situation[,]" *i.e.*, Buyer did not have resources to pay the full purchase price contained in the LOI unless Buyer entered into and received proceeds from the prospective lease/purchase agreement with Allegheny, but Allegheny would not enter into the lease/purchase agreement unless Buyer could assure Allegheny that the Property was off the market.

would not actually be met. Seller's net receipt of cash would be less than the LOI purchase price by an amount equal to the proposed capital improvements credit despite the provision of the LOI that the property was to be sold "AS IS."

In mid-July, Buyer increased its cash at closing offer to $103.5 million and lowered its capital credit request to $2.5 million. On July 30th, Seller's agent, Devon Glenn, asked Buyer to put the "earn-out" proposal in writing. Upon receiving same, Seller requested Buyer to give "teeth" to the proposal. The trial court found that by "teeth," Seller meant it wanted to be able to realize a percentage of any profit Buyer might get from consummating the Allegheny lease/purchase transaction. Buyer declined to put "teeth" into the "earn-out" proposal and on August 12, 1996, Glenn took the Buyer's purchase offer of $103.5 million cash at closing with a subsequent potential "earn-out" payment of $3.25 million to Prudential's investment committee for approval. The committee rejected Buyer's purchase offer that same date.

From the time the parties executed the LOI, Seller repeatedly assured Buyer that the property was off the market and that Buyer was the only prospective purchaser. The court found that Seller did, in fact, keep the Property "off the market at least from May 13, 1996 until August 12, 1996." After August 12th, Seller continued to negotiate with Buyer and continued to assure Buyer that it was not "shopping the deal" to other prospective purchasers, when, in fact, Seller allowed the Government of Singapore Investment Corporation (GSIC) to tour the Property on August 21st to determine whether GSIC had any interest in purchasing the Property. For a period of approximately three weeks thereafter, Seller conducted negotiations with both prospective purchasers, GMH and GSIC, without telling either entity about its negotiations with the other.

When Seller rejected GMH's latest proposal on August 12th, Seller told GMH that it was not interested in an "earn out" proposal and would require an all cash offer. Thus, on August 16th, GMH made a new oral offer of $105.5 million, all cash at closing. Seller did not immediately act thereon because GSIC was also expected to make an offer. On August 27th, an internal memorandum of Seller stated that "we will have GSIC's offer by the end of the week . . . we should be prepared to consider both proposals from GMH and GSIC and respond accordingly by Friday."

On August 30th, GSIC forwarded a letter of intent to Seller offering to purchase the Property for $108.5 million, all cash at closing. That date, Seller rejected GMH's $105.5 million all cash offer, but untruthfully continued to assure GMH that there existed no other bidder. . . .

. . . On September 9th, GMH's Chief Financial Officer, Bruce Robinson, spoke with Devon Glenn who told Robinson that "if he wanted to make sure that GMH got the property, he must offer . . . $107,250,000 because that was the number Devon Glenn knew he could get the deal approved at."

However, the next day, September 10th, Joseph told Robinson that "there were three people interested in the property and he was concerned they were going to put in bids on the property. . .". Joseph, at that time, advised Robinson that GMH's next offer had to be in writing and did not disclose to GMH that GSIC had already submitted a written $108.5 million bid on the Property. Immediately after speaking with Joseph, Robinson called the leasing agent for the Property, Janet Giuliani. Giuliani informed Robinson that GSIC had toured the Property.

The next day, September 11th, Mr. Holloway and Mr. Robinson decided that they would meet Seller's "offer" of $107.25 million. Also that date, before putting their "acceptance" of Seller's "offer" in writing, the pair met with representatives of Allegheny. The meeting had been called by Allegheny. At the beginning of the meeting, Holloway told the Allegheny representatives that "GMH had a deal with Prudential, that GMH and Prudential had agreed to a price, and GMH was moving toward closing." At the conclusion of the meeting, Allegheny told GMH that they had an agreement in principle to the lease/purchase transaction but that further negotiations were necessary to resolve some outstanding issues, namely "clarification from GMH on when GMH would be able to put tenants into the Bala buildings and whether GMH was able to give Allegheny an additional $10 [per square foot] allowance [on a 185,000 square foot space] for tenant improvement."[8] The court found these issues did not appear to be material or significant to the ultimate completion of the GMH/Allegheny transaction.

Later in the day, Mr. Robinson called Mr. Joseph to inform him that GMH had "accepted" Prudential's "offer" of $107.25 million and would put the acceptance in writing. Joseph suggested that the writing be in a letter of interest format. Thus, on September 11th, Robinson forwarded a letter to Devon Glenn which stated, in pertinent part:

> This letter summarizes certain revised terms and conditions which we have discussed regarding the sale of [the Property] by Prudential Insurance Company of America ("Seller") to GMH Associates, Inc. ("Purchaser").
>
> 1. Purchase Price. The Purchase Price for the Property will be $107,250,000 ("Purchase Price") payable as follows:
>   (a) $1,000,000 in immediately available funds . . . upon full execution of the contract for the sale and purchase of the property . . .
>   (b) The balance of the Purchase Price would be paid upon closing . . .
> 2. Due Diligence and Inspection Contingencies
>   (a) Both Purchaser and Seller acknowledge that there is an outstanding environmental issue . . . Purchaser and Seller both agree to have their respective representatives meet in order to come to a mutually agreeable resolution to this issue. . . .
>
> All other terms and conditions of the letter of interest dated May 13, 1996 between Purchaser and Seller shall remain in full force and effect except for the items mentioned above, and the contract and closing dates of which shall now be changed to October 31, 1996.

8. Thus, it appears that Allegheny wanted to negotiate a $1.85 million credit from GMH toward tenant improvements.

If you are in agreement with the above please so indicate by signing the enclosed copy of this letter in the space provided below and return to us as soon as possible.

Sincerely Yours,
GMH ASSOCIATES, INC.

By: [*Signature*]
Bruce F. Robinson

AGREED TO AND ACCEPTED:
By: _____
Name:
Title:
Date Executed:

On September 12th, Devon Glenn called Joseph Grubb, GSIC's agent. Glenn informed Grubb that Prudential had received an offer from GMH that was a "higher net number than GSIC's offer."[9] Mr. Glenn further told Grubb that if GSIC agreed to pay $806,158 toward tenant improvements and brokerage commissions (TIBCs) then Prudential would sign GSIC's letter of intent. GSIC agreed to the proposal which, as the trial court found, made GSIC's "offer approximately $500,000 more than GMH's number, including TIBCs."

That same date, Glenn and Joseph informed Holloway and Robinson that Prudential had rejected GMH's bid and had agreed to sell the Property to GSIC.

GMH subsequently sued Prudential, CB Commercial Real Estate and Douglas Joseph. The complaint alleged Breach of Contract, Breach of Duty to Negotiate in Good Faith, and Promissory Estoppel against Prudential. It further alleged Fraudulent Misrepresentation, Fraudulent Nondisclosure, and Civil Conspiracy against all defendants. . . .

Following a non-jury trial, the court found for GMH on all its claims and awarded damages to GMH for lost profits in the amount of $20,340,623. It also awarded GMH $10,000,000 in punitive damages — $7,000,000 assessed against Prudential and $3,000,000 assessed against CB Commercial. . . .

The trial court authored a lengthy opinion in support of its determination. Among other things, the court concluded that GMH and Prudential entered into an enforceable oral contract for the sale of the Property on September 11th; that Prudential defrauded GMH and failed to negotiate in good faith in procuring the oral contract; that GMH relied to its detriment on Prudential's representations; that Prudential breached the September

---

9. As the trial court explained: The reason GMH's $107.25 million number was a higher net number than GSIC's $108.5 million number was because, in its LOI, GMH agreed to pay tenant improvements and broker's commissions, which were $1.6 million. GSIC had no such provision in its offer. Therefore, comparing "apples to apples," GMH's number was $107.25 [million] plus $1.6 million, or $108,850,000, and GSIC's was $350,000 less.

11th oral contract with GMH when it subsequently sold the property to GSIC; and that GMH was entitled to damages in the nature of lost profits.

Prudential now appeals, contending that the court's verdict is not sustainable under any of the causes of action GMH presented. We agree.

A. BREACH OF CONTRACT

Contrary to the trial court's determination, we find that no oral contract for the sale of the Property arose. . . .

It appears the court's conclusion that an enforceable oral contract was formed between the parties was based, in part, on its finding that $107.25 million was Prudential's "will sell" price. The court found Mr. Robinson credible and credited his testimony that on September 9th, Devon Glenn asserted he could "close the deal" at a purchase price of $107.25 million; that the price quoted was "not a moving target" and represented the "number that we will sell the property to you for." Further the court found that GMH "met" Prudential's "will sell" offer on the basis of the content of the September 11th letter of interest, which stated that the purchase price would be $107.25 million. Thus, the court implicitly found that on September 9th, Prudential orally "offered" to sell the Property to GMH for $107.25 million and that on September 11th, GMH "accepted" Prudential's offer, in writing, by forwarding the letter of interest containing the agreed upon purchase price. Based on these findings, the court concluded that an enforceable oral contract for the sale of the Property arose on September 11th.

We find that the court's determination was legal error. First, we cannot agree that Glenn's statements to Robinson on September 9th constituted an offer to sell. . . . Robinson testified that during his conversation with Glenn on September 9th, Glenn said "I'm not saying you can't *offer* a lower number and that we won't *accept* a lower number. However, if you want to make sure you get the property, you must *offer* the $107,250,000 because that's the number I know *I can get the deal approved at.*" We find that Prudential, through Glenn, was soliciting an offer from GMH which would then be taken to Prudential's decision makers for approval and acceptance.

Assuming *arguendo* that Glenn's statements on September 9th did, in fact, constitute an offer to sell the property for a sum certain, we would find the offer was revoked the next day when Joseph informed Robinson that there were other likely bidders competing for the Property; that GMH's next offer had to be in writing; and that GMH's next offer ought to be its best offer. It is hornbook law that an offeree's power to accept an offer is terminated by a revocation of the offer by the offeror. Restatement (Second) of Contracts §36 (1981).

Moreover, GMH's purported acceptance of Prudential's offer, made via the unexecuted letter of interest dated September 11th, included a clause stating that the parties would agree to discuss an open and apparently unresolved environmental issue regarding the property. . . . We additionally note that, on its face, the unexecuted letter of interest, which the court concluded was GMH's "acceptance," does not purport to be an acceptance at all, but, in fact, is drafted as an offer. We conclude that GMH's offer to buy the Property was rejected by Prudential and that no contract was formed.

Further, it is clear that the parties always intended and agreed that any binding transaction between them for the conveyance of the Property would be accomplished by a written contract. This intention is stated and agreed to by the parties in the executed LOI of May 13th and is adopted by reference in GMH's unexecuted September 11th letter of interest.

Our supreme court has recently reiterated that "where the parties have agreed orally to all the terms of their contract, and a part of the mutual understanding is that a written contract embodying these terms shall be drawn and executed by the respective parties, such oral contract may be enforced, though one of the parties thereafter refuses to execute the written contract." Shovel Transfer & Storage, Inc. v. PLCB, 739 A.2d 133, 138 (Pa. 1999). *See also* Mazzella v. Koken, 739 A.2d 531, 536 (Pa. 1999) ("where the parties have agreed on the essential terms of a contract, the fact that they intend to formalize their agreement in writing but have not yet done so does not prevent enforcement of such an agreement"). Relying on decisional precedent which embodies this proposition, the trial court concluded that an enforceable contract arose on September 11th despite the fact that no written contract was ever executed. . . . We find that the court's conclusion in this regard was error.

The essential terms that must be identified and agreed to in order to form a valid contract for the sale of real estate are the naming of the specific parties, property and consideration or purchase price. *See* Detwiler v. Capone, 55 A.2d 380, 385 (Pa. 1947). . . . We conclude that there was no mutual assent between the parties as to essential terms or the subject matter of the transaction and that all issues surrounding the structure of the proposed transaction had not been closed.

First, the original LOI contemplated a $109.25 million all cash at closing purchase price. At the same time that GMH informed Prudential that there was a "glitch" in procuring Allegheny's involvement, it also informed Prudential that its due diligence had uncovered $3 million in necessary capital improvements. Despite the LOI's "AS IS" language, GMH sought a $3 million capital improvements credit. . . . the evidence is that when GMH's "earn out" proposal was rejected and the parties began to focus on an all cash price, the parties were still $1.5 million apart on the amount of any capital improvements credit. The evidence does not suggest that gap was ever closed. Thus, we conclude that an essential term, namely, the purchase price amount, as affected by the capital improvements credit, had never been agreed to by the parties and thus that no enforceable contract arose.

Second, the September 11th "acceptance" letter of interest specifically incorporated the terms of the original LOI of May 13th. The May 13th LOI provided that "the parties have not attempted in this letter to set forth all essential terms of the subject matter of this transaction, and such essential terms shall be the subject of further negotiations." Moreover, the September 11th letter expressly provided that the parties would continue to negotiate regarding an unresolved environmental issue. Because recognized issues remained unresolved, no mutual assent existed sufficient to bind the parties.

Third, the executed LOI of May 13th contained an express condition precedent that was never met. The parties agreed that any written contract they might negotiate would not bind Seller unless it was approved by Seller's senior corporate officers, law department and board finance committee. It is undisputed that no corporate approval was given to the terms of the Buyer's September 11th proposal and thus, we conclude that no enforceable contract arose. . . .

B. FRAUD

The trial court concluded that "Prudential obtained the oral agreement of September 11th by fraud." Specifically, the court found as fact that all defendants, between August 15th and September 12th, continually assured GMH that Prudential was not negotiating with other prospective buyers, when in fact, Prudential was actively negotiating with GSIC during that period. The court concluded that these assurances were fraudulent misrepresentations. Similarly, the court concluded that after August 15th, the defendants' failure to inform GMH that Prudential was negotiating with GSIC amounted to fraudulent nondisclosure of the fact that the Property was no longer "off the market." Thus, the court concluded that the oral contract of sale created on September 11th, was procured through fraud.

Initially, because we find that no contract was created, we correspondingly conclude that no fraud was committed in its alleged procurement. However, even if the elements of an oral contract had been created on September 11th, we would nonetheless be constrained to conclude that defendants' collective failure to disclose, between August 15th and September 12th, that the Property was no longer "off the market," as well as their affirmative statements that GMH was the exclusive bidder, were immaterial to the transaction at hand, *i.e.*, GMH's decision to offer $107.25 million and Prudential's decision to reject that offer. Thus, we would conclude that no fraud was committed. . . .

C. DUTY TO NEGOTIATE IN GOOD FAITH

The court determined that Prudential breached a duty to negotiate in good faith by failing to keep the Property off the market.

Our courts have not determined whether a cause of action for breach of duty to negotiate in good faith exists in Pennsylvania. Jenkins v. County of Schuylkill, 658 A.2d 380, 385 (Pa. Super. Ct. 1995). The Third Circuit Court of Appeals has predicted that Pennsylvania would recognize such an action. *See* Flight Systems, Inc. v. EDS Corp., 112 F.3d 124, 129 (3d Cir. 1997).

This court has previously quoted the following principle with approval: "The full extent of a party's duty to negotiate in good faith can only be determined, however, from the terms of the letter of intent itself." *Jenkins*, 658 A.2d at 385. . . .

Here, the parties' May 13th LOI expressly provided that either party could terminate negotiations at any time for any reason without incurring liability to the other prior to the execution of a written contract. It did not contain any provision regarding the duty to negotiate in good faith. Further, the LOI included no provision regarding the Property's "off the market" status. Thus, we conclude, if our courts were to recognize the existence of such a cause of action, that the duty to negotiate in good faith was not breached in this case by Prudential's failure to keep the property "off the market" or to reveal that it was entering negotiations with GSIC.

D. Promissory Estoppel

The doctrine of promissory estoppel allows a party, under certain circumstances, to enforce a promise even though the promise is not supported by consideration. . . .

The trial court found that the doctrine of promissory estoppel applied to GMH's claims that (1) Prudential promised to keep the Property off the market while negotiations with GMH continued; and (2) Prudential promised to sell the Property to GMH for $107.25 million.

We conclude the court erred in finding these "promises" were enforceable for the same reasons we find that no contract arose and that no fraud was committed. First, the parties agreed that the Property would stay off the market, *inter alia*, as long as GMH was meeting the deadlines it proposed to Prudential. The Property was, in fact, off the market for three months, but GMH could not close within that time. . . . Since Prudential kept the Property off the market for three months during which time the proposed transaction was not consummated, we do not find the doctrine of promissory estoppel available to bind it to continue to keep the Property off the market seemingly indefinitely.

Second, we find that any offer Prudential made on September 9th, to sell the Property to GMH for $107.25 million, was revoked by Prudential's representations of September 10th. Thus, we conclude that there existed no enforceable "promise" to sell the property to GMH for a sum certain. . . .

G. Conclusion

For the foregoing reasons, we find that the court's verdict is not sustainable under any of the causes of action set forth by GMH. Accordingly, we reverse the judgment entered in favor of GMH and remand with directions to enter judgment notwithstanding the verdict in favor of appellants. Jurisdiction is relinquished.

EAKIN, J., dissenting. While my colleagues' analysis is well reasoned, I find sufficient support in the record for the findings of the learned trial court, and therefore am constrained to dissent.

Problem 3B

Gina, a real estate investor, is interested in buying an office building owned by Andrew and Tammy as partners. Gina has several preliminary conversations with Andrew concerning the property. She wants to induce him to take the property off the market while she thinks about the deal. At the same time she wants to lock in a good price in the event that she decides to go through with the purchase. Gina prepares a letter of intent to purchase the property from Andrew. The letter she prepares is set out below.

Gina Peters
1010 Boiler Lane
Big City, Golden State, USA

September 1, 2017

Re: ("Property") Blackstone Office Building, 201 Rocky Ripple Ave., Big City, Golden State, USA

Mr. Andrew Cain
2637 Bulldog Court
Big City, Golden State, USA

Dear Mr. Cain:
The following is to serve as a Letter of Intent to acquire from you that certain Property described above.

    1. *Buyer* Gina Peters

    2. *Seller* Andrew Cain

    3. *Purchase Price:* Purchase price shall be the sum of $3,500,000, which shall be payable:

        A. $500,000 cash deposit to be deposited with an escrow agent, selected by Buyer, said deposit to be deposited in an interest-bearing account, interest accruing to the benefit of the Buyer. Said deposit to be paid upon execution of a formal Contract to Purchase, executed by both parties.

B. $3,000,000 payable in cash at closing.

4. *Acceptance of Letter of Intent*: Seller shall have twenty-four hours to accept this Letter of Intent, by delivering written notice of acceptance to Buyer by hand delivery or return email.

24h to accept LOI

time to K

5. *Contract of Sale*: Within thirty (30) days of your acceptance of this Letter of Intent by written notice to the Buyer specified above, the parties will enter into a contract embodying the terms of this Letter of Intent, and such other provisions as the parties and/or their counsel deem necessary or appropriate.

6. *Rights of Inspection*: Seller shall furnish Buyer upon execution of the Contract of Sale, copies of any mortgages or liens encumbering the subject property, a current rent roll, copies of all leases and contracts pertaining to the property, a current survey, and profit and loss operating statements relative to the property for the past three years. Buyer shall have twenty (20) days from the date of delivery of said documents to review the same. In addition, Buyer shall have twenty (20) business days from the date of execution of the Contract of Sale within which to inspect the property and all improvements thereon, and to conduct a termite inspection of the improvements plus any environmental audits on the property. If the Seller is not notified in writing prior to the termination of the twenty (20) business day period that Buyer wishes to terminate the Contract of Sale, the earnest money deposit will be forfeited to Seller and will be non-refundable.

Loss of $/delay

7. *Closing*: Closing with respect to the sale will take place on or before November 20, 2017.

8. *Off the Market:* Seller shall keep the property off the market during the full time period covered by this Letter of Intent.

Please confirm that the foregoing is acceptable to you so that we may proceed to prepare a formal Purchase and Sale Agreement for your review.

Very truly yours,

Gina Peters

Two hours after Gina hand delivered the Letter of Intent to Andrew he emailed an acceptance to her. Three days later Andrew delivered three years of property information and reports to Gina, as provided for under paragraph 6 of the Letter. Gina and her staff reviewed this information, and Gina had several conversations about the property with Andrew. During the conversations, which were recorded, Gina said, "Everything looks great. I like the numbers. We can do this deal." Andrew listened and is heard to say at the end, "Great." On day 20 after signing the Letter, Gina prepared a purchase contract for Andrew to sign. She sent Andrew a text message indicating that a person from her office would be at his office in about two hours with a contract. What Gina did not know at the time was that Andrew had continued to discuss the potential sale of the property to a person named Brian, whose interest had been "hot and cold" during the past year. Andrew sent a text message to Brian indicating that Gina was currently writing up a contract on the property to present to him shortly. In response, Brian submitted a standard-form contract offering Andrew $3.6 million in cash for the building. Andrew accepted Brian's contract in writing thirty minutes before Gina delivered her signed contract to him.

When Gina learned of the contract with Brian, she called Andrew and said, "I thought we had a deal! I'm suing you for breach of contract." Andrew denies the breach and prepares to close with Brian. In the meantime it turns out that, unknown to Andrew, his partner Tammy had learned of Gina's text message with respect to preparing to deliver the contract to Andrew. Fifteen minutes before Andrew signed Brian's contract, Tammy posted on the firm's Facebook page stating, "Finally sold the Blackstone Building to Gina Peters after more than a year of trying to unload it from our investment portfolio. Looking to party this weekend!" Will Gina prevail in her claim against Andrew? How might Brian and Tammy be involved? Does it make a difference if Tammy is a business partner with Andrew but the property is titled in Andrew's name only?

AMERICAN CANADIAN EXPEDITIONS, LTD. v. GAULEY RIVER CORPORATION

Supreme Court of Appeals of West Virginia, 2007
655 S.E. 2d 188

Albright, Justice. This case involves the appeal by the plaintiff below, American Canadian Expeditions, Ltd. (hereinafter referred to as "Appellant"), of the May 18, 2006, order of the Fayette County Circuit Court granting summary judgment to the defendants below, Gauley River Corporation and Mountain River Tours, Inc. (hereinafter referred to as "Appellees"). . . .

FACTUAL AND PROCEDURAL BACKGROUND

The parties to this appeal are white water rafting businesses. On May 1, 2002, Appellant entered into a real estate option contract with Appellees, giving Appellant exclusive right for a three-year period to purchase certain tracts of real estate in Fayette County, West Virginia.[1] At the same time, the parties also executed a "Deed of Easement."[2] The easement provided Appellant and its customers access to the river over the property. As consideration for the option and easement, Appellant paid $75,000. Under the terms of the option contract, another $175,000 would be due upon exercising the option; the option terminated on April 1, 2005. Logging or standing timber was not mentioned in either of the agreements.

In July 2002, Appellees contracted for the removal of timber from a portion of the option property and logging began in August 2002. The logging operation was completed before the end of the year. Appellees received nearly $42,000 for the timber removed. Appellees maintain that the logging was done while Appellant was regularly using the option property for its white water rafting business, and that the logging operation was clearly visible to anyone on the property.

Appellant filed suit in February 2004 seeking damages for the loss of timber and for damage the logging operation allegedly caused to the option property. During the pendency of this suit, Appellant supplied notice to Appellees of intent to exercise the option to purchase. The notice was later supplemented by letter advising Appellees that the exercise of the option was not a waiver of any claim for damages, including the removal of timber. A closing was held on April 1, 2005, at which time legal title to the subject property was conveyed to Appellant.

On May 18, 2006, the circuit court granted summary judgment in favor of Appellees in the property damage suit [concluding that] Appellant had failed to show that it had either a legal or equitable interest in the real property at the time the timber was removed and sold. . . .

DISCUSSION

This appeal raises various issues regarding rights related to an option contract. Central among these issues is whether the holder of an option contract to purchase land has an in personam right to a claim of damages to the property occurring during the life of the option but before the option is exercised. Appellant essentially suggests that a type of conditional equitable conversion should be adopted in this jurisdiction whereby the holder of an option would be treated as an equitable or beneficial owner of the property

---

1. The option contract concerned three tracts of land, with the largest measuring an approximate 212.5 acres, a second approximately 75 acres, the third approximately 27.5 acres.

2. Both legal instruments were prepared by Appellees' counsel; Appellant had not retained legal representation at the time the agreements were executed.

from the date of the option contract when and if the holder exercises the option. By allowing equitable ownership rights to revert back to the date of the option contract, the holder of the option attains the right through exercise of the option to claim damages from the giver of the option for any detrimental changes occurring to the land during the life of the option contract. . . .

Historically, our law affords no property interest in the holder of an option for the purchase of land before the option is exercised. As explained in Pollock v. Brookover, 53 S.E. 795, 796 (W. Va. 1906), an option contract

> is not a contract to sell, nor an agreement to sell, real estate, because there is no mutuality of obligation and remedy; but it is a contract by which the owner agrees with another person that he shall have the right to buy, within a certain time, at a stipulated price. It is a continuing offer to sell, which may or may not, with the time specified, at the election of the optionee, be accepted. The owner parts with his right to sell to another for such time, and gives to the optionee this exclusive privilege. It is the right of election to purchase, which has been bought and paid for, and which forms the basis of the contract between the parties. Upon the payment of the consideration, and the signing of the option, it becomes an executed contract—not, however, an executed contract selling the land, but the sale of the option, which is irrevocable by the optionor, and which is capable of being converted into a valid executory contract for the sale of land. . . .

. . . The Court in *Pollock* relied upon the following legal principle announced in Rease v. Kittle, 49 S.E. 150 (W. Va. 1904), in order to reach its conclusion: "Before payment or tender of the purchase money within the time stipulated [in an option contract], such contract does not vest in the person to whom the offer of sale is made any title to the land, *either legal or equitable*. . . ." *Id.* at 150 (emphasis added). The following discussion from the *Rease* case sheds further light on the ambit of this holding:

> A contract of this kind is in no sense a sale of the land, and vests no equitable title in the optionee. It amounts, at the most, to an irrevocable privilege of purchase. It is unlike an accepted offer of sale which constitutes a contract of sale, giving mutuality of remedy to both parties, by which either may enforce the specific performance of it. "An option contract to purchase is but a continuing offer to sell, and conveys no interest in the property." Caldwell v. Frazier, 68 P. 1076 (Kan. 1902). This was the case of a lease with an option of purchase, which, as above shown, is in all respects similar to the contract involved here. Between the offer and acceptance, the improvements on the property were destroyed by fire, and the plaintiff sought performance of the contract, with the improvements restored, or with an abatement in price equal to the value of the lost improvements. The court held that he had no interest in the property at the time of the fire, and, having accepted the contract after the loss, he must pay the full price.

Id. at 153-54. Along these same lines in the later case of Rutherford v. MacQueen, 161 S.E. 612 (W. Va. 1931), this Court found that the holder of an option to purchase real estate was not entitled to the benefit of insurance moneys collected by the giver of the option for fire damages occurring on the property before the option was exercised. . . . Another case involving property subject to an option contract which was destroyed by fire is Tate v. Wood, 289 S.E.2d 432 (W. Va. 1982). As the holders of the option had not exercised their option, the Court in *Tate* observed that without an executory contract for sale of land, the doctrine of equitable conversion, placing beneficial ownership and risk of loss on the vendee, did not apply. However, because an express provision of the lease-option contract at issue in *Tate* stated that the giver of the option would refund one-half of the cost of any improvements the holders of the contract made to the property if the holders did not exercise the option, the holders were entitled to damages based upon the agreement of the parties.

As our review above discloses, even though option holders have no ownership interest in the subject land, they do possess rights stemming from the contract. The basic enforceable personal right attained by Appellant under the option contract was the right to purchase the property at a certain price within a prescribed period.

Applying this rule, we hold that: During the option period of a real estate option contract, the optionee has no ownership interest in the property, or the timber on it, absent specific language in the option contract to the contrary. Therefore, Appellant's enforceable rights under the terms of this option contract were limited to being able to purchase the property at the agreed upon price within the agreed upon period. As with any contract, additional terms and conditions may be negotiated by the parties to an option contract and enforcement of those terms and conditions would be governed by contract law. No additional terms or conditions were stipulated in the option contract at issue. Having no equitable or legal ownership interest in the timber under our established law. and preserving no special right under the contract, the only remedy to Appellant's objection to the damage which may have occurred to the property during the option period was to not exercise the option. Clearly, the law contains no requirement for optionees to exercise their option and thus be forced to accept the damages and acquire ownership of unsuitable, if not unusable, property. Accordingly, we hold that the basic enforceable personal rights of the holder of an option to purchase real estate include the right to purchase the property at a certain price within a prescribed period. As with any contract, additional terms and conditions may be negotiated by the parties and enforcement of those terms and conditions would be governed by contract law.

While the result in this case may appear harsh, it is based on the principles which parties entering into option contracts have relied upon for over a hundred years and cannot be said to come as a surprise. A harsh result does not necessarily imply an unfair or unjust process. . . .

Affirmed.

Problem 3C

Karen has a business idea for developing a micro-brewery to produce a local ale. She has put together some investor partners and an entity for purposes of acquiring a property and developing the micro-brewery. Karen has identified a parcel of land located in an industrial zone (per the local zoning code). Currently the property is used as a warehouse. Karen plans to acquire the property, refurbish it, and equip it so that she can produce beer and ale on location. She also plans to include an onsite pub, café, and gift shop. The current zoning does not permit the uses Karen has described so she will have to go to the planning and zoning board to obtain special approval for her project. Many of the surrounding properties in this area of town are abandoned industrial buildings that have not been used productively for more than a decade. Given that the property Karen is interested in is located in an economic revitalization zone, with little redevelopment accomplished so far, Karen feels fairly confident that local planning and zoning officials will approve her project. She recognizes that approval may be based on complying with zoning and planning conditions that will impact the details of her plans, but she feels that as long as these are reasonable, the project should still be profitable.

Karen understands that she could enter into a contract to purchase this property and if she does this the contract will need to provide for a number of planning and zoning contingencies that may also impact financing and other aspects of the deal. This could make for a complicated contract. Therefore, Karen is hoping to get a number of issues figured out prior to actually signing a contract. She has talked with the property owner, who she believes is motivated to sell the property. Karen wants to avoid getting contractually obligated to a deal before she has more details worked out, but she also does not want the seller to keep the property on the market and risk losing the opportunity to some other potential buyer. Karen comes to you to ask about alternatives to going right to a contract; in particular, she is interested in either a letter of intent or taking an option on the property. She wants your advice.

Draft a letter to Karen explaining the legal effect of letters of intent and options, and explain how they relate to a full contract of purchase. In your letter advise her of the potential benefits and risks of each approach. Also offer your advice on the best way to protect her interest in going forward and provide a rationale for your opinion.

4

Executory Contracts

The executory contract period of a real estate transaction is a busy time for the parties, full of risk and activity. The time period generally begins at the moment the parties reach an agreement, usually memorialized in the execution of a formal writing. Typically, it ends at the closing of the contract with the satisfactory completion of all the various contractual undertakings of each party. Thus, the time horizon we are considering is the duration of the parties' contractual relationship with each other.

Identifying the specific points of opening and closure to the contract is not always a clean and easy matter. Sometimes it can be outright messy. As we discuss in Chapter 3, it is not always clear when the parties have reached the point of having entered into an enforceable agreement. Moreover, even when the parties attempt to write out a formal contract of purchase and sale, they are sometimes unsuccessful. Thus, what sometimes looks like the moment of agreement between the parties may still be only the potential for such a legally recognizable relationship. At the other end of the time span, the difficulties inherent in determining the commencement of a contract can also arise when trying to pinpoint the ending of that relationship. Sometimes the parties to an agreement will intentionally leave certain aspects of their contractual relationship open beyond what otherwise passes as the closing ceremony. Likewise, the courts have developed legal doctrines that can prolong some aspects of a contractual relationship beyond the formalities of the closing process. Despite these "gray areas," it is still useful to begin the study of this time period by thinking of it as a specific time horizon with specific and measurable moments of commencement and closure.

During the executory contract period, the parties are busy performing their obligations. It is a time that allows for more detailed investigation of the property and for the gathering of evidence to demonstrate one's own compliance with the contract.

A. EXECUTING AN ENFORCEABLE CONTRACT

The main purpose of the contract in a real estate transaction is to arrange for the orderly transfer of an interest in real property to the buyer in exchange for the money or other consideration given to the seller. In its most simple formulation, one might think in terms of a deed conveying title swapped for cash.

1. The Need for a Writing

A basic legal rule is that an agreement for the purchase and sale of real property must comply with the *statute of frauds.* The requirements for a writing to satisfy the statute are often muddy, both because the legal rules suffer from indeterminacy and because the disputes are fact-specific. Statute of frauds defenses are often raised in connection with the many modern real estate transactions that go awry and end up in court. Usually this happens when parties forgo the assistance of lawyers in planning their transaction. High volumes of litigation have generally failed to resolve the lack of clarity concerning the requirements of the statute.

To satisfy the statute of frauds, the writing must include essential terms such as the names of the parties, the description of the property, and the intent to buy and sell. The writing must be signed by the party to be charged. It need not include all contract terms, and thus the *parol evidence rule* may be a factor when considering the enforceability of alleged contract terms that are not part of the written agreement.

Paper contracts are no longer required for the sale of real property, or more generally. The *Electronic Signatures in Global and National Commerce Act,* 15 U.S.C. §§7001 to 7031, passed by Congress in 2000, validates the use of electronic contracts and electronic records and authorizes electronic signatures. This legislation, sometimes referred to as the *E-sign Act,* preempts any state law to the contrary; it operates notwithstanding "any statute, regulation, or other rule of law." *Id.* §7001(a). At the state-law level, in 1999 the Uniform Law Commission promulgated the Uniform Electronic Transactions Act (UETA). Under an express provision of the E-sign Act, federal preemption of state law is removed if a state adopts UETA. *Id.* §7002(a)(1).

Thus, in all states a traditional state statute of frauds, which may be interpreted to require a traditional writing, is either overridden by UETA or preempted by E-sign. These acts overlap significantly, but they are not identical in scope and substance. UETA is more comprehensive and detailed with respect to a number of topics. The acts do not force parties to use electronic records, electronic signatures, or other electronic processes. UETA applies only to transactions in which the parties have "agreed to conduct transactions by electronic means." UETA §5(b). "Whether the parties agree to conduct a transaction by electronic means is determined from the context and surrounding circumstances, including the parties' conduct." *Id.*

Both UETA and the E-sign Act validate an electronic signature for purposes of a variety of transactions. This means that a seller could send a contract proposal for the sale of real estate to a buyer as an e-mail attachment and the buyer could form a legally binding commitment by e-mailing back an approval that is meant to signify intent to be bound. In addition, telephone calls are electronic communications, and thus voice mail or a message left on an answering machine may operate as a legal signature. Naturally, there are continuing issues of when a signature or a mark, even an electronic mark, signifies intent to be bound, and there are issues to be raised about the authenticity of an e-signature.

Some oral contracts for the purchase and sale of real property can be enforced on the theory of *part performance* or *equitable estoppel.* In each case, there must be proof of an oral agreement between the parties. In the alternative, a claim may be raised on the theory of *promissory estoppel,* which is a contract substitute. As a contract substitute, one would not have to prove an underlying oral contract using this theory, but would have to demonstrate the facts supporting detrimental reliance.

STERLING v. TAYLOR
Supreme Court of California, 2007
152 P.3d 420

CORRIGAN, Justice. The statute of frauds provides that certain contracts "are invalid, unless they, or some note or memorandum thereof, are in writing and subscribed by the party to be charged. . . ." Civ. Code §1624. In this case, the Court of Appeal held that a memorandum regarding the sale of several apartment buildings was sufficient to satisfy the statute of frauds. Defendants contend the court improperly considered extrinsic evidence to resolve uncertainties in the terms identifying the seller, the property, and the price.

We reverse, but not because the court consulted extrinsic evidence. Extrinsic evidence has long been held admissible to clarify the terms of a memorandum for purposes of the statute of frauds. Statements to the contrary appear in some cases, but we disapprove them. A memorandum serves only an evidentiary function under the statute. If the writing includes the essential terms of the parties' agreement, there is no bar to the admission of relevant extrinsic evidence to explain or clarify those terms. The memorandum, viewed in light of the evidence, must be sufficient to demonstrate with reasonable certainty the terms to which the parties agreed to be bound. Here, plaintiffs attempt to enforce a price term that lacks the certainty required by the statute of frauds.

I. FACTUAL AND PROCEDURAL BACKGROUND

In January 2000, defendant Lawrence N. Taylor and plaintiff Donald Sterling discussed the sale of three apartment buildings in Santa Monica owned by the Santa Monica Collection partnership (SMC). Defendant was a general partner in SMC. Plaintiff and defendant, both experienced real estate investors, met on March 13, 2000, and discussed a series of transactions including the purchase of the SMC properties. At this meeting, plaintiff drafted a handwritten memorandum entitled "Contract for Sale of Real Property."

The memorandum encompasses the sale of five properties; only the SMC properties are involved here. They are identified in the memorandum as "808 4th St.," "843 4th St.," and "1251 14th St.," with an aggregate price term of "approx. 10.468 × gross income[,] estimated income 1.600.000, Price $16,750.00." Although defendant had given plaintiff rent rolls showing the income from the properties, neither man brought these documents to the March 13 meeting. Plaintiff dated and initialed the memorandum as "Buyer," but the line he provided for "Seller" was left blank. Plaintiff contends the omission was inadvertent. Defendant, however, asserts he did not sign the document because he needed approval from a majority of SMC's limited partners. . . .

On April 4, 2000, defendant sent plaintiff three formal purchase agreements with escrow instructions, identifying the properties by their legal descriptions. SMC was named as the seller and the Sterling Family Trust as the buyer. The price terms totalled $16,750,000. Defendant signed the agreements as a general partner of SMC. Plaintiff refused to sign. Defendant claims plaintiff telephoned on April 28, saying the purchase price was unacceptable. Plaintiff asserts that after reviewing the rent rolls, he determined the actual rental income from the SMC buildings was $1,375,404, not $1,600,000 as estimated on the March 13 memorandum. Plaintiff claims he tried to have defendant correct the escrow instructions, but defendant did not return his calls. Plaintiff wanted to lower the price to $14,404,841, based on the actual rental income figure and the 10.468 multiplier noted in the memorandum.

Plaintiff did not ask for the $16,750.00 purchase price stated in the memorandum. He admits that he "accidentally left off one zero" when he wrote down that figure. Defendant also acknowledges that the price recorded on the memorandum was meant to be $16,750,000.

[In March 2001 the trustees of the Sterling Family Trust sued Taylor, SMC, and related entities, alleging breach of a written contract to sell the properties for a total price of $14,404,841. Defendants sought summary judgment, claiming that the alleged contract violated the statute of frauds because it established no agreement on price. The trial court granted summary judgment, ruling that the price term was too uncertain to be enforced and the writings did not comply with the statute of frauds. The Court of Appeal reversed, holding that defendants' evidence raised a triable issue as to whether the parties had agreed on a formula for determining the purchase price.]

II. DISCUSSION

Defendants contend the Court of Appeal improperly considered extrinsic evidence to establish essential contract terms. They insist the statute of frauds requires a memorandum that, standing alone, supplies all material elements of the contract. Plaintiffs, on the other hand, argue that extrinsic evidence is routinely admitted for the purpose of determining whether memoranda comply with the statute of frauds.

arguing over extrinsic evidence

Both sides of this debate find support in California case law, sometimes in the same opinion. Part A of our discussion explains that plaintiffs' view is correct. The statute of frauds does not preclude the admission of evidence in any form; it imposes a writing requirement, but not a comprehensive one. In part B, however, we conclude that defendants are nevertheless entitled to judgment. The Court of Appeal properly considered the parties' extrinsic evidence, but erroneously deemed it legally sufficient under the statute of frauds to establish the price sought by plaintiffs.

extrinsic evidence allowed

A. THE MEMORANDUM REQUIREMENT OF THE STATUTE OF FRAUDS

The statute of frauds does not require a written contract; a "note or memorandum . . . subscribed by the party to be charged" is adequate. Civ. Code §1624, subd. (a). In Crowley v. Modern Faucet Mfg. Co., 282 P.2d 33, 35 (Cal. 1955), we observed that "a written memorandum is not identical with a written contract; it is merely evidence of it and usually does not contain all of the terms." Indeed, in most instances it is not even necessary that the parties intended the memorandum to serve a contractual purpose.

A memorandum satisfies the statute of frauds if it identifies the subject of the parties' agreement, shows that they made a contract, and states the essential contract terms with reasonable certainty. Only the essential terms must be stated, "'details or particulars' need not [be]. What is essential depends on the agreement and its context and also on the subsequent conduct of the parties. . . ." Rest. 2d Contracts §131, com. g (1981).

When memo satisfies SoF

This court recently observed that the writing requirement of the statute of frauds "'serves only to prevent the contract from being unenforceable' [citation]; it does not necessarily establish the terms of the parties' contract." Casa Herrera, Inc. v. Beydoun, 83 P.3d 497, 503 (Cal. 2004.) Unlike the parol evidence rule, which "determines the enforceable and incontrovertible terms of an integrated written agreement," the statute of frauds "merely serve[s] an evidentiary purpose." Id. As the drafters of the Second Restatement of Contracts explained:

PoE vs SoF

> The primary purpose of the Statute is evidentiary, to require reliable evidence of the existence and terms of the contract and to prevent enforcement

through fraud or perjury of contracts never in fact made. The contents of the writing must be such as to make successful fraud unlikely, but the possibility need not be excluded that some other subject matter or person than those intended will also fall within the words of the writing. Where only an evidentiary purpose is served, *the requirement of a memorandum is read in the light of the dispute which arises and the admissions of the party to be charged*; there is no need for evidence on points not in dispute.

Rest. 2d Contracts §131, com. c, italics added.

Thus, when ambiguous terms in a memorandum are disputed, extrinsic evidence is admissible to resolve the uncertainty. Extrinsic evidence can also support reformation of a memorandum to correct a mistake.

Because the memorandum itself must include the essential contractual terms, it is clear that extrinsic evidence cannot *supply* those required terms. It can, however, be used to *explain* essential terms that were understood by the parties but would otherwise be unintelligible to others. . . .

To clarify the law on this point, we disapprove the statements in California cases barring consideration of extrinsic evidence to determine the sufficiency of a memorandum under the statute of frauds. The purposes of the statute are not served by such a rigid rule, which has never been a consistent feature of the common law. Corbin observes:

> Judicial dicta abound to the effect that the writing must contain all of the "essential terms and conditions" of the contract, and it is often said that these must be so clear as to be understood "without any aid from parol testimony." But the long course of judicial decision shows that "essential terms and conditions" is itself a term of considerable flexibility and that the courts do not in fact blind themselves by excluding parol testimony when it is a necessary aid to understanding. . . .
>
> Some confusion is attributable to a failure to keep clearly in mind the purpose of the statute and the informal character of the evidence that the actual words of the statute require; some is no doubt due to differences in the attitude of the judges as to the beneficence of the statute and the wisdom of its existence. Further, there are differences in the strictness of judicial requirements as to the contents of the memorandum. It is believed that sometimes these apparent differences can be explained by the degree of doubt existing in the court's mind as to the actual making and performance of the alleged contract. The better and the more disinterested is the oral testimony offered by the plaintiff, the more convincing the corroboration that is found in the surrounding circumstances, and the more limited the disputed issue because of admissions made by the defendant, the less that should be and is required of the written memorandum.

4 *Corbin on Contracts* §22.2, at 706-07, 709 (rev. ed. 1997; fns. omitted). . . .

We emphasize that a memorandum of the parties' agreement is *controlling* evidence under the statute of frauds. Thus, extrinsic evidence cannot be

Controlling evidence

[handwritten margin note: extrinsic ev. can't be at odds w/ memo]

employed to prove an agreement at odds with the terms of the memorandum. This point was made in Beazell v. Schrader, 381 P.2d 390 (Cal. 1963). There, the plaintiff sought to recover a 5 percent real estate broker's commission under an oral agreement. The escrow instructions, which specified a 1.25 percent commission, were the "memorandum" on which the plaintiff relied to comply with the statute. However, he contended the instructions incorrectly reflected the parties' actual agreement, as shown by extrinsic evidence. The *Beazell* court rejected this argument, holding that under the statute of frauds, "the parol agreement of which the writing is a memorandum must be one whose terms are consistent with the terms of the memorandum." *Id.* at 393. Thus, in determining whether extrinsic evidence provides the certainty required by the statute, courts must bear in mind that the evidence cannot contradict the terms of the writing.

B. THE SUFFICIENCY OF THIS MEMORANDUM

As noted above, it is a question of law whether a memorandum, considered in light of the circumstances surrounding its making, complies with the statute of frauds. Accordingly, the issue is generally amenable to resolution by summary judgment. We independently review the record to determine whether a triable issue of fact might defeat the statute of frauds defense in this case.

A memorandum of a contract for the sale of real property must identify the buyer, the seller, the price, and the property. Defendants contend the memorandum drafted by plaintiff Sterling fails to adequately specify the seller, the property, or the price. . . .

[handwritten margin note: memo lacks reqs]

As defendants forthrightly conceded in the trial court, "[t]he problem here is the price term." The Court of Appeal concluded that the lines in the memorandum stating "approx. 10.468 × gross income[,] estimated income 1.600.000, Price $16,750.00" were ambiguous, given the use of the modifier "approx." before the multiplier, the omitted zero in the price, and the uncertain meaning of "gross income." The court then considered Sterling's testimony that "approx." was meant to modify the total price, not the multiplier; that the missing zero was merely an error; and that "gross income" was used by the parties to refer to actual gross annual income. It decided that this evidence, if accepted by the trier of fact, could establish an agreement to determine the price based on a formula, which would be binding under Carver v. Teitsworth, 2 Cal. Rptr. 2d 446, 450 (Ct. App. 1991). In *Carver*, a bid for either a specified price or $1,000 over any higher bid was deemed sufficiently certain. . . .

[handwritten margin note: ambiguity w/ price term]

The Court of Appeal erred by deeming Sterling's testimony sufficient to establish his interpretation of the memorandum for purposes of the statute of frauds. Had Taylor testified that the parties meant to leave the price open to determination based on a rental income figure that was yet to be determined, this would be a different case. Then, the "admissions of the party to be charged" might have supported a reasonably certain price term derived from a negotiated formula. Rest. 2d Contracts §131, com. c. Here, however, Taylor insists the price was meant to be $16,750,000, and Sterling agrees that was the number he intended to write down, underlined, as the "Price."

$16,750,000 is clearly an approximate product of the formula specified in the memorandum, applied to the income figure stated there. On the other hand, Sterling's asserted price of $14,404,841 cannot reasonably be considered an approximation of $16,750,000. It is instead an approximate product of the formula applied to an actual income figure not found in the memorandum. The writing does not include the term "actual gross income," nor does it state that the price term will vary depending on proof or later agreement regarding the actual rental income from the buildings. In effect, Sterling would employ only the first part of the price term ("approx. 10.468 × gross income") and ignore the last parts ("estimated income 1.600.000, Price $16,750.00"). He would hold Taylor to a price that is 10.468 times the actual rental income figure gleaned from the rent rolls, but only "approximately" so because of Sterling's computational errors.

Thus, two competing interpretations of the memorandum were before the court. Taylor's is consistent with the figures provided in the memorandum, requiring only the correction of the price by reference to undisputed extrinsic evidence. Sterling's price is not stated in the memorandum, and depends on extrinsic evidence in the form of his own testimony, disputed by Taylor, that the parties intended to apply the formula to actual gross rental income instead of the estimated income noted in the memorandum. Even if the trier of fact were to accept Sterling's version of the parties' negotiations, the price he seeks is not reflected in the memorandum; indeed, it is inconsistent with the price term that appears in the memorandum. Under these circumstances, we conclude the evidence is insufficient to establish Sterling's price term with the reasonable certainty required by the statute of frauds.

The statute of frauds demands written evidence that reflects the parties' mutual understanding of the essential terms of their agreement, when viewed in light of the transaction at issue and the dispute before the court. The writing requirement is intended to permit the enforcement of agreements actually reached, but "to prevent enforcement through fraud or perjury of contracts never in fact made." Rest. 2d Contracts, §131, com. c, p. 335. The sufficiency of a memorandum to fulfill this purpose may depend on the quality of the extrinsic evidence offered to explain its terms. . . . Here . . . the extrinsic evidence offered by plaintiffs is at odds with the writing, which states a specific price and does not indicate that the parties contemplated any change based on actual rental income. Therefore, the evidence is insufficient to show with reasonable certainty that the parties understood and agreed to the price alleged by plaintiffs. The price terms stated in the memorandum, considered together with the extrinsic evidence of the contemplated price, leave a degree of doubt that the statute of frauds does not tolerate. The trial court properly granted defendants summary judgment.

III. DISPOSITION

The judgment of the Court of Appeal is reversed with directions to affirm the trial court judgment in its entirety.

KENNARD, Justice, concurring and dissenting, joined by Justice WERDEGAR. I agree with the majority that extrinsic evidence is admissible to resolve the meaning of an ambiguity in a written memorandum required by the statute of frauds as evidence of an agreement, and that conflicts in the evidence are for the trier of fact to resolve. The majority, however, goes astray when it takes it upon itself to resolve an existing conflict in the evidence. In my view, the ambiguity in the language of the memorandum at issue should be resolved by the trier of fact. . . .

Problem 4A

(a) Gary and Jean, a married couple, own property in Charleston. On August 1, they enter into a contract to sell the property to Katie and Andrew for a price of $600,000 and undertake to convey good and marketable fee simple title to the property by delivery of a warranty deed at a closing to be held on November 1. On August 10, Gary and Jean take out a 60-day loan in the amount of $100,000 secured by a mortgage against the property. Katie and Andrew learn about this loan on August 15 and object in writing to the placing of the mortgage lien against the property. They insist that the action by Gary and Jean is improper because, as sellers, they have already contracted away the ability to deal further with the property. Gary and Jean respond by saying that Katie and Andrew are wrong. Which party is correct, and why?

(b) Assume that only Gary signed the contract of sale with Katie and Andrew on August 1. Jean was out of town that weekend and did not find out about Katie and Andrew until a week later. On October 12, during the contract period, a major business from the northeastern United States announces that it will relocate to the Charleston area and that it expects to hire 3,000 new employees. This news drives the price of housing up and Gary realizes that their home is now worth $900,000. Katie and Andrew are amazed at their good fortune; the property they contracted to buy at $600,000 has already appreciated by $300,000. On October 30, Gary sends a notice to Katie and Andrew stating, "My wife, Jean, refuses to sign off on the contract and likewise as to any deed, thus I will not be able to go any further with the discussions we have been pursuing concerning the sale of my home, unless, of course, you are willing to increase your offer price to $900,000." Katie and Andrew are shocked when they receive this note. Are Gary and Jean permitted to do this? Will they have to pay damages? Can Katie and Andrew specifically enforce the contract? If Gary and Jean can escape an obligation under the agreement, how might a buyer reduce the risk of a similar loss in a future deal?

(c) Would Katie and Andrew have an ability to avoid the contract if the news had gone the other way? For example, assume that during the contract period, the Defense Department announces a major cost savings move in which it will close all military facilities in the Charleston area. The result of this news on housing prices is that prices fall. Gary and Jean's home has a new market value of $400,000, down from the contract price of $600,000. Can Katie and Andrew just walk away from the deal without legal consequences? Does it make a difference if Katie and Andrew cancel the contract before Jean signs it? That is, if the value of the house drops and Jean decides to sign the contract before Katie and Andrew withdraw the contract, can they still cancel it? Should it make any sense to treat the situations differently based on when and whether Jean signs? What is the problem with treating them the same, or with treating them differently?

2. Other Requirements for an Enforceable Contract

In addition to the statute of frauds requirement of a writing for the sale of real property, we must remember that the entire domain of contract law generally applies to real estate transactions. This means that there will be issues of adequate consideration, offer, acceptance, unconscionability, anticipatory repudiation, breach, warranty, and damages, among others. This is important to keep in mind, because it is easy to forget when the subject matter of a contract is real property. For instance, the law governing deeds, leases, titles, mortgages, foreclosures, liens, real covenants, and priority rights can be very different from that governing contract law, or from the law applicable to personal property. The underlying law applicable to your subject matter can nonetheless generally be the subject of contract. This means that when parties to a transaction structure their relationship, they are given the opportunity to impose obligations and benefits on each other in a manner prescribed by contract law principles. To do this effectively, however, requires a working knowledge of the relevant property law so that the appropriate risks, obligations, and consequences of a proposed transaction can be accounted for in the parties' agreement. Thus, a person needs to know the types of deeds that are available to convey real property, and also the rules and consequences, under real property law, related to those deeds, before he can intelligently invoke contract law to structure a relationship involving the property.

In today's real estate markets, most transactions will include some non-real property elements, which means that the contract of purchase and sale will have to account for more than just real property law. Even in the simplest residential home sale, for example, the transfer of basic appliances such as a stove or refrigerator is covered under the law pertaining to the sale of goods, and the transfer of the furnace and central air conditioning units might well fall into yet another classification as fixtures. Some forms of residential housing offer even more complication. The purchase and sale of a cooperative apartment, for instance, actually involves the transfer of stock, which is considered personal property subject to a security interest under Article 9 of the Uniform Commercial Code (UCC), rather than a real estate mortgage.

Problem 4B

Gina has contracted to buy Donald's diner for $750,000. The diner sits on a two-acre lot and is equipped with a commercial kitchen. Gina is borrowing $700,000 from Niagara Bank to purchase the diner, the loan is to be secured by all of the property being transferred. The contract of sale includes the transfer to Gina of "all of the real property together with all of the furniture, appliances, dishes, flatware, stock, and inventory of the diner now located on the premises." Donald has his lawyer prepare a deed to deliver to Gina at closing. Gina is satisfied with the deed and ready to close, but the attorney for Gina's lender objects. The attorney for Niagara Bank questions the ability of Donald to transfer by a single warranty deed all of the furniture, appliances, dishes, flatware, stock, and inventory.

Why do you think the Niagara Bank attorney is concerned? If you were Gina's attorney, how might you resolve the situation so that the bank will approve the closing?

While discussing the issue raised above, the Niagara Bank attorney raises another question. He wants to know about the diner's famous chicken and rib barbeque sauce recipe. He tells Gina that the secret family recipe is an important asset of the diner and the bank thought it was included in the sale. Gina responds that she too thought it was included in the deed transfer of the property. Assuming Donald agreed to transfer the recipe as part of the deal, can it be done in the same deed as is used for the real estate transfer?

MORAN v. ERK
Court of Appeals of New York, 2008
901 N.E.2d 187

READ, Judge. On December 13, 1995, defendants Mehmet and Susan Erk signed a real estate contract to purchase the home of plaintiffs James J. and Kathleen D. Moran, a 5,000-square-foot ranch-style house located in Clarence, New York. The contract, which was executed by the Morans on December 22, 1995, provided for a purchase price of $505,000, and contained a rider with an "ATTORNEY APPROVAL CONTINGENCY" stating as follows:

> This Contract is contingent upon approval by attorneys for Seller and Purchaser by the third business day following each party's attorney's receipt of a copy of the fully executed Contract (the "Approval Period"). . . . If either party's attorney disapproves this Contract before the end of the Approval Period, it is void and the entire deposit shall be returned.

Both the contract and the rider were form documents copyrighted and approved by the Greater Buffalo Association of Realtors, Inc. and the Bar Association of Erie County.

After signing the contract, the Erks developed qualms about purchasing the Morans' house. They discussed their misgivings with each other and with friends and family, and ultimately decided to buy a different residence. As a result, they instructed their attorney to disapprove the contract, and she did so on December 28, 1995, which was within the three-day period for invoking the attorney approval contingency.

The Morans — who had moved out of their Clarence residence in September 1995 — kept the house on the market until it was eventually sold for $385,000 in late 1998. Shortly thereafter, they sued the Erks in Supreme Court, alleging breach of contract. They sought to recover as damages the difference between the contract price of $505,000 and the eventual sale price of $385,000, as well as "carrying costs" for marketing the Clarence property for almost three years beyond the date of the 1995 contract with the Erks.

After a bench trial, Supreme Court found in the Morans' favor, and entered a judgment against the Erks for $234,065.75, which represented the difference between the contract price and the eventual sale price, plus statutory interest. . . . [T]he Appellate Division affirmed in a short memorandum opinion. We subsequently granted the Erks' motion for leave to appeal and now reverse.

Attorney approval contingencies are routinely included in real estate contracts in upstate New York. Requiring a real estate contract to be "subject to" or "contingent upon" the approval of attorneys for both contracting parties ensures that real estate brokers avoid the unauthorized practice of law, and allows both contracting parties to have agents representing their respective legal interests. Where a real estate contract states that it is "subject to" or "contingent upon" the approval of each party's attorney, this language means what it says: no vested rights are created by the contract prior to the expiration of the contingency period. *See* Black's Law Dictionary 828 (8th ed. 2004), contingent interest ("An interest that the holder may enjoy *only upon the occurrence of a condition precedent*") (emphasis added).

Here, as previously noted, the contract between the Erks and the Morans explicitly stated that "[t]his Contract is *contingent upon approval by attorneys for Seller and Purchaser* by the third business day following each party's attorney's receipt of a copy of the fully executed Contract," and further provided that "[i]f either party's attorney disapproves this Contract before the end of the Approval Period, *it is void*" (emphases added). The Morans argue that the contract nonetheless created an implied limitation upon an attorney's discretion to approve or disapprove the contract. We do not ordinarily read implied limitations into unambiguously worded contractual provisions designed to protect contracting parties. The Morans, however, contend — and the lower courts apparently agreed — that the implied covenant of good faith and fair dealing implicitly limits an attorney's ability to approve or disapprove a real estate contract pursuant to an attorney approval contingency. This argument misconstrues the implied covenant of good faith and fair dealing under New York law.

The implied covenant of good faith and fair dealing between parties to a contract embraces a pledge that "neither party shall do anything which will have the effect of destroying or injuring the right of the other party to receive the fruits of the contract." 511 W. 232nd Owners Corp. v. Jennifer Realty Co., 773 N.E.2d 496, 500 (N.Y. 2002). Yet the plain language of the contract in this case makes clear that any "fruits" of the contract were *contingent* on attorney approval, as any reasonable person in the Morans' position should have understood.

Further, considerations of clarity, predictability, and professional responsibility weigh against reading an implied limitation into the attorney approval contingency. Clarity and predictability are particularly important in the interpretation of contracts. . . . But the bad faith rule advocated by the Morans, which derives from McKenna v. Case, 507 N.Y.S.2d 777 (App. Div. 4th Dept. 1986), advances none of those objectives.

In *McKenna*, a short memorandum opinion, the Appellate Division held that an attorney's disapproval pursuant to an attorney approval contingency "would terminate plaintiff's rights under the contract, *unless said disapproval is occasioned by bad faith.*" *Id.* at 777 (emphasis added). The court further stated,

> While the issue of "bad faith" usually raises a question of fact precluding summary judgment, the uncontradicted proof demonstrates conclusively that defendant acted in bad faith by instructing his attorney to disapprove the contract. Defendant, by interfering and preventing his attorney from considering the contract, acted in bad faith and, therefore, the condition that the contract be approved by seller's attorney must be deemed waived and the contract formed. *Id.* at 777-78.

Reading a bad faith exception into an attorney approval contingency would create[,] as the *McKenna* court itself recognized, a regime where "question[s] of fact precluding summary judgment" would "usually [be] raise[d]" by a disappointed would-be seller or buyer *any time* an attorney disapproved a real estate contract pursuant to an attorney approval contingency. In an area of law where clarity and predictability are particularly important, "this novel notion would be entirely dependent on the subjective equitable variations of different Judges and courts instead of the objective, reliable, predictable and relatively definitive rules" of plain-text contractual language. Ely-Cruikshank Co. v. Bank of Montreal, 615 N.E.2d 985, 988 (N.Y. 1993).

The circumstances of this case illustrate the chanciness inherent in a bad faith rule. The Erks' attorney disapproved the contract for the sale of the

Morans' Clarence house in late 1995. The Erks soon bought a house in a different community, and continued on with their lives, relying on their attorney's disapproval of a contract that declared that such disapproval rendered it "void." Some three years after their last contact with the Morans, the Erks were served with the complaint in this breach-of-contract lawsuit. Now—10 years after their attorney disapproved the contract within a three-day disapproval period—the Erks are fighting a six-figure judgment for putatively breaching an unwritten covenant because of something Mrs. Erk may have said or neglected to say in a single conversation with her attorney.

Indeed, any inquiry into whether a particular attorney disapproval was motivated by bad faith will likely require factual examination of communications between the disapproving attorney and that attorney's client. *See, e.g., McKenna,* 507 N.Y.S.2d at 777 ("defendant acted in bad faith *by instructing his attorney to disapprove the contract*" (emphasis added)); Moran v. Erk, 844 N.Y.S.2d at 807 ("the evidence supports the court's determination that defendants acted in bad faith *by instructing their attorney to disapprove the contract*" (emphasis added)). That is, the disapproving attorney will be subpoenaed to testify about communications the disclosure of which might be detrimental to that attorney's client; a direct conflict with an attorney's duty to preserve a client's confidences and secrets. *See* 22 N.Y.C.R.R. 1200.19(a) (defining "secret" as "information gained in the professional relationship that the client has requested be held inviolate or the disclosure of which would be embarrassing or would be likely to be detrimental to the client"). This is precisely what occurred here, where the lower courts' findings of bad faith were expressly grounded in the deposition testimony of the Erks' attorney. Moreover, the threat to attorney-client confidentiality under a bad faith regime could harm the attorney-client relationship itself in the context of real estate transactions. A diligent attorney, cognizant of the risk of being subpoenaed to testify as to the basis for a disapproval, would face a perverse incentive to avoid candid communications with his or her client regarding a transaction in which the attorney is supposed to represent the client's legal interest.

All these potential problems vanish when an attorney approval contingency is interpreted according to its plain meaning, as our sister state of New Jersey has long done. *See* New Jersey State Bar Assn. v New Jersey Assn. of Realtor Bds., 452 A.2d 1323, 1325 (N.J. Super. Ct. 1982) (approving "broad construction" of attorney approval clause "enabling an attorney to disapprove a contract or lease for any reason or reasons which would not be subject to review"), *mod. on other grounds and aff'd,* 461 A.2d 1112 (N.J. 1983). We therefore hold that where a real estate contract contains an attorney approval contingency providing that the contract is "subject to" or "contingent upon" attorney approval within a specified time period and no further limitations on approval appear in the contract's language, an attorney for either party may timely disapprove the contract for any reason or for no stated reason. Since no explicit limitations were placed on the attorney approval contingency in the contract in this case, the Erks' attorney's timely disapproval was valid, and the contract is void by its express terms.

Accordingly, the order of the Appellate Division should be reversed, with costs, and the complaint dismissed.

B. EQUITABLE CONVERSION AND ALLOCATION OF RISK

One of the most significant legal consequences of entering a binding contract between the buyer and the seller of real property involves the doctrine of *equitable conversion*. In simple terms, this doctrine splits title to the property between the seller and the buyer at the moment the contract is signed. The seller is still the owner of the property and is said to retain *legal title* to the realty, while the buyer is said to acquire *equitable title*. This splitting of the title by way of the doctrine of equitable conversion has a number of legal consequences. To start with, it means that the buyer has an interest in the property even though the contract has not been fully performed. Both parties have the right to deal with their respective interests — that is, to buy, sell, assign, pledge, mortgage, devise, and insure, among other things. A seller may not want the buyer to have such abilities, because they could affect the ultimate risk of completing a successful transaction. For similar reasons, a buyer may want to limit the seller's right to transfer his legal title and interest in the property to a third party while the contract remains executory.

Another important consequence of equitable conversion relates to risk allocation during the executory contract period. The basic problem is to determine who should be responsible for a loss to the property during this time period when title is split between the expectant owner with equitable title and the seller with legal title. Common situations involve the destruction of building improvements by fire, hurricane, or similar natural disasters. Also included are disputes over special taxes or assessments levied after the signing of the contract but before the closing and actual transfer of title. Similar problems arise when there is a zoning change or a public condemnation proceeding implemented with respect to the property during this time. These and many other scenarios raise the question of which party should pay the cost or take the loss as a result of actions, events, or information that affect the value of the property during this stage of the transaction. The same type of question would arise if some new discovery enhanced the value of the property during this time period, such as the discovery of gold. In such a case, who gets the benefit of this value-enhancing benefit?

The rules that have developed generally start with the proposition that at the moment of equitable conversion, the buyer takes on the risks associated with anything that happens during the executory period. Over the years, courts were confronted with a variety of fact patterns that made them reevaluate the application of the risk allocation function of the doctrine. The courts took a number of approaches that included putting the risk on the party in possession or control of the property or assigning risk after the fact to the party who might have been the least-cost avoider. Most courts retained the basic pro-seller risk rule, but modified it around the edges to protect buyers under some circumstances. Most notably, equitable conversion operates to transfer the risk of loss to the buyer only if the contract is specifically enforceable at the time of the loss. Based on this precept, courts have often come up with reasons why, in retrospect, specific performance may be said not to have been available to the seller. Perhaps the seller had unperformed contract obligations, or there were title defects that had not yet been cured, or the buyer had not yet obtained financing as specified in an express contract condition.

In most states, common-law rules presently govern risk of loss, but there is one significant legislative reform. The Uniform Vendor and Purchaser Risk Act (UVPRA), drafted by contracts scholar Samuel Williston, may well be the most succinct uniform act in American legal history. The Act in its entirety states:

Uniform Vendor and Purchaser Risk Act (1935)

Section 1. Risk of Loss.

Any contract hereafter made in this State for the purchase and sale of realty shall be interpreted as including an agreement that the parties shall have the following rights and duties, unless the contract expressly provides otherwise:

(a) If, when neither the legal title nor the possession of the subject matter of the contract has been transferred, all or a material part thereof is destroyed without fault of the purchaser or is taken by eminent domain, the vendor cannot enforce the contract, and the purchaser is entitled to recover any portion of the price that he has paid;

(b) If, when either the legal title or the possession of the subject matter of the contract has been transferred, all or any part thereof is destroyed without fault of the vendor or is taken by eminent domain, the purchaser is not thereby relieved from a duty to pay the price, nor is he entitled to recover any portion thereof that he has paid.

Section 2. Uniformity of Interpretation.

This act shall be so interpreted and construed as to effectuate its general purpose to make uniform the law of those states which enact it.

Section 3. Short Title.

This act may be cited as the Uniform Vendor and Purchaser Risk Act.

Beginning in the 1930s, 12 states, including California and New York, enacted the UVPRA, some with minor modifications.

With the variety of rule choices for risk of loss that have developed, both judicial and statutory, only one thing is certain. A cautious lawyer does not subject his client to the risk of guessing which of the many rules a future court would apply to any particular case. The most important risk allocation rule for the practicing lawyer is that the parties are free to address the issues in their contract. This means that counsel for the parties should draft liberally with specific provisions addressing all manner of foreseeable risk. Generally, many types of risk are foreseeable, including fire, earthquake, hurricane, tornado, zoning changes, environmental regulation changes, bankruptcy, death, and interest rate changes, to name a few.

Each party to a real estate contract has an *insurable interest,* and this is generally true regardless of how the party's contract allocates risk of loss. When a property loss occurs during the contract executory period and one or both parties have insurance covering the relevant risk, one might suppose there would be little trouble and both parties could easily proceed to consummate the deal. Unfortunately, this is not so. Courts often have great trouble sorting things out when there is an insured loss and the parties' contract does not specifically address insurance matters. Ideally, the party who has the risk of loss should obtain insurance, but this doesn't always happen. The most common scenario is the seller having property insurance but the buyer assuming the risk of loss, either under the implied doctrine of equitable conversion or under an express contract provision. A standard principle of insurance law states that an insurance contract is a personal contract between the insurance company and the insured, giving rise to no third-party rights. Following this characterization, the traditional judicial response was to ignore the seller's insurance policy when the contract was silent on the matter, permitting the seller to collect insurance proceeds *and* enforce the contract against the buyer for the full price. Although some states still follow this rule, most states perceive this outcome as a windfall for the seller coupled with a devastating, undeserved loss to the buyer, and thus they have reformed their laws to protect the buyer under these circumstances. The insurance proceeds are held in trust by the seller for the buyer, and if the transaction goes forward to close, the buyer receives a credit on the price equal to the proceeds minus the amount of the insurance premium previously paid by the seller. This device of an implied trust overrides the maxim that insurance is a personal contract of indemnity, in effect making the insurance proceeds into a substitute res that runs with the land.

BRUSH GROCERY KART, INC. v. SURE FINE MARKET, INC.
Supreme Court of Colorado, 2002
47 P.3d 680

Coats, Justice. . . .

In October 1992 Brush Grocery Kart, Inc. and Sure Fine Market, Inc. entered into a five-year "Lease with Renewal Provisions and Option to

Purchase" for real property, including a building to be operated by Brush as a grocery store. Under the contract's purchase option provision, any time during the last six months of the lease, Brush could elect to purchase the property at a price equal to the average of the appraisals of an expert designated by each party.

Shortly before expiration of the lease, Brush notified Sure Fine of its desire to purchase the property and begin the process of determining a sale price. Although each party offered an appraisal, the parties were unable to agree on a final price by the time the lease expired. Brush then vacated the premises, returned all keys to Sure Fine, and advised Sure Fine that it would discontinue its casualty insurance covering the property during the lease. Brush also filed suit, alleging that Sure Fine failed to negotiate the price term in good faith and asking for the appointment of a special master to determine the purchase price. Sure Fine agreed to the appointment of a special master and counterclaimed, alleging that Brush negotiated the price term in bad faith and was therefore the breaching party.

During litigation over the price term, the property was substantially damaged during a hail storm. With neither party carrying casualty insurance, each asserted that the other was liable for the damage. The issue was added to the litigation at a stipulated amount of $60,000. The court appointed a special master . . . accepted his appraised value of $375,000. The court then found that under the doctrine of equitable conversion, Brush was the equitable owner of the property and bore the risk of loss. It therefore declined to abate the purchase price or award damages to Brush for the loss.

Brush appealed the loss allocation, and the court of appeals affirmed on similar grounds. . . . Noting that allocation of the risk of loss in circumstances where the vendee is not in possession had not previously been addressed by an appellate court in this jurisdiction, the court of appeals went on to conclude that a "bright line rule" allocating the risk of loss to the vendee, without regard to possession, would best inform the parties of their rights and obligations under a contract for the sale of land. . . .

III. The Risk of Casualty Loss in the Absence of Statutory Authority

In the absence of statutory authority, the rights, powers, duties, and liabilities arising out of a contract for the sale of land have frequently been derived by reference to the theory of equitable conversion. This theory or doctrine, which has been described as a legal fiction, is based on equitable principles that permit the vendee to be considered the equitable owner of the land and debtor for the purchase money and the vendor to be regarded as a secured creditor. The changes in rights and liabilities that occur upon the making of the contract result from the equitable right to specific performance. Even with regard to third parties, the theory has been relied on to determine, for example, the devolution, upon death, of the rights and liabilities of each party with respect to the land, *see* Chain O'Mines v. Williamson, 72 P.2d 265, 266 (Colo. 1937), and to ascertain the powers of creditors of each party to reach the land in payment of their claims.

The assignment of the risk of casualty loss in the executory period of contracts for the sale of real property varies greatly throughout the jurisdictions of this country. What appears to yet be a slim majority of states, *see* Randy R. Koenders, Annotation, *Risk of Loss by Casualty Pending Contract for Conveyance of Real Property Modern Cases*, 85 A.L.R.4th 233 (2001), places the risk of loss on the vendee from the moment of contracting, on the rationale that once an equitable conversion takes place, the vendee must be treated as owner for all purposes. Once the vendee becomes the equitable owner, he therefore becomes responsible for the condition of the property, despite not having a present right of occupancy or control. In sharp contrast, a handful of other states reject the allocation of casualty loss risk as a consequence of the theory of equitable conversion and follow the equally rigid "Massachusetts Rule," under which the seller continues to bear the risk until actual transfer of the title, absent an express agreement to the contrary. A substantial and growing number of jurisdictions, however, base the legal consequences of no-fault casualty loss on the right to possession of the property at the time the loss occurs. This view has found expression in the Uniform Vendor and Purchaser Risk Act, and while a number of states have adopted some variation of the Uniform Act, others have arrived at a similar position through the interpretations of their courts.

This court has applied the theory of equitable conversion in limited circumstances affecting title, . . . and refused to apply it in some circumstances, *see Chain O'Mines,* 72 P.2d 265 (holding that even if the doctrine applies to option contracts, no conversion would take place until the option were exercised by the party having the right of election). . . . It has never before, however, expressly relied on the theory of equitable conversion alone as allocating the risk of casualty loss to a vendee.

In Wiley v. Lininger, 204 P.2d 1083 (Colo. 1949), where fire destroyed improvements on land occupied by the vendee during the multi-year executory period of an installment land contract, we held, according to the generally accepted rule, that neither the buyer nor the seller, each of whom had an insurable interest in the property, had an obligation to insure the property for the benefit of the other. We also adopted a rule, which we characterized as "the majority rule," that "the vendee under a contract for the sale of land, being regarded as the equitable owner, assumes the risk of destruction of or injury to the property *where he is in possession,* and the destruction or loss is not proximately caused by the negligence of the vendor." *Id.* at 1085-86 (emphasis added). The vendee in possession was therefore not relieved of his obligation to continue making payments according to the terms of the contract, despite material loss by fire to some of the improvements on the property.

limited prec.

. . . While it may have been unnecessary to determine more than the obligations of a vendee in possession in that case, rather than limit the holding to that situation, this court pointedly announced a broader rule. The rule expressly articulated by this court limited the transfer of the risk of loss to vendees who are already in possession. Had this not been the court's deliberate intention, there would have been no need to mention possession at all because a rule governing all vendees would necessarily include vendees in possession. Whether or not a majority of jurisdictions would actually limit the transfer of risk in precisely the same way, the rule as clearly stated and adopted by this court was supported by strong policy and theoretical considerations at the time, and those considerations apply equally today.

Those jurisdictions that indiscriminately include the risk of casualty loss among the incidents or "attributes" of equitable ownership do so largely in reliance on ancient authority or by considering it necessary for consistent application of the theory of equitable conversion. . . . Under virtually any accepted understanding of the theory, however, equitable conversion is not viewed as entitling the purchaser to every significant right of ownership, and particularly not the right of possession. As a matter of both logic and equity, the obligation to maintain property in its physical condition follows the right to have actual possession and control rather than a legal right to force conveyance of the property through specific performance at some future date.

The equitable conversion theory is literally stood on its head by imposing on a vendee, solely because of his right to specific performance, the risk that the vendor will be unable to specifically perform when the time comes because of an accidental casualty loss. . . .

By contrast, there is substantial justification, both as a matter of law and policy, for not relieving a vendee who is entitled to possession before transfer of title, of his duty to pay the full contract price, notwithstanding an accidental loss. In addition to having control over the property and being entitled to the benefits of its use, an equitable owner who also has the right of possession has already acquired virtually all of the rights of ownership and almost invariably will have already paid at least some portion of the contract price to exercise those rights. By expressly including in the contract for sale the right of possession, which otherwise generally accompanies transfer of title, the vendor has for all practical purposes already transferred the property as promised, and the parties have in effect expressed their joint intention that the vendee pay the purchase price as promised.

rule

. . . In the absence of a right of possession, a vendee of real property that suffers a material casualty loss during the executory period of the contract, through no fault of his own, must be permitted to rescind and recover any payments he had already made. *Cf.* Uniform Vendor and Purchaser Risk Act §1.

Furthermore, where a vendee is entitled to rescind as a result of casualty loss, the vendee should generally also be entitled to partial specific performance of the contract with an abatement in the purchase price reflecting the loss. Where the damage is ascertainable, permitting partial specific performance with a price abatement allows courts as nearly as possible to fulfill the expectations of the parties expressed in the contract, while leaving each in a position that is equitable relative to the other. Partial specific performance with a price abatement has long been recognized in this jurisdiction as an alternative to rescission in the analogous situation in which a vendor of real property is unable to convey marketable title to all of the land described in the contract.

Here, Brush was clearly not in possession of the property as the equitable owner. . . . The casualty loss was ascertainable and in fact stipulated by the parties, and neither party challenged the district court's enforcement of the contract except with regard to its allocation of the casualty loss. Both the court of appeals and the district court therefore erred in finding that the doctrine of equitable conversion required Brush to bear the loss caused by hail damage.

IV. CONCLUSION

Where Brush was not an equitable owner in possession at the time of the casualty loss, it was entitled to rescind its contract with Sure Fine. At least under the circumstances of this case, where Brush chose to go forward with the contract under a stipulation as to loss from the hail damage, it was also entitled to specific performance with an abatement of the purchase price equal to the casualty loss. The judgment of the court of appeals is therefore reversed and the case is remanded for further proceedings consistent with this opinion.

Problem 4C

(a) On September 12, Buyer and Seller enter into a contract for the purchase and sale of a 3,000-square-foot house. The closing date is set for December 1. During the executory contract period Buyer applies for a mortgage loan to cover 50 percent of the financing of the purchase price of $400,000. ABC bank agrees to make the loan to Buyer. Prior to the closing on the contract, ABC bank, as a result of a series of bad loans, is taken over and placed in receivership. Consequently, ABC is unable to provide funds for the scheduled closing on the contract. Buyer seeks to escape from the contract on the grounds that the risk of this occurrence was on the seller. What result, under what assumptions? Should the court use mutual mistake to provide a remedy? If it does so, what effect would the availability of the remedy have on the allocation of risk between the parties?

(b) Buyer and Seller are negotiating a contract for purchase and sale of a seven-year-old single-family house. They have exchanged various contract language to cover a number of risks and contingencies. One provision being discussed is specifically titled a "Risk of Loss" clause. It reads as follows:

> The risk of loss or damage to the Property by casualty or condemnation prior to the Closing Date is Seller's. If the Property is damaged by some casualty prior to the Closing Date, Seller agrees to the cost of repairing or restoring the Property, up to a value which does not exceed thirty percent (30%) of the valuation of the Property so damaged. Should aggregate damage exceed thirty percent (30%) of the Purchase Price hereof, then this Agreement may be rescinded at the option of either party.

vagueness

ambiguity

What comments, criticisms, or changes might you want to make if you represented the buyer? The seller? Or would this language be adequate for most cases?

Problem 4D

Gary owns a one-acre parcel of property with a four-bedroom home on it. He contracts to sell it to Jean for $400,000. They value the lot at about $100,000 and the structure at $300,000. According to the terms of the contract, "The owner of the Property shall have the risk of loss during the executory contract period." During the executory contract period, while Gary is in possession, the house burns to the ground as a result of a fire that was not caused by either party.

(a) If Gary has $300,000 of insurance on the property (to cover the value of the improvements to the land) and Jean does not have any insurance, does Jean have to proceed under the contract? Is she entitled to the insurance proceeds if she pays the contract price? Does Gary have any obligation to rebuild the structure? If Gary sought to rebuild the structure, would it have to be an exact duplicate of the prior home, or could he use lower-cost or different materials? Who, if anyone, would supervise and approve the work?

(b) If Jean has $300,000 of insurance to cover the improvements but Gary does not (he previously cancelled his policy), should Jean be able to pocket the money and walk away from the transaction?

(c) What if both parties have insurance, but neither one has an adequate policy of coverage? Assume Gary has kept his policy in force, but has not updated it for several years, so his coverage is only $225,000 for the improvements. Jean has also insured the property, but took a deal on a low-cost policy that covers less than 100 percent of a loss by fire, so she can only get a maximum of $275,000. In this case, what should each party's obligation be, and why? Should the insurance companies have to pay out a total of $500,000 under their policies even though the property loss is $300,000?

(d) In the above situations, who is meant to be benefited by the insurance? Should the presence of insurance coverage be relevant to the questions of contract interpretation and the allocation of risk? Does the contract term drafted by the parties clarify the problem in any of the foregoing situations? Would it make a difference in the above situations if the jurisdiction had enacted the Uniform Vendor and Purchaser Risk Act?

C. MAJOR CONTRACT CONDITIONS

During the executory contract period, there are many ways to allocate risk between the parties. In addition to the use of implied rules such as equitable conversion, risk can be allocated by express promises as well as by warranties, representations, and conditions. Transactional lawyers often use the term "covenants" instead of promises; they mean the same thing (historically, a covenant was a promise made under seal.) Promises allocate risk by mapping out the parties' mutual expectations and obligations. They can also reduce risk by assigning specific tasks to each party. The seller may, for example, undertake or promise to get title search work done on the property, while the buyer agrees to file applications for permits that are needed.

In addition to promises for contractual undertakings, a number of contract warranties and representations will likely be made between the parties. The term _warranty_ has different meanings in different context. In contract law, warranty generally means an affirmation of fact or a promise to pay damages if something is not as described, or if a certain event occurs that defeats a party's expectations. A _representation_ is a present statement of fact. When a representation is made in a contract, it is one type of warranty. Sometimes the term representation is used to describe an affirmation of fact that precedes and induces the contract. All of these contract terms are designed to address areas of informational risk. A seller, for instance, tells a buyer that the house he is selling is free of radon gas problems and that it is located in "Elite School District #1." If this information is important to the buyer, he might want to have the contract address it specifically. The buyer may want a contract provision that says, "Seller hereby represents and warrants that this property is free of any and all radon gas problems meaning that any government calibrated reading levels would register at '0'; and, Seller further represents and warrants that the property is located within the Elite School District #1 and eligible for all of the benefits thereof." By putting these express provisions in the contract, the buyer gains a direct cause of action against the seller should the information prove to be false. It also provides some basis for arguing that the particular items of information were material to the buyer's decision to purchase the property. If the information proves to be incorrect, the buyer may have a cause of action for breach of warranty.

Contracts of purchase and sale contain many conditions (conditions are often called "contingencies" in real estate contracts). In drafting contracts, conditions serve to allocate risk and establish an orderly timing for the performance of specific tasks. They also help to reduce economic exposure and cost by sometimes allowing one party to hold back on certain actions or expenses until the other party has first accomplished a preliminary prerequisite or objective. Should the preliminary objective fail to occur, no further action or investment may be required. A typical contract condition will make the buyer's obligation to go forward with a purchase conditional on being approved for an appropriate home mortgage loan. This means that if the buyer cannot get such a loan, the buyer does not have to proceed under the contract toward closing. Similarly, when a contract has such a mortgage loan condition, the seller will usually make his obligation to obtain costly title information conditional upon the buyer's first being approved for a loan.

Not all conditions provide for termination of the contract in the event that a condition does not occur. Generally, though, the major conditions related to financing, title, and land use will provide for such a termination. Other conditions may spell out different consequences in the event that they fail to take place. Contract conditions can be used to order other rights and obligations between the parties even as they proceed with an exchange.

Timing issues may be resolved by resort to the classification of conditions. Does language create a condition precedent, a condition subsequent, or simultaneous conditions, or is it merely poor drafting that results in no condition at all?

With respect to conditions and other performance requirements under a contract, most courts strictly enforce the time for performance if the contract states a date certain and provides that "time is of the essence." Some states have relaxed the "time is of the essence" rule, which requires careful and explicit drafting for the parties to make time of the essence. When time is essential, to enforce strict compliance with stated dates, one must avoid taking steps that might be interpreted as evidence of waiver or estoppel with respect to time being of the essence.

If a contract term is interpreted as establishing a condition precedent or a simultaneous condition, the parties will generally be released from any further obligations; but if the contract language in question is interpreted as a promise, there may be a different result. In the case of a breached promise, when the breach does not destroy the entire value of the exchange, the parties may be obligated to proceed under the contract with only an allowance for the breach of the promise or warranty. The allowance might be in the form of a price abatement or an award of damages to account for the diminished value of a given performance, but the end result is that, as is not the case with an unmet condition, performance may still be required.

Whenever the buyer and the seller begin the process of drafting a contract, they must keep in mind the effects that their agreement may have on third parties. Prior to executing the purchase and sale agreement, for instance, the seller probably has already entered into an agreement with a broker to sell his property. To a certain extent, the seller may have already committed himself to undertakings with the broker that will not be subject to alteration in the purchase and sale contract. Answering the question of what happens under the contract between the buyer and the seller does not always tell one what happens with respect to third parties like the broker.

In the next part of this chapter, we consider the condition for mortgage financing in more detail. In Chapters 8 and 9, we discuss contract conditions related to marketable title, including the provision for the preparation of a survey. Taken together, the conditions for mortgage financing, title examination, and survey preparation are probably the most important examples of the use of contract conditions in the residential transaction. The lessons to be learned from these examples can be applied to many other contract areas one will encounter when participating in more complex real estate transactions.

In most real estate transactions, the exchange will require some form of financing. The buyer seldom does a transaction for all cash, although this is sometimes the case. Usually, the buyer does not have all the necessary cash, but has some money on hand, plus the credit to borrow the remaining capital. When a buyer undertakes to borrow funds in the financial markets or from the seller, there will be a charge for the extension of credit. The value of the transaction must, therefore, cover the cost of financing. Additionally, the cost of credit for any particular real estate investment must be weighed against alternative investment opportunities. Thus, the buyer must think in terms of both the accounting and economic profit potential from the proposed investment. Tax motivations may also play a factor in determining the profitability of an exchange. Similarly, the buyer's asset and liquidity position may restrict or limit the availability of credit even in a situation where additional borrowing might prove to be profitable.

To understand the buyer's position more clearly, one should start with the rule that in the absence of any contract financing terms, the transaction would most likely be construed to be an "all-cash" exchange. An *all-cash exchange* means that the buyer undertakes to buy the property at the stated price and takes on all the risk of having the full amount of money in hand at closing.

When the buyer obtains financing from the seller, the transaction is usually documented as a *purchase-money mortgage* (PMM). Generally, people in real estate refer to a PMM only when the seller is the one providing financing. Figure 4-1 illustrates the general understanding of the PMM transaction. The seller of the property not only undertakes to convey the property to the buyer, but also agrees to act as the lender on the deal. Seller, therefore, extends credit to the buyer to facilitate buyer's acquisition of the property. In doing this, the seller should obtain a formal mortgage and promissory note setting out the terms of the credit arrangement and providing seller with a right to foreclose in the event that buyer defaults on the terms of the credit agreement. Buyer therefore, pays an agreed-upon amount of cash at closing, and covers the remaining purchase obligation by executing the PMM and note establishing the terms of credit.

The term PMM sometimes refers more broadly to include a mortgage loan made by a third-party lender to enable the buyer to acquire the property. Under the broader definition, the PMM in real property has the same scope as the purchase-money security interest (PMSI) under Article 9 of the UCC (*see* §9-107). Although PMMs are very common, not all extensions of mortgage credit are purchase-money transactions. For instance, home equity loans are not PMMs. Likewise, people sometimes grant a mortgage on their property in order to finance other purchases or activities.

The PMM is unlike the PMSI under UCC Article 9 in that it may or may not have a special priority status. Under real property law, the priority of a claim against real estate is governed by the recording statutes and related legal principles. In some states this means that a PMM will generally be given whatever priority it has with respect to other creditor claims based on when it was recorded in the public records. Some other states, however, will grant a special priority to a PMM that is made contemporaneously with any third-party financing, even if recorded later. This is different from the PMSI under Article 9, which provides a uniform system for PMSI lenders to obtain a super priority over the competing claims of secured creditors that are prior in time. In the real property context, priority for a later creditor, even if a PMM creditor, can generally be earned only by getting the party with the earlier priority to agree to a subordination of his claim.

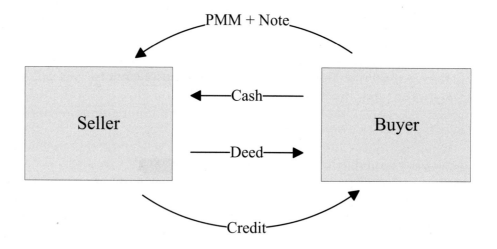

Figure 4-1
Purchase-Money Mortgage Transaction

LOUISIANA REAL ESTATE COMMISSION v. BUTLER
Court of Appeal of Louisiana, 2005
899 So. 2d 151

EZELL, Judge. This is a concursus matter arising out of a contract to buy a home. The buyers, Dr. Brett Butler and his wife, Elizabeth, appeal the decision of the trial court awarding the sellers, Dr. Edward Crocker and his wife Trudy, a $12,500 deposit for the failure to complete the transaction. For the following reasons, we affirm the decision of the trial court.

The Crockers owned a home in Lake Charles which was listed for sale through ERA Moffett Realty. Through their own realtor, the Butlers found the home and eventually submitted a purchase agreement, offering to buy the home for the sum of $770,000. The agreement was signed by both parties, and a deposit of $12,500 was given by the Butlers. The contract stated that the sale was contingent on the Butlers obtaining financing for the home, the amount of which was "to be determined," at an eight and one half percent interest rate. The Butlers applied for a loan through Red River Bank. The loan was denied. Thereafter, the Butlers sought the return of their deposit. The Crockers refused. Based on this dispute, the Louisiana Real Estate Commission filed this concursus proceeding in the trial court below. The trial court found that no specific amount of funding was set out by the contract as a condition, only that the desired interest rate be secured. Noting that there was no evidence that the rate was not obtained, the trial court found that the Crockers were entitled to keep the deposit. From this decision, the Butlers appeal. . . .

The general rules of contract interpretation are found in Articles 2045 through 2057 of the Louisiana Civil Code. . . . "In case of doubt that cannot be otherwise resolved, a provision in a contract must be interpreted against the party who furnished its text." La. Civ. Code art. 2056.

The agreement to purchase or sell in this matter contained two pertinent provisions. The first provision, paragraph two, stated[1]

> THIS SALE is conditioned upon the ability of the PURCHASER(s) to borrow upon this property as security the sum of $**To Be Determined** by a Mortgage loan or loans at an initial Fixed rate of interest not to exceed 8¹/₂% per annum payable in equal monthly installments, or upon such other terms that may be acceptable to PURCHASER, so long as such terms create no additional cost to seller and do not affect the closing date.

The other provision, included in paragraph seven, states that "PURCHASER represents that PURCHASER has the funds necessary to satisfy Purchasers obligations, including the down payment, under this Agreement."

The Butlers contend that because they applied for a loan of ninety percent of the value of the home and were rejected that they have met

---

1. Bold emphasis indicates handwritten portions of the agreement.

the requirements of the contract. We disagree. Nowhere within the four corners of the contract is listed any specific monetary amount the Butlers must have obtained loan approval for. On the contrary, the only condition set forth by the document is that a loan be approved at an eight and one half percent interest rate. There is no evidence that they could not obtain financing at some amount at the desired rate. If the Butlers had wanted to require a specific amount of financing, they could have simply inserted whatever amount they desired into the blank where they wrote instead "to be determined." Taken in conjunction with the provision in paragraph seven which represents that the Butlers had sufficient funds to complete the transaction, including any down payment, it is clear that the Butlers failed to meet the obligations set out for them in the contract. Moreover, if there was any ambiguity in the contract, as the party who furnished the text in question, the "to be determined" provision in the contract must be interpreted against the Butlers. La. Civ. Code art. 2056. There is no error in the trial court's ruling awarding the Crockers the deposit.

The Butlers next assert that the agreement should be declared null and void for lack of consent, as a mutual misunderstanding existed as to the loan amount they would seek. This is based on Mr. Butler's self serving assertion that, at the time the contract was signed, he only intended to put forth a ten percent down payment and seek financing for the remainder. However, as noted above, if he had actually intended to set a limit as to the maximum amount he would finance, he, as the writer of the contract, could simply have inserted the ninety percent amount into the contract. Furthermore, Charmayne Crawford, one of the realtors handling the sale, testified that forty percent of all purchase agreements contain the "to be determined" language and that she felt, based on the language, that the Butlers would have no trouble obtaining funds, but were only seeking a set interest rate. There is no evidence in the record of a mutual misunderstanding as to the terms of the contract. . . .

For the above reasons, we affirm the decision of the trial court. Costs of this appeal are assessed against Brett and Elizabeth Butler.

ALH HOLDING COMPANY v. BANK OF TELLURIDE
Supreme Court of Colorado, 2000
18 P.3d 742

COATS, Justice. . . .

. . . The Petitioner, ALH Holding Company, sold real property to Linda Crocker and Robert Hackley (the "buyers") for $165,000. In connection with the sale, the buyers borrowed $110,000 from ALH in exchange for a promissory note secured with a vendor's purchase money deed of trust in favor of ALH. The buyers also borrowed $55,000 from the Respondent, the Bank of Telluride, and similarly signed a promissory note secured with a purchase money deed of trust in favor of the Bank. Both ALH and the Bank knew, before the closing, that the other would be loaning money to the purchaser and that both loans would be secured by deeds of trust conveying interests in the same property. Telluride Mountain Title Company closed the transaction for both parties on June 29, 1993, and on the following day recorded the deeds of trust. The deed of trust in favor of the Bank was recorded before that of ALH.

Default

After the buyers defaulted on both notes, the Bank initiated a public trustee's foreclosure sale of its interest in the property, characterizing its own deed of trust as a superior lien to that of ALH. ALH brought an action against the Bank, seeking a preliminary injunction and a declaratory judgment resolving the respective priorities of the two deeds of trust. The parties stipulated to certain facts and moved for a determination of the question of priority as between the two deeds of trust pursuant to C.R.C.P. 56(h). The district court concluded that as a matter of Colorado law, a vendor's purchase money deed of trust takes priority over a third-party's purchase money deed of trust, and it entered judgment in favor of ALH.

With one member dissenting, a panel of the court of appeals reversed. . . .

This court granted ALH's petition for a writ of certiorari to consider whether the court of appeals properly applied the state's recording statute and if not to indicate the principles upon which the priority of interests should be determined.

II

Recording statutes in this country have long operated to alter the priority of various property rights on the basis of notice, recording, or some combination of the two. Colorado has had a recording statute since 1861. *See* §9, Colo. G.L., p. 65 (1861). The statute has undergone numerous revisions from its original form and is currently codified at section 38-35-109(1) of the Colorado Revised Statutes. At the time applicable to the events in this case, the recording statute included the following language:

Stat

> All deeds, powers of attorney, agreements, or other instruments in writing conveying, encumbering, or affecting the title to real property, certificates, and certified copies of orders, judgments, and decrees of courts of record may be recorded in the office of the county clerk and recorder of the county where such real property is situated. No such unrecorded instrument or document shall be valid as against any class of persons with any kind of rights who first records, except between the parties thereto and such as have notice thereof. This is a race-notice recording statute.

Where a security agreement, or mortgage, is executed between a purchaser and a vendor as part of the same transaction in which the purchaser acquires title to the property, the execution of the deed and the mortgage are considered simultaneous acts. Chambers v. Nation, 497 P.2d 5, 7 (Colo. 1972); Bank of Denver v. Legler, 350 P.2d 1059, 1061 (Colo. 1960). As a matter of law, such a purchaser never has an unencumbered title to property in which he can assign further rights. *See Chambers*, 497 P.2d at 7; *Legler*, 350 P.2d at 1061. Therefore, even a third party who loans money to the purchaser that is applied to the purchase, and who takes back a mortgage on the purchased property, cannot acquire rights to the property from the purchaser unencumbered by the vendor's mortgage, regardless of the order in which the documents are signed. *Legler*, 350 P.2d at 1061.

By acquiring its rights to the property in the same transaction, with full knowledge that the loan of the vendor, ALH, would be secured by a deed of trust, the Bank necessarily had notice of ALH's unrecorded instrument within the meaning of the recording statute. Whether or not the Bank's deed of trust was actually signed before that of ALH at the closing, the Bank's deed of trust could not have the legal effect of acquiring rights to the property before the execution of ALH's instruments, of which the Bank was aware. The statute, therefore, could not resolve the question of priorities in favor of the Bank. . . .

III

When the priority of rights in real property is not dictated by the operation of the recording statute, the rule in Colorado has long been that security interests, or mortgages, given in exchange for money applied to the purchase of the property have priority over all other liens. The rationale for the rule derives, here again, from the fact that execution of the deed and mortgage are considered simultaneous acts, such that the title never rests in the buyer unencumbered by the mortgage. As between the owner of property who never parts with the title except in exchange for a mortgage from the purchaser and a third party who lends money to the purchaser for part of the purchase price and accepts a mortgage on the property in return, the same logic demands that the vendor's mortgage have priority. . . .

Although Colorado has never expressly adopted the Restatement (Third) of Property §7.2, the . . . cases, which support the priority of a vendor purchase money mortgage over third-party purchase money mortgages, are consistent with the Restatement. . . . As the Comments to the Restatement explain (*id.* cmt. 6):

> [T]he equities favor the vendor. Not only does the vendor part with specific real estate rather than money, but the vendor would never relinquish it at all except on the understanding that the vendor will be able to use it to satisfy the obligation to pay the price. This is the case even though the vendor may know that the mortgagor is going to finance the transaction in part by borrowing from a third party and giving a mortgage to secure that obligation. In

the final analysis, the law is more sympathetic to the vendor's hazard of losing real estate previously owned than to the third party lender's risk of being unable to collect from an interest in real estate that never previously belonged to it.

Furthermore, nothing in these cases suggests that the parties cannot avoid the effect of the priority afforded vendor purchase money deeds of trust by subordinating the vendor's lien to that of the third-party lender by agreement. . . .

IV

Although the Bank's deed of trust was recorded before that of ALH, the Bank was not entitled to the benefits of the recording statute because it had notice of ALH's unrecorded instrument prior to acquiring rights of its own in the property. Furthermore, in the absence of a statutory determination of the relative priorities of the two deeds of trust, or any agreement of the parties resolving the matter, the deed of trust of ALH, the vendor, has priority over the deed of trust of the Bank concerning the same real property. The judgment of the court of appeals is therefore reversed, and the case is remanded.

Problem 4E

(a) Teresa and José contract for the purchase and sale of a property. Teresa agrees to buy the property on the condition that she can obtain suitable financing in the amount of $180,000, which will be a 90 percent loan against the contract price of $200,000. Teresa goes to Big Bank for a loan and is told that the bank valued the property at $170,000 and, therefore, would loan only $153,000 (90 percent) against the property. As a result, Teresa must back out of the purchase. A week later José sells the property to Mary Ann for $240,000. Big Bank discovers that it made an error in its appraisal. What, if anything, do you think Teresa should be able to do, and what might have been done to protect against this outcome?

(b) Assume instead that when Teresa notifies José of Big Bank's refusal to make the requested loan, José responds that he will make the loan to her as a purchase-money mortgage (PMM) transaction. Teresa is uncomfortable with buying the property this way. She comes to you for advice. What do you perceive as the benefits and risks if she buys with José extending a PMM? If Teresa wants to decline José's offer, may José treat her refusal to go forward as a breach of contract?

(c) Assume instead that the contract calls for Teresa to apply for mortgage financing within two days after signing the contract. Furthermore, it requires Teresa to notify José when she has done so. The contract also states that "time is of the essence." On day three, after not hearing from Teresa, José contacts her to see whether she has applied for the loan. Teresa indicates that she has been unable to get to the bank but will do so in the next day or two. Two days later José contacts Teresa again, and she explains that she had to attend to some personal matters but will take care of it the next day. José calls the next day, and Teresa has still not applied for the loan. Later that same day José sends her a written communication cancelling the contract, stating that he is doing so because of Teresa's failure to comply with the loan application provision. Teresa wants to know whether José's cancellation is valid.

Problem 4F

Buyer and Seller enter a contract for the purchase and sale of a single-family residential home. As a condition to purchase, Buyer drafts a contract term to deal with inspection of the home for any defects. The parties agree on language that they put in their contract. The contract provision reads as follows:

> Purchaser reserves the right to have the Property inspected. All inspections shall be made within 10 business days of the date of this contract. Inspections shall be at the expense of the Purchaser and shall be made by qualified and licensed inspectors and contractors within this state. Inspections may include but are not limited to heating, cooling, electrical, plumbing, roof, walls, ceilings, floors, foundation, basement, crawl space, well, septic, water analysis, and wood-eating infestations. If the Purchaser does not make a written objection within 17 business days from the date of this contract Purchaser will be deemed to have accepted the Property. Objections must be accompanied by copies of the written inspection reports. If an inspection report reveals a major problem with the Property, the seller can either fix the problem at its own expense or if seller elects not to fix the problem either party can terminate the contract.

(a) Under the contract in this case, the price of the home is $150,000. Buyer has an inspection done, and it is reported that there is a leak in the roof, termite damage to a structural beam, and a wet area in the basement. The estimated cost to repair all these items is $1,000. Under the inspection provision of the contract, should Buyer be able to terminate this contract?

(b) If Buyer mails a written objection to Seller on the 16th business day after entering the contract but it is not delivered to Seller until the 19th business day, is it an effective objection?

(c) Assume that Buyer submits a timely objection to Seller. The objection is based on a termite inspection that reports damage to a roof support beam and recommends replacement of the beam at a cost of $700. On receipt of this objection, Seller hires a separate qualified and licensed inspector who reports evidence of prior termite activity in the identified beam but goes on to say that the activity is old and has left the beam structurally sound. Consequently, Seller's inspector concludes that the beam is not in need of replacement or repair. Seller presents its report to Buyer, refuses to make a repair, and insists that Buyer close on the contract. What result?

(d) Assume that the property is located in Syracuse, New York, where the winters are long, cold, and very snowy. The transaction is taking place in the winter, and Buyer is getting inspections during February. At this time of the year, the ground has been frozen hard for several months, and there is three feet of snow on the ground. Buyer has the home inspected for radon gas emissions and detects a level slightly above the federal government guidelines for this type of naturally occurring radioactive gas. Buyer makes a timely objection to Seller. A radon abatement system could cost between $1,000 and $1,500 to install. Seller responds with a copy of a radon test report done in the summer months that indicates a radon level below the federal government guidelines. If both tests were done properly, what might explain this difference? Can Buyer terminate the contract if Seller refuses to install an abatement system? What if, instead of repairing or correcting the problem, Seller takes $1,000 off the sale price; can Buyer be forced to close on the contract?

(e) Assume a wintertime transaction in Minnesota with freezing temperatures. The home inspector informs Buyer that the air conditioning system cannot be tested without risk of serious damage when outside temperatures are below 50°F. Buyer goes forward with the contract and closes on the deal in March. By June, the outside temperature is warm enough to try out the central air conditioning and Buyer learns for the first time that the system does not work. What do you think Buyer can do or should be able to do at this point? How could Buyer have protected himself under the terms of the inspection contract provision as written?

Problem 4G

Drafting contract conditions that are effective in accomplishing the stated client's objectives is an important skill, but it is not easy to do. Suppose that Robin is negotiating to buy Jim's small farm of 300 acres and 500 dairy cows at a cost of $800,000. One issue that has come up is the health of the cows. Robin wants some assurance that the cows will survive the first year. In addition, the parties are contemplating that Robin will pay the price in several installments. It is now October, and the parties hope to sign a contract on November 15. Jim wants a last payment of $200,000 on December 1 of the following year. Robin is willing to make this payment then, but only if all 500 cows are still alive at the end of next year. Jim is willing to refund $1,000 per cow for any cow that dies in the time period, up to a maximum amount of $100,000, but he wants full payment on December 1.

   (a) How would you use the language of conditions to draft the last installment payment provision to meet Robin's objective? To meet Jim's?

   (b) How might you use the language of promises and warranties to further
provide protection to Robin as to the health of the cows and their ability to live
through the first full year after the closing of the contract? Draft some language
to accomplish this objective.

5

Condition of the Property

When contracting for the purchase and sale of real property, one must be concerned with the condition of the subject real estate. The contract must address matters that relate to both the quantity and the quality of the property being exchanged. The parties want to have a degree of certainty regarding the amount of land or improvements being transferred as well as the physical characteristics of the property. This is important because both matters will affect the value — and, therefore, the appropriate price of the transaction. This may seem easy and straightforward, but there are many potential problem areas in the context of a real estate transaction.

A. QUANTITY

PERFECT v. McANDREW
Court of Appeals of Indiana, 2003
798 N.E.2d 470

Sharpnack, Judge. Clyde and Ella Mae Perfect (the "Perfects") appeal the trial court's judgment granting specific performance of a contract to sell real estate to Michael E. McAndrew. . . .

The relevant facts follow. In the spring of 1999, McAndrew became interested in purchasing real estate in Dearborn County, Indiana from the Perfects.[1] Based upon acreage listed in the deed conveying the property to the Perfects, the Perfects thought that the property consisted of 81.1 acres. On April 20, 1999, McAndrew offered to purchase the real estate from the Perfects for $250,000. The offer described the property as "Anderson Rd,

---

1. The property is actually owned only by Ella Mae Perfect. However, Ella Mae gave Clyde authority to handle the transaction for her. For purposes of this opinion, we will refer to the Perfects as the owners of the property.

117

81.1 acres owned by Perfects." On April 21, 1999, the Perfects countered with a purchase price of $252,500. On April 23, 1999, McAndrew, his wife, and Ashley Howe and Betsy Bates, real estate agents with StarOne Realtors, met with Clyde Perfect to view the property and its boundaries. Clyde could not walk the property because of an injury to his knee. However, he rode his tractor along much of the boundary while the others walked. When they encountered an area that Clyde could not traverse with his tractor, Clyde described the remaining boundaries to the McAndrews and the real estate agents. The McAndrews and the real estate agents then walked the remaining boundaries. McAndrew never had any conversations with the Perfects regarding the acreage of the property. After inspecting the property, McAndrew accepted the Perfects' counteroffer of $252,500.

The contract provided, in part, that:

> [McAndrew] shall apply for financing within 10 calendar days after acceptance of this Contract and will make a diligent effort to obtain financing. If [McAndrew] or [McAndrew's] lender does not notify Listing REALTOR or [the Perfects], in writing, that a loan commitment has been obtained, denied or waived by May 20, 1999, then [the Perfects] may, by written notice to selling REALTOR or [McAndrew], terminate this Contract.

The contract also provided for the following contingencies:

1. Satisfactory septic approval (to [McAndrew]).
2. Satisfactory to [McAndrew] survey to be [paid] by [McAndrew] and [the Perfects] equally.
3. Satisfactory to [McAndrew] verification of easements on property.
4. [The Perfects] to remove all debris—junk around barn area and along property line as discussed.
5. Satisfactory to [McAndrew] verification of lot lines A.S.A.P.

On May 11, 1999, McAndrew advised Bates that he had secured a loan. McAndrew received a written loan commitment on May 21, 1999, and signed the commitment on May 25, 1999. On approximately June 20, 1999, the Perfects removed the junk and debris from the property. The survey was completed on June 24, 1999, and indicated that the property contained 96.2815 acres rather than 81.1 acres. After receiving the survey, Clyde "was quite surprised and thought about it for a while and decided [he] didn't want to give away 15 acres."

On July 8, 1999, the Perfects attempted to renegotiate the contract with three different proposals: (1) McAndrew would purchase the 96.2815 acres for an additional $35,000; (2) McAndrew would purchase 81 acres for $230,000 and the Perfects would keep 15.30 acres with west frontage on Anderson Road; or (3) McAndrew would purchase sixty acres on the east side of the property for $200,000. McAndrew rejected the new proposals and sought to close on the property pursuant to the contract. On August 4, 1999, the Perfects sent a letter to Howe attempting to terminate the contract because McAndrew had failed to provide a timely written notice of a loan commitment. Prior to this letter, the Perfects had not advised McAndrew or Howe of any problems regarding the timeliness of McAndrew's loan commitment. The Perfects then refused to convey the property to McAndrew.

McAndrew filed a complaint against the Perfects for specific performance. . . .

Spnkc prt

I

The first issue is whether the trial court's finding that the parties intended an "in gross" sale of real estate is clearly erroneous. The Perfects argue that the trial court erred when it determined that the parties intended an in gross sale of the property because: (1) the property was discussed in terms of 81.1 acres, not 81.1 acres "more or less;" (2) all of the parties were surprised to discover that the property was actually 96.2815 acres and surprise is not an element contemplated by in gross sales; and (3) the parties' actions demonstrated that acreage was important to the bargain. McAndrew argues that nothing indicated that the sale of the land was based upon a price per acre and the phrase "more or less" in describing the acreage is not determinative of whether the sale is an in gross sale or a price per acre sale. Further, McAndrew argues that the parties' actions demonstrated that the acreage of the property was not important to the bargain.

□ args

In general, where property is "sold in lump, and for a gross sum," such that "it appears by words of qualification, as 'more or less,' that the statement of the quantity of acres in the deed is mere matter of description and not of the essence of the contract, the buyer takes the risk of the quantity" so long as there is no fraud, concealment, or misrepresentation. Tyler v. Anderson, 6 N.E. 600, 601 (Ind. 1886); *see also* Cravens v. Kiser, 4 Ind. 512, 513 (1853) ("Where land is sold by metes and bounds, and estimated to contain a specific quantity, or for 'more or less,' and a gross sum is paid for the entire tract, the vendee will not be entitled to an abatement in price should the number of acres fall short of the estimated quantity," unless there is fraud or concealment on the part of the vendor.). However, where property is "sold at so much per acre, and there is a deficiency in the number [of acres] conveyed, the purchaser will be entitled to a compensation." Hays v. Hays, 25 N.E. 600, 601 (Ind. 1890) (holding that the purchaser was entitled to compensation where the property was sold at $100 per acre and estimated to contain 28 $^{40}/_{100}$ acres but actually contained only 23 $^{40}/_{100}$ acres). . . .

in gross

The Perfects argue that . . . because the contract here did not contain the phrase "more or less," the sale here was a per acre sale. McAndrew responds that the sale was an in gross sale despite the lack of the phrase "more or less." In *Hays*, our supreme court discussed the use of the phrase "more or less" and concluded that:

The question of quantity, in its most complicated form, usually arises in sales of land in compact bodies, sold under some specific name, or by particular description, and as containing, by estimation, a given number of acres, or a given number of acres more or less. The difficulty arises in determining whether the sale was intended to be in gross or by the acre. If in gross, the mention of the quantity of acres after another and certain description, whether by metes and bounds, or other known specifications, is not a covenant or agreement as to the quantity to be conveyed. In such cases the statement of acreage is regarded as mere matter of description, and not of contract. *But the terms "by estimation," "more or less," or other expressions of similar import, added to a statement of quantity, can only be considered as covering inconsiderable or small differences, one way or the other, and do not, in themselves, determine the character of the sale.* Even where the sale has been in gross, and not by the acre, if it appear that the estimated number of acres was in fact the controlling inducement, and that the price, though a gross sum, was based upon the supposed area, and measured by it, equity will interfere to grant relief, and rescind the contract on the ground of gross mistake.

Hays, 25 N.E. at 600 (emphasis added). Thus, while the phrase "more or less" may assist in determining if the sale was an in gross sale or a price per acre sale, the language is not determinative.

. . . Here, the contract described the land as "Anderson Rd, 81.1 acres owned by Perfects." Before accepting the Perfects' counteroffer, McAndrew walked the property with Clyde, and Clyde pointed out the boundaries. McAndrew never had any conversations with the Perfects regarding the acreage of the property. In fact, Clyde testified that he never discussed the acreage with McAndrew and did not counteroffer with a price per acre. Thus, there is no evidence that the parties ever discussed a per acre price for the property. There is also no indication that the estimated acreage was the controlling inducement in the contract. Although the contract describes the property as "Anderson Rd, 81.1 acres owned by Perfects," the evidence indicates that the estimated acreage was merely a manner of describing the property. The evidence indicates that the parties contemplated a sale of the entire tract for a lump sum, not a price per acre.

II

The next issue is whether the trial court's finding that there was no mutual mistake of fact is clearly erroneous. The trial court found that "on the issue of what land was intended to be bought and sold there was a meeting of the minds. There was no ambiguity, no fraud, no misrepresentation, and no equitable circumstances that would indicate otherwise." The Perfects argue that the trial court's finding is clearly erroneous because this "is a classic example where mutual mistake of fact renders the contract voidable by either party." The Perfects argue that the parties thought that the property was 81.1 acres and that the parties were surprised to learn that the property actually contained 96.2185 acres. McAndrew argues that the acreage was not the "essence of the agreement," and, thus, no mutual mistake of fact exists.

The doctrine of mutual mistake provides that "where both parties share a common assumption about a vital fact upon which they based their bargain, and that assumption is false, the transaction may be avoided if because of the mistake a quite different exchange of values occurs from the exchange of values contemplated by the parties." Bowling v. Poole, 756 N.E.2d 983, 988-989 (Ind. Ct. App. 2001). . . .

[H]ere, there is no evidence that the parties were mistaken about the actual tract of land to be sold. In fact, Clyde testified that "there wasn't any question about which piece of property [they] were dealing for. The only question [was] how many acres it really [was]." There is also no evidence that the exact acreage was the essence of the parties' agreement. [I]t is not enough that McAndrew and the Perfects were mistaken about the acreage. Rather, to constitute a mutual mistake of fact, the fact complained of must be one that is "of the essence of the agreement" and "must be such that it animates and controls the conduct of the parties." Bowling, 756 N.E.2d at 989. . . . Consequently, we cannot say that the trial court's finding that no mutual mistake of fact existed here is clearly erroneous.

III

The next issue is whether the trial court's judgment improperly added a provision to the contract. The Perfects argue that the clear contract language requires the sale of 81.1 acres but the trial court ordered the sale of 96.2185 acres, thus adding a term to the written contract. McAndrew argues that the trial court did not add a new term to the contract. Rather, according to McAndrew, the trial court correctly determined that the Perfects intended to sell and McAndrew intended to buy the entire tract. . . .

Here, although the trial court did not specifically find the "Anderson Rd, 81.1 acres owned by Perfects" language to be ambiguous, it considered extrinsic evidence in interpreting the language. The description of the property is ambiguous because it could be interpreted to mean the entire tract of land on Anderson Road owned by the Perfects or to mean only 81.1 acres of the land. Because the description is ambiguous, the trial court appropriately considered extrinsic evidence regarding the transaction. The extrinsic evidence indicated that the parties intended that the Perfects sell and McAndrew purchase the entire tract, not just 81.1 acres. Further, the evidence indicated that the sale was an in gross sale and not a price per acre sale. *See supra* Part I. Consequently, the trial court did not add a term to the contract, but rather properly interpreted an ambiguous contract with the aid of extrinsic evidence.

For the foregoing reasons, we affirm the trial court's judgment in favor of McAndrew on his complaint for specific performance.

Problem 5A

Moses looks at a house listed for sale. Later he submits a contract with an offer price of $250,000 that is accepted by the seller. The contract describes the land by proper legal description and also includes the words "being a ½ acre lot including a residential home of 2,500 square feet, more or less." Moses uses this information to apply for a loan. After closing on the contract, it is discovered that the house is actually only 2,100 square feet.

(a) Can Moses recover damages from the seller for this shortfall? If so, how should the court measure the damages?

(b) What if Moses' lender notifies him that it is calling the loan due because the shortfall in square footage has made the loan insecure? (In other words, the loan is being called due because the lender had relied upon an appraisal that calculated the market value based on the 2,500 square feet identified in the contract.)

(c) If you were representing Moses before he submitted a signed contract to the seller, what steps would you take to reduce the risk of an error in quantity with respect to the size of the house? Could problems also arise with respect to the size of the lot where the house is situated?

B. QUALITY

Issues of property quality are also important to the parties in an exchange. Quality issues arise in many different situations. Primary areas of concern include the structural soundness of improvements, the condition of building operating systems and appliances, the environmental safety of improvements and land, the availability of amenities such as utilities and vehicular access, and previous uses of the property that may affect value or desirability. We address some of these problem areas in this section. In Chapters 8 through 12 we explore a number of issues related to the quality of title.

1. *Express Allocations of Risk of Quality*

CLAIR v. HILLENMEYER
Court of Appeals of Kentucky, 2007
232 S.W.3d 544

NICKELL, Judge. Paul E. Hillenmeyer and his wife, Mary W. Hillenmeyer (hereinafter collectively referred to as "Hillenmeyer"), filed suit against Jeffrey K. Clair and his wife, Susan C. Clair (hereinafter collectively referred to as "Clair"), in the Grant Circuit Court for damages incurred as a result of Clair's repudiation of a real estate sale and purchase agreement. . . .

In April 2004 Hillenmeyer listed for sale a certain parcel of real estate located in Dry Ridge, Grant County, Kentucky. Clair made an offer to purchase the property for $219,000 on June 9, 2004, which offer was promptly accepted by Hillenmeyer. A standard contract to purchase was prepared and executed by all parties. Several stipulations were set forth therein which were required to be satisfied prior to the closing of the transaction. Of singular importance to this appeal was a restriction added by Clair that the septic system servicing the property be repaired.[2] According to the deposition testimony offered to the trial court, the septic system was malfunctioning in some way, allowing waste water to percolate to the surface of the yard. This condition was readily observable upon inspection of the property and was not concealed from view in any way. Thus, after viewing the property and determining to make an offer thereon, Clair added the *caveat* regarding repair of the system.

Following execution of the contract to purchase, a meeting occurred in the yard of the subject property between Clair, Hillenmeyer, their respective Realtors, and Jeff Franxman, a local plumber familiar with septic systems. The purpose of this meeting was to obtain suggestions for modifications and repairs to the faulty septic system. Franxman offered several alternatives, but the discussions focused upon a single alternative which involved installation of a secondary leach field which would be accessed via a manually operated valve system. This secondary field would be used when the original leach field became overburdened or "broke out" above ground. The only feasible location for this addition was near the home where Clair intended to construct an addition.[4] The meeting adjourned, and the parties left to discuss the situation. There is no indication further discussions occurred between the parties regarding this proposal or any other alternatives. Furthermore, no repairs or alterations were commenced on the system.

Shortly after the meeting, on August 6, 2004, Clair's real estate agent, Ellen Heile, notified Hillenmeyer of Clair's intention to withdraw from the purchase contract. Therefore, Heile stated Clair was dissatisfied with the proposed modification . . . .

On December 3, 2004, Hillenmeyer filed suit in the Grant Circuit Court alleging breach of the purchase contract and seeking damages as a result thereof. . . . The trial court granted summary judgment to Hillenmeyer and . . . fixed damages at $39,976.20.[8] This appeal followed. . . .

2. The specific language of the handwritten restriction added by Clair reads: "Seller will repair septic system to meet code & allow Purchaser to attend while repairs are performed."

4. One of the other handwritten additions to the purchase contract was a provision allowing Clair to begin construction of a new sunroom and detached garage off the rear of the home after closing, but before receiving actual physical possession of the property. The change in possession was to occur some 30 days after closing.

8. During the course of the litigation, Hillenmeyer was able to find a new buyer for the home, albeit for the lower sales price of $205,000. The damage award included the $14,000 difference in sales price, attorneys fees, costs, additional repair expenses, and the earnest money deposit from the first sale.

First, Hillenmeyer consistently claimed the septic system on the property was up to "code" which was all that Clair required. In Hillenmeyer's own words, however, "all parties were left guessing" as to what "code" was referred to in the contingency. The resolution of this question is clearly a material fact for the jury to decide in order to determine who, if anyone, breached the purchase contract, and if there was a valid defense therefor. Further, even if this question could be answered based upon the evidence presented to the trial court, there remained a genuine dispute between the parties as to whether the system met any particular code in light of the alleged failures within the system. Resolution of these questions should have been reserved for the finder of fact.

Next, Hillenmeyer argued the system itself worked as designed. Any perceived failures or defects were not from a faulty design or a result of damage within the system, but rather were a direct result of running more water through the system than it was designed to handle. Additionally, Hillenmeyer argued the presence of water from a septic system above ground is a normal occurrence and is not indicative of any system flaw. However, the deposition testimony of Franxman reveals such is not a normal happening and would indicate to him the system had failed.[9] These contradictory positions reveal a genuine issue as to whether there was a failure within the system. If there was no failure, Hillenmeyer's position is superior. Conversely, if a failure did exist, Clair could reasonably be found to have a valid defense on the breach of contract issue. Again, this reveals an issue to be resolved by the finder of fact. . . .

Finally, the trial court relied on Clair's refusal to accept the proposed addition to the septic system and their failure to make a counter proposal in ruling Clair could not prevail at trial. Clair testified the proposed manual valve system was unacceptable, over-burdensome, and not what had been originally bargained. Hillenmeyer argued, and the trial court agreed, that Clair's satisfaction with any proposed repair was not required under the contract, only that Clair be allowed to be present when repairs were effectuated. However, the language of the purchase contract directly contravenes Hillenmeyer's position and undermines the trial court's ruling that Clair could not prevail at trial under any circumstances. The preprinted portion of the purchase contract specifically states that if inspection of the property revealed a defect which was timely reported to Hillenmeyer, then Hillenmeyer shall "either (a) repair the defects *in a manner acceptable to the Buyer* who reported the defects, or (b) provide other assurances *reasonably acceptable to Buyer* that the defects will be repaired with due diligence and in a manner acceptable to the inspectors or contractors who reported the same" (emphases added). There is no question the defect was known to all parties. Its inclusion as a handwritten clause in the contract is further proof it was

9. It is important to note that Franxman was a neutral third-party in this controversy, and his consultation was obtained upon agreement by all of the parties.

called to Hillenmeyer's attention. Contrary to the trial court's finding, the handwritten clause does not eliminate, but merely supplements, the preprinted clause regarding repairs.[11] Thus, a jury could reasonably have found that Clair's satisfaction with any proposed repairs was, in fact, required by the contract. The question would then become whether the proposed extension of the system was reasonable and whether Clair's rejection of the proposed fix was reasonable. These were questions of material fact for the jury to answer. . . .

For the foregoing reasons, Hillenmeyer failed to show Clair could not prevail under any circumstances at trial. Therefore, we do not believe from the record before us that Hillenmeyer was entitled to judgment as a matter of law. Thus, we hold the circuit court erred in granting summary judgment. . . .

Accordingly, the judgment of the Grant Circuit Court is reversed and remanded for proceedings consistent with this opinion.

Problem 5B

Hernandes is buying a home from Gorky. The property is located in a region of the country known to have problems with wood-destroying organisms such as termites. In the written contract of purchase, Hernandes bargains for a termite inspection and a representation from Gorky that "the property is free of all wood-destroying organisms." Gorky obtains a termite inspection report from Pestfree Company, which he delivers to Hernandes. The report indicates the presence of no wood-destroying organisms, but also contains standard-form disclaimers and qualifiers related to the inaccessibility of certain parts of the premises and to the fact that internal walls and structures cannot be seen with a visual check. The parties close the transaction. About one month later, Hernandes notices little black droppings along some of the edge boards of the house, and a close inspection of some "dust" build-up reveals the presence of additional droppings. During the regularly scheduled pest control service visit, Hernandes consults with Pestfree Company's employee. Hernandes is told that these droppings are evidence of termite activity in the home. This is followed up a week later by a more detailed examination of the property by Pestfree, at which time termite damage is discovered in some of the structural beams and braces of the home. The company estimates, based on the discovered damages, that the termites have most likely been present for about a year. They add, however, that this is sometimes difficult to determine. After evaluating the report,

---

11. The general rule of interpretation of contracts is that effect must be given to all terms of the contract, if possible. When inconsistencies appear on the face of the document, handwritten or typewritten additions or alterations intentionally added by the parties will prevail over preprinted terms, and handwriting prevails over typewriting. . . . Here, no ambiguity exists between the preprinted and handwritten portions of the contract. Therefore, all provisions must be given effect.

Hernandes comes to you for advice. Evaluate his potential claims against Gorky and Pestfree Company. What if Hernandes had received all of this information prior to closing on the contract, could he have been released from the agreement?

Problem 5C

Alires and his wife contract to purchase a home from McGehee for $300,000. McGehee has lived in the home for 28 years. In looking at the home prior to contracting, Alires asks McGehee whether the basement ever gets water in it. McGehee responds that at one time a pipe burst and there was water. He also informs Alires that he and his wife have difficulty walking up and down steps at their age so they seldom go into the basement. In fact, he notes that he and his wife have not been in the basement in the past three years. McGehee says that the Alireses can inspect the basement if they wish to do so. In the contract, the Alireses reserve the right to conduct mechanical, structural, and wood infestation inspections of the house prior to closing. The McGehees agree to pay up to $550 for repairs if defects are found. If the cost of repairs exceeds that amount, either the Alireses or the McGehees can pay the excess amount, or the contract can be cancelled. The contract specifically provides that if inspections are not performed regarding all or part of the property,

> Buyer is bound by whatever information an inspection would have revealed, and waives any claim, right, or cause of action relating to or arising from any condition of the property that would have been apparent had inspections been performed.

At the same time as executing the contract, McGehee signs a document provided by the broker in which he checks off items on a Property Condition Disclosure form indicating the following:

- The property does not have radon gas above the government specified level.
- The property does not have lead paint.
- The property has not been used for manufacture of any illegal drugs.
- The property does not have water in the basement.

McGehee is instructed to sign the Property Disclosure Form so it can be provided to the buyer at the time of contracting. McGehee is told it is a standard form that is simply required in order to sell the property. The Alireses are provided with a copy of the disclosure form, along with other information concerning the property, before signing the contract of purchase and sale with the McGehees. Thirty days later the parties close on the contract.

Instead of obtaining an inspection prior to closing, one week after closing, Alires hires a contractor to examine the basement because Alires has observed some cracks in the basement walls. The contractor inspects the basement and quickly concludes that there is a water problem in the basement, and that the cracking will continue to get worse over time. There is evidence of water having been in the basement in the past. The contractor indicates that this is relatively easy to determine with a routine inspection, and he offers the observation that water probably comes in after a heavy rain, but not on a regular basis.

The Alireses seek a remedy against the McGehees. The McGehees assert that they have no obligation to the Alireses. How would you analyze this problem, and who should win in any legal dispute?

2. Disclosing Inaccurate Information

PETRILLO v. BACHENBERG
Supreme Court of New Jersey, 1995
655 A.2d 1354

POLLOCK, Justice. The issue is whether under the circumstances of this case the attorney for the seller of real estate owes a duty to a potential buyer. Plaintiff, Lisa Petrillo, alleges that because of the negligence of defendant Bruce Herrigel, an attorney, she received a misleading copy of a percolation-test report that induced her to sign a contract to purchase property. At the close of plaintiff's case, the Law Division concluded that Herrigel did not owe a duty to plaintiff to provide a complete and accurate report. The Appellate Division reversed, 623 A.2d 272 (N.J. Super. Ct. 1993). It determined that an attorney for a seller has a duty not to provide misleading information to potential buyers who the attorney knows, or should know, will rely on the information. We granted Herrigel's petition for certification to determine whether he owed such a duty to plaintiff. We now affirm the judgment of the Appellate Division.

I

In 1987, Rohrer Construction (Rohrer) owned a 1.3-acre tract of undeveloped land in Union Township, Hunterdon County. Herrigel represented Rohrer in the sale of the property. Rohrer hired Heritage Consulting Engineers (Heritage) to perform percolation tests concerning a contract of sale to Land Resources Corporation (Land Resources). Percolation tests reveal, among other things, the suitability of soil for a septic system. Union Township requires two successful percolation tests for municipal approval of a septic system.

In September and October 1987, Heritage provided Rohrer and Herrigel with copies of reports describing two series of percolation tests. The first report, dated September 24, 1987, revealed that of twenty-two tests, only one had been successful. A November 3, 1987, report showed that of eight tests conducted in October, one had been successful.

Rohrer's contract with Land Resources failed. Subsequently, Rohrer listed the property with a local real estate broker, Bachenberg & Bachenberg, Inc. In October 1988, William G. Bachenberg, Jr. (Bachenberg) of Bachenberg & Bachenberg, Inc. asked Herrigel for information concerning the listing. Herrigel told Bachenberg that "he had some perc results," and sent him a two-page document consisting of one page from each of the two Heritage reports. The first page was page one from the September 24, 1987, report; it reflected one successful test and five unsuccessful tests. The second page was culled from the November 3, 1987, report; it listed one successful and one unsuccessful test. Read together, the two pages appear to describe a single series of [eight] tests, two of which were successful. In fact, the property had passed only two of thirty percolation tests. The document, subsequently described as the "composite report," became part of Bachenberg's sales packet. . . .

Bachenberg listed the property for sale at $160,000. In February 1989, Petrillo expressed an interest in purchasing the property to build and operate a child day-care facility. That month, at their first meeting, Bachenberg gave Petrillo a sales packet, which included the composite report.

In June 1989, Petrillo agreed to pay Bachenberg his asking price. Herrigel represented Bachenberg in negotiating the terms of the contract with Petrillo's attorney. Nothing in the record indicates that Herrigel informed Petrillo's attorney of the test results that had been omitted from the composite report. At the insistence of Petrillo's attorney, the contract provided Petrillo with forty-five days to conduct independent soil and water tests, including percolation tests. The contract provided further that Petrillo could rescind if the percolation tests were not satisfactory to her.

In August 1989, Petrillo hired an engineering firm, Canger & Cassera, to conduct soil tests and site planning. Based on the composite report, Canger & Cassera recommended that they start site-planning work simultaneously with the conduct of percolation tests by a sub-contractor, PMK, Ferris & Perricone (PMK). PMK conducted six percolation tests, all of which failed. Consequently, PMK concluded that the site was inadequate for a septic system. Canger & Cassera stopped working on the preliminary site plan. On August 22, 1989, Petrillo notified Bachenberg that the contract was null and void.

In response, Bachenberg contracted with Heritage to design a septic system that would satisfy the municipality. Heritage designed the system, which the Hunterdon County Board of Health approved. Petrillo, however, refused to accept the design, and requested permission to conduct additional percolation tests. Bachenberg denied her request. During the course of their negotiations, Herrigel sent Petrillo the complete copies of the September 24 and November 3 Heritage reports.

The parties could not settle their differences. Bachenberg refused to return Petrillo's $16,000 down payment, claiming that she had breached the contract. Petrillo sued . . . for the return of the down payment and for the costs of her engineering fees. . . .

In the complaint, Petrillo alleged, among other things, that Herrigel's failure to provide the complete Heritage reports violated a duty that he owed to her. She claimed further that the violation had caused her to incur engineering expenses that she would not have incurred if she had known all the facts. Specifically, she contended that if she had known that the property had passed only two of thirty percolation tests, she would not have signed the contract or hired Canger & Cassera and PMK.

At the close of plaintiff's case, the trial court dismissed Petrillo's complaint against Herrigel. The court concluded that Petrillo had not alleged facts sufficient to support a duty extending from Herrigel to her. . . .

Before us, however, is the Appellate Division's reversal of the dismissal of Petrillo's claims against Herrigel for negligent misrepresentation. The Appellate Division determined that a seller's attorney owes a duty to a non-client buyer "who the attorney knows or should know would rely on the attorney in his or her professional capacity." 623 A.2d at 278. It stated that "a buyer of real estate has a cause of action against an attorney for the seller who provides misleading information concerning the subject of the transaction." *Id.* at 280. The court concluded that a jury could have found that when Herrigel gave Bachenberg the composite report, Herrigel should have known that Bachenberg would provide the report to a prospective purchaser, such as Petrillo, who would rely on the report in deciding whether to purchase the property. *Ibid.*

II

As a claim against an attorney for negligence resulting in economic loss, Petrillo's claim against Herrigel is essentially one for economic negligence. Formerly, the doctrine of privity limited such claims by non-clients against attorneys and other professionals. Jay M. Feinman, *Economic Negligence: Liability of Professionals and Businesses to Third Parties for Economic Loss* 29 (1995). More recently, other doctrines have replaced privity as a means of limiting a professional's duty to a non-client. *See, e.g.,* Biakanja v. Irving, 320 P.2d 16 (Cal. 1958) (adopting a "balance of factors" test).

The determination of the existence of a duty is a question of law for the court. Whether an attorney owes a duty to a non-client third party depends on balancing the attorney's duty to represent clients vigorously, Rules of Professional Conduct, Rule 1.3 (1993), with the duty not to provide misleading information on which third parties foreseeably will rely, Rules of Professional Conduct, Rule 4.1 (1993). *See also* Restatement of the Law Governing

Lawyers §73 comment b (Tentative Draft No. 7, 1994) (discussing rationale for imposing duty to non-clients); Stephen Gillers, *Regulation of Lawyers* 656–64 (3d ed. 1992) (discussing duty to non-clients). Because this matter arises on the grant of defendant Herrigel's motion to dismiss, we accord Petrillo the benefit of all favorable inferences that may be drawn from her proofs.

Although we have not previously addressed the issue of attorney liability to third parties, the Appellate Division has recognized that attorneys may owe a limited duty in favor of specific non-clients. In Stewart v. Sbarro, 362 A.2d 581 (N.J. Super. Ct. 1976), an attorney for the buyers of a corporation agreed to obtain the buyers' signatures on a bond and mortgage indemnifying the sellers against liability for existing corporate debt. The attorney failed to obtain the required signatures. As a result, the debt was unsecured, rather than secured. When the buyers filed a bankruptcy petition, the sellers sued their own attorney, the buyers, and the buyers' attorney for the unpaid debt. The Appellate Division determined that the buyers' attorney could be liable in negligence for breaching a duty to the sellers. It reasoned that when an attorney should foresee that a third party may rely on the attorney's promise to act, a duty attaches. *Id.* at 587.

Similarly, in Albright v. Burns, 503 A.2d 386 (N.J. Super. Ct. 1986), the Appellate Division held that an attorney was liable to a decedent's estate when the attorney knowingly facilitated improper transactions involving the holder of the decedent's power of attorney. The court stated that "a member of the bar owes a fiduciary duty to persons, though not strictly clients, who he knows or should know rely on him in his professional capacity." *Id.* at 389.

More recently, in R. J. Longo Construction Co. v. Schragger, 527 A.2d 480 (N.J. Super. Ct. 1987), the Appellate Division considered a case involving township attorneys who had prepared bid documents for a sewer-construction contract. The attorneys had failed to obtain certain easements mentioned in the bid package. Consequently, the successful bidder, plaintiff, R. J. Longo Construction Co. (Longo), which had begun construction on notice to proceed from the town, was forced to stop work. As a result, Longo suffered losses and sued the attorneys. The trial court dismissed the claims against the township attorneys because of the absence of privity. The Appellate Division reversed. It held that Longo was an intended third-party beneficiary of the defendant attorneys' employment contracts with the township. The court determined that the attorneys owed the contractor a fiduciary duty and that they were liable for the foreseeable consequences of their negligent misrepresentations on which plaintiff reasonably and foreseeably relied. *Id.* at 481.

Other jurisdictions similarly have relaxed traditional privity requirements when an attorney induces specific non-clients to rely on the attorney's representations. For example, in Greycas, Inc. v. Proud, 826 F.2d 1560, 1561-62 (7th Cir. 1987), *cert. denied*, 484 U.S. 1043 (1988), Greycas, a finance company, agreed to lend funds to an Illinois borrower if the borrower provided an attorney's opinion letter stating that the borrower's collateral was not subject to prior liens. The borrower asked an attorney, his brother-in-law, to prepare the needed opinion letter. The attorney prepared the letter based solely on the borrower's representations and submitted it to Greycas, which promptly issued the funds. After the borrower defaulted, Greycas learned that most of the borrower's collateral was subject to superior liens and that the loan was largely unsecured. Greycas sued the attorney for negligent misrepresentation. The court concluded under Illinois law that the attorney owed Greycas a duty not to negligently misrepresent the status of the borrower's collateral notwithstanding the lack of privity. *Id.* at 1564-65.

The New York Court of Appeals has likewise held that an attorney may owe a duty to specific non-clients who rely on the attorney's representations. *See* Prudential Insurance Co. of America v. Dewey Ballantine, Bushby, Palmer & Wood, 605 N.E.2d 318 (N.Y. 1992). In *Prudential*, a lender sued a borrower's attorney for negligently preparing an opinion letter that was provided to the lender as a condition to a debt restructuring. An attorney could be liable to a non-client for negligent misrepresentation, the court conceded, if the nature of the relationship between the attorney and the non-client was "so close as to approach that of privity." *Id.* at 320. The court stated the criteria for finding a duty:

> (1) an awareness by the maker of the statement that it is to be used for a particular purpose; (2) reliance by a known party on the statement in furtherance of that purpose; and (3) some conduct by the maker of the statement linking it to the relying party and evincing its understanding of that reliance.

Id. at 321-22. The court concluded that the attorney knew that the lender would rely on the opinion letter and intended to induce that reliance. *Id.* at 322. *See also* Vereins- und Westbank, AG v. Carter, 691 F. Supp. 704, 708-16 (S.D.N.Y. 1988) (holding under New York law that lawyer owes duty to non-clients to whom lawyer furnishes legal opinion on behalf of client).

Thus, when courts relax the privity requirement, they typically limit a lawyer's duty to situations in which the lawyer intended or should have foreseen that the third party would rely on the lawyer's work. *See* Feinman, *supra*, at 131-34. For example, a lawyer reasonably should foresee that third parties will rely on an opinion letter issued in connection with a securities offering. *See* Norman v. Brown, Todd & Heyburn, 693 F. Supp. 1259, 1265 (D. Mass. 1988) ("As a general matter, tax opinion letters are drafted so that someone can rely upon them."). The purpose of a legal opinion letter is to induce reliance by others. If an attorney foresees or should foresee that reliance, the resulting duty of care can extend to non-client third parties.

In other contexts, courts have imposed a duty on an attorney who prepares an instrument with the intent that third parties will rely on it. Thus, in Molecular Technology Corp. v. Valentine, 925 F.2d 910, 915-17 (1991), the Sixth Circuit Court of Appeals determined that a lawyer who prepared a private offering statement for his client's corporate debentures owed a duty of care to potential investors whom the attorney knew, or should have known, would rely on the statement. The court held that Michigan law "imposes a duty in favor of all those third parties who defendant knows will rely on the information and to third parties who defendant should reasonably foresee will rely on the information." *Id.* at 916.

Likewise, in Century 21 Deep South Properties, Ltd. v. Corson, 612 So. 2d 359 (Miss. 1992), a buyer of real property sued alleging negligence of the attorney for the seller, who had conducted a title search on which the buyer had detrimentally relied. The Mississippi Supreme Court held that "an attorney performing title work will be liable to reasonably foreseeable persons who, for a proper business purpose, detrimentally rely on the attorney's work." *Id.* at 374.

Similarly, section 73 of the proposed Restatement of the Law Governing Lawyers, *supra*, pertaining to "duty to certain non-clients," provides:

> For the purposes of liability . . . , a lawyer owes a duty to use care . . . (2) To a non-client when and to the extent that the lawyer or (with the lawyer's acquiescence) the lawyer's client invites the non-client to rely on the lawyer's opinion or provision of other legal services, the non-client so relies, and the non-client is not, under applicable law, too remote from the lawyer to be entitled to protection. . . .

We also recognize that attorneys may owe a duty of care to non-clients when the attorneys know, or should know, that non-clients will rely on the attorneys' representations and the non-clients are not too remote from the attorneys to be entitled to protection. The Restatement's requirement that the lawyer invite or acquiesce in the non-client's reliance comports with our formulation that the lawyer know, or should know, of that reliance. No matter how expressed, the point is to cabin the lawyer's duty, so the resulting obligation is fair to both lawyers and the public.

III

The imposition on attorneys of defined liability to third parties comports with general principles of tort law. . . .

IV

The objective purpose of documents such as opinion letters, title reports, or offering statements, and the extent to which others foreseeably may rely on them, determines the scope of a lawyer's duty in preparing such documents. . . .

Here, Herrigel did not prepare an opinion letter. Giving Petrillo the benefit of all reasonable inferences, however, we infer that Herrigel extracted information from existing percolation-test reports, created the composite report, and delivered the report to a real estate broker. Our initial inquiry, as with an opinion letter or comparable document, is to ascertain the purpose of the report.

Although Herrigel may have intended that the composite report would demonstrate only that the property had passed two percolation tests, his subjective intent may not define the objective meaning of the report. The roles and relationships of the parties color our assessment. In making that assessment, we cannot ignore the fact that Herrigel is an attorney who, in connection with his client's efforts to sell the property, provided the report to a real estate broker. We infer that when he delivered the report to Bachenberg, Herrigel knew, or should have known, that Bachenberg might deliver it to a prospective purchaser, such as Petrillo. Herrigel did nothing to restrict a prospective purchaser's foreseeable use of the report. In neither the report, a covering letter, nor a disclaimer did Herrigel even hint that the report was anything but complete and accurate.

Significantly, Herrigel's involvement continued after he delivered the report to Bachenberg. After Bachenberg purchased the property, Herrigel acted as his lawyer and negotiated the terms of the contract for the sale of commercial property to Petrillo. Although compiling an engineering report to help a client sell real estate may not be part of a lawyer's stock-in-trade, representing the seller of real estate is a traditional legal service. By representing Bachenberg on the sale to Petrillo, Herrigel confirmed the continuity of his involvement as a lawyer. On these facts, Herrigel's continuing involvement permits the inference that the objective purpose of the report was to induce a prospective purchaser to buy the property. His involvement supports the further inference that Herrigel knew that Bachenberg intended to use the report for that purpose.

Furthermore, a purchaser reading the composite report reasonably could conclude that the property had passed two of [eight], not two of thirty, percolation tests. Based on that conclusion, a purchaser reasonably could decide to sign a purchase contract, although the purchaser would not have signed the contract if he or she had seen the complete set of percolation reports. So viewed, Herrigel should have foreseen that Petrillo would rely on the total number of percolation tests in deciding whether to sign the purchase contract. In sum, a jury reasonably could infer that the composite report misrepresented material facts.

By providing the composite report to Bachenberg and subsequently representing him in the sale, Herrigel assumed a duty to Petrillo to provide reliable information regarding the percolation tests. Herrigel controlled the risk that the composite report would mislead a purchaser. Fairness suggests that he should bear the risk of loss resulting from the delivery of a misleading report. We further conclude that Herrigel should have foreseen that a prospective purchaser would rely on the composite report in deciding whether to sign the contract and proceed with engineering and site work.

Herrigel easily could have limited his liability. Most simply, he could have sent complete copies of both reports to Bachenberg. Alternatively, Herrigel could have sent a letter to Bachenberg stating that the property had passed two successful percolation tests as required by Union Township. Or he could have stated either in a letter to Bachenberg or in the composite report that the report evidenced only that the property had yielded two successful percolation tests and that no one should rely on the report for any other purpose. Because Herrigel did nothing to limit the objective purpose of the composite report, he should have foreseen that Petrillo, as a prospective purchaser, would rely on the facts set forth in the report. Accordingly, Herrigel's duty extends to Petrillo. . . .

. . . The recognized duty hardly constitutes lawyers as "guarantors of the accuracy of surveys or other similar experts' reports that they merely transmit [as claimed by the dissent *infra*]." We do not hold that Herrigel guaranteed the accuracy of the tests. Our holding goes no further than to state that Herrigel had a duty not to misrepresent negligently the contents of a material document on which he knew others would rely to their financial detriment. In many situations, lawyers, like people generally, may not have a duty to act, but when they act, like other people, they should act carefully.

The judgment of the Appellate Division is affirmed.

STEIN, J., concurring. [Concurring opinion omitted.]

GARIBALDI, J., dissenting. The majority imposes on an attorney a duty of care to a non-client broader than that imposed on an attorney under the proposed Restatement of the Law Governing Lawyers §73 (Tentative Draft No. 7, 1994), under the Restatement (Second) of Torts §552 (1977), and under our case law, including Rosenblum v. Adler, 461 A.2d 138 (N.J. 1983). Such an extension will lead to defensive lawyering; it will make legal services more cumbersome, more costly, and less accessible to clients. . . .

Problem 5D

Abby is negotiating to purchase an office building from Jesse, the current owner who bought the building 20 years ago. Based on land values and cash flow from current leases along with other economic indicators, Abby offers $17.5 million for the property. Jesse considers this a fair offer and accepts the deal. The contract includes a provision allowing Abby to have the building inspected for "structural soundness" and to have the standard inspections for mechanicals in the building, such as the electric, heating, cooling, plumbing, elevators, fire alarms, and so on.

The inspections are completed and the deal is closed. About a year after owning the property, Abby decides to refurbish and renovate some of the office space so that it will be more appealing to tenants. In the course of the renovation work, the presence of asbestos is discovered. On closer exam-ination, it turns out that the entire building contains asbestos, which was applied as a fire retardant at the time of the original construction. The law requires that the asbestos be removed, at an estimated cost of $1.8 million.

(a) Should Abby be able to recover anything from Jesse?

(b) Assume that Abby discovers the asbestos prior to closing the transac-tion. She tries to back out of the deal, but Jesse wants to enforce the contract. What are the parties' arguments? Who should prevail, and why?

(c) Assume that Debbie is the attorney for Jesse and that she is aware of the high probability of asbestos being in the building based on her review of some of the original building construction blueprints. Debbie advises Jesse to avoid raising the issue or undertaking to confirm her suspicions for fear that it will "open a can of worms" and that the client's best interest will not be served thereby. Further assume that, based on some court decisions from other jur-isdictions, Debbie feels that the language of "structural soundness" does not imply environmental or health issues. During the contract negotiations, noth-ing is said about the asbestos issue and Debbie negotiates hard for the "struc-tural soundness" language. Might Debbie be found to have a duty of some sort to Abby? What if Debbie knew that Abby and her lawyers were concerned about such issues even if they never specifically asked a direct question concerning the presence or absence of asbestos? What if Abby, in the presence of Debbie, asked Jesse a direct question about the presence of asbestos on the property and Jesse replied, "Don't worry about it. I did a detailed examination a year ago and there is no problem. Your only concern should be to confirm the structural soundness of the building, which I think you will find more than satisfactory." Knowing Jesse's statement to be false, would Debbie have any duty to Abby at that time? What would be the appropriate action for Debbie to take with Jesse?

3. Material Defects and Duty to Disclose

Statutes and regulations at both the federal and state level increasingly bear on issues of quality of real property being sold, especially when it is sold by developers or merchants. At the local level, for example, a home seller who builds a house with material violations of the building code may be required, at the buyer's insistence, to remedy the defect.

At the federal level, one significant law bearing on property quality is the Interstate Land Sales Full Disclosure Act, 15 U.S.C. §§1701-1720. Adopted by Congress in 1968, the Act applies to the sale of unimproved lots in subdivi-sions with 25 or more lots. Builders' sales of completed new homes are not subject to the Act. Although the principal application of the Act is to resi-dential properties, it also covers developers who plan industrial and com-mercial subdivisions. Jurisdiction under the Act is triggered whenever the developer uses any of the means of interstate commerce, including mail and advertising that circulates in more than one state. Basically, the Act is a disclosure statute, requiring the developer to file a registration known as a *statement of record* for approval by the government before offering any lots for sale. As part of marketing, the developer must give each prospective purcha-ser a detailed "property report" that contains required disclosures about the lots and the overall real estate development. Because the Act is designed to protect lot buyers, it has antifraud provisions and provides penalties for viola-tions. Under general notions of contract law, a representation made by the developer in the property report may be enforceable by purchasers. One significant buyer remedy for a developer's violation of the Act is the buyer's statutory right to revoke her lot purchase contract at any time within two years after signing the contract. The Act and its regulations are quite complicated, and compliance by developers may be costly in terms of legal and adminis-trative expense. The main point to keep in mind is that merchant sellers must consider whether the Act applies to their project or whether they are entitled to one of the Act's full or partial exemptions. Lot buyers, in contrast, should be aware of their rights to information and remedies under the Act.

Some defects in the quality of a property arise from prior uses of the property, including illegal activity on or near the property. Defects of this type are difficult to determine. The next three cases explore the duty to disclose defects arising from illegal use of the property and from stigma associated with the property. These cases not only address the duty to dis-close, they raise serious questions regarding the ability to learn about a property and to anticipate potential "defects" that may not be easy to uncover. Some forms of defects are psychological and may not have any negative impact on the physical structure of a building or the quality of the land. How is a lawyer to account for these situations? Can they truly be said to be "property" defects? How do these cases impact the lawyer's duty of inquiry? What kinds of questions and investigations should a lawyer representing a buyer undertake with respect to non-physical defects? Con-versely, what steps should a lawyer representing a seller take to shield her client from the risk of liability or having to defend a claim?

BLOOR v. FRITZ
Court of Appeals of Washington, Division 2, 2008
180 P.3d 805

ARMSTRONG, Judge. . . .

Robert Fritz owned a home and approximately five acres of land on Spirit Lake Highway in Cowlitz County. He and his wife, Charmaine, moved from the home in 2001 and hired LAM Management, to manage the property as a rental. Lance Miller and Jayson Brudvik are co-owners and operators of LAM. Miller and Brudvik are also licensed real estate agents for LC Realty.

In January 2004, Jason and Charles Waddington, Pam Jackson, and Sarah Holton occupied the Spirit Lake property under a rental agreement through LAM. On January 30, the Cowlitz-Wahkiakum Joint Narcotics Task Force executed a search warrant at the property. Task force members discov-ered a marijuana growing operation in the house's basement and implements of methamphetamine manufacturing on and under the house's rear deck and in a hot tub on the deck. Although the task force processed the site as a methamphetamine lab, no one from the task force or any other law enforcement agency notified the Cowlitz County Health Department, the Washington State Department of Health, or any other state agency of the methamphetamine lab. The State charged Jason Waddington with manufacturing marijuana and Charles Waddington with manufacturing methamphetamine.

On January 31, the task force issued a press release that identified the Spirit Lake property as the site of the drug search, identified the people involved, and stated that the task force had removed a marijuana growing operation and implements of a small methamphetamine lab from the property. On February 1, the *Longview Daily News* published an article that reported the information in the press release.

Charmaine learned of the police activity at the property and contacted numerous law enforcement agencies to find out what had occurred at the property. On February 2, she contacted the task force and spoke with Judy Connor, the support staff specialist. Connor told Charmaine that the police had arrested people on the property and that the task force had confiscated a marijuana growing operation and implements of a methamphetamine lab.

The following day, Charmaine spoke with Detective Darren Ullmann, a member of the task force who had been present at the search. Ullmann told Charmaine that the task force had removed implements of a methamphetamine lab from the property. Charmaine shared this information with Robert [Fritz]. Miller also contacted law enforcement to learn the status of the property and the arrests in the first few days of February.

LAM initiated eviction proceedings against the Waddington tenants, and they left the property in February or March 2004. LAM subsequently re-rented the property for a short period of time but evicted those tenants in May 2004. The Fritzes then decided to sell the property.

In preparation for the sale, the Fritzes cleaned the house, painted it, and changed the floor coverings. During this time, Charmaine spoke with John and Jenae Cyr, who lived across the street from the property. Charmaine told the Cyrs that she and her husband felt they were lucky that the Waddington tenants had not cooked methamphetamine inside the house but had cooked it only on the back porch.

Eddie and Eva Bloor moved to Cowlitz County from Missouri in 2004 and began looking for a home to purchase. Brudvik showed them the Spirit Lake property. The Bloors decided to make an offer to buy the property. Miller represented both the Fritzes and the Bloors in the transaction.

. . . The Fritzes accepted the Bloors' offer and the transaction closed in August 2004. The Bloors moved into the home shortly thereafter.

In September, the Bloors' son heard from a member of the community that the property was known as a "drug house." The Bloors began investigating and found an online version of the February 1 *Daily News* article. Eva contacted the task force, where Sergeant Kevin Tate confirmed that the task force had confiscated a methamphetamine lab at the property. She then contacted the Cowlitz County Health Department, where Audrey Shaver confirmed that nobody had reported the lab to the health department and that it would investigate the matter to determine what action it would take.

On October 22, Shaver told the Bloors that the health department had determined that the property was contaminated by the methamphetamine manufacturing and was not fit for occupancy. She told the Bloors that they could not remove their personal property from the house because of the risk of cross-contamination. The Bloors left the residence as instructed, leaving nearly all their personal belongings in the house and garage.

The health department posted an order prohibiting use of the property. The order stated that the Bloors were financially responsible for the cost of remediation, that a certified decontamination contractor would have to perform the remediation, and that use of the property was subject to criminal charges. Occupancy of buildings contaminated by methamphetamine manufacturing is dangerous to the health and safety of occupants.

The Bloors stayed with relatives until they could secure a place to live, eventually moving to Spokane. They had to repurchase clothing, bedding, furniture, and other necessities. They were unable to both support themselves and make their monthly mortgage payments. The Bloors experienced emotional distress and anxiety due to the loss of their home, personal effects, and keepsakes.

The Bloors sued the Fritzes, Miller, LAM Management, LC Realty, and Cowlitz County. After a bench trial, the trial court ruled for the Bloors, awarding them damages jointly and severally against all the defendants for emotional distress, loss of personal property, loss of income, loss of use of the property, and damage to the Bloors' credit. . . . [In addition, the trial court] . . . ordered the contract between the Bloors and the Fritzes rescinded, requiring the Fritzes to [refund] the purchase price [and pay other charges related to the Bloors' mortgage financing] and the Bloors to return the property to the Fritzes. . . .

MILLER AND LC REALTY'S APPEAL

I. KNOWLEDGE OF METHAMPHETAMINE MANUFACTURING

Miller argues that substantial evidence does not support the trial court's findings regarding his knowledge of the methamphetamine manufacturing at the Spirit Lake property. . . . The trial court's findings included the following:

> Miller concealed his knowledge that the Property had been used for illegal drug manufacturing when he announced his listing of the Property, and during his marketing of the Property for the Fritzes. Miller knew of the history of illegal drug manufacturing and of the potential contamination, knew that the Fritzes had not disclosed it on their Disclosure Statement, and failed to disclose his personal knowledge of the history of use of the Property for illegal drug manufacturing, or of the potential contamination of the Property to the public, . . . or to the Bloors.

The Bloors were damaged by Miller's failure to disclose the history of drug manufacturing at the Property. As shown by the investigation made by Eva Bloor upon receiving information that drug activity had occurred at the Property, Miller's failure to disclose his knowledge of the drug activity on the Property to the Bloors misled the Bloors and deprived them of essential information needed by them to learn of the true condition of the Property. Had Miller revealed his knowledge of the drug activity on the Property, the Bloors would have probably made inquiry to law enforcement and the health department, which they did upon receiving information of the history of such activity at the Property.

. . . .

Eva Bloor testified that, if the Fritzes had disclosed the illegal drug manufacturing at the home, she might have changed her mind about buying the property. She would have asked questions about the drug manufacturing, including what the drug was. She also would have inquired with the health department. That the Bloors began investigating the property's history as soon as they learned of the illegal drugs supports a finding that if they had known earlier, they would have investigated before closing the purchase. Again, substantial evidence supports this finding of fact.

II. FAILURE TO DISCLOSE A MATERIAL FACT

Miller next argues that the trial court erred in concluding that he failed to disclose his knowledge of the methamphetamine manufacturing as RCW 18.86.030 requires.

Under RCW 18.86.030(1)(d), a real estate agent has a duty to disclose "all existing material facts known by the [agent] and not apparent or readily ascertainable to a party; provided that this subsection shall not be construed to imply any duty to investigate matters that the [agent] has not agreed to investigate." A "material fact" is "information that substantially adversely affects the value of the property or a party's ability to perform its obligations in a real estate transaction, or operates to materially impair or defeat the purpose of the transaction." RCW 18.86.010(9). . . .

. . . Miller violated his duty to disclose known material facts about the property . . . .

[The trial court determination that the Fritzes and Miller are jointly and severally liable to the Bloors is affirmed.]

VAN CAMP v. BRADFORD
Court of Common Pleas of Ohio, Butler County, 1993
623 N.E.2d 731

MICHAEL J. SAGE, Judge. This matter comes before this court on three motions filed by the defendants. The defendants in this case are Connie Bradford, the original owner/seller; Campbell Realty World (hereinafter "Realty World"), the . . . listing agency; William Campbell, the owner of

Realty World; Martin Patton, the agent of Realty World; West Shell Realtors, Inc., the cooperating agency (hereinafter "West Shell"); and Robert Hoff, the cooperating agent of West Shell. Counsel have agreed that these motions are to be treated as Civ.R. 56(C) motions for summary judgment.

I

This case arises from the sale of a residence located at 6027 Arcade Drive, Fairfield, Ohio. On or about October 30, 1991, a renter's daughter was raped at knifepoint in the residence owned by defendant Bradford. On or about December 20, 1991, another rape occurred in a neighboring home at 2499 E. Highland Drive; that same day, defendant Bradford listed the house for sale with defendant Realty World.

Plaintiff Kitty Van Camp submitted a written offer to purchase the home on February 4, 1992. Before closing and during a walk-through inspection of the premises with defendant Bradford, and defendant Patton and defendant Hoff present, plaintiff noticed bars on the basement windows. In response to plaintiff's inquiry regarding the purpose and necessity of the bars on the windows, defendant Bradford stated that a break-in had occurred sixteen years earlier, but that there was currently no problem with the residence. Plaintiff stated that she would like to remove the bars for cosmetic purposes, but Bradford advised her not to do so, as it was in plaintiff's best interests to leave the bars in place.

Figure 5-1
The house purchased by Kitty Van Camp

The closing on the property took place on February 21, 1992. At this time, the perpetrator of the crimes was still at large. While moving into the home, a neighbor informed plaintiff that the daughter of the last occupant had been raped in October, and that another brutal rape had occurred shortly before Christmas, in 1991. Two more rapes occurred in June and August 1992 at a nearby home, 5886 Coachmont Drive, Fairfield. Plaintiff's house was burglarized on April 8, 1992, and threatening phone calls were received by plaintiff in July 1992. Police reports submitted by plaintiff confirm that all of these crimes did in fact take place.

Plaintiff, after being informed of the rapes in her home and the surrounding neighborhood, confronted defendant Campbell, who acknowledged that he, defendant Patton, and defendant Hoff were all aware of the rapes, including the rape at the subject property.

Plaintiff filed her complaint on May 25, 1992, alleging that the defendants knew of the unsafe character of the residence and neighborhood, failed to disclose, and concealed these material facts, which would have influenced her decision to buy the property. Plaintiff seeks damages from all defendants for mental stress and anguish, for the decreased value of the property, for fraud and negligence, and for equitable relief.

The defendants have filed for summary judgment, arguing primarily that the doctrine of caveat emptor is a complete defense in a suit seeking recovery for the "stigma" attached to or the "psychological impairment" of a piece of property. Defendants also claim that a cause of action for property defects that are neither a physical or legal impairment does not exist in Ohio.

II

The rule that a seller is generally under no duty to disclose material facts about the subject matter of a sale unless a specific exception exists originates from the doctrine of *caveat emptor*. Powell, *The Seller's Duty to Disclose in Sales of Commercial Property* (Summer 1990), 28 Am. Bus. L.J. 245, at 248. At least since 1956, the principle of *caveat emptor* has been consistently applied in Ohio to sales of real estate relative to conditions discoverable by the buyer, or open to observation upon an investigation of the property. Traverse v. Long, 135 N.E.2d 256 (Ohio 1956). One of the earliest Ohio cases upholding this principle held that since repairs to an area of filled-in land were clearly visible upon inspection, the plaintiffs knew of the defect and *caveat emptor* was an applicable defense to their claim. *Id.* Similarly, in 1974, the Franklin County Court of Appeals held that since the seller generally has no affirmative duty to disclose patent material defects, the defendants were not liable for failing to disclose that the residence in question was serviced by well water and not city water, since the well itself and the defects in the well were both readily observable. Klott v. Assoc. Real Estate, 322 N.E.2d 690, 692 (Ohio Ct. App. 1974).

Five years later, however, the Supreme Court of Ohio held that latent defects do give rise to a duty on the part of the seller, and constitute an exception to the application of *caveat emptor*. Miles v. McSwegin 388 N.E.2d 1367, 1369 (Ohio 1979). When latent defects are coupled with misrepresentations or concealment, the doctrine of *caveat emptor* does not preclude recovery for fraud. Finomore v. Epstein, 481 N.E.2d 1193 (Ohio Ct. App. 1984). Fraudulent concealment exists where a vendor fails to disclose sources of peril of which he is aware, if such a source is not discoverable by the vendee. *Klott*, 322 N.E.2d at 692. Thus, the Supreme Court of Ohio held that the plaintiffs could sue for termites discovered after the real estate agent made the representation that the house was a "good solid home," especially since the seller was personally aware of the problem prior to the sale. *See Miles*. The nature of the defect and the ability of the parties to determine through a reasonable inspection that a defect exists are key to determining whether or not the defect is latent. *Miles*, 388 N.E.2d at 1369.

In the 1983 case of Kaye v. Buehrle, 457 N.E.2d 373 (Ohio Ct. App. 1983). the Summit County Court of Appeals affirmed a directed verdict in favor of the defendants and upheld the validity of a real estate "as is" disclaimer clause. Such disclaimer clauses bar suit for passive nondisclosure, but will not protect a defendant from positive misrepresentation or concealment. *Id.* The court found, however, that the defendants did not make any statement or false representation regarding the condition of the basement, which suffered extensive flooding after the plaintiffs purchased the property.

The following year, the Cuyahoga County Court of Appeals held that *caveat emptor* did not preclude the purchaser of two tracts of land from recovering for fraud due to a latent defect in the form of a blemished title, since a misrepresentation had accompanied the latent defect. *See Finomore*. The plaintiff in that case testified that the owner had told him that the lots were "free and clear," yet the evidence indicated that a small mortgage on the property was outstanding at the time of the sale. . . .

Virtually all of the case law regarding the buyer's duties under *caveat emptor* focuses on physical property defects. Thus, the case at bar is unique in that it presents issues regarding duty and liability for a so-called psychological defect in the property, namely, that the property was rendered unsafe for habitation by the plaintiff due to the serious crimes that had occurred in and near the residence.

The stigma associated with the residence at 6027 Arcade Drive is analogous to the latent property defects that have become an exception to the strict application of *caveat emptor*. Due to the intangible nature of the defect at issue here, a prospective buyer would have been unable to determine from a walk-through of the house in 1992 that it was the site of a serious, unsolved violent crime. Clearly, any psychological stigma that may be attached to a residence is even more undiscoverable than the existence of termites in a home, *see Miles*, or a defect in the title to the property, *see Finomore*, both of which have been deemed latent defects despite the fact that they could have been discovered through a professional inspection or title search.

Defendants' argument that the defect at issue here was readily discoverable lacks merit. Checking police records in order to ascertain the relative safety of a neighborhood or a particular residence would not be an action undertaken by even the most prudent of purchasers. When viewed in conjunction with a potential misrepresentation or concealment on the part of defendant Bradford regarding the relative safety of the home, the latent nature of the defect at issue here renders the defense of *caveat emptor* inapplicable.

III

The case sub judice raises the question whether Ohio should recognize a cause of action for residential property tainted by stigmatizing events that have occurred on and near the premises. The only reported case involving a psychological property defect was heard in California by the Third District Court of Appeals, and involved a house that had been the site of multiple murders ten years prior to its sale to the plaintiff. Reed v. King, 193 Cal. Rptr. 130 (Ct. App. 1983). The Third District held that the plaintiff buyer did have a cause of action capable of surviving the seller's motion to dismiss. The determinative issue in that case was whether the failure to disclose the murders was material. *Id.* . . .

Clearly defining the cause of action for stigmatized property is necessary in order to protect the stability of contracts and prevent limitless recovery for insubstantial harms and irrational fears: misrepresentation, concealment or nondisclosure of a material fact by a seller of residential property in response to an affirmative inquiry is evidence of a breach of duty on the part of the seller. After inquiry, if the buyer justifiably relied on the misrepresentation or nondisclosure, or was induced or misled into effecting the sale to his/her detriment and damage, the buyer has met the burden of proof required to withstand a summary judgment motion.

Fraud may be committed by suppression or concealment, as well as by expression of a falsehood. Even an innocent misrepresentation may, under the appropriate circumstances, justify rescission in the interests of fairness.

The misrepresentation, however, must be regarding a material fact. . . .

The misrepresentation or nondisclosure of the seller must cause justifiable reliance on the part of the buyer, and damage must result as a consequence of the fraudulent transaction. Both of these requirements will serve as effective limitations on seller liability and will function to prevent the bringing of meritless claims. In determining whether reliance is justifiable, courts consider the various circumstances involved, such as the nature of the transaction, the form and materiality of the representation, the relationship of the parties, the respective intelligence, experience, age, and mental and physical condition of the parties, and their respective knowledge and means of knowledge. *Finomore,* 481 N.E.2d at 1195. When a fiduciary relationship exists, as between a realty agent and a client, the client is entitled to rely upon the representations of the realty agent. *Id.* In the absence of a fiduciary relationship, the law requires a person to exercise proper vigilance in his dealings, so that where one is put on notice as to any doubt as to the truth of a representation, the person is under a duty to reasonably investigate before relying thereon. The prevailing trend in misrepresentation cases, however, is to place a minimal duty on the buyer to investigate and discover the true facts about the property. *See* Powell, *supra* at 258.

A seller who is under a duty to disclose facts and fails to do so will be held liable for damages directly and proximately resulting from his silence. A person injured by fraud is entitled to such damages as will fairly compensate him for the wrong suffered. . . .

The defendants in this case have argued that the prevailing trend across the nation regarding property disclosure is evidenced by the nondisclosure statutes that have been enacted in twenty states and the District of Columbia. . . .

These statutes generally state that sellers of real estate are not liable for failing to disclose stigmatizing events, such as the fact that a homicide, suicide, felony or death by AIDS occurred in the residence. Ohio has not adopted a nondisclosure statute of this nature.

It is the opinion of this court that the nondisclosure statutes as enacted in other states still require a good faith response to an inquiry regarding a potential psychological impairment: these statutes were enacted solely to insulate sellers from liability for any failure to voluntarily and automatically disclose information regarding potential stigmas associated with property. . . .

Nondisclosure statutes are not designed to allow sellers to make false representations regarding property defects in response to affirmative questioning by the buyer. . . .

Thus, since the nondisclosure statutes of other states merely protect sellers from the burden of voluntary disclosure regarding psychological defects, and since several states have specific provisions designed to uphold honesty in residential sales transactions, the duty described in this opinion is well within the range delineated and envisioned by other state legislatures.

VI

A cause of action for stigmatized property, as previously defined and limited, is warranted in the case at bar. . . .

Construing the evidence in the light most favorable to the plaintiff, the court finds that the plaintiff has met her initial burden of proof. . . .

Reasonable minds could construe the plaintiff's question regarding the bars on the basement windows as an affirmative inquiry directed at ascertaining the safety of the premises, and defendant Bradford's statements regarding the reason for the bars to be a misrepresentation or a nondisclosure of their current purpose. Upon the plaintiff's inquiry, defendant Bradford was simply required to tell the truth. A more difficult case would arise had there been no evidence to indicate that the plaintiff had solicited information regarding the safety of the residence.

Further, both the plaintiff and defendant Bradford are single mothers with teenage daughters. This fact alone may be sufficient to make disclosure of the rape a material fact with regard to the sale of the property at Arcade Drive, or at least may be sufficient to demonstrate that defendant Bradford should have known that the plaintiff was "peculiarly disposed" to attach importance to the subject of female-targeted crimes. Thus, a potential misrepresentation in response to plaintiff's affirmative inquiry regarding a material fact placed a duty of honesty upon the seller, and plaintiff has shouldered her initial burden in coming forward.

Numerous questions of material fact remain regarding the conversation that took place between plaintiff and defendant Bradford, and these questions preclude a granting of summary judgment. . . .

By contrast, however, the court finds as a matter of law that the inquiry of plaintiff was directed solely to the homeowner, defendant Bradford: she alone responded to plaintiff's question regarding the safety of the residence. The real estate defendants had no duty to affirmatively speak up and disclose their knowledge of the crimes simply because they were in the room at the time the inquiry was made. . . .

STAMBOVSKY v. ACKLEY
Supreme Court of New York, Appellate Division, 1991
572 N.Y.S.2d 672

RUBIN, Justice. Plaintiff, to his horror, discovered that the house he had recently contracted to purchase was widely reputed to be possessed by poltergeists, reportedly seen by defendant seller and members of her family on numerous occasions over the last nine years. Plaintiff promptly commenced this action seeking rescission of the contract of sale. Supreme Court reluctantly dismissed the complaint, holding that plaintiff has no remedy at law in this jurisdiction.

The unusual facts of this case, as disclosed by the record, clearly warrant a grant of equitable relief to the buyer who, as a resident of New York City, cannot be expected to have any familiarity with the folklore of the Village of Nyack. Not being a "local," plaintiff could not readily learn that the home he had contracted to purchase is haunted. Whether the source of the spectral apparitions seen by defendant seller are parapsychic or psychogenic, having reported their presence in both a national publication (Readers' Digest) and the local press (in 1977 and 1982, respectively), defendant is estopped to deny their existence and, as a matter of law, the house is haunted. More to the point, however, no divination is required to conclude that it is defendant's promotional efforts in publicizing her close encounters with these spirits which fostered the home's reputation in the community. In 1989, the house was included in a five-home walking tour of Nyack and described in a November 27th newspaper article as "a riverfront Victorian (with ghost)." The impact of the reputation thus created goes to the very essence of the bargain between the parties, greatly impairing both the value of the property and its potential for resale. . . .

While I agree with Supreme Court that the real estate broker, as agent for the seller, is under no duty to disclose to a potential buyer the phantasmal reputation of the premises and that, in his pursuit of a legal remedy for fraudulent misrepresentation against the seller, plaintiff hasn't a ghost of a chance, I am nevertheless moved by the spirit of equity to allow the buyer to seek rescission of the contract of sale and recovery of his down payment. New York law fails to recognize any remedy for damages incurred as a result of the seller's mere silence, applying instead the strict rule of caveat emptor. Therefore, the theoretical basis for granting relief, even under the extraordinary facts of this case, is elusive if not ephemeral.

"Pity me not but lend thy serious hearing to what I shall unfold." William Shakespeare, *Hamlet*, Act I, Scene V [Ghost].

From the perspective of a person in the position of plaintiff herein, a very practical problem arises with respect to the discovery of a paranormal phenomenon: "Who you gonna call?" as the title song to the movie "Ghostbusters" asks. Applying the strict rule of caveat emptor to a contract involving a house possessed by poltergeists conjures up visions of a psychic or medium routinely accompanying the structural engineer and Terminix man on an inspection of every home subject to a contract of sale. It portends that the prudent attorney will establish an escrow account lest the subject of the transaction come back to haunt him and his client—or pray that his malpractice insurance coverage extends to supernatural disasters. In the interest of avoiding such untenable consequences, the notion that a haunting is a condition which can and should be ascertained upon reasonable inspection of the premises is a hobgoblin which should be exorcised from the body of legal precedent and laid quietly to rest.

It has been suggested by a leading authority that the ancient rule which holds that mere non-disclosure does not constitute actionable misrepresentation "finds proper application in cases where the fact undisclosed is patent, or the plaintiff has equal opportunities for obtaining information which he may be expected to utilize, or the defendant has no reason to think that he is acting under any misapprehension." Prosser, *Law of Torts* §106, at 696 (4th ed., 1971). However, with respect to transactions in real estate, New York adheres to the doctrine of caveat emptor and imposes no duty upon the vendor to disclose any information concerning the premises unless there is a confidential or fiduciary relationship between the parties or some conduct on the part of the seller which constitutes "active concealment." *See* 17 East

80th Realty Corp. v. 68th Associates, 569 N.Y.S.2d 647 (App. Div. 1991) (dummy ventilation system constructed by seller); Haberman v. Greenspan, 368 N.Y.S.2d 717 (Sup. Ct. 1975) (foundation cracks covered by seller). Normally, some affirmative misrepresentation or partial disclosure is required to impose upon the seller a duty to communicate undisclosed conditions affecting the premises.

Caveat emptor is not so all-encompassing a doctrine of common law as to render every act of non-disclosure immune from redress, whether legal or equitable.

> In regard to the necessity of giving information which has not been asked, the rule differs somewhat at law and in equity, and while the law courts would permit no recovery of *damages* against a vendor, because of mere concealment of facts *under certain circumstances*, yet if the vendee refused to complete the contract because of the concealment of a material fact on the part of the other, equity would refuse to compel him so to do, because equity only compels the specific performance of a contract which is fair and open, and in regard to which all material matters known to each have been communicated to the other.

Rothmiller v. Stein, 38 N.E. 718, 721 (N.Y. 1894) (emphasis added). . . . Where fairness and common sense dictate that an exception should be created, the evolution of the law should not be stifled by rigid application of a legal maxim.

The doctrine of caveat emptor requires that a buyer act prudently to assess the fitness and value of his purchase and operates to bar the purchaser who fails to exercise due care from seeking the equitable remedy of rescission. . . . It should be apparent, however, that the most meticulous inspection and the search would not reveal the presence of poltergeists at the premises or unearth the property's ghoulish reputation in the community. Therefore, there is no sound policy reason to deny plaintiff relief for failing to discover a state of affairs which the most prudent purchaser would not be expected to even contemplate. *See* Da Silva v. Musso, 428 N.E.2d 382, 386 (N.Y. 1981). . . .

Where a condition which has been created by the seller materially impairs the value of the contract and is peculiarly within the knowledge of the seller or unlikely to be discovered by a prudent purchaser exercising due care with respect to the subject transaction, nondisclosure constitutes a basis for rescission as a matter of equity. Any other outcome places upon the buyer not merely the obligation to exercise care in his purchase but rather to be omniscient with respect to any fact which may affect the bargain. No practical purpose is served by imposing such a burden upon a purchaser. To the contrary, it encourages predatory business practice and offends the principle that equity will suffer no wrong to be without a remedy.

Defendant's contention that the contract of sale, particularly the merger or "as is" clause, bars recovery of the buyer's deposit is unavailing. . . . [A] fair reading of the merger clause reveals that it expressly disclaims only representations made with respect to the physical condition of the premises and merely makes general reference to representations concerning "any other matter or things affecting or relating to the aforesaid premises." As broad as this language may be, a reasonable interpretation is that its effect is limited to tangible or physical matters and does not extend to paranormal phenomena. Finally, if the language of the contract is to be construed as broadly as defendant urges to encompass the presence of poltergeists in the house, it cannot be said that she has delivered the premises "vacant" in accordance with her obligation under the provisions of the contract rider. . . .

In the case at bar, defendant seller deliberately fostered the public belief that her home was possessed. Having undertaken to inform the public at large, to whom she has no legal relationship, about the supernatural occurrences on her property, she may be said to owe no less a duty to her contract vendee. It has been remarked that the occasional modern cases which permit a seller to take unfair advantage of a buyer's ignorance so long as he is not actively misled are "singularly unappetizing." Prosser, *Law of Torts* §106, at 696 (4th ed. 1971). Where, as here, the seller not only takes unfair advantage of the buyer's ignorance but has created and perpetuated a condition about which he is unlikely to even inquire, enforcement of the contract (in whole or in part) is offensive to the court's sense of equity. Application of the remedy of rescission, within the bounds of the narrow exception to the doctrine of caveat emptor set forth herein, is entirely appropriate to relieve the unwitting purchaser from the consequences of a most unnatural bargain.

Accordingly, the judgment of the Supreme Court, New York County . . . should be modified . . . and the first cause of action seeking rescission of the contract reinstated, without costs.

SMITH, Justice, dissenting. I would affirm the dismissal of the complaint by the motion court. . . .

> It is settled law in New York that the seller of real property is under no duty to speak when the parties deal at arm's length. The mere silence of the seller, without some act or conduct which deceived the purchaser, does not amount to a concealment that is actionable as a fraud. The buyer has the duty to satisfy himself as to the quality of his bargain pursuant to the doctrine of caveat emptor, which in New York State still applies to real estate transactions.

London v. Courduff, 529 N.Y.S.2d 874, 875 (App. Div.), *app. dism'd*, 534 N.E.2d 332 (N.Y. 1988).

Problem 5E

Giorgio is interested in buying a home from Clara. The home is located in the town of Dewitt, a suburb of the city of Syracuse, New York. The home has a mailing address of Fayetteville, New York, which is an adjoining suburb. It is a spacious three-bedroom, four-bath home on an acre of land with three fireplaces and all the amenities that Giorgio has been looking for. The asking price is $260,000, but Giorgio is confident he can get it for $240,000. In fact, he ends up with a contract to purchase at his offer price.

(a) Assume that during one of the times Giorgio looks at the home, he asks about the size of the rooms and total square footage. Clara replies that the total is 3,000 square feet. After moving in Giorgio determines that the home is 2,600 square feet. Should Giorgio have a cause of action against Clara? Does Clara's state of mind (intent) affect your view? What if Clara said she didn't know but the broker volunteered the 3,000-square-foot number? Would the broker be liable? What if the broker knew it was 2,600 but Clara said 3,000, and the broker remained silent (did not correct the error)? What if Giorgio never asked about the square footage but it was erroneously stated on the multiple listing service description of the home? Would it be vital that Giorgio prove that he read the erroneous description? How can a broker or seller provide the buyer with information about the home without worrying about the problems of unintended errors or about what has to be disclosed?

(b) What if Giorgio asks about the school district that his home is located in? The home is in Dewitt but has a mailing address of Fayetteville. Clara has no children, so she is uncertain. The broker says, "They are both very good school districts, but since your mailing address is Fayetteville, it's a pretty safe bet that you are in that school district." Giorgio, not having any children himself, takes that as a good enough answer. Ten months later, Giorgio decides to sell the house and he has a prospect who is very interested. The prospect is a young family currently living in a smaller home in Fayetteville. They want to buy a bigger home, but they want to keep their children in the same school district. They tell Giorgio they want to buy the home for $243,000 and Giorgio agrees to sell. They plan to meet later that night to draw up the written contract. That night, Giorgio gets a call from the family saying they decided not to buy the house because they called the Fayetteville school district and were told that the house is located just across the district boundary line and therefore is within the Dewitt school district. Six months pass and Giorgio has had no other prospects even look at this house. Can Giorgio recover from the broker? What if the broker who was there and made the comment was Clara's listing broker and not Giorgio's broker? Would that make any difference?

(c) Assume that Clara is an HIV-infected person in the later stages of the disease and she is selling the home in order to move into a hospice. The contract with Giorgio is a good deal for her. Furthermore, her companion of ten years who lived with her in the home died of AIDS at home about three months earlier. One day while Giorgio is viewing the home with Clara's broker in preparation for moving in, and while Clara is out, the broker says, "You know it's too bad that Clara's friend died of AIDS in this house and now Clara is preparing herself for the same fate. It's sad, but I suppose you should know that about the place before you move in." Giorgio decides not to go ahead with the deal. Clara sues her broker for breach of privacy, disclosure of confidential information, and damages for a lost sale. Should Clara be able to recover? Did the broker have a duty to disclose? What if the broker was responding to conversation but not a direct question, such as if Giorgio had been saying, "I can't wait to move out here to the suburbs, I'm sick of the city with its drug users, crack houses, and other things. . . . I'm scared to death that half the people in my neighborhood have AIDS because there are so many junkies sharing needles over at this abandoned housing project." What if a fear of AIDS, even an unfounded one, is shown to have a substantial impact on the value of a property?

(d) Assume that the house, the school district, and everything else are all in good shape and Clara is in perfect health. About a week prior to entering the contract with Giorgio, Clara gets a notice from the town zoning board informing her that a local not-for-profit organization has bought the house two doors down from Clara's. They have applied to turn the home into a group residence for five teenage boys and girls with mental and physical disabilities. One trained adult supervisor will be on location 24 hours a day. The notice says the board has granted preliminary approval for the zoning modification, with a public hearing scheduled two weeks from now. Does Clara have to disclose this to Giorgio?

(e) Assume that a week after entering the contract, the town tax authority sends Clara a notice of special assessment. Clara and her neighbors are being assessed $2,000 per lot to pay for the installation of new sewer lines that will directly benefit each home on her street. Is nondisclosure of the tax notice material if the sewer work in fact adds value to the house? If the assessment is made against the property during the executory contract period, who should pay the $2,000 cost?

4. Implied Warranties

Express warranties are traditional elements of a real estate transaction because they form a part of the parties' bargain in fact. *Implied warranties* arise from the situation or context in which a transaction takes place. As the term indicates, the implied warranty is read into an exchange on the basis of reasonable or fair expectations given the nature of the exchange. The implied warranty has been more problematic in real estate sales where, up until the 1950s, *caveat emptor* was clearly the ruling doctrine.

Since the 1950s, we have witnessed the gradual decline of the doctrine of *caveat emptor*. Courts have increasingly analogized a home sale to a sale of goods, thereby creating implied warranty protections for homebuyers and home dwellers. This implied warranty protection has been extended, in some cases, beyond the physical structure of the home to include such things as the quality of the water and soil related to the home. The cases in this area have recognized that housing markets and the methods of housing production and sales have changed over the years. Now most homes are mass-produced using prefabricated materials and, thus, home building very much resembles other forms of commercial product production. These market changes have exerted considerable pressure on real estate law to abandon old common-law principles in favor of new approaches that comport with modern commercial realities. This shift should also serve to alert lawyers to a related legal matter. As real estate development is increasingly seen as a commercial production process — similar to that of many other complex products such as automobiles — it not only becomes subject to more general contract and commercial law principles, but it also opens the door to tort law implications. Products liability, strict liability, damages for emotional distress, and punitive damages seem more and more appropriate for application to real estate transactions as our society becomes increasingly comfortable with the idea of conceptualizing real estate development as similar to other forms of commercial manufacturing and production.

The movement toward treating real estate development like other forms of commercial production is not just a process occurring in the courts. There are legislative measures addressing this area as well. A number of states, for instance, have passed statutes that read warranties into the sale of new housing, and some states have disclosure statutes that require sellers of used homes to inform buyers of material latent defects known to the seller.

The homebuilding industry has also responded to issues of property quality. Many builders offer their own express warranties to buyers of new homes, but more significant are standardized warranties given or guaranteed by third parties. The most prominent such warranty is backed by the Residential Warranty Corporation (RWC), founded in 1981, with headquarters in Harrisburg, Pennsylvania. It offers warranties on new homes, including manufactured homes, as well as remodeling projects.

In addition to the warranties for new homes, many realty companies offer insurance on used homes to help relieve buyers' fears of unknown problems with the home they are thinking of purchasing. Although this adds some cost to the transaction, it gives the buyer a vehicle for fixing certain home repair problems without cost during the covered time period, which is usually one year. One key problem with both the new and used warranty programs is that the actual insurance policy must be read carefully to see what types of repairs are covered and what types are excluded.

LOFTS AT FILLMORE CONDOMINIUM ASSOCIATION v. RELIANCE COMMERCIAL CONSTRUCTION, INC.
Supreme Court of Arizona, 2008
190 P.3d 733

HURWITZ, Justice. We consider today whether a homebuilder who is not also the vendor of the residence can be sued by a buyer for breach of the implied warranty of workmanship and habitability. We conclude that absence of contractual privity does not bar such a suit.

I.

William Mahoney and The Lofts at Fillmore, L.L.C. (collectively, "the Developer") contracted with Reliance Commercial Construction, Inc. ("Reliance") to convert a building owned by the Developer into condominiums. The Developer later sold condominium units to individual buyers, who formed The Lofts at Fillmore Condominium Association ("the Association"). Claiming various construction defects, the Association subsequently sued the Developer and Reliance for breach of the implied warranty of workmanship and habitability.

The superior court granted summary judgment to Reliance. The court of appeals affirmed, finding the implied warranty claim barred because the Association had no contractual relationship with Reliance. . . .

We granted the Association's petition for review because the issue presented is of statewide importance. . . .

II.

A.

. . . In Richards v. Powercraft Homes, Inc., 678 P.2d 427 (Ariz. 1984), . . . we held that suit on the implied warranty of workmanship and habitability may be brought not only by the original buyer of the home, but also by subsequent buyers. *Id.* at 430.

Richards involved claims by homebuyers against a builder-vendor — a company that built and then sold homes to residential purchasers. Reliance, in contrast, only built The Lofts condominiums; the Developer owned the property throughout and sold the residences to members of the Association. The issue before us is whether the absence of privity bars the Association's suit on the implied warranty against Reliance.

B.

The threshold question is whether a builder who is not also the vendor of a new home impliedly warrants that construction has been done in a workmanlike manner and that the home is habitable.[1]

Although prior Arizona cases do not directly address this issue, they provide important guidance. It has long been the rule "that implied warranties as to quality or condition do not apply to realty." Voight v. Ott, 341 P.2d 923, 925 (Ariz. 1959). In Columbia Western Corp. v. Vela, 592 P.2d 1294, 1299 (Ariz. Ct. App. 1979), the court of appeals recognized this rule, but distinguished *Voight*: "In our opinion *Voight* is authority for the proposition that no implied warranties arise from the *sale* of realty, but is not dispositive of the issue of implied warranties arising out of the *construction* of new housing which ultimately becomes 'realty.'" *Id.* at 1296. . . .

. . . Given its careful distinction of *Voight*, *Columbia Western* thus rests on the premise that an implied warranty arises from the *construction* of a new home, whether or not the builder is also a vendor of the home.[2] . . .

Thus, although *Columbia Western* and *Richards* involved builder-vendors, both opinions — and our prior cases — make clear that an implied warranty arises from construction of the home, without regard to the identity of the vendor. Moxley v. Laramie Builders, Inc., 600 P.2d 733 (Wyo. 1979), which we cited with approval in *Richards*, makes this point expressly:

> We can see no difference between a builder or contractor who undertakes construction of a home and a builder-developer. To the buyer of a home the same considerations are present, no matter whether a builder constructs a residence on the land of the owner or whether the builder constructs a habitation on land he is developing and selling the residential structures as part of a package including the land. It is the structure and all its intricate components and related facilities that are the subject matter of the implied warranty. Those who hold themselves out as builders must be just as accountable for the workmanship that goes into a home . . . as are builder-developers.

Id. at 735. We therefore conclude that Reliance gave an implied warranty of workmanship and habitability, even though it was not also the vendor of the condominiums. We next turn to the issue of whether suit on this warranty can be brought by residential homebuyers, like those in the Association, who had no direct contractual relationship with the builder.

---

1. The parties have apparently assumed that the condominium conversion constituted new home construction. We also so assume without deciding the issue.

2. All parties to this case have assumed that there is a single implied warranty of workmanship and habitability, as opposed to two separate warranties. *See* Nastri v. Wood Bros. Homes, Inc., 690 P.2d 158, 163 (Ariz. Ct. App. 1984) (holding that the Arizona decisions establish one implied warranty). We therefore today make a similar assumption, without deciding the issue. We also assume arguendo, as have the parties, that suit could properly be brought against the Developer on an implied warranty theory.

C.

The courts below held that *Richards* abrogated the common law requirement of privity in contract actions only when the builder of the new home is also the vendor. We disagree.

We stressed in *Richards* that, given the policies behind the implied warranty — to protect innocent buyers and hold builders responsible for their work — "any reasoning which would arbitrarily interpose a first buyer as an obstruction to someone equally deserving of recovery is incomprehensible." 678 P.2d at 430. We also noted that such a rule "might encourage sham first sales to insulate builders from liability." *Id.* And, we emphasized

> that the character of our society is such that people and families are increasingly mobile. Home builders should anticipate that the houses they construct will eventually, and perhaps frequently, change ownership. The effect of latent defects will be just as catastrophic on a subsequent owner as on an original buyer and the builder will be just as unable to justify improper or substandard work.

Id. Identical concerns guide us today. In today's marketplace, as this case illustrates, there has been some shift from the traditional builder-vendor model to arrangements under which a construction entity builds the homes and a sales entity markets them to the public. In some cases, the builder may be related to the vendor; in other cases, the vendor and the builder may be unrelated. But whatever the commercial utility of such contractual arrangements, they should not affect the homebuyer's ability to enforce the implied warranty against the builder. Innocent buyers of defectively constructed homes should not be denied redress on the implied warranty simply because of the form of the business deal chosen by the builder and vendor.[3]

D.

Reliance argues that failure to require privity in implied warranty actions will expose residential homebuilders to expanded liability and disrupt an important sector of the Arizona economy. But homebuilders who do not sell directly to the public already are liable for defective construction. As noted above, builders have long been directly liable to those with whom they contract for breach of the implied warranty of good workmanship. Therefore, a developer-vendor sued for defective construction will typically seek indemnity from the builder; such a defendant may also choose to assign his claim against the builder to the plaintiff. *See* Webb v. Gittlen, 174 P.3d 275, 276 (Ariz. 2008) (noting that unliquidated non-personal injury claims are

---

3. We have no occasion today to decide whether privity is a requirement for enforcement of implied warranties in the context of non-residential construction. . . .

generally assignable). Our decision today thus does not impose liability on builders where none existed in the past.[4]

Reliance also argues that failure to require privity will chill salutary attempts between developers and builders to allocate responsibility for contract damages arising out of construction defects. But nothing in our opinion today prevents or discourages such agreements; we hold only that the Association may bring suit directly against Reliance. Reliance may not rely upon an agreement it has with the Developer respecting allocation of eventual responsibility for defective construction to escape its obligations to the Association on the implied warranty.[5]

III.

For the foregoing reasons, we hold that the superior court erred in dismissing the Association's implied warranty claim for lack of privity. We therefore vacate the opinion of the court of appeals, reverse the judgment of the superior court, and remand to the superior court for further proceedings consistent with this opinion.

4. Arizona law also provides builders with protections against actions by those claiming construction defects. *See* A.R. §§12-1361 to -1366 (requiring putative plaintiffs to give builders notice and an opportunity to repair defective construction); *id.* §12-552 (imposing eight-year statute of limitations from substantial completion of the dwelling, regardless of whether defective construction is discovered during that period).

5. We recognize that if the developer-vendor is financially unable to satisfy a judgment for breach of the implied warranty, the builder may be left with the entire monetary responsibility, notwithstanding any allocation agreements. But under such circumstances, the costs of remedying defective construction most appropriately fall on the builder, rather than on innocent end users.

6
Closing the Contract

Closing the contract of purchase and sale represents the culmination of the earlier stages of the transaction. In some respects, it is actually a two-phase process. The first phase consists of everything that goes into preparing for the completion of the exchange as contracted. The second phase involves the paperwork that is required post-closing, such as the recording of documents in the public records. In each phase there are a number of concerns that require the attorney's attention.

From the buyer's point of view, the primary document is the deed of conveyance, which has to be examined for the quantity and quality of estate transferred and for any typographical errors that could result in title problems, such as a mistyped legal description or an incorrect spelling of the grantor or grantee's name.

Six important elements of conveyance must be complied with and accomplished at closing. To have an effective conveyance, (1) the deed must be in writing, (2) it must name a grantor and a grantee, (3) it must adequately describe the real property to the exclusion of all others, (4) there must be an intent to convey by the grantor, (5) there must be actual or constructive delivery, and (6) the grantee must accept the deed. Recording of the document is not required to create the interest. Recording is done to protect the grantee's interest from various third parties. We discuss recording in Chapter 10.

Problem 6A

Celia is preparing to move from her home of twenty years into an assisted living apartment building. In preparation for the move she contacts her lawyer, Phil, and decides that she wants to transfer her home to her daughter Marie. She tells Phil that she does not want her son, Gregg, to get any of the real property. Phil has Celia execute a deed of conveyance to her daughter Marie.

The deed conveys the property to Marie in fee simple absolute. At the same time Phil has Celia execute an updated version of her last will and testament. The will leaves various personal property and funds in relatively small bank accounts to be divided evenly between Marie and Gregg. The will also has a catch-all provision at the end leaving all property, real and personal, not otherwise transferred prior to death, to Marie and Gregg "share and share alike." Phil takes the will and the deed back to his office and places them into his vault for safe keeping. Two years later Celia dies. Phil opens the files and presents Marie with the deed to the property. Gregg objects to Marie getting the real property and claims to be a co-owner of the real property. What issues are involved here? Does the analysis change if someone records the deed in the public records prior to Gregg raising an objection?

A. ATTORNEY'S CONDUCT AT CLOSING

ST. LOUIS v. WILKINSON LAW OFFICES, P.C.
Supreme Judicial Court of Maine, 2012
55 A.3d 443

ALEXANDER, Justice. Theresa L. St. Louis and Dale T. St. Louis appeal from a judgment entered in the Superior Court (Penobscot County, *Cuddy, J.*) in favor of Wilkinson Law Offices, P.C. (Wilkinson Law) on their negligent misrepresentation claim. The judgment for Wilkinson Law was entered after the close of the St. Louises' case in a nonjury trial.

The St. Louises argue that the court erred in finding that they had failed to prove their claim of negligent misrepresentation because (1) an attorney from Wilkinson Law, acting as a closing agent, effectively made misrepresentations concerning the terms of a prepayment penalty when the attorney displayed, read, and quoted a summary document that erroneously stated the prepayment penalty terms, and (2) the attorney expanded upon the misrepresentations by participating in a discussion at the closing concerning the prepayment penalty. The St. Louises also argue that, as a matter of law and of policy, any closing agent, whether an attorney or not, must be held to a standard of knowing and understanding the contents of closing documents, given the "public importance" of closings. We affirm the judgment.

Dale T. St. Louis acquires and develops or improves real estate for a living. As part of his business, Dale and his wife, Theresa, had participated in twenty to twenty-five closings related to construction financing or sale of property prior to December 2007. None of those transactions had involved commercial loans and, to Dale's knowledge, none had involved notes containing prepayment penalties. The St. Louises typically participated in closings without an attorney present to represent them and had never had a problem in the past.

In 2007, a mortgage broker from Northstar Mortgage contacted Dale offering to help him acquire funding or refinancing for projects. This mortgage broker had worked with Dale on refinancing two residential loans, neither of which included prepayment penalty terms. These residential loans closed without issue. A representative from Wilkinson Law had conducted those closings. The St. Louises did not select Wilkinson Law to perform this service, although Wilkinson Law's fee was paid through the closing costs paid by the St. Louises.

Dale wanted to obtain a loan for a third property. Northstar Mortgage proposed several options, one of which the mortgage broker represented as including a prepayment penalty if the loan, a commercial loan in the amount of $273,000, was repaid early. The lender for this loan was Silver Hill Financial, LLC. Dale agreed to the Silver Hill loan option, understanding from the broker that the prepayment penalty would result in little more than a $13,000 penalty when he repaid the loan, which he planned to do as quickly as possible after construction was complete and the property sold.

The St. Louises attended the closing on the Silver Hill loan, which took place at their home on December 6, 2007. The Northstar Mortgage mortgage broker with whom Dale had worked on the loan also attended the closing. The St. Louises received no closing documents in advance of the closing and did not seek advice of counsel beforehand. As with the two previous closings, Wilkinson Law was engaged by a party other than the St. Louises to act as the settlement agent and was paid as part of the closing costs. Sarah Wilkinson, an attorney from Wilkinson Law, conducted this closing.

Along with the closing documents, Sarah Wilkinson had before her a document, apparently prepared by Silver Hill, entitled "Funding Instructions."[3] There is no evidence that Wilkinson Law prepared the Funding Instructions. The Funding Instructions contained a section entitled "Funding Details." At the closing, Sarah Wilkinson said something to the effect that, "these are my closing instructions," and she read each of the items stated in the Funding Details to the St. Louises. The last of the items in the Funding Details was "Prepayment terms: 5 percent of unpaid principal balance if prepaid during first 5 yrs." Dale believed that this term was consistent with what the mortgage broker had said the prepayment penalty would be.

Because Theresa was unaware of any prepayment penalty provision, the mortgage broker and Dale talked about what the prepayment penalty meant, and Dale told Theresa that he was aware of it and that it was fine. Dale later testified at trial that he, the mortgage broker, and Sarah Wilkinson said "it was a five percent penalty and would be thirteen thousand dollars." Dale admitted, however, that he did not know exactly what Sarah Wilkinson said during the conversation, as opposed to what he and the mortgage broker,

---

3. Although one could infer from the record that the Funding Instructions were prepared by the lender, Silver Hill Financial, LLC, the trial court did not make a finding in this regard.

who did the majority of the talking, had said. Sarah Wilkinson apparently did agree that "five percent was thirteen thousand and change." Wilkinson also stated that a prepayment penalty is "standard procedure" in commercial loans.

Because they believed it was a routine closing, the St. Louises then signed the closing documents, including the promissory note, without reading the documents, despite having had the opportunity to do so. Sarah Wilkinson did not specifically point out the prepayment penalty provision in the promissory note before the St. Louises signed the note, but instead handled the closing documents in the same manner as in other closings the St. Louises had attended. The prepayment penalty stated in the promissory note was not consistent with the five percent prepayment penalty stated in the Funding Details.

When the St. Louises subsequently prepared to sell the property and pay off the loan in early 2009, the prepayment penalty was not approximately $13,000 as expected, but was instead $100,473. The St. Louises incurred additional damages of $11,269. The St. Louises filed a complaint against Wilkinson Law and Stephen F. Jordan, LLC, d/b/a Northstar Mortgage ("Northstar"), in February 2010. Subsequently, the St. Louises filed an amended complaint, alleging, as relevant here, negligent misrepresentation against Wilkinson Law. The St. Louises filed no action against Silver Hill Financial. The court held a one-day nonjury trial in September 2011.

At the close of the St. Louises' case, both Wilkinson Law and Northstar moved for judgment as a matter of law pursuant to M.R. Civ. P. 50(d). The court denied Northstar's motion and granted Wilkinson Law's motion. In findings stated on the record, the court indicated that Wilkinson Law did not make misrepresentations during the closing or otherwise affirmatively state what the closing documents actually contained. Instead, the court found that Wilkinson Law had accurately recited what was in the Funding Details. The court also stated that "[i]n light of the burden under Rule 50 and giving all inferences in this matter in favor of Plaintiff, nonetheless, the [c]ourt is persuaded that, as to the Count One as against the Wilkinson Law Office the burden has not been met, and the motion is granted."

The trial continued with respect to Northstar, and the court entered a judgment in favor of the St. Louises against Northstar. The court concluded that Northstar (1) breached a contractual agreement with the St. Louises to obtain financing that included a five percent prepayment penalty, and (2) engaged in negligent misrepresentation with respect to the terms of the prepayment penalty.[5] The court awarded the St. Louises $98,142.67 in total damages, plus interest and costs. No appeal was taken from the judgment against Northstar.[6]

---

5. The court found for Northstar on the St. Louises' claim for breach of fiduciary duty.
6. At oral argument, counsel represented that the judgment against Northstar will not be paid because Northstar is no longer in business.

The court's judgment further stated that it had been entered at trial in favor of Wilkinson Law "for failure to prove substantive elements of the claim, including that a misrepresentation was made." After final judgment was entered, the St. Louises brought this timely appeal from the judgment entered in favor of Wilkinson Law. . . .

B. NEGLIGENT MISREPRESENTATION CLAIM

We have discussed the tort of negligent misrepresentation as follows:

> One who, in the course of his business, profession or employment, or in any other transaction in which he has a pecuniary interest, supplies false information for the guidance of others in their business transactions, is subject to liability for pecuniary loss caused to them by their justifiable reliance upon the information, if he fails to exercise reasonable care or competence in obtaining or communicating the information.

Chapman v. Rideout, 568 A.2d 829, 830 (Me. 1990) (adopting the formulation of the tort as stated in the Restatement (Second) of Torts §552(1) (1977)); *accord* Rand v. Bath Iron Works Corp., 832 A.2d 771 (Me. 2003).

Whether a party made a misrepresentation and whether the opposing party justifiably relied on a misrepresentation are questions of fact. *See* McCarthy v. U.S.I. Corp., 678 A.2d 48, 53 (Me. 1996). Additionally, liability only attaches if, when communicating the information, the party making the alleged misrepresentation "fails to exercise the care or competence of a reasonable person under like circumstances," an inquiry that is likewise for the fact-finder. *Rand, supra* at 774-75. "[T]he defendant's knowledge is largely immaterial for negligent misrepresentation"; "the fact-finder's primary task is to ascertain whether the defendant's conduct was reasonable." *Id.* at 775.

In this case, the court found the following facts, which we review for clear error: (1) there is no indication in the record as to who prepared the Funding Details; (2) Wilkinson Law, acting as the closing agent, simply made a "recitation" and a "representation and an affirmation as to what was on the summary sheet"; (3) in this regard, Wilkinson Law made an "accurate statement"; (4) the court was "not at all persuaded . . . that the statements made on behalf of the Wilkinson Law Office represented an affirmation as to what the documents contained or didn't contain," despite finding that "the information contained in the loan documents themselves were inconsistent with what's on the summary sheet." Ultimately, the court was "persuaded that, as to the [negligent misrepresentation count] against the Wilkinson Law Office the burden has not been met."

The court's finding that Wilkinson Law did not make a misrepresentation, given that its agent, who happened to be an attorney, was merely, and accurately, stating the information from the Funding Details, is supported by competent record evidence. In describing the role that the Wilkinson Law attorney played at the closing, the St. Louises consistently testified only that she stated the terms contained on the Funding Details sheet.

The St. Louises contend that the Wilkinson Law attorney was obligated to provide full and fair disclosure as to matters on which she chose to speak. We do not need to address whether this closing agent, who happened to be an attorney, but who was an agent of another party and who did not represent the St. Louises, was under such an obligation under the facts of this case. The St. Louises only claimed misrepresentation. The evidentiary record supports the court's finding that the attorney only addressed what information the Funding Details contained and not whether the underlying documents that the Funding Details purportedly summarized actually contained that information. There is no dispute that the attorney fairly disclosed the terms stated in the Funding Details.

Additionally, the St. Louises contend that the Wilkinson Law attorney expanded upon the misrepresentation that the terms of the loan included a five percent prepayment penalty by participating in a discussion at the closing. However, the court did not make that finding, and the record does not support that claim. To the extent that the Wilkinson Law attorney participated in a conversation, in response to Theresa's inquiry about the prepayment penalty, the record shows that the only specific comment attributable to the attorney was that prepayment penalties are standard in a commercial loan situation, which is not an alleged misrepresentation in this appeal. Additionally, contrary to the St. Louises' characterization, the record does not indicate that the attorney affirmatively stated "that the amount of exposure" to the St. Louises from the prepayment penalty was "just over $13,000." The record actually indicates that the attorney agreed with others at the table that "five percent was thirteen thousand and change," which is simply a correct mathematical calculation.

Because the court's factual finding that Wilkinson Law did not make a misrepresentation is supported by competent record evidence and a contrary finding is not compelled by the record, the St. Louises have not met their burden of persuasion on appeal. Accordingly, the court did not err in entering a judgment in favor of Wilkinson Law.[7] . . .

In re OPINION 710 OF THE ADVISORY COMMITTEE ON PROFESSIONAL ETHICS
Supreme Court of New Jersey, 2008
939 A.2d 794

PER CURIAM. We granted the New Jersey State Bar Association's (NJSBA) petition to review Advisory Committee on Professional Ethics (ACPE)

---

7. Because we affirm the judgment on the narrow grounds stated above, we do not reach the St. Louises' policy-based contentions.

Opinion 710, entitled *Misrepresenting Purchase Price or Other Material Fact Regarding a Real Estate Transaction,* 186 N.J.L.J. 1198 (2006). The ACPE received an inquiry seeking an advisory opinion on the ethical propriety of a real estate transaction that the inquirer posited "'is a fraudulent practice perpetrated on the ultimate investor.'" Opinion 710, *supra,* 186 N.J.L.J. at 1198. In the factual scenario provided by the inquirer,

> [a] contract for the sale of residential property has been prepared by a realtor and signed by both seller and buyer for a set purchase price with a mortgage contingency. Either during attorney review or thereafter, the lawyers for the seller and the buyer are requested to amend the contract by increasing the purchase price and the mortgage contingency amount in like amounts. In addition, the attorneys are asked to amend the contract to provide that the seller give a credit to the purchaser at closing in the same amount, calling it a "seller's concession" or "seller's payment of purchaser's closing costs."

Id. In that scenario given to the ACPE, the inquirer further declared that the amendments to the contract are intended to "increase the size of the purchaser's mortgage loan," with the understanding that "the originating lender or the secondary investors may be deceived as to the true market price of the house." *Id.* The ACPE assumed that the seller's concession in that scenario did not involve legitimate or actual costs "payable by the buyer." *Id.* The ACPE therefore reviewed a factual supposition in which a lawyer actively participated in a real estate transaction likely to perpetrate a fraud on the ultimate investor, namely the mortgage lender, a purchaser of the mortgage on a secondary market, or a buyer of mortgage-backed securities. *Id.* Unsurprisingly, the ACPE concluded that such a practice would violate Rules of Professional Conduct 1.2(d) ("A lawyer shall not counsel or assist a client in conduct that the lawyer knows is illegal, criminal or fraudulent. . . ."), 4.1(a) ("In representing a client a lawyer shall not knowingly: (1) make a false statement of material fact or law to a third person; or (2) fail to disclose a material fact to a third person when disclosure is necessary to avoid assisting a criminal or fraudulent act by a client."), and 8.4 ("It is professional misconduct for a lawyer to . . . (c) engage in conduct involving dishonesty, fraud, deceit or misrepresentation. . . ."). Opinion 710, *supra,* 186 N.J.L.J. at 1198.

The ACPE issued a clarification to Opinion 710 in response to numerous inquiries concerning the propriety of seller's concessions. In its clarification, the ACPE explained that the opinion, which was based on the particular facts submitted by the inquirer,

> addresses fictional and deceptive increases in purchase prices unrelated to the actual circumstances or costs of closing, and contrary to the expectations of the lender or the ultimate holder of the mortgage. As stated in the Opinion, a prohibited transaction is one that is not premised on "a legitimate charge

against the seller on account of any actual costs assumed by it and otherwise payable by the buyer." Accordingly, the Opinion does not implicate a contract of sale that explicitly states that the seller shall provide the buyer with a credit against legal and legitimate costs or expenses related to the sale, which would otherwise be absorbed by the buyer, such as actual closing costs.

Clarification of Advisory Comm. on Prof'l Ethics Opinion 710, 187 N.J.L.J. 2, 2 (2007).

Essentially, the ACPE was asked a very simple question—whether the Rules of Professional Conduct are violated when a seller and a buyer engage in a seller's concession for the purpose of perpetrating a fraud on the ultimate investor. We are confident that attorneys in this state know that they cannot participate in deceptive transactions. Opinion 710 stands for the unremarkable proposition that fraudulent transactions by attorneys in connection with real estate closings will run afoul of the Rules of Professional Conduct. It does not suggest that disclosed seller's concessions are, in and of themselves, fraudulent or unethical. With that in mind, lawyers versed in their ethical responsibilities have nothing to fear from ACPE Opinion 710.

For those reasons, we affirm ACPE Opinion 710 as clarified.

Problem 6B

Clarence is representing M&S, LLC in a closing on a deal in which it is selling a $2.3 million office building to Fred. M&S is a limited liability company that Mary founded with Suzann, a friend of hers from her days back in business school. Mary is chief operating officer of the company, and Suzann is chief executive officer and chairman of the board. Prior to the closing, Suzann signed the closing statements and the required seller affidavits. In a rush to fly to Chicago on business, however, Suzann did not see the deed, which was accidentally paper-clipped to another document on her desk. As a result, when Clarence showed up at Mary's office to close the transaction with Mary and Fred, there was no signed deed. Fred's lawyer, Lucy, asked to see the documents for review. This is when it was noticed that Suzann had not signed the deed. Clarence then pulled the blank form of deed out of the file and gave it to Mary to sign for the company. Mary signed the deed of conveyance and presented it to Fred. Fred gave it to Lucy to review. Lucy asked Clarence why the deed was signed by Mary when all the other closing documents had been signed by Suzann. After Clarence explained the situation, Lucy asked the question, "Is this deed going to be effective if it is signed by the COO rather than the CEO of M&S?" Lucy explained her concern. She does not want Fred to part with $2.3 million if the deed will not be effective. At the same time, Mary informs Clarence that if they do not close today, she and Suzann will not have the cash funds needed to pay off an obligation that has to be paid by close of business of the same day. What advice would you give to Clarence in this situation?

Problem 6C

Nancy is a young associate in a large law firm. She is in the real estate department and is handling part of a transaction for one of the partners in the firm. The client is a major developer and is in the process of acquiring a significant piece of property. The deal is for $11 million. The closing will take place in the law firm's conference room and is scheduled for 4:00 P.M. on Friday. The attorney for the seller is Tanya, a senior partner in another large firm in town. Tanya arrives late for the closing, and once they get started Nancy finds that several points of the deal still remain unresolved, despite careful pre-closing planning and earlier conversations during the day. As a result of these factors, Nancy and Tanya don't finish the closing paperwork until 7:00 P.M. that night. Because it is too late to take the documents directly to the recording office, Tanya turns to Nancy and says, "I will leave the documents in your able hands for recording first thing bright and early Monday morning." Nancy says, "Sure, let's just get it over with so we can go home." Tanya looks at Nancy again and says, "You will undertake to hold the documents over the weekend and record them first thing Monday morning." Nancy says, "Yes." Then Tanya leaves and Nancy finishes up additional work at the office.

On Monday morning, Nancy is in the office at 6:30 A.M. and is getting some work done while waiting to go to the recording office when it opens at 9:00 A.M. Around 8:50 A.M., the senior partner comes into the office and asks Nancy if she has recorded the documents on the deal with Tanya. Nancy is explaining that she was not able to do it on Friday when the partner interrupts and says, "Good, don't record them. The client just called, mad as can be, saying that Tanya and her clients pulled a fast one on the soil test information and he doesn't want to finish the deal until things get reworked. It seems this all broke loose over the weekend. Lucky break for us, because the client is adamant that we not record in order to preserve the strongest position we can." By the time this is all explained, it is about 9:20 A.M. and the phone rings for Nancy. It is Tanya, checking to see if Nancy has fulfilled her obligation to record the documents as promised.

(a) What should Nancy's obligation be? Does she have an ethical obligation to Tanya or to the firm's client or to both?

(b) What should Nancy do if the partner says, "Look, the firm made no promises to Tanya, and this client is worth a good $1 million in billables per year to the firm. You know what the client wants, and I want the client to be happy. Just get it resolved and don't tell me anything more about *your* problems."

Problem 6D

Sean Paul is buying a $1.2 million home from Elizabeth with mortgage financing provided by your client, First Bank. Brokers represented both parties in preparing the contract and giving advice on closing. Before closing you'll prepare the loan documents that Sean Paul will sign. At closing you'll review the deed from Elizabeth to Sean Paul to ensure that First Bank will have a proper first lien on the property. You will also be looking at other closing documents, including the property survey, the title insurance commitment, the settlement statement, and buyer's and seller's affidavits. Neither Sean Paul nor Elizabeth will have an attorney at closing. Based on your prior experience with such closings, you can anticipate that Sean Paul and Elizabeth, as well as the real estate brokers, will engage you in conversation and ask you questions about the transaction and about the documents that are being signed and reviewed at closing. To make your legal representation and obligations clear to all the parties in the room, the senior partner in your firm has asked you to prepare a disclosure and non-representation letter to bring with you to the closing. The senior partner wants to review your letter before the closing. Draft a letter of disclosure and non-representation that will adequately clarify your role in the transaction and limit your firm's exposure to liability to all persons who are not your client.

B. DOCTRINE OF MERGER

Closing is the time when we must deal with the *doctrine of merger*. Basically, this doctrine provides that everything that came before closing is merged into the documents exchanged at closing. As a consequence, all rights, warranties, and obligations from the executory contract are no longer operative between the parties. The contract is no longer "executory"; at closing, it is "executed." Any causes of action based on the pre-closing contracts or negotiations no longer exist. Once closing occurs, the parties are left with only those rights, warranties, and promises expressed in the closing documents. As with most legal rules, there are important exceptions to the doctrine of merger. Common exceptions include fraud, mutual mistake, ambiguity, collateral rights, and a promise that by its terms cannot be performed until after closing. Fraud is a highly malleable concept, with different meanings in different contexts; but a useful general definition is (1) a knowing misrepresentation or concealment (2) of a material fact (3) made for the purpose of inducing reliance (4) that in fact results in reasonable reliance (5) to the injury or loss of the relying party.

PANOS v. OLSEN
Court of Appeals of Utah, 2005
123 P. 3d. 816

BENCH, Associate Presiding Judge. . . .

In July 2001, Panos sold Olsen a vacant lot (Lot 29) in Sandy, Utah. Panos continued to own and reside in his home on Lot 24, which is adjacent and southeast to Lot 29. At the time of sale, the parties entered into a real estate purchase contract. The contract included addenda that detailed several additional terms and restrictions, including a prohibition against any building on the lot higher than thirty-two feet when measured "from the road." Panos asserts that the purpose of the height restriction was to preserve his unobstructed view from his property.

At closing, Panos signed a warranty deed granting Olsen title to Lot 29. The deed contained language relating to the height restriction: "SUBJECT TO THE FOLLOWING BUILDING RESTRICTIONS: THE ROOF LEVEL OR HIGHEST PROTION [*sic*] OF ANY BUILDING OR PERMANENT STRUCTURE PLACED OR CONSTRUCTED UPON SAID LAND SHALL NOT BE HIGHER THAN 32 FEET. MEASURED FROM THE EXISTING STREET LYING WEST AND ADJACENT TO SAID LAND." No other specifications were contained in the deed concerning the height restriction. The road lying west and adjacent to Lot 29 is a portion of Elm Ridge Road. The road runs north to south and is sloped in that direction. As a result, height measurements from the road vary depending on the starting point.

About a year before Panos sold Lot 29, he ordered a survey of both Lots 29 and 24 (Panos survey). He ordered the survey to determine, inter alia, the greatest height at which a potential home could be built upon Lot 29 so as to preserve his view. The Panos survey measured from a base point at the Salt Lake County brass cap monument (monument), lying southwest of Lot 29 on Elm Ridge Road. Panos contends that the monument must be the starting point for any height measurements in the deed.

The parties dispute whether the Panos survey was provided to Olsen and also whether they agreed that the monument would be the starting point for measuring the height restriction. Although Panos alleges that his survey and measurement from the monument were critical and specifically discussed by the parties, neither the deed nor the contract reference the monument or any other specific point for measuring the height restriction.

After closing, Olsen began construction of a home. When it was completed, the Panos survey was updated to include elevation information of the Olsen home, measured from the monument. The updated Panos survey indicated that the newly constructed Olsen home was approximately 34.91 feet above the monument, in violation of the height restriction by 2.91 feet.

Olsen hired David Jenkins, an engineer, to conduct a survey (Olsen survey) of the Olsen home to determine whether it was in compliance with the height restriction. Jenkins used a point on the street gutter, near the northwest corner of Lot 29 on Elm Ridge Road, to measure the height restriction. The gutter point utilized in the Olsen survey is higher in elevation than the monument utilized in the Panos survey. As a result, Jenkins found the Olsen home to be only 31.96 feet high and, therefore, in compliance with the height restriction.

Based on the Panos survey, Panos filed a complaint alleging breach of contract, seeking an injunction, and requesting a declaratory judgment. Olsen filed a motion for summary judgment, arguing that the merger doctrine applies to the deed and that the Olsen home is in compliance based on the Olsen survey. . . . The trial court granted Olsen's motion for summary judgment. . . . ruling that the merger doctrine applies and that the Olsen home satisfies the height restriction specified in the deed.

. . . Panos now appeals the entry of summary judgment in favor of Olsen. . . .

I. MERGER DOCTRINE

In determining the nature and content of the parties' agreement, the trial court determined that the merger doctrine applies to the contract and the deed. We agree. Under the merger doctrine, a deed is the final, integrated agreement of the parties and it abrogates all prior agreements, whether written or oral. *See* Maynard v. Wharton, 912 P.2d 446, 449–50 (Utah Ct. App. 1996); Verhoef v. Aston, 740 P.2d 1342, 1344 (Utah Ct. App. 1987) ("[A] basic tenet of contract law is that prior negotiations and agreements merge into the final written agreement on the subject.").

The Utah Supreme Court has explained the doctrine of merger as follows:

> The doctrine of merger . . . is applicable when the acts to be performed by the seller in a contract relate only to the delivery of title to the buyer. Execution and delivery of a deed by the seller then usually constitute full performance on his part, and acceptance of the deed by the buyer manifests his acceptance of that performance even though the estate conveyed may differ from that promised in the antecedent agreement. Therefore, in such a case, the deed is the final agreement and all prior terms, whether written or verbal, are extinguished and unenforceable.

Stubbs v. Hemmert, 567 P.2d 168, 169 (Utah 1977); *see also* Secor v. Knight, 716 P.2d 790, 793 (Utah 1986). The merger doctrine is "an admittedly harsh rule of law." *Secor*, 716 P.2d at 794. We adhere to the merger doctrine because it "preserves the integrity of the final document of conveyance and encourages the diligence of the parties." *Id.* at 795. Parties to real estate transactions have a duty "to make certain that their agreements have in fact been fully included in the final document," *id.*, and that "any agreements involving conveyance [or encumbrance] of title are incorporated into the final closing document, which is usually a warranty deed,"*Maynard*, 912 P.2d at 451.

In this matter, the height restriction specified in the deed is the final, integrated agreement of the parties. Panos, however, relies upon two exceptions to the merger doctrine: ambiguity and mutual mistake. Panos contends that parol evidence, including the parties' prior discussions, must be considered in construing the deed. Such parol evidence allegedly includes the parties' agreement that the height restriction measurement would originate from the monument, not the gutter.

II. Merger Doctrine Exceptions

Under Utah law, the "merger doctrine has four discrete exceptions: (1) mutual mistake in the drafting of the final documents; (2) ambiguity in the final documents; (3) existence of rights collateral to the contract of sale; and (4) fraud in the transaction."*Id.* at 450. Panos only contends that two exceptions apply: (1) ambiguity and (2) mutual mistake. We hold that neither exception applies in this case.

A. Ambiguity

Panos asserts that the deed contains a latent ambiguity, in that the deed does not indicate the precise location from which to measure the height restriction. "Deeds are construed according to ordinary rules of contract construction." Homer v. Smith, 866 P.2d 622, 629 (Utah Ct. App. 1993). "Whether a contract is ambiguous is a question of law." Village Inn Apts. v. State Farm Fire & Cas. Co., 790 P.2d 581, 582 (Utah Ct. App. 1990). We interpret contract terms "in accordance with their plain and ordinary meaning" within the four corners of the document. *Id.* at 583. . . .

Without a specific reference point where the measurement must originate, Panos claims that the height restriction is ambiguous because the words used "may be understood to reach two or more plausible meanings." Crowther v. Carter, 767 P.2d 129, 131 (Utah Ct. App. 1989). As Elm Ridge Road is sloped, measurement taken from the higher portion of the road would result in the Olsen home being in compliance with the height restriction and measurement taken at the lower portion would result in a violation of the height restriction. Panos argues that this results in multiple meanings and thus, a latent ambiguity. We disagree.

The height restriction is "32 feet" and is to be "measured from the existing street lying west and adjacent to said land." This language is unambiguous and does not have multiple meanings. The terms "existing street lying west and adjacent to said land" mean, as conceded by the parties, the portion of Elm Ridge Road, lying west and adjacent to Lot 29. As no other words are used to narrow the precise location on Elm Ridge Road where the measurement is to originate, any point of measurement originating on the portion of Elm Ridge Road, lying west and adjacent to Lot 29, satisfies this part of the height restriction. We "will not rewrite a [deed] to supply terms which the parties omitted." Hal Taylor Assocs. v. Unionamerica, Inc., 657 P.2d 743, 749 (Utah 1982). Although the terms are broad in their application, it does not mean the terms are ambiguous.

The word "from" used in the height restriction also does not specify a more precise location on the street where the measurement is to originate. In its plain meaning, the word "from" indicates a place as a starting point. Therefore, the height restriction measurement need only have a starting point someplace on the portion of Elm Ridge Road, lying west and adjacent to Lot 29. If the parties intended a more precise measurement point on Elm Ridge Road, the parties could have so indicated. . . . [W]e hold that the height restriction language is not ambiguous as a matter of law.

B. MUTUAL MISTAKE

Panos also asserts that the lack of a more precise location for measuring the height restriction constitutes a mutual mistake that precludes merger. We disagree. Although mistakes can bar the application of merger, "not every mistake will suffice." Embassy Group, Inc. v. Hatch, 865 P.2d 1366, 1371 (Utah Ct. App. 1993). "A mistake precludes merger when one of the parties demonstrates [that] a *mutual* mistake in the drafting of the contractual documents has occurred." *Id.* (emphasis added). "Mutual mistake" is defined as "a mistake in which each party misunderstands the other's intent." *Black's Law Dictionary* 1017 (7th ed. 1999). The Utah Supreme Court has required that "when a party denies merger due to mistake, he has the burden to show mistake by *clear and convincing evidence*." Neeley v. Kelsch, 600 P.2d 979, 981 (Utah 1979). "The party denying merger must demonstrate that (1) the instrument does not conform to the intent of both parties, [or] (2) the claimant was mistaken as to the content of the instrument and the other party knew of the mistake but kept silent, or (3) the claimant was mistaken as to actual content due to fraudulent affirmative behavior." *Embassy Group,* 865 P.2d at 1372. Panos fails to demonstrate any of these arguments. Before the trial court and on appeal, Panos asserts only that the instrument does not conform with the intent of the parties. We, therefore, limit our review to this argument. Based on our review, Panos fails to provide clear and convincing evidence that the deed, specifically the height restriction, did not conform to the intent of both of the parties.

III. REFORMATION

Additionally, Panos argues that the "deed should be reformed pursuant to the principles of equity to reflect the agreement of the parties, even if an important provision is not mentioned at all." We disagree. The Utah Supreme Court set forth two grounds before reformation of an agreement is permissible: (1) "mutual mistake of the parties" or (2) "ignorance or mistake by one party, coupled with fraud by the other party." Hottinger v.

Jensen, 684 P.2d 1271, 1273 (Utah 1984). As Panos has failed to establish mutual mistake and also does not allege any claims of fraud in his pleadings, Panos fails to satisfy any grounds for reformation. Therefore, the trial court did not err in denying such relief. . . .

Conclusion

The merger doctrine applies to the deed. Although the height restriction in the deed is broad in its application, it is not ambiguous. As a result, any point on the portion of Elm Ridge Road lying west and adjacent to Lot 29 may be used as the originating measuring point in satisfying the height restriction. We conclude that the ambiguity and mutual mistake exceptions to the merger doctrine are inapplicable. We also conclude that reformation was properly denied by the trial court. Finally, Olsen is awarded reasonable attorney fees on appeal.

Accordingly, we affirm the trial court's grant of summary judgment in favor of Olsen and remand to the trial court for a determination of Olsen's reasonable attorney fees incurred on appeal.

Problem 6E

Sophia owned 40 acres of rural property. On November 1, she contracted to sell ten acres of the property to Bartelo for $250,000, with closing specified to take place on or before February 15. The parties signed an earnest money contract, which satisfied all requirements of the statute of frauds. Bartelo, a wealthy individual who had won a major lottery prize three years ago, planned to pay all cash for the property. The parties closed on February 15, with Sophia conveying the ten-acre tract to Bartelo by warranty deed in exchange for Bartelo's full payment of the price.

(a) Prior to signing the earnest money contract, while the parties were negotiating, Sophia disclosed to Bartelo the following facts: the 40-acre parcel was subject to a mortgage loan, with an amount due of approximately $148,000; the mortgage had a maturity date of September 1 of the following year, when the debt was payable in full; Sophia was not able to obtain a release of the mortgage to clear title because she did not have the right to prepay the mortgage debt and the mortgagee was not willing to accept prepayment. The contract provided: "Title shall be good and marketable, free of all liens except the existing mortgage on the property, which Seller promises to pay in full upon maturity. Seller also promises to obtain a release of mortgage and record same no later than 20 days after maturity date." The deed does not mention the mortgage, and no other document executed at closing mentions the mortgage. Sophia fails to pay the mortgage debt the following September. Bartelo discovers this and complains. Is Bartelo entitled to sue Sophia for breach of the promise made in the earnest money contract, or is Bartelo limited to whatever rights he may have under the warranty deed?

(b) In March, Bartelo's finances have taken a turn for the worse. He wants to borrow money, using his new property as collateral, but he is unable to get a suitable mortgage loan due to the existing mortgage owed by Sophia. Bartelo hires an attorney, who advises him that his warranty deed includes a covenant that there are no liens on the property, and that the mortgage violates that covenant. The attorney sends Sophia a letter, demanding that she pay off the mortgage within five days and stating that she will be responsible for damages incurred by Bartelo if she fails to do so. If Sophia does not or cannot comply, should Bartelo have a cause of action for breach of the covenant in the warranty deed?

(c) Sophia had a residence on the 30 acres that she was retaining, and she did not want the conveyed property to be used for commercial purposes. During negotiations, Bartelo agreed to this limitation, and the earnest money contract provided: "No trade or business of any kind shall be conducted on the property." The warranty deed delivered at closing did not contain this or any other restriction. Two years later, Bartelo opens a commercial nursery on the ten-acre parcel. Should Sophia have the right to force him to stop this use?

(d) In (c), suppose that Bartelo had sold the parcel to Eve. Eve opened the nursery, and she was unaware of the restriction in the earnest money contract. Should Sophia have the right to close Eve's nursery?

(e) The ten-acre parcel had a portable storage building, which Sophia wanted to keep. She and Bartelo agreed that she could remove it, and the earnest money contract provided: "Seller has the right to remove the portable storage building from the property." Sophia did not do so prior to the closing. On March 1, she hired a crew to relocate the building to her property. Before they began work, Bartelo intercepted them. He insists that the building belongs to him because Sophia did not remove it prior to closing. What result?

(f) Suppose the portable storage building was dilapidated. Bartelo considered it an eyesore. He had bargained for the earnest money contract to provide: "Seller will remove the portable storage building from the property." Again, Sophia did not do so before the closing. Can Bartelo insist that Sophia comply with her promise after the closing?

(g) In the situations above, if you represented Sophia or Bartelo, what might you do in the contract or at closing to avoid or reduce the risk of messy arguments about the application of the doctrine of merger?

C. ESCROWS

The term *escrow* is sometimes confusing to laypersons because of the different ways it is used in real estate transactions. It may refer to a means of collecting funds for the payment of taxes and insurance, a method to handle the real estate closing, or a technique to resolve a closing contingency or problem. Each of these three common uses of escrow serves a distinct purpose.

The first type of escrow, the *loan escrow,* is used by lenders to collect and hold money from the debtor for paying annual real property taxes and fire and hazard insurance premiums. Lenders desire loan escrows for two reasons. First, with the escrow the lender does not have to worry about a default by the borrower in paying taxes, which could lead to a tax lien or tax sale that jeopardizes the lender's security. Similarly, for hazard insurance, the lender wants to control the payment of insurance premiums so it is certain that the property remains properly insured. In the event of a casualty, the lender will insist that the insurance proceeds be used either to restore the improvements or to pay all or part of the mortgage loan. Second, the lender typically holds escrow funds in a non-interest-paying account.

The second form of escrow, an *escrow closing,* means that the parties have appointed an escrow agent to conduct the closing. The escrow is usually documented by a written escrow agreement, which is signed by the buyer, the seller, and an escrow agent, and spells out the duties of all three parties. The escrow agent administers the contract of purchase and sale and has fiduciary duties to both the buyer and the seller.

The third type of escrow, a *contingency escrow,* is a process used to resolve a problem that arises at or before closing. Often the problem concerns the physical condition of the property being purchased. When the problem consists of an unperformed obligation of the seller, the escrow usually consists of withholding part of the purchase price from the seller pending correction of the problem.

It is important that the contingency escrow agreement be carefully drafted so that disputes are avoided with respect to satisfaction of its requirements. In general, a good contingency escrow agreement should be in writing and should address six concerns.

1. The agreement should clearly identify the matter at issue, such as a leaky pipe, a broken light fixture, or a document in need of correction.
2. The agreement should qualify and limit the dollar amount attributed to correcting the problem. For example, it might establish $400 as the amount of the purchase price that will be placed in escrow in contemplation of the seller fixing or replacing a broken light fixture.
3. The agreement should identify the action needed to be taken by each party and the time period in which action must be taken and completed.
4. The agreement should establish the proof that will be needed to demonstrate compliance. For example, if a leaking pipe needs to be fixed, what kind of proof is needed to demonstrate that it was properly fixed? Is the seller's word enough, or is a receipt showing

payment for the work adequate? Does the work have to have been done by a master plumber rather than a handyman?

5. The agreement should establish a right of inspection. Is there a right of inspection and by whom, and on what terms?

6. The agreement needs to address the release of any funds or documents that are being held by an escrow agent under the terms of the agreement. It should establish the conditions for release of funds and documents, and provide for the escrow agent to obtain a written release from both parties as to the agent's obligations under the agreement. In the event of any party to the escrow agreement refusing to sign a release, the escrow agent should be authorized to have the matter turned over to an agreed-upon arbitrator or placed into a court proceeding for the parties to settle.

MILLER v. CRAIG
Court of Appeals of Arizona, Division 1, 1976
558 P.2d 984

NELSON, Judge. This action was brought by the plaintiffs, George W. Miller and his wife, Johanna Miller (appellants here), to recover $5,000 in earnest money deposited in escrow with the defendant, Harry E. Craig (appellee here). The Millers' claim was based on alternate theories of conversion and breach of fiduciary duty. On appeal they seek reversal of a summary judgment granted in favor of Craig and allege error in the trial court's failure to grant their own motion for summary judgment. For the reasons stated below we find that the judgment in favor of the defendant, Craig, must be reversed and that the cause be remanded for entry of judgment in favor of the plaintiffs, Millers. . . .

In 1970 the Millers entered into an agreement with Mary E. Crouse[1] to sell their interest in a tavern located in the City of Phoenix. Pursuant to that agreement Craig, an attorney at law, was retained to draft the documents necessary to complete the sale and to act as the parties' escrow agent.

Prior to closing, a dispute arose between the parties. Ms. Crouse filed suit seeking rescission of the sales contract and recovery of $5,000, the amount deposited by her with Craig as earnest money. Millers counterclaimed for specific performance of the contract and for damages. The trial court resolved the controversy in favor of Crouse and judgment was entered entitling her to "recover of the defendants (the Millers) the sum of FIVE THOUSAND ($5,000) DOLLARS. . . ."

Thereafter, Crouse, through her attorney, presented defendant Craig with a copy of the judgment and demanded return of the $5,000 deposit. Craig, without notifying the Millers or attempting to ascertain whether they

---

1. Ms. Crouse is not a party to this action.

would seek review of the judgment, disbursed the money to Crouse.[3] The judgment in favor of Crouse was subsequently reversed and judgment was entered for the Millers in the amount of the escrow deposit, as directed by the court in Miller v. Crouse, 506 P.2d 659 (Ariz. Ct. App. 1973).

After several unsuccessful attempts to recover the deposit from Craig, Millers initiated the present action. The parties filed cross-motions for summary judgment. Craig's motion was granted and judgment dismissing Millers' cause with prejudice was entered.

Two questions are presented for our consideration. First, whether Craig's transfer of the $5,000 to Crouse was a breach of his fiduciary duty as escrow agent. Second, if it was a breach, whether he is excused from the consequences thereof by reason of the following clause contained in the escrow agreement: "We, and each of us, agree that the said Harry E. Craig acting in the beforementioned capacity shall not become liable to either or both of us for anything whatsoever so long as said Agent acts with reasonable prudence in connection with his position, ..."

We answer the first question in the affirmative, the second in the negative. . . .

. . . With respect to those who have retained him, an escrow agent is a trustee and can properly execute his duties only as they are set out by the terms of the escrow agreement. Malta v. Phoenix Title & Trust Co., 259 P.2d 554 (Ariz. 1953). Deviation from those terms without the mutual consent of the parties concerned will subject the agent to liability for damages caused by his departure. Tucson Title Insurance Co. v. D'Ascoli, 383 P.2d 119 (Ariz. 1963).

In the present case the sales contract, incorporated by reference in the escrow agreement, provided that the $5,000 earnest money was part of the purchase price and that the sale was to be completed upon transfer of Millers' Number 7 beer and wine license. Alternatively, the contract provided that the Millers might retain as liquidated damages the sum paid into escrow by Crouse should she fail to comply with the terms of the agreement. The contract contained no other provision authorizing disbursement of funds. It is clear, therefore, that Craig, by transferring the $5,000 without first securing plaintiff's consent, deviated from and exceeded his authority under the escrow agreement.

Craig contends the transfer was pursuant to a judgment on which he properly relied and therefore his conduct cannot be construed as a breach of duty. We disagree. The judgment in favor of Crouse dealt not with a specific

---

3. Judgment in favor of Crouse was entered and filed November 24, 1971. In a letter dated November 29, 1971, containing a copy of the November 24 judgment, Crouse through her attorney demanded that defendant Craig return the $5,000 held by him as escrow agent. In response to the demand, the defendant, on November 30, 1971 and December 17, 1971, forwarded checks totaling $5,000 to Crouse's attorney. Denial of plaintiffs' motion to amend the November 24 judgment or for a new trial was entered January 7, 1972. Plaintiffs' notice of appeal to Division I of the Court of Appeals was filed February 4, 1972.

res, the earnest money deposit, but merely entitled her to recover $5,000 from the Millers. It did not authorize a disbursement of funds held in escrow.

At the time of the Crouse demand, Craig should have inquired of the Millers regarding their intentions relative to an appeal. If they were not going to appeal he should have sought their permission to return the funds to Crouse. If they intended to appeal, as subsequent events indicated was their intention, he should have notified Crouse that he would retain the funds in escrow pending the outcome of the appeal or pending execution. If none of these arrangements were satisfactory to either or both parties, Craig should have sought relief in the trial court, either in the pending action, or by interpleader. *See generally* Rule 22(a), Rules of Civil Procedure, 16 A.R.S.; 28 Am. Jur. 2d *Escrow* §40 (1966).

Finally, Craig argues that even if a fiduciary obligation was breached, it was done so in a "reasonable manner," exempting him from liability under the terms of the escrow agreement, *supra*, by which he is to be held harmless for acts done with "reasonable prudence." We find this contention absolutely without merit. As stated above, the duties of an escrow agent are defined in the escrow agreement and will be strictly construed. Any deviation therefrom without the requisite authority is per se unreasonable and cannot be done with "reasonable prudence." *Cf.* Tucson Title Insurance Co. v. D'Ascoli, *supra*; Malta v. Phoenix Title & Trust Co., *supra*. . . .

. . . Craig was fiducially responsible to both parties and it was incumbent upon him to determine whether *in fact* the controversy had been finally resolved so that he could properly disburse the money. Having failed in that duty, he is liable for his unauthorized disbursement.

The judgment of the Superior Court is reversed. The cause is remanded with directions to enter judgment for the Millers.

Problem 6F

Dennis is selling a beach house to Helen for $2.1 million. Dennis and Helen are both lawyers; Dennis is representing himself and Helen has hired you to represent her. Dennis has an outstanding mortgage against the property with Big Bank in the amount of $800,000, which he will pay off at closing using part of the purchase price. His bank will deliver a satisfaction of mortgage to allow Helen to purchase the property free and clear of its lien. With the bank's satisfaction of mortgage, Helen will be able to provide her lender, E-Bank, with the first lien mortgage that it requires for the transaction.

At closing the parties confirm that all of the many documents are in order, with one exception. The local Beach Front Coastal Management Board has not yet issued a proper water run-off certification for the property. This certification is required before a new occupant can move into a property, and it involves a test to certify the run-off and discharge capacity coming from the property to the waterfront. The inspector has completed the test and informed the parties by telephone that it passed, but the certification document provided at closing used the wrong legal description and tax identification number for the property. At closing, held late on a Friday, the parties discovered this error in the document prepared by the Board and contacted the Board's office. Dennis and Helen were told that the office would see about issuing a new and corrected certificate sometime on Monday, but no guarantees. The Board's office told them not to worry as these mistakes happen every now and then but eventually it all gets worked out. Dennis would like to wrap up the transaction today because he has plans to leave town for a week right after the closing. Helen also wants to close today because she is concerned about losing her loan commitment if she does not, as this is the last day of her 60-day commitment. E-Bank would like to facilitate the transaction, but it is concerned about making certain the property passes the certification test, as without proper documentation the value of the property could be diminished and make E-Bank's loan more risky.

Given that all parties want to close the deal today (on Friday afternoon), Helen asks you to draft an escrow agreement that will be suitable for permitting this to happen. In the escrow agreement Dennis is willing to close with $25,000 from the proceeds of the sale to be held in escrow by Helen's attorney (you), with funds being released upon issuing of the certificate within three business days. Under the terms of the escrow, the parties agree that Helen will take possession immediately after closing. Other than these key deal points, the parties have all turned to you to draft an escrow agreement at the closing so that they can sign it and finish up and then go home to enjoy their evening and the weekend. Draft an escrow agreement that you believe properly covers the situation and all of the elements that need to be covered in an escrow arrangement. Also be certain to address your own obligations under the escrow agreement and to disclose all information that you may be required to disclose in acting as the escrow agent for the arrangement. In drafting the agreement you should be conscious of the real world dynamic that all parties are waiting in your conference room to review the agreement and approve and sign it. Their time is valuable and they expect you, as an expert, to produce a seemingly perfect document in the shortest possible amount of time.

7

Contract Remedies

The remedies for breach or default under a real estate contract are similar to the remedies provided by basic contract law, and both the parties may turn to a variety of remedies. The primary categories of remedies for the breach of real estate contracts are damages, forfeiture of the buyer's part payments (sometimes analyzed as liquidated damages), equitable remedies, and tort remedies related to the contract. In addition, in this chapter we also explore some related concepts, such as slander of title and the filing of a lis pendens. Keep in mind that other types of legal actions, beyond those discussed herein, may be appropriate in given situations. Because real estate transactions involve a variety of human relationships and can become complex, at times the lawyer should consider additional remedies. For instance, you may wish to prevent someone from proceeding under a contract by seeking an injunction to prohibit her from taking any further action. At times, when rights under a contract are in dispute, a party's best course of action may be to seek a declaratory judgment that determines the parties' respective rights. There may be a need for an ejectment action to recover possession of property from a wrongdoer, or for a quiet title action to resolve a title dispute. There can even be situations, in the process of doing a transaction, where tempers flare up, leading to tortious or criminal behavior such as assault, trespass to land, or even outright physical violence. In these cases, a lawyer will pursue appropriate remedies and actions depending on the nature of the specific problem that arises.

A. DAMAGES AND FORFEITURE OF PAYMENTS

Damages to compensate a party include recovery for loss of expectation value on the transaction, out-of-pocket expenses, and lost profits, among other things. These damage remedies are all designed to make the injured party whole in an economic sense. The loss to the injured party is considered fungible in that an award of money is deemed capable of providing appropriate relief for the loss. Though often left unsaid, the concept of fungibility is the cornerstone of this category of remedy, because it allows us to equate the loss of rights under the contract with an award of cash as damages. In a sense, money is used as a mediating device to make the injured party whole, either by replacing the monetary objective of the contract with a cash award or by giving the injured party the monetary resources deemed sufficient to go back out into the marketplace to find a suitable replacement for the thing (the real estate) that was the object of the original contract.

Fungibility plays another important role in determining loss-of-bargain damages. The general measure of damages is the difference between the contract price and the fair market value of the property at the time of the breach, not at the time set for performance or some other date. The reference to fair market value implies fungibility because it supposes that we can find independent and objective criteria of value by looking at other comparable opportunities that are available in the market. Things that are fungible have a ready market for sale and resale. Value is set by the prices that willing buyers and sellers voluntarily pay or take for these items in an open market of exchange. The more fungible and more competitive the market is, the more objective and reliable the value of a thing will be. This is because a competitive market is assumed to leave the seller powerless in the sense that every seller takes her terms from the market. If a seller, offering a similar product, charges more or sells on less favorable terms than other sellers in the market, her sales will rapidly diminish as buyers move their purchases to other sellers. Thus, sellers in a competitive market must either take their terms from the market (respond to the demands of buyers) or adequately distinguish their products. The idea that buyers will simply ignore a seller who seeks to do business at too high a price or on unfavorable terms implies two additional assumptions of competitive markets. First, information is assumed to be generally well known and easily available to all market participants; second, buyers and sellers are free to move and shift their resources as they shop for the best deals. These market assumptions are important for purposes of remedies, because the less true they are in any given context, the more likely it is that money damages will not provide the injured party with satisfactory compensation. In such situations, we tend to prefer other types of remedies.

For real estate contracts, sellers usually prefer to avoid the complexities of collecting damages based on loss of the expectation interest. Instead, sellers rely on a clause in the contract stating that if the buyer defaults, the seller has the right to terminate the contract and retain the earnest money or deposit already paid by the buyer. The amount of earnest money is highly negotiable both for residential and commercial transactions, and in most communities there is no standard amount. A typical range for earnest money is between 3 and 10 percent of the purchase price. The seller is allowed to retain the buyer's payment without having to prove actual damages under one of two theories. Either forfeiture of the deposit is rationalized as valid as a consequence of the buyer's default, or the clause is considered to be a valid attempt by the parties to liquidate damages.

Liquidated damages are damages that the parties to a contract agree to and quantify in advance of any breach. For real estate contracts, liquidated damages are very commonly used as a remedy for the seller. Either or both parties can agree to pay liquidated damages, and occasionally a seller will promise to pay liquidated damages if she breaches the contract. Not every liquidated damages clause is enforceable. Courts supervise their use to make sure they are consistent with the objectives stated earlier. The amount of liquidated damages must appear to be reasonable in light of all the circumstances. A court will refuse to enforce unreasonably large liquidated damages. Moreover, the actual damages from a potential breach must be difficult to predict at the time of contracting. For real estate contracts, it usually is difficult or impossible to determine actual damages in advance for either party.

UZAN v. 845 UN LIMITED PARTNERSHIP
Supreme Court, Appellate Division, First Department, 2004
778 N.Y.S.2d 171

MAZZARELLI, Justice. This appeal presents the issue of whether plaintiffs, who defaulted on the purchase of four luxury condominium units, have forfeited their 25% down payments as a matter of law. Because the governing purchase agreements were a product of lengthy negotiation between parties of equal bargaining power, all represented by counsel, there was no evidence of overreaching, and upon consideration of the fact that a 25% down payment is common usage in the new construction luxury condominium market in New York City, we hold that upon their default and failure to cure, plaintiffs forfeited all rights to their deposits. . . .

FACTS

In October 1998, Defendant 845 UN Limited Partnership (sponsor or 845 UN) began to sell apartments at The Trump World Tower (Trump World), a luxury condominium building to be constructed at 845 United Nations Plaza. Donald Trump is the managing general partner of the sponsor. Plaintiffs Cem Uzan and Hakan Uzan, two brothers, are Turkish billionaires who sought to purchase multiple units in the building. In April 1999, plaintiffs and an associate executed seven purchase agreements for apartments in Trump World. Only four of those units (the penthouse units) are the subject of this lawsuit and appeal. As relevant, Cem Uzan defaulted on contracts to buy two penthouse units on the 90th floor of the building, and

Figure 7-1
The Trump World Tower from the East River

Hakan defaulted on contracts to purchase two other penthouse units on the 89th floor.[2]

The building had not been constructed when plaintiffs executed their purchase agreements. In paragraph 17.4 of those contracts, the sponsor projected that the first closing in the building would occur on or about April 1, 2001, nearly two years after the signing of the agreements. . . .

NEGOTIATIONS PRECEDING EXECUTION OF THE PURCHASE AGREEMENTS

Plaintiffs were represented by experienced local counsel during the two month long negotiation for the purchase of the apartments. There were numerous telephone conversations between counsel, and at least four extensively marked up copies of draft purchase agreements were exchanged. In consideration for plaintiffs' purchase of multiple units, the sponsor reduced the aggregate purchase price of the penthouse units by more than $7 million from the list price in the offering plan for a total cost of approximately $32 million. Plaintiffs also negotiated a number of revisions to the standard purchase agreement, including extensions of time for payment of the down payment. As amended, each purchase agreement obligated plaintiffs to make a 25% down payment: 10% at contract, an additional 7½% down

---

2. The transactions for three of the seven total units closed in July of 2001. Antonio Betancourt, an associate of the Uzans, purchased two units on the 59th floor of the building, and plaintiff Cem Uzan purchased a unit on the 80th floor.

payment twelve months later, and a final 7½% down payment 18 months after the execution of the contract. . . .

The executed purchase agreements provide, at paragraph 12(b), that:

> [u]pon the occurrence of an Event of Default . . . [i]f Sponsor elects to cancel . . . [and i]f the default is not cured within . . . thirty (30) days, then this Agreement shall be deemed canceled, and Sponsor shall have the right to retain, as and for liquidated damages, the Down payment and any interest earned on the Down payment. . . .

DEFAULT, FAILURE TO CURE, AND THIS ACTION

On September 11, 2001, terrorists attacked New York City by flying two planes into the World Trade Center, the city's two tallest buildings, murdering thousands of people. Plaintiffs, asserting concerns of future terrorist attacks, failed to appear at the October 19, 2001 closing, resulting in their default. By letter dated October 19, 2001, plaintiffs' counsel stated:

> [W]e believe that our clients are entitled to rescind their Purchase Agreements in view of the terrorist attack which occurred on September 11 and has not abated. In particular, our clients are concerned that the top floors in a "trophy" building, described as the tallest residential building in the world, will be an attractive terrorist target. The situation is further aggravated by the fact that the building bears the name of Donald Trump, perhaps the most widely known symbol of American capitalism. Finally, the United Nations complex brings even more attention to this location.

That day 845 UN sent plaintiffs default letters, notifying them that they had 30 days to cure. On November 19, 2001, upon expiration of the cure period, the sponsor terminated the four purchase agreements.

Plaintiffs then brought this action. They alleged that Donald Trump had prior special knowledge that certain tall buildings, such as Trump World, were potential targets for terrorists. Plaintiffs also alleged that Trump World did not have adequate protection for the residents of the upper floors of the building. . . .

THE ROLE OF THE 25% DOWN PAYMENT

In his affidavit in support of the cross motion, Donald Trump stated that he sought 25% down payments from pre-construction purchasers at the Trump World Tower because of the substantial length of time between contract signing and closing, during which period the sponsor had to keep the units off the market, and because of the obvious associated risks. Trump also affirmed that down payments in the range of 20% to 25% are standard practice in the new construction luxury condominium submarket in New York City. He cited three projects where he was the developer, The

Trump Palace, 610 Park Avenue and Trump International Hotel and Tower, all of which had similar down payment provisions. Trump also noted that:

> [i]n new construction condominium projects, purchasers often speculate on the market by putting down initial down payments of 10% and 15% and watching how the market moves. If the market value increases, they will then make the second down payment. If the market prices drop, they may then walk away from their down payment. . . .

Defendant also presented a compilation of sixteen recent condominium offering plans, all of which required down payments of either 20% or 25% of the purchase price for the unit. . . .

The Order Appealed

After hearing oral argument on the motion, the court granted defendant partial summary judgment, finding that plaintiffs forfeited the portion of their down payment amounting to 10% of the purchase price, pursuant to Maxton Builders, Inc. v. Lo Galbo, 502 N.E.2d 184 (N.Y. 1986). The court held that the remainder of the down payment was subject to a liquidated damages analysis to determine whether it bore a reasonable relation to the sponsor's actual or probable loss. Defendant appeals from that portion of the order which denied it full relief.

Discussion

More than a century ago, the Court of Appeals, in Lawrence v. Miller, 86 N.Y. 131 (1881), held that a vendee who defaults on a real estate contract without lawful excuse cannot recover his or her down payment. It reaffirmed this holding in *Maxton, supra,* again in 1986. The facts of *Lawrence* are common to real estate transactions, and parallel those presented here. In that case, plaintiff made a $2000 down payment on the purchase of certain real estate, and then defaulted. The seller refused to extend plaintiff's time to perform the contract, retained the down payment, and ultimately sold the property to another purchaser. In plaintiff's subsequent action for a refund of the down payment, the Court of Appeals affirmed a judgment dismissing the complaint, stating:

> To allow a recovery of this money would be to sustain an action by a party on his own breach of his own contract, which the law does not allow. When we once declare in this case that the vendor has done all that the law asks of him, we also declare that the vendee has not so done on his part. And then to maintain this action would be to declare that a party may violate his agreement, and make an infraction of it by himself a cause of action. That would be ill doctrine.

Lawrence, 86 N.Y. 131, 140.

For over a century, courts have consistently upheld what was called the *Lawrence* rule and recognized a distinction between real estate deposits and general liquidated damages clauses.[3] Liquidated damages clauses have traditionally been subject to judicial oversight to confirm that the stipulated damages bear a reasonable proportion to the probable loss caused by the breach. By contrast, real estate down payments have been subject to limited supervision. They have only been refunded upon a showing of disparity of bargaining power between the parties, duress, fraud, illegality or mutual mistake. *See* Cipriano v. Glen Cove Lodge # 1458, 801 N.E.2d 388 (N.Y. 2003).

In *Maxton*, plaintiff had contracted to sell defendants a house, and accepted a check for a 10 percent down payment. When defendants canceled the contract and placed a stop payment on the check, plaintiff sued for the down payment, citing the *Lawrence* rule. Defendants argued that plaintiff's recovery should be limited to its actual damages. In ruling for the vendor, the Court of Appeals identified two legal principles as flowing from *Lawrence*. First, that the vendor was entitled to retain the down payment in a real estate contract, without reference to his actual damages. Second, the "parent" rule, upon which the first rule was based, that one who breaches a contract may not recover the value of his part performance.

The Court noted that the parent rule had been substantially undermined in the 100 years since *Lawrence*. Many courts had rejected the parent rule because of criticism that it produced a forfeiture "and the amount of the forfeiture increases as performance proceeds, so that the penalty grows larger as the breach grows smaller." *Maxton*, 502 N.E.2d 187.

The Court also noted that since *Lawrence*, the rule of allowing recovery of down payments of not more than 10% in real estate contracts continues to be followed by a "majority of jurisdictions," including in New York. . . .

After acknowledging that "[R]eal estate contracts are probably the best examples of arms length transactions," the Court broadly concluded:

> Except in cases where there is a real risk of overreaching, there should be no need for the courts to relieve the parties of the consequences of their contract. *If the parties are dissatisfied with the rule of (Lawrence), the time to say so is at the bargaining table.*

Maxton, 502 N.E.2d 189 (emphasis supplied).

Applying the reasoning of these cases to the facts of the instant matter, it is clear that plaintiffs are not entitled to a return of any portion of their down payment. Here the 25 percent down payment was a specifically negotiated element of the contracts. . . .

Finally, there was no evidence of a disparity of bargaining power, or of duress, fraud, illegality or mutual mistake by the parties in drafting the down payment clause of the purchase agreements. . . .

3. A liquidated damage clause is a contractual provision by which the parties stipulate to a fixed sum to be paid in the event of a breach.

Accordingly, the order of the Supreme Court, New York County (Alice Schlesinger, J.), entered July 21, 2003, which, to the extent appealed from, denied defendant 845 UN Limited Partnership's motion for summary judgment, should be reversed. . . .

The Clerk is directed to enter judgment in favor of defendant appellant dismissing the complaint as against it.

Problem 7A

Juan and Alicia contract with Developer to purchase a condominium unit in a luxury high-rise building currently under construction in Center City. They have selected a unit with scenic views of the city and many desirable features. The contract price is $1.75 million. The construction is scheduled to be completed within the next twelve months. The contract requires a $30,000 deposit with an additional $20,000 due in 90 days. The buyers will be credited with the deposit amounts at closing.

The contract includes the following two clauses:

Liquidated Damages. The parties hereto agree that actual damages from a breach will be difficult to calculate, and they hereby agree that the contract deposit amount shall serve as the agreed-to damages in the event of Buyer's default, and in such event said deposit shall be forfeited to Seller.

Time is of the essence: The parties hereto agree that the timely performance of all terms and obligations under this contract is essential to the successful completion of the project, including the obligation of the developer to meet its financial commitment to its construction lender.

When the parties sign the contract on September 1, Juan and Alicia make a deposit of $30,000. When the date arrives for making the second deposit, they deliver a check for $20,000 to Developer's office. Ten days later when Developer deposits the check it is returned for insufficient funds. Developer immediately declares Juan and Alicia to be in default on the contract and notifies them that it is keeping their initial deposit as liquidated damages, and demands payment of the additional $20,000 that they should have paid.

(a) Is Developer entitled to the $30,000 initial deposit as liquidated damages?

(b) Is Developer entitled to the additional $20,000 as liquidated damages? As an alternative theory, what if Developer sues Juan and Alicia to collect on the unpaid check?

(c) Should it matter whether Juan and Alicia issued the check on insufficient funds by mistake (thinking that they had the funds in their account at the time) or they issued the check knowing that they did not have current funds in their checking account?

(d) Assume Juan and Alicia had decided not to go through with the deal on day 60 because market values were dropping and they located a larger unit in a comparable nearby building for $300,000 less. They want to walk away from the deal and limit their loss under the contract, so they notify Developer that they will not make the second deposit and will not buy the property. At that point, would the contract language preclude Developer from collecting the second deposit, from seeking actual damages, or from seeking specific performance?

B. EQUITABLE REMEDIES

There are four major equitable remedies that courts frequently award to protect parties to real estate contracts: specific performance, reformation, rescission, and equitable liens.

1. *Specific performance.* Perhaps the most important of the equitable remedies is specific performance. Under the traditional view of *mutuality of remedy*, both the buyer and the seller are generally entitled to specific performance. Some recent judicial trends have limited the blanket acceptance of the traditional conception of mutuality of remedy and have instead looked at the actual expectations of the parties and the nature of the breach to determine the appropriate remedy. Following the new trend, for example, a seller could not obtain a right of specific performance merely because the buyer would be in a position to invoke such a remedy. The seller would need to make out a case for specific performance on her own behalf, not simply by asserting the *doctrine of mutuality.*

Central to the remedy of specific performance is the requirement that the party seeking the remedy must be *ready, willing,* and *able* to perform. This means that the plaintiff must have satisfied all contract conditions and requirements that were her obligations before she can demand performance from the other side. Furthermore, she must stand ready, willing, and able to perform throughout the proceeding.

Sometimes a party seeks the remedy of specific performance when there are minor breaches in the contract, such as slight title defects, shortages in area, or defects in the property's physical condition. If the defect is minor, and therefore does not materially affect the buyer's intended use, the buyer might simply waive the nonconformity and proceed with the closing of the deal. However, if the problem is more than negligible, the buyer will want to pay less than the contract price and will ask for specific performance with an abatement of price to reflect the loss of value from the problem. Conversely, if the buyer balks at the minor defect or flaw, it may be the seller who wants to force the buyer to close on the contract under the original terms with the price abatement applied. Using the discretion of equity, a number of courts have granted specific performance coupled with price abatement when an improvement on the property is damaged by fire or when some other imperfection is noted.

2. *Reformation.* If the language of a written contract has an error or mistake, one of the parties may seek a correction through reformation. Typically, reformation is granted only if the plaintiff can establish a mutual

mistake. When a mistake is mutual, the language of the contract fails to reflect the parties' actual intent. For example, a drafting error that results in an incorrect statement of the price or description of the property is subject to correction by reformation.

3. *Rescission.* Contracts often include conditions that give parties an express right to terminate, or rescind, the contract. When an express right is lacking, a court of equity may grant rescission based upon grounds such as fraud, misrepresentation, or mutual mistake of fact. Like other equitable remedies, the granting of rescission is subject to the court's discretion. Normally, rescission is granted only if the problem is sufficiently material that continuation of the contract is not appropriate or feasible.

4. *Equitable liens.* By operation of law, a seller obtains a *vendor's lien* on the title to the real property to secure the unpaid purchase price. Prior to closing, the vendor's lien attaches to the buyer's equitable title, which the buyer has as a consequence of the doctrine of equitable conversion. After closing, if the seller has not received full payment, the lien attaches to the title conveyed by the deed. The buyer has a reciprocal right, known as a *vendee's lien,* to secure the return of the down payment or the payment of reliance damages in the event the sale does not close.

DIGUIUSEPPE v. LAWLER
Supreme Court of Texas, 2008
269 S.W.3d 588

WALDROP, Justice. This case involves a claim for specific performance of a real estate purchase contract. After a trial in which the jury found that the seller breached the contract, the trial court rendered judgment in favor of the buyer and ordered specific performance. The court of appeals reversed on the basis that the buyer did not obtain a finding of fact or prove that he was ready, willing, and able to perform. . . . We affirm the judgment of the court of appeals with respect to the claim for specific performance. . . .

I. FACTUAL AND PROCEDURAL BACKGROUND

In October 1998, Nick DiGiuseppe d/b/a Southbrook Development Co. entered into a contract with Richard Lawler to purchase approximately 756 acres of Lawler's land near Frisco, Texas, for $40,000 an acre. The contract made closing of the purchase contingent on obtaining acceptable rezoning of the property from the City of Frisco to accommodate DiGiuseppe's development plans, and provided that closing would occur on the fifteenth day after successful completion of rezoning. The purchase contract also provided for a three-stage deposit of earnest money with the title company: (1) $100,000 upon the signing of the contract; (2) $100,000 upon the submission to the City of Frisco of the application to rezone the property;

and (3) $400,000 upon "approval by the planning and zoning commission of the City of Frisco of zoning acceptable to Purchaser of the 'Land' as applied for." DiGiuseppe made the first two earnest money deposits. However, a dispute arose as to whether the events that would trigger the requirement for the third deposit had occurred.

In late November 1999, after numerous meetings and a number of revisions to the rezoning application, the Planning and Zoning Commission approved new zoning for the property at issue. This new zoning was approved by the City Council on January 4, 2000. Although the new zoning differed from the zoning that the parties had applied for in their original application, it was acceptable to DiGiuseppe.

On January 12, 2000, Lawler faxed a letter to DiGiuseppe notifying him that Lawler considered DiGiuseppe in default of the purchase contract for failing to make the third earnest money deposit. Lawler took the position that the requirement for the third ($400,000) earnest money deposit had been triggered when the Planning and Zoning Commission had approved zoning that DiGiuseppe found acceptable. The January 12 letter also declared the contract "cancelled" and demanded release of the earnest money on deposit to Lawler. DiGiuseppe objected to Lawler's notification that the contract was terminated, taking the position that the third earnest money installment had not been triggered because the new zoning was not approved "as applied for." He also declared that he was moving forward with the transaction and demanded that Lawler continue to move toward closing.

Acting on the belief that the contract with DiGiuseppe was terminated, Lawler signed a new purchase contract for the property with DRHI, Inc. on February 1, 2000. DiGiuseppe, acting on the belief that the contract was not terminated, proceeded with finalizing his side of the transaction and demanded that Lawler close. The transaction did not close. Both parties alleged the other was responsible for the failure to close. DiGiuseppe then filed the purchase contract in the deed records. On April 14, 2000, Lawler filed suit against DiGiuseppe in Collin County District Court seeking a declaration that the purchase contract was terminated, requesting damages for breach of contract, and also seeking to quiet title as a result of the filing of the purchase contract in the deed records. DiGiuseppe counterclaimed for breach of contract, quantum meruit, breach of a duty of good faith and fair dealing, statutory fraud, promissory estoppel, and specific performance.

The purchase contract limited the remedies available to the parties in the event of a breach. In the event DiGiuseppe failed to close, Lawler's "sole and exclusive" remedy was to retain the earnest money as liquidated damages, and he expressly waived any right to claim any other damages or specific performance from DiGiuseppe. In the event Lawler defaulted in performing his obligations under the contract for any reason other than DiGiuseppe's default or a proper termination of the contract under its provisions, DiGiuseppe could choose between two remedies: (1) terminate the contract and receive a full and immediate refund of the earnest money, or

(2) "seek to enforce" specific performance of the contract. DiGiuseppe also expressly waived any right to claim damages.

The case was ultimately tried to a jury and the parties' breach of contract claims were submitted on broad-form questions inquiring as to whether either party failed to comply with the contract. The jury answered favorably to DiGiuseppe that Lawler had failed to comply with the contract and that DiGiuseppe had not failed to comply. A damages question was also submitted and the jury found that DiGiuseppe had suffered $295,696.93 in damages. Although disputed at trial, no question was requested by either party or submitted to the jury with respect to specific performance or whether DiGiuseppe was ready, willing, and able to perform under the contract at the time he alleged the transaction should have closed. . . .

On DiGiuseppe's post-verdict motion, the trial court rendered a take-nothing judgment against Lawler and granted DiGiuseppe specific performance of the purchase contract together with an award of attorneys' fees in the amount of $75,000. The trial court also appointed a receiver to take possession of the property and effectuate a closing of the purchase contract in accordance with its terms.

The court of appeals reversed the trial court's order granting specific performance, holding that DiGiuseppe had failed to conclusively establish, or to request and obtain a finding of fact on, an essential element of his claim for specific performance; that he was ready, willing, and able to perform under the terms of the purchase contract. . . .

DiGiuseppe sought review in this Court on two grounds: (1) the purchase contract provided for the remedy of specific performance in the event of a breach by Lawler regardless of whether DiGiuseppe obtained a finding of fact that he was ready, willing, and able to perform; and, (2) in the alternative, if he is not entitled to specific performance, the court of appeals erred in failing either to award the damages found by the jury or to allow DiGiuseppe to recover the $200,000 in earnest money he paid. . . .

II. Specific Performance

An essential element in obtaining the equitable remedy of specific performance is that the party seeking such relief must plead and prove he was ready, willing, and able to timely perform his obligations under the contract. In 1938, we stated: "The doctrine is fundamental that a party seeking the remedy of specific performance . . . must show himself to have been ready, desirous, prompt, and eager. These principles have been long recognized and respected by the Courts of Texas." Ratcliffe v. Mahres, 122 S.W.2d 718, 721–22 (Tex. Civ. App.-El Paso 1938, writ ref'd). . . . "[T]o be entitled to specific performance, the plaintiff must show that it has substantially performed its part of the contract, and that it is able to continue performing its part of the agreement. The plaintiff's burden of proving readiness, willingness and ability is a continuing one that extends to all times relevant to the contract and thereafter." 25 Richard A. Lord, *Williston on Contracts* §67:15, at 236–37 (4th ed. 2002). . . .

A corollary to this rule is that when a defendant refuses to perform or repudiates a contract, the plaintiff may be excused from actually tendering his or her performance to the repudiating party before filing suit for specific performance. In such a circumstance, a plaintiff seeking specific performance is excused from tendering performance presuit and may simply plead that performance would have been tendered but for the defendant's breach or repudiation. Corzelius v. Oliver, 220 S.W.2d 632, 634 (Tex. 1949). . . .

. . . Notably, the evidence on DiGiuseppe's readiness and ability to perform — all from the testimony of DiGiuseppe — was equivocal and conflicting. DiGiuseppe testified that he did not have the funds to close at the time originally specified by the purchase contract, or any written commitments from third parties to fund the closing at that time, and that he could not close.[8] He later testified that he "had the means to close the contract."[9]

---

8. The following exchange occurred during examination by Lawler's counsel:

Q. Mr. DiGiuseppe, you personally did not have the money to close this contract, did you?
A. I did not.
Q. When you assigned — when you entered into this contract, you had a right to assign it, right?
A. That's right.
Q. And so you were going to have to find a third party or parties to assign this contract in order for it to close, correct? . . .
A. Yes.
Q. You couldn't close the contract?
A. No.
Q. How did you intend . . . to close this contract?
A. Well, normally what I do is — dealing with a piece of property like this, I'll put it under contract, do the work, do the zoning. And through that process, I usually put together parties to be the investors in the deal. And they, then, close on the contract, and they would fund the development of the property and so on. And I would be the development arm of that entity usually.
Q. You never had any written agreement from any third parties to close this contract, did you?
A. I haven't gotten a written agreement with the parties that were going to close it with me, no. That's not the way I do business.
Q. You don't use contracts?
A. No. What I mean is if somebody tells me they are going to do something, I expect them to do it.
Q. Well, in your deposition, didn't you tell me that you felt that there would be three different home builders that might participate and provide that money to close this deal? . . .
A. Three different home builders were going to close the deal with me, yes.
Q. But you didn't have any written agreement from them that they were going to close the deal?
A. Not a written agreement, no. . . .
Q. When you sent the letter that said you were ready, willing and able to close this contract, you, individually, couldn't close that contract, could you?
A. I, individually, never intended to close that contract.
Q. You didn't have the funds to close the contract, did you?
A. Not personally, no.

9. The following exchange occurred during examination by DiGiuseppe's counsel:

Q. Mr. DiGiuseppe, you had the means to close the contract, didn't you?
A. Yes. In fact, a month later, we closed one that was $24 million.

DiGiuseppe does not raise an issue with respect to the state of the applicable law, but contends that the parties' contract alters the manner in which the law applies to this case. He concedes that he did not request a finding by the jury on the issue of whether he was ready, willing, and able to perform under the terms of the purchase contract. He complains that the court of appeals misinterpreted and misapplied the remedy provisions of the purchase contract. He argues that, because the parties had agreed in the purchase contract that one of his available remedies would be to seek to enforce specific performance, he had a right to specific performance in the event Lawler breached or defaulted on the contract without the need for any further proof. According to DiGiuseppe, the only *material* disputed fact issue — by virtue of the language of the remedy provision in the contract — is whether Lawler failed to comply with the contract. . . .

Lawler responds that specific performance was not automatic under the purchase contract in the event he defaulted. He asserts that the purchase contract's reference to DiGiuseppe having the right to "seek to enforce" specific performance does not equate to a right to automatically receive specific performance. . . .

We agree with Lawler and the court of appeals that the remedy provision at issue here does not entitle DiGiuseppe to obtain specific performance merely upon a showing of a breach or default by Lawler. The provision at issue limits the available remedies to either (1) terminating the contract and receiving a refund of earnest money, or (2) seeking to enforce specific performance. It does not in any way alter the requirements for obtaining specific performance in the event DiGiuseppe decides to seek such a remedy. . . .

V. Conclusion

We affirm the holding of the court of appeals that the contract at issue in this case does not alter DiGiuseppe's obligation to prove and secure a finding of fact that he was ready, willing, and able to perform his obligations under the purchase contract as a prerequisite to obtaining the equitable relief of specific performance. . . .

Green, Justice, joined by Jefferson, O'Neill, and Johnson, dissenting. The Court requires an innocent buyer, otherwise excused from his contractual obligations by the seller's breach, to nevertheless prove, in a suit for specific performance, that he could have fully performed those obligations had the seller not breached. This makes no sense for at least two reasons. First, it provides the breaching seller information he was not entitled to under the contract. A seller entering into a real estate transaction is rarely entitled to know the details of how the buyer intends to finance the transaction. At closing, the buyer will either perform or not, and in the latter event, the contract will provide remedies for the breach. But if the seller breaches the contract before closing and the buyer sues to enforce the deal, the Court now says the buyer must prove to a fact-finder, at a trial many months or years after the sale was originally supposed to close, that he was, at the time specified by the contract, "ready, willing, and able" to perform. To do this, the innocent buyer will necessarily be required to reveal his plan for financing the transaction — information a seller generally would not be privy to under agreed contract terms.

Second, and perhaps most important, the Court's holding makes no sense because a finding that the buyer was ready, willing, and able to perform at the closing time specified in the contract is irrelevant. Although the Court does not say what the trial court is supposed to do with such a finding, presumably it would order a date for the transaction to close within a reasonable time. But what if the buyer was able to close on the original contract date and is unable to close on the court-appointed date? The whole exercise is rendered meaningless. The only thing that makes sense is to do precisely what the trial court did in this case, which is to set a closing date within a reasonable time after a finding that the seller breached. . . .

Problem 7B

A proposed draft for a contract to purchase 160 acres of unimproved rural land includes the following clause: "In the event Seller fails to comply with this purchase agreement for any other reason than inability to deliver merchantable title, Buyer shall have the right to demand specific performance." No other clause deals with remedies for either party, except for a standard clause allowing Seller to retain the earnest money if Buyer defaults. What effect does this specific performance clause have on the parties' rights, compared to a contract that is silent on the topic? If you were representing Seller, would you accept this clause as is, or do you recommend revision? What if you were representing Buyer?

DeVENNEY v. HILL
Supreme Court of Alabama, 2013
918 So. 2d 106

SEE, Justice. John J. "Jack" DeVenney and Shirley Ann DeVenney, husband and wife, sued Mason Hill, H. Frank Thomas III, David Eason, and Community Bank & Trust ("the Bank"). The trial court entered a summary judgment in favor of Hill, Thomas, and the Bank on all the claims against them and a summary judgment in favor of the DeVenneys against Eason on all claims against him. The DeVenneys appeal the summary judgment entered in favor of Hill, Thomas, and the Bank. We affirm in part, reverse in part, and remand.

I. FACTS AND PROCEDURAL HISTORY

The DeVenneys live in Wetumpka. They owned 33.7 acres of land, described in the deed as "original lots 294 and 295, East Wetumpka, Alabama" ("the land").

In 2002, Eason approached Mrs. DeVenney about buying the land for $205,000. Mrs. DeVenney refused his offer. Eason then offered Mrs. DeVenney $250,000. Mrs. DeVenney accepted the offer, provided that the DeVenneys would keep a 250-foot by 250-foot lot by the road ("the retained lot") and that Eason would excavate the retained lot for the DeVenneys. On April 8, 2002, Eason and Mrs. DeVenney entered into a "sales agreement," reflecting that Eason agreed to buy the land, excluding the retained lot, for $250,000 within 90 days; the sales agreement said nothing about the oral agreement to excavate the retained lot.

At some point when he was negotiating the sale of the land with Mrs. DeVenney, Eason approached Hill about financing his purchase of the land. Eason had borrowed money from Hill and Thomas for other business transactions. Eason and Hill eventually agreed that Hill and Thomas would purchase the land directly from the DeVenneys for $200,000[1] and that Eason would then buy the land from Hill and Thomas for $275,000. Hill and Thomas considered themselves equal partners in this transaction, and both were experienced in real estate. . . .

Eason approached Mrs. DeVenney one or two days before the scheduled closing and offered her an additional $50,000 if she would allow him an extra month after the closing to pay $150,000 of the purchase price. Mrs. DeVenney agreed, and the total purchase price was thus orally increased to $300,000, $100,000 of which was due at the closing.

The closing was on April 19, 2002, at the office of the closing attorney, John Thornton. The DeVenneys met Hill and Thomas for the first time at the closing. Thornton's office and the Bank prepared all the closing documents. Hill and Thomas borrowed $202,350 from the Bank and out of that amount brought $200,000 to the closing. Eason brought to the closing two checks: one for $150,000 and the other for $50,000; both were postdated May 19, 2002.

The DeVenneys, Eason, Hill, Thomas, and Thornton were present during the closing. Thornton explained to all the parties that Hill[2] was actually buying the land. The DeVenneys did not object. Mrs. DeVenney, however, insisted that the sales agreement she had entered into with Eason reflect that Eason was to excavate the retained lot. Thornton added the following hand-written clause at the bottom of the sales agreement: "David Eason agrees to

---

1. Eason and Mrs. DeVenney agreed to a purchase price of $250,000, but Eason apparently told Hill and Thomas that the purchase price would be $200,000.

2. Hill and Thomas do not dispute that they acted as partners in the transaction. Although only Hill was named in the deed, Hill and Thomas considered themselves to be joint buyers of the land. Hill and Thomas jointly obtained a loan from the Bank for this transaction. Hill was acting in this case on behalf of the Hill and Thomas partnership. . . .

excavate and level the 250 x 250 lot to a commercially feasible grade to the satisfaction of seller within 90 days." Eason and the DeVenneys signed below the clause. Thornton also added on the side of the sales agreement the following handwritten clause: "Contract assigned to Mason Hill." Eason signed at the bottom of this clause. . . .

Thornton gave the DeVenneys a $100,000 check and showed everyone the two postdated checks in the amount of $150,000 and $50,000. Thornton also explained to the DeVenneys that the checks were not good that day, and Mrs. DeVenney acknowledged that she was depending on Eason to make the checks good. Thornton agreed to hold the checks until May 19, 2002, and the DeVenneys, Eason, and Thornton executed an agreement reflecting that Thornton would deliver the checks to the DeVenneys on May 19, 2002. Thornton made a copy of the checks for the DeVenneys.

The postdated checks to the DeVenneys were never honored. The DeVenneys sued Hill and Thomas, the Bank, and Eason. They alleged breach of contract against Hill and Thomas in Hill and Thomas's capacity as assignees of the contract; they asserted a vendor's lien against Hill and Thomas; and they sought specific performance of the contract from Hill and Thomas. The DeVenneys asserted only a vendor's lien against the Bank. They stated that the Bank was a party because of its status as a mortgagee, and the DeVenneys sought to establish a vendor's lien superior to the Bank's mortgage lien. The DeVenneys asserted against Eason various fraud claims, a vendor's lien claim, and the claims under §6-5-101 et seq., Ala. Code 1975 (statutory deceit, fraud, and/or fraudulent suppression). . . .

The trial court entered a summary judgment in favor of the DeVenneys and against Eason on all the claims against Eason. The trial court also entered a summary judgment against the DeVenneys and in favor of Hill, Thomas, and the Bank on all the claims the DeVenneys stated against Hill, Thomas, and the Bank. . . .

III. BREACH-OF-CONTRACT CLAIM AGAINST HILL AND THOMAS

The DeVenneys argue that the trial court erred in failing to enter a summary judgment in their favor on their breach-of-contract claim against Hill and Thomas. . . .

The DeVenneys presented substantial evidence indicating that Eason properly assigned the sales agreement to Hill and Thomas.[11] Thus, as assignees, Hill and Thomas were obligated to perform the terms of the assigned contract. *See* Meighan v. Watts Constr. Co., 475 So.2d 829, 834 (Ala. 1985). . . .

---

11. We note that Hill and Thomas argue that the sales agreement was never assigned and that they should not have to perform the terms of the agreement; yet, under the scenario they present, they would retain the land and reap the benefits of the agreement. A party cannot reap the benefits of a contract, yet seek to avoid the burdens of performing his obligations under the terms of the contract.

Although Eason paid the remaining portion of the purchase price, $150,000, with a postdated check, Hill and Thomas, as assignees and purchasers, had a contractual duty to make sure that the payment was made good. *See Meighan*, 475 So.2d at 834 (holding that the assignee impliedly promises to perform the duties of the assigned contract). The DeVenneys presented substantial evidence tending to show that because Eason was no longer a party to the transaction, his payment must have been made on behalf of the purchasers, Hill and Thomas. The HUD-1 statement reflects that each amount deposited by the purchasers was "paid by or in behalf of borrower."

Thus, we conclude that the sales agreement was properly assigned to Hill and Thomas, as partners. We also conclude that the additional $50,000 fee for delaying collection of part of the purchase price was not a term of the sales agreement as assigned but that the excavation of the retained lot was a term of the assigned sales agreement. Therefore, the trial court erred in entering a summary judgment in favor of Hill and Thomas on the breach-of-contract claim brought against them in their status as assignees of the sales agreement. We, therefore, reverse the summary judgment in favor of Hill and Thomas on the breach-of-contract claim, and we remand the case for further proceedings.

IV. Vendor's Lien Claim Against Hill, Thomas, and the Bank

The DeVenneys argue that the trial court erred in failing to enter a summary judgment in their favor on the equitable claim of a vendor's lien against Hill, Thomas, and the Bank. The DeVenneys argue that they have an equitable vendor's lien against Hill, Thomas, and the Bank because, they say, they transferred the land to Hill but did not receive the full purchase price. Hill, Thomas, and the Bank argue that the DeVenneys waived their equitable claim of a vendor's lien and that the trial court correctly entered a summary judgment in their favor. We agree that the DeVenneys waived their equitable claim to a vendor's lien, and we affirm the summary judgment in favor of Hill, Thomas, and the Bank on the vendor's lien claim.

There are three types of vendor's lien: (1) the grantor's implied lien where the law imposes a lien in favor of a vendor who has conveyed real property without taking any security for the payment of the purchase price; (2) the grantor's express lien where the grantor secured the lien by express contract; and (3) the grantor's retention of title where the vendor retains his title as security for the vendee to perform the contract. An implied vendor's lien arises if (1) there is a sale of real property and (2) unsecured purchase money remains unpaid. In this case, the DeVenneys agreed to sell the land; they conveyed the deed to Hill; and Hill and Thomas did not fully pay the purchase price. Thus, the law could impose a vendor's lien. *See* Bridgeport Land & Improvement Co. v. American Fire-Proof Steel Car Co. of Alabama, 10 So. 704 (Ala. 1892) (holding that the vendor's lien is a creature of equity and that the reason for attaching the lien is that it goes against good conscience for one person to keep another person's land without having paid the agreed consideration).

However, the implied vendor's lien may be waived, and the purchaser has the burden of showing any waiver of the implied vendor's lien. Lindsey v. Thornton, 173 So. 500 (Ala. 1937). The lien may be waived (1) by the vendor's affirmative intention, *Lindsey,* (2) by reliance, not on land, but on a substituted, independent security, Armour Fertilizer Works v. Zills, 177 So. 136 (Ala. 1937); Kinney v. Ensminger, 10 So. 143 (Ala 1891), or (3) by reliance on the personal responsibility of the vendee, *Armour; Kinney.* The courts should look at all the facts and circumstances in a case to determine whether the vendor waived the lien. *Armour.*

In this case, Thornton explained at the closing that the postdated check of $150,000 was not good at that time. Mrs. DeVenney testified at her deposition that she told Thornton that she understood that she was looking to Eason to make the $150,000 check good. Further, Mrs. DeVenney understood that the DeVenneys were essentially financing $150,000 for 30 days after the closing. Thus, facts and circumstances indicate that Mrs. DeVenney was relying on the personal responsibility of Eason, who was paying on behalf of Hill and Thomas, for the rest of the purchase money. The appearance of reliance on personal responsibility creates a rebuttable presumption of waiver. Walker v. Carroll, 65 Ala. 61 (1880). *See also Lindsey, supra* (holding that the giving of other security creates a prima facie presumption of waiver, but that the presumption may be rebutted). The DeVenneys have not shown any facts to rebut the presumption that they were relying upon Eason's personal responsibility for the unpaid portion of the purchase price.

In Fowler v. Falkner, 73 So. 980 (Ala. 1917) (holding that where the vendor was induced by the vendee to accept third-party notes as part of the purchase price, the vendor did not waive the lien where the notes were not of the agreed-upon value, and the vendee had fraudulently misrepresented the value of the notes), and Madden v. Barnes, 45 Wis. 135 (1878) (holding that the vendor did not waive the lien where a check was refused for insufficient funds by the vendee's bank; the vendee's check was fraudulent because the presentment of a check presupposes that there are sufficient funds in the bank account), the recipients of the payments had no reason to believe that the respective notes and check were not good. The DeVenneys, on the other hand, knew at the time of the closing that the $150,000 check was not good. The DeVenneys understood that they were essentially making a $150,000 loan for 30 days and that they were relying on the personal responsibility of Eason to make good the payment. Under these circumstances, we find that the DeVenneys waived their implied vendor's lien against Hill, Thomas, and the Bank.[14]

---

14. The DeVenneys' personal reliance on Eason to later fund a portion of the purchase price on behalf of Hill and Thomas waived the implied vendor's lien, but regardless of on whom the DeVenneys relied to fund a portion of the purchase price, Hill and Thomas as assignees and purchasers were ultimately responsible to pay all of the purchase price. *See Meighan,* 475 So.2d at 834.

V. Conclusion

We conclude that the trial court erred in entering a summary judgment in favor of Hill and Thomas on the breach-of-contract claim. The summary judgment on the breach-of-contract claim against Hill and Thomas as assignees of the sales agreement is reversed, and we remand for further proceedings consistent with this opinion. We affirm the summary judgment in favor of Hill, Thomas, and the Bank on the implied vendor's lien claim.

Problem 7C

Robin agrees to buy a home from Jim for $100,000, with the contract stating that Jim will pay $50,000 in cash at closing on November 1 and the remaining $50,000 on the first anniversary of the closing date. In the contract they agree that at the closing of the contract, Robin will sign a purchase-money mortgage with Jim to secure the additional payment of $50,000. At closing there are a number of documents to be signed by the parties and some confusion arises as to title and survey matters. In the course of the closing they resolve all of the title and survey matters and then finish up. In the midst of the confusion, however, Robin never signed the mortgage form. On December 10, Jim calls you, his attorney, to ask what to do if Robin does not want to sign a mortgage now. In particular, he wonders what other possible legal grounds he may have to secure the payment of the remaining amount due in the event that Robin does not pay.

C. SLANDER OF TITLE AND LIS PENDENS

The tort action called *slander of title* is designed to protect the value of property. Changes in, or the perception of changes in, this bundle of rights have an effect on the property's value. Therefore, a property owner has an interest in protecting the legitimate nature of a property's title and its related reputation. If anyone maligns or disparages the reputation of the property, the owner can take steps to protect its reputation and value in a manner similar to that offered to defend her own good name — that is, the law recognizes a cause of action for slander of title that is similar to a slander action between individuals.

A *lis pendens* is a method of asserting a potential claim or conflicting interest against title to real estate when litigation is filed and pending. The lis pendens is a notice filed in the public records for real estate that gives notice that a legal action is currently pending, the outcome of which may have an impact on the status of title of the specifically described property. By definition, the lis pendens is designed to put a *cloud* on the owner's title (giving it an unmarketable title) and thereby make it difficult or impossible to transfer or otherwise deal with the property. It also serves the purpose of giving notice to any potential BFPs, thereby destroying their ability to take without knowledge of the pending dispute.

EXECUTIVE EXCELLENCE, LLC v. MARTIN BROTHERS INVESTMENTS, LLC
Court of Appeals of Georgia, 2011
710 S.E.2d 169

McFadden, Judge. These consolidated appeals arise out of the rescission of two written contracts for the purchase and sale of real property. The sellers and property owners were Executive Excellence, LLC, its principal owner Richard R. Fritts, and Sterling Trust Company (collectively "sellers"). The buyers under assignments were Southern Tradition Investments, LLC and Martin Brothers Investments, LLC (collectively "buyers"). . . .

. . . Executive, operated by Fritts, was the owner of a 15-acre tract of undeveloped land in Hall County. A separate four-acre tract was owned by Sterling Trust as Custodian for the Benefit of Richard R. Fritts. On or about December 26, 2006, Fritts executed two contracts to sell the respective tracts to a third party, Sund Enterprises. Although Sterling Trust was listed as the seller on the contract for the four-acre tract, the contract was not executed by any authorized representative of Sterling Trust.

Sund Enterprises later assigned its rights under the contract to purchase the 15-acre tract to Southern Tradition and assigned its rights under the contract to purchase the four-acre tract to Martin Brothers. Both contracts contained a zoning contingency that provided as follows:

> This contract is conditioned on the ability of the Buyer to obtain the rezoning of said property to zoning classification pursuant to the *City of Oakwood (Zoned C-2) or Hall County (Zoned HB)* Zoning Resolutions so as to permit the construction of Commercial/Highway Business on the property. . . . Buyer agrees to apply for said rezoning within Sixty (60) days of the date of this agreement and Seller agrees to cooperate with the Buyer in obtaining such rezoning. . . . *It is expressly understood that in the event a final determination is not made on said application by the City of Oakwood or Hall County, on or before April 1, 2007, either party may rescind this contract by notifying the other party as provided for herein.*

(Emphasis supplied). . . .

Southern Tradition and Martin Brothers failed to obtain a final determination on their rezoning applications by the April 1, 2007 deadline. On April 25, 2007, counsel for Executive sent a letter to counsel for Southern Tradition rescinding the contract based upon the failure of the zoning contingency. Subsequently, on May 16, 2007, counsel for Sterling Trust sent a letter to counsel for Martin Brothers, advising that the purported contract was null and void since it was not approved or accepted by Sterling Trust and, to the extent that a contract existed, it was rescinded due to the failure of the zoning contingency.

Southern Tradition and Martin Brothers continued to pursue a rezoning of the properties and enforcement of the contracts. At the Hall County Board of Commissioners meeting held on April 26, 2007, the agent for Southern Tradition and Martin Brothers allegedly stated to third parties that they intended to pursue enforcement of the contracts for the properties "in order to teach [Fritts] a lesson and that [they] had enough money to do so." At a subsequent Board of Commissioners meeting on May 24, 2007, the Hall County attorney, who also was a partner at the law firm representing Southern Tradition and Martin Brothers, openly stated that there was active litigation involving the properties. On October 8, 2007, the agent for Southern Tradition and Martin Brothers allegedly stated to third parties that they "had enough money to keep the [properties] tied-up in litigation for the next 5 to 10 years."

Southern Tradition filed suit against Executive, asserting claims for contract reformation, specific performance, and attorney fees. . . . In addition, Martin Brothers alleged that Fritts had fraudulently misrepresented that he had authority to execute the contract to sell the property on behalf of Sterling Trust. In conjunction with filing the lawsuits, Southern Tradition and Martin Brothers filed notices of lis pendens identifying the lawsuits, the relief sought, and the properties subject to the lawsuits.

Executive, Fritts, and Sterling Trust . . . filed counterclaims seeking damages and attorney fees for slander of title, pertinently alleging that Southern Tradition and Martin Brothers had maliciously impugned their title to the properties by filing the notices of lis pendens and by making the statements to third parties at the Board of Commissioners meetings. . . .

Under OCGA §51-9-11, "[t]he owner of any estate in lands may bring an action for libelous or slanderous words which falsely and maliciously impugn his title if any damage accrues to him therefrom." To establish a claim for the slander of title tort in accordance with the statute, the plaintiff must prove: (1) publication of slanderous or libelous statements; (2) that the statements were false and malicious; (3) that the plaintiff sustained special damages thereby; and (4) that the plaintiff possessed an estate in the property slandered or libeled. See Premier Cabinets v. Bulat, 583 S.E.2d 235 (Ga. Ct. App. 2003). In this case, the slander of title claim alleged that Southern Tradition and Martin Brothers had wrongfully filed and maintained notices of lis pendens against the properties and had also made false and malicious representations to third parties regarding the property dispute.

A. LIS PENDENS

The notices of lis pendens filed by Southern Tradition and Martin Brothers in conjunction with their complaints were privileged and therefore, could not serve as the basis for the slander of title claim. The privilege is set out at OCGA §51-5-8:

> All charges, allegations, and averments contained in regular pleadings filed in a court of competent jurisdiction, which are pertinent and material to the relief sought, whether legally sufficient to obtain it or not, are privileged. However false and malicious such charges, allegations, and averments may be, they shall not be deemed libelous.

A valid and effective lis pendens filed in a court of competent jurisdiction to provide notice that certain real property is directly involved in the pending suit falls within the purview of this statutory privilege. *See* Alcovy Properties v. MTW Investment Co., 441 S.E.2d 288 (Ga. Ct. App. 1994). Here, the lis pendens were properly filed in the trial court in conjunction with the lawsuits that were based upon the property contract disputes. The lis pendens identified the properties that were directly involved in the pending suits. As such, the lis pendens were proper, privileged, and could not be deemed as constituting a slander of title. *See id.*

Executive, Fritts, and Sterling Trust nevertheless contend that Southern Tradition and Martin Brothers committed the tort by continuing to maintain the lis pendens after they filed a voluntary dismissal without prejudice as to their claims in the lawsuit. Their contention is without merit.

"The phrase 'lis pendens' means, literally, pending suit." Vance v. Lomas Mtg. USA, 426 S.E.2d 873, 875 (Ga. 1993). In this regard, our Supreme Court has held that a valid notice of lis pendens remains in effect until a final judgment has been entered in the action and the time for appeal has expired. *See id.* . . .

Although Southern Tradition and Martin Brothers filed a voluntary dismissal without prejudice as to their claims presented in the lawsuits, such did not finalize all claims in the lawsuit since the counterclaim for slander of title filed by Executive, Fritts, and Sterling Trust remained pending for resolution. . . . There is no merit to appellants' argument that Southern Tradition and Martin Brothers were required to physically remove the notices of lis pendens from the records. . . .

B. STATEMENTS TO THIRD PARTIES

The slander of title claim was further based upon statements allegedly made by the agents of Southern Tradition and Martin Brothers to third parties at Hall County Board of Commissioners meetings. . . .

Southern Tradition and Martin Brothers contend that the alleged statements were not false and did not reflect upon or impugn appellants' title to the property.

We agree with the trial court that the attorney's alleged statement at the May 24, 2007 meeting did not amount to actionable slander of title.

Appellants contend that the attorney's statement falsely informed third parties that there was active litigation involving the properties, when in fact the lawsuits had not yet been filed. The lawsuits were filed on May 30, 2007 and May 31, 2007 respectively, approximately one week after the alleged statement was made. Nevertheless, "[d]efamation law overlooks minor inaccuracies and concentrates upon substantial truth. A statement is not considered false unless it would have a different effect on the mind of the listener from that which the pleaded truth would have produced." Vito v. Inman, 649 S.E.2d 753, 756 (Ga. Ct. App. 2007). It is undisputed that the parties were then embroiled in a contract dispute over the purchase and sale of the properties when the alleged statement was made. The lawsuits were filed shortly thereafter, presenting active litigation. Under these circumstances, the attorney's statement presented a minor factual error which did not go to the substance of the statement and did not render the communication false for defamation purposes. *See id.*

We also agree with the trial court that the April and October 2007 statements do not constitute slander to title. As previously noted, an action for slander to title must be based on the uttering of false words. Here, the trial court correctly held that neither of the statements in question was false. At the time the statements were made, whether or not the contracts were still enforceable or had been lawfully terminated was in dispute between the parties. . . .

We agree with the trial court's finding . . . that the slander to title claim . . . was without merit. . . .

Miller, Presiding Judge, concurring in part and dissenting in part. I respectfully dissent. . . .

The sellers' slander of title claim pertinently alleged that the agent for Southern Tradition and Martin Brothers made statements to third parties that Southern Tradition and Martin Brothers intended to pursue enforcement of the contracts for the properties "in order to teach [Fritts] a lesson" and that they "had enough money to keep the [properties] tied-up in litigation for the next 5 to 10 years." Southern Tradition and Martin Brothers contend that the alleged statements were not false and did not reflect upon or impugn the sellers' title to the property. The majority finds this argument persuasive. I disagree.

While the majority appears to view the statements narrowly, the legal standard for evaluating a slander of title claim requires that the statements be viewed in context, considering the circumstances in which the statements were made. See Webster v. Wilkins, 456 S.E.2d 699, 700 (Ga. Ct. App. 1995). When viewed in this context, the statements falsely insinuated that the contracts for the properties were enforceable, when in fact, the contracts had been terminated and were unenforceable based upon their plain, unambiguous terms. Accordingly, to the extent that the statements asserted a false claim of entitlement to enforce the contracts after their lawful terminations,

a jury would be authorized to find that the statements were false and that Southern Tradition and Martin Brothers had asserted a false claim to the properties.

Moreover, based upon the statements, a jury would be authorized to find that Southern Tradition and Martin Brothers were acting out of malice, with a purpose to harass the sellers and to bind their property. In addition, the statement's reference to bind or "tie[]-up" the properties recognized that a cloud on the title would exist during the pendency of the litigation. As such, the statements could reasonably be construed as having the effect of maliciously impugning the sellers' title to the properties. . . .

D. TORT REMEDIES RELATED TO THE CONTRACT

Although contract damages are generally only compensatory in nature, in the right situation a party to a real estate transaction can obtain tort damages. These damages can emerge from the direct contract relationship between a buyer and a seller, or they can relate to the undertakings and contractual relationships entered into with third parties involved in the real estate transaction.

SEXTON v. ST. CLAIR FEDERAL SAVINGS BANK
Supreme Court of Alabama, 1995
653 So. 2d 959

KENNEDY, Justice. The plaintiffs, William Jack Sexton and Marsha C. Sexton, sued St. Clair Federal Savings Bank ("St. Clair"), alleging breach of contract and breach of fiduciary duty. The Sextons appeal from a partial summary judgment (1) in favor of St. Clair on the Sextons' fiduciary relationship claim and (2) holding that the Sextons could not recover certain damages on their breach of contract claim.

This case arose out of a loan agreement between the Sextons and St. Clair, through which the Sextons borrowed approximately $160,000 from St. Clair to build a residence. The loan was secured by a construction mortgage. The loan agreement provided that St. Clair was to disburse the loan proceeds in increments approximating the stage of construction of the residence.

Several weeks after construction had started, St. Clair notified the Sextons that the stage of construction did not justify the amount of proceeds that had been drawn by the Sextons' builder. St. Clair advised the Sextons that, given the situation, it would not permit any more draws on the loan proceeds at that time. According to the Sextons, they learned that all but $17,000 of the loan proceeds had been disbursed by St. Clair and that

approximately $93,000 of the monies disbursed had not been used by their builder on the construction of the residence.

The Sextons were unable to complete the construction, and they ceased making the required payments on the construction loan. St. Clair sued, seeking an order of foreclosure, the sale of the uncompleted residence to satisfy the indebtedness on the loan, and any deficiency that might exist after the sale. The Sextons counterclaimed, alleging that St. Clair had failed to monitor construction and to disburse the loan proceeds in proportion to the stage of construction consistent with the loan agreement. They alleged that St. Clair had thereby breached the loan agreement and had breached a fiduciary duty to them. In addition to punitive damages, the Sextons sought compensatory damages for what they claimed were their "direct, consequential, and incidental losses, including an amount for their mental anguish, emotional suffering, annoyance [and] inconvenience," and they sought to recover purported lost profits from their sale of investment property. They alleged that they sold that investment in an effort to raise money to complete the construction. . . .

As to the first issue raised by the Sextons—whether they can recover mental anguish-type damages—the trial court stated that in limited circumstances damages for mental anguish can properly be awarded on a breach of contract claim. The trial court correctly stated:

> Damages cannot be received for mental anguish arising from a breach of contract. There are exceptions to that general rule and they are as follows: "[W]here the contractual duty or obligation is so coupled with matters of mental concern or solicitude, or with the feelings of the party to whom the duty is owed, that a breach of that duty will necessarily or reasonably result in mental anguish or suffering, it is just that damages therefore be taken into consideration and awarded. . . . Another exception is where the breach of the contract is tortious, or attended with personal injury, damages for mental anguish may be awarded."

C.R. 211, *quoting* B & M Homes, Inc. v. Hogan, 376 So. 2d 667, 671 (Ala. 1979) (as *B & M Homes* quoted earlier cases). The court . . . concluded that, based on undisputed material facts, as a matter of law "the case . . . does not fall into those narrow exceptions.". . .

The Sextons argue that the trial court erred in so holding, and they emphasize the special nature of the breach of a contractual provision involving one's residence, as it relates to the applicability of the exception based on a "contractual duty" that is "coupled with matters of mental concern or solicitude.". . .

In the *B & M Homes* case, the plaintiffs sued a home builder, who had agreed to construct their new residence, but who did not do so in a workmanlike manner. The finished structure had "major defects." The plaintiffs sued on contract theories, and demanded damages for mental anguish. This

Court applied the exception, stating: "It was reasonably foreseeable . . . that faulty construction of [the plaintiffs'] house would cause them severe mental anguish. The largest single investment the average American family will make is the purchase of a home. The purchase of a home by an individual or [a] family places the purchaser in debt for a period ranging from twenty (20) to thirty (30) years." *Id.*

The contract provision alleged to have been breached in this case deals with the Sextons' residence. We observe, also, that this provision was apparently aimed at preventing the very kind of situation that the plaintiffs allege occurred here: the squandering of the means to build that residence, the construction loan proceeds. That provision states: "[T]he bank is authorized to disburse funds under its control [from the] construction loan account, together with the net proceeds of the loan, only in proportion to its Inspector's Report of Progress or by Architect's or Superintendent's Certificate accompanied by a proper affidavit from the contractor." A St. Clair employee testified that it is within the bank's "normal process" for bank personnel to discuss the "monitoring procedures" with construction loan borrowers, and he agreed that this was done "in part[,] in order so that the [construction loan borrower] will have some confidence in entering into [a construction loan] agreement—so that they will know that they are having some type of protection." C.R. 275–76. Consistent with this testimony, William Jack Sexton testified that a bank employee had gone "over the loan papers" with him and that the employee had "pointed out that the bank would monitor [disbursements]." According to Sexton, the employee told him "that the wording [of the loan agreement] was that it should not—the funds wouldn't be used for any other expenditures other than for our own home—personal home."

St. Clair argues that the contract allegedly breached contemplated matters regarding an anticipated residence, rather than a residence occupied by the plaintiffs.[2] St. Clair says that therefore this case is not generally "characteristic of the cases that fit the exception to the general rule," which, it says, involves situations in which the contract relates to a current residence.

We agree that the exception based on a "contractual duty" that is "coupled with matters of mental concern or solicitude" has been applied in situations involving contracts relating to a plaintiff's current residence. *See, e.g.,* Orkin Exterminating Co. v. Donavan, 519 So. 2d 1330 (Ala. 1988). However, the contract at issue in the *B & M Homes* case, where the Court held that the exception applied, related to construction of a future residence. Similarly, in Lawler Mobile Homes, Inc. v. Tarver, 492 So. 2d 297 (Ala. 1986), where the Court held that the exception applied, the contract related to the sale and delivery of a mobile home, the plaintiffs' future residence. Like the

---

2. St. Clair also emphasizes that "the Sextons never had to fear being cast out on the street, being battered by the outside elements or having to find temporary substitute shelter." Such a point would be relevant on the question of the degree of the Sextons' alleged mental anguish, a question not before us.

plaintiffs in this case, the plaintiffs in *Lawler Mobile Homes* were living else-where at the time of the contract, and the contract in *Lawler Mobile Homes* did not relate to the residence in which they were residing at the time of contract. . . .

Applying the reasoning of those cases to the situation here, we hold that a reasonable construction lender could easily foresee that a borrower could undergo extreme mental anguish if that lender breached a provision such as the one these plaintiffs allege was breached. Here, the provision alleged to have been breached, although it appears as part of a contract to lend money, unquestionably relates to the construction of the Sextons' residence. Clearly, the contractual duty created by that provision — to monitor the construction of the Sextons' residence and the disbursements related to that construction — "is so coupled with matters of mental concern or solicitude, or with the feelings of the part[ies] to whom [that] duty is owed, that a breach will necessarily or reasonably result in mental anguish or suffering." *B & M Homes*, 376 So. 2d at 671 (quoting earlier cases). . . .

Affirmed in part; reversed in part; and remanded.

Problem 7D

Amber, a single mother with two children, contracts to purchase a home from Jason for $400,000. Jason is developing a 50-lot subdivision with single-family homes on each lot. At the time of the contract with Amber, Jason has already sold 44 lots and has completed homes on 40 of them. Furthermore, 39 families have already moved into homes in the subdivision, several families more than two years ago. The homes in the subdivision are all on two-acre lots and have well water. The lot Amber purchased is typical, and Jason had to drill down 100 feet to reach the water table to supply well water to the house.

Jason acquired the property, 100 acres of vacant land, from Energy, Inc. five years ago. Energy was conducting hydrofracking operations under the 100 acres that it sold to Jason, as well as under adjoining properties. The hydro-fracking process involves pumping water and chemicals under pressure deep into the ground to release petroleum and natural gas situated in the rock layers. At the time of selling the property to Jason, Energy had discontinued operations with respect to the 100 acres, and it advised Jason against using well water in his proposed development project. Energy advised that this was a precautionary approach and that Jason would need to take special steps in order to protect the water if he were to start drilling. They suggested that if Jason were to develop the property he should connect it with the city water supply.

Two months after moving into her new home Amber observed a difference in her well water. The water appeared cloudy and tasted bad. Jason told Amber to let the water stand in a jug in the refrigerator overnight and that it would taste, look, and smell fine in the morning. She tried this and it seemed to work. A few weeks later she learned that the substance in her water was a chemical used in the process of hydrofracking.

Amber looks into the matter and learns that there may be potential health problems for children from well water with high concentrations of the identified chemical. Amber is nervous about her children and loses sleep and gets headaches worrying about her water. She misses work several times.

Amber asks Jason to fix the problem by connecting the subdivision to the city water supply so that the home owners will not need to rely on well water. Amber worries about her children's health, so she starts buying spring water from the store. She keeps receipts to show that she spent $20 per week for bottled water.

Amber discovers that the city can hook her up to its water supply from a line that passes under a nearby street at a cost of $15,000. The city says that if Jason had set this up at the time he was building the subdivision the hookups would have cost $3,200 per lot, because they would have laid the line along ditches they were then digging for other utilities. The city also says that Jason was informed of this before he started any construction and before he contracted with Amber and others in the subdivision. Jason opted to work with well water because he had a well-digging business and could supply water to the homes by this method for $2,200 per lot.

(a) What type of contract damages, if any, might Amber recover? (Assume that she has been buying bottled water for 30 weeks at the time she brings this suit.)

(b) Should Amber be able to recover tort damages in connection with her contract problems? What issues should be addressed in such a case, and how might one go about setting the amount of recovery?

(c) Should Amber be able to file a lis pendens on Jason's six unsold lots in the subdivision?

8
Allocating Title Risk

A. TITLE UNDER THE REAL ESTATE CONTRACT

Title to the property is an important concern in every sale of real estate. Uncertainty about title constitutes a major form of historical risk. The risk of title error is historical in the sense that reaching a judgment about title involves the evaluation of evidence about the past. One of the primary reasons the real estate contract has an executory period is for the parties to handle title matters. Most parties do not obtain a title search prior to contracting; instead, they sign a contract on the assumption that most title issues will be manageable. All contracts deal with title by either an express term or an implied term.

In contracting about title, the starting point is the norm that the buyer has the right to *marketable title.* Some courts say the buyer has the right to *merchantable title,* a term that is synonymous with marketable title. The right to marketable title is an implied term of the contract, based on the parties' probable expectations. Marketable title disputes arise in many different contexts. Courts have used the term to address the merits of purchasers' objections to all of the following matters: defects in the record chain of title, outstanding possessory rights, future interests, mortgages, liens, easements, real covenants and equitable servitudes, zoning ordinances and other land use regulations, eminent domain, adverse possession claims, boundary disputes, encroachment of improvements, and access to land.

The marketable title provision operates to allocate risk between the parties. By entering into the contract, the seller impliedly promises that his title is marketable. This means that he has taken on the risk that a defect may be discovered that makes title unmarketable. If this happens, the seller has failed in his obligation under the contract and is responsible for damages.

In addition to being an implied promise, marketable title is an implied condition. The buyer's obligations to pay the purchase price and close the transaction are conditioned on title being marketable. If this condition fails, the buyer has no further obligation and does not have to go forward. The seller's title must be marketable only at the closing, not earlier. Moreover, when the land is subject to a mortgage or other lien, the seller may use the purchase price to satisfy that encumbrance.

Most written contracts, however, are not silent on the issue of title. Many contracts have an express promise by the seller of marketable title; instead of changing the implied term, the parties simply recognize it. Often contracts use equivalent terms — requirements that title be "good," "perfect," "satisfactory," "clear," or "with no defects" generally are treated as synonyms for "marketable title." Sometimes the contract language sets forth procedures for the title search, including time parameters for the buyer to make title objections.

On the other hand, many contracts define the quality of title that the seller must furnish and the buyer must accept. The parties specify what the seller's obligations are and what is acceptable to the buyer. This is sometimes referred to as *contract title*. Contract title may be more lenient than marketable title, or it may be more strict.

Two common types of contract title are *insurable title* and *record title*. When the buyer plans to obtain a title insurance policy, the contract often describes the type of policy that will be satisfactory to the buyer. The contract may provide that a title insurance company's willingness to issue that policy fully satisfies the seller's title obligations. In effect, the parties replace the courts, as the arbiter of marketability, with the insurance company.

Record title requires proof of the status of title, gathered solely from deeds and other instruments that are recorded in the public records for recording interests in real property. This means that the seller's title cannot depend on an unrecorded instrument, such as a deed that hasn't been recorded, a will that hasn't been probated, or a claim based on adverse possession.

A marketable title is not necessarily a *record* title. After a contract is signed, the title search sometimes reveals that the seller lacks record title to some or all of the real property but has evidence of title by adverse possession. When the parties have failed expressly to allocate the risk of adverse possession title, courts must come up with an implied rule for them. There is a split of authority on the question of whether title by adverse possession is marketable when the seller has not successfully litigated the adverse possession claim, but has strong evidence of the underlying elements. One position, followed by the courts in California and some other states, is that marketable title must be based on the records. If title depends on possible testimony of witnesses who might be called in an adverse possession case, this raises a reasonable doubt as a matter of law. Under this approach, the duty is on the seller to disclose, prior to contracting, the fact that he is relying on adverse possession to shore up his title. This approach, however, goes beyond a requirement that the seller disclose a known fact. Some sellers cannot disclose their plan to rely on adverse possession because they are ignorant of the state of their title.

The alternative judicial position, followed by New York and other states, is that title by adverse possession is marketable, provided that the seller can clearly establish the requisite elements. It is thus a question of fact whether such a title is marketable. The rationale for this view is that many titles are not perfectly shown by the public records but are subject to flaws that pose only a very remote risk of loss. This rule, in contrast to its opposite, can be seen as putting a disclosure duty on the buyer. The seller need not disclose reliance on the law of adverse possession; rather, the buyer who wants a clear title of record, not depending at all on the statute of limitations, must expressly bargain for such a term.

Problem 8A

(a) Sara contracts to sell Simpleacre to Baker. The contract says nothing about the quality of title Baker is to receive. A title search reveals that in a deed recorded in 1930, a prior owner of the land conveyed the land "so long as liquor is not sold on the premises." Is title marketable? Does Sara's present use of Simpleacre matter? Does Baker's intended use of Simpleacre matter?

(b) Would it make a difference if in the contract Sara promised to deliver "a fee simple title of record"?

(c) What if the contract has a condition that "title must be satisfactory to Buyer's attorney"? Does this allow Baker to terminate even if the risk of loss from the anti-liquor provision is remote?

1. Encumbrances and Encroachments

An *encumbrance* is a nonpossessory right or interest in the property held by a third party that reduces the property's market value, restricts its use, or imposes an obligation on the property owner. Encumbrances include easements, real covenants, equitable servitudes, marital property rights, mortgage liens, tax liens, and other liens and charges. An encumbrance does not negate the present existence of the seller's estate itself. For example, a defect in the nature of an outstanding cotenant's interest is not an encumbrance; it means the seller does not own 100 percent of the fee simple absolute estate. Courts generally define *marketable title* as an estate that is totally free from encumbrances. Yet there are a good number of cases holding that a particular encumbrance does not impair marketability. In many states, the law is not settled in this area. The result often turns upon the specific details of the parties' transaction.

An *encroachment* is an unauthorized extension of an improvement across a boundary line. This constitutes a trespass by the improver. Three types of encroachments are of concern to a purchaser. The improvements on the property under contract may encroach on neighboring tracts or on a street, or neighboring improvements may encroach on the property. Often the term *encroachment* is also used to describe a different locational problem. Improvements may be wholly located on the property in question, but they may improperly extend upon an easement, a setback area established by restrictive covenants or zoning, or other restricted space. All three types of encroachments generally render title unmarketable. When the seller's improvements encroach on the neighbor's land or a protected area, the purchaser may be required to remove the improvement or pay for damages. When the neighbor's improvements encroach, the purchaser may have lost title to the area covered by the encroachment under the law of adverse possession, or by virtue of principles of equity.

STALEY v. STEPHENS
Court of Appeals of Indiana, First District, 1980
404 N.E.2d 633

ROBERTSON, Presiding Judge. Paul R. and Suzanne B. Staley (Sellers) commenced an action against Paul L. and Carolyn A. Stephens (Buyers) as a result of Buyers' refusal to complete the purchase of Sellers' property. In their answer, Buyers counterclaimed for damages predicated upon Sellers' failure to tender marketable title. At the close of Sellers' evidence, Buyers moved for judgment on the evidence. . . . The trial court granted the motion and found for the Buyers on Sellers' complaint, and additionally, found against the Buyers on their counterclaim. We affirm in part and reverse in part.

There are in essence two issues with which this court must deal. The first concerns the question of how a slight infringement on a side line set back requirement effects marketable title as a matter of law. Secondly, we must address the trial court's denial of Buyers' counterclaim before Buyers had the opportunity to present any evidence on their claim.

. . . [T]he parties contracted for the purchase of a home, and Buyers tendered to the real estate agent $1,000 as earnest money.[1] The Buyers were to receive, at the closing, an abstract of title disclosing marketable title to the real estate. At the time of the original subdivision, the tract was divided into ten lots. A restrictive covenant of this original subdivision required a ten foot side line set back. At a later date, Lot #10 of the original subdivision was further subdivided, and at the time of re-platting, the side line set back requirements of the Town of New Haven were incorporated by reference into this further subdivision. At that time, the New Haven zoning ordinance

1. During the pendency of this action, the earnest money was delivered to the court, which held the funds pending disposition of the cause.

required a side yard set back line of 8.5 feet. Sellers' property was located in this second subdivision.

A survey was made of the property as called for by the purchase agreement, and revealed that a portion of Sellers' house was only 8.4 feet from the side line, in violation of the New Haven zoning ordinance. It further provided, in the restrictive covenants of this subdivision, that any lot owner could enforce at law or equity any attempt to violate or any violation of the covenants by either injunctive relief or by the recovery of damages.

Upon notification of this defect, Buyers requested that Sellers obtain waivers from the other landowners waiving this side line set back violation. Sellers refused to do this, whereupon Buyers determined that the title was not acceptable and refused to complete the purchase.

The parties stipulated quite a number of the facts, and among the stipulations was that the Allen County Bar Association had adopted a standard of marketability which indicated that violation of side line set back requirements contained in restrictive covenants should be waived as to residential lots if the improvements in question were completed and in place for at least two years prior to the date of the examination of the title. This standard of marketability, however, was not agreed to by the parties, even though the house was built in 1970.

We first note that the "two year statute of limitations" as adopted by the Allen County Bar Association has no legal effect, unless a contract is specifically referenced to that period, and merely serves as a guide to the parties and the Bar Association itself. The applicable statute of limitations as passed by the General Assembly calls for a twenty (20) year period within which actions must be brought upon contracts in writing other than those for the payment of money. Ind. Code 34-1-2-2.

. . . Kenefick v. Schumaker, 116 N.E. 319 (Ind. App. 1917), provides the basis for what little modern law there is on the subject of marketable title. In *Kenefick*, the court, after reviewing the standard espoused by commentators and applied in other jurisdictions, determined that the controlling test and more reasonable rule is that a title "which has no defects of a serious nature, and none which affect the possessory title of the owner, ought to be adjudged marketable." *Id.* at 323. . . .

What we are faced with in this case is a violation of between one-tenth of a foot and one foot six-tenths depending upon which restrictive covenant would be found controlling. The question that must be addressed is whether a title is marketable as a matter of law, notwithstanding a clear violation of a restrictive covenant.

A court of equity will not compel a purchaser to accept a title which is so doubtful that it may expose him to litigation, though the court may believe it to be good. Smith v. Turner, 50 Ind. 367 (1875). . . .

When viewed in this regard, it is evident that although the title defect is small, it is nonetheless a cloud on the title that may expose Buyers to the possibility of litigation due to the remedies available to other landowners in the subdivision. Even though a damage recovery may be nominal, Buyers would still incur the cost of defending against any litigation. Absent waivers from all landowners holding Buyers harmless, the possibility of litigation on the matter will not end until the running of the twenty year statute of limitations. Consequently, with the admitted cloud on the title, we are not prepared to say that the title was marketable as a matter of law. Therefore, . . . the trial court did not err in granting Buyers' motion for judgment on the evidence as to Sellers' complaint.

The second issue with which we must deal concerns the trial court's ruling on Buyers' counterclaim prior to the presentation of any evidence by the Buyers.

. . . We fail to perceive how a motion for judgment on the evidence can be granted as to the counterclaim, when Buyers, who had the burden of proof, were not able to present any evidence as to their claim. . . .

Judgment affirmed in part; reversed in part.

Problem 8B

(a) Stanford contracts to sell his home to Belinda, promising to convey "good title to the property free of all liens and encumbrances." The title search reveals that the driveway leading to Stanford's garage straddles the boundary line. The neighboring lot is presently vacant, but the neighbor and Stanford each have express recorded easements to use the entire driveway. Does Belinda have a valid objection to title? To make a valid objection, must she prove that the easement for the common driveway reduces the value of Stanford's property? Suppose that Stanford can prove that it has no effect on value whatsoever, what result?

(b) Belinda, your client, wants out of her contract. She confides that the common driveway doesn't trouble her in the least — she wants out because her brother-in-law has convinced her that she is paying way too much for the property. What advice do you give her? Will you write a letter to Stanford's attorney that terminates the contract? What should the letter say?

2. Effect of Public Regulation on Title

Zoning and other forms of land use regulation often have a critical impact on property value. When the parties have failed expressly to allocate the risks associated with zoning and other types of public land use regulations, disappointed buyers have sometimes sought judicial protection by arguing that title is unmarketable. For this reason, in many states there is often some confusion about the relationship between zoning and title or marketable title. One view treats title narrowly, looking only at evidence bearing on fee simple ownership of an estate and the existence of encumbrances consisting only of servitudes and liens. Other courts have taken a broader view of marketable title, using this concept to protect buyers whose expectations concerning property use and value are frustrated when certain zoning problems are encountered. This approach ignores traditional conceptions of what the term *title* means in property law, but achieves an outcome that may be defensible for reasons of policy.

SCOTT v. TURNER
United States Court of Appeals, Third Circuit, 2009
345 Fed. Appx. 761, 2009 WL 2965006

SMITH, Circuit Judge. This case arises from a 2006 land sale agreement between Peter and Anne Scott ("the Scotts") and Stephen and Nancy Hoke Turner ("the Turners"). The Scotts sued the Turners, claiming that they breached a contract to purchase land located in Freedom Township in Adams County, Pennsylvania. . . .

Section 403 of Freedom Township's Municipal Subdivision and Land Development Ordinance ("the Ordinance") requires roadways in the Township to meet certain specifications, including minimum right-of-way widths of 50 feet and minimum cartway widths of 32 feet. On February 11, 1993, landowners Bradley and Mary Yohe obtained a variance to these requirements from the Freedom Township Board of Supervisors ("the Board"). That variance permitted a 16 foot wide gravel "right-of-way" connecting one segment of the Yohes' lot to Pumping Station Road. The variance excused the right-of-way's non-conformance with the Ordinance so long as certain conditions were met. First, the variance was limited to the "period of time during which the [Yohes] own[ed] all of the land." The variance did "not extend to subsequent owners." Second, if the land in question were ever "subdivided to provide for more than three residential building lots," then the variance would be "void," and the right-of-way would have to be upgraded to conform with the Ordinance.

In December of 1993, the Yohes sold a portion of their land ("Lot 2") to the Scotts, while retaining part of it ("Lot 1") for themselves. The Scotts built a residence on Lot 2, which was serviced by the right-of-way through Lot 1. The Yohes later subdivided Lot 1, such that there are currently four residential lots on the tract of land described in the variance.

In October of 2006, the Scotts agreed to sell Lot 2 and an adjoining lot to the Turners for $1.25 million. That agreement required the Scotts to convey "good and marketable" title to the land. Pursuant to the agreement, the Turners paid a $50,000 deposit into escrow. Upon learning of the variance, however, the Turners refused to complete the sale. The Scotts sued the Turners for breach of contract; the Turners counterclaimed for the return of their deposit. Both parties moved for summary judgment. The District Court held that the Scotts, not the Turners, had breached the agreement by failing to provide "marketable title" to the land. The Court granted summary judgment in favor of the Turners and ordered the return of their deposit. The Scotts appealed.

Pennsylvania courts have defined "marketable" title as title "that is free from liens and encumbrances and which a reasonable purchaser, well informed as to the facts and their legal bearings . . . would in the exercise of that prudence which businessmen ordinarily bring to bear upon such transactions, be willing to accept and ought to accept." Barter v. Palmerton Area School Dist., 581 A.2d 652, 654 (Pa. Super. Ct. 1990). Under Pennsylvania law, title is unmarketable if it would expose "the party holding it to litigation." Swayne v. Lyon, 67 Pa. 436 (1871). We agree with the District Court that the Scotts' title was unmarketable because the variance permitting the gravel right-of-way expired, leaving the property owner exposed to a lawsuit by the Township to conform the right-of-way to the Ordinance. . . .

The Scotts admit that there are presently four residential lots on the land described in the variance. Therefore, the variance has expired. Given the non-conforming right-of-way and the expired variance, the township could sue the owners of the property and force them to upgrade the road at any time. As a result, the Scotts' title was unmarketable, and the Turners' refusal to consummate the sale was not a breach of contract. Rather, the Scotts breached the land sale agreement by failing to provide marketable title. We will therefore affirm the District Court's order granting summary judgment for the Turners.

Problem 8C

Susan and Ben contract to buy a three-bedroom house with no garage. The title search reveals neighborhood restrictive covenants that require a 20-foot setback from the side property lines. The zoning ordinance requires only 10-foot setback lines. A survey indicates that the house is 20.2 feet from one sideline and 30.8 feet from the other sideline. Nevertheless, Susan and Ben notify the seller that they are terminating the contract, stating that the restrictive covenants render title unmarketable. They claim they planned to add a garage to the house, and the 20-foot setback does not allow sufficient room. What result if:

(a) The contract requires the seller to convey "good and clear record title"?

(b) The contract says nothing at all about title?

(c) The contract requires the seller to submit to the buyer a "title report satisfactory to the buyer's attorney"?

3. Buyer's Remedies for Title Defects

Under contract law generally, when one party breaches, the other party is entitled to collect damages for loss of expectation, provided they are proven. The reason for the breach does not matter. For real estate contracts, the general rule applies, but with a major caveat. When the buyer seeks damages because the seller is unable to convey marketable title, many states follow the "English rule" announced in Flureau v. Thornhill, 96 Eng. Rep. 635 (C.P. 1776), which limits recovery to the earnest money plus any expenses incurred in reliance on the contract such as title examination costs. The buyer cannot recover expectation damages unless he can prove that the seller who is unable to convey marketable title has acted in bad faith. In contrast, other states have adopted the "American rule," which awards expectation damages under the normal rules of contract law.

JONES v. WARMACK
District Court of Appeal of Florida, First District, 2007
967 So. 2d 400

THOMAS, Judge. In the case we have before us, Appellant ("Buyer") appeals the trial court's entry of summary judgment below, which effectively authorizes Appellee ("Seller") to keep $200,000 in earnest money deposits paid by Buyer. Buyer argues that it is entitled to a return of its deposits because it was, in fact, Seller who first breached the agreement between the parties by failing to provide marketable title. We agree with the trial court that Seller's actions did not constitute an anticipatory breach of the contract, and affirm.

The dispute in this case involves an Assignment Agreement ("the Agreement") entered into between the parties, whereby Seller assigned his rights and interests in two identical underlying land purchase contracts ("the contracts") to Buyer in consideration for $14 million. The Agreement required Buyer to make three earnest money deposits to an escrow agent on dates certain. Buyer timely made the first two deposits totaling $200,000. According to the terms of the Agreement, Buyer's third deposit of $200,000 was due on February 8, 2005.

In both contracts, Section 4 states:

> 4. TITLE: Seller has the legal capacity to and will convey marketable title to the Property by statutory warranty deed, . . . free of liens, easements and encumbrances of record or known to Seller, but subject to property taxes for the year of closing; covenants, restrictions, and public utility easements of record; and . . . zoning, density, release of leases; provided there exists at closing no violation of the foregoing and none of them prevents Buyer's intended use of the Property as Commercial. . . .
>
> (b) Title Examination: Buyer will, within 15 days from receipt of the evidence of the title deliver written notice to Seller of title defects.

The contracts further provide that Seller had a "Curative Period" of ten days from the date of this notice to cure all title defects, but also note, "Seller may elect not to cure defects if Seller reasonably believes any defect cannot be cured within the Curative Period." If incurable defects were found, the contracts specifically gave Buyer ten days to either terminate the Agreement or accept title with the existing defects. The Agreement further specified that if one party breached or defaulted on any of the terms, the other party was entitled to the earnest money deposits.

On January 25, 2005, Seller timely provided a title commitment disclosing all requirements for, and exceptions to, the title insurance to be issued on the property. The next day Buyer provided Seller with a list of nine objections to the title.

On February 3, 2005, Seller responded to Buyer's objections, stating that although most of the listed objections would be cured at closing, some objections could not be cured.[1] In a letter to Buyer's counsel, Seller reminded Buyer that he now had ten days to decide whether to accept title or terminate the Agreement.

During this ten-day period, on February 8, 2005, Buyer's third deposit became due, and Buyer did not make the payment. On February 11, 2005, counsel for Seller notified Buyer that because Buyer failed to make the deposit required under the Agreement, Buyer was in default, the Agreement was terminated, and Seller was entitled to keep the $200,000 in earnest money deposits.

Later that same day, counsel for Buyer faxed a correspondence to Seller stating that Buyer did not accept the title as written and that Buyer wished to cancel the Agreement. Buyer argued that it was entitled to a refund of its $200,000 in deposits because this notification occurred within the ten-day time period set forth in the contracts.

Buyer filed suit below, seeking a declaratory judgment that it was entitled to a refund of its deposits. The trial court granted Seller's motion for summary judgment and entered its final judgment determining that Seller was entitled to the $200,000 in earnest money deposits.

We are asked to determine which party breached the Agreement first. If one party to an agreement has breached the agreement, the other party's failure to continue with the agreement is not considered a default of the contract. Buyer alleges that Seller committed an anticipatory breach of the Agreement when Seller failed to cure the title defects. If such a breach occurred, Buyer's failure to pay the third deposit is not a default. . . . Conversely, if Seller's actions did not constitute a breach, then Buyer's failure to pay the deposit would be a default of the Agreement, and Seller would be entitled to the deposits. . . .

Because the parties agreed that Seller had the right to choose whether to cure any title defects, and Buyer had the right to accept or reject title, Seller did not breach the contract. Under the language of the contracts as a whole, the parties did not intend the title to be without defect but, rather, to be the best title to which Buyer would agree; or stated a different way, a marketable title that satisfied Buyer.

1. The title objections that could not be cured included a power line easement, a mineral rights reservation in favor of the State of Florida, and objections to the plat.

We can find no reason for the remedial structure of section 4(b) to be included in the contracts other than to provide a means to resolve any objections regarding title. This provision gives Buyer the opportunity to raise objections, and Seller the option to cure those objections. The provision further gives Buyer the final say in accepting or rejecting Seller's cures. We do not accept Buyer's argument that Seller's delivery of a title with defects was an immediate breach of the Agreement, and all other provisions were superfluous. There is no language in the Agreement suggesting that, despite this remedial provision, defects in the title will terminate the Agreement.

We also note that under the terms of the Agreement, Buyer maintained his right to have ten days to consider the title offered by Seller. The act of paying the deposit was entirely separate and distinct from the decision to accept or reject the title. At the moment Seller informed Buyer that some defects would not be cured, Buyer had two contractual responsibilities: (1) pay the third deposit by the due date; and (2) inform Seller on or before the tenth day if the Agreement would be accepted or terminated. Buyer's adherence to one responsibility did not excuse performance of the other.

Accordingly, we agree with the trial court that the only breach that occurred was Buyer's failure to pay the third deposit. Thus, under the terms agreed to by the parties, Seller is entitled to the $200,000 in earnest money deposits.

Problem 8D

Andy contracts to buy a two-year-old house from Sara for $200,000. Neighborhood covenants and a zoning ordinance both require that all parts of the house be set back at least ten feet from the side boundary lines. A survey discloses that the eaves of the house are only eight feet from a side boundary line.

(a) Andy decides that the risk posed by the encroachment is remote and he notifies Sara that "I elect to waive the title defect." Meanwhile, Sara decides that she prefers not to sell the house to Andy for $200,000. She responds, "Title is not marketable and for that reason the contract is terminated." She tenders Andy his earnest money. Can Andy refuse and get specific performance?

(b) Andy decides that the risk posed by the encroachment is significant, but he still wants the house. He notifies Sara that he wants a price abatement equal to the cost of remodeling the roof to cause the eaves not to encroach. He has an estimate from a home improvement contractor to do the job for $8,000. Sara objects. What result?

(c) What result in (a) and (b) if the parties signed a contract of sale stating: "If Purchaser furnishes Seller with a written statement of objections to title, and Seller fails to satisfy any valid objections within a reasonable time, then, at the option of Purchaser, upon written notice to Seller, this contract may be cancelled and shall be null and void"?

B. DEED COVENANTS OF TITLE

A *deed* is an instrument that conveys an interest in real estate. Deeds tend to be more standardized than contracts of sale. Printed forms are very often used, not only for residential sales but also for commercial transactions. Deed forms vary substantially from state to state. In many states, a statute specifies a deed form that may be used, with many printed forms following the statutory suggestions.

1. Warranty Deeds and Quitclaim Deeds

Among the most important provisions of a deed are its covenants of title, or warranties of title. Their function is to allocate between the parties the risk of problems related to the quality of title that arise at any time after delivery of the deed. The parties should be certain that the deed they use accurately reflects their expectations about title and about what should happen if, after closing, a title problem of some sort is discovered.

At common law, no title covenants are implied; they must be express. The buyer, as grantee, must be sure that the deed spells out whatever guarantees of title the seller has undertaken as an express or implied part of their contractual arrangements. This principle is still the baseline American rule, unless changed by statute. In most states today, however, use of a certain phrase or a statutory deed form creates implied title covenants, which the statute specifies. These statutes vary widely from state to state, which is one reason why a lawyer licensed and knowledgeable about local real estate practice should draft or review the parties' deed.

Most deeds have general warranties of title. This means that the grantor's promises as to title are "general" in the sense that they cover the entire chain of title up to the time of delivery. With a *general warranty deed*, there are no time restrictions as to the title defects that are subject to the warranties. This gives the grantee the maximum amount of protection, with the grantor taking on all the title risk.

A *special warranty deed* offers less protection to the grantee than a general warranty deed. Unlike the general warranty deed, in which the grantor assumes all the title risk, the special warranty deed reflects a sharing of title risk between the parties. The warranties under a special warranty deed are limited to title matters arising while the grantor owned the property. All the grantor is promising is that since the moment he acquired title, he has not done anything to dilute or impair that title. Thus, while the general and special warranty deeds may contain all of the same warranty covenants, the scope of coverage is narrower under the special warranty deed. In some states, the term *limited warranty deed* is used instead of *special warranty deed*.

A *quitclaim deed* is a deed that has no covenants of title. In contrast to the general warranty deed and the special warranty deed, the grantee bears *all* risk associated with quality of title. If it turns out that the property is subject to liens, encumbrances, or other title defects, the grantor is not liable. Indeed, if the grantor did not own the property at all and a third party has paramount title, the grantor is not responsible — the grantee bears the entire loss.

In thinking about deed covenants, we should consider the prevalence of title insurance in modern real estate transactions. During the past several decades, the institution of title insurance has made deed warranties of title significantly less important than they were years ago. When title insurance is used, the insurance company as third party is being compensated to undertake the risk of title defects. When the buyer obtains a good title insurance policy, the nature and strength of the deed warranties of title are not as great a concern. At the same time, it is a mistake to believe that title insurance replaces the need to obtain a high-quality warranty deed. As we will see when we study title insurance in Chapter 11, title insurance policies have exceptions and exclusions that eliminate coverage for certain types of defects, along with other policy limitations on recovery. When an actual loss is not covered by title insurance, the grantee may have an alternative route of recovery by suing the grantor on the warranties in the deed. For this reason understanding the various deed covenants remains important.

EGLI v. TROY
Supreme Court of Iowa, 1999
602 N.W.2d 329

LARSON, Justice. When these plaintiffs, the Eglis, discovered a home being built on land they thought was theirs, they brought an action against the parties building the house, the Troys, as well as other adjoining neighbors, the Ransons, who the Eglis claim were also asserting dominion over some of the Egli land. The Eglis' action was brought under Iowa Code chapter 650 (1995) to establish ownership of the land by acquiescence.

The Troys and Ransons brought in their seller, Rosemary Greve, on a third-party petition asserting breach of a special warranty deed given to the Ransons (who later conveyed part of it to the Troys). The district court, Robert J. Curnan, Judge, entered summary judgment against the Troys and Ransons on their third-party claim against Mrs. Greve. Later, the court [received evidence and] ruled in favor of the Eglis on their claim that the property in question was bounded by a fence line. This is so, according to the court, because the fence line had been established for over ten years and the adjoining owners had acquiesced in the fence as a boundary. We affirm the acquiescence ruling but reverse the summary judgment in favor of the third-party defendant. . . .

The Eglis claim they own [two triangular parcels of land in Dubuque County] because they and their predecessors on the east side of the fence have treated the fence as the boundary, and the Troys, Ransons, and their predecessors on the west side of the fence have acquiesced in that boundary line for over ten years. . . .

When the Ransons purchased their property from Elmer and Rosemary Greve in 1988, part of it was purchased for cash, with a warranty deed, and the balance was purchased on an installment contract. The contract was paid off in 1996. In the meantime, Elmer Greve had died. When the Ransons paid off the contract, a court officer's deed was given to convey Elmer's share of the land to the Ransons. Rosemary Greve conveyed her interest by the special warranty deed now at issue. The deed provided in part:

> Grantors do Hereby Covenant with Grantees and successors in interest to Warrant and Defend the real estate against the lawful claims of all persons claiming by, through or under them, except as may be above stated.

The Ransons, relying on the covenants of this deed, seek protection in the event they lose on the Eglis' claim of title by acquiescence. The district court granted Greve's motion for summary judgment, ruling that Greve could not be held liable under any covenants of the deed because the suit by the Eglis was not a claim by "persons claiming by, through or under" her. . . .

We have not previously considered special warranty deeds under similar circumstances. . . . The Arkansas Supreme Court has stated a special warranty deed "simply warrants the title against all defects therein done *or suffered by* the grantor." Reeves v. Wisconsin & Arkansas Lumber Co., 42 S.W.2d 11, 12 (Ark. 1931) (emphasis added).

The issue before us is whether a grantor who has allegedly acquiesced in the establishment of an encumbrance on real estate is responsible for a claim "by, through or under" the vendor, as these third-party petitioners claim. We believe the warranty in this case covers claims permitted by the vendor as well as those affirmatively created by her. If that were not so, encumbrances such as mechanics' liens, which are imposed by others, would be excluded from the warranty. We do not believe that would be a reasonable interpretation of the warranting language.

The third-party defendant, Greve, . . . argues principally that, even assuming acquiescence can give rise to a claim covered by the warranty, any title acquired by her neighbors across the fence through acquiescence occurred long before she and her husband acquired title in 1964. Therefore, according to her, any acquiescence in the boundary line during the time the Greves owned the property would be irrelevant.

The acquiescence, if any, cannot be pinpointed in terms of time. In fact, the district court, in denying the Eglis' motion for summary judgment (in which they attempted to fix a pre-1964 acquiescence as a matter of law) stated, "the court cannot find as a matter of law that the boundaries were established by acquiescence prior to the Greves' 1964 purchase of the . . . property." . . .

... A genuine issue of material fact was generated as to whether the Greves were responsible for any part of the ten-year period of acquiescence. It was therefore error for the court to grant summary judgment in favor of Greve. We reverse and remand for further proceedings on the third-party petition. ...

SJ not approp.

2. Types of Covenants

The law of deeds recognizes six widely recognized covenants of title, each of which may be made general or special by incorporating the proper language for a general warranty or special warranty. Although the parties to a warranty deed are free to tailor their own covenants of title, expressing them as they please, in most transactions a combination of the six standard covenants suffices.

Three of the covenants of title are classified as *present covenants*, which means that the covenant speaks only to the state of affairs at the moment the deed is delivered. If a present covenant is breached, it is breached upon delivery. Thus, the statute of limitations generally begins to run at deed delivery. Present covenants do not run with the land; a grantee may sue only his immediate grantor on a present covenant, even though the statute of limitations has not expired on a covenant in a prior warranty deed in the chain of title. The following are present covenants.

Seisin. Under the covenant of seisin, the grantor promises he is seized of the estate the deed purports to convey. Historically, a person with seisin was in actual possession, claiming a freehold estate. Today, most courts view the covenant of seisin as a promise of good title to the estate.

Right to Convey. Under the covenant of right to convey, the grantor promises that he has the legal right to convey the estate the deed purports to convey.

Covenant against Encumbrances. Under the covenant against encumbrances, the grantor promises that there are no encumbrances on the land. It is generally accepted that the buyer's knowledge of encumbrances at the time of delivery of the deed does not preclude recovery against the grantor under this covenant. However, when the encumbrance is visible, many courts find an implied exception from the covenant against encumbrances.

The next three covenants of title are called *future covenants*. They protect the grantee from certain specified events that may occur after the deed is delivered in the future. Future covenants, in contrast to present covenants, run with the land, meaning that they protect successors in interest to the property. The present owner may sue not only his immediate grantor on a future covenant but also any remote grantor in the chain of title on future covenants contained in the remote grantor's warranty deed.

Covenant of Quiet Enjoyment. Under the covenant of quiet enjoyment, the grantor promises that the grantee may possess and quietly enjoy the land.

The covenant of quiet enjoyment is breached if the grantee is actually or constructively evicted from all or part of the land by the grantor, by someone claiming under the grantor, or by someone with paramount title.

Covenant of Warranty. Under the covenant of warranty, the grantor warrants the title to the grantee. Typically, the clause uses the terms "warrant and forever defend" the conveyed land. In most states, this covenant has the same scope as the covenant of quiet enjoyment; it is breached by an actual or constructive eviction of the grantee from all or part of the property. Upon breach, the grantor must pay damages for the grantee's loss of possession.

Covenant for Further Assurances. The remedy for breach of the first five covenants is damages, with most states limiting the grantor's liability to the purchase price received plus statutory interest. Under the covenant of further assurances, the grantor promises to give whatever "further assurances" may be required in the future to vest the grantee with the title the deed purports to convey. In appropriate cases, if the grantor refuses to give further assurances, thus breaching the covenant, the remedy of specific performance is available as an alternative to damages.

Strategically, one may have to frame a legal dispute in terms of breach of a future covenant if the statute of limitations has run on a present covenant. Likewise, if a grantee's immediate grantor has no assets, framing the issue as a future covenant breach permits one to sue an earlier owner in the chain of title because future covenants run with the land. Because the ability to recover on deed covenants often is limited, it is important for a buyer to obtain title insurance. This gives an injured party two possible routes to recovery — two bites at the apple, as they say.

Problem 8E

Nicole sells her 640-acre ranch to Kristin, delivering at closing a general warranty deed that contains all six standard title covenants, with no express exceptions. Four months after closing, Kristin discovers two problems. At the time of the conveyance, real estate taxes for the prior year were due and unpaid. Also, a footpath across the ranch goes from a neighbor's parcel to a lake that borders the ranch. It turns out that the neighbor, Ned, has an easement to use the footpath. Kristin demands that Nicole pay the taxes, along with a penalty assessed for late payment; plus, she wants damages due to the effect of the easement on the ranch. Nicole refuses, saying Kristin should have inspected and checked out these problems prior to closing and that merger applies.

(a) Who should prevail? Should it matter whether either party knew prior to closing that: (1) taxes were unpaid; (2) there was a footpath across the ranch; or (3) Ned periodically used the footpath?

(b) The state in which the ranch is located has a two-year statute of limitations for bringing an action on a deed covenant. Assume that Kristin first learns of the footpath easement two and one-half years after the closing when Ned proves that he has an unrecorded grant of easement, signed by Nicole's predecessor in title. Kristin has not seen Ned walking the footpath because he has been in Africa on assignment for the past three years and has left his home vacant. How, if at all, does the passing of time affect your analysis of the situation?

(c) What difference, if any, might it make in (a) and (b) if the transfer from Nicole to Kristin was by special warranty deed rather than by a general warranty deed?

BOOKER T. WASHINGTON CONSTRUCTION & DESIGN COMPANY v. HUNTINGTON URBAN RENEWAL AUTHORITY
Supreme Court of Appeals of West Virginia, 1989
383 S.E.2d 41

NEELY, Justice. The City of Huntington sold a parcel of city land to the Huntington Urban Renewal Authority so the latter could redevelop the property for residential use under a federal low interest loan program. The City sold this land by a general warranty deed for one dollar. The Authority executed an agreement to sell the land to the plaintiff/appellee, the Booker T. Washington Building Construction & Design Company, so the latter could improve the property and sell it to a private homeowner. The construction company built a residence but was unable to sell the property to its prospective purchaser because a title search revealed that the Authority had only a life estate in the property. The construction company never acquired title to the property.

The City purchased the property in 1981 from several members of the Mickens family. However, the deed to the City did not include conveyance by persons who were remaindermen under the will of Clarence E. Mickens. On 6 April 1984, the Booker T. Washington Company filed this action in the Circuit Court of Cabell County alleging the City and the Authority breached the contract because the Authority could not convey good and marketable title to the property as required by the contract. The construction company alleged that it suffered lost profits, interest, litigation expenses and other consequential damages. The construction company also alleged a willful and wanton refusal by defendants to cure the defect in the title and sued the City and the Authority for punitive damages. The City was dismissed as a defendant because it was not a party to the contract. However, on 6 September 1984, the Authority sued the City as a third-party defendant, calling upon the City to defend the title and to indemnify the Authority for any damages awarded against it and for costs and legal expenses.

On 4 January 1986, the City filed an action to condemn the property. By an Amended Final Order entered on 7 October 1986, the Circuit Court of

Cabell County declared fee simple title to be vested in the City.[3] The City then argued that because it eventually passed good title through its condemnation action, it should be dismissed as a defendant. The Circuit Court of Cabell County agreed and granted summary judgment in favor of the City, dismissing it from the suit.[4] The Authority appeals, assigning as error the circuit court's order granting summary judgment.

The City argues that the filing of the lawsuit by the Booker T. Washington Company was not a sufficient ouster to violate the general warranty covenant. . . .

The requirement that there be an eviction or equivalent disturbance of the enjoyment of the property as a necessary element for a breach of the covenant distinguishes this covenant from the express covenant of seisin. . . . The Authority argues that the lawsuit by the Booker T. Washington Company constituted a constructive eviction while the City argues that no constructive eviction took place. . . .

In the case now before us, the Booker T. Washington Company sued the Authority for a breach of contract based on the Authority's inability to convey a marketable title. The Authority then filed its third-party action against the City for a breach of the general warranty covenant contained in the deed from the City to the Authority. There is one old case from another jurisdiction where the grantor purported to convey a fee but had only title to a life estate and the court held that the covenant of quiet enjoyment was not broken until the life estate expires and the covenantee is evicted. *Maupin on Marketable Title to Real Estate* 379 n.22 (3d ed. 1921). However, that decision is not binding authority for us, and we believe such a holding to be untenable in this day of frequent land transactions. Certainly today, . . . the right to enjoy one's property necessarily includes the right to sell the property.

. . . Therefore, we hold that when the grantee of real property under a fee simple, general warranty deed contracts to sell the fee to a purchaser and, in fact, the grantee has only a life estate, if the purchaser sues the grantee for an inability to convey marketable title, the covenant of general warranty in the deed to the grantee is broken, and the covenantor, upon proper notice, is obligated to defend the title or be answerable to the grantee in damages.

However, two inter-related questions remain: What action was the City bound to take in defending the title?; and, What is the City's potential liability for damages? The Booker T. Washington Company has sought damages from the Authority not for the value of the remainder estate, but consequential damages including lost profits and the value of improvements apparently resulting from the Authority's alleged breach of contract. The

3. Although there was no conveyance by the City to the Authority after the property was condemned, when a vendor acquires title after a conveyance by general warranty deed, the subsequently acquired title inures to the benefit of the purchaser as if it had passed by the original deed. Clark v. Lambert, 47 S.E. 312 (W. Va. 1904).

4. The court also granted summary judgment in favor of the fourth-party defendant, the law firm that prepared the Abstract of Title for the City.

City eventually passed good title to the Authority at the successful conclusion of its condemnation action. What further liability, if any, does the City have to the Authority?

The general rule regarding the measure of damages in an action for breach of the covenant of general warranty was stated in Moreland v. Metz, 24 W. Va. 119 (1884):

> If a covenant of warranty is broken in Virginia or West Virginia, the measure of damages, when the land is entirely lost to the vendee, is the purchase money with interest from the date of the actual eviction, the costs incurred in defending the title and such damages as the vendee may have paid or may be shown to be clearly liable to pay the person who evicted him. But if the actual value of the land at the time of the sale be proven to be greater than the purchase-money with interest, & c., perhaps this actual value might be recovered in lieu of the usual measure of recovery.

Id. at 137–38.[10] If the purchaser suffers only a partial eviction, the measure of damages is the portion of the purchase money that represents the relative value of the land (or interest) lost compared to the value of the whole land (or interest). Butcher v. Peterson, 26 W. Va. 447, 455 (1885). . . .

In the case *sub judice*, the City did eventually correct the deficiency in the title through its condemnation action and passed fee simple title to the Authority. The general warranty covenant given the Authority by the City does not mean that the City must completely indemnify the Authority. The action against the Authority by Booker T. Washington Company is based on a breach of contract to which the City is not a party, and the plaintiff is claiming several types of consequential and punitive damages. Although these damages might stem from the inability of the Authority to convey marketable title, they are not damages that can be awarded the Authority against the City for a breach of the latter's general warranty. The damages for which the City might be liable under its general warranty of title are limited to the value of the remainder estate at the time of conveyance as determined from the actual value of the fee simple estate (the consideration paid is prima facie but not conclusive evidence of the actual value of the fee) and the costs and reasonable attorneys' fees expended by the Authority to determine the actual state of the title to the land.

Because the City was successful in condemning the land and eventually passed fee simple title, the City thereby mitigated its damages. However, because the City was put on notice (by being named a party defendant) that the title was allegedly defective, it should have initiated the condemnation action (or taken other ameliorative action) immediately rather than

---

10. The minority rule, followed by some of the New England states, is that the measure of damages for a breach of general warranty is the value of the land at the time of eviction, including the value of any improvements made before the eviction. 24 W. Va. at 138-39; 6A *Powell on Real Property* at 81A-148; Maupin, *supra* at 424-27.

waiting more than a year and a half before doing so. Therefore, should the Booker T. Washington Company recover damages from the Authority, the City will be liable to the Authority for interest on the value of the remainder estate from the date an answer was due on the plaintiff's original complaint until the final order in the condemnation action. In addition, the City will also be liable to the Authority for costs and reasonable attorneys' fees incurred by the Authority not to defend the breach of contract action, but to determine that the title to the property was defective. . . .

. . . If the Authority had desired to protect itself against the eventuality of a lawsuit and recovery against it by the construction company, it should have purchased title insurance before buying the property from the City. Commercial parties should know enough to purchase title insurance, particularly when planning to improve property. The concept of a general warranty deed is in many ways obsolete today, when title insurance can be purchased at a modest price with an almost absolute guarantee against title defects because title insurance lawyers seldom make mistakes.

Accordingly, the Circuit Court of Cabell County's award of summary judgment to the City of Huntington is reversed and the case is remanded for further proceedings consistent with this opinion.

Problem 8F

In 2009, Alice sells Orangeacre to Brian for $100,000 using a general warranty deed with all six covenants of title. In 2011, Brian sells Orangeacre to Chris for $120,000 using a special warranty deed with all six covenants of title. In 2012, Chris sells Orangeacre to Donna for $140,000 using a quitclaim deed. In 2013, Nasty, a neighbor, relocates his fence, moving it ten feet past the boundary line described in the deeds to Orangeacre. It turns out that Nasty has had paramount title to the ten-foot strip since 2007. Does Donna have a cause of action against any of the prior owners for loss of the ten-foot strip? If so, is there a limit to the amount of damages she may recover?

MAGUN v. BOMBACI
Superior Court of Connecticut, Judicial District of New Haven, 1985
492 A.2d 235

HIGGINS, Judge. The plaintiffs purchased the subject real estate, with dwelling house and improvements located thereon, by general warranty deed from the defendants on August 4, 1978. Among other provisions, the deed provided ". . . *with the buildings and all other improvements thereon.* . . ." (emphasis added.) The premises were conveyed free and clear of all encumbrances, except as mentioned in the deed. The deed contained no reference

Dribbly at issue

to the location of the driveway and/or sewer lines, or any other improvement.

From the evidence, it is established that part of the driveway and portions of the sewer lateral line were, in fact, located on property adjacent to the subject premises. This is the condition that existed when the defendants purchased the property in 1973 from the Stone Construction Company and when they sold the property to the plaintiffs in 1978. The evidence does not establish that the defendants had any definitive information concerning the driveway and sewer line problems until after they sold the property to the plaintiffs.

Issues w/ start Dribbly

The plaintiffs base their claim for damages on the theory in law that this factual situation raises a breach of the covenant against encumbrances.

An encumbrance includes every right to or interest in land which may subsist in third persons to the diminution of the value of the land, but consistent with the passing of the fee. Aczas v. Stuart Heights, Inc., 221 A.2d 589, 593 (Conn. 1966). It must be a lawful claim or demand enforceable against the grantee. Straite v. Smith, 111 A. 799 (Conn. 1920). The location of the driveway and sewer lines partially on the property belonging to another does not constitute an encumbrance against the fee herein conveyed.

encumbrance Definition

The habendum clause in the deed granted to the plaintiffs "the above . . . bargained premises with the appurtenances thereof. . . ." The plaintiff claims that sewer and driveway that encroach or are located on another's property are so related to the reasonable use of the bargained for property that they constitute appurtenances thereof. In effect, the plaintiffs claim that the defendants' lack of ownership of a portion of these alleged appurtenances constitutes an encumbrance on the property conveyed.

∏s argument

For something to pass appurtenant to land, two conditions must be satisfied: it must be something ①which the grantor has the power to convey, and ② which is reasonably necessary to the enjoyment of the thing granted. Whittelsey v. Porter, 72 A. 593 (Conn. 1909). Although the evidence would satisfy the second prong of this test, the defendants in no way had any power to convey that part of the driveway and sewer line located on property of another.

2 inlings

① at issue

It is evident that this situation has resulted from misapprehension of the parties as to what the actual factual situation was. The complaint in no sense raises any question of fraud or misrepresentation, nor, indeed, does the evidence tend to sustain any such theory of recovery.

The court recognizes that there are cases that appear to hold that the encroachment of a building on the purchaser's land upon adjacent property does constitute a violation of the covenant against encumbrances. Jones v. Carlson, 17 Conn. Supp. 109 (1950); Gamorsil Realty Corporation v. Graef, 220 N.Y.S. 221 (Sup. Ct. 1926); Fehlhaber v. Fehlhaber, 140 N.Y.S. 973 (App. Term. 1913). It appears, however, that the result in Burke v. Nichols, 41 N.Y.

670, 1 Abb. App. 260 (N.Y. 1866), is more nearly in conformity with Connecticut precedent as spelled out in *Whittelsey*. In that case, the house on the conveyed property encroached on adjoining land. The purchaser claimed that this encroachment constituted a breach of the covenants of the deed. That court disagreed and held that the rule was that land does not pass as an appurtenant to land. Since the adjoining land was not conveyed or described by the deed, the plaintiff had no claim against the defendant by reason of the failure of title to that portion of the house and fence that stood thereon. The court noted that no action could have been maintained for the breach of any of the covenants of the deed.

This court opines that this may be the core reason why many wise purchasers require a survey to establish the location of the improvements on land sought for purchase.

Accordingly, this court concludes that the evidence fails to establish a cause of action upon which relief can be granted. Judgment is hereby rendered in favor of the named defendants.

Problem 8G

Harold contracts to buy a house from Susan under a contract that guarantees that title is marketable, subject to "easements and restrictions of record." The contract provides for a general warranty deed, with all six covenants, to be delivered at closing. The contract says nothing about a survey of the lot, but Harold orders one. The surveyor prepares a survey, which reveals an underground water line, running from the city's water distribution system under the street through the side yard of Susan's lot, connecting to the house of an adjoining neighbor. The water line appears to be approximately 40 years old, and there is no recorded easement or other recorded document referring to or authorizing the water line across Susan's lot. Does Harold have the right to object to title prior to closing? If Harold completes the purchase without making an objection, can he then make a claim under the deed covenants?

Problem 8H

Your client, Maggie, agrees to buy Gina's home for $250,000, with the contract providing, "Seller will convey the property in fee simple by a warranty deed." Prior to signing the contract Maggie was concerned about the possibility of the neighborhood turning from owner-occupied housing to rental housing. Maggie determined that the current zoning is for single-family residential use, but this does not preclude long-term rentals to a single family, and might not be interpreted to preclude short-term or vacation rentals. Gina and Maggie discuss this issue several times, and at closing Gina tenders a special warranty deed conveying the property to Maggie "in fee simple so long as the property is never used for rental."Gina figures that the language of the deed should satisfy Maggie's concerns. Maggie is concerned about the deed and also is upset because home prices in the community have fallen during the contract executory period. She believes Gina's home is now worth $240,000 at the most. During the closing, Maggie turns to you and asks if she can avoid closing. What's your advice?

9

Land Descriptions

A. TYPES OF DESCRIPTIONS

Both real estate contracts and deeds must contain a description of the land. This is also true for other instruments that involve real property, such as mortgages, leases, covenants, and easements. The land description, often called the *legal description*, is a crucial part of the transaction. One of the requirements imposed by the statute of frauds is a written description; it is not sufficient that the parties orally agree to the location and size of the parcel.

There are three methods of land description in widespread use today. The oldest method is the *metes and bounds description*, which describes every boundary line of the parcel. It tells the reader how to draw a square, rectangle, or other geometric shape on the face of the earth. The description starts at a point of beginning, which is usually a corner of the parcel adjoining a public road. Each boundary line is defined by length and ''course'' (direction given by reference to a compass). See Figure 9-1. Surveyors indicate the course by divergence from the north-south line. In most communities today, surveyors use true north-south, rather than magnetic north-south.

All boundaries do not have to be straight lines. Many parcels adjoin bodies of water, where the boundary is defined by some aspect of the water's edge, which is irregular. On dry land, surveyors draw curved boundary lines, defining the curve by reference to an imaginary circle, which is specified by arc, chord, and radius. For an example, see the survey at page 246.

The second method of legal description is the *Government Survey System*. Developed by Thomas Jefferson for the Northwest Territories in 1785, the system divides land into townships and sections, using a system of square and rectangular grids. The federal government subsequently extended the scheme to much of the midwestern and western parts of the United States. The starting point for every government survey description is the intersection of a principal meridian (P.M.), a line of longitude which runs north-south, and a baseline (B.L.), a line of latitude which runs east-west. Each

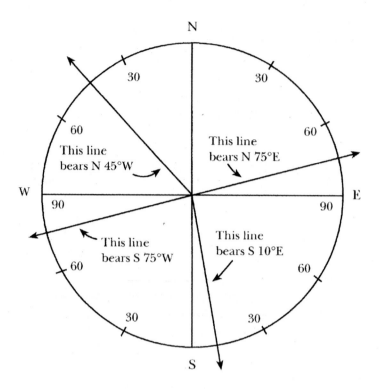

The circle has 360 degrees. Each degree contains 60 minutes, and each minute contains 60 seconds. All survey lines that are not due north, south, east, or west are described by the angle of divergence from the north-south axis.

Figure 9-1
Directions of Survey Lines

principal meridian and baseline is identified by a distinctive number or name. See Figure 9-2.

Under the government survey system, the basic units of area are *townships* and *sections*. Each township is a square with sides that are approximately six miles (we say "approximately" because small corrections are occasionally necessary to accommodate projection of the system on the globe). Each township is located by reference to the intersection of a principal meridian and baseline.

Notice that the term *range* denotes distance east-west along the baseline, and *township* denotes distance north-south along the principal meridian. An unfortunate feature of the government survey system is its use of the word "township" with two meanings: a unit of area (36 square miles) and a unit of distance (6-mile north-south increments).

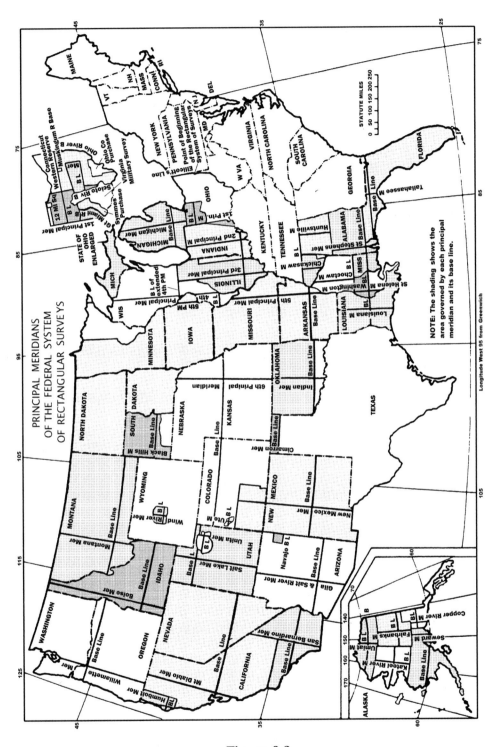

Figure 9-2
Map of Principal Meridians of Government Survey System

Each township is divided into 36 sections. This means that each section is a one-mile square, which contains 640 acres. The sections within each township are numbered. Section 1 begins in the northeast corner of the township, and numbers proceed back and forth, as follows, so that sections bearing consecutive numbers are always contiguous. See Figure 9-3.

6	5	4	3	2	1
7	8	9	10	11	12
18	17	16	15	14	13
19	20	21	22	23	24
30	29	28	27	26	25
31	32	33	34	35	36

Figure 9-3
Numbering System for Sections of a Township

Using the government survey system, one particular township in Arkansas is described as "Township 3 North, Range 2 West, 5th Principal Meridian." This describes the township in Figure 9-4.

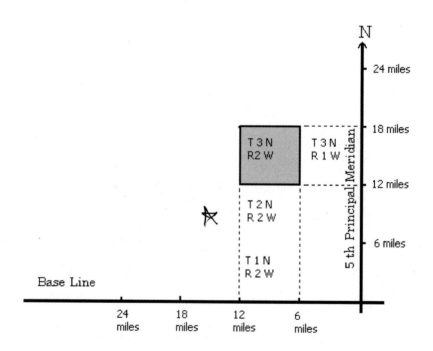

Figure 9-4
Location for Townships from P.M. and B.L.

Farmland, ranchland, and other rural lands are commonly sold in full sections and subparts of sections. The subparts typically used are half sections, quarter sections, and smaller square and rectangular units. In the Arkansas township mentioned above, one may convey part of a particular section using the following description: "The southern half of the northeast quarter of Section 17, Township 3 North, Range 2 West, 5th Principal Meridian." Abbreviations are commonly used. Thus, this description may be written as: "S NE, §17, T.3N., R.2W., 5th P.M." Look at Figure 9-5 to see if you can identify this land. It is customary to add the name of the county and state where the land is located, but legally this is not necessary. (Do you understand why?)

The third method of legal description is by reference to subdivision maps, or *plats*, which are filed as part of the public land records. Lots in the subdivision are then described by referring to the recorded plat. Much urban and suburban land, both residential and commercial, is described by this method.

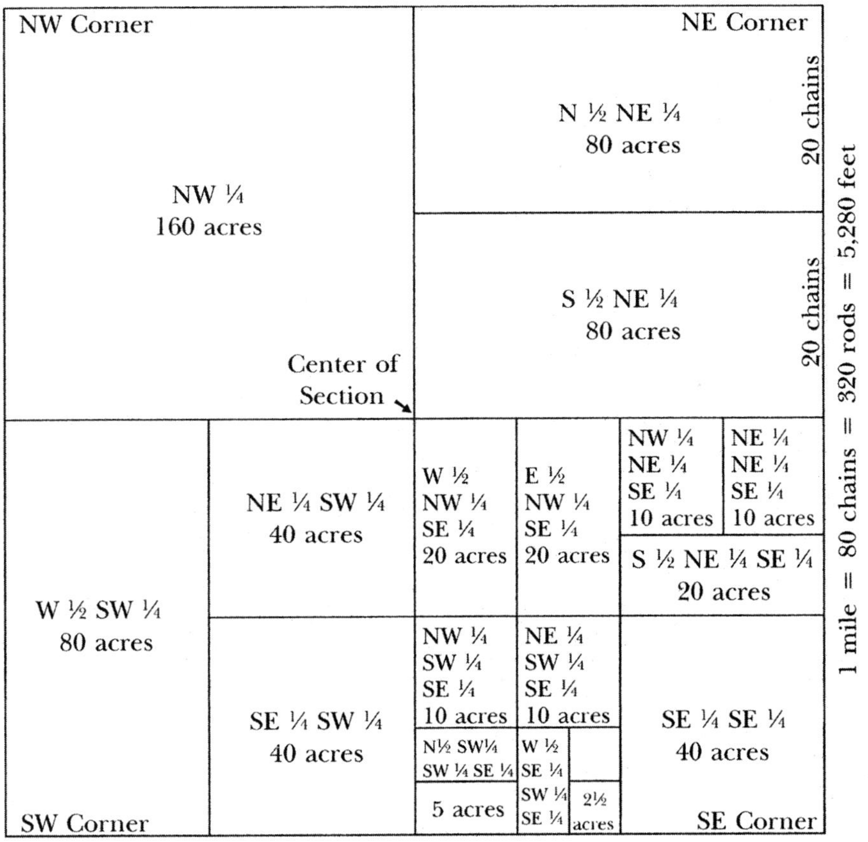

Figure 9-5
Section of Land (640 acres), Government Survey System

A good land description, it is often said, describes one and only one parcel of land. It permits the reader to find the described parcel, to the exclusion of all other parcels of land in the world. As a matter of logic, this means that all the boundary lines of the parcel must be capable of identification on the ground. One must be able to tell where one parcel stops and the neighboring parcels begin. The land near the boundary counts as part of the described land just as much as the land near the middle.

Boundaries must be identified to describe adequately a parcel of land. Thus, all good land descriptions are metes and bounds descriptions, either directly or because they are reducible to metes and bounds descriptions. Descriptions under the government survey system and by reference to subdivision plats, when properly crafted, work because they enable a reader to draw all the boundary lines. In each case, the reader must look not only at the deed but also at the government survey system reference points or the recorded subdivision plat; when this is done, the reader in effect has found a metes and bounds description for the subject parcel. The virtue of government survey descriptions and subdivision plat descriptions is efficiency. Both function as a type of shorthand, as they incorporate by reference an external, reliable system.

Problem 9A

What is the size, shape, and location of land described as follows?

N ½ of NE ¼, Section 20, T.2N., R.3E., 6th P.M.

Prepare a sketch that shows how to locate this tract, beginning at the intersection of the relevant principal meridian and baseline. In which state is this land located?

B. THE SURVEY

MITCHELL G. WILLIAMS & HARLAN J. ONSRUD, WHAT EVERY LAWYER SHOULD KNOW ABOUT TITLE SURVEYS
in Land Surveys: A Guide for Lawyers and Other Professionals 3 (American Bar Association 3d ed. 2012)

WHAT IS A SURVEY?

The word *survey* is derived from an old French word meaning "to look over" and refers to the process of evaluating real property evidence in order to locate the physical limits of a particular parcel of land. The real property evidence considered by the surveyor typically consists of physical field evidence, written record evidence, and field measurements. The surveyor, having made an evaluation of the evidence, forms an opinion as to where he believes a court would locate the boundary lines of the property. The typical modern-day surveyor sees himself as an expert evaluator of evidence, and would expect to arrive at the same opinion of boundary location regardless of who commissioned the survey. The surveyor's opinion is founded on experience and applicable legal precedents; unlike the attorney, the surveyor does not see himself primarily as an advocate for his client. . . .

. . . The evaluation of land surveying evidence is not a "science" in the sense that there is one procedure to follow which will yield the "correct" result. Surveyors occasionally disagree on the proper location of a boundary line — not necessarily because one surveyor measures better than the other, but more commonly because each surveyor has weighed the evidence differently and they have formed different opinions. Just as two lawyers may draw different conclusions from the same line of cases, surveyors may disagree about the appropriate location for a boundary. Because a survey is a professional opinion, it is subject to review by a court in the event that a boundary dispute reaches litigation. For the same reason, attorneys should remember that a survey and supporting documentation provided by one professional surveyor may be far superior or far inferior to that provided by another. Almost any field technician with basic training can make measurements with an acceptable degree of precision and replicability. In those instances in which locating the bounds of a land parcel requires an extensive amount of evidence evaluation, an individual with the requisite amount of education, knowledge, and experience should be employed to accomplish the survey with competence.

WHY A SURVEY?

There are six fundamental reasons for requiring land surveys in real estate transactions:

1. THE EXISTENCE OF THE PROPERTY

Nearly all titles to land in the United States depend on an original grant or patent and subsequent conveyance instruments. Each of these instruments contains descriptions of the land conveyed. It is a fundamental principle that for a deed to be valid it must contain a sufficient description. Whether a metes-and-bounds description or a description by reference to a parcel on a map is sufficient to transfer the property often depends upon whether a knowledgeable surveyor can interpret the description to reasonably locate the property physically on the ground. In determining whether the land description is sufficient, the surveyor determines whether the description forms a mathematically closed figure and whether the description reasonably conforms to the physical evidence on the earth's surface. The first determination is done by numeric calculation, the second by physical measurements in the field.

2. THE RELATIONSHIP OF THE PROPERTY TO ADJOINING PROPERTIES

Merely locating the lines described in a deed on the ground is not adequate to establish the physical limits of a property owner's interest. All parcels of land exist in relation to the parcels surrounding them. Surrounding parcels may include privately or publicly owned lands, rights-of-way, easements, roads, streams, and other bodies of water. At some point in the past, all adjoining land parcels were held in common by a single grantor. Over time, parcels were partitioned off or subdivided to arrive at the current ownership configuration. As a general rule, the description in a senior deed or prior conveyance controls over any discrepancy in a later one. If the drafter made an error or created an ambiguity in describing a parcel being partitioned off from a larger parcel, or made an error in a later attempt to "correct" or refine an earlier description, the legal descriptions of adjoining parcels may be inconsistent. The two descriptions of their "common" boundary may in fact either overlap or have a gap between them. Failure to discover overlaps may leave the holder of the junior deed owning much less property than the junior deed on its face would indicate. The presence of gaps or gores also poses problems when attempting to consolidate several adjacent parcels under a single owner for development purposes. When consolidation is attempted, one must definitively establish ownership to these leftover land strips. If a gap or gore exists along a street line or right-of-way, it has the potential of creating a landlocked parcel.

3. THE RELATIONSHIP OF OCCUPIED LINES TO RECORD LINES

Not infrequently, the boundary lines of a parcel as physically occupied or possessed by its owner differ from the distances and direction or the monuments called for in the deed. Discrepancies between possession and the record deed lines may range from minor variations in fence line locations to substantial encroachments of multistory buildings. A land survey should always show the occupied lines together with the deed record lines and the extent of any mismatch. Significant mismatches may suggest potential claims of ownership by senior right or adverse possession or a change in a boundary line by mutual agreement and acquiescence. . . .

4. THE LOCATION OF PHYSICAL IMPROVEMENTS

This reason for requiring a survey is related to the previous one, but deals with the relationship of all physical improvements on the parcel to the boundary lines of the parcel, not just those improvements near the exterior limits of the parcel. Features that surveyors are often requested to locate include fences, walls, driveways, pavements, buildings, structures, utilities, wells, and natural features such as streams and ponds. This information is necessary to determine the presence of features that may limit the value or use of the property, and to determine conformity to setback lines contained in recorded documents and with local ordinances regarding minimum building setbacks. It is also necessary to confirm that the improvements do not encroach upon easements or rights-of-way. . . .

5. Unrecorded Easements and Other Facts Not of Record

There are numerous unrecorded rights that can affect title to land which may not show up in a title search but will become obvious upon an inspection of the property. The right of a neighbor to use utility lines, drainage ditches, sewer lines, and unrecorded travel easements across the property may have arisen by prescription or other methods of unwritten land transfer. A visual inspection of the property will usually give some physical indication as to whether such adverse rights may exist; for example, the presence of manholes or vent pipes suggests underground sewers or other utilities. Typically, only a survey in which unrecorded physical features are referenced to the property lines will induce a title insurance company to remove its exception in regard to "any state of facts an accurate survey might show."

6. Water Boundaries.

Water boundaries are a complex subject, and details of ownership, usage rights, and location vary from state to state. . . . In general, a boundary defined by a body of water—for example, a creek, river, bay, or oceanfront—moves with changes in the course of the creek, river, or high-water mark over time, provided that the change is gradual; changes due to sudden causes, such as severe flooding or hurricanes, or changes due to actions by the property owner, whether gradual or not, such as building a dam, dredging, or filling, do *not* result in the movement of the boundary. It can be difficult to determine what caused a change in the course of a stream or in the high-water mark without historical research into old maps, deeds, and surveys. If the water in question is "navigable," a number of additional issues arise. A body of water is navigable if it in fact can physically be used for commerce or navigation, *e.g.*, a river or a lake connected to other navigable waters, or if it is subject to the ebb and flow of the tide, *e.g.*, oceanfront or bayfront property and tidelands. . . .

Types of Surveys

The above six reasons for obtaining a survey are fundamental in the case of a title survey. There are, however, many types of land surveys: boundary surveys, title surveys, topographic surveys, plot plans, subdivision maps, "as-built" surveys, and so forth. Each serves a different purpose, and they are not interchangeable. . . . Some attorneys believe that if they acquire an "as-built" survey, they have acquired the highest quality survey available. An "as-built" survey, however, is merely a detailed map of a building or other improvement and its relation, as built, to the *plans* it was built from. . . . The purpose of an "as-built" survey is to determine if the completed project

types

As-built Survey

accords with previously approved plans and specifications. . . . An attorney who uses one of these types of survey to advise a client about boundary and title questions flirts with malpractice.

THE PRESUMED PRIORITY OF CONFLICTING TITLE ELEMENTS THAT DETERMINE BOUNDARY LOCATION

A surveyor looks to legal principles as a guide in evaluating the evidence for a boundary line location. One such principle is the presumed priority of conflicting title elements that determine boundary line location. A right of ownership can arise from two sources: by written means (such as a deed or written boundary line agreement) or by unwritten means (such as adverse possession). The resolution of conflicts between written and unwritten rights is one of the most difficult problems for both surveyors and lawyers. . . . When such a conflict occurs, it is necessary to decide which terms were intended to control and which terms were informational. Which term is controlling generally depends upon its order of importance as determined by the courts. One summarized listing of a judge-made priority ranking among the terms of a deed is as follows:

1. Call for a survey
2. Call for monuments
   a. Natural
   b. Artificial
   c. Record boundaries (in the event of a gap)
3. Calls for directions and distances
4. Calls for directions
5. Calls for distance
6. Call for coordinates
7. Call for area

If the results obtained by adhering to the above ranking are clearly contrary to the overall intent expressed in the deed, however, the intent expressed in the deed will control.

The above priorities are based on assumptions about the relative certainty of each type of evidence. The presumption that directions should control when in conflict with distances is based on the assumption that one can determine angles and bearings more precisely than distances. In some jurisdictions, however, directions were historically observed with an imprecise magnetic compass and distances were measured with a precise steel tape; in these jurisdictions, courts held that distances should control over directions when in conflict. It makes sense that when the reasons for adhering to the presumed priority ranking no longer exist, the presumed ranking should fail and the best available evidence should prevail.

SAMPLE EVALUATION OF A PROPERTY LINE FACT SITUATION

In order to illustrate the land surveyor's use of the foregoing rankings in arriving at an opinion as to where property ownership lines are likely to lie, we present the following hypothetical facts. Alice owns the large parcel of land shown in [Figure 9-6]. The parcel was surveyed and corners monumented in 1932. There are no conflicts between Alice's lines and those of her neighbors. Alice sells a portion of her parcel to Betty in 1960. The land description in Betty's deed from Alice reads as follows:

Beginning at the NW corner of Alice's property as marked by a 2″ iron pipe; thence East along the centerline of White Road 400 feet to the center of the Jones Creek culvert; thence South 200 feet along Jones Creek; thence West 400 feet; thence North 200 feet to the point of beginning.

The information shown in [Figure 9-6] reflects the state of facts disclosed by a field survey. There are no fences, tree lines, hedges, or evidence of possession along the lines of Betty's parcel. There is no field or record evidence to suggest that Jones Creek has significantly changed its course since 1960.

How might a surveyor reasonably evaluate this evidence? One of the surveyor's obligations in accomplishing a land survey is to locate the title lines and then locate occupation lines with respect to those title lines. Under the given facts, it is proper to consult only the terms of Betty's deed description in locating the title lines.

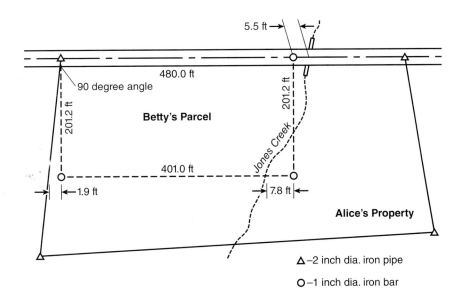

Figure 9-6
Sketch of Alice's Parcel

- The call for the 2-inch iron pipe is a call for an artificial monument, and if the surveyor can establish that the iron pipe actually found is the pipe called for in the deed, it fixes the location of the point of beginning. The found 1-inch diameter iron bars shown in [Figure 9-6] are not called for in the deed and, therefore, are not legally artificial monuments. There is nothing to suggest that they were set during a survey except that the bars are of a material and size typically used by surveyors in marking property corners and the bars are in the approximate locations where a current survey would place Betty's property corners. These uncalled-for monuments should be accepted as marking the southerly line of Betty's parcel only if the lines of this parcel are so uncertain that most surveyors would not locate the title lines in the same locations.

- In the first course, the call "to the center of the Jones Creek culvert" is controlling as a natural monument called for in the deed. The 400-foot distance called for is informational. It provides an approximate distance to aid in finding the physical corner called for.

- In the second course, the creek as a natural monument called for in the deed delineates the property line. Thus, the eastern line of Betty's parcel is synonymous with Jones Creek. If the called-for distance of 200 feet is accepted as controlling, it would be necessary to trace the sinuosities of the stream to find the southeast corner of Betty's parcel. . . .

- The call "thence West 400 feet" does not additionally say "to the east line of Alice's property." It appears unreasonable to assume, however, that Alice had intended to retain the small sliver of land that would result if the uncalled-for monument in the southwest corner is held as controlling. Additionally, when measured along Betty's southerly line, the creek is less than 400 feet away from Alice's west property line. Therefore Betty's parcel appears to be defined on its west end by Alice's west property line.

- The only side of Betty's parcel that has yet to be located is the southerly boundary. When considering the overall written intentions of the parties to the deed, it appears that the parties intended to partition off a parcel in the northwest portion of Alice's property bounded by Jones Creek on the east, bounded by Alice's west line on the west, and having dimensions of approximately 400 feet by 200 feet.

- The sequence of the calls in a description is generally held by the courts to be immaterial. Therefore, reading the description backwards, one possible location for Betty's southwest corner is at a distance of 200 feet from the point of beginning along Alice's west property line. It would then appear reasonable to define the southerly line of Betty's parcel by a line extended from this monument and running easterly parallel to White Road. This would result in a configuration for the parcel in close agreement with the overall written intent of the parties.

- In the alternative, the court might find the southerly line of Betty's parcel to lie a perpendicular distance of 200 feet from and run parallel with the centerline of White Road. Because the grantor had the responsibility for making the description clear and failed to do so, any ambiguity in the description should be resolved in favor of the grantee. This configuration also closely agrees with the overall written intent of the parties. This is the solution that a large number of surveyors would probably reach.
- In some eastern states, particularly in rural areas, uncalled for monuments tend to carry substantial weight in the courts. In such jurisdictions, the court would probably strive to hold a straight line passing through the two 1-inch diameter bars as defining Betty's southerly property line. Due to the inconsistency in the dimensions between the monuments along the east and west bounds, however, it appears unlikely that a surveyor set the bars. They probably were set by a lay person to mark the approximate locations of the property corners and never intended to mark the precise actual locations of the corners. Under these facts, the 1-inch iron bars should not be held as marking the location of Betty's southerly line.

The primary purposes in presenting the preceding example are to illustrate the thought processes that a surveyor goes through in evaluating property line evidence and to stress that the location of property lines is more often a matter of legal opinion than scientific fact. . . .

Problem 9B

Study the survey set forth in Figure 9-7 (page 246) from the standpoint of a potential purchaser. How much does the survey tell you about the tract it describes? Review the six reasons listed by Williams and Onsrud for obtaining a survey. Does the survey satisfy all six criteria?

C. LEGAL ADEQUACY OF DESCRIPTION

Under the statute of frauds, all writings that affect title to land must contain a written description of the land. This is true not only for deeds but also for other instruments that usually are recorded—for example, easements, covenants, and mortgages—as well as instruments that usually are not recorded, such as leases and contracts of sale.

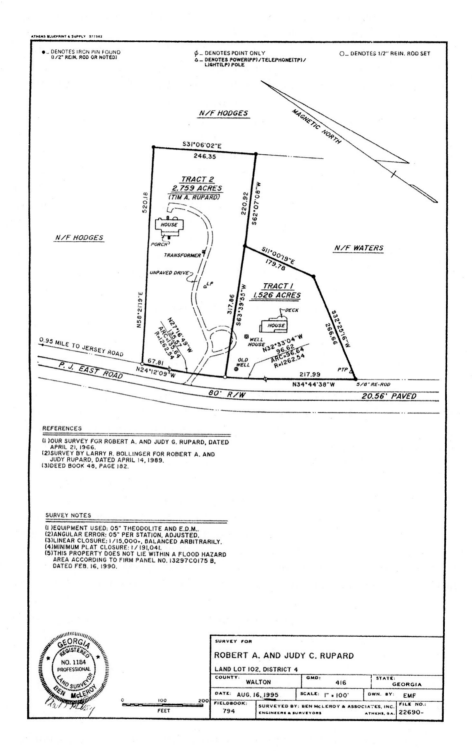

Figure 9-7
Sample Survey

Most statutes of fraud in the United States are tailored on the English model, enacted in 1677. The English statute of frauds treated contracts and conveyances in separate sections, and this separation remains a feature of modern U.S. statutory law governing real estate transactions. With respect to contracts for the sale of interests in land, the statute of frauds for contracts requires a memorandum, which as one of its elements must include a written description of the land. With respect to conveyances, a separate statute specifies the formal requisites for deeds and other instruments of conveyance; again, one of the requisites is a written land description. In most states, neither the contract statute of frauds nor the conveyance statute of frauds provides any express standard for assessing the sufficiency of the land description. This responsibility devolves to the courts. In most states, the judicially enunciated standards and interpretational rules appear to be the same, whether the description at issue is contained in a contract or a conveyance. A minority of states impose requirements on contract descriptions that are more lenient than those imposed on conveyances.

Compliance with the relevant statute of frauds is not the only concern for an attorney who deals with a land description to be used in a real estate transaction. A description may be good enough to comply with the statute but nevertheless cause problems. It may contain ambiguities or other flaws, it may be difficult to interpret, or its meaning may turn on extrinsic evidence that either is not readily accessible or is indeterminate. The problem, for example, may be only a simple error in the direction of line — the description reads "south 40° west 80 feet" when it must say "south 40° *east* 80 feet." Such an error, which may seem slight and hard to catch by proofreading, can have a drastic effect and make the description very different from what the parties intended. Whenever a description is less than totally clear, an owner may have to resort to costly and time-consuming litigation to obtain a definitive conclusion as to what the description really means. In the preceding example, the parties may mutually agree to correct the mistake in direction, but in the absence of agreement a party who wishes to enforce the deal will have to bring an action for reformation. This takes time and money and requires clear and convincing evidence of the true agreement. A good real estate attorney wants to avoid, not invite, judicial scrutiny of land descriptions. She aims not only to satisfy the minimum requirements of the statute of frauds, but also to employ a land description that is as clear, definite, and easy to interpret as is reasonably possible.

1. Descriptions in Contracts of Sale

When the parties to a contract of sale describe the land by means other than a formal legal description, anything can happen in court. In this area generalizations are risky, but two different judicial attitudes are displayed that can be viewed as polar extremes. One view strictly enforces the statute of frauds, requiring that the writing completely describe the tract by permitting the location of all boundaries, with no ambiguity and no need to look to extrinsic evidence. Under this view, all competent surveyors would arrive at the same outcome in applying the writing to the ground. At this end of the spectrum are decisions, reported in a number of states, that invalidate descriptions that fail to specify the county and state where the tract is located. The opposite view cares more about enforcing the parties' bargain in fact than about compliance with legal formality. It posits that when the parties have some written description of the land, the contract should be enforced if the land can be identified with reasonable certainty by supplementing the writing with extrinsic evidence (including oral testimony). Extrinsic evidence that doesn't contradict the writing may be used liberally. Many states cannot neatly be labeled as following one extreme or the other. Rather, the case law of a given state often reflects both strands, with decisions that may be reconciled on their facts but that are difficult to rationalize in terms of overall policy.

TR-ONE, INC. v. LAZZ DEVELOPMENT CO.
Supreme Court of New York, Appellate Division, 2012
945 N.Y.S.2d 416

PER CURIUM. In an action to recover damages for breach of contract, the plaintiff appeals from an order of the Supreme Court, . . . which granted the motion of the defendants Lazz Development Co., Inc., and Louis Larizza for summary judgment dismissing the complaint insofar as asserted against them.

On May 20, 2004, the plaintiff and the defendant Lazz Development Co., Inc. (hereinafter Lazz), entered into an agreement giving Lazz the exclusive right and option to buy property described as "approximately 48 acres of vacant land located at 89 Mount Tom Road, Pawling, New York." The agreement explained that "[t]he exact size and location of the parcel subject to this option is located primarily in the Village of Pawling and is to be defined and determined by a Survey map to be obtained by Optionee [Lazz] at its expense and which description will be agreed upon by the parties and then added as an exhibit to the contract of sale." The purchase price was set forth as a minimum of $1,600,000 with the ultimate price dependent on the future development of the property. . . .

The agreement was sufficiently detailed to identify the purchase price to be paid. . . . However, on the face of the agreement, it is impossible to identify the subject property with the degree of certainty necessary to satisfy the statute of frauds. *See* Cooley v. Lobdell, 47 N.E. 783 (N.Y. 1897).

By showing that the agreement was too vague to satisfy the statute of frauds, the defendants Lazz and Louis Larizza (hereinafter the respondents) made a prima facie showing of entitlement to judgment as a matter of law, tendering sufficient evidence to demonstrate the absence of any material issues of fact. . . .

Holding

Accordingly, the Supreme Court properly granted the respondents' motion for summary judgment dismissing the complaint insofar as asserted against them. The order is affirmed, with costs.

Problem 9C

Clarisse owned and lived on a 960-acre farm, which she inherited from her parents. To raise money to afford a comfortable retirement, she agreed to sell her farm to Mega Farms, Inc., for $5,760,000. When negotiating the deal, Clarisse told Mega Farms that she wanted to live in her farmhouse for the rest of her life and use the surrounding gardens, lawns, and orchard. Mega Farms' representative orally agreed. An attorney representing Mega Farms drafted the contract of purchase and sale, which the parties then signed. The contract contains a sufficient legal description of the 960-acre farm, pursuant to the government survey system. A special stipulation provides, "Seller reserves a life estate in her home and 20 acres of land immediately surrounding her home."

(a) Since the signing of the contract, farmland values per acre have declined markedly. Mega Farms refuses to close, arguing that the contract is unenforceable because the description of the life estate is too vague. Clarisse brings an action for specific performance. Who prevails, and why?

(b) Should it make a difference if, instead of specific performance, Clarisse seeks to recover damages or to retain Mega Farms' deposit?

(c) Suppose instead that the market value of farmland has not declined, and it is Clarisse who wants out of the contract. She raises the issue of vagueness. Mega Farms responds by saying she can draw the boundaries for the 20-acre tract any way she wants.

(d) Would it make a difference in any of the above situations if the contract said, "her home and surrounding 20 acres of land, shape and boundaries to be agreed upon by the parties"? Or if the contract said, "her home and surrounding 20 acres of land, shape and boundaries to be drawn by Seller"?

(e) Assume that the contract closes and a dispute arises one year later. Mega Farms seeks to evict Clarisse from the property. Clarisse asserts her right to be on the property because she has a life estate. It turns out that the actual deed signed by Clarisse at closing and recorded in the public records does not mention the life estate at all. The deed simply purports to convey a full fee simple to Mega Farms. Should Clarisse be able to avoid eviction based on the language in the contract? Would it make a difference if the deed failing to mention the life estate was not, for some reason, recorded in the public records?

2. Descriptions in Deeds and Other Recorded Instruments

When land is described in a deed conveying fee title or in other recorded instruments, a prime characteristic of the writing is its permanence. It becomes part of the chain of title for the property, to be retrieved and evaluated for many decades. This raises special concerns with respect to the quality of the land description, concerns that are not present in short-term contractual arrangements such as earnest money contracts, brokers' agreements, and many leases. For this reason, should the standards for validity and the introduction of extrinsic evidence be stricter for conveyances than for contracts? Or, instead, should the standards depend not on the type of instrument but on the presence of successors in interest? In other words, should a court be more willing to admit extrinsic evidence when the dispute is between the original parties who used the language, with no concerns for the expectations of third parties who may have relied on the written records?

We should also consider the fact that for recorded instruments, interpretation may occur many years after the writing was made, when the original parties are dead and gone. Proper interpretation may turn not only on the inferred intent of parties who cannot be consulted, but also on community norms and customs from the historical period in question. Even when it is clear that the deed is legally sufficient, difficult issues of interpretation may arise. For example, an ancient deed that conveys rural land "up to the hills" might mean the boundary is located at the foot of the hills or at the crest. *See* Padilla v. City of Santa Fe, 753 P.2d 353 (N.M. 1988) (1930 deed written in Spanish referring to "las lomas" boundary goes to crest; insufficient evidence of custom that Spanish deeds of this era conveyed only to bottom of hills).

WALTERS v. TUCKER
Supreme Court of Missouri, 1955
281 S.W.2d 843

HOLLINGSWORTH, Judge. This is an action to quiet title to certain real estate situate in the City of Webster Groves, St. Louis County, Missouri. Plaintiff and defendants are the owners of adjoining residential properties fronting northward on Oak Street. Plaintiff's property, known as 450 Oak Street, lies to the west of defendants' property, known as 446 Oak Street. The controversy arises over their division line. Plaintiff contends that her lot is 50 feet in width, east and west. Defendants contend that plaintiff's lot is only approximately 42 feet in width, east and west. The trial court, sitting without a jury, found the issues in favor of defendants and rendered judgment accordingly, from which plaintiff has appealed.

The common source of title is Fred F. Wolf and Rose E. Wolf, husband and wife, who in 1922 acquired the whole of Lot 13 of West Helfenstein Park,

[handwritten: Disagreement on lot size.]

[handwritten: Both get title from the Wolfs]

as shown by plat thereof recorded in St. Louis County. In 1924, Mr. and Mrs. Wolf conveyed to Charles Arthur Forse and wife the following described portion of said Lot 13:

> The West 50 feet of Lot 13 of West Helfenstein Park, a Subdivision in United States Survey 1953, Twp. 45, Range 8 East, St. Louis County, Missouri, ...

Plaintiff, through mesne conveyances carrying a description like that above, is the last grantee of and successor in title to the aforesaid portion of Lot 13. Defendants, through mesne conveyances, are the last grantees of and successors in title to the remaining portion of Lot 13.

At the time of the above conveyance in 1924, there was and is now situate on the tract described therein a one-story frame dwelling house (450 Oak Street), which was then and continuously since has been occupied as a dwelling by the successive owners of said tract, or their tenants. In 1925, Mr. and Mrs. Wolf built a 1½-story stucco dwelling house on the portion of Lot 13 retained by them. This house (446 Oak Street) continuously since has been occupied as a dwelling by the successive owners of said portion of Lot 13, or their tenants.

Despite the apparent clarity of the description in plaintiff's deed, extrinsic evidence was heard for the purpose of enabling the trial court to interpret the true meaning of the description set forth therein. At the close of all the evidence the trial court found that the description did not clearly reveal whether the property conveyed "was to be fifty feet along the front line facing Oak Street or fifty feet measured Eastwardly at right angles from the West line of the property . . ."; that the "difference in method of ascertaining fifty feet would result in a difference to the parties of a strip the length of the lot and approximately eight feet in width"; that an ambiguity existed which justified the hearing of extrinsic evidence; and that the "West fifty feet should be measured on the front or street line facing Oak Street." The judgment rendered in conformity with the above finding had the effect of fixing the east-west width of plaintiff's tract at about 42 feet.

Plaintiff contends that the description in the deed is clear, definite and unambiguous, both on its face and when applied to the land; that the trial court erred in hearing and considering extrinsic evidence; and that its finding and judgment changes the clearly expressed meaning of the description and describes and substitutes a different tract from that acquired by her under her deed. Defendants do not contend that the description, on its face, is ambiguous, but do contend that when applied to the land it is subject to "dual interpretation"; that under the evidence the trial court did not err in finding it contained a latent ambiguity and that parol evidence was admissible to ascertain and determine its true meaning; and that the finding and judgment of the trial court properly construes and adjudges the true meaning of the description set forth in said deed.

Plat ought to be viewed North to South

Q: What you call "measured width"

Attached hereto is a reduced copy of an unchallenged survey of Lot 13, as made by plaintiff's witness, Robert J. Joyce, surveyor and graduate (1928) in civil engineering at Massachusetts Institute of Technology, for use in this litigation. Inasmuch as the two properties here in question front northward on Oak Street, the plat is made to be viewed from the bottom toward the top, which in this instance is from north to south [see Figure 9-8].

It is seen that Lot 13 extends generally north and south. It is bounded on the north by Oak Street (except that a small triangular lot from another subdivision cuts off its frontage thereon at the northeast corner). On the south it is bounded by the Missouri Pacific Railroad right of way. Both Oak Street and the railroad right of way extend in a general northeast-southwest direction, but at differing angles.

Joyce testified: The plat was a "survey of the West 50 feet of Lot 13 of West Helfenstein Park." In making the survey the west boundary line of Lot 13 was first established. Lines 50 feet in length (one near the north end and one near the south end of the lot, as shown by the plat) were run eastwardly at right angles to the west line of the lot, and then a line was run parallel to the west line and 50 feet, as above measured, from it, intersecting both the north and south boundaries of the lot. This line, which represented 50 feet in width of Lot 13, made a frontage of 58 feet, 2³/₈ inches, on Oak Street, and 53 feet, 8³/₄ inches, on the railroad right of way. The line, as thus measured, comes within 1 foot, 1³/₄ inches, of the west front corner of the stucco house (446 Oak Street), within 1 foot, 7 inches, of the west rear corner thereof, and within less than 1 foot of a chimney in the west wall.

The trial court refused to permit the witness to testify, but counsel for plaintiff offered to prove that, if permitted, witness would testify that the methods used by him in making the survey were in accordance with the practices and procedures followed in his profession in determining the boundaries of lots such as was described in the deed. The witness further testified that the method used by him was the only method by which a lot such as that described in the deeds in question could be measured having precisely and uniformly a width of 50 feet; and that a 50 foot strip is a strip with a uniform width of 50 feet.

Defendants also introduced in evidence a plat of Lot 13. It was prepared by Elbring Surveying Company for use in this litigation. August Elbring, a practicing surveyor and engineer for 34 years, testified in behalf of defendants:

> In view of the fact that the deed (to the west 50 feet of Lot 13) made reference to the western 53 feet, and in view of the fact that the line which would have been established construing the dimension to be 50 feet at right angles, coming within a foot or so of an existing building (the stucco house), we felt that the line was intended to have been placed using the frontage of 50 feet on Oak Street and thence running the line (southward) parallel to the western line of Lot 13.

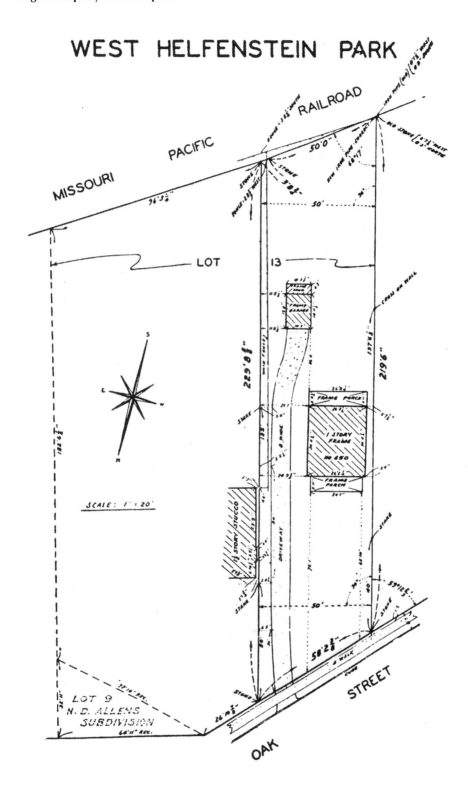

Figure 9-8
Map from Walters v. Tucker

The line so run, as being the east line of plaintiff's tract, was 8.01 feet west of the northwest corner of the stucco house and 8.32 feet west of its southwest corner. The Elbring plat does not show the actual width of plaintiff's tract as thus measured. But, concededly, there is no point on it where it approximates 50 feet in width; and, while it "fronts" 50 feet on Oak Street, its actual width is between 42 and 43 feet.

Both plats show a concrete driveway 8 feet in width extending from Oak Street to plaintiff's garage in the rear of her home, which, the testimony shows, was built by one of plaintiff's predecessors in title. The east line of plaintiff's tract, as measured by the Joyce (plaintiff's) survey, lies 6 or 7 feet east of the eastern edge of this driveway. Admittedly, the driveway is upon and an appurtenance of plaintiff's property. On the Elbring (defendants') plat, the east line of plaintiff's lot, as measured by Elbring, is shown to coincide with the east side of the driveway at Oak Street and to encroach upon it 1.25 feet for a distance of 30 or more feet as it extends between the houses. Thus, the area in dispute is essentially the area between the east edge of the driveway and the line fixed by the Joyce survey as the eastern line of plaintiff's tract.

Plaintiff adduced testimony to the effect that she and several of her predecessors in title had asserted claim to and had exercised physical dominion and control over all of the 50 feet in width of Lot 13, which included the concrete driveway and 6 or 7 feet to the east thereof. Defendants adduced testimony to the effect that they and their predecessors in title had asserted claim to and had exercised physical dominion and control over all of Lot 13 east of the driveway. The view we take of this case makes it unnecessary to set forth this testimony in detail. . . .

The law is clear that when there is no inconsistency on the face of a deed and, on application of the description to the ground, no inconsistency appears, parol evidence is not admissible to show that the parties intended to convey either more or less or different ground from that described. But where there are conflicting calls in a deed, or the description may be made to apply to two or more parcels, and there is nothing in the deed to show which is meant, then parol evidence is admissible to show the true meaning of the words used. . . .

No ambiguity or confusion arises when the description here in question is applied to Lot 13. The description, when applied to the ground, fits the land claimed by plaintiff and cannot be made to apply to any other tract. When the deed was made, Lot 13 was vacant land except for the frame dwelling at 450 Oak Street. The stucco house (446 Oak Street) was not built until the following year. Under no conceivable theory can the fact that defendants' predecessors in title (Mr. and Mrs. Wolf) thereafter built the stucco house within a few feet of the east line of the property described in the deed be construed as competent evidence of any ambiguity in the description. Neither could the fact, if it be a fact, that the Wolfs and their successors in title claimed title to and exercised dominion and control over a portion of the tract be construed as creating or revealing an ambiguity in the description.

Whether the above testimony and other testimony in the record constitute evidence of a mistake in the deed we do not here determine. Defendants have not sought reformation, and yet that is what the decree herein rendered undertakes to do. It seems apparent that the trial court considered the testimony and came to the conclusion that the parties to the deed did not intend a conveyance of the "West 50 feet of Lot 13," but rather a tract fronting 50 feet on Oak Street. And, the decree, on the theory of interpreting an ambiguity, undertakes to change (reform) the description so as to describe a lot approximately 42 feet in width instead of a lot 50 feet in width, as originally described. That, we are convinced, the courts cannot do.

The judgment is reversed and the cause remanded for further proceedings not inconsistent with the views expressed.

McGHEE v. YOUNG

District Court of Appeal of Florida, Fourth District, 1992
606 So. 2d 1215, review denied, 620 So. 2d 761 (Fla. 1993)

POLEN, Judge. This appeal concerns a dispute between neighbors regarding the boundary line between their property. Appellants, the McGhees, own lot 2 of the Rustic Hills development in Martin County. The McGhees filed a complaint for ejectment against Evelyn Young, the owner of lot 1. Lot 1 adjoins lot 2, with the south boundary of lot 1 forming the north boundary of lot 2. In its final judgment the trial court determined that the legal boundary between lots 1 and 2 was a line that corresponded with the location of certain monuments found in the ground, and was approximately equidistant from each parties' home, rather than, as appellants now contend, the line that corresponded to the metes and bounds descriptions contained in the parties' deeds and the recorded plat of Rustic Hills, which line cuts through Young's home, garage, and septic tank drain field.

The parties are in agreement for the most part as to the facts of this case, with one significant exception. The parties agree that the deeds to their respective lots contain metes and bounds descriptions that correlate to the plat of survey of Rustic Hills. They agree that the original surveyor of the land placed 4″ by 4″ concrete monuments in the ground while taking metes and bounds measurements of the placement of these monuments. The parties' deeds contain these metes and bounds descriptions and reference the minor plat of Rustic Hills, although this plat was not filed until sometime after several lots in the subdivision, including these two, were conveyed from the developer.

Where the parties disagree is on the location of those original concrete monuments placed in the ground. There was substantial competent evidence to support the trial court's finding that the monuments were located along the line that became the fence line between the McGhees' lot 2 and Young's lot 1, the boundary which the trial court ultimately determined to be the legal boundary.

Having determined that the placement of the monuments in the ground differed from the metes and bounds descriptions contained in the deeds and depicted in the minor plat of Rustic Hills, the question became [which should control, the monuments, or the descriptions as contained in the deeds and subsequently recorded in the plat?] The trial court applied the reasoning contained in Tyson v. Edwards, 433 So. 2d 549 (Fla. 5th DCA), *review denied*, 441 So. 2d 633 (Fla. 1983). . . .

In *Tyson* Judge Cowart noted the distinction between the role and practice of the surveyor and that of the lawyer, architect, or design engineer. The latter group is accustomed to reducing abstract ideas to paper and then relying upon the written document to achieve the original goal as written. In this case the written document is always considered authoritative and any deviation or discrepancy between this written document and what is actually done, is resolved in favor of "changing the physical to conform to the intention evidenced by the writing." *Id.* at 552. The surveyor, however, plays a different role and has a different practice with respect to his profession. While the original surveyor has a right or responsibility to establish new boundaries when he surveys previously unplatted land or subdivides a new tract, the sole duty of all subsequent or following surveyors is to locate the points and lines of the original survey by locating existing boundaries. *Id.* No following surveyor may establish a new corner or line, or correct erroneous surveys of earlier surveyors, when they track the original survey in locating existing boundaries. This is so because "man set monuments as landmarks before he invented paper and still today the true survey is what the original surveyor *did on the ground by way of fixing boundaries by setting monuments* and by running lines ('metes and bounds'), and the paper 'survey' or plat of survey is intended only as a map of what is on the ground." *Id.* (emphasis added). . . .

Applying *Tyson* to the instant case leads to the conclusion that the monuments, as located on the ground, control over the written descriptions of what the surveyor intended to do, that intention being evidenced in the deeds to the parcels as well as the later recorded minor plat of Rustic Hills. The correctness of this position is strengthened by a consideration of the ramifications of the alternative position. As Judge Cowart noted:

> Even if it were true [that application of this rule of law would require the "redrawing" of several lot lines], it is far better to redraw lines on a piece of paper to make them consistent with occupancy on the ground than to uproot and move all of the property owners who have in good faith erected homes, fences and other improvements in conformity with monuments on the ground, in order to make their actual occupancy and possession conform to what is erroneously shown on a piece of paper recorded in the courthouse.

Id. at 554 n.2. . . .

In summary, we conclude that the trial court correctly applied the principles recited in *Tyson* in determining that the monuments located on the ground between lot 1 and lot 2 should control as to the location of the legal boundary line. Although the McGhees argue that the trial court erred in finding that the monument located at point "L" was the *original* monument, the record contains substantial competent evidence to support the court's finding. The final judgment is affirmed.

SCHWARTZ, ALAN R., Associate Judge, dissenting. In my judgment, this case is not governed by Tyson v. Edwards, 433 So. 2d 549 (Fla. 5th DCA 1983), *review denied*, 441 So. 2d 663 (Fla. 1983), but by Rivers v. Lozeau, 539 So. 2d 1147 (Fla. 5th DCA 1989), *review denied*, 545 So. 2d 1368 (Fla. 1989). I would reverse on the authority of that decision.

Problem 9D

Julio has lived on a parcel of ranchland that he purchased 20 years ago. The deed to Julio describes the property as follows: "Beginning at the northwest corner of Section 14, Township 2 South, Range 3 West, 6th P.M.; thence south 20 chains; thence east 40 chains, thence north 20 chains, thence east 20 chains to the point of beginning." Your client is Francesca, who is negotiating with Julio to buy his property. Do you believe this deed is adequate to convey title to Julio? Does it matter whether any monuments can be found at or near the apparent boundaries of the property? Does it matter whether Julio obtained a survey 20 years ago when he bought the property? What course of action do you recommend?

Problem 9E

Your new client Goldy has just arrived at your law office with a boundary line problem and a confession to make. She owns a house in the suburbs on a one-acre lot. The neighborhood is about 25 years old. Three years ago, Goldy added a redwood fence to the backyard. She did the work herself but made a mistake. When she started, she looked for monuments for the back corners of her lot, but couldn't find them, so she guessed at the corners. Well, she guessed wrong. After she completed the fence and started clearing brush and digging to make flower beds along the fence line, she found iron pins for both corners approximately one yard in from the fence corners. Goldy moved the iron pins, pounding them into the ground just outside the two fence corners. Now everything's fine, right? Last week, Goldy's backyard neighbor, Spanky, stopped by. Spanky is selling his house, and his buyer insisted on a new survey. The surveyor, according to Spanky, says the iron pins are in the wrong location and should be on the other side of the fence.

Spanky asked Goldy who built her fence and whether she has any survey of her property. Goldy told Spanky she got a survey when she bought her house ten years ago, she hasn't had a surveyor on her lot since then, and she built the fence herself. This is all Goldy said to Spanky. Goldy believes either Spanky or his buyer will soon make trouble about the fence and boundary.

Goldy has told you her story. It's time for you to start talking. What's your advice and counsel for Goldy? Does it matter whether you are in Florida, where *McGhee* is precedent, or in a jurisdiction where a different rule applies or where the rule is unclear?

10

Public Records

The system of public records helps to resolve competing claims to land. To understand the system, it is important to have a firm grasp of how the common-law system resolves competing claims. At common law, the basic rule is "first in time, first in right." At common law, there is one exception to letting time decide priorities — between a prior equitable claim and a subsequent legal claim held by a bona fide purchaser without notice of the prior claim, the subsequent purchaser wins. The rationale is that because both grantees have an equity but only one has legal title, the legal title should control to break the tie.

All states have recording acts. These acts vary considerably from state to state, but they have a number of common features. The acts set up a system that provides for the recording of instruments that affect title to land. A deed or other instrument must be acknowledged before it qualifies for recording. Most instruments are acknowledged before a notary public ("notarized"), but other public officials, such as judges, also may acknowledge a person's signature of an instrument.

The recording system has two basic functions, the first being *title assur-* ① *ance.* The point here is risk reduction. Buyers and other persons who deal with property don't want their expectations about the quality of title to be defeated. The recording system reduces risk by providing a method for determining who owns a tract of land.

The second basic function of the recording system is to establish prior- ② ities when there are successive transfers of interests. Often successive transfers do not directly conflict (as when *A* sells Blackacre twice), but it is necessary to rank them. *Priority* means that the law determines who among various claimants has the superior, prior interest.

A. TITLE SEARCH PROCESS

Title search practices vary widely from state to state, and sometimes counties in the same state have different local practices. Notwithstanding local variations, the basic process for searching title has four common steps. First, the title examiner must discover the *chain of title*. Every parcel of land has a chain of title, the first link being the sovereign and the last link being the present owner. The best possible title search traces title back to the sovereign, reconstructing the entire chain of title. In most states, this is not done for most title searches. Custom, sometimes backed by state bar title standards or by legislation, dictates that the search typically goes back a set period, such as 50 or 60 years. In complex transactions or when significant values are involved, however, title searches may go back farther than the customary period, including going all the way back to the sovereign.

After the searcher has constructed the chain of title (at this stage, it's best to say the apparent chain of title), the second step is to look for *adverse recorded transfers* by the present owner and by all prior owners in the chain of title. To find these adverse transfers, the searcher checks the records of deeds and other instruments in the county where the land is located. An adverse transfer may upset the apparent chain of title by showing that a prior owner conveyed the land twice or that the apparent present owner has conveyed to someone else. Other adverse transfers do not jeopardize the conclusion that the apparent present owner actually owns the estate.

The third step is for the searcher to study full copies of all recorded instruments previously uncovered, both links in the chain of title and adverse transfers. Instruments in the chain may contain reservations, exceptions, easements, covenants, declarations (such as the declaration of condominium), or other matters. The searcher must read all the instruments that affect the chain of title to determine their content. The searcher must determine whether a deed transfers a full fee simple absolute title or something less and assess the content of servitudes, including locating the position of any easements. Formalities of all recorded instruments, such as the parties' names, the land descriptions, and acknowledgments must be examined. The searcher may find that some of the adverse transfers do not currently affect title. For example, the records often show satisfactions of prior debt obligations.

The fourth and last step is for the searcher to consult other records, in addition to recorded instruments, for adverse interests. These sources vary from state to state, but there are always other records that must be examined. Federal claims, such as tax liens and bankruptcy records, are kept completely outside of the state recording system. Many state-law-created claims against land are reflected in sets of records other than the land records; common examples are ad valorem taxes, lis pendens, judgment liens, and mechanic's liens. A title examiner will also check tax records, a survey, the zoning code, and other sources of information to gather the most complete file of information regarding the status of title to a property.

Also note that no matter how complete and diligent your title search, there are certain title risks that are impossible to discover from the records, such as forged deeds, fraudulent transactions, unrecorded interests, and improperly recorded interests. Consequently, after completing a title search, it is important to manage the risk of error with some form of title assurance. (Methods of title assurance are covered in Chapter 11.)

1. Index Systems

With thousands and thousands of recorded instruments on file, even in modest-sized counties, an index system is essential to find the relevant documents for a title search. In most states, the index system uses only the names of the parties to the deeds and other instruments. Typically, the indexes are printed and separately bound for each calendar year or for sets of years. A searcher uses the name indexes (often called *"grantor-grantee"* indexes) to construct a chain of title for the land by working backward from the present owner. When the searcher finds a deed into the present owner, the searcher takes the name of the grantor in that deed (the immediately prior owner) and looks for that name in the grantee indexes to find how that owner acquired the property. After the searcher constructs a chain of title of sufficient length, he uses the grantor indexes to check for the presence of adverse record transfers by each owner.

The other index system is the *tract index*, which divides all the land in the county into parcels and organizes deeds and other instruments according to the parcel or parcels they affect. Tract indexes are much better and easier to use than name indexes. Most states, however, organize their public land records only by name indexes, which are often required by state statute. Only six states have tract indexes in all counties. Several states have tract indexes for selected counties, sometimes initiated as a pilot program.

2. Electronic Title Searching

One of the most important recent developments in title searching involves the greatly increased availability of electronic recording systems. Now, many communities have electronic recording and searching capability for official public records involving real property. Today, many title searches are done online, electronically, depending upon the county and state and the nature of the property. In addition to mastering the search tools of the electronic system, the electronic searcher must fully understand the organization of the underlying land title records, including the details of the indexing system. As with a traditional paper search, the title examiner is looking for all matters that might affect title to the property. Knowledge of the underlying recording system and the search engine enables you to do an accurate and complete search and also informs you of the types of errors and risks that may arise for any particular search. The scope of the electronic records matters a great deal. Like paper records, the electronic records generally are not comprehensive, so it is necessary to consult other sets of relevant records. In addition, in many communities the electronic records go back only a given number of years, whereas the county's paper records usually go back to the beginning of the polity, making it possible to search title back to the sovereign.

Advances in technology, coupled with law reform, have allowed electronic title searching to flourish. Two major statutes facilitate the electronic filing of documents in lieu of traditional filing of paper originals: the Uniform Electronic Transactions Act (UETA) and the Uniform Real Property Electronic Recording Act (URPERA). These acts give legal validity to documents completed and recorded electronically. The search process of electronic title records follows the same basic steps as the traditional search of paper records at the county recording office; the difference is that the search can now be done electronically.

3. Sample Search

Duncan Doubtful has contracted to sell a house and tract of land to Hope Goodtitle, and a title search is necessary to see whether title is marketable. A title search thus is assigned to an attorney or other title professional, whom we will call Sara Searchwell. To get started, Searchwell may ask Doubtful how he got the land and, if by deed, for a copy of the deed. If Doubtful has title insurance, Searchwell will want a copy of the policy. As it turns out, Doubtful is unhelpful — he is unavailable, uncooperative, or simply not the type of guy who keeps any important papers where he can find them. Thus, all Searchwell knows is that Doubtful claims to be the present owner and that the contract has a legal description of the land: "Lot 7, Block 3, Shaky Heights Subdivision, according to the plat recorded in Vol. 19, Page 45 of the Plat Records of Luck County, State of Orange."

Like most states, Orange has name indexes for its records. Searchwell begins to use them by looking for Doubtful in the grantee indexes. After looking through several volumes, beginning with the current year and working back, she finds a deed to Doubtful in 2010:

Date	Grantees	Grantors	Type	Book	Brief legal
. . .	. . .	. . .	. . .	. . .	. . .
5–14	Doty, Stan	Freeman, Amy	Deed	54–17	Ten Oaks Subd
9–23	Doubtful, Duncan	Cramer, Christine	Deed	54–5	Shaky Hts Subd
6–20	Douglas, Betty	Stamp, Scott	Mortg	55–3	Lexington Rd
. . .	. . .	. . .	. . .	. . .	. . .

Figure 10-1
Partial Grantee/Grantor Index

She determines that Doubtful got his deed from a grantor named Christine Cramer. Now Searchwell must start looking for Cramer as a grantee prior to the conveyance to Doubtful — that is, Searchwell must make sure that Cramer had title to the property prior to granting it to Doubtful. When she finds Cramer as a grantee, she will then learn of Cramer's grantor and that will be the next link to trace back in the chain of title. If the remainder of the search is this easy (which is unlikely), all links in the chain of title may be documented by recorded deeds. Often, however, an apparent gap surfaces. Searchwell quickly traces title back to Gregory Brown, who in 1990 deeded the lot to Christine Cramer, but she then encounters a problem going further back. She can't find any person named Brown as a grantee for this property in any of the grantee index books for this century. Searchwell doesn't give up, but she has to do some detective work. Maybe Brown acquired the land by inheritance or devise, evidenced by local probate court records. In most states, probate transfers of land are documented only in the probate court records, without cross-reference or other indication in the land records. Perhaps Brown acquired the land by a deed that he never recorded. It's possible that a judicial decree quieted title in Brown, with the decree not reflected by a recorded instrument. Brown, for example, may have prevailed in court on a claim of title by adverse possession. If Brown is alive and can be located, Searchwell might ask him how he got the land. If Sara is unable to construct a chain of title of sufficient length, the present owner's title will not be marketable.

Searchwell does her work and finds probate court records showing that Brown inherited the land in 1970 from his aunt, Charlotte Agee. Returning to the recorder's office to plow through the grantee indexes for Agee, she finds a deed from Zippy Homebuilders, Inc., to Agee in 1950. In accordance with local title underwriting standards, searches in Orange usually go back only 50 years, so Searchwell stops here. Her chain of title is long enough to meet the local standard, without determining whether Zippy Homebuilders' title can be traced through the records back to the sovereign. The chain of title that Searchwell has put together looks like this:

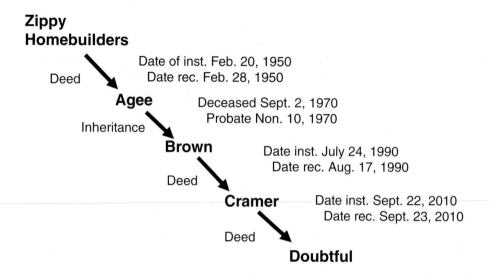

Figure 10-2
Partial Chain of Title

Now it's time for Searchwell to check for adverse record transfers. She uses the grantor indexes, beginning by looking under "Doubtful, Duncan" in the index volumes for 2010, when he acquired the property, through the present. She finds two entries, both mortgages: in 2010, to borrow money to buy the house, Doubtful granted a mortgage to Mean Mortgage Co., and in 2014 he granted a mortgage to Home Equity Loans of America. Searchwell then checks for any adverse transfers by Cramer, using the indexes for the years 1990 through 2010, finding a mortgage given in 1990 when Cramer bought the house. Repeating the process for Brown for the years 1970 through 1990, she finds nothing. For Agee, she finds a mortgage granted in 1950, a utility easement granted in 1951, and a set of restrictive covenants, which she and other neighbors entered into in 1952. Searchwell finds releases, which are recorded, for the two older mortgages (Agee's and Cramer's). Searchwell studies all the recorded documents, including the subdivision plat, which is a key part of the present legal description and is referred to in all instruments in the chain of title. The plat was recorded in 1949, the year before Charlotte Agee bought the house from Zippy Homebuilders. The plat apparently was recorded when the neighborhood was first developed; very probably Agee was the first owner of the house, having bought it new from the developer. Searchwell finds all the instruments, including the plat, to be in order. There is no indication that the old easement and covenants have expired. Searchwell checks the other sets of records in Luck County that reveal liens and other encumbrances, finding that the taxes are paid currently and finding no evidence of other problems. Her title report, therefore, is as follows:

> Duncan Doubtful has an estate in fee simple absolute, subject to (i) Easement from Charlotte Agee to Luck Power Co., dated May 4, 1951, recorded May 11, 1951, Vol. 45, Page 13, Deed Records, Luck County, Orange; (ii) Covenants dated Jan. 5, 1952 recorded March 23, 1952, Vol. 46, Page 32, Deed Records, Luck County, Orange; (iii) Mortgage from Duncan Doubtful to Mean Mortgage Co., dated Sept. 22, 2010, recorded Sept. 23, 2010, Vol. 132, Page 2, Deed Records, Luck County, Orange; (iv) Mortgage from Duncan Doubtful to Home Equity Loans of America, Inc., dated June 1, 2014, recorded June 4, 2014, Vol. 135, Page 340, Deed Records, Luck County, Orange.

Searchwell, as a prudent title examiner, is careful to disclose and qualify the scope of her search, and thus the limits of her opinion. Her title opinion states that she has not inspected the property, and unrecorded interests that affect title may exist. She has not ordered or seen a survey, and her search is not designed to disclose the boundary and title problems that an accurate survey would show. She stopped her search in 1950, and there is the possibility that older interests, validly recorded, are presently outstanding.

Date filed	Grantors	Grantees	Type	Book-Page
5–13–1949	Zippy Homebdrs		Plat	19–45
2–28–1950	Zippy Homebdrs	Agee, Charlotte	Deed	40–325
2–28–1950	Agee, Charlotte	Big Bank	Mortg	40–326
5–11–1951	Agee, Charlotte	Luck Power Co	Easement	45–13
3–23–1952	Agee, Charlotte	Shady Hts Owners	Covts	46–32
11–5–1961	Big Bank		Release	59–452
8–17–1990	Brown, Gregory	Cramer, Christine	Deed	95–320
8–17–1990	Cramer, Christine	Second Savings	Mortg	95–321
9–23–2010	Cramer, Christine	Doubtful, Duncan	Deed	131–598
9–23–2010	Second Savings		Release	132–1
9–23–2010	Doubtful, Duncan	Mean Mortgage	Mortg	132–2
6–4–2014	Doubtful, Duncan	Home Equity	Mortg	135–340

Figure 10-3
Shaky Heights Subdivision, Block 3, Lot 7
Plat Book Vol. 19, Page 45

If Searchwell has the opportunity to search title to Doubtful's property using a tract index, using either a private title plant or one of the few public tract index systems, the operation will be much faster and easier. With a properly maintained tract index, Searchwell looks up Shaky Heights Subdivision, and under that heading finds Block 3, Lot 7. Each tract typically has its own page in the index; tracts with many recorded instruments have several index pages. The page for Block 3, Lot 7 is as shown in Figure 10-3. Notice that everything Searchwell found and needed is referenced there, in one place, with the exception of the probate transfer from Agee to Brown. A tract index system, like name indexes, often fails to show probate transfers. Notice also that the tract index starts with the subdivision plat. If Searchwell wants to search further back, she needs to find out how the system is organized for pre-1949 records. Perhaps there is a tract index page for a larger parcel of land, which Zippy Homebuilders acquired and subdivided in the late 1940s. Perhaps the tract index system does not go back to a patent from the sovereign, and early name indexes must be consulted.

Searchwell obtained the same information for the buyer, Hope Goodtitle, whether she used name indexes or tract indexes. In our example, both systems worked satisfactorily, without flaws or errors. How is the title search used? Goodtitle will require that Doubtful obtain releases of his two mortgages at or before the closing. The lenders will agree to furnish those releases, of course, only if the existing loan balances are paid at or before closing. Does Goodtitle have the right to object to the easement or the covenants? How would you find out? (If you do not remember how to attack this question, review Chapter 8.)

B. TYPES OF RECORDING ACTS

Recording statutes modify the common-law "first in time, first in right" rule. Subsequent takers of interests sometimes beat prior valid interests that are unrecorded. The statutes expand the common-law rule that a subsequent legal *bona fide purchaser* (BFP) cuts off a prior equity. There are three basic types of recording acts, which specify when the subsequent taker defeats the prior taker.

The key idea for the *race statute* is that "the first to record wins." The race statute (sometimes called a "pure race" statute) evokes the image of two competing grantees in a footrace to the recorder's office. The first grantee to record wins, regardless of whether he has notice of the other claimant and regardless of which interest is prior in time. Only three states — Delaware, Louisiana, and North Carolina — have a race statute as their general recording act. There is a split of authority as to whether the subsequent grantee must pay value to cut off a prior unrecorded interest. The North Carolina statute explicitly requires the payment of value, the Louisiana statute explicitly does not, and Delaware law is not clear. Several states use a race approach for certain specialized types of conveyances. Ohio, for example, has a pure race system for mortgages.

The key idea for the *notice statute* is that "the last BFP wins." Under a notice statute, a subsequent purchaser who takes without notice of the prior unrecorded interest wins. If there are competing purchasers, each of whom claims to qualify as a BFP by paying value and taking without notice, the last BFP to take a conveyance wins. Notice is evaluated at the time the grantee pays value. There are three types of notice:

Actual Notice. The purchaser has actual knowledge of the prior interest.

Constructive Notice. The purchaser is deemed to have notice of all recorded interests, whether or not the grantee in fact searches title.

Inquiry Notice. If the purchaser has knowledge of facts suggesting that someone might have an unrecorded interest, the grantee has a duty to inquire and is charged with knowing whatever that inquiry would have revealed. The most important aspect of inquiry notice is a duty to inspect the land; the purchaser generally takes subject to the rights of parties in possession and other unrecorded interests that are visible from inspection.

The *race-notice statute* is a hybrid of the first two types of recording acts. The key idea is that among later competing claimants "the first BFP to record wins." The subsequent purchaser must both record before the holder of the prior-in-time interest records (as under a race statute) and take without notice of the prior interest (as under a notice statute). This means the BFP must do three things to prevail: pay value, without notice of the prior claim, and record first. Thus, the race-notice statute is less protective of BFPs than either a race statute or a notice statute. If there are competing purchasers, each of whom claims to qualify as a BFP, the first BFP to record his instrument wins. Almost all states have either a notice act or a race-notice act; these two types are about equally common.

The recording act, no matter which type, only protects a BFP against an off-the-record interest that is capable of being recorded — that is, a *recordable interest.* If a prior in time claimant asserts a property right that he is not permitted to place on the record, the recording act has no application to that claimant's dispute with a subsequent purchaser. Instead, common law must resolve the dispute, and it generally applies the "first-in-time, first-in-right" baseline.

Recording acts define what instruments should be recorded. Their scope varies from state to state, but in every state there are some interests in land that are not required to be recorded. There are two types of *nonrecordable interests*: those that cannot be created by instrument, such as claims of adverse possession, prescriptive easements, and marital property rights; and instruments that are not eligible for recording. For example, in many states, short-term leases are not recordable. The consequence of having nonrecordable rights in land is that a purchaser is bound by them, even though their existence is not ascertainable by a search of the records.

Often a prudent purchaser can detect these unrecorded interests by inspecting the land (for example, the adverse possessor may have remained in open, visible possession after expiration of the limitations period), but this is not always the case.

Problem 10A

A conveys Greenacre to B on April 1. B does not then record his deed. On April 5, A sells Greenacre to C, delivering a deed to Greenacre in exchange for C's payment of the purchase price. When C pays the purchase price, he knows that A conveyed Greenacre to B four days earlier. On April 6, C records his deed. On April 7, B records his deed.

(a) Who owns Greenacre under (1) a race statute, (2) a notice statute, or (3) a race-notice statute?

(b) Does it make a difference if the A-to-B transaction is a sale or a gift? (The term *conveys* does not tell us whether B paid anything.)

Problem 10B

A conveys Whiteacre to B on May 1. B does not record his deed and does not take possession of Whiteacre. On May 5, A sells Whiteacre to C, delivering a deed to Whiteacre in exchange for C's payment of the purchase price. When C pays the purchase price, he has no notice of A's prior conveyance to B. On May 6, B records his deed. On May 7, C records his deed.

(a) Who owns Whiteacre under (1) a race statute, (2) a notice statute, or (3) a race-notice statute?

(b) Suppose neither B nor C has recorded his deed, and it's now May 31. Who owns Whiteacre under each of the three types of statutes?

C. BONA FIDE PURCHASER STATUS

1. Notice from Records

A purchaser has constructive notice of any interest that is validly recorded. In most contexts, this straightforward proposition is easy to apply. The recorded instrument directly creates an estate or other interest in land, and any subsequent purchaser is therefore bound by it. Some records, however, refer to matters and transactions that are not themselves recorded, raising issues about the scope of constructive notice. A recorded deed may have a recital to a mortgage that is not recorded, or it may say that the grantor acquired the property from his mother by inheritance. A *lis pendens* that is recorded refers to ongoing litigation the outcome of which may affect title to real property; the pleadings and other filings can be located not in the real property records, but at the office of the relevant court. Parties sometimes decide to not record an entire instrument, but only a shorter memorandum; for instance, the parties to a commercial lease may record a Memorandum of Lease, which keeps the amount of rent and other details off record.

PELFRESNE v. VILLAGE OF WILLIAMS BAY
United States Court of Appeals, Seventh Circuit, 1990
917 F.2d 1017

POSNER, Circuit Judge. The district court dismissed Donald Pelfresne's suit against a municipality and a number of its officials and employees as barred by the Anti-Injunction Act, 28 U.S.C. §2283, and then refused to allow him to amend his complaint. The appeal presents interesting questions, rarely encountered in a federal court, of property law.

In November 1984 the Village of Williams Bay in Walworth County, Wisconsin brought suit in the Circuit Court of Walworth County against Michael Schiessle. The suit sought a court order to raze four single-family houses located on property owned by Schiessle in Williams Bay that were in disrepair and believed to be unsafe. The Village filed a notice of lis pendens (pending litigation) in the Walworth County registry of deeds.

The next month, December 1984, Schiessle conveyed the property to Lommen Eley and John Koch to hold in trust for him, whereupon the Village named Eley and Koch as additional defendants in its suit. The suit was dismissed in July of the following year (1985) on technical grounds and promptly refiled, but no new notice of lis pendens was filed. In February 1986 Eley and Koch conveyed the property to Anita Catania, but the conveyance was not recorded.

On June 25, 1986, judgment was entered for the Village in the refiled suit. The judgment ordered the buildings razed and also awarded the Village damages and costs totaling $629.42. The clerk of the circuit court, pursuant to statute, prepared the judgment docket card that appears at the end of this opinion. Wis. Stat. §806.10(1). The card notes the damages and costs but not the raze order.

In September 1987, months after the judgment in the circuit court action had become final upon the exhaustion of the defendants' appellate remedies, both the release of the notice of lis pendens in the first suit (the one that had been dismissed) and the deed to Catania were recorded in the Walworth County registry of deeds, along with another deed from Catania, this one made in 1986 or 1987 (the record is unclear which) to Allen Veren. Schiessle continued as the beneficial owner.

The day after these instruments were recorded, Pelfresne bought the property for $60,000 and ten days later he brought this suit, basing federal jurisdiction on diversity of citizenship. (He is a citizen of Michigan, while all the defendants are citizens of Wisconsin.) The suit depicts him as a bona fide purchaser for value who under Wisconsin law was not bound by the raze order contained in the judgment that had been entered against Schiessle, Eley, and Koch in June 1986. . . .

. . . The Anti-Injunction Act forbids a federal court to enjoin state court proceedings and the prohibition has been interpreted to bar an injunction against the enforcement of a judgment obtained in such proceedings, even though such an injunction is directed not against the state court itself but against the victorious party in state court proceedings, who is trying to enforce the judgment he obtained. . . .

[The district judge dismissed the complaint under the Anti-Injunction Act]. . . .

However, a stranger to the state court litigation — hence one who cannot be regarded as a litigant in state court, disappointed or otherwise — is not barred. . . .

. . . Only a party, or, what amounts to the same thing in contemplation of the law, one who is in privity with a party, is barred by the Anti-Injunction Act. County of Imperial v. Munoz, 449 U.S. 54, 59, 60 n.3 (1980).

The question of privity is central to this case. Pelfresne concedes that if the raze order issued by the Circuit Court of Walworth County is a lien on the property that he bought, then he is in privity with the defendants in the circuit court action. He further concedes that it is a lien on the property enforceable against him if he knew about the raze order when he bought the property, or if, though he did not know about it, he is treated by Wisconsin law as if he did: in legalese, if he had "constructive notice" of the order.

He may well have had actual notice. Schiessle has been the beneficial owner of the property throughout the elaborate series of transfers that preceded the sale to Pelfresne and that appear to have been motivated by a desire to escape the raze order, and Pelfresne is Schiessle's nephew. Either they are in cahoots or the uncle has tried to pull a fast one on his nephew; the fact that Pelfresne brought this suit to enjoin the raze order just ten days after he bought the property supports the former hypothesis. But there has been no finding of actual notice as yet, so we proceed to the question of constructive notice.

At first glance "constructive notice" may seem another of those unworthy legal fictions that contribute to the law's poor reputation among laymen. It means no notice, and its purpose and effect may therefore seem to be to pretend that a person who did not know something did know it. In fact, however, it is a mainstay of the system of protecting interests, both prior and subsequent, in land by means of a system of public records. One who records his interest in the proper records office is thereby protected against subsequent claimants and need not attempt to publicize that interest in any other way, and he is also protected against any prior claimants who by failing to record their interests had failed to provide notice in the prescribed manner.

But was the Village's raze order properly recorded? It was if it was within the "chain of title" of the property, a term that "includes instruments, actions and proceedings discoverable by reasonable search of the public records and indices affecting real estate in the offices of the register of deeds and in probate and of clerks of courts in the counties in which the real estate is located." Wis. Stat. §706.09(4). A purchaser of real estate has constructive notice of a prior interest if "there appears of record in the chain of title of the real estate affected . . . an instrument affording affirmative and express notice of such prior outstanding interest conforming to the requirements of definiteness of sub. (1)(b)." §706.09(2)(b). We go to subsection (1)(b) to discover those requirements and read there that "any conveyance, transaction or event not appearing of record in the chain" does not place a purchaser on constructive notice unless the conveyance, etc. "is identified by definite reference in an instrument of record in such chain" and that to be definite the reference must specify "the nature and scope of the prior outstanding interest created." In other words, even an instrument that appears in the chain of title will place a subsequent purchaser on notice of an interest created by that instrument only if it specifies the interest's nature and scope.

If the instrument in Pelfresne's chain of title is the judgment in the circuit court action, then since the judgment includes the raze order, the requirement of definite reference is satisfied and Pelfresne loses. That is what the district judge thought. If on the other hand the instrument is the judgment docket card, then Pelfresne's hand is greatly (though, as we shall see, not necessarily decisively) strengthened, for the card contains no definite reference — no reference, period — to the raze order.

To be in the chain of title, an instrument must, according to the passage from section 706.09(4) quoted earlier, be one "affecting real estate." So we must decide whether it is the judgment or the judgment docket that affects real estate, i.e., that creates a lien. We think it is the latter. Every judgment that is "properly docketed" creates, under Wisconsin law, a lien against real estate owned by the person or persons against whom the judgment is entered. Wis. Stat. §806.15(1). The Wisconsin courts take this specification literally: no docket, no lien. Wisconsin Mortgage & Security Co. v. Kriesel, 211 N.W. 795 (Wis. 1927). "[P]roperly docketed" means written up on a judgment docket card that is entered, alphabetically by the name of the defendant, in the judgment docket, in effect an index of judgments. Wis. Stat. §806.10(1). The card in this case was filed in triplicate, one card under the name of each of the three defendants in the Village's suit, and the card mentions no raze order. The judgment entering that order therefore was not docketed; did not create a lien, other than for $629.42, the monetary part of the judgment, which was entered on the card; therefore did not (with the same qualification) affect real estate; therefore (again with the same qualification) was not in the chain of title of Pelfresne's predecessors in title.

This may seem a cruel blow to the interests of creditors. It is not. The Village, the judgment creditor, could have filed the judgment containing the raze order in the registry of deeds. "[E]very conveyance, and every other instrument which affects title to land in this state, shall be entitled to record in the office of the register of deeds of each county in which land affected thereby may lie." Wis. Stat. §706.05(1). "[I]nstrument which affects title to land" is broadly construed. It includes equitable as well as legal judgments. Cutler v. James, 24 N.W. 874 (Wis. 1885). Although we can find no previous case involving raze orders, we think it must also include an equitable judgment that, in ordering the demolition of buildings, affected the defendants' title to the property that included those buildings. Surely the statutory term "land" includes the buildings on it, though this too is a question on which we find no cases.

The clincher is Wis. Stat. §66.05(8)(b), the statute under which the raze order was issued. It provides (in subsection (8)(b)(3)) that the order binds subsequent owners "if a lis pendens was filed before the change of ownership." This implies that a raze order creates an interest affecting land, and hence extinguishes the rights of subsequent purchasers, even if bona fide, provided it is properly recorded. No doubt this is why in its initial suit the Village filed a notice of lis pendens with the register of deeds. Once that suit was over, the notice was properly removed. The Village neglected to file a notice of lis pendens in the refiled suit; had it done so, then perhaps after it obtained the judgment it would, as it should, have replaced the notice of lis pendens with the judgment.

The fact that the docket card contains no space for an equitable judgment is telling. Such judgments, which affect the land directly, should be filed with the register of deeds. The clerk's docket is designed for money judgments, which merely by virtue of being entered and properly docketed become liens against any land that the defendant should happen to own; because of that automaticity, the filing of a mere money judgment in the registry of deeds would clog that registry with paper unnecessarily.

This may seem to conclude the case triumphantly for Pelfresne. Not so. Remember what section 706.09(2)(b) says: the purchaser takes subject to any interest of which he has "affirmative and express notice" from an instrument in the chain of title. The recording system is for the protection of purchasers (including creditors) who are "bona fide" in the sense not only of purity of heart but also of some minimum degree of carefulness. The docket card showing the money judgment against Pelfresne's predecessors was an instrument in the chain of title, and the language of "affirmative and express notice" has been held not to extinguish the traditional duty of "reasonable inquiry." Kordecki v. Rizzo, 317 N.W.2d 479, 483 (Wis. 1982). Anyone searching title on Pelfresne's behalf would first have gone to the registry of deeds and there found, in the file for the property that Pelfresne wanted to buy, the identity of the previous owners, including Schiessle, the equitable or beneficial owner, and Eley and Koch, two in a string of holders of the legal title. The next step, a step required by the statutory definition of chain of title as including instruments recorded in the office of the clerk of the circuit court for the county in which the property is located, was to look up these names in the judgment docket card file of the clerk's office. There one would have found—and there Pelfresne's title searcher, who had already found the deed to Eley and Koch in the registry of deeds, did in fact find—the card for the Village's judgment. Although the judgment was for a small amount of money, the fact that it was entered jointly against three recent owners of the land that Pelfresne was buying should have set the alarm bells to ringing. Almost certainly it was a judgment arising out of their ownership.

The duty of reasonable inquiry is a function in part of the burden of inquiry. It would have been a matter of minutes for Pelfresne's title searcher to look up the judgment and find the raze order in it. Especially when we consider the personal relationship between Pelfresne and Schiessle, the indications that Pelfresne was on inquiry notice of the raze order are very strong, and that is notice enough as we have seen to put him in the chain of title from the defendants in the Village's suit. A finding of inquiry notice, however, like other assessments of reasonableness, is one of fact. . . . We shall therefore remand for a determination of whether Pelfresne was on inquiry notice. Also open on remand of course is whether he had actual notice.

Affirmed in part, reversed in part, and remanded.

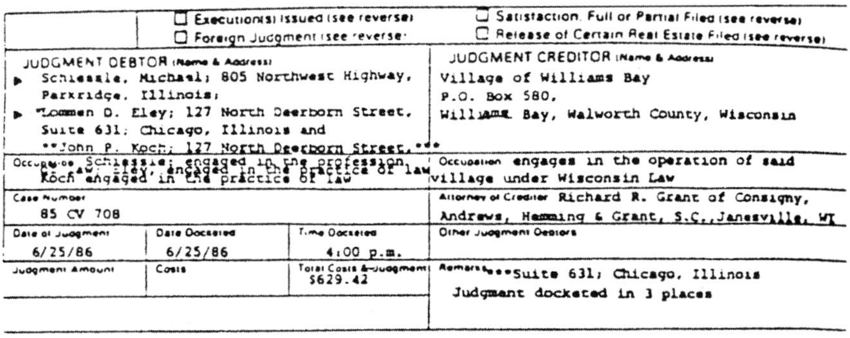
☐ Execution(s) Issued (see reverse)
☐ Foreign Judgment (see reverse)
☐ Satisfaction, Full or Partial Filed (see reverse)
☐ Release of Certain Real Estate Filed (see reverse)
JUDGMENT DEBTOR (Name & Address)
▶ Schiessle, Michael; 805 Northwest Highway, Parkridge, Illinois;
▶ *Lommen D. Eley; 127 North Deerborn Street, Suite 631; Chicago, Illinois and
John P. Koch; 127 North Deerborn Street,*
JUDGMENT CREDITOR (Name & Address)
Village of Williams Bay
P.O. Box 580,
Williams Bay, Walworth County, Wisconsin
Occupation Schiessle; engaged in the profession of law; Eley, engaged in the practice of law Koch engaged in the practice of law
Occupation engages in the operation of said village under Wisconsin Law
Case Number 85 CV 708
Attorney of Creditor Richard R. Grant of Consigny, Andrews, Hemming & Grant, S.C., Janesville, WI
Date of Judgment 6/25/86
Date Docketed 6/25/86
Time Docketed 4:00 p.m.
Other Judgment Debtors
Judgment Amount
Costs
Total Costs & Judgment $629.42
Remarks ***Suite 631; Chicago, Illinois
Judgment docketed in 3 places

Figure 10-4
Docket Card in Favor of Village of Williams Bay As Creditor

Problem 10C

Carla, the present owner of Pinkacre, has contracted to sell Pinkacre to David. Together, Carla and David hire a local attorney, Toby, to search title and handle the closing. Toby finds, as one link in the chain of title, a deed from Aaron, recorded in 2010, conveying Pinkacre to Byron "subject to a mortgage dated June 1, 2006, to Junior Morgan, securing a promissory note in amount of

$40,000." Toby conducts a complete search, finding no recorded mortgage to Morgan and no other evidence of record concerning Morgan's note or mortgage. The subsequent deed from Byron to Carla does not mention the mortgage to Morgan. Carla says she has not paid the mortgage loan and knows nothing about it. Toby decides that title is marketable and closing takes place, with Carla conveying Pinkacre to David by warranty deed. One month later, Morgan returns from a long stay at the Gray Bar Hotel somewhere in the Caribbean and demands that David pay the promissory note. David refuses. Morgan threatens to foreclose. Does Morgan have the right to foreclose? Assume the debt evidenced by the promissory note is not time-barred and Morgan has a valid but unrecorded mortgage, executed by Aaron, which secures payment of the note.

2. Defects in Recorded Instruments

Occasionally an instrument is recorded even though it does not meet the formal statutory requirements for recordation. When this happens, usually the defect relates to acknowledgment; all states limit recordation to documents that are properly acknowledged. Most courts, examining the language of their recording acts, have concluded that a defectively acknowledged deed does not impart constructive notice, because it should not be there. This means that the grantee who claims under the defective instrument has some risk of losing to a subsequent BFP. Some states have distinguished defects that are apparent on the face of the instrument, called *patent defects*, from defects that cannot be detected by studying the instrument, called *latent defects*. An instrument with a patent defect does not impart constructive notice, but one with a latent defect does so. A few states have reformed their recording statutes to eliminate the risk stemming from defective acknowledgment.

Recorded instruments may be defective for reasons other than improper acknowledgment. Deeds that are forged and deeds that were signed by the grantor but were not delivered to the grantee are deemed void, even though these defects are not ascertainable by looking at the deed itself. Labeling these deeds "void" means that the original owner can recover the land, even though the grantee under the void deed has sold the land to a BFP. In contrast, less serious defects are said to render a deed "voidable," but not void. For example, if a grantor is induced by fraud or misrepresentation to sign and deliver a deed, this makes the deed voidable, not void. This permits the grantor to recover the property as long as the grantee continues to own it, but protects a subsequent BFP who relies on the first grantee's apparent title. This distinction between void deeds and voidable deeds is closely analogous to the principles that apply to the bona fide purchase of personal property. *See* UCC §2-403.

In re *SIMPSON*
United States Bankruptcy Court, Northern District of Georgia, 2016
544 B.R. 913

WENDY L. HAGENAU, U.S. Bankruptcy Court Judge. . . . The parties dispute whether a security deed contains the requisite signatures and formalities to comply with Georgia law. The Court holds it does not, the defect in the deed is patent and, under Georgia law, the deed does not provide constructive notice to a bona fide purchaser. . . .

. . . On October 24, 2004, Debtor [Tammy Patricia Simpson] executed a second priority security deed for real property located at 2520 Brookwood Drive, NE, Atlanta, Georgia 30305 ("Security Deed") in favor of First Horizon Home Loan Corporation ("First Horizon") securing the repayment of a home equity line of credit. . . . First Tennessee is the current holder of the Security Deed.

The Security Deed was <u>recorded</u> with the Fulton County Superior Court on November 8, 2004 on pages 248 through 259 of Deed Book # 38801 ("Deed Book"). The signature page of the Security Deed is located on page 256 of the Deed Book ("Signature Page"). The pages immediately following the signature page include a page titled "GA Borrower Acknowledgment and Waiver" on page 257 ("Waiver Page") and a page titled "Rider to the Deed of Trust/Mortgage/Security Deed" on page 258 ("Rider"). Page 259, which is the last page in the collection of documents associated with the Security Deed, consists of a description of the property subject to the Security Deed.

The Signature Page is the source of the dispute between the parties. The page consists of two distinct sections. The top half of the page contains a section for the Debtor's signature and the attestation of Debtor's signature by witnesses, and the bottom half of the page is comprised of an acknowledgment clause. The Signature Page appears in [Figure 10-5].

The top of the page begins with the words, "*IN WITNESS WHEREOF, Borrower has signed, sealed and delivered this Security Deed. Signed, sealed and delivered in the presence of :*". Below these words is a line marked "*Witness*" which is signed with an illegible signature. Below that is a second line marked "*Witness*" which is blank. Across from the top witness line is a line marked "*TAMMY P SIMPSON, Borrower*" which is signed by the Debtor. The bottom half of the page contains language of acknowledgment, which reads "*Before me on this ___ day of ____, ____, personally appeared TAMMY P SIMPSON who acknowledged that he/she/they signed this Georgia Deed to Secure Debt as his/her/their own act.*" The official witness signature follows this language and includes the printed name, signature, and seal of notary Charles Weldon, but does not include the date.

The Debtor filed her bankruptcy petition under Chapter 7 of the Bankruptcy Code on April 3, 2015. . . . [T]he Trustee filed this Adversary

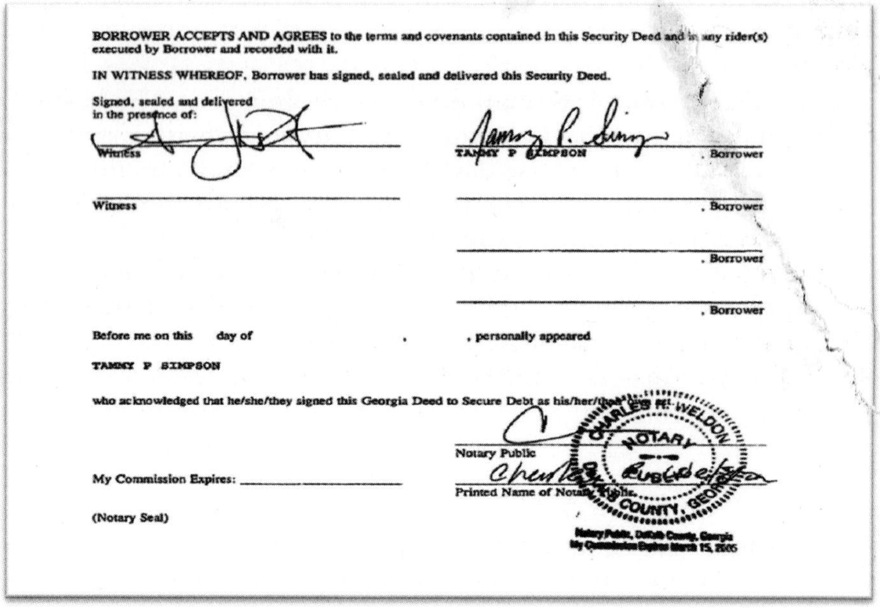

Figure 10-5
Signature Page

Proceeding . . . to avoid the security interest held by First Tennessee on Debtor's interest in the property. . . .

Under 11 U.S.C. §544(a)(3), a bankruptcy trustee may avoid "any transfer of property of the debtor or any obligation incurred by the debtor that is voidable by a bona fide purchaser of real property . . . that obtains the status of a bona fide purchaser and has perfected such transfer at the time of the commencement of the case, whether or not such a purchaser exists." A bona fide purchaser is not bound by any deed of which he does not have constructive notice. Under Georgia law, a security deed with a patent defect, even if recorded, does not provide constructive notice to a bona fide purchaser. U.S. Bank, N.A. v. Gordon, 709 S.E.2d 258 (Ga. 2011). A patent defect is one that is "obvious and easily detectable", while a latent defect "is not apparent on the face of the deed". Gordon v. Wells Fargo Bank, N.A. (In re Codrington), 430 B.R. 287, 292 (Bankr. N.D. Ga. 2009), aff'd, 716 F.3d 1344 (11th Cir. 2013). In other words, "[i]f the document appears proper on its face, and only matters outside the document create the issue, the deficiency is latent, but if the issue is identifiable on the face of the document, it is patent." Gordon v. Wells Fargo Bank, N.A. (In re Knight), 504 B.R. 668, 672 (Bankr. N.D. Ga. 2014).

A security deed must be attested or acknowledged as provided by law in the manner set forth for mortgages under Georgia law.

See O.C.G.A. §§44–2–14, 44–14–61. In order for a security deed to be "duly recorded", it must be attested or acknowledged by an "official witness" such as a judge of a court of record, a notary public, or a clerk or deputy clerk of a superior court or a city court, and it must also be attested or acknowledged by an additional "unofficial" witness. *See* O.C.G.A. §§44–2–1, 44–14–33.

The parties agree that the sole question to be decided is whether the Security Deed is patently defective. The Trustee asserts the Security Deed is patently defective because it lacks the attestation or acknowledgment of an official witness. The Trustee claims the official witness signature on the Security Deed is not a proper attestation or acknowledgment. First Tennessee argues the notary's signature should be construed as an attestation, and that the location of the signature on the page does not matter for that purpose. There is no dispute regarding the validity of the unofficial witness signature.

SUFFICIENCY OF SIGNATURES UNDER 2004 GEORGIA LAW

At the time the Security Deed was executed, Georgia law required signatures of both an official witness and an unofficial witness, and allowed for acknowledgment as well as attestation as alternate means of authentication. *See* O.C.G.A. §44–14–33 (2004 Ga. Code Archive).[1] Attestation and acknowledgment are distinct acts. Attestation is the act of witnessing the actual execution of a paper and subscribing one's name as a witness to that fact. *See* White v. Magarahan, 13 S.E. 509, 510 (Ga. 1891).[2] Acknowledgment is the act of a grantor going before a competent officer and declaring the paper to be his deed. *Id.* . . .

Georgia law does not require specific words or phrases for attestations or acknowledgments. However, certain commonly used recitals can be used to both identify and differentiate between attestations and acknowledgments. The form of attestation in common use recites that the witness saw the maker sign, or that he signed in the witness' presence. *See* Daniel F. Hinkel, *Pindar's Ga. Real Estate Law & Proc.* §19:63 (7th ed.). Though there are no specific words that are required for a valid attestation, the use of words or phrases such as "witness" or "signed in the presence of" have been deemed sufficient to indicate that a witness attested to the execution of a document.

---

1. O.C.G.A. §44–14–33 was amended, effective July 1, 2015, to read: "In order to admit a mortgage to record, it shall be signed by the maker, attested by an officer as provided in Code Section 44–2–15, and attested by one other witness." Legislative history indicates that while "the [former] language allow[ed] for acknowledgment as well as attestation", the change removing the acknowledgment language from the statute is meant to "clarify that only attestation will suffice in recording and executing [deeds]." Ga. H.R. Daily Rep., 2015 Reg. Sess. No. 40 (Apr. 7, 2015).

2. *Magarahan* was overruled by Leeds Bldg. Prods. Inc. v. Sears Mortg. Corp., 477 S.E.2d 565 (Ga. 1996), to the extent that a latently defective attestation would destroy the constructive notice of an otherwise improperly recorded deed.

An acknowledgment is generally identified by language found in the form of a "jurat" or certificate of acknowledgment, which is an explicit certification by a notary public that a person signing a document appeared before the notary and swore or affirmed that the assertions in the document were true. *See* 91 *Am. Jur. Proof of Facts* 3d 345 §8 (2006). Like attestation clauses, there are no specific words or precise form required for a certificate of acknowledgment; it only needs to state the fact of the acknowledgment and identify the person making the acknowledgment. Id.; *see also Magarahan*, 13 S.E. at 510.

The portion of the Signature Page signed by notary Charles Weldon begins with the language: "Before me on this day . . . personally appeared TAMMY P. SIMPSON who acknowledged that he she they signed this Georgia Deed to Secure Debt as his/her/their own act." This language indicates a certificate of acknowledgment. The attestation language begins at the top of the page, but is interrupted by the certificate of acknowledgment midway down the page. Mr. Weldon signs on the space designated for a notary's signature in the jurat. Based on the placement of the notary's signature within the certificate of acknowledgment on the Signature Page the Court concludes the signature of the official witness, notary Charles Weldon, is an attempted acknowledgment and not an attestation. . . .

VALIDITY OF NOTARY CHARLES WELDON'S ACKNOWLEDGMENT

A notary public is authorized under Georgia law to attest to the signature or execution of deeds and to take acknowledgments. *See* O.C.G.A. §§45–17–8(a), 45–17–1(2). When documenting a notarial act, such as an attestation or an acknowledgment, a notary "shall sign on the notarial certification . . . exactly the name indicated on the notary's commission and shall record on the notarial certification the exact date of the notarial act." O.C.G.A. §45–17–8.1(a). If however the notarial act is an attestation of deeds or other instruments pertaining to real property, the requirement that the notary record the exact date shall not apply. O.C.G.A. §45–17–8.1(b). The Signature Page shows that notary Charles Weldon signed his name and affixed his seal on the signature line provided in the certificate of acknowledgment, but failed to fill in the date. Because his signature has been construed as an acknowledgment, rather than an attestation, the exception to the date requirement in O.C.G.A. §45–17–8.1(b) does not apply. Therefore, the Court must determine whether the failure to include the date of acknowledgment invalidates the acknowledgment, rendering the Security Deed patently defective.

Case law addressing the validity of an acknowledgment that is missing a date is limited. When the issue does arise, courts tend to strictly hold notaries public to whatever duties are required by statute, including the requirement that a notary record the date when performing notarial acts other than attestations. *See, e.g.*, Hurt v. Norwest, 580 S.E.2d 580 (Ga. Ct. App. 2003) (acknowledgment of affidavit of indigence invalid where the signature of the notary not dated). Other circuits that have addressed the issue in the context of deeds have reached the same conclusion. *See, e.g.*, Davis v. World Savings Bank (In re Androes), 382 B.R. 805 (Bankr. D. Kan. 2008) (mortgage avoidable by trustee due to notary's failure to include date of notarial act in acknowledgment where required by statute); First Sec. Bank of Utah, N.A. v. Styler, 147 B.R. 248 (D. Utah 1992) (acknowledgment of deed defective where it does not indicate the date, along with other missing information).

This Court concludes that the failure of Mr. Weldon to insert the date of his notarial act of acknowledgment invalidates the acknowledgment. While this may seem technical, the date of the notarial act is particularly important in the context of the acknowledgment since the acknowledgment need not occur on the same date as the execution of the deed. The date of acknowledgment can be important for numerous reasons affecting the validity and authenticity of the deed. The failure to record the date in an acknowledgment must be treated similarly to the way other deed defects are treated under Georgia law: a deed that shows on its face it was "not properly attested or acknowledged, as required by statute, is ineligible for recording." U S. Bank, N.A. v. Gordon, 709 S.E.2d 258, 261 (Ga. 2011). The Court is persuaded based on the plain language of O.C.G.A. §45–17–8.1(a) & (b) and case law interpreting the validity of acknowledgments in various contexts that in order to be valid, the notary's acknowledgment must include the date of the notarial act. . . .

Accordingly, it is hereby ordered . . . that judgment is granted for the Trustee. First Tennessee's security interest is avoided pursuant to 11 U.S.C. §544, and the Security Deed is preserved for the benefit of Debtor's bankruptcy estate under 11 U.S.C. §§550 and 551.

Problem 10D

Caroline Messersmith and Frederick Messersmith owned land in Golden Valley as tenants in common. Caroline executed and delivered to Frederick a quitclaim deed to the property, which Frederick did not record. Five years later, on May 7, Caroline executed a mineral deed conveying to Herbert Smith an undivided one-half interest of all oil, gas, and other minerals in and under the property. Smith paid her $1,400. A notary public was not present when she signed the deed. Smith took the deed to a notary, who called Caroline over the telephone and then placed on the deed the usual notarial acknowledgment, including the notary's signature and seal. For a valid acknowledgment, state law requires that the grantor personally appear before the notary to acknowledge her execution of the deed.

On May 9 Smith executed a mineral deed conveying to Herbert E. B. Seale an undivided one-half interest of all oil, gas, and other minerals in and under the property. Seale paid value to Smith and had no actual notice of

Frederick's quitclaim deed. Both the deeds to Smith and to Seale were recorded on May 26. Frederick recorded his deed on July 9 of the same year. Frederick brought an action to quiet title to all of the property. Seale claims title to one-half of the mineral estate. What result, and why, under a (1) race statute, (2) notice statute, and (3) race-notice statute?

3. Notice from Possession

In notice and race-notice states, a purchaser takes subject to rights of parties in possession and other unrecorded interests that are visible from an inspection of the property. Even though holders of these interests could have recorded and failed to do so, they are protected by their state's view of inquiry notice. Possession by someone other than the seller gives rise to a duty of inquiry. The rule envisions a dialogue between the purchaser and the possessor. The purchaser is bound by whatever rights would have been uncovered by diligent inquiry of the possessor.

There is one general exception to the duty to inquire of possessors. When possession is consistent with record title, there is no duty of inquiry. Thus, when there is a recorded lease, there is no duty to ask the tenant why he is there. In many states, there is also an exception to inquiry notice for possession by a grantor who recently deeded the property to the seller. The rationale is that it is not unusual for a grantee to let the seller remain in possession for a reasonable period of time after the conveyance. When this exception applies, it protects the purchaser as BFP from the possessing grantor's claim either that he has unrecorded rights, such as a life estate, or the right to rescind the transfer for some reason such as fraud.

In re WEISMAN
United States Court of Appeals, Ninth Circuit, 1993
5 F.3d 417

REINHARDT, Circuit Judge. We are faced with the question whether under California law a husband's occupation of his family residence with his second wife can create a duty in a bona fide purchaser for value or a bankruptcy trustee to inquire as to whether his former wife still retains the ownership interest in that property that appears of record. Guided by reality, our answer is yes.

I. FACTUAL AND PROCEDURAL BACKGROUND

Debtor Sheila Weisman (formerly Sheila Peters) married defendant Marc Peters in 1963. They bought a house, which is the subject of the instant dispute, in Campbell, California in 1967. The couple lived in the Campbell residence until March 1985, when Sheila Peters moved out. The couple's marriage was dissolved that fall, but the judgment of dissolution was not recorded. Pursuant to their property settlement, Marc Peters had the right to purchase his former wife's interest in the house they had previously shared. He did so by refinancing and using the loan as the purchase price. However, the lender required Sheila Weisman, who had married debtor Marc Weisman in November 1985, to remain on the title to the property.

As a result of the refinancing transaction, title to the Campbell residence was transferred from Marc Peters and Sheila Peters, as community property, to Marc Peters and Sheila Weisman (a married woman), as tenants in common.[2] The deed reflecting the transfer was dated June 23, 1986, and was recorded July 2, 1986. Marc Weisman then executed a quit claim deed in favor of Sheila Weisman on June 24, 1986, which was also recorded on July 2, 1986. After receiving payment from Marc Peters for her interest in their former home, Sheila Weisman executed a quit claim deed in favor of him on June 25, 1986. The deed was delivered on August 27, 1986, but was not recorded until December 8, 1988. Marc Peters married Nianne Neergaard in August 1986 and the couple has lived in the Campbell residence since that time.

In August 1988, Sheila Weisman and her second husband, Marc Weisman, filed a voluntary bankruptcy petition under Chapter 7 of the Bankruptcy Code (liquidation). A trustee, plaintiff Jerome Robertson, was appointed. After learning that Sheila Weisman was a record title holder to the Campbell residence, the trustee filed a complaint against Marc Peters for authorization to sell that property, as permitted by the Bankruptcy Code. After hearing oral argument, the bankruptcy court found for defendant Peters. The district court reversed the bankruptcy judge's finding as clearly erroneous and entered judgment for the trustee. Peters appealed. . . .

II. ANALYSIS

The Bankruptcy Code, 11 U.S.C. section 544(a)(3), gives a bankruptcy trustee "strong arm powers" to avoid transfers of real property of the debtor that would be voidable under state law by a bona fide purchaser (BFP) of the property from the debtor. . . . Here, California law applies and will determine whether the trustee can set aside Sheila Weisman's (hereinafter "Weisman") unrecorded transfer of all of her interests in the house to Marc Peters (hereinafter "Peters").

California is a race-notice jurisdiction and requires every conveyance of real property to be recorded in order to be valid against a subsequent purchaser of the same property. Cal. Civil Code §1214. However, an unrecorded instrument is valid as between the parties thereto and those who have notice of it. Cal. Civil Code §1217. Although 11 U.S.C. section 544(a)(3) creates the

---

2. Although Sheila Weisman was remarried, her interest in the house was held as separate property.

legal fiction of a perfect BFP and explicitly renders the trustee's actual notice of prior grantees irrelevant, *In re* Professional Investment Properties, 955 F.2d 623, 627 n.2 (9th Cir. 1992), we have held that constructive or inquiry notice obtained in accordance with California Civil Code section 19 can defeat a trustee's claim. *In re* Probasco, 839 F.2d 1352, at 1354-56 (9th Cir. 1988).

The resolution of this case turns on California Civil Code section 19. It provides: "Every person who has actual notice of circumstances sufficient to put a prudent man upon inquiry as to a particular fact, has constructive notice of the fact itself in all cases in which, by prosecuting such inquiry, he might have learned such fact."

In this context the question is whether a prudent purchaser, in light of the information reasonably available to him on the date the Weismans filed their bankruptcy petition, would have made an inquiry into the possibility that Peters owned his residence outright. A "prudent purchaser" describes someone who is shrewd in the management of practical affairs and whose conduct is marked by wisdom, judiciousness, or circumspection. *See Probasco*, 839 F.2d at 1356. Such a purchaser will be charged with knowledge of 1) the nature of the property; 2) its current use; 3) the identities of the persons occupying it; 4) the relationship among them; and, 5) the relationship between those in possession and the person whose purported interest in the property the purchaser intended to acquire. . . .

. . . If, under the circumstances, the trustee should have made an inquiry as to whether Weisman had transferred all of her interests in the Campbell residence to Peters, then . . . the trustee [is charged] with knowledge of the unrecorded deed that did just that. Such knowledge would prevent the trustee from prevailing in this strong arm action. *See Probasco*, 839 F.2d at 1354-56.

Resolution of the question whether the trustee was under a duty to make an inquiry depends in part on the interplay of several long established and related principles of California real estate law:

1. Open, notorious, exclusive, and visible possession of real property by one other than the vendor is notice sufficient to put a prospective purchaser on inquiry of any rights held by the occupant, unless there is no duty under the circumstances to make inquiry.
2. There is no duty to inquire upon a subsequent purchaser regarding any unknown claims or interests by a person in possession of real property where the occupant's possession is consistent with the record title.
3. Where possession is inconsistent with the record title and thereby creates a duty to inquire, a prospective purchaser is charged with constructive notice of all facts that would be revealed by a reasonably diligent inquiry, regardless of whether the purchaser has ever seen the property.

The essential dispute between the parties is whether Peters' and Neergaard's possession of the house was consistent or inconsistent with the record title in Peters' and Weisman's names. The trustee argues that the possession was consistent because, as a cotenant, Peters had the right to possess the whole of the property. The trustee maintains it was immaterial that Weisman lived elsewhere and that Neergaard resided on the property. Peters contends possession was inconsistent with title because of a combination of 1) the change in title from Marc Peters and Sheila Peters to Marc Peters and Sheila Weisman, a married woman, demonstrating that the couple had divorced and Sheila had remarried, and 2) the presence of Peters' second wife, Neergaard, on the property with him. Peters argues that knowledge of these facts would have caused a prudent purchaser to conduct an inquiry.

The trustee places great reliance on the case of Schumacher v. Truman, 66 P. 591 (Cal. 1901), as did the district court. There, a husband and wife owned a parcel of real property. They entered into an unrecorded agreement giving the husband complete management and control over the property. Later the couple divorced and they took title as tenants in common. The husband then subleased his interest in the property to a tenant, who took up exclusive occupation of the property. The wife sold her interest in the property to a third party. The husband argued that anyone in the wife's chain of title took an interest in the property subject to the unrecorded agreement giving him exclusive management and control. The California Supreme Court disagreed and held that there was no constructive notice of the unrecorded agreement between the wife and husband. It reasoned that the exclusive possession by the husband's tenant was consistent with record title and, therefore, a prospective purchaser had no duty to make further inquiry. The tenant's possession was considered to be the equivalent of sole occupation by the ex-husband, and it could be presumed that sole possession by him was in the interest and benefit of the absent cotenant, his ex-wife. *Id.* at 592.

That same presumption is inapplicable here. Inquiry becomes a duty for a prospective purchaser of property when the visible state of affairs is inconsistent with the alleged rights of the person who has proposed to sell the property in question. . . . Here, the trustee is charged both with knowing that Neergaard resided on the property with Peters and that she was his second wife. He is also, of course, charged with knowledge of Weisman's remarriage because that information is on the recorded deed to the Campbell residence.

Peters and his second wife, Neergaard, occupied their family home for all the world to see. They did so as a married couple. Record title placed a one-half ownership interest in their home in the hands of Weisman, Peters' former wife, who herself had already remarried. Under the circumstances the bankruptcy court could reasonably find that Peters' and Neergaard's possession of their residence was sufficiently inconsistent with record title that a prudent purchaser would have inquired whether Peters had previously obtained *all* the ownership interests or whether Weisman still retained a 50 per cent interest in Peters' and Neergaard's house.

In determining inconsistency, we take a practical approach. The state of affairs at the Campbell residence would have made a prudent purchaser suspicious that Weisman, divorced and remarried, no longer actually owned any interest in the home occupied by her former husband and his new wife. Circumstances have changed since 1901. No longer are wives and former wives statutorily disabled from managing and controlling their property, *see, e.g.,* Kirchberg v. Feenstra, 450 U.S. 455, 457 & n.1 (1981), and certainly they are not ordinarily willing to allow a former husband to enjoy exclusive use of their property by living in it with a second wife. Nor are former husbands particularly anxious these days to have a former wife own half of the home in which they reside with her successor. As we approach the end of the century the nature of financial arrangements between divorced spouses is generally far different than it was when the century began.[11] In any event, the circumstances relating to Peters' home were such as to give rise to a duty to inquire on the part of a prudent purchaser.

A reasonable inquiry into the true ownership of the Campbell residence would have confirmed the suspicions that would have been aroused by a realistic analysis of the visible circumstances at the property. Inquiry would have revealed that Peters, in fact, had full title and that Weisman had no interest to sell. . . . [T]he trustee is charged with that knowledge and, therefore, does not qualify as a BFP able to set aside, under 11 U.S.C. section 544(a)(3), the unrecorded transaction whereby Weisman gave Peters complete ownership of the house in which he, but not she, continued to reside. Accordingly, the district court erred in reversing the bankruptcy court.

III. Conclusion

The bankruptcy court did not clearly err in finding that, given the discrepancies between Peters' and Neergaard's possession of their residence and record title, a prudent purchaser would have inquired of Peters as to whether his former wife continued to own an interest in her former home. Consequently, the judgment of the district court is reversed and the case remanded to the bankruptcy court for the entry of judgment in favor of Peters.

---

11. It was at the turn of the century that a three-judge panel of the California Supreme Court decided Schumacher v. Truman, the principal case relied upon by the trustee.

Problem 10E

Boone Bungalow Homes developed a senior living facility consisting of 32 bungalows and amenities, including a swimming pool, fitness center, and clubhouse. The bungalows are occupied by residents, who entered into written Resident Agreements. Under the agreement, the resident pays a lump sum for the right to occupy the premises and use the common facilities until death. At that time, the agreement terminates, and Boone markets the bungalow to another resident and returns a specified percentage of the lump sum to the prior resident's estate. Four years after Boone completed construction of the bungalows, it refinanced its original project financing with a $3.8 million mortgage loan from Main Bank. Two years later Boone defaulted, and Main Bank foreclosed, buying the property at the foreclosure sale. None of the Resident Agreements are recorded, and Main Bank did not have actual notice of those agreements when it made the loan. Since the foreclosure sale, three of the residents have died. Their estates have demanded that Main Bank refund the appropriate percentage of the lump sum payments, which Main Bank refuses to do. What result?

4. Shelter Rule

CHERGOSKY v. CROSSTOWN BELL, INC.
Supreme Court of Minnesota, 1990
463 N.W.2d 522

KEITH, Justice. This case raises the question whether a person who assumed the obligations of an unrecorded contract for deed at the time he acquired an interest in a piece of real property in Richfield, Minnesota, may assert priority over the unrecorded contract for deed after purchasing a mortgage on the property from a bona fide purchaser who recorded the mortgage before the contract for deed was recorded.

George and Dorothy Chergosky, appellants, brought this suit against Crosstown Bell, Inc. (Crosstown), and Alfred Teien for breach of a contract for deed agreement on the Richfield property. The Chergoskys also named Griffith and the law firm of Katz, Davis & Manka as parties to determine the priority of their interests in the property. On cross motions for summary judgment, the district court held that Crosstown breached the contract for deed. The district court found damages against Crosstown in the amount of $97,850.65 plus prejudgment interest and costs and disbursements, and pierced the corporate veil to hold Teien also personally liable. The district court further held that the Chergoskys' claim was superior to those of both Griffith and Katz, Davis & Manka.

Crosstown, Teien, and Griffith appealed from the summary judgment entered in favor of the Chergoskys. The court of appeals upheld the trial court's award of damages to the Chergoskys and the imposition of personal liability on Teien but reversed the trial court's ruling on the priority issue and held that Griffith's mortgage was superior to the Chergoskys' contract for deed because Griffith acquired the mortgage through a bona fide purchaser. Chergosky v. Crosstown Bell, Inc., 454 N.W.2d 654, 656-57 (Minn. App. 1990). We accepted the Chergoskys' petition for further review.

I

On November 4, 1971, Alfred and Donna Teien, the record owners of the property at 6244 Cedar Avenue in Richfield, leased the property as well as a building and garage to be constructed thereon to Northwestern Bell Telephone Company (Northwestern Bell) for a term of 20 years. The lease gave Northwestern Bell the option to purchase the property for $650,000 at the end of ten years. Alfred Teien later formed Crosstown Bell, Inc., a Minnesota corporation, of which Teien was the sole shareholder and officer. The Teiens transferred title to the Richfield property to Crosstown on April 27, 1972, and assigned the Northwestern Bell lease to Crosstown as well. Crosstown acquired permanent financing from Union Central Life Insurance Company, which took a first mortgage on the property that it recorded on September 12, 1972.

In 1977, in need of money, Alfred Teien contacted a friend, George Chergosky. Crosstown entered into a contract for deed conveying the vendee's interest in the Richfield property to George Chergosky and his wife Dorothy, made effective January 1, 1977. The purchase price of $550,000 included $50,000 up front and monthly payments of $5,504.89. The contract for deed gave Crosstown the option to repurchase the property from the Chergoskys, which would be required if Northwestern Bell exercised its purchase option. The Chergoskys did not record the contract for deed until August 19, 1985.

On December 7, 1978, Alfred and Donna Teien borrowed $120,000 from Summit State Bank of Bloomington (Summit), and as security Crosstown gave a mortgage on the Richfield property that Summit recorded on December 18, 1978. Summit did not have notice of the Chergoskys' contract for deed at the time it took the mortgage.

In June 1982, Northwestern Bell notified Crosstown of its intention to exercise its lease purchase option. Crosstown disputed the timeliness of the notice, and in January 1983, brought a declaratory judgment action alleging that Northwestern Bell had not exercised its purchase option in a timely manner.

While this litigation was pending, on March 31, 1983, Robert Griffith, a long-time friend of Teien, acquired a 70% undivided interest in the Richfield property in exchange for past and present loans he made to Teien personally and to Crosstown. At the time Griffith, Teien, and Crosstown entered into this contract Griffith clearly had notice of the Chergoskys' contract for deed.

On August 22, 1985, while the litigation with Northwestern Bell still was pending, Griffith purchased the $120,000 note as well as other notes with a face value of $370,000 for $350,000 from Metropolitan Bank, Summit's assignee. As part of this transaction, Griffith received an assignment of the $120,000 second mortgage on the Richfield property, which Griffith recorded in November 1985.

On October 18, 1985, the trial court ordered Crosstown to convey marketable title to the Richfield property to Northwestern Bell, and ordered Northwestern Bell to pay the option purchase price into the court. *See* Crosstown Bell, Inc. v. Northwestern Bell Tel. Co., 381 N.W.2d 911 (Minn. App. 1986) (affirming the trial court's order). The subject matter of this dispute is the funds which remain on deposit with the court after satisfaction of the first mortgage pursuant to court order.

II

As the holder of the second mortgage, Griffith claims priority over the Chergoskys to the remaining proceeds from the sale of the Richfield property because he acquired the mortgage through a bona fide purchaser who recorded its mortgage before the Chergoskys recorded their contract for deed. . . .

Under the Minnesota Recording Act, a bona fide purchaser who records first obtains rights to the property which are superior to a prior purchaser who failed to record. . . .

Generally, a bona fide purchaser of property which was subject to a prior outstanding unrecorded interest may pass title free of the unrecorded interest to a subsequent purchaser who otherwise would not qualify as a bona fide purchaser under the recording act. Henschke v. Christian, 36 N.W.2d 547, 550 (Minn. 1949). This bona fide purchaser filter rule protects the alienability of property. Without this rule the bona fide purchaser would be deprived of the full benefit of the purchase — the right to transfer good title to a subsequent purchaser. *See, e.g.,* 8 G. Thompson, *Commentaries on the Modern Law of Real Property* §4315, at 380 (1940 & photo. reprint 1963).

Summit paid valuable consideration for its mortgage, took the mortgage without notice of the Chergoskys' contract for deed, and recorded the mortgage before the Chergoskys recorded their contract for deed. As between the Chergoskys' contract for deed and the second mortgage in the hands of Summit, Summit has priority. Generally, the filter principle then would operate to pass Summit's superior interest to Metropolitan and then to Griffith.

III

We first must examine the nature of the March 31, 1983, contract between Griffith, Teien, and Crosstown, to determine whether Griffith's rights and obligations under that contract affect his ability to claim the priority of a bona fide purchaser even though he had actual knowledge of the contract for deed when he acquired the mortgage.] . .

When the intention of the parties to a contract is totally ascertainable from the writing, construction is for the court. . . .

. . . Read as a whole to harmonize the different parts of the instrument, the contract provides that Griffith assumes 70% of the obligations of the contract for deed but that Crosstown and Teien will be liable to Griffith for any amounts that he pays under the contract for deed. We thus conclude as a matter of law that Griffith assumed 70% of Crosstown's obligations under the contract for deed in the March 31, 1983 contract with Crosstown and Teien.

IV

The issue then becomes whether Griffith, who has assumed obligations to the Chergoskys based on the contract for deed, can rely on the bona fide purchaser filter principle to assert priority to the Richfield property over the Chergoskys. The bona fide purchaser filter principle is subject to a well-recognized exception, which prevents the grantor or former owner of the property, who held the property subject to a prior equity, from acquiring the rights of a bona fide purchaser. Walker v. Wilson, 469 So. 2d 580, 582 (Ala. 1985); Clark v. McNeal, 21 N.E. 405, 407 (N.Y. 1889).[4] Professor Cribbet wrote that this exception "prevents a holder of the title from using the [bona fide purchaser] as a 'filter' to cleanse his defective ownership." J. Cribbet, *Principles of the Law of Property* 287-88 (2d ed. 1975). . . . By asserting priority to the Richfield property, Griffith, in effect, is attempting to build title on his own default or at least on the default of Crosstown/Teien, with whom Griffith is closely associated and who, along with Griffith, is the co-owner of the vendor's interest in the property. *See* Conner v. How, 29 N.W. 314 (Minn. 1886). In *How*, Mayo, who had purchased property and assumed the two mortgages on the property, defaulted on the first mortgage and then bought the property from the purchaser at the foreclosure sale. We held that Mayo remained liable on the second mortgage because he could not "build up a title upon his own default." *Id.* at 316.

We agree with the trial court that the same principles apply in this case. Griffith was obligated to the Chergoskys under the contract for deed. Griffith, prior to his acquisition of the second mortgage, held his 70% interest in the Richfield property subject to the Chergoskys' contract for

---

4. The Rhode Island Supreme Court applied this exception to the brother and wife of the original mortgagors who acquired a mortgage through a bona fide purchaser. Rogis v. Barnatowich, 89 A. 838 (R.I. 1914). In *Rogis*, a church gave a first mortgage which was not recorded until after a second mortgage, given by the church and two of its members, was recorded. The court held that the brother and wife of these two members, who acquired the second mortgage from a bona fide purchaser, were not entitled to succeed to the rights of the bona fide purchaser. *Id.* at 840.

deed and with a personal obligation to the Chergoskys under the contract for deed. Having assumed the obligations of the contract for deed, Griffith cannot rely on the bona fide purchaser filter rule to obtain an interest in the property which is superior to the Chergoskys.

The bona fide purchaser filter rule is essential to the sound functioning of the secondary mortgage market. We emphasize that it is the unique facts concerning the March 31, 1983 contract, in which Griffith assumed 70% of the vendor's obligations to the Chergoskys under the contract for deed, that place this case in the well-recognized but limited exception to the bona fide purchaser filter principle.

We reverse the court of appeals and reinstate the trial court's judgment in favor of the Chergoskys on the priority issue.

Problem 10F

(a) Oprah, in need of money to launch a TV show, borrowed $50,000 from Creditor, giving Creditor a mortgage on Newacre to secure the loan. Creditor did not record its mortgage, and Oprah remained in possession of Newacre. One year later, Oprah sold Newacre to Amy for $200,000, without informing her of the mortgage. Amy promptly recorded. Then Creditor recorded its mortgage. The following year, Amy contracts to sell Newacre to Bart for $250,000. Bart closes the purchase, paying the purchase price in full. Creditor has never been paid. Is Creditor's mortgage on Newacre valid as against Bart?

(b) Assume the same transaction, except that one year after the sale from Amy to Bart, Bart contracts to sell Newacre to your client, Daffy, for $300,000. Your title search reveals Creditor's mortgage, as well as the chain of deeds from Oprah to Bart. Should you raise an objection to Bart's title?

5. Payment of Value

The second requirement for a grantee to qualify as a BFP, in addition to lack of notice of the prior interest, is payment of value. This is true under both types of notice-based statutes and under the North Carolina pure race statute. Two sets of issues concerning value are raised; one concerns measurement, the other concerns timing.

The measurement issue relates to how much consideration is needed. The requirement of valuable consideration is intended to disqualify a donee who receives a gift, either by deed or as heir or devisee, but it is not always easy to distinguish purchasers and donees. Standard deed forms often recite that the grantee has paid "ten dollars and other good and valuable consideration," and such forms are often used for gifts. Nominal consideration, however, does not suffice to make a donee into a BFP. Nevertheless, the consideration doesn't have to be full market value, it just has to be substantial. Many courts treat a deed recital of the payment of consideration with some respect, saying it gives rise to a presumption that valuable consideration was given.

With regard to timing, the standard traditional doctrine is that the purchaser is not a BFP before he actually pays the consideration to the seller. This means that a binding promise to pay, although it may be consideration in the general contract-law sense, is not enough for the recording act. For example, when a purchaser signs an executory contract, paying the seller a normal amount of earnest money, the purchaser is not yet a BFP. Only at closing, when he pays the remainder of the purchase price, does he become a BFP. The significance of this rule is that the purchaser bears the risk that third parties might record their claims or otherwise give notice of their claims after the contract is signed but prior to closing.

Mortgagee as Purchaser. In all states, lenders as well as buyers qualify as BFPs. Some recording acts specifically state that mortgagees are entitled to defeat prior unrecorded interests. Other states with acts that refer only to "purchasers" have interpreted the term to include mortgagees. The money they lend to the mortgagor is valuable consideration, given in exchange for the mortgage. A mortgage given to secure antecedent debt raises special problems. If the mortgagee does not give new value when it takes the mortgage, in most states the mortgagee is not a purchaser. If the mortgagee gives new value by, for example, extending the term of the loan, it is a BFP who takes free of prior unrecorded interests of which it lacks notice.

Problem 10G

Eight months ago Larry rented his single-family house to Teresa and Thomas, pursuant to a written one-year lease. During lease negotiations, Teresa and Thomas asked for and got an option to purchase the house for $210,000 at the end of the lease term. The written lease, which the tenants promptly recorded, contains an integration clause and fails to mention the option. The purchase option is set forth in a side letter agreement, which was not acknowledged or recorded. The side letter is sufficient to satisfy the statute of frauds.

Two months ago, Larry agreed to sell the house to Pamela for $240,000 pursuant to an unacknowledged, unrecorded contract of sale. When Pamela inspected the house, Teresa and Thomas weren't there, although Larry told her that the furnishings in the house belonged to the tenants. Under the contract between Larry and Pamela, the one-year lease is a permitted encumbrance, and at closing Larry is to assign his interest in the lease to Pamela. Larry "forgot" to tell Pamela about the tenants' purchase option.

(a) Pamela closes the purchase without learning of the tenants' purchase option and records her deed. At the end of the one-year lease, the tenants notify Pamela that they are exercising their option to purchase for $210,000. What result?

(b) After signing the contract, Pamela decides to introduce herself to Teresa and Thomas — soon she'll be their new landlord. Early during their conversation, they mention their option and the likelihood that they'll exercise it. Pamela says she knows nothing about their option and plans not to honor it. What result? Does it matter what type of recording act the state has?

(c) Assume that Pamela never inspected or visited the house prior to signing the contract of sale with Larry. Does this change the analysis in (a) or (b)?

(d) Assume that Teresa and Thomas's lease is not recorded, but that Larry supplied Pamela with a copy of the lease (but not the side letter) while they were negotiating the contract of sale. Does this change the analysis in (a) or (b)?

D. SPECIAL PROBLEMS: INTERESTS THAT ARE HARD OR IMPOSSIBLE TO FIND

The prevalent use of name indexes to organize recorded instruments can make a deed or other instrument that is recorded difficult or even impossible for a searcher to find. There is something called a *wild deed*, which means an instrument is literally recorded and properly indexed, but it cannot be found by use of the name indexes because there is a missing link. Because the wild deed is completely impossible to find, courts have treated it as unrecorded despite the fact that it's physically recorded as well as name indexed.

The *late recorded deed* and the *early recorded deed* are like the wild deed, in that the name index system impairs the searcher's access to them. A deed or other instrument is late recorded when there is a substantial gap in time between delivery and recordation, and in the meantime the record owner has transferred ownership to someone else. The difficulty is that the searcher will stop looking in the grantor indexes for adverse transfers after the time the record owner transferred to someone else.

The early recorded deed is the flip side of the late recorded deed. A person transfers an interest in land he does not own and subsequently acquires an estate in that land. This is much like a familiar transaction in stock whereby a person "sells short," contracting to sell stock he does not own with the understanding that he will acquire it to make good on the undertaking. In the land context, when the grantor eventually gets title, the doctrine of estoppel by deed operates to transfer that title to the prior grantee. An explanation often given by courts is that without estoppel, the grantor would have breached his deed warranties of title. The estoppel-by-deed rule prevents this breach by passing the appropriate title to the grantee. For this reason, a number of courts have refused to apply estoppel by deed in transactions involving early recorded quitclaim deeds.

Jurisdictions are about evenly split on whether late recorded deeds and early recorded deeds are treated as validly recorded, thus imparting constructive notice to subsequent purchasers. Unlike the wild deed, late and early recorded deeds can be found if the searcher does the extra work of checking index books for years before and after the dates each record owner acquired and parted with title.

A title search not only has to account for fee ownership, but it must also uncover any servitudes, such as *easements* and *restrictive covenants,* that bind the property. Most servitudes are created by express language, set forth in documents in the property's chain of title, and thus pose no special problems of searching. However, our system of land law permits the creation of several types of servitudes by implication, such as easements implied from prior existing use, easements by necessity, and reciprocal negative easements. Typically, such servitudes are created at the time land is sold in the process of subdivision, when the grantor retains neighboring land that is either burdened or benefited by the implied servitude. Although the implied servitude may serve the worthwhile purpose of effectuating the intent of the parties to the sale, when third parties subsequently come on the scene, these implied rights are hard to detect in the search process. Similar title search problems are raised by prescriptive easements, easements by estoppel (also called irrevocable licenses), and express restrictions that are imposed upon the grantor's retained land (here, the problem arises when the recording office fails to index the deed as affecting not only the conveyed parcel but also the retained parcel). For all of these types of servitudes, there are some cases that protect the purchaser as BFP and others that fail to do so on the theory that the purchaser had some type of constructive or inquiry notice.

Occasionally the recorder's office makes a mistake in the recording process. As a result, a subsequent purchaser may not be able to find a prior instrument that was filed for recording, or actually recorded. The question then becomes: Who bears the risk of losing his interest in the real property—the recording party or the subsequent purchaser who did not and perhaps could not find the prior instrument? In some states, when the error is attributable to a recording employee's negligence, a suit for damages is possible. Sometimes the public employee is bonded, but typically the bond is for a small amount. In other states, sovereign immunity bars such an action.

MidCOUNTRY BANK v. KRUEGER
Supreme Court of Minnesota, 2010
782 N.W.2d 238

ANDERSON, G. BARRY, Justice. At issue in this appeal is whether a mortgage was "properly recorded" under Minn. Stat. §507.32 (2008), thereby giving constructive notice to a subsequent purchaser of land and a mortgagee.

Respondent MidCountry Bank brought an action in district court to foreclose a mortgage on property owned by appellant Cherolyn Hinshaw (the "Hinshaw property")....

...On March 21, 2000, Frederick and Nancy Krueger purchased the Hinshaw property in Belle Plaine, Minnesota. Four years later, the Kruegers obtained a loan from MidCountry to purchase two different parcels of land (the "Krueger properties") and to build a house on the acquired property.

To provide security for the loan, the Kruegers executed and delivered a mortgage to MidCountry that encumbered not only the Krueger properties but also the Hinshaw property purchased four years earlier. On May 19, 2004, the deed to the Krueger properties and the MidCountry mortgage were delivered to the Scott County Recorder's Office to be recorded.

RECORDING PROCESS

The Scott County Recorder provided deposition testimony concerning the process for recording real-property instruments. Scott County uses the TriMin computer system to electronically store all official property records. The day after a document is delivered to the recorder's office to be recorded, a label is placed on the document showing the date, time of receipt, and the document number to fulfill the requirements of Minn. Stat. §386.41 (2008). After the labeling procedure is complete, information about the document is entered into the TriMin system, beginning with the names of the grantor and grantee, the date of the document, and the legal description of the property contained in the document.

When a deed and a mortgage are brought in together to be recorded, such as here, the recorder will "clone" the legal description from the first document entered into the system, and apply that legal description to the second document so that the information does not have to be reentered. [The recorder assumes that the legal descriptions are the same for the bundled documents.] After the recorder enters the information into the system, the documents are scanned so that an image of each document is available on the TriMin system. Scott County has been scanning real estate documents presented for recording since approximately 1991. The public can access the records at the recorder's office or via the county recorder's website. But the information contained on the county recorder's website is only for reference purposes and is not considered the official record for county property recording purposes. In addition, images of documents that may have a Social Security number are not available on the website due to privacy concerns. Images of such documents are, however, available on the county recorder's official in-house system.

Minnesota Statutes §§386.03-.05 and 386.32 (2008) require a county to maintain a grantor-grantee index, a consecutive index, and a tract index. The TriMin system satisfies these requirements because it is searchable by (1) grantor-grantee name (the grantor-grantee index), (2) tract/legal description (the tract index), and (3) document number. If a search is conducted by the name of the grantor or grantee, any document under the grantor or grantee name will be listed. The search also displays the type of instrument, the document number, the date it was recorded, and a brief legal description of the property. On the county recorder's official in-house system, users of the system have several options that allow them to review specific information, such as the legal description of property and images of documents.[5]

Scott County Recorder's Office and the MidCountry Mortgage

When the deed to the Krueger properties and the MidCountry mortgage were delivered to the Scott County Recorder's Office to be recorded, the deed and the mortgage were labeled as received on May 19, 2004, and were marked as document numbers A657035 and A657036, respectively. The deed to the Krueger properties was entered into the TriMin system prior to the MidCountry mortgage. But because the deed transferred only the two Krueger properties, the deed only contained the legal descriptions of those two Krueger properties. Only those two descriptions were entered into the TriMin system as being related to that document. The next document was the MidCountry mortgage, and the recorder's office cloned the legal descriptions from the deed for the legal descriptions in the TriMin system for the mortgage. Because the legal descriptions in the deed referenced the two Krueger properties and only those legal descriptions were cloned for the mortgage, the only way that the TriMin system showed the mortgage as encumbering the third property – the Hinshaw property – was by the imaged copy of page three of the mortgage, which stated that it encumbered the Hinshaw property in addition to the Krueger properties.

Kruegers' Conveyance of the Hinshaw Property to Hinshaw and Foreclosure

Two years after the MidCountry mortgage was delivered to the Scott County Recorder's Office to be recorded, the Kruegers conveyed the Hinshaw property to Hinshaw, but without any recorded documentary disclosure of the mortgage to MidCountry.[6] Hinshaw executed a mortgage on the property and delivered it to [appellant PHH Home Loans.] . . . The Kruegers defaulted on the MidCountry mortgage, which encumbered not only the Krueger properties, but also the Hinshaw property. MidCountry brought

---

5. For instance, a user of the in-house system has the option of placing an "X" next to a document in order to enter into a document number inquiry screen to view additional information. From there, a user can push the "F8" key to view more specific information about the legal description of the land, or the "F13" key to view an image of the document.

6. The Kruegers apparently did not disclose to Hinshaw that the Hinshaw property was still encumbered by the MidCountry mortgage, and did not obtain a satisfaction, release, or consent from MidCountry.

an action in district court to foreclose on the Krueger properties and the Hinshaw property. . . .

The licensed abstracter that had conducted title examinations of the Hinshaw property prior to Hinshaw's purchase of the Hinshaw property from the Kruegers testified, as part of the foreclosure discovery process, that she had performed two title examinations prior to the sale of the Hinshaw property. She had performed those searches by using the tract index (*i.e.*, searched by entering the legal description of the property), and those searches did not indicate that the MidCountry mortgage was recorded against the Hinshaw property. She did not check the grantor-grantee index (i.e., did not search by grantor or grantee name), because she testified that she does not routinely check that index when performing title examinations, but will if requested. . . .

. . . [The district] court held that the [MidCountry] mortgage was not properly recorded, and granted summary judgment in favor of Hinshaw and PHH because neither could be charged with actual, implied, or constructive notice of the MidCountry mortgage.

MidCountry appealed and the court of appeals reversed, [concluding that the MidCountry's mortgage was properly recorded.] . . . We granted review.

I.

Hinshaw and PHH argue that because the MidCountry mortgage was not properly indexed in the Scott County Recorder's Office as required by Minn. Stat. §§386.03-.05, the mortgage was not properly recorded under Minn. Stat. §507.32, and they should not be charged with constructive notice of its existence. . . .

The Minnesota Recording Act gives priority to those who purchase property in good faith, for valuable consideration, and who first record their interests, by providing that

> [e]very conveyance of real estate shall be recorded in the office of the county recorder of the county where such real estate is situated; and every such conveyance not so recorded shall be void as against any subsequent purchaser in good faith and for a valuable consideration of the same real estate . . . whose conveyance is first duly recorded.

Minn. Stat. §507.34 (2008). . . . The only dispute here is whether Hinshaw and PHH had constructive notice of the MidCountry mortgage as a matter of law. . . .

A.

Hinshaw and PHH contend that proper recording of an instrument depends on whether a document is properly indexed by a county recorder's office because a county recorder is required by law to keep three property indexes under Minn. Stat. §§386.03-.05. Their argument rests on the premise that information contained in the indexes is part of the record, and that indexing is part of the recording process.

Our prior opinions support Hinshaw and PHH's implicit premise that information contained in the indexes is part of the record, and that indexing is part of the recording process. We have said that "[t]he entries required by law to be made in the reception books [(indexes)], and the transcribing of the instrument into the record book, constitute the full record." Whitacre v. Martin, 53 N.W. 806, 807 (Minn. 1892). . . . Because information in the indexes is considered part of the record of a document, the only logical conclusion we can draw is that indexing is part of the recording process.

The court of appeals concluded that if an instrument bears the certificate of recording required by Minn. Stat. §386.41, that is presumptive proof that the instrument was properly recorded. The conclusion of the court of appeals is correct, but incomplete. Minnesota Statutes §386.41 provides that

> [e]very county recorder shall endorse upon each instrument recorded, over the recorder's official signature, OFFICE OF THE COUNTY RECORDER, . . . COUNTY, MINNESOTA, CERTIFIED, FILED, AND/OR RECORDED ON, the date and time when it was recorded and the document number and/or book and page in which it was recorded; and every *instrument shall be considered as recorded at the time so noted.* (Emphasis added.)

We agree with the court of appeals that if an instrument bears the recording label required by section 386.41, that is presumptive proof that the instrument was properly recorded. But that presumption rests on the understanding that the subsequent steps in the recording process will be completed. Thus, while there is no dispute that the Scott County Recorder's Office affixed a label to the MidCountry mortgage on May 19, 2004, containing the endorsement and information required by Minn. Stat. §386.41, Hinshaw and PHH are not precluded from attempting to rebut the presumption that the mortgage was properly recorded.

To be clear, Minn. Stat. §386.41 does not state, and we do not read it as meaning, that an instrument is properly recorded so long as it bears the endorsement of the county recorder, nor does section 386.41 exclude indexing from the recording process. Where, as here, the public records are available, further analysis is required before concluding that an instrument was properly recorded. This analysis requires examining the record of the instrument, which includes the indexes. Nevertheless, as Minn. Stat. §386.41 states, an instrument is considered recorded as of the date and time specified on the recording label.

B.

We turn next to Hinshaw and PHH's contention that proper recording requires proper indexing, and that Minn. Stat. §§386.03-.05 and 386.32

establish the requirements for proper recording. Minnesota Statutes chapter 386 requires that a county recorder's office keep (1) a *grantor-grantee reception index* that includes the date and time an instrument was received to be recorded, the names of the grantor and grantee, where the land is situated, the instrument number, and the type of instrument; (2) a *consecutive index* of all records showing the number of the instrument consecutively and the time of its reception . . . and (3) a *tract index* that includes the legal description of the affected land. . . .

Hinshaw and PHH argue that these statutes require the indexes to record the legal descriptions of property affected by a recorded instrument. They contend that Scott County's indexing system failed to do this, and thus the system did not show that the Hinshaw property was encumbered by the MidCountry mortgage. They maintain that even though the document number appeared in the grantor-grantee index under the Krueger name, the TriMin system did not list the description of the Hinshaw property in connection with the mortgage. According to Hinshaw and PHH, the indexing system failed to provide the "where situated" information required under Minn. Stat. ch. 386, making the MidCountry mortgage not properly recorded. . . .

[We] note that the MidCountry mortgage was not listed in the tract index as encumbering the Hinshaw property. Additionally, if a title searcher looked under the mortgage's document number A657036 in the document number inquiry screen and pressed the "F8" key, the legal descriptions of the Krueger properties were listed, but not the Hinshaw property. Based on these omissions, the mortgage did not meet all of the indexing requirements of sections 386.03-.05 and 386.32. On the other hand, it did meet some of the requirements. Most importantly, the mortgage was listed in the historically primary grantor-grantee index under the names of both Frederick Krueger and Nancy Krueger. Further, the index provided information about the nature of the instrument (*i.e.*, that the document was a mortgage), the mortgage's document number, and the date it was recorded. The "where situated" or legal description column gave the general location of the land as "Belle Plaine." Given the limited amount of space available for the column in the grantor-grantee index screen, it would have been impossible to provide there the full legal description of all the properties the MidCountry mortgage encumbered.[11]

An index is intended to be a springboard in helping the record searcher find the word-for-word record of the document that is on file with the county recorder's office as required by Minn. Stat. §386.19 (2008). The MidCountry mortgage was listed in the grantor-grantee index under both of the Kruegers' names, and was described as situated in "Belle Plaine." The title

11. A screen print of the grantor-grantee index indicates that only 12 spaces are available in the "where situated" or legal description column. The legal description of all three of the properties encumbered by the MidCountry mortgage would take approximately 300 spaces.

searcher could have typed an "X" by the listing for the mortgage and entered into a document number inquiry screen that contained additional information about the mortgage. While viewing that screen, a title searcher could have viewed an image of the MidCountry mortgage and found on page three that it encumbered the Hinshaw property. Because the mortgage was listed in the grantor-grantee index under the Kruegers' names with a description of the land as located in "Belle Plaine," and there was an image of the document itself, which provided the correct legal description of each property that the mortgage encumbered, we conclude that the mortgage was properly recorded. Although the mortgage was properly recorded, it was imperfectly indexed; one screen revealed the mortgage while another screen showed the legal description of the Krueger properties and nothing for the Hinshaw property. . . .

We conclude that the indexes are the starting point for a subsequent purchaser or title examiner, and that Hinshaw and PHH are charged with notice of the facts contained in the MidCountry mortgage itself because the mortgage was indexed in the grantor-grantee index under the correct names (the Kruegers) and an image of the document itself was available through the grantor-grantee index. We are not dealing with a misindexed document (*e.g.*, a document indexed under the wrong grantor's or grantee's name), nor are we dealing with an unindexed document (i.e., a document that was not indexed at all). Instead, the mortgage here was indexed, although imperfectly. But we do not consider "properly recorded" as coterminous with "properly indexed." Rather, "properly recorded" requires a reference in the indexes sufficient to locate the document and a record of the document itself, and that between the indexes and the record, there is sufficient evidence that the document pertains to the property. Here, the MidCountry mortgage was listed in the grantor-grantee index, and an image of the document was available via this index. In spite of the incomplete legal description of the encumbered property in the index, the contents of the mortgage itself were available and compensated for the deficiencies in the indexes for constructive notice purposes. Therefore, although the mortgage may have been imperfectly indexed, it was "properly recorded." Because we conclude that the MidCountry mortgage was properly recorded, Hinshaw and PHH are charged with constructive notice of its existence, and therefore were not good faith purchasers.

C.

Hinshaw and PHH cite cases from other jurisdictions in an effort to show that an instrument must be properly indexed in order to be considered properly recorded for constructive notice purposes. *E.g.*, Noyes v. Horr, 13 Iowa 570 (1862); Hanson v. Zoller, 187 N.W.2d 47 (N.D.1971). But these cases are from states that have different recording statutes, different indexing systems, and different case law precedent. Further, courts in other jurisdictions have rejected Hinshaw and PHH's position. *See, e.g.,*

First Citizens Nat'l Bank v. Sherwood, 583 Pa. 466, 879 A.2d 178 (2005). Looking to other jurisdictions for guidance is not instructive here.

D.

Hinshaw and PHH also raise a policy argument in support of their position. They contend that if they are charged with constructive notice and are required to read the entire record, including the terms of the Mid-Country mortgage imaged into an electronic system, then subsequent purchasers cannot rely on the recording and indexing performed by county recorders. Instead, purchasers would have to assume that the recording indexes are inaccurate and must read the full text of every document referenced in any index. They argue that this inefficiently places the risk of loss on subsequent purchasers when the risk of loss should be placed on the party seeking to have an instrument recorded with the county recorder's office because only that party would know what and where to check, and how to identify a problem. Further, Hinshaw and PHH argue that by not equating proper indexing with proper recording, title examinations will be more burdensome and real estate closings will be more expensive.

We understand Hinshaw and PHH's policy argument, but think it is overstated. Reviewing the legal descriptions contained in a mortgage that is indexed under the names of the grantor and grantee is not overly burdensome, nor is checking documents that potentially relate to the property at issue. The electronic storing of real property records significantly reduces the burden of searching in comparison with the burden that existed prior to electronic access to county property records. Our conclusion that the Mid-Country mortgage was properly recorded for constructive notice purposes merely affirms what we believe the rule has been in this state for over 90 years: purchasers are presumed to have read and are charged with constructive notice of the entire record, including information contained in the indexes and the contents of the recorded document itself if it appears in the grantor-grantee index under the correct name.[14]

---

14. The requirement that a subsequent purchaser and title abstracter must examine the records of the instrument themselves and a subsequent purchaser is imputed with notice of the instrument's contents appears to continue today in Minnesota. For example, the Legislature established the Minnesota Electronic Real Estate Recording Task Force "to study and make recommendations for the establishment of a system for the electronic filing and recording of real estate documents." Act of Apr. 14, 2000, ch. 391, §1, 2000 Minn. Laws 500, 500-01. The Electronic Real Estate Recording Task Force prepared and submitted a report in 2001 to the Legislature, as required by the Act of Apr. 14, 2000; in the report, the task force noted the continued connection between the indexes and the transcription of the original document (which is now an electronic or imaged copy of the document) in an electronic records system: "The copy of the document and both indexes are public records, so anyone who wants to know who currently owns a particular parcel of property, or wishes to trace its history of ownership, may do so by searching the indexes and *then examining the documents* located through the search." Elec. Real Estate Recording Task Force, *Workplan Report to the Legislature* 13 (Jan. 15, 2001) (emphasis added). . . .

Because we hold that the MidCountry mortgage was properly recorded, thereby charging Hinshaw and PHH with constructive notice, MidCountry's mortgage takes priority over Hinshaw's and PHH's interests in the Hinshaw property. Accordingly, we affirm the court of appeals. . . .

Problem 10H

Thrifty Rentals, Inc., a Colorado corporation, deeds a tract of land with a small building, located on N. Pine St., to John Martz. Martz files the deed at the recorder's office, paying the recording fee. Two months later, Jake obtains a judgment lien against Thrifty Rentals, Inc., and properly records it. The recording act requires that the recorder's office maintain name indexes. It also stipulates that an instrument provides constructive notice to third parties from the date of its recordation.

(a) Is the judgment lien valid as against Martz if the recording officer made any of the following mistakes with respect to the deed from Thrifty to Martz, which remained uncorrected until after Jake's recording?

1. She indexed the grantor's name as "Thrift Rentals, Inc."
2. She indexed the grantor's name as "Shrifty Rentals, Inc."
3. She indexed the grantee's name under "J" as "John, Martz" rather than "Martz, John."
4. She indexed the names properly, but the column of the index that contains a short property description refers to "N. Martz St." when it should refer to "N. Pine St."

(b) Does it matter whether Jake has actually searched the records to determine whether Thrifty has record title to the land?

11
Title Products

The recording system is the backbone of title assurance. When someone searches title, it always involves searching the county land records. It also often involves inspecting the land (or hiring a surveyor to inspect the land) to look for unrecorded interests or other title-related problems. In the last chapter, we saw that searching titles requires the meticulous following of a number of steps, coupled with the application of legal knowledge. Local practices can vary considerably, and within local communities individual searchers often develop their own systems for collecting and organizing title data.

The title search process and the final product are two different things. The search process can result in several different types of final products, each giving a different set of rights to the purchaser. The three main products are (1) title abstracts, (2) attorneys' title opinions or title certificates, and (3) title insurance policies. In each case, the search and the final product are used to manage risk. The search provides information about the quality and quantity of the property interest involved in the transaction, and the title products discussed in this chapter provide some assurance as to the accuracy of the information. Each title product starts with and depends upon a detailed search of the property records.

The title assurance products shift risk by placing some of the risk of inaccurate information or erroneous conclusions on a third party. Each of the three major title assurance products provides a different approach to risk protection. In other words, the persons who issue these products undertake varying degrees of liability. With each title assurance product, however, it is the ability to pursue damages that gives the recipient of the title product a degree of protection with respect to the risk of a title problem.

A. TITLE ABSTRACTS

A *title abstract* is a written distillation of the record search process. It summarizes all recorded deeds and other recorded items in the chain of title, including encumbrances. A complete abstract takes the chain of title back to the sovereign, but today many searches (and thus many abstracts) go back only a customary period, such as 20, 50, or 60 years. Typically, the person making an abstract studies each recorded document, putting pertinent information on blank abstract forms, which are either printed standardized forms or forms tailor-made by the abstractor.

After doing this research and note-taking, the abstractor prepares the finished product. Most abstracts are arranged chronologically, with a synopsis or summary of all items found, including those believed to have no present operative effect on title (for example, a mortgage lien for which there is a release or discharge of record). Generally, the abstract contains a certification that it contains all instruments of record that affect the land. The purpose of the abstract is to give the purchaser sufficient information to decide whether record title is acceptable. Most abstracts do not directly opine on the present state of title by saying, for example, that Jones has record title to a fee simple absolute subject to one lien and one restrictive covenant. Instead, interpretation of the abstracted instruments is left to the reader, who must review the entire abstract and infer the present condition of title.

In some localities, attorneys prepare abstracts, but in most states abstracts are made by nonlawyer professionals. In some states, title abstractors must be careful not to overstep their boundaries or they may find themselves liable for the unauthorized practice of law. Under this view, the abstractor's role is to supply a summary of the records and avoid opining as to what those records mean with respect to the quality of title. Most purchasers who receive abstracts prepared by nonlawyers need to supplement the abstract by having a lawyer evaluate the abstract for them. This review of the abstract may be informal, with the lawyer informing the client of the abstract's contents and any areas of concern that it may raise. Alternatively, the purchaser's lawyer may use the abstract as the basis for writing a title opinion or title certificate to be given to the client.

Roughly half the states, most of them in the West, regulate the business of abstracting. Bonding of abstractors to cover liability for erroneous abstracts is typically required. Some states require licensing of abstractors, with the passage of an examination. Several states require that an abstract company maintain its own private title plant and develop its own index.

An abstractor's liability to a client for an erroneous abstract is generally based on negligence, which is a professional malpractice standard. Traditionally, only the purchaser of an abstract may rely upon it. Other parties who obtain and read the abstract, who are not in privity of contract, cannot sue the abstractor if they become disappointed with the abstract's contents. As in other areas of law, courts have substantially eroded the privity shield, extending abstractor liability to third parties under some circumstances. The most expansive rejection of privity allows a tort action for negligent misrepresentation when a subsequent buyer of the land receives and relies upon the abstract to her detriment, even though that buyer is several contract steps removed from the abstractor. A more limited rejection of privity relies on third-party beneficiary theory when it is clear that the person contracting with the abstractor plans to deliver the abstract to a third party, such as a buyer or mortgagee, who can be expected to rely on it. For example, an owner who is trying to sell her land might order an abstract for the purpose of convincing a prospective buyer that she has good title.

Problem 11A

Last year Jessica purchased her dream home, a single-family residence on a one-acre lot, from Roger for $700,000. In the contract of purchase, Roger promised to deliver to Jessica an abstract of title to the property showing all recorded documents in the chain of title. Roger hired an abstract company, who delivered the abstract to Jessica before the closing. Six months after closing, Jessica is sued by Margaret, who asserts a superior right to the property by showing that the title into Roger was by a forged deed. Margaret, it turns out, is the wife of Roger. They had separated, but not divorced, two years earlier, and Roger was living in the home at the time of the sale to Jessica. Margaret moved to another state at the time of the separation, and she recently discovered that Roger "sold" her undivided one-half interest in the property without her consent. It turns out that Roger forged and recorded a quitclaim deed fully "conveying" Margaret's interest to him, and then he executed a deed from himself conveying the property to Jessica, which was also recorded. Everything looked normal and legitimate on the public records, and the abstractor had no notice of any irregularities.

(a) Assuming that Jessica loses the property to the "true owner," Margaret, does Jessica have a cause of action against the abstract company for her loss?

(b) Assume that the abstract company failed to notice and disclose the recorded quitclaim deed that Roger had executed and filed on the public records, but its abstract identified all other relevant documents of title. Does this make any difference in your analysis of the company's liability to Jessica as a result of the forged deed?

(c) Assume that Margaret wins in her litigation against Jessica and that Jessica then asserts a claim for damages against the abstract company, which the company pays. Does the abstractor then have a cause of action against Roger?

(d) If you were representing the abstract company, is there any language you might add to the contract for the abstract to protect the company against the risk of liability in situations like these?

B. ATTORNEYS' TITLE OPINIONS AND CERTIFICATES

An attorney who writes a title opinion or title certificate is performing an important task and is held to a high standard of care. The client has hired the attorney based on the belief that she has the professional skills and judgment needed to protect the client's expectations concerning the real estate transaction.

A title opinion or certificate does not guarantee the client that title is in fact marketable. It only reflects the attorney's professional *opinion* that based on the evidence she has, it appears to be marketable. This means that when a title problem arises causing grief or loss to the client, the attorney is not necessarily liable just because the opinion has turned out to be wrong. Just as a physician does not guarantee that a certain operation or treatment will help a patient, a title attorney does not guarantee that title is perfect, with no chance of unpleasant surprises in the future. With our system of public records, coupled with the many types of off-record claims that may have validity, an attorney's undertaking to guarantee title would be foolhardy. All the title attorney promises, by implication if not expressly, is that she has done competent, professional work, complying with the norms established by and followed in the legal community where she practices. If there is a recorded interest that the attorney does not locate, or if she locates an instrument but reaches the conclusion that it does not affect or no longer affects the subject property, she is liable only if her failure to find or failure properly to evaluate is negligent. Attorneys aren't infallible, though perhaps too often they pretend to be. When an attorney makes a mistake in a title matter, the client may be able to prove that the mistake constitutes negligence or malpractice, but this depends on the circumstances.

The attorney should take great care in drafting her title opinion or certificate. Obviously a writing is preferable to an oral opinion. Additionally, her opinion should include a specific statement of the records she has reviewed, along with any limitations and qualifiers with respect to the conclusions. In many deals, an attorney opinion will be a closing requirement, with the exact language of the opinion subject to intense negotiation. In addition to opinions about the status of title, attorneys are often asked to opine as to other matters, such as the legal status and authority of parties to engage in the transaction, the validity and enforceability of the documents, the priority of a particular interest, and the effective coverage and protection of a title insurance commitment and policy.

NORTH BAY COUNCIL, INC., BOY SCOUTS v. BRUCKNER
Supreme Court of New Hampshire, 1989
563 A.2d 428

SOUTER, Justice. In this action for legal malpractice in failing to make adequate disclosure of a cloud on the title to real property, the plaintiff appeals a defendant's verdict rendered after jury trial in the Superior Court (Smith, J.). Because a verdict should have been directed for the plaintiff on the issue of liability, we reverse and remand for a new trial on damages.

The title problem underlying this action was first brought to the court's notice in North Bay Council, Inc. v. Grinnell, 461 A.2d 114 (N.H. 1983), upon which we rely in part for an understanding of facts and procedural history. In 1951, William Morse Cole conveyed a tract of some 1200 acres in Orford and Piermont to Kaiora Camp, Inc. The recorded deed from Cole to the camp contained this paragraph:

> RESTRICTIONS: It is a condition of this conveyance that the Grantee herein and is (sic) successor shall not, for a period of TEN YEARS from the date of this deed, use the land and premises herein conveyed for any purpose other than agriculture, lumbering, and a SUMMER CAMP for children under secondary school age; and that any other Commercial Enterprise such as maintaining a Public House of entertainment and/or recreation, a Public Boat Livery or a Public Store, is excluded from the provileges (sic) under this conveyance; but the term Commercial Enterprise shall not be construed to include the building and rental or sale of a dwelling or dwellings for single-family use standing not less then (sic) two hundred feet from all other dwellings on said land; and further, the Grantee and its successors herein, shall not sell any part of the property herein conveyed until it shall have first offered it for purchase to the Grantor, his heirs or assigns, at the highest price at which they have received a Bona Fide Offer.

Cole died in 1961, and the following year Kaiora Camp agreed to sell the land for $125,000 to Bay Shore Council, Inc., Boy Scouts of America, the corporate predecessor in interest of the plaintiff, North Bay Council, Inc. . . . In anticipation of its purchase, the plaintiff acted through a Massachusetts lawyer associated with it as a director or trustee, Charles Demakis, who hired the defendant, Karl T. Bruckner, Esq., to provide an abstract of title and an opinion about its quality. The title examination disclosed Cole's restrictions set out above, but it revealed no indication that the property had been released from the restrictions, or that the restrictions had been waived by those entitled to their benefit, or that the obligation imposed by the right of first refusal had been satisfied by Kaiora Camp.

Because time was short, the defendant gave no written opinion prior to the closing, but he did communicate with Demakis over the telephone. The defendant testified that he apprised Demakis of the language creating the right of first refusal for the benefit of Cole, his heirs and assigns, and gave his opinion that the resulting restriction had expired by its own terms ten years after the date of Cole's deed. The plaintiff proceeded to accept conveyance of the land and thereafter received the title abstract certified by the defendant, which quoted the paragraph of restrictions in Cole's deed, together with the defendant's written opinion that the plaintiff then had "good" title to the tract, subject to several listed encumbrances not relevant here, but without mention of the first refusal.

Although Kaiora Camp paid no heed to Cole's restrictions when it conveyed the land to the plaintiff, the first refusal right attracted attention in 1979, when the plaintiff was negotiating a sale of the major part of the property to Webville Enterprises, Inc. . . . Webville's lawyer discovered the first refusal provision, which he viewed as creating a cloud on the plaintiff's title, and soon thereafter Cole's heirs, his two daughters, learned about it. The heirs declined at that time to purchase the tract, but after the plaintiff had begun action to quiet the title in North Bay Council, Inc. v. Grinnell *supra*, they claimed the right to purchase at the price the plaintiff had paid in 1962. North Bay Council, Inc. v. Grinnell, 461 A.2d at 115.

In that earlier action, the superior court construed the first refusal right as enduring beyond ten years from the date of Cole's deed, but subject to the rule against perpetuities, so as to limit its enforceability to twenty-one years from Cole's death in 1961. *Id.* at 116. The heirs nevertheless lost their bid to enforce the right at the 1962 price when the court found them chargeable with laches in asserting their claim, *id.* at 117, and the appeal to this court was ostensibly limited to the application of the rule against perpetuities and the doctrine of laches, *id.* at 116. Our affirmance of the superior court's judgment left the plaintiff in a position to sell the property and to begin this malpractice or negligence action against the defendant.

The plaintiff's declaration faults the defendant, not in examining the title or in abstracting the record, but in advising that the title was good, subject only to the exceptions not relevant here. The nub of the claim is negligence in failing to advise that the language creating the first refusal right constituted an objectionable cloud on Kaiora Camp's title. As a consequence of its reliance on the title opinion, the plaintiff is said ultimately to have incurred damages resulting from delay in disposing of the property until the title could be cleared through the prior litigation. The case was tried to a jury, which returned a verdict for the defendant. . . .

A plaintiff is entitled to a directed verdict on liability only if no rational trier of fact viewing the evidence most favorably to the defendant could fail to find on undisputed facts that each element of liability has been proven. . . . The elements of liability in a legal malpractice action to which this rule may be applied require demonstration of a relationship, as of client and attorney, upon the latter of whom the law imposes a duty to exercise care, skill and knowledge in providing legal services to the client; a breach of that duty; and a connection of legally recognized causation between the breach and resulting harm to the client. . . .

The obligation of the lawyer giving an opinion on title to real estate reflects the normal concern of a client intending to buy land, who, in the absence of a different agreement with an intending seller, seeks ideally to acquire property free from third-party interests. Given the fact that no transaction in life can promise entire certainty of consequences, the buyer's actual objective is to limit the risk of harm from third-party claims to some practically achievable minimum. . . .

Accordingly, a lawyer evaluating title to real property for an intending buyer is bound by the standard of professional due care to disclose and explain the significance of any feature of the title, subject to discovery within the requisite scope of the lawyer's title examination, that would lead a reasonably prudent purchaser to refuse to take conveyance of the property, at least when paying full value for it. IV *American Law of Property* §18.7 (1952). Under the standard of the prudent purchaser, features subject to such disclosure and advice include not only actual defects and encumbrances, but any apparent defects and encumbrances subject to reasonable objection as creating risks of adverse claims or losses that the prudent buyer would refuse to run, which are thus spoken of as clouds on the title. *See* Dowd v. Gagnon, 187 A.2d 63, 65 (N.H. 1962).

As the second element of its case on liability, therefore, the plaintiff had to demonstrate that a reasonably prudent buyer in 1962 would not have paid full value for property with a record title that included Cole's 1951 first refusal provision, in the absence of any indication of record that its terms had been released, waived or satisfied, and that the defendant failed to explain that, on the state of the entire record, the terms of the 1951 deed thus rendered the title unmarketable. The plaintiff had the burden, that is to say, to demonstrate the significance of the preemptive 1951 deed language; its inconsistency, standing alone, with marketability of title in 1962; and the defendant's failure to give adequate advice to this effect.

The first step in thus establishing breach of duty, to demonstrate the significance of Cole's restriction, presented a matter to be resolved by the court, under the rule that interpretation of the terms of a deed is an issue of law. The trial court committed error, however, not only by leaving it to the jurors to place the final construction on Cole's language, but also by charging them that the specific issue of interpretation was whether the right of first refusal created in 1951 was enforceable at the time of Kaiora Camp's conveyance to the plaintiffs. As we have seen, a cloud is sufficient to render title unmarketable, and a cloud is defined by reference, not to the ultimate enforceability of a third party's demand, but to the reasonableness of a buyer's objection to a potential third-party claim. Thus, the appropriate question was not whether Cole's heirs could have enforced the right of first refusal in 1962, but whether Cole's language, considered in light of the entire record title, raised a reasonable question about the plaintiff's ability to convey free of preemptive third-party rights. Another way to phrase the appropriate question would have been to ask whether the first refusal provision could reasonably be read to provide a colorable basis for a third-party claim that, if pressed, would cause damage to the buyer, whatever its ultimate resolution might be.

When the question about the meaning of the 1951 language is posed this way, the deed restriction does not present a difficult problem of interpretation. The paragraph headed "Restrictions" contains four clauses separated by semi-colons. The terms of the first restrict the uses of the land to agriculture, lumbering and a children's summer camp, for a period ten years from the date of the deed. The second and third clauses forbid any other commercial uses of the land except as sites for single-family houses at least two hundred feet apart. The fourth clause creates the right of first refusal. The plaintiff argues that if the ten-year limitation contained in the first clause also applied to the second and third, the latter two would be redundant, since there would be no need to forbid a commercial use such as running a public house if the only permissible uses were agriculture, lumbering and camping for children. On this reasoning, therefore, the ten-year limitation applies to the first clause in which it is contained, but not to the second or third, with the result that the land was open to commercial residential development after ten years. Finally, if there is thus good reason to infer that the time limitation has no application to the second and third clauses, then the contextual basis to hold the limitation applicable to the fourth clause creating the right of first refusal must at best be doubtful. (And the doubt would not disappear even upon realizing that Cole's wife joined in his deed in order to give Kaiora Camp a ten-year right of first refusal over certain other land that she owned.)

What is significant is not whether this analysis would ultimately have been held to be right or wrong (even though it is consistent with the results reached by the superior court when it construed the fourth clause in the earlier litigation). What is important is that the analysis rests on a textual basis placing it within the realm of reasonable argument that there was no express limit of time within which Cole or his heirs were entitled to first refusal.

. . . A gambler might have bought from the camp under these circumstances, but the evidence indicated that no prudent purchaser would have done so, let alone for full value, subject to the risk that some time in the future Cole or his heirs could demand conveyance of the property to them at the price paid by the plaintiff to the camp. No contrary opinion was presented to the jurors, who could not reasonably have found otherwise.

The third step in considering breach of duty is to inquire whether the defendant did whatever was reasonably necessary to apprise the plaintiff of the title's unmarketability, and on this question we perceive no conflict in evidence for the jury to resolve. The title opinion rendered after the closing and supposedly confirming the defendant's prior advice made no reference whatever to the provision in question or to the absence of any recorded indication of release, waiver or compliance, or to the risk of at least a colorable third-party claim inherent in this state of the title. Moreover, the defendant's own account of his conversation with Demakis before the closing indicates that at best he mentioned the 1951 language and advised that the period of its enforceability had expired. No one could have found that he had advised of the risk created by the provision. . . .

The remaining element of liability required proof that the failure to give adequate advice was a cause of the litigation and delay that the plaintiff claims as the source of monetary damages. . . . Because the object of hiring a title attorney to advise about risks inherent in the title is to enable a buyer to act prudently either in declining to take title subject to those risks, or at least in assessing the risks intelligently if the buyer should decide to take title anyway, proof of the causal link between negligent title advice and subsequent damage required evidence of the buyer's reliance upon the advice. . . .

In this case, the burden to prove reliance is not subject to complication by claims of comparative or contributory negligence, and there is no evidence that the damages flowed from any title defect other than the cloud that the defendant failed to identify as such. Hence it is fair to say here that causation may be established by proof that the plaintiff completed the purchase in sole reliance on the defendant's opinion that the title was free from the cloud under consideration, and that the subsequent delay and litigation were within the risk of harm that the defendant's opinion failed to disclose. On neither point was there any evidence on which the jury could reasonably have found in the defendant's favor. . . .

. . . As we observed before, the risk was that the individuals arguably entitled to exercise the right of first refusal in 1962 would claim that they had not received the offer to which they had been entitled and would demand the conveyance that they could then have obtained, or its economic equivalent. That, of course, is exactly what Cole's heirs subsequently demanded and would have received, but for the successful defense of laches sustained by this court in the prior appeal. No reasonable juror could have reached any other conclusion. . . .

Reversed and remanded.

Problem 11B

Anthony sold a 160-acre tract of land to Melissa in 1983. In the deed of conveyance, Anthony reserved all subsurface rights to oil, gas, and minerals. Since then, Melissa has maintained a single-family residence on the property and has farmed the 159 acres not immediately surrounding the home. This year Melissa contracted to sell the property to Frank for $600,000. The contract is silent on the matter of marketability of title but calls for Melissa to convey the property in fee simple absolute. At closing she presented Frank with such a deed, making no exception for any oil, gas, or mineral rights. At closing, Frank's lawyer, Lisa, objected to the marketability of the title because she examined title and found the reservation of rights in Anthony. Melissa responds by asserting that she acquired full marketable title to the property by virtue of adverse possession.

(a) Is Lisa's objection to a lack of marketable title valid, given that Melissa is presenting a fee simple absolute deed?

(b) Assume that Melissa takes a hard position on marketable title and insists that Frank must close on the contract or lose his $25,000 deposit. Lisa maintains her position that the title to the property is unmarketable because of the cloud created by the oil, gas, and mineral reservation in Anthony. Consequently, Frank refuses to close and sues Melissa for return of his deposit. The trial court deciding the case determines that Melissa has indeed attained full fee simple absolute title to the property, including the rights to oil, gas, and minerals, and denies Frank's claim to return of the deposit. Is Lisa liable to Frank for the loss of his deposit?

(c) Assume instead that Melissa responds to Lisa's concern about marketability simply by agreeing to release Frank from the contract and returning his deposit. Two months later Melissa sells the property to Lone Star Gas for $700,000. Lone Star Gas immediately brings a quiet title action to address the issue of Melissa's rights in the oil, gas, and minerals, and the court determines that Melissa had the right to transfer as a result of adverse possession. Lone Star does some testing and confirms that there is a large natural gas reserve in the shale beneath the property, making the property worth at least $4 million. Can Frank sue Lisa for making him miss out on a lost opportunity? After all, if he closed on the contract with Melissa, he would own a highly valuable natural gas property.

(d) Suppose that at closing Lisa, instead of worrying about the lack of marketable title, simply reviewed the facts and agreed that Melissa did have a right to convey the full fee simple absolute title to the property, including rights to oil, gas, and minerals. As a result of Lisa's conclusion, Frank closes on the purchase. Two days later, Anthony sues Frank to quiet title to his reserved rights. Anthony sues because Lone Star Gas approached him with an offer to buy his rights for $400,000, provided he can demonstrate good title. Lone Star is acquiring oil, gas, and mineral rights from a number of property owners in the area, as it plans to undertake a major hydrofracking operation. Assume that the court determines that Anthony has a valid reservation and that Melissa did not acquire those rights by adverse possession or any other means. In such a case, can Frank sue Lisa for damages as a result of Lisa being wrong about the marketability of Melissa's title to the property at the time of closing?

C. TITLE INSURANCE

Unlike so much of our property law inherited from England, title insurance is an American invention, with its roots in Philadelphia during the 1870s. Title insurance is a form of title assurance that serves as an alternative to an abstract of title or a lawyer's opinion. Gradually, title insurance has captured a greater and greater share of the title assurance market. Since the 1960s, this growth has accelerated and has become national rather than regional, the primary cause being movement of capital. Real estate finance markets became national, and interstate purchasers of mortgage loans demanded a national product for title assurance. Out-of-state lenders and institutional buyers of mortgages were (and are) not willing to rely on the opinions of local title attorneys with whom they are not familiar. Title insurance provides a vehicle for stating an opinion of title within the context of an insurance policy. The policy is written consonant with a set of underwriting standards and issued by a corporation that is regulated and required to have reserve assets. It is easier to learn about a few regulated title insurance companies than it is to learn about numerous individual attorneys. This is one of the commercial appeals of title insurance. It is standardized, the players are generally well known, and they are regulated with information available concerning asset reserves and loss records. Though all of this makes title insurance highly marketable in an integrated economy, it is still important to know something about the skill of the people working for the title company who make the determinations as to status of title. A client, after all, is more interested in getting an accurate statement of title than she is in knowing that there are assets to reach in the event that litigation is needed over a disputed title problem.

Title insurance has two main functions: the insurer searches the records and discloses its findings, and it insures undisclosed risks. These are the two reasons why purchasers and mortgagees buy title insurance. The first function, search and disclose, is also fulfilled by title abstracts and attorneys' title opinions. The insured purchaser or lender pays to acquire valuable information in order to reduce historical risk. The insured wants to know that she is getting good record title and wants to know what encumbrances, if any, burden that title.

The second function, insurance of undisclosed risk, represents risk spreading, the classic function of all types of insurance products. A title abstract or an attorney's title opinion may be wrong, even though the abstractor or attorney was careful. When an erroneous abstract or opinion causes loss to a purchaser, the abstractor or attorney is liable only if the purchaser can prove malpractice. This is the critical difference between these products and title insurance. The insurer has absolute liability for insured defects. A title insurance company pays claims for losses stemming from insured risks, regardless of whether it was at fault (negligent) in searching title.

In modern transactions, approximately 25 percent of closings involve a title-related issue or problem; consequently, informed purchasers and lenders have a strong preference for title insurance. The distinction between the legal standard of liability, fault-based for abstracts and title opinions versus no-fault for title insurance, is critical. When a purchaser or lender suffers a loss because title turns out not to be as expected, she wants to be paid without having to prove negligence or malpractice, which, even in a simple case, may be hard to do. In addition, wholly apart from the liability standard, there are compelling institutional reasons for favoring title insurance. An insurance company is required to meet state-prescribed solvency standards, and it is used to paying claims when they are found to be covered risks. Abstractors and attorneys, when found liable for defective title work, will not always be solvent. Most, but not all, abstractors are bonded; most, but not all, attorneys carry malpractice insurance in some amount. It doesn't make sense to use or rely on an attorney's malpractice carrier when there is the practical alternative of a solvent, regulated insurance company.

For these reasons, a real estate attorney should almost always use title insurance, rather than a title abstract or a title opinion. This is true regardless of the type of transaction — whether the client is a homebuyer, a purchaser of commercial property, a developer, or a lender; and whether the client's investment is small, such as a modest house or condominium, or large. In fact, given the changing nature of the housing and mortgage markets, a strong case can be made that a lawyer who fails to obtain title insurance for a homebuyer or lender is guilty of malpractice. *See* Robin Paul Malloy & Mark Klapow, *Attorney Malpractice for Failure to Require Fee Owner's Title Insurance in a Residential Real Estate Transaction*, 74 St. John's L. Rev. 407 (2000); Robin Paul Malloy, *Using Title Insurance to Avoid Malpractice and Protect Clients in a Changing Marketplace*, 11 The Digest 51 (2003). This argument recognizes that real estate markets are no longer local or even regional. Integrated financial and sales markets have made real estate markets national, and in some respects (by way of secondary mortgage market activities) international in scope. As a result, the standard of professional conduct has been elevated to a national rather than local one, and title insurance has become the expected professional norm.

It is also important to remember that a title insurance policy is no substitute for continuing to seek the best possible warranty deed from the seller. A title policy provides insurance coverage for matters covered by the policy. In some situations, however, a title issue may not come within the policy, and in this situation a buyer would then look to a cause of action on the deed warranties.

1. The Commitment and the Policy

In a typical transaction with title insurance, there are two primary documents of legal significance: the title insurance commitment and the policy. Suppose a buyer has contracted to buy a tract of land, with title insurance to be obtained. Prior to closing, while the contract is executory, the buyer (or someone else) contacts a title insurer and orders a *title insurance commitment,* also often called a *title insurance binder* or *preliminary title report*. Only after doing a title search will the company issue a commitment or binder. If it has a title plant for the county where the land lies, it searches "in house"; otherwise, it contracts out, ordering a title search from a local abstractor or local attorney.

Upon completing the title search, the company issues its written commitment. The commitment is the company's promise to issue a policy, on a designated standard form, provided that it receives the insurance premium and that certain other specified conditions are met. A title *policy* is only issued after closing.

Insurance policies issued today are standardized. The vast majority of policies are on forms promulgated by a trade organization called the American Land Title Association (ALTA). In Texas, the state department of insurance has promulgated its own forms, and in California, the forms of the California Land Title Association (CLTA) are sometimes used. A title policy can insure a variety of real property interests, not only fee simple estates but also interests such as leaseholds, life estates, and joint tenancies. As mentioned earlier, both buyers and lenders often obtain title insurance. Different policy forms are used; the buyer obtains an Owner's Policy, the lender a Loan Policy or a Mortgagee Policy. In today's marketplace, companies have introduced multiple variations for their policies, so it is important for the lawyer to attend carefully to the particular terms of the specific commitment and policy to be used in her transaction. Not only do companies offer various standard forms, including long-forms and short-forms, they also differentiate their products by offering special endorsements for those forms. Deciding what you want is much like buying a new car — for example, if you want to buy a Honda, you have decided on the make, but you have plenty of decisions to make with respect to model and trim.

To determine whether a particular title problem is insured, you must study the policy of title insurance carefully. Policies are laid out in several different parts, which must be read in combination. The key parts are (1) the insuring provisions, (2) the conditions and stipulations, (3) the exclusions from coverage, (4) the exceptions from coverage (typically listed on Schedule B), and (5) the endorsements, if any.

The most common and significant exclusions and exceptions, usually expressed in standardized language, are:

1. Survey exception. There is no coverage for matters an accurate survey would show, such as encroachments, boundary line disputes, or shortages in area.
2. Zoning and building laws.
3. Rights of parties in possession not shown by the public records.
4. Rights or claims of which the insured has knowledge prior to issuance of the policy.

5. Taxes or assessments for the current year, which are not yet due and payable, and taxes or assessments that are not shown as existing liens by the public records.
6. Liens for work performed on the property and materials incorporated into the property (mechanic's and materialmen's liens).

All policies have some title risks that are not insured. With respect to the scope of coverage, the company and the insured have opposing interests. The company wants to minimize the risk of claims that must be paid, and the insured wants maximum protection. The scope of coverage is negotiable and, especially in commercial transactions, is often negotiated by the company and the insured purchaser or lender. For most policies, the exclusions and exceptions are the key determinant of coverage. As a general rule of thumb, if a title matter affects the insured land and the policy does not exclude it from coverage, then it is an insured risk. The insuring provisions, as well as the conditions and stipulations, are boilerplate that is seldom touched. Broad exclusions and exceptions minimize coverage; narrow exclusions and exceptions expand coverage.

The primary benefit of title insurance coverage is that the insured can recover if there is an actual loss as a result of someone else asserting a claim or interest that turns out to be superior to the stated interest of the insured. Title insurance also covers the insured for actual loss resulting from a document that is improperly signed, sealed, acknowledged, or delivered; or if there is fraud, forgery, incapacity, or impersonation involved in the transaction. The insured is also covered against improper filing of documents, meaning that the title company will generally take on the responsibility to record all closing documents. Any errors made in the title search or loss as a result of a wild deed or other undiscoverable title defect would also be covered unless otherwise eliminated from coverage. Many policies also protect a *legal right of access* to and from the property. It is important to note, however, that legal access and physical access may not be the same thing. For example, land with a legal right of access may be submerged under flood waters for nine months of the year and yet remain legally accessible. The other major benefit to title insurance is that the policy also covers attorneys' fees, in that the title company will defend against claims. This can be valuable if the title company is willing to pursue a matter, but the policy gives the company the alternative of simply paying a claim up to the full amount of the coverage. Obviously, the company will assess the cost of litigation against the cost of paying the submitted claim and other potential claims on similarly situated properties, which they might have to address.

When both a lender and an owner policy are issued, the title insurance liability exposure is not cumulative. The lender is paid to the amount of the outstanding debt and then the owner is paid. Together, the title insurance company is only liable up to the full amount of the stated title insurance coverage.

VESTIN MORTGAGE, INC. v. FIRST AMERICAN TITLE INSURANCE COMPANY
Supreme Court of Utah, 2006
139 P.3d 1055

WILKINS, Associate Chief Justice. Vestin Mortgage, Inc. (Vestin) sought to recover under two policies of title insurance issued by First American Title Insurance Company (First American). The claim arises from the adoption of a special improvement district (SID) by the municipality in which the real property lies. First American said the notice of intent to create the SID recorded by the municipality was not a defect in title covered by the policies and moved to dismiss Vestin's complaint. The district court agreed and granted the motion. Vestin appealed to the court of appeals, which affirmed. Vestin now challenges the decision of the court of appeals on certiorari. We affirm.

BACKGROUND

Vestin, or its predecessor, made two loans to The Ranches, L.C., each secured by trust deeds on real property located in Eagle Mountain, Utah. In connection with the loans, First American issued two title insurance policies that insured Vestin's interest under the trust deeds.

Between the dates of the two loans, Eagle Mountain adopted a resolution declaring its intention to create a SID, adopted a resolution creating the SID, and recorded a "Notice of Intention" with the county recorder's office in Utah County, in accordance with Utah Code section 17A-3-307. The notice disclosed that the town council had adopted a resolution declaring the council's intention to create the SID, the project's total anticipated cost, and the council's intention to assess real property within the boundaries of the SID to pay for the improvements. The notice also included a copy of the ordinance that was adopted creating the SID. The property securing the Vestin loans lies within the SID.

Some months after the title policies were issued, Eagle Mountain adopted the "Assessment Ordinance" which levied the assessment on real property within the SID. This ordinance included a provision which indicated, for the first time, that if the property were sold, the property's share of the assessment would be accelerated and due in full upon the sale instead of being payable in small annual amounts over an extended period of time.

About two years after the second policy was issued by First American, The Ranches defaulted on the two loans and Vestin took title to the property pursuant to its trust deeds through a nonjudicial foreclosure. Vestin then entered into a contract to sell the property, and in conjunction with this potential sale, Vestin received an updated title report regarding the property. Vestin alleges that it is at this time that it first learned of the assessment levied against the property by the SID and that the assessment became immediately due and payable upon the sale of the property. After Vestin disclosed this information to the buyer, the buyer refused to proceed with the sale of the property. Vestin filed a claim with First American in which Vestin contended that the policies insured against the assessment. First American denied the claim. . . .

ANALYSIS

The sole issue before us is whether the title insurance policies unambiguously applied only to actual assessments for a special improvement district and did not include an obligation to provide notice of an intent to create the district and levy the assessments. We conclude that only actual assessments are covered and therefore affirm the decision of the court of appeals. . . .

We begin our analysis by looking at the plain language of the policies, paying particular attention to the insuring clauses as did the court of appeals. There are three insuring clauses within the policies that are relevant to Vestin's claim. These are the policy jacket cover, F.A. Form 31, and CLTA Form 104. We will review them in turn.

I. THE POLICY JACKET COVER

The policy jacket cover states that First American "insures . . . against loss or damage . . . sustained or incurred by the insured by reason of" and then goes on to list nine insurable events or conditions. The condition at issue here is number two, addressing "[a]ny defect in or lien or encumbrance on the title." Vestin argues that the creation of the SID and the filing of the Notice of Intention did in fact create a defect in the title. First American, on the other hand, argues that neither the creation of the SID nor the filing of the Notice of Intention created a defect. Instead, the actual levying of the assessment created the defect in the title, and the assessment was actually levied by the city of Eagle Mountain after the policies had been issued and thus falls outside the coverage of the policies.

Unlike other insurance contracts, title insurance does not insure against future events. Thus, in order for a defect, lien, or encumbrance to fall within the insurance policy's coverage, it must have been in existence as of the effective date of the policy. At a minimum, an existing assessment that has been recorded would be considered a defect in the title and would be covered unless it had been otherwise exempted or excluded. The more difficult question, and the one before us now, is whether the recorded notice of the possibility of a future assessment also rises to the level of a defect, lien, or encumbrance. We conclude that it does not.

Neither the creation of the SID nor the filing of the Notice of Intention creates a lien on real property that affects the title. Utah Code section 17A-3-323 (2005) provides that an assessment becomes a lien on the property assessed on the day the ordinance levying the assessment becomes effective.

In Vestin's case, the effective date of the ordinance that levied the assessment was after the date on which the policies were issued by First American. No lien could have attached as a result of this SID at the time First American provided the policies.

Additionally, neither the creation of the SID nor the Notice of Intention is an encumbrance on the property. No claim or liability attached to the title or property arises by virtue of the creation of the SID or Notice of Intention. Likewise, no defect in the title is occasioned by the creation of the SID or the Notice of Intention. . . .

It is important to remember that the "defect," "lien," or "encumbrance" mentioned in the policy jacket cover had to be *in* or *on* the *title*. The SID and Notice of Intention simply had no effect in or on the title. The policies unambiguously applied only to actual assessments and did not include an obligation to disclose the SID or Notice of Intention.

II. F.A. FORM 31 AND CLTA FORM 104

We also look to the other two insuring clauses for any obligation to provide notice of the creation of a SID and possible assessment. The first, F.A. Form 31, provides in part that First American will insure

> against loss which the Insured shall sustain by reason of any of the following matters:
>
> (1) Any incorrectness in the assurance which the Company hereby gives:
> (a) That there are no covenants, conditions, or restrictions under which the lien of the mortgage referred to in Schedule A can be cut off, subordinated, or otherwise impaired.

In addition, the CLTA Form 104, as it appears in the policy at issue, states that First American will insure

> against loss or damage which such insured shall sustain by reason of any of the following . . .
>
> 5. The existence of any subsisting tax or assessment lien which is prior to the insured mortgage except: NONE
>
> 6. The existence of other matters affecting the validity or priority of the lien of the insured mortgage, other than those shown in the policy except: NONE

Neither of these forms obligated First American to disclose information regarding the SID or the possibility of a future assessment. We find no ambiguity in this regard in either of these two forms. The forms, at their core, insure the mortgage liens that Vestin held in the property. Specifically, the forms insure against loss or damage that Vestin would sustain due to the *mortgage* being "cut off, subordinated, or otherwise impaired," the loss of priority, and "other matters affecting the validity" of the mortgage lien.

Neither the creation of the SID nor the Notice of Intention affected the priority or validity of the mortgage lien, nor was the mortgage lien "cut off, subordinated, or otherwise impaired." Once The Ranches defaulted on the loans, Vestin was able to exercise its rights under the trust deeds without any consequence arising from the SID and to take ownership through a non-judicial foreclosure. Nothing in the Notice of Intention or in the SID affected the mortgage lien or affected the title Vestin acquired. Only the actual assessment ordinance has affected Vestin in any way, and only as to the ability to sell the property, not as to the validity of title. Vestin still holds a valid title to the property. . . .

III. THE EXCLUSION AND EXCEPTION SECTIONS OF THE POLICIES

Vestin also seeks to extend coverage through the exclusions and exemptions that are enumerated in the policies, in particular through the governmental police power exception. As the court of appeals concluded, "Because the existence of the SID and the notice of Eagle Mountain's intention to levy assessments do not affect Vestin's title and, therefore, are not covered by the policies, the exclusions to the policies and the recorded police power exception to those exclusions are not applicable." We agree. If there is *no* coverage, then an exception that prevents application of an exclusion from coverage has no application.

CONCLUSION

A notice of intent to create a special improvement district and to levy assessments in the future did not give rise to coverage under the title policies or to an obligation on the title insurer to disclose that notice as part of the contract of insurance. The decision of the court of appeals is affirmed.

2. Title Insurance and the Contract of Purchase

In many contracts to buy land, the purchaser intends to obtain title insurance as the primary or sole method of title protection. Typically, the purchaser has made this decision before entering into the contract of purchase, and therefore the contract expressly refers to title insurance. In addition to requiring a title commitment prior to closing, a contract may include language such as:

> Seller at Seller's expense shall furnish an Owner's Policy of Title Insurance issued by [*insert name of designated title insurance provider*] in the amount of the purchase price and dated at or after closing. The Policy shall guarantee Buyer's title to be good and indefeasible in accordance with the standard form of policy used by said company.

A contract may also call for the issuance of a lender's title insurance policy if an institutional lender will be providing financing and taking a mortgage against the property as part of the transaction. The buyer of the property and the lender making a loan to be secured by the property both have an interest in trying to manage the risk of a title defect by acquiring title insurance. When the property is purchased and financed, the insured parties have an expectation that certain insurable risks will be covered by the title insurance commitment and the policy that will follow. A question that sometimes arises, however, concerns the nature of the risk that is expected to be covered by title insurance. For instance, does it include the risk of a defect in the closing process itself, such as dealing with a forged document delivered pursuant to the contract?

KEYINGHAM INVESTMENTS, LLC v. FIDELITY NATIONAL TITLE INSURANCE COMPANY

Court of Appeals of Georgia, 2009
680 S.E. 2d 442, affirmed, 702 S.E. 2d 851 (Ga. 2010)[*]

BLACKBURN, Presiding Judge. In this breach of contract action, Keyingham Investments, LLC and Peter St. Martin (d/b/a Real Estate Solutions Providers, Inc.) appeal from the trial court's order granting summary judgment to Fidelity National Title Insurance Company and denying summary judgment to them. Keyingham and Martin argue that the plain language of the title commitment contract required Fidelity to issue a title insurance policy that covered their losses caused by a forgery at closing. We agree and reverse. . . .

The undisputed facts show that Thoughtforce International, Inc., Sam Dobrow, and Real Estate Solutions Providers, Inc. (the "lenders") agreed to loan $106,000 to a man they thought was Michael Shanahan. In exchange, they were to receive a security deed conveying a security interest in the subject real property, in which the real Michael Shanahan had an ownership interest. Prior to closing, the lenders received a commitment from Fidelity to insure the subject property against defects in the title upon the satisfaction of certain conditions. The commitment was executed on behalf of Fidelity by its agent closing lawyers. The commitment conditions included the following:

> Documents satisfactory to the Company creating the interest in the land and/or mortgage to be insured must be signed, delivered and recorded:
>   a) Execution, recording and delivery of a Security Deed in the original amount of 106000, in favor of THOUGHTFORCE INT, INC, 34%, SAM

* [We have reproduced the Court of Appeals opinion rather than the Supreme Court opinion because the former provides a more detailed statement of the facts and a fuller analysis of the parties' arguments–Eds.]

DOBROW 16%, REAL ESTATE SOL. PRO. INC. 50%, to secure subject property.

Pursuant to this commitment, the law firm acting as Fidelity's agent prepared the closing documents for the $106,000 loan transaction, including the security deed. At the closing on May 12, 2004, the law firm checked the identity of the man who claimed to be Michael Shanahan and, satisfied with the identity documents produced, including a driver's license with photo, proceeded with the closing. Unbeknownst to either the law firm or the lenders, this man in fact was not Shanahan but was an imposter with false identification papers. After the documents were executed and reviewed, the law firm disbursed the funds from the closing, including payment to Fidelity of the insurance premium for the title policy to be issued under the commitment. The law firm then forwarded the executed security deed to the county clerk for recordation in the county's property files. The recordation took place on June 1, 2004, and the recorded deed was returned to the law firm.

The loan then went into default, and the parties, including the law firm as agent for Fidelity, learned of the fraud perpetrated at the closing. At Fidelity's express instruction, the law firm refused to issue the title policy referenced in the title commitment. The lenders made a claim under the commitment agreement in September 2004, which Fidelity denied. On June 2, 2005, two of the lenders (Thoughtforce and Dobrow) assigned to Keyingham their interests in the promissory note, in the security deed, and in the claim against Fidelity.

On June 6, 2005, Keyingham and Martin d/b/a Real Estate Solutions Providers, Inc. sued Fidelity for breach of contract and other claims, seeking to recover the $106,000 (plus interest) lost in the transaction. Plaintiffs moved for partial summary judgment for liability on the breach of contract claim, arguing that Fidelity was liable as a matter of law for its failure to issue the policy as promised in the title commitment. Fidelity cross-moved for summary judgment. . . . Concluding that the forgery meant that the conditions of the title commitment were not met, the trial court entered partial summary judgment in favor of Fidelity and against the lenders on the breach of contract claim (concomitantly denying plaintiffs' motion for summary judgment on the same claim), which judgment the lenders appeal.

The parties agree that this appeal rises and falls on whether the conditions set forth in the title commitment (also known as a binder) were met. If they were met, then according to Fidelity's own agent attorney, the promised "long form"[3] policy should have issued that would have covered the forgery

---

3. "Long form" policies are issued after the recorded deed is received back from the county clerk, as opposed to "short form" policies that are issued at the real estate closing.

in this case.[4] If they were not met, then Fidelity was not so obligated and therefore would not have been liable for its refusal to issue the policy.

The key condition at issue required that "[d]ocuments satisfactory to the Company creating the interest in the land and/or mortgage to be insured must be signed, delivered and recorded." Fidelity argues that the modifying phrase "creating the interest in the land and/or mortgage to be insured" meant that a forged document, which would neither pass nor create any interest in the land, would prevent this condition from being fulfilled. We disagree.

"An insurance contract that is clear and unambiguous must be enforced by the court as made. The binder in this case is unambiguous." Glass v. Stewart Title Guaranty Co., 354 S.E.2d 187, 189 (Ga. Ct. App. 1987). The plain meaning of the binder condition here was that documents, which were satisfactory to Fidelity, and whose language created the interest in the land or mortgage to be insured, had to be signed, delivered, and recorded. In other words, the question to be resolved in applying the commitment's conditions was did the language or form of the executed documents here, satisfy Fidelity's agent. It is not whether those accepted documents, in fact, created the insured's interest in the property as was held by the trial court. The entire purpose of title insurance is to protect the insured against defects, including fraud or forgeries, in the chain of title. The protection for the insurer in this process is in the review and acceptance of the documents by the insurer's agent prior to any liability attaching under the binder. . . .

The security deed was drafted by Fidelity's agent law firm to Fidelity's satisfaction. This deed was then signed, delivered, and recorded, all under the supervision of Fidelity's agent and to its satisfaction. The commitment's conditions were undisputedly fulfilled to the satisfaction of Fidelity, who cannot now complain that such documents failed to satisfy its requirements.

Significantly, unlike the title commitment in *Glass, supra,* the title commitment here did not require that the documents or the security deed had to be executed by a particular person, but only that they had to be executed to the satisfaction of Fidelity's agents. Thus, in *Glass,* when the title commitment required that the deed be signed by Sherrill Y. Wilson, the forged signing of that deed by another person did not fulfill the requirements of the condition. *Id.* Here, the condition at issue did not require that the described documents had to be executed by a named individual; the commitment contract did not specify *who* had to execute those documents, only that they be acceptable to Fidelity's agents, which they were. Thus, the condition was fulfilled when Fidelity's agents reviewed, approved and accepted the closing documents and recorded them. Fidelity then became

---

4. When asked "[i]f the long form policy had been issued before this fraud was discovered, do you have an opinion about whether that policy would have covered this claim?", Fidelity's agent attorney answered: "[T]he answer is, that if assuming there was no knowledge of the forgery and the policy had been issued, Fidelity would have been bound to pay."

obligated to issue the promised title policy, and is thus liable to its insured under the commitment agreement as though it had in fact issued the policy.

Fidelity maintains that absent receipt of a valid interest in the land, the three lenders could not receive title insurance on that land. This argument, however, ignores *that one of the very purposes of title insurance is to protect a party from the consequences of forgery in the chain of title,* which necessarily results in the party not receiving an interest in the land. *See* 16 *Powell on Real Property* §92.04[3] (2008) ("certain risks, referred to as 'off-record' risks, because they are not usually discernable from an inspection of the public record, are considered to be insured by the title insurance policy"; Lawyers Title Ins. Corp. v. First Fed. Sav. Bank & Trust, 744 F. Supp. 778, 786 n.7 (E.D. Mich. 1990) ("[i]t is ironic that in its promotional materials, Lawyers Title repeatedly represents to prospective customers that a primary purpose of title insurance is specifically to protect buyers from the risks of forged instruments").

Analogously, Black v. Pioneer Nat. Title Ins. Co. 225 S.E.2d 689 (Ga. Ct. App. 1976), held that a title insurance policy protected the purchasing landowners when they did not receive fee simple title to the middle portion of the tract they purchased, as it was discovered that a third party (not the seller) actually owned that portion in fee simple. Thus, although the insured parties received no interest whatsoever in this middle portion owned by a third party, the insured parties were able to recover under the title insurance policy that insured their interests in the deed that claimed to give them a fee simple title to this middle portion. *Id.*

Because the plain language of the title commitment condition was fulfilled, the trial court erred . . . in failing to award . . . judgment to the plaintiffs on the question of liability under the breach of contract claim . . . .

Problem 11C

Go back to the facts of Problem 11A and Problem 11B, dealing with an abstract and a lawyer's title opinion respectively, and assume that instead of those title products an insurance company had issued a standard owner's policy of title insurance. How does this affect your analysis of risk and potential liability for asserted losses? Would it make a difference if the insurance company issued a standard title insurance commitment, but not issued a policy because the problem surfaced before the company completed that postclosing step?

Problem 11D

Lamar contracts to buy an apartment complex from Candi. Paragraph 3 of the contract states: "Seller shall deliver, at closing, a general warranty deed conveying said property, subject to (1) covenants, restrictions, utility agree-ments, and easements of record, if any, now in force, provided same are not now violated; and (2) any state of facts an accurate survey may show, provided same does not render title unmarketable." Paragraph 7 of the contract states: "Seller shall order and obtain, at Seller's expense, and Purchaser shall accept, a title insured by a reputable title insurance company selected by Seller." Candi picks Reputable Title Insurance Co., which searches and prepares a title insurance commitment.

(a) Reputable finds and lists, as a special exception, a restrictive covenant recorded in 1985 that restricts occupancy of the apartment units to "adults only," purportedly for the benefit of a neighboring retirement community. The Fair Housing Act, since its amendment in 1988, prohibits discrimination against families with children in the rental and sale of housing. A number of families with children presently live in Candi's apartment complex. Lamar objects to the special exception for the 1985 covenant, but Reputable refuses to remove it. Can Lamar terminate the contract? If so, may Lamar obtain expectancy damages?

(b) Reputable finds and lists, as a matter that requires curative action prior to closing, a problem in the chain of title. Twenty-two years ago, before the apartments were built, Thomas, who then owned the land, died and was survived by his wife. She promptly conveyed the property, by properly recorded warranty deed. There are no probate court records showing a trans-fer, by will or intestate succession, to his wife. The chain of title since that deed, which eventually leads to Candi, is fine. Candi's attorney persuades Reputable that the risk of missing heirs or devisees showing up is remote, and thus curative action is not necessary. Therefore, Reputable issues a new commitment, deleting any requirement concerning, or reference to, Thomas or his estate. At closing, Lamar's attorney asks if the Thomas probate matter has been cleaned up. He is not satisfied by the answer that "it hasn't, but Reputable is issuing a clean policy." He claims title is not marketable, and he and his client, Lamar, leave the closing. Is he correct? Is title marketable?

(c) Suppose you represent the prospective buyer of an apartment com-plex, and the seller submits for your review a draft contract, with Paragraphs 3 and 7 as quoted at the beginning of this problem. Are they acceptable to you? Are there any changes you want to propose?

3. Ethical Problems: Conflicts and Confidentiality

The business of insuring titles is the practice of law, and not surprisingly attorneys are heavily involved in the title insurance industry. Title companies are often owned and managed by attorneys, and companies often hire attor-neys as employees to work "in house." Usually, no special ethical problems are raised in connection with this practice — the company attorney has duties to only one client, the company.

Real estate attorneys who are not insurance company employees often participate in providing title insurance. There are a number of different arrangements in use. The attorney or her law firm may be an agent for a title insurance company, with an underwriting agreement giving the agent a percentage of the insurance premium in exchange for services such as the agent's title search, issuance of commitment, and supervision of the closing. Alternatively, the attorney or firm may own a corporation that functions as an agent. Instead of an agent with broad powers and responsibilities, the attorney may do title work as "examining counsel," submitting an abstract or a certificate to the insurer and receiving a share of the premium as compensation. Another relationship is that of closing attorney, where the insurance company pays the attorney to attend the closing and handle all the closing items necessary for the policy to be written, including receipt of the premium. Closing attorneys usually are paid a flat fee rather than a percentage of the premium. In some states, like Florida, the real estate attorneys operate their own title insurance fund so that members can directly compete with other commercial insurance companies. In many cases, the lawyers involved in title insurance work are recognized or rewarded for having a good record or few errors or claims.

Ethical problems often result when attorneys represent persons other than or in addition to the insurance company. Imagine that your law firm is an agent for a title insurance company. If you have a client buying property and she needs title insurance, which insurer would you like your client to use? Thus, it is not surprising that in many transactions, an attorney who represents a buyer or lender has an economic interest in the title insurance used in the same transaction. Most, but not all, of the ethical problem areas involve multiple representation, or the appearance of multiple representation, and related issues of disclosure and informed consent.

Problem 11E

Donna represents a commercial developer, RP Contractors (RP), which is buying 120 acres of undeveloped land to build a shopping center. RP will develop the land in multiple phases, beginning with the east 50 acres. RP informs Donna that about a year ago the seller of the property granted an easement along the west boundary of the property to the County Water Department. RP tells her that the easement should be 20 feet in width, but RP does not know the exact location. RP wants Donna to do a title search and issue a title opinion as part of his purchase. Instead, Donna gets RP's approval to order title insurance. She engages Quick Title Insurance Inc., a local company with whom she and her firm have no affiliation. When Donna receives the title commitment prior to closing, she reviews it and notices that it does not mention any easement to the County Water Department.

(a) What action, if any, should Donna take at the present time?

(b) Assume that Donna personally searches the land records for the past year, and finds the County Water Department easement recorded in the proper office. A local attorney—one of Donna's friends—is the issuing agent for the insurer and, in his search, evidently missed the easement. What should Donna do? What are her ethical obligations to her client? To the insurance company? To her friend?

Problem 11F

Assume the above facts from Problem 11E, but this time Donna not only represents RP but is also an agent for Republic. In connection with RP's land acquisition Donna provides a title search and issues the title insurance commitment and policy for Republic. Donna's only comments to RP about title insurance were: "Don't worry, I can save you some money on the title work because I am an agent for Republic Title and I can give you a 10 percent discount." After taking on the representation of RP, Donna assigns the title search to a new associate at her firm. This is only the second time that Donna's associate has done a title search and prepared the title insurance commitment. The associate does not find any easements affecting the property and makes the judgment that the seller has marketable title. The associate prepares the commitment and eventually the postclosing title insurance policy showing a "clean" title. Donna signed the commitment and policy as an agent for Republic. Three months after closing, RP comes to see Donna, telling her about a problem with the County Water Department having workers starting to clear vegetation from a strip of the east 50 acres of the property. The County Water Department claims it has a 40-foot-wide utility easement running along the land that it is clearing. RP reminds Donna that she was told about an easement, but RP reiterates that he thought it was located along the west property line and that it would not impact his project. Donna rechecks the title records, and finds that the County Water Department easement was properly recorded prior to the signing of the contract of sale between RP and his seller. The new associate just plain missed it. What should Donna do? Did Donna meet her ethical obligations in agreeing to represent RP and issuing insurance as an agent for Republic? What were her ethical obligations in taking on the legal representation, and in supervising her associate? What are her ethical duties to each client at this point now that the error has surfaced?

12
Improving the Efficiency of the Title System

The recording system, despite its faults, is a mainstay of American land law, destined to remain in place for the foreseeable future. Proposals for structural reform, such as the Torrens registration system discussed below, have generally failed. Instead, successful reforms have conceded the present structure of the recording system, seeking incremental improvements by ameliorating some of the system's worst features.

The weaknesses of the recording system fall into two general categories. First, stale recorded interests accumulate over time. The system makes it easy and inexpensive to record virtually any type of instrument. This is a virtue in that it encourages all owners to use the system, thereby getting protection and furnishing information that will be valuable to subsequent purchasers, but in the long run it is also a vice that impedes efficiency. Stale interests of record, often decades old, cloud titles.

The old interests usually are economically devalued. They were valuable to their holders when initially created and recorded, but as time passes, their value wanes. Often the only remaining value of old interests is as an impediment to title — they have blockage value only. Because the present possessor lacks marketable title to the old clog, the owner (or apparent owner) of the old interest can block a transaction, insisting on compensation before signing a quitclaim deed or release.

An additional problem with stale interests is that their owners become hard to identify. For example, it may be difficult or impossible to find the present owners — heirs or successors — of old undivided interests, old rights of entry for breach of conditions, and old covenants related to land use.

The second major group of recording system weaknesses comprises the off-the-record risks. Deeds and other instruments may be void or voidable for reasons such as nondelivery, incapacity, fraud, and adverse possession.

Attempts made over the years to improve the functioning of the recording system consist of changes in title practices and statutory reforms. With respect to title practices, title standards and the evolution of title insurance have improved operation of the system. The law of adverse possession strengthens titles to land by barring potential claims of persons who are not in possession of a parcel after a specified period of time has elapsed, provided that certain conditions are met. Title standards, along with statutory reforms (*e.g.*, title curative acts, marketable title acts, and Torrens statutes), are examined in this chapter.

A. TITLE STANDARDS

A title standard provides guidance for attorneys and other professionals who examine title to real property. In the absence of title standards, each title examiner must make up his own mind as to whether the real property records are sufficient to establish title. The point is assessment of risk. It is often said that there is no such thing as a "perfect title." Every title with an appreciable number of instruments of record will have some oddities, quirks, unusual features, or possible open questions, which at least in theory might rise to the level of a title defect or cloud on title. There are many close cases, in which the title examiner must exercise judgment, just as highly trained professionals in other fields must exercise judgment (for example, a surgeon reaching an opinion as to whether a patient is likely to benefit from a particular type of surgery).

In the context of title examination, however, one distinctive consideration often informs that judgment. Title examination is iterative. The records in the chain of title are durable, and therefore most titles are reexamined at some point in the future, sometimes frequently if there are many subsequent sales or financings. A competent title examiner thus realizes that if he approves title and his client later sells or mortgages the property, his title work will be reevaluated by another title professional. This sometimes leads title examiners to be "overly meticulous" to minimize the risk that a subsequent examiner will object to an arguable flaw that he forgave.

The main purpose of title standards is to eliminate technical objections, which are highly unlikely to impair the rights of buyers and lenders. They also are designed to forestall objections that stem from a misapprehension of the law. They have the practical effect of making more titles marketable, thereby reducing the number of title objections raised by attorneys and title insurance companies.

Many states have official title standards, approved by state bar associations. Sometimes city or county bar associations adopt title standards to address particular issues of local concern. In most states, title standards do not have the force of law. They reflect the consensus of the practicing bar on how to solve particular problems involved in the process of title examination. Usually the standards address issues on which there is general statewide consensus among title attorneys. Drafters of standards usually avoid issues on which there are significant differences of opinion held by experienced practitioners.

State bar title standards began in the 1930s, starting with Connecticut in 1938 and Nebraska the next year. After 23 states adopted standards, the American Bar Association and the University of Michigan Law School collaborated to draft model standards. This resulted in the publication of Simes and Taylor's *Model Title Standards*. The volume consists of 101 separate standards organized in 12 chapters, covering topics such as abstracts, the period for searching records, name variances, marital property rights, and quitclaim deeds. The model standards have been highly influential, forming the basis for the promulgation of state bar standards in four additional states, plus informing the revisions of standards in states that already had a set of standards. Most state bar associations periodically review and revise their title standards, although some states have no recent revisions, which raises a concern as to possible obsolescence given changes both in practice and law over time.

LEWIS M. SIMES & CLARENCE B. TAYLOR, MODEL TITLE STANDARDS (1960)

STANDARD 2.1. EXAMINING ATTORNEY'S ATTITUDE.

The purpose of the examination of title and of objections, if any, shall be to secure for the examiner's client a title which is in fact marketable and which is shown by the record to be marketable, subject to no other encumbrances than those expressly provided for by the client's contract. Objections and requirements should be made only when the irregularities or defects reasonably can be expected to expose the purchaser or lender to the hazard of adverse claims or litigation.

Comment: Title Standards are primarily intended to eliminate technical objections which do not impair marketability and some common objections which are based upon misapprehension of the law. The examining attorney, by way of a test, may ask himself after examining the title, what defects and irregularities he has discovered by his examination, and as to each such irregularity or defect, who, if anyone, can take advantage of it as against the purported owner, and to what end. . . .

STANDARD 3.1. PERIOD OF SEARCH.

[In this standard, it is assumed that record titles in the jurisdiction are so long that it is unreasonably burdensome to trace title back to the government, or that if land titles do not originate with the United States or with the state, it is impracticable to trace titles back to their origin. Of course, if the Model Marketable Title Act, or similar legislation, were in force, then the length of search, for most purposes, would be determined by such legislation. This standard is not as satisfactory as a marketable title act, since defects in title prior to the period of search as stated in the title standard constitute a risk which a vendee must assume. Whereas, if a marketable title act is in force, defects in title prior to the period of the act are extinguished.]

A record title covering a period of fifty years or more is marketable: provided that the basis thereof is a warranty deed, one or more quitclaim deeds supported by a reasonable record proof that they convey the full title, a patent from the United States, or a conveyance from the state, a probate proceeding in which the property is reasonably identifiable, a warranty mortgage deed if subsequently regularly foreclosed, or any other instrument which shows of record reasonable probability of title and possession thereunder; provided further that the period actually searched does not refer to or indicate prior instruments or defects in title, in which case such prior instruments may be used in turn as a start, and that the period actually searched discloses instruments which confirm and carry forward the title so established.

Comment: In applying this standard, it is necessary to trace the record title back to a "root" or "start," which may be, and generally is, more than fifty years back. Any defects in the record title subsequent to the date of recording of the "root" or "start" must be considered by the examiner. . . .

STANDARD 5.1. RULE OF IDEM SONANS.

Differently spelled names are presumed to be the same when they sound alike, or when their sounds cannot be distinguished easily, or when common usage by corruption or abbreviation has made their pronunciation identical. . . .

STANDARD 5.2. USE OR NON-USE OF MIDDLE NAMES OR INITIALS.

The use in one instrument and non-use in another of a middle name or initial ordinarily does not create a question of identity affecting title, unless the examiner is otherwise put on inquiry.

STANDARD 5.3. ABBREVIATIONS.

All customary and generally accepted abbreviations of first and middle names should be recognized as the equivalent thereof. . . .

STANDARD 5.5. EFFECT OF SUFFIX.

Although identity of name raises the presumption of identity of person, the addition of a suffix such as "Jr." or "II" to the name of a subsequent grantor may rebut the presumption of identity with the prior grantee.

Comment: Ordinarily it is said that the suffix is no part of the name. Thus, where the grantee in one instrument is "John Lawrence, M.D." and the grantor in the next instrument is merely "John Lawrence," it would be presumed that they are the same person. But if the grantee in one instrument is "John Lawrence, Sr." and the grantor in the next instrument is "John Lawrence, Jr.," the presumption that they are the same person would be rebutted. Or, if the grantee in one instrument is "John Lawrence," and, in another instrument, the grantor is "John Lawrence, Jr.," and it appears that there are both a father and a son of the name of John Lawrence, the presumption of identity is rebutted.

UNITED STATES v. MORALES
United States District Court, Middle District of Florida, 2014 Sex trafficking case
36 F. Supp. 3d 1276

Roy B. Dalton, Jr., District Judge. . . .

This matter is before the Court concerning the Petitioner Linda Morales' claim to the one-half interest in real property located at 8 Crossings Trail, Ormond Beach, Florida 32174 (the "Property"), which this Court ordered preliminarily forfeited to the Government pursuant to 18 U.S.C. §2428 . . . .

Upon de novo review of the record as a whole and the parties' objections, the Court agrees entirely with Magistrate Judge Spaulding's comprehensive and well-reasoned report and recommendation. . . . Thus, the report and recommendation is due to be adopted. . . .

REPORT AND RECOMMENDATION
Karla R. Spaulding, United States Magistrate Judge.

On November 5, 2012, a jury convicted Luis E. Morales ("Luis Morales") of one count of child sex trafficking, in violation of 18 U.S.C. §1591(a), and five counts of transporting minors in interstate commerce with the intent that they engage in sexual activity, in violation of 18 U.S.C. §2423(a). These crimes occurred between November 2009 and January 2011. . . .

II. Statement of Facts

On June 27, 1988, Linda Morales purchased the Property as a joint owner with John Palfrey ("Palfrey"), her then husband. The 1988 Deed listed as the grantees "John D. Palfrey and Linda M. Palfrey, his wife." In August 1990, Palfrey and Linda Morales divorced. As part of the distribution of the marital property, Palfrey executed a quitclaim deed in October 1990 transferring his interest in the Property to Linda Morales. . . .

In November 1997, Linda Morales married Luis Morales. She and Luis Morales resided together at the Property from November 1997 until Luis Morales's arrest in 2012. . . .

In July 2007, Linda Morales became seriously ill and feared that she might die. She wished to arrange for the Property to pass to Luis Morales if she died. On July 24, 2007, Linda Morales executed a quitclaim deed transferring the Property from the grantor, "Linda M. (Palfrey) Morales," to the grantees, "Linda M. Morales and Luis Enrique Morales." She signed the 2007 Deed in the name Linda Marie Morales. . . . Linda Morales and Luis Morales orally agreed that Luis Morales would only acquire an ownership interest in the Property if Linda died.

By April 8, 2011, Linda Morales had recovered from her illness. On April 8, 2011, Luis and Linda Morales executed a quitclaim deed transferring the Property from the grantors, "Linda M. (Palfrey) Morales and Luis Enrique Morales," to the grantee, "Linda M. (Palfrey) Morales." . . . At the time of the execution of the 2011 Deed, no charges had been filed against Luis Morales. . . .

IV. ANALYSIS

Federal law decides what interests are subject to forfeiture, but state property law defines what those interests are in the first instance. . . .

As a preliminary matter, the United States concedes that, at the time of the commission of the crimes giving rise to the forfeiture, Linda Morales had a one-half interest in the whole of the Property.[6] The United States does not seek the forfeiture of Linda Morales's one-half interest in the Property. . . .

The United States argues that the 2007 Deed created a valid tenancy by the entireties in the Property held by Luis and Linda Morales and that this tenancy by the entireties continued through the period of the crimes of conviction, November 2009 through January 2011. The United States submits that the very nature of a tenancy by the entireties prevents Linda Morales from validly claiming that her interest in the Property was superior to Luis Morales's interest in the Property. *See* United States v. Kennedy, 201 F.3d 1324, 1331 (11th Cir. 2000).

Linda Morales makes a number of arguments in response. She . . . submits that the 2007 Deed is invalid. In the alternative, she argues that the 2007 Deed did not convey a legal interest in the Property to Luis Morales. I will address these arguments in turn.

---

6. Even though Linda Morales is now the sole owner of the Property, the United States can forfeit the interest in the Property, if any, that Luis Morales held at the time of the commission of the crimes of conviction under the "relation back" doctrine found in 21 U.S.C. §853(c) . . . .

2. WHETHER THE 2007 DEED IS VALID

In Florida, an estate or interest of freehold is validly created or conveyed by a deed when (a) the instrument is in writing, (b) signed by the party creating or conveying the estate or interest, (c) in the presence of two subscribing witnesses. Fla. Stat. §689.01. The title-holding spouse of real estate, including homestead, may create a tenancy by the entirety by conveying a deed to both spouses as joint holders of title. Fla. Stat. §689.11(1). The Florida Constitution expressly permits homestead property to be conveyed in this manner. *See* Fla. Const., art. X, §4(c).

The 2007 Deed satisfies these requirements. It is in writing, it is signed by Linda Morales and it is subscribed to by two witnesses. Nevertheless, Linda Morales argues that the 2007 Deed is invalid because (1) there are discrepancies in the names used to transfer title to the Property; and, (2) she did not intend to make a gift of an interest in the Property to Luis Morales and Luis Morales did not pay consideration to obtain an interest in the Property. Neither of these arguments is meritorious for the reasons discussed below.

A. Discrepancies In The Names Used In Deeds Conveying The Property

As discussed above, Linda Morales took title to the Property from her former husband, John Palfrey, in the 1988 Deed, which listed the grantee as Linda M. Palfrey. In the 2007 Deed, Linda Morales, using the name Linda M. (Palfrey) Morales, conveyed the Property to Linda M. Morales and Luis Enrique Morales. She signed the 2007 Deed in the name Linda Marie Morales.[8] Linda Morales contends that the 2007 Deed is invalid because she used the name Linda M. (Palfrey) Morales as the grantor, which is not the same name used in the 1988 Deed conveying the Property to Linda M. Palfrey, and because she signed the 2007 Deed using the name Linda Marie Morales, which name is not included in either deed.

In support of this argument, Linda Morales relies on the Declaration of Allison G. Edwards. Ms. Edwards avers that she is an attorney who practices real estate law. She formerly owned a title company and handled closings on sales of residential and commercial property. As such, she attests that she is familiar with many issues that can render property deeds defective under Florida law and make a property transaction non-insurable. After reviewing the 1990 Deed and the 2007 Deed, Ms. Edwards opines that only Linda M. Palfrey, the grantee in the 1990 Deed, could have conveyed valid title to the Property through the 2007 Deed, because Linda M. Palfrey was the only person who acquired legal title to the Property through the 1990 Deed. She asserts that "Florida law requires strict compliance as to names. If there is any possibility that the one later identified as the grantor may not be the same as the grantee originally described, the deed is invalid."

Linda Morales cites Barnett Bank of S. Fla., N.A. v. Westbrook Atkinson Realtors, 564 So. 2d 570 (Fla. 4th Dist. Ct. App. 1990), as further support for

---

8. She also used the name Linda Marie (Palfrey) Morales in the body of the deed.

Ms. Edwards's opinion. The Barnett Bank case arose from a dispute about the name specified as the beneficiary of a letter of credit. One of the terms of the letter of credit was that payment would be made upon delivery of a letter from the beneficiary, Edna May Walker. Individuals who held powers of attorney executed by Edna Wilson Walker attempted to obtain payment under the letter of credit. The Fourth District Court of Appeal found that the bank did not err in refusing to make payment under these circumstances because there was no "written or oral substantiation to explain that Edna *May* Walker and Edna *Wilson* Walker were one and the same." *Id.* at 570.

In contrast to the facts in *Barnett Bank*, in the present case Linda Morales does not dispute that she was the grantee named in the 1990 Deed and that she was the grantor named in the 2007 Deed. Rather, in her Declaration, she avers that, in 1990, John Palfrey, her former husband, transferred title to the Property to her. She further attests that, in 2007, she "attempted to arrange for [the Property] to pass to [Luis Morales]," and references the date of the 2007 Deed. Therefore, there is no factual dispute presented in this case that Linda Palfrey, Linda M. (Palfrey) Morales, Linda Marie Morales and Linda Morales are the same person. Under these circumstances, the differences in the names used do not invalidate the 2007 Deed. *See, e.g., Fla. Uniform Title Standards,* http://www.lawdb.com/Fl_Uniform_Title_Standards.pdf, Standard 10.3 (last visited April 28, 2014) (woman may validly convey real property she acquired in her maiden name by using her married name as grantor, with reference to her maiden name);[9] *c.f.* Bacon v. Feigel, 80 Fla. 566, 567–69, 86 So. 424 (Fla. 1920) (indicating that evidence of identity would be accepted to prove that grantee, Robert A. Bacon, was the same person as the subsequent grantor of the property, R.A. Bacon). . . .

B. TITLE CURATIVE ACTS

One consequence of the high volume of instruments presented for recording in many localities is that inevitably some contain various sorts of defects. The acknowledgment may be missing or defective, the grantee may have failed to pay the recording fee or a transfer tax, the instrument may lack a seal, or delivery may be suspect. Some of these defects may be observable from a close inspection of the instrument. Other defects are off-the-record in the sense that the instrument looks fine and only an investigation into the circumstances of the underlying transaction can reveal the problem. Many of these defects are violations of the statutory requirements for recording — the instrument, which is in fact recorded, was not entitled to be recorded, but it slipped into the system anyway.

9. Florida courts have relied on the Uniform Title Standards in resolving disputes about the validity of deeds conveying real property. *See, e.g.,* DGG Dev. Corp. v. Estate of Capponi, 983 So.2d 1232, 1234 (Fla. 5th Dist. Ct. App. 2008); Cunningham v. Haley, 501 So.2d 649, 653 n. 3 (Fla. 5th Dist. Ct. App. 1986).

Defective instruments of record pose two types of risk for parties dealing with the system. First, a party to the defectively documented transaction may have the right to attack the transaction, seeking rescission or some other remedy that affects title to the land. This risk goes to the core of marketable title. A careful, conservative title searcher who finds a technical defect will often raise an objection, even if the risk of loss is unlikely. Second, the defective instrument's recordation status is doubtful. When the defect, such as improper acknowledgment, is of the nature that the instrument was not entitled to be recorded, many courts hold that the instrument does not impart constructive notice. This presents a risk for the grantee under the instrument, as well as subsequent grantees whose chain of title includes the defective instrument. A BFP who lacks actual notice of the instrument has the ability to obtain superior rights to the property.

In response to the problems stemming from defective instruments of record, many states have passed title curative acts, which provide that instruments bearing certain defects are conclusively presumed valid after the passage of a specified number of years after recordation. The acts' features, including the time periods, differ markedly from state to state.

With curative legislation, more titles are marketable because searchers may safely disregard evidence of old defects. This increases the efficiency of the title assurance system, without imposing any significant costs—it is extremely rare that shoring up the record title by eliminating old formal defects cuts off substantive rights of claimants to the land.

Problem 12A

A title search for a client, Gomer, who is interested in buying an 82-acre farm, reveals the following information:

1. A deed in the chain of title, recorded eight years ago, appears to be properly executed and to be acknowledged by a notary, but the space in the acknowledgment form where the date of acknowledgment is to be inserted was left blank.
2. A deed in the chain of title, recorded 22 years ago, purports to convey a fee simple estate from John Wallace to Susan Dollar; however, the deed is executed only by the grantee, Susan Dollar, with the acknowledgment likewise reciting execution by Susan Dollar.
3. The immediately prior deed in the chain of title, recorded 27 years ago, purports to convey a fee simple estate from Donald Mitchem to John Wallis, Jr. The title searcher, having asked the present record owner and several neighbors about the Wallace (Wallis) family, has been unable to establish whether John Wallace and John Wallis, Jr. are the same person.

(a) Is title to the farm marketable if the state:

 (i)   has no relevant title standards or legislation?

(ii)   has adopted the Model Title Standards reproduced earlier in this chapter?

(iii) has adopted a title curative act, which provides: "When any instrument shall have been recorded . . . and the instrument contains any of the following defects: . . . (5) the instrument is not acknowledged; . . . (7) any defect in the execution, acknowledgment, recording or certificate of recording the same; such instrument shall, from and after the expiration of five (5) years from the filing thereof for record, be valid as though such instrument had, in the first instance, been in all respects duly executed [and] acknowledged. . . ."? Okla. Stat., Title 16, §27a.

(b) Suppose that you are Gomer's attorney. Gomer tells you he really wants to buy the farm and doesn't want to make title objections just for the sake of making title objections. If title is really okay, he wants you to proceed to closing. Does this client information affect your evaluation of title? How do you advise Gomer?

(c) Suppose that you are Gomer's attorney. Gomer tells you he has cold feet and now realizes that in the signed contract, he agreed to pay way too much for this lousy farm. Does this client information affect your evaluation of title? How do you advise Gomer?

C. MARKETABLE TITLE ACTS

Twenty states presently have marketable title acts. The primary goals of this remedial legislation are to limit the period of time covered by title searches and to render more titles marketable by eliminating stale interests. A period of 40 years is most common, but some states specify 30 or 50 years. The marketable title act operates to extinguish interests and defects that are older than the "root of title," which is the most recent deed or other instrument in the record chain of title that is more than 30 (or 40 or 50) years old. Without marketable title legislation, in states where searches customarily go back only an agreed-upon number of years, there is the risk of older, undiscovered interests that are still valid. For example, a nineteenth-century deed may have conveyed a defeasible fee simple, with the future interest still outstanding. Thus, it is a calculated risk not to trace title back to the sovereign. This risk may be justified, given the real-world probability that ancient rights, not appearing of record during the past 40 years, either do not exist or will never be asserted. A marketable title act seeks to reduce the risk even further by cutting off ancient claims that do not appear of record during the specified period.

The aim of marketable title legislation is to render unnecessary searches of records prior to the root of title. An interest created prior to the root of title no longer affects title unless it is referred to in a post-root instrument, or re-recorded, or reflected by possession after the root of title. Unfortunately, all marketable title acts have exceptions, which substantially undercut the fundamental goal. Many older interests are sheltered by exceptions, the most common ones being: (1) interests of the United States government; (2) interests of state and local governments; (3) utility and railroad easements; (4) mineral rights; and (5) visible easements. As a practical matter, the list of exceptions means that the searcher who stops at the root of title is actually taking a significant risk of missing an interest that is still valid.

Consider how marketable title acts compare to a related problem under the Uniform Commercial Code (UCC). Under the UCC, security interests in goods and other personal property are perfected by the filing of financing statements. UCC §9-515 handles the problem of stale security interests by making a financing statement effective for a period of five years from the date of filing. A secured party who wants continued protection must file a continuation statement. Can a plan like the Article 9 system work for real estate?

A number of states have specialized statutes, more limited in scope than marketable title acts, which address the problem of outstanding mineral interests that cloud title. Regular adverse possession statutes have little impact with respect to minerals because possession of the land surface is typically not viewed as adverse to the rights of the mineral owner. These specialized acts, often called mineral lapse acts or dormant mineral interest acts, apply when mineral rights are severed from the surface estate and the mineral interest owner does not explore or produce for a long period of time, such as 20 years. Such acts function by transferring the mineral rights to the surface owner, thus making the surface owner's title fully marketable. Ancient mortgage statutes address the problem of a very old recorded mortgage for which there is no recorded release of lien. Generally, a period of 30 or 40 years applies, measured from the date of final maturity stated in the mortgage or, if the mortgage does not specify such a date, from the date of execution. Some states impose time limitations on the exercise of rights of entry and possibilities of reverter. One type of statute prohibits such interests from remaining in effect for more than a stated number of years, typically 30 or 40. The period begins running when the future interest is created and runs regardless of whether a breach of the limitation or condition has occurred.

MATISSEK v. WALLER
District Court of Appeal of Florida, Second District, 2011
51 So. 3d 625

CRENSHAW, Judge. Joseph Gerhard Matissek and Kelly Beth Matissek, homeowners in the deed restricted community of Hidden Lakes Estates, in Pasco County, Florida, appeal a final judgment directing them to bring

Dd MRTA
extinguish restrictions

an airplane hangar built on their property in compliance with the Hidden Lakes Estates' deed restrictions. The issue that we must decide is whether the Marketable Record Titles to Real Property Act (MRTA), chapter 712, Florida Statutes (2008), extinguished both the original and amended restrictions placed upon the Matisseks' property. We find the MRTA did extinguish these restrictions, and therefore the Matisseks have a free and clear, marketable record title to their property. Accordingly, the circuit court erred as a matter of law by failing to enter a final summary judgment in favor of the Matisseks on this basis, and we reverse.

THE ORIGINAL AND AMENDED RESTRICTIONS

On April 16, 1971, developer Hidden Lakes Estates, Inc. (HLEI) platted a parcel of land known as "Hidden Lakes Estates Unit One." This plat was recorded at Plat Book 10, Pages 80–81 of the Public Records of Pasco County, Florida. HLEI designed Hidden Lakes Estates to be an airpark community that would include its own airport and permit its residents to construct aircraft hangars on their property. In support of this plan, HLEI also recorded restrictions, titled "Hidden Lake Estates Restrictions," to be placed upon all lots in Unit One. Of particular importance, provision (9) of the restrictions required that "[a]ll buildings shall be constructed of masonry or similar materials." The restrictions also stated in provision (27) that "[t]he Developer reserves the right to modify restrictions on any lot or lots," and in provision (31) that "[t]he Developer, or its assigns, reserves the right to make reasonable modifications and clarifications to any and all restrictions set forth herein." HLEI recorded these restrictions on May 18, 1971, at O.R. Book 544, Pages 248–51, of the Public Records of Pasco County, Florida.

On August 15, 1977, HLEI recorded an amendment to the original restrictions pursuant to its authority under provision (31). The amended restrictions deleted provisions (14), (27), and (31), amended provisions (5), (8), and (18), and stated that the "remaining restrictions shall remain in full force and effect." This amendment, which will be referred to as Amendment 1, was recorded at O.R. Book 904, Pages 126–27.

On November 7, 1977, HLEI recorded another amendment to amend both the original restrictions and Amendment 1 pursuant to provision (31) of the original restrictions.[3] This amendment, which will be referred to as Amendment 2, provided a list of restrictions that "shall be controlling and binding on all future owners of properties" in Hidden Lakes Estates. The list of restrictions included the same provision (9) that was in the original restrictions. HLEI recorded this amendment at O.R. Book 915, Pages 1910–13.

3. Though it is not pertinent to our findings, we observe that this amendment does not address the earlier deletion of provision (31) in Amendment 1.

Between recording the original restrictions in 1971 and Amendments 1 and 2 in 1977, HLEI gave Peter Dreher an indenture for lots 23, 24, 25, and 26 in Unit One of Hidden Lakes Estates. The indenture, recorded on June 28, 1974, simply stated that these lots, as recorded in Plat Book 10, Pages 80–81, were "[s]ubject to easements and restrictions of record." Mr. Dreher then conveyed the indenture for lots 23, 24, and 25 to Stephen Covert, which was recorded on April 14, 1980. Though this indenture referred to the plat recorded at Plat Book 10, Pages 80–81, it did not refer to any restrictions. After this conveyance, lot 25 and a portion of lot 24 changed hands three times — from Mr. Covert to Radial Development Corporation (RDC), from RDC to Charles and Johnnie Coward, and from the Cowards to Agnes Rice, respectively. Each of these conveyances was properly recorded in Pasco County, and each of these conveyances described the parcel from the plat recorded at Plat Book 10, Pages 80–81. Two of the conveyances — from Mr. Covert to RDC and from RDC to the Cowards — contained a general statement that the parcel was "[s]ubject to easements of record," and the third conveyance from the Cowards to Ms. Rice made no mention of any restrictions.

The Matisseks' Acquisition of the Subject Property

Finally, on December 18, 1995, the Matisseks became the fee simple owners of lot 25 and a portion of lot 24. The warranty deed granting them the subject property from Ms. Rice did not cite to the original plat, nor did it mention any restrictions on the property. During the summer of 2007, Mr. Matissek began constructing an airplane hangar on the property and submitted his plans to Pasco County to get a permit to build a pre-engineered hangar containing a steel frame and steel paneling. Unfortunately for Mr. Matissek, fellow Hidden Lakes Estates resident Roland Waller noticed the construction and believed Mr. Matissek's plan to place a metal exterior on his hangar violated provision (9) of the Hidden Lakes Estates' restrictions requiring all buildings to be constructed of masonry or similar materials. Mr. Waller communicated to Mr. Matissek that if he did not bring the hangar in compliance with the Hidden Lakes Estates' restrictions, an injunction would be sought. Despite this warning, Mr. Matissek continued with the construction of his hangar, and Mr. Waller filed a complaint in January 2008 seeking a mandatory injunction requiring the hangar's removal.[4] We note that during the pendency of Mr. Waller's action, Mr. Matissek applied a stucco finish covering the hangar's metal exterior.

---

4. As Mr. Waller notes in his communications to Mr. Matissek, the Hidden Lakes Estates did not create a standing homeowners association to enforce the deed restrictions. Rather, Mr. Waller pursued this action as an interested party with an ownership interest in Unit One of Hidden Lakes Estates.

THE SUMMARY JUDGMENT MOTION

The Matisseks filed a motion for summary judgment arguing the MRTA extinguished HLEI's 1971 restrictions and 1977 amended restrictions. The circuit court denied the motion, and the matter proceeded to trial. The circuit court found at the conclusion of the proceedings that the MRTA extinguished the 1971 restrictions but did not extinguish the 1977 amended restrictions because the amended restrictions were recorded after the root of title created by the 1974 conveyance of the property from HLEI to Mr. Dreher. Accordingly, the circuit court found that Mr. Matissek's hangar did not comply with the 1977 amended restrictions and entered a final judgment directing Matissek to bring the hangar in compliance by either removing the hangar or by constructing "masonry walls of block, brick, prestressed concrete or other masonry materials to the building."

On appeal, the Matisseks argue the circuit court misapplied the MRTA because the 1977 amended restrictions could not stand alone and the original 1971 restrictions could only be preserved through specific identification in the muniments of title under section 712.03(1) or by recording a proper notice under sections 712.03(2), 712.05, and 712.06, which was never done. Therefore, they contend the circuit court erred by denying the motion for summary judgment because the original 1971 restrictions and 1977 amended restrictions were extinguished by the MRTA as a matter of law. . . .

BACKGROUND OF THE MRTA

The Florida Legislature enacted the MRTA in 1963 to simplify and facilitate land transactions. *See* Blanton v. City of Pinellas Park, 887 So. 2d 1224, 1227 (Fla. 2004). To effectuate this legislative purpose, section 712.10 requires the MRTA "be liberally construed . . . by allowing persons to rely on a record title as described in [section] 712.02 subject only to such limitations as appear in [section] 712.03." Section 712.02, titled "Marketable record title; suspension of applicability," provides:

> Any person having the legal capacity to own land in this state, who, alone or together with her or his predecessors in title, has been vested with any estate in land of record for 30 years or more, shall have a marketable record title to such estate in said land, which shall be free and clear of all claims except the matters set forth as exceptions to marketability in [section] 712.03.

Similarly, section 712.04, titled "Interests extinguished by marketable record title," provides:

> Subject to the matters stated in [section] 712.03, such marketable record title shall be free and clear of all estates, interests, claims, or charges whatsoever, the existence of which depends upon any act, title transaction, event or omission that occurred prior to the effective date of the root of title.

Subsection (1) of the exceptions listed under section 712.03 states:

> Such marketable record title shall not affect or extinguish the following rights:
>
> (1) Estates or interests, easements and use restrictions disclosed by and defects inherent in the muniments of title on which said estate is based beginning with the root of title; provided, however, that a general reference in any of such muniments to easements, use restrictions or other interests created prior to the root of title shall not be sufficient to preserve them unless specific identification by reference to book and page of record or by name of recorded plat be made therein to a recorded title transaction which imposed, transferred or continued such easement, use restrictions or other interests; subject, however, to the provisions of subsection (5).

Finally, the "root of title" is defined under section 712.01(2) as

> any title transaction purporting to create or transfer the estate claimed by any person and which is the last title transaction to have been recorded at least 30 years prior to the time when marketability is being determined. The effective date of the root of title is the date on which it was recorded.

THE APPLICATION OF THE MRTA TO THE MATISSEKS' PROPERTY

In this case, the circuit court determined that the effective date of the root title of the Matisseks' property was June 28, 1974, when HLEI gave Peter Dreher an indenture for lots 23, 24, 25, and 26. The parties do not dispute this finding, nor do we. Because this action commenced in January 2008, and because the next recorded title transaction after the original indenture occurred in 1980, the 1974 indenture was the last title transaction to have been recorded prior to the circuit court's determination of the subject property's marketability.

The circuit court also found that the 1971 restrictions, which predated the 1974 root of title, were extinguished by the MRTA in accordance with section 712.04. We agree with the circuit court's determination because there is nothing in the record which would provide an exception to the marketability under section 712.03. Standing alone, the 1974 indenture was insufficient to preserve the 1971 restrictions because the indenture's vague provision that the conveyance was "[s]ubject to easements and restrictions of record" did not comply with the "specific identification" language of section 712.03(1). Rather, "'specific identification' to the title transaction can be made in one of two ways: (1) by reference to the book and page in the public records where the title transaction that imposed the restriction can be found, or (2) by reference to the name of a recorded plat that imposed the restriction." Sunshine Vistas Homeowners Ass'n v. Caruana, 623 So. 2d 490, 491-92 (Fla. 1993) (quoting §712.03(1), Fla. Stat. (1989)). Although the 1974 indenture does cite to the original plat recorded on April 16, 1971, the indenture does not reference the book or page of the title transaction or the name of the plat that imposed the original restrictions on May 18, 1971. *See* Martin v. Town of Palm Beach, 643 So. 2d 112, 114 (Fla. 4th DCA 1994) (finding use restrictions created prior to the root of title are extinguished by section 712.02 unless the use restrictions are disclosed and specifically identified in a muniment of title); *but cf. Caruana*, 623 So. 2d at 490 (finding the MRTA did not extinguish plat restrictions recorded in 1925 because subsequent muniments of title recorded in 1951, 1977, and 1990 contained specific identifications referencing the 1925 plat).

Despite finding that the MRTA extinguished the 1971 restrictions, the circuit court then simply concluded, without explanation, that the MRTA "[did] not cut off the 1977 deed restrictions." The Matisseks contend this was error because the 1977 amendments could not exist independently of the original 1971 restrictions and should either have been extinguished or been found simply inapplicable to their property. . . .

We agree that the 1977 amended restrictions, just like the 1971 restrictions, do not provide an exception under section 712.03 that would prevent HLEI's interest in the property from being extinguished under section 712.04. The 1977 amendments address revisions to the 1971 restrictions and do not concern a chain of title to any property, let alone the Matisseks' property. Thus, the amendments are not considered to be "muniments of title," and subsection 712.03(1) is inapplicable.[7] Similarly, the 1977 amendments do not apply under subsection 712.03(4) because the amendments are not "title transactions" as defined in section 712.01(3),[8] and the legislature did not intend that a covenant or restriction be considered an estate, interest, claim, or charge affecting title.

We also find that the 1977 amended restrictions in this case were recorded outside of the chain of title of the Matisseks' property . . . .

[I]t is hard to see in this case how the Matisseks would have known of the masonry restriction under provision (9) because the 1974 root of title and the subsequent title transactions to Mr. Covert, RDC, the Cowards, and Ms. Rice fail to comply with the "specific identification" language of subsection 712.03(1). None of the conveyances reference either the original 1971 restrictions or the 1977 amended restrictions.

Therefore, we find the circuit court erred by denying the Matisseks' motion for summary judgment as a matter of law because the MRTA extinguished the original 1971 restrictions and 1977 amended restrictions placed upon the Matisseks' property. Accordingly, we reverse the entry of final judgment in favor of Mr. Waller and direct the circuit court on remand to

7. A muniment of title is any documentary evidence upon which title is based. Muniments of title are deeds, wills, and court judgments *through which a particular* land *title passes and upon which its validity depends.* . . . Muniments of title do more than merely "affect" title; they must carry title and be a vital link in the chain of title.

Cunningham v. Haley, 501 So. 2d 649, 652 (Fla. 5th DCA 1986).

8. "'Title transaction' means any recorded instrument or court proceeding which affects title to any estate or interest in land and which describes the land sufficiently to identify its location and boundaries." §712.01(3).

enter a final summary judgment finding that the Matisseks have a marketable record title to their property that is free and clear of any of HLEI's earlier restrictions.

Problem 12B

In the preceding case, the court holds that the Matisseks are not bound by the covenants and restrictions. Are the other residents in the development also free of the restrictions? If the covenants and restrictions apply to some people but not all as a consequence of the marketable title act, what impact will this have on the uses of the property within the development and the market values of various parcels? Is this a good outcome from a community perspective?

Problem 12C

Bruno, a real estate attorney, has an angry client, Sam Strip. Bruno represented Strip in connection with his purchase, for $680,000, of a 4.2-acre tract of undeveloped land situated on the outskirts of Megapolis, in the path of suburban growth. The land is zoned light commercial, and Strip plans to build a strip shopping center. The transaction closed nine months ago, and Bruno personally conducted the title search. Most attorneys in Megapolis search titles back for a 50-year period. Bruno found title to be clear and marketable, searching back to a "root of title" consisting of a warranty deed recorded 57 years ago that conveyed a 185-acre tract that included Strip's 4.2-acre tract. Prior to closing, Bruno orally told Strip that title was good. Also prior to closing, Bruno advised Strip that he could purchase an owner's policy of title insurance for $2,800, but Bruno pointed out he would have to buy title insurance in the near future to satisfy the project lenders and he could save money by not purchasing a policy now. Strip made what he thought was an easy decision to save money, since his lawyer was not insisting that he buy title insurance.

Now Strip, wanting to break ground on the shopping center, has a major-league problem. Sixty-one years ago, the then-owner of the property conveyed a pipeline easement to Napper Natural Gas Company, and this easement cuts right across the 4.2-acre tract. The easement is properly recorded and an underground pipeline is in place, but at the present time no evidence of the pipeline is visible at the surface of the 4.2-acre tract. The center cannot be developed unless the gas company can be persuaded to relocate its easement. Strip claims Bruno is responsible for his title problem and needs to solve it or pay damages. Is Bruno liable if:

(a) Megapolis is in a state with no relevant title standards or legislation?

(b) Megapolis is in a state with the Model Title Standards (reproduced earlier in this chapter)?

(c) Megapolis is in a state with the Model Title Standards, plus the state legislature has enacted the following statute: *"Abstracts; Effect of Title Standards.* In the compilation or examination of an abstract of title to real estate, it shall not be considered negligence for a registered abstracter or an attorney to follow the Title Standards promulgated by the Nebraska State Bar Association."* Neb. Rev. St. §76-557.

(d) Megapolis is in a state with a Marketable Title Act that contains the list of five exceptions described in text at page 337.

D. TORRENS SYSTEM: TITLE REGISTRATION

The reforms to the title assurance system discussed in this chapter are all alike in that they keep the basic elements of the recording system intact. Parties are encouraged to record instruments, which then serve as evidence of title that is available for inspection by other interested parties. Recording officers do not issue opinions concerning title or concerning the nature, legitimacy, or effect of any of the records.

In contrast, the Torrens system of title registration does not seek to reform or improve the operation of the recording system. Instead, it aims to be a complete replacement. For each registered parcel of land, the government issues a certificate of title that is intended to be conclusive. The principle is the same as for title to automobiles; under modern certificate of title acts, the government-issued certificate is proof of title, subject to any liens noted thereon. Compared to the system used for automobiles, the Torrens title system for land is necessarily much more complex, because of the many different types of interests in land recognized by our legal system, but the principle is the same. A Torrens certificate is much more than evidence of title, it *is* title — just as in the real estate game *Monopoly*, in which you own Boardwalk if you hold the one and only Boardwalk title deed, and otherwise you don't. In this sense, a Torrens certificate fits the image that many laypersons have of deeds to land — that for each parcel there is only one, and if it's not a forgery, it's by definition good. As real estate lawyers, of course, we know that the layperson's understanding is incorrect, and it is our task to make our clients understand the risks and issues inherent in the real situation.

The Torrens system is named for its inventor, Sir Robert Richard Torrens, who in the 1850s developed a system for Australia, modeled after the existing registry used in England to document ownership, liens, and encumbrances of ships. Currently, most countries in the world have government-run land title registration systems. The United Kingdom's system is one of the best known and is regarded as highly successful. Beginning with Illinois in 1895, twenty U.S. states adopted Torrens legislation. Early in the last century Torrens was thought to have great promise, but its potential was never realized. In ten of the states, Torrens statutes were repealed or lapsed.

Of the remaining states, the Torrens system is in substantial use today only in Hawaii, Massachusetts, Minnesota, and Ohio.

Four reasons are commonly given for Torrens's lack of success in the United States. First, U.S. Torrens systems are voluntary, allowing owners to decide whether to register their land or to continue to use the existing recording system. Most owners have elected not to register because registration requires a judicial proceeding, similar to a quiet title action, usually costing thousands of dollars. In other countries like the UK, registration is mandatory, often triggered when an owner of unregistered land sells or transfers ownership. Second, all Torrens systems have indemnity funds to back up their guarantees of title shown on title certificates. When people suffer losses due to mistakes in registration of the certificate, they are entitled to compensation from the indemnity fund, but most states had inadequately capitalized funds and procedures that made it difficult to obtain compensation. Third, although in principle a Torrens certificate is supposed to be absolutely conclusive as to title, all Torrens systems have some exceptions that allow certain interests not shown on a certificate to be valid. Common exceptions to conclusiveness are governmental interests, short-term leases, possessory rights, and certain types of equitable interests. Finally, when Torrens began, the United States already had well-established recording systems, unlike many other countries such as the UK, which had no public land records prior to Torrens. In the United States, many existing users of the recording system (lawyers, abstractors, and title insurance companies) preferred to retain what they were familiar with. Their opposition to the new Torrens system probably contributed to the weaknesses described above.

In re COLLIER
Supreme Court of Minnesota, 2007
726 N.W.2d 799

ANDERSON, PAUL H., Justice. Joshua Collier purchased a parcel of Torrens property with the knowledge that M & I Bank FSB had an unregistered mortgage and purchase interest in the property. After purchasing the property, Collier filed a petition in Ramsey County District Court, seeking an adjudication and declaration of rights in the property. Collier's petition named M & I as a party. M & I moved for summary judgment, and the district court granted its motion, concluding that M & I's interest in the property was superior to Collier's interest because Collier was not a good faith purchaser under Minnesota's Torrens Act. The Minnesota Court of Appeals reversed the district court, concluding that Collier's actual knowledge of M & I's unregistered interest did not preclude him from being a good faith purchaser. The court of appeals then held that Collier's interest in the property was superior to M & I's interest. We reverse.

In September 2000, Joseph Conley obtained a loan from Great Northern Mortgage Corporation. The loan was secured by a mortgage on a parcel of Torrens property Conley owned. The Torrens property subject to Great Northern's mortgage is located in Ramsey County, Minnesota, and was described in the mortgage as Lot 2, Stipe's Rearrangement. It is this property that is the subject of this action. Later in September, Great Northern assigned the mortgage and its rights in the loan to appellant M & I Bank FSB. M & I or its title company filed the mortgage with the Ramsey County Recorder's office, but did not file the mortgage with the county's Registrar of Titles.

In 2002, Conley defaulted on his loan. M & I then filed a power of attorney to foreclose on the mortgage and served notice of the foreclosure on Conley. The Ramsey County Sheriff's office held a mortgage foreclosure sale on the property and M & I purchased it for $118,000. M & I filed a Sheriff's Certificate of Sale in the Ramsey County Recorder's office, but failed to file its purchase interest with the Registrar of Titles. Shortly thereafter, respondent Joshua Collier learned of the foreclosure sale through a notice published by the Ramsey County Sheriff's office. Collier contacted M & I and offered to purchase M & I's interest in the property on behalf of a real estate investment company. M & I declined Collier's offer to purchase the property.

Collier subsequently conducted a title search on the property, and thereby learned that M & I had not filed its mortgage or purchase interest with the Ramsey County Registrar of Titles. Knowing that the property was Torrens property, Collier concluded that M & I did not have a validly recorded interest in it. Collier then contacted Conley on his own behalf and offered to purchase any interest Conley may have had in the property. Conley agreed to sell Collier any such interest for $5,000 and conveyed his interest to Collier by a warranty deed. On the same day he received the deed from Conley, Collier obtained a loan from Dennis Wager, repayment of which was secured by a mortgage on the property Collier had just purchased from Conley. Collier then filed the Conley warranty deed and the Wager mortgage with the Registrar of Titles. . . .

This case involves the Minnesota Torrens Act and Torrens property, and because the Torrens property system is distinct from the abstract property system, we begin our analysis with a brief overview of the two property systems and the policy underlying the Torrens system. Until Minnesota adopted the Torrens system in 1901, all real property in the state was abstract property. Hersh Props., LLC v. McDonald's Corp., 588 N.W.2d 728, 733 (Minn. 1999). Under the abstract system, transactions that affect real property are recorded with the county recorder in the county where the property is located. *Id.* The documents recording the transactions become public records and are a source for prospective purchasers to ascertain the status of title. *Id.* These documents are typically summarized in a single document, called an abstract of title, so that prospective purchasers, mortgagors, mortgagees, and others may have a source to research the status of the title. *Id.* But in addition to the recorded documents, under the abstract system, a title may be affected by factors not reflected in the recorded documents. *Id.* Therefore, a prospective purchaser or mortgagee must carefully investigate a property's history and condition in order to ascertain marketability of the title to that property.

In 1901, the Minnesota legislature adopted an alternative to the abstract system — the Torrens system. *See* Act of Apr. 11, 1901, ch. 237, 1901 Minn. Laws 348. The Torrens Act is codified at Minn. Stat. ch. 508. Under the Torrens system, a party seeking to register an ownership interest in property applies for a court adjudication of ownership and a court decree that converts abstract property into Torrens property. *See* Minn. Stat. §508.22 (2004). A court-appointed officer, the examiner of titles, oversees the registration process. Minn. Stat. §§508.12, 508.13 (2004). After the court adjudicates ownership and any other existing interests in the property, the registrar of titles creates a certificate of title, which is issued to the owner. *See* Minn. Stat. §§508.34, 508.35 (2004). After the issuance of a certificate of title, any conveyance, lien, instrument, or proceeding that would affect the title to the now registered Torrens property must be filed and registered with the registrar of titles in the county where the property is located in order to affect the title to the Torrens property. Minn. Stat. §508.48 (2004).

We have said that "[t]he purpose of the Torrens system was to create a title registration procedure intended to simplify conveyancing by eliminating the need to examine extensive abstracts of title by issuance of a single certificate of title." *Hersh Props.*, 588 N.W.2d at 733. Under the Torrens system, time-consuming and expensive title searches, which characterize the abstract system, are alleviated because the purchaser of Torrens property may, subject to limited exceptions, determine the status of title by inspecting the certificate of title.

M & I argues that Collier's actual knowledge of M & I's unregistered mortgage and subsequent foreclosure on the property negates the good faith requirement in section 508.25, and therefore, its interest in the property is superior to Collier's. Collier argues that his actual knowledge of M & I's unregistered interest does not affect his status as a good faith purchaser, making his interest superior to M & I's.

Collier correctly asserts that Minnesota's Torrens Act places great emphasis on the acts of filing and registration. The Torrens Act provides that "[e]very conveyance, lien, attachment, order, decree, or judgment, or other instrument or proceeding, which would affect the title to unregistered land under existing laws, if recorded . . . shall, in like manner, affect the title to registered land *if filed and registered.*" Minn. Stat. §508.48 (emphasis added). "All interests in registered land, less than an estate in fee simple, *shall be registered* by filing with the registrar. . . ." Minn. Stat. §508.49 (2004) (emphasis added). When conveying, mortgaging, leasing, or otherwise dealing with registered land, "[t]he act of registration shall be the operative act to convey or affect the land." Minn. Stat. §508.47, subd. 1 (2004). Minnesota

Statutes §508.54, which specifically addresses mortgages, requires that mortgage interests in Torrens property "be registered and take effect upon the title only from the time of registration."

Although the Torrens Act makes clear that the acts of filing and registration are critical in the Torrens system, M & I's failure to file its interests in the property with the registrar of titles does not end our inquiry under the Torrens Act. Section 508.25 also provides that "every subsequent purchaser of registered land who receives a certificate of title *in good faith* and for a valuable consideration shall hold it free from all encumbrances and adverse claims" except from interests noted on the certificate of title. (Emphasis added.) Based on this language, we conclude that our inquiry must focus on whether Collier's actual knowledge of M & I's unregistered interest in the property affects his status as a good faith purchaser under section 508.25.

The relevant language of section 508.25 remains unchanged from when the Torrens Act was first codified in Minnesota. *See* Minn. Rev. Laws §3393 (1905). Although the legislature never defined the meaning of good faith in that section, we conclude that good faith must mean something; if not, the language would be rendered a nullity. *See* Minn. Stat. §645.17(2) (2004) (directing courts to presume that the legislature intends an entire statute to be "effective and certain"). Our analysis indicates that since the passage of the Torrens Act, the meaning of good faith has been established through both case law and real estate practice. As far back as 1913, we presumed that the good faith language in the Torrens Act contained a notice or knowledge component, when we stated that "one who purchases from the registered owner for a valuable consideration, in reliance upon [a Torrens] judgment and *without notice or anything to put him on inquiry,* takes the title free from all 'incumbrances and adverse claims.'" Henry v. White, 143 N.W. 324, 326 (Minn. 1913) (emphasis added) (quoting Minn. Rev. Laws §3393). . . .

It also appears that real estate practitioners in Minnesota have come to support and rely on our precedent that actual notice of another's unregistered interest in Torrens property can negate the good faith requirement found in section 508.25. For example, in his amicus brief, Hennepin County Examiner of Titles Edward A. Bock, Jr.,[4] asserts that our precedent . . . "has provided sound guidance for the operation of the Torrens system for over 75 years." Bock claims that some degree of flexibility makes the Torrens Act more useful and efficient. He asserts that if a prospective purchaser could purchase Torrens property and then file his purchase documents with the registrar of titles when he has actual notice of another's unregistered interest, it "would establish a pure 'race' situation providing no benefit to good faith purchasers." Bock claims that such a system would "encourag[e] unscrupulous persons to seek opportunities to profit at the expense of others." He also asserts that our failure to uphold our [prior]

4. Bock oversees the registration of Torrens property in Hennepin County, which is the largest county in the state in terms of population and has more Torrens property than any other county in the state.

ruling . . . would create business risks. He claims that in the ordinary course of business, it may be days between a real estate closing and filing of the documents with the registrar of titles. During this interval, one who knows of the closing could take advantage of the delay. . . .

We conclude that under section 508.25, a purchaser of Torrens property who has actual knowledge of a prior, unregistered interest in the property is not a good faith purchaser. Here, Collier gained actual knowledge of M & I's interest in the property through the Ramsey County Sheriff's office's publication of the notice of foreclosure sale and through his subsequent negotiations with M & I to purchase the property. We also conclude that Collier's knowledge constitutes actual notice. . . .

In rendering this decision, we decline any entreaty by M & I and amicus to define the outer contours of actual notice; rather, we limit our holding to the facts of this case. Also, because we conclude that Collier is not a good faith purchaser, we do not reach the issue of whether Collier's purchase of Conley's interest in the property for $5,000 constitutes "valuable consideration" under section 508.25.

Based on the foregoing analysis, we hold that the district court properly granted summary judgment in favor of M & I, and that the court of appeals erred when it reversed the district court's ruling on M & I's summary judgment motion. Therefore, we reverse and remand to the district court for further proceedings consistent with this opinion.

Problem 12D

Your client, Speedy Builders, is negotiating the purchase of an undeveloped 65-acre tract of land from Reo Realty, Inc. Speedy plans to develop a residential subdivision on the land. You prepared and submitted to Reo Realty a first draft of a contract of purchase, which specifies the agreed-upon contract price of $3.1 million. The title provision in the contract (which you drafted) calls for the seller to purchase an owner's policy of title insurance for the buyer. Reo Realty asked that you delete this provision, claiming that the land is registered under the state's Torrens system and that it has a "clean" certificate of title. According to Reo Realty, Speedy does not need title insurance. What is your response? Does it matter which of the states with Torrens systems the land is in?

E. ELECTRONIC LAND RECORDS

The law and practice concerning land records and title searches developed over hundreds of years with the exclusive use of paper documents. The modern electronic revolution, which has transformed all forms of information throughout society, not surprisingly also touched our land records. In most states it has already resulted in significant changes in some aspects of recording and searching, and further major changes are inevitable. They hold the promise of making our title systems much more efficient, inexpensive, user-friendly, and error free.

Most changes in the United States to date have taken place at the state or local level, as initiatives undertaken by state agencies or organizations or county land records offices. One exception, which impacts the land records at the stage of document preparation and execution, is the federal *E-sign Act* and its state-law analogue, the Uniform Electronic Transactions Act (UETA), approved in 1999 and discussed in Chapter 4. This legislation gives legitimacy to electronic signatures and electronic records as a general matter. More particularly directed to the recording process is the Uniform Real Property Electronic Recording Act, approved by the Uniform Law Commission in 2005 and now adopted by more than 30 states. It authorizes recording offices to receive and record documents and information in electronic form. Any state-law requirements that an instrument be an original, on paper, or in writing are satisfied by an electronic document. Electronic signatures and electronic acknowledgments now serve the same purpose as the traditional paper analogues. The act also specifically authorizes the recording office to accept electronic documents for recording and to index and store those documents.

Problem 12E

In most states, the existing public land records do not provide free, open access to the public. Persons who want to do electronic title searches must either purchase a subscription or otherwise pay to search and use the database. But there are exceptions, including the land records in Florida. All Florida counties have searchable online databases. In order to get an idea of how electronic records tend to be organized and how one finds relevant records, here is a search for you to do using the online records for Broward County, Florida. Although the Broward County online records go back to 1978 — a period long enough that many searches can be completed without going to the county office to view older, paper documents — this problem is not asking you to do an entire search. Your task is only to locate and read several instruments of record.

Your client is interested in buying a house located at 1720 NW 42nd St, Oakland Park, FL 33309, that is listed on a "homes for sale" website. The website shows the prospective seller's name as Joanne McKeage. Go to the Broward County online records at http://www.broward.org/recordstaxes treasury/records/pages/publicrecordssearch.aspx.

Select "Search Records" and do a "Name" search for Joanne McKeage to determine if she is an owner of real property located at the address.

(a) When did Joanne McKeage acquire an ownership interest in the property? Identify the type of instrument, the date of execution, the date of recordation, and the name of the grantor(s). What estate does McKeage own?

(b) If you were able to find the instrument requested in (a) above, go back one step further in the chain of title to determine when the immediately prior owner(s) acquired title. You should find a quitclaim deed, which you should study. What was the purpose of the quitclaim deed? Does it raise any questions as to marketability of title?

(c) Ascertain whether the online records show a mortgage granted by Joanne McKeage when she acquired the property. If there is a recorded mortgage, identify the name of the lender, the date of execution, the date of recordation, and the amount of the debt.

(d) An adequate title search of this property would consist of additional steps, including going further back in the chain of title, looking for adverse transfers from McKeage and prior owners, finding and studying the subdivision plat where the home is located, checking tax records, and looking into other matters.

13
Housing Products

To understand the lawyer's role in real estate transactions, we must have some basic knowledge about the housing products that are on the market today. The marketplace should enhance opportunities for all people to enjoy the benefits of high-quality and affordable housing, while continuing to expand the types of products that are available. In this chapter, we focus on ownership products, because rental properties present themselves as commercial undertakings for most real estate lawyers. Also, residential landlord and tenant issues generally are discussed in appropriate detail in the basic course on property law. A complete study of housing products would also survey the many different affordable-housing initiatives that provide housing opportunities for significant numbers of American families, but to keep this chapter to manageable length, we have concentrated on standard products offered by for-profit providers.

In the United States during the twentieth century, the proportion of American families who owned homes rose gradually. Since World War II, when the national rate of home ownership stood at 43.6 percent, opportunities for ownership have greatly expanded. In 2004, homeownership rates reached a high-water mark of 69.2 percent. With the financial collapse that began in 2007 ownership rates steadily dropped, falling to 65.4 percent in 2012 and 63.5 percent in 2016. Homeownership rates vary by a number of factors including race, with whites and Asians consistently having the highest rates of ownership in recent years. Key factors for housing design and products, looking forward, relate to the shrinking size of the typical household and the gradual but dramatic aging of the general population. Currently, the overall population of the United States includes approximately 18 to 20 percent of families having a family member with a mobility impairment. This has an impact on housing accessibility and design. Mobility impairment increases with age, so an aging population will require greater attention to accessibility issues. Projections indicate that at some time between the years 2020 and 2030, the population of the United States that is age 60 and older will be approximately 20 to 25 percent. The types of products, services, amenities, and financing options needed for our changing population are different from what the market has provided in the past.

Private housing markets will properly respond to market forces to provide for our future housing needs only if they are competitive and dynamic. An issue that constantly confronts housing experts is the degree to which public regulation is needed for private markets to function properly. While this is a complex issue that raises many political and ideological questions, the *White* case, set out below, offers a glimpse into some of the concerns. The *White* case raises questions regarding matters such as the definition of a competitive market for housing and its financing, the availability of good information, the problem of transaction costs, and the tension between legitimate business practices (undertaken for sound economic reasons) and illegal activities such as racially motivated *redlining*. The *White* case includes discussion of the law preventing racial discrimination in housing. This discussion is furthered in the subsequent case of *Texas Department of Housing and Community Affairs*. While reading these cases, keep in mind that even though they involve issues of racial discrimination, they have implications for discrimination in housing markets generally, including concerns for the housing needs of an aging population, housing for households composed of multiple unrelated adults (often regulated as undesirable near college and university campuses), and the housing needs of people with disabilities.

M & T MORTGAGE CORP. v. WHITE
United States District Court, Eastern District of New York, 2010
736 F. Supp. 2d 538

GARAUFIS, District Judge. This court has reviewed [and adopts] the unopposed Report and Recommendation of Magistrate Judge Viktor V. Pohorelsky dated March 18, 2010. [This decision relates to two cases that were resolved together involving plaintiffs Leo White, Linda Council, and Kimberly Council.]

. . . Both cases arise out of materially similar transactions, which consist of the plaintiffs' purchase of a dwelling from the defendant Better Homes Depot, Inc. ("Better Homes" or "BHD") financed by a mortgage issued by the defendant Madison Home Equities, Inc. ("Madison" or "MHE"). The allegations sound primarily in fraud, conspiracy, deceptive trade practices, and federal housing discrimination in connection with those transactions. . . . For the reasons that follow, the undersigned finds that genuine issues of material fact remain, and respectfully recommends that [motions for summary judgment be denied.]

. . . The transactions in question both occurred in 1999, when Leo White and the Councils separately purchased residential properties in Brooklyn, New York from Better Homes, with financing provided by

Madison. At issue are the defendants' alleged representations that the properties were or would be converted into legal four-family (White) and two-family (the Councils) homes, that Certificates of Occupancy would be obtained, and that the premises would be substantially repaired and renovated. Their respective experiences with the defendants—including their discussions, the transactions at issue, and the events that ensued—are separately described below.

LEO WHITE

At the time that White first approached Better Homes about purchasing a home, he was a 21-year-old African-American hotel doorman earning roughly $2,100 per month. He had not graduated high school. White was interested in purchasing a multi-family dwelling in the Bedford-Stuyvesant section of Brooklyn. To enable him to carry the mortgage that would be necessary, White wanted to have rent-paying tenants. Thus, he planned to live with his family on one floor, and collect rent from tenants on the other floors. Because White's aunt had previously purchased a home from BHD financed by an MHE mortgage, she took White to BHD and MHE offices to begin inquiries about buying and financing a home. Over a period of approximately one month, White had numerous meetings with Better Homes and Madison agents, including Glen John and Charles Styles, and was shown an estimated 20 houses. Although he initially agreed to purchase a different property, White ultimately settled on the purchase of a house at 164 Macon Street.

The premises at 164 Macon Street, which were built around 1899, consisted of a basement and four floors. The apartments on the first and second floors each have one bedroom, while the third and fourth floor apartments each have two bedrooms. It appears that the property did not have a Certificate of Occupancy ("CO") for use as a four-family dwelling at the time; White testified that the existing CO was for use as a three-family house. White testified, however, that BHD promised to perform any necessary repairs so that the property could be legally categorized as a four-family dwelling. White also testified that he was told by BHD and MHE agents—including John, Styles, Eric Fessler (the President of Better Homes), and Nadine Malone (the President of Madison Home Equities)—that he would be able to rent the three other units in the home, and realize approximately $3,600 per month in rental revenue. Never having purchased a home before, however, White did not independently verify that information. Nor did he obtain an independent engineering inspection or appraisal, or independently investigate the house's market value or condition. White was not represented by an attorney when he signed the contract of sale, and does not remember speaking with or consulting anyone about its terms prior to signing. He did not object to any of the contract terms, and testified that he had read through and understood the document.

The MHE mortgage that White used to finance the purchase of 164 Macon Street was insured by the Federal Housing Administration (the "FHA"). The rental income he expected to realize was included on his mortgage application, subject to verification in the appraisal. At the behest of Madison, the residence was appraised by Robert Dosch, an employee of CLA Appraisals. His appraisal report contained the following provision: "The appraiser has based his or her appraisal report and valuation conclusion for an appraisal that is subject to satisfactory completion, repairs, or alterations on the assumption that completion of the improvements will be performed in a workmanlike manner." The appraisal amount in his report essentially matched the purchase price, and was calculated on the basis that the legal occupancy status of the property was a four-family dwelling. Dosch's appraisal indicated that White would be able to rent each unit for $1,200 per month.

White remained without counsel until the closing, when he was represented by C. Peter David, an attorney who had been recommended to him by BHD or MHE. Better Homes had informed White that David's legal services were included as part of his down payment. White stated that at the closing David told White that he had looked through the paperwork, and that everything was proper.

Prior to the closing, Better Homes performed a number of cosmetic repairs or renovations on White's home, including installation of ceramic flooring and stoves, painting, carpeting, sheet-rocking, and fixing a leak, and White indicated his satisfaction with the work. Roughly one year after moving in, however, the roof began to leak. White also experienced leaks in some of the piping, and encountered other problems with the chimney and windows. Shortly thereafter, the boiler broke, costing White approximately $2,000. White did not ask Better Homes to make repairs. Ultimately, although White did not realize the level of rental income he had anticipated, he continuously had at least one paying tenant in the premises, and frequently more.[2] When he failed to make his mortgage payments, foreclosure proceedings were initiated and W[h]ite filed a bankruptcy petition in 2003.

THE COUNCILS

The Councils, who are also African-American, learned of Better Homes after seeing signs on a house listing BHD as the seller, as well as from newspaper advertisements. Because the Councils were unable to remain in the apartment they occupied at the time, there was some urgency in finding a house or, at a minimum, another place to live. Although similarly inexperienced in real estate transactions, Linda Council and her daughter,

2. In 2003, he was collecting approximately $3,000 in monthly rental income, while in 2006 he was collecting $2,400 per month from the three rental units.

Kimberly, had both earned college degrees and had done post-graduate work when they first came into contact with BHD and MHE. Linda worked for the United States Postal Service, and together with Kimberly, they were earning approximately $74,000 per year.

After contacting BHD by telephone, they were shown several properties by Mitch Lewis, a Better Homes agent. They ultimately became interested in a house at 102 Etna Street. The property was undergoing extensive repair and renovation, and the basement was being redone. Linda Council expressed to Lewis her interest in obtaining rental income from the basement unit, and both Linda and Kimberly testified that Lewis represented to them that they would be able to rent out the basement for up to $1,200 a month. While the house was undergoing renovation, Better Homes and Lewis "always made it clear that they would fix the house . . . to [their] specifications and what had to be done to the house." Linda Council said she was specifically told that the dwelling was a two-family house, that the basement would be fixed and thus able to be rented out. She was assured that "everything was going to be done that needed to be done, that the house would be up to HUD's codes, everything would be in working condition." Like White, however, the Councils did not have an independent engineering inspection or appraisal performed, nor did they independently investigate the house's market value or condition.

In contrast to White, the Councils were represented by an attorney, Stephen Weinstock, prior to signing the contract of sale. . . .

At the closing, when Linda Council inquired whether signing the closing documents was in their best interests and whether their rights would be protected, she was given the same assurances she was given when the contract of sale was signed. Council stated she was not given enough time to read all the closing documents, but was told by Weinstock, "Don't worry about it. HUD has a stamp of approval on the house being the way it's supposed to be." He assured the Councils that the terms of the mortgage were "aboveboard," and that the transaction was "endorsed by HUD." Better Homes paid the closing costs, and the Councils ultimately executed a number of documents at or prior to closing without objection.

Better Homes performed repairs and renovations at the Councils' property both before and after the closing. . . . Roughly one year after moving in, the roof began to leak. Council contacted Better Homes, but the leak was not fixed until 2004.

Kimberly Council lived with her family in the basement for approximately three years, but was forced to move out because it became "unlivable." The Councils testified that they were never able to rent out the basement to a paying tenant because it remained unfinished, did not function properly, was "falling apart," and was uninhabitable. In addition, the basement was cited by the Buildings Department in a summons for an "illegal conversion" because the house was not a legal two-family home. . . .

OTHER FACTS RELEVANT TO THE TRANSACTIONS

The contracts of sale signed by White and the Councils state that their houses were being sold "as is" — except that at closing, the plumbing, heating, and electrical systems would be in working order, and the roof would not have leaks. The contracts state that "[e]xcept as otherwise expressly set forth in this contract, none of Seller's covenants, representations, and warranties or other obligations contained in this contract shall survive closing." Finally, the contracts contain a standard merger clause: "All prior understandings, agreements, representations and warranties, oral or written, between Seller and Purchaser are merged in this contract; it completely expresses their agreement and has been entered into after full investigation, no party relying upon any statement made by anyone else that is not set forth in this contract." Riders to the contracts of sale contain representations concerning the legal occupancy of the respective dwellings. For White, the rider states that the "seller represents that the premises is a legal four family dwelling," and for the Councils an identical representation is made that the premises are a legal one-family dwelling. . . .

[The court held that fact issues precluded summary judgment as to the plaintiffs' claims for fraud, conspiracy, and deceptive trade practices.]

FEDERAL DISCRIMINATION CLAIMS

The plaintiffs also bring federal discrimination claims under the Fair Housing Act (FHA) and the Equal Credit Opportunity Act (ECOA). The FHA forbids, *inter alia*, "discriminat[ing] against any person in the terms, conditions, or privileges of sale or rental of a dwelling, or in the provision or services or facilities in connection therewith, because of race, color, religion, sex, familial status, or national origin." 42 U.S.C. §3604. The FHA also makes it unlawful for "any person or other entity whose business includes engaging in residential real estate-related transactions to discriminate against any person in making available such a transaction, or in the terms or conditions of such a transaction, because of race, color, religion, sex, handicap, familial status, or national origin." 42 U.S.C. §3605. Similarly, the ECOA makes it unlawful for a creditor to discriminate against a loan applicant on the basis of race, color, sex, national origin, religion, marital status, or age. 15 U.S.C. §1691. Broadly speaking, FHA and ECOA claims may be prosecuted on the basis of (i) disparate treatment, i.e., that plaintiffs were treated differently because of their membership in a protected class, or on the basis of (ii) disparate impact, i.e., that the defendant's practices have a proportionally greater negative impact on minority populations. FHA plaintiffs who allege disparate treatment must show (1) "that they are members of a protected class; (2) that they sought and were qualified to rent or purchase the housing; (3) that they were rejected; and (4) that the housing opportunity remained available to other renters or purchasers." Mitchell v. Shane, 350

F.3d 39, 47 (2d Cir. 2003). The proof required for an ECOA claim is essentially the same, but focuses on the loan rather than the rental or purchase of a dwelling, and varies the fourth FHA element with a requirement that the lender "showed a preference for a non-protected individual." Powell v. American General Finance, Inc., 310 F. Supp. 2d 481, 487 (N.D.N.Y. 2004).

[T]he plaintiffs cannot show and do not allege that the defendants did not rent or sell housing or extend credit to them. Nor have they shown (a) how or why they were treated *differently* from other groups, since they have not alleged or shown how the defendants have treated other groups, or (b) the impact of the defendants' practices or policies. There is an argument on this basis that they cannot make out a *prima facie* case under the ECOA or the FHA. The plaintiffs contend, however, that the defendants practice a form of discrimination by lending or providing housing to a group of persons on less favorable terms than those borrowers would have received if they were outside that particular class of persons. The nature of this type of discrimination, inasmuch as the plaintiffs were not *denied* a loan or a housing opportunity on account [of] race, but were allegedly *targeted* for unfavorable terms in connection with housing and a loan on account of race, should therefore trigger alternative legal considerations reflective of this different species of discrimination. . . . *See, e.g.,* Matthews v. New Century Mortgage Corp., 185 F. Supp. 2d 874, 886-87 (S.D. Ohio 2002) (allowing [a] reverse-redlining FHA claim to proceed with evidence that borrowers received loans on "grossly unfavorable terms" and were "discriminated against in the terms of their credit based on" race); Barkley v. Olympia Mortg. Co., 2007 WL 2437810, at 14 (E.D.N.Y. Aug. 22, 2007) (allowing FHA reverse-redlining claim to proceed with evidence of "intentional targeting"). As the court observed in *Barkley*, limiting a plaintiff to proof only of disparate impact or disparate treatment in lieu of evidence of intentional targeting "would allow predatory lending schemes to continue as long as they are exclusively perpetrated upon one racial group." The court thus concluded that the broader approach was consistent not only with the FHA's aim of ending discrimination in making housing *unavailable* (denying access), but also with its goal of ending discrimination in the terms and conditions of the housing that *is* made available. *Id.* (citing cases). Courts have thus softened the requirements for establishing a *prima facie* case when reverse-redlining forms the substance of the discrimination claim, and have allowed such plaintiffs to show that they (i) were members of a protected class; (ii) applied for and were qualified for the housing or the loan; (iii) received grossly unfavorable terms; and (iv) were intentionally targeted or intentionally discriminated against. *See Barkley,* 2007 WL 2437810, at 13–15. . . .

Firstly, as African-Americans, the plaintiffs are members of a protected class. Secondly, the evidence is clear that they applied to purchase a home and to borrow money. The evidence is less clear, at least with respect to Leo White, that he was *qualified* for the loan. It strikes the court as somewhat imprudent to extend nearly $300,000 in credit to a 21 year-old hotel bellman with little work experience, a monthly salary close to $2,000, no high school diploma, and roughly 3% down. Nevertheless, the court does not wish to substitute any judgment it has in lending practices for that of the defendants. Since White had held that job for two years, and thus had a regular income, in addition to whatever rental income he would be able to bring in, there are legitimate arguments both ways as to his qualification for the loan. With two earners and a combined yearly salary approaching $75,000, there is also enough evidence that the Councils were qualified for their loan. Next, genuine issues of fact remain with respect to the third element — in these cases, receiving unfair or unfavorable terms or conditions. In *Barkley*, Judge Dearie found that a "grossly inflated appraisal" could constitute significantly unfavorable terms and conditions. As the facts appear to be in dispute on whether and how the appraisals were grossly and fraudulently inflated, this element entitles neither party to summary judgment.

With respect to the fourth element, merely allowing the plaintiffs to show evidence of intentional targeting or discrimination does not mean they have presented adequate evidence that they were, in fact, intentionally targeted because they were African-American. The plaintiffs argue that the buyers in 47 of the 52 comparable sales (including the 2 sales to White and the Councils) were racial minorities.[27] A perusal of the addresses for the Schedule A and Schedule B properties as well as the records for the 50 other comparable sales, indicates that most are in heavily minority neighborhoods. It is no accident that Better Homes was not selling real estate on Park Avenue or Central Park West. But that over 90% of similarly-situated home buyers were minorities is not conclusive proof that, as a matter of law, the plaintiffs were intentionally targeted by BHD or MHE. Moreover, that over 90% of comparable sales were made to racial minorities does not indicate that the purchasers in those sales also received grossly unfavorable terms. In other words, just because White and the Councils may have received inflated appraisals and hollow promises, does not indicate one way or the other whether the 50 other buyers also received inflated appraisals and misrepresentations. Thus, the court is hesitant to place too much value on the 90% figure; all it shows is that a great majority of comparable sales were made to racial minorities, not that all of those buyers received grossly unfavorable terms as well. While the plaintiffs may have been the ones who first contacted BHD (rather than the other way around), this does not mean that they were not "targeted" in the broader sense, or that generally speaking, the defendants did not take advantage of unsophisticated, first-time minority home buyers. Employing African-American agents such as John and Styles, who appealed to potential purchasers that their job was a "personal mission" to

---

27. The plaintiffs appear to lump together racial minorities broadly, though the plaintiffs in both cases are African-American. The court is unsure what proportion of the 47 minority buyers is African-American, the specific protected class to which the plaintiffs belong. Regardless, the defendants do not appear to have taken issue with the plaintiffs' calculation and inclusion of other racial minorities.

help minorities achieve the American Dream of home ownership, could show some degree of intentional targeting, as could advertising in heavily minority neighborhoods. Similar, though not identical, practices were held in *Hargraves v.* Capital City Mortgage Corp., 140 F. Supp. 2d 7, 21–22 (D.D.C. 2000), to create a genuine issue of material fact with regard to intentional targeting on the basis of race. *See also* Honorable v. Easy Life Real Estate Sys., Inc., 182 F.R.D. 553, 561 (N.D. Ill. 1998). But selling real estate predominantly to minorities does not indicate, as a matter of law, that the plaintiffs were intentionally targeted as African-Americans. A jury might well conclude that White and Council were targeted not on the basis of being African-American, but because they were vulnerable, low-income, unsophisticated, first-time home buyers who *happened* to be African-American. It is unfortunate that buyers fitting that profile may be found in proportionally greater numbers in the African-American community, but that observation does not mean that the plaintiffs were targeted *because* of their race. Either way, that decision should be the fact-finder's call. . . .

CONCLUSION

Both sides seek to minimize the facts in dispute, but it is rather clear from the facts acknowledged and opposed that much remains in dispute, and that genuine issues of material fact remain. . . . No party is entitled to judgment as a matter of law, and both sides should be entitled to present their theories of the case and ask the jury to make the legitimate, rational inferences that the claims might require and the evidence might warrant. . . .

TEXAS DEPARTMENT OF HOUSING AND COMMUNITY AFFAIRS v. INCLUSIVE COMMUNITIES PROJECT, INC.
Supreme Court of the United States, 2015
135 S. Ct. 2507

KENNEDY, Justice. The underlying dispute in this case concerns where housing for low-income persons should be constructed in Dallas, Texas—that is, whether the housing should be built in the inner city or in the suburbs. This dispute comes to the Court on a disparate-impact theory of liability. In contrast to a disparate-treatment case, where a "plaintiff must establish that the defendant had a discriminatory intent or motive," a plaintiff bringing a disparate-impact claim challenges practices that have a "disproportionately adverse effect on minorities" and are otherwise unjustified by a legitimate rationale. Ricci v. DeStefano, 557 U.S. 557, 577 (2009). The question presented for the Court's determination is whether disparate-impact claims are cognizable under the Fair Housing Act (or FHA), 82 Stat. 81, as amended, 42 U.S.C. §3601 *et seq.*

I

A

Before turning to the question presented, it is necessary to discuss a different federal statute that gives rise to this dispute. The Federal Government provides low-income housing tax credits that are distributed to developers through designated state agencies. 26 U.S.C. §42. Congress has directed States to develop plans identifying selection criteria for distributing the credits. §42(m)(1). Those plans must include certain criteria, such as public housing waiting lists, §42(m)(1)(C), as well as certain preferences, including that low-income housing units "contribut[e] to a concerted community revitalization plan" and be built in census tracts populated predominantly by low-income residents. §§42(m)(1)(B)(ii)(III), 42(d)(5)(ii)(I). Federal law thus favors the distribution of these tax credits for the development of housing units in low-income areas.

In the State of Texas these federal credits are distributed by the Texas Department of Housing and Community Affairs (Department). Under Texas law, a developer's application for the tax credits is scored under a point system that gives priority to statutory criteria, such as the financial feasibility of the development project and the income level of tenants. The Texas Attorney General has interpreted state law to permit the consideration of additional criteria, such as whether the housing units will be built in a neighborhood with good schools. Those criteria cannot be awarded more points than statutorily mandated criteria.

The Inclusive Communities Project, Inc. (ICP), is a Texas-based nonprofit corporation that assists low-income families in obtaining affordable housing. In 2008, the ICP brought this suit against the Department and its officers in the United States District Court for the Northern District of Texas. As relevant here, it brought a disparate-impact claim under §§804(a) and 805(a) of the FHA. The ICP alleged the Department has caused continued segregated housing patterns by its disproportionate allocation of the tax credits, granting too many credits for housing in predominantly black inner-city areas and too few in predominantly white suburban neighborhoods. The ICP contended that the Department must modify its selection criteria in order to encourage the construction of low-income housing in suburban communities.

The District Court concluded that the ICP had established a prima facie case of disparate impact. It relied on two pieces of statistical evidence. First, it found "from 1999–2008, [the Department] approved tax credits for 49.7% of proposed non-elderly units in 0% to 9.9% Caucasian areas, but only approved 37.4% of proposed non-elderly units in 90% to 100% Caucasian areas." 749 F. Supp. 2d 486, 499 (N.D. Tex. 2010). Second, it found "92.29% of [low-income housing tax credit] units in the city of Dallas were located in census tracts with less than 50% Caucasian residents." *Ibid.*

The District Court then placed the burden on the Department to rebut the ICP's prima facie showing of disparate impact. After assuming the Department's proffered interests were legitimate, the District Court held that a defendant—here the Department—must prove "that there are no other less discriminatory alternatives to advancing their proffered interests." Because, in its view, the Department "failed to meet [its] burden of proving that there are no less discriminatory alternatives," the District Court ruled for the ICP. *Id.* at 331. . . .

While the Department's appeal was pending, the Secretary of Housing and Urban Development (HUD) issued a regulation interpreting the FHA to encompass disparate-impact liability. *See* Implementation of the Fair Housing Act's Discriminatory Effects Standard, 78 Fed. Reg. 11460 (2013). The regulation also established a burden-shifting framework for adjudicating disparate-impact claims. Under the regulation, a plaintiff first must make a prima facie showing of disparate impact. That is, the plaintiff "has the burden of proving that a challenged practice caused or predictably will cause a discriminatory effect." 24 CFR §100.500(c)(1) (2014). If a statistical discrepancy is caused by factors other than the defendant's policy, a plaintiff cannot establish a prima facie case, and there is no liability. After a plaintiff does establish a prima facie showing of disparate impact, the burden shifts to the defendant to "prov[e] that the challenged practice is necessary to achieve one or more substantial, legitimate, nondiscriminatory interests." §100.500(c)(2). HUD has clarified that this step of the analysis "is analogous to the Title VII requirement that an employer's interest in an employment practice with a disparate impact be job related." 78 Fed. Reg. 11470. Once a defendant has satisfied its burden at step two, a plaintiff may "prevail upon proving that the substantial, legitimate, nondiscriminatory interests supporting the challenged practice could be served by another practice that has a less discriminatory effect." §100.500(c)(3).

The Court of Appeals for the Fifth Circuit held, consistent with its precedent, that disparate-impact claims are cognizable under the FHA. 747 F.3d 275, 280 (2014). On the merits, however, the Court of Appeals reversed and remanded. Relying on HUD's regulation, the Court of Appeals held that it was improper for the District Court to have placed the burden on the Department to prove there were no less discriminatory alternatives for allocating low-income housing tax credits. *Id.* at 282–283. . . .

B

De jure residential segregation by race was declared unconstitutional almost a century ago, Buchanan v. Warley, 245 U.S. 60 (1917), but its vestiges remain today, intertwined with the country's economic and social life. Some segregated housing patterns can be traced to conditions that arose in the mid-20th century. Rapid urbanization, concomitant with the rise of suburban developments accessible by car, led many white families to leave the inner cities. This often left minority families concentrated in the center of the Nation's cities. During this time, various practices were followed, sometimes with governmental support, to encourage and maintain the separation of the races: Racially restrictive covenants prevented the conveyance of property to minorities, *see* Shelley v. Kraemer, 334 U.S. 1 (1948); steering by real-estate agents led potential buyers to consider homes in racially homogenous areas; and discriminatory lending practices, often referred to as redlining, precluded minority families from purchasing homes in affluent areas. By the 1960's, these policies, practices, and prejudices had created many predominantly black inner cities surrounded by mostly white suburbs. . . .

In April 1968, Dr. Martin Luther King, Jr., was assassinated in Memphis, Tennessee, and the Nation faced a new urgency to resolve the social unrest in the inner cities. Congress responded by adopting the Kerner Commission's recommendation and passing the Fair Housing Act. The statute addressed the denial of housing opportunities on the basis of "race, color, religion, or national origin." Civil Rights Act of 1968, §804, 82 Stat. 83. Then, in 1988, Congress amended the FHA. Among other provisions, it created certain exemptions from liability and added "familial status" as a protected characteristic. *See* Fair Housing Amendments Act of 1988, 102 Stat. 1619.

II

The issue here is whether, under a proper interpretation of the FHA, housing decisions with a disparate impact are prohibited. Before turning to the FHA, however, it is necessary to consider two other antidiscrimination statutes that preceded it.

The first relevant statute is §703(a) of Title VII of the Civil Rights Act of 1964, 78 Stat. 255. The Court addressed the concept of disparate impact under this statute in Griggs v. Duke Power Co., 401 U.S. 424 (1971). There, the employer had a policy requiring its manual laborers to possess a high school diploma and to obtain satisfactory scores on two intelligence tests. The Court of Appeals held the employer had not adopted these job requirements for a racially discriminatory purpose, and the plaintiffs did not challenge that holding in this Court. Instead, the plaintiffs argued §703(a)(2) covers the discriminatory effect of a practice as well as the motivation behind the practice. . . .

In interpreting §703(a)(2), the Court reasoned that disparate-impact liability furthered the purpose and design of the statute. . . . [T]he Court held §703(a)(2) of Title VII must be interpreted to allow disparate-impact claims. . . .

The second relevant statute that bears on the proper interpretation of the FHA is the Age Discrimination in Employment Act of 1967 (ADEA), 81 Stat. 602 *et seq.*, as amended. . . .

The Court first addressed whether this provision allows disparate-impact claims in Smith v. City of Jackson, 544 U.S. 228 (2005). There, a group of older employees challenged their employer's decision to give proportionately greater raises to employees with less than five years of experience.

Explaining that *Griggs* "represented the better reading of [Title VII's] statutory text," *id.* at 235, a plurality of the Court concluded that the same reasoning pertained to §4(a)(2) of the ADEA. The *Smith* plurality emphasized that both §703(a)(2) of Title VII and §4(a)(2) of the ADEA contain language "prohibit[ing] such actions that 'deprive any individual of employment opportunities or *otherwise adversely affect* his status as an employee, because of such individual's' race or age." *Id.* at 235. . . .

Together, *Griggs* holds and the plurality in *Smith* instructs that antidiscrimination laws must be construed to encompass disparate-impact claims when their text refers to the consequences of actions and not just to the mindset of actors, and where that interpretation is consistent with statutory purpose. . . .

Turning to the FHA, the ICP relies on two provisions. Section 804(a) provides that it shall be unlawful:

> To refuse to sell or rent after the making of a bona fide offer, or to refuse to negotiate for the sale or rental of, or otherwise make unavailable or deny, a dwelling to any person because of race, color, religion, sex, familial status, or national origin. 42 U.S.C. §3604(a).

Here, the phrase "otherwise make unavailable" is of central importance to the analysis that follows.

Section 805(a), in turn, provides:

> It shall be unlawful for any person or other entity whose business includes engaging in real estate-related transactions to discriminate against any person in making available such a transaction, or in the terms or conditions of such a transaction, because of race, color, religion, sex, handicap, familial status, or national origin. §3605(a).

Applied here, the logic of *Griggs* and *Smith* provides strong support for the conclusion that the FHA encompasses disparate-impact claims. Congress' use of the phrase "otherwise make unavailable" refers to the consequences of an action rather than the actor's intent. . . .

In addition, it is of crucial importance that the existence of disparate-impact liability is supported by amendments to the FHA that Congress enacted in 1988. By that time, all nine Courts of Appeals to have addressed the question had concluded the Fair Housing Act encompassed disparate-impact claims.

When it amended the FHA, Congress was aware of this unanimous precedent. And with that understanding, it made a considered judgment to retain the relevant statutory text. Indeed, Congress rejected a proposed amendment that would have eliminated disparate-impact liability for certain zoning decisions.

Against this background understanding in the legal and regulatory system, Congress' decision in 1988 to amend the FHA while still adhering to the operative language in §§804(a) and 805(a) is convincing support for the conclusion that Congress accepted and ratified the unanimous holdings of the Courts of Appeals finding disparate-impact liability. . . .

Recognition of disparate-impact claims is consistent with the FHA's central purpose. The FHA, like Title VII and the ADEA, was enacted to eradicate discriminatory practices within a sector of our Nation's economy. *See* 42 U.S.C. §3601 ("It is the policy of the United States to provide, within constitutional limitations, for fair housing throughout the United States").

These unlawful practices include zoning laws and other housing restrictions that function unfairly to exclude minorities from certain neighborhoods without any sufficient justification. Suits targeting such practices reside at the heartland of disparate-impact liability. *See, e.g.*, Huntington v. Huntington Branch, NAACP, 488 U.S. 15, 16-18 (1988) (invalidating zoning law preventing construction of multifamily rental units); United States v. Black Jack, 508 F.2d 1179, 1182-88 (C.A.8 1974); (invalidating ordinance prohibiting construction of new multifamily dwellings); Greater New Orleans Fair Housing Action Center v. St. Bernard Parish, 641 F. Supp. 2d 563, 569, 577–78 (E.D. La. 2009) (invalidating post-Hurricane Katrina ordinance restricting the rental of housing units to only "blood relative[s]" in an area of the city that was 88.3% white and 7.6% black). The availability of disparate-impact liability, furthermore, has allowed private developers to vindicate the FHA's objectives and to protect their property rights by stopping municipalities from enforcing arbitrary and, in practice, discriminatory ordinances barring the construction of certain types of housing units. Recognition of disparate-impact liability under the FHA also plays a role in uncovering discriminatory intent: It permits plaintiffs to counteract unconscious prejudices and disguised animus that escape easy classification as disparate treatment. In this way disparate-impact liability may prevent segregated housing patterns that might otherwise result from covert and illicit stereotyping.

But disparate-impact liability has always been properly limited in key respects that avoid the serious constitutional questions that might arise under the FHA, for instance, if such liability were imposed based solely on a showing of a statistical disparity. Disparate-impact liability mandates the "removal of artificial, arbitrary, and unnecessary barriers," not the displacement of valid governmental policies. *Griggs, supra* at 431. The FHA is not an instrument to force housing authorities to reorder their priorities. Rather, the FHA aims to ensure that those priorities can be achieved without arbitrarily creating discriminatory effects or perpetuating segregation. . . .

. . . [H]ousing authorities and private developers [must] be allowed to maintain a policy if they can prove it is necessary to achieve a valid interest. To be sure, the Title VII framework may not transfer exactly to the fair-housing context, but the comparison suffices for present purposes.

It would be paradoxical to construe the FHA to impose onerous costs on actors who encourage revitalizing dilapidated housing in our Nation's cities merely because some other priority might seem preferable. Entrepreneurs must be given latitude to consider market factors. Zoning officials, moreover, must often make decisions based on a mix of factors, both objective (such as cost and traffic patterns) and, at least to some extent, subjective (such as preserving historic architecture). These factors contribute to a community's quality of life and are legitimate concerns for housing authorities. The FHA does not decree a particular vision of urban development; and it does not put housing authorities and private developers in a double bind of liability, subject to suit whether they choose to rejuvenate a city core or to promote new low-income housing in suburban communities. As HUD itself recognized in its recent rulemaking, disparate-impact liability "does not mandate that affordable housing be located in neighborhoods with any particular characteristic." 78 Fed. Reg. 11476.

In a similar vein, a disparate-impact claim that relies on a statistical disparity must fail if the plaintiff cannot point to a defendant's policy or policies causing that disparity. A robust causality requirement ensures that "[r]acial imbalance . . . does not, without more, establish a prima facie case of disparate impact" and thus protects defendants from being held liable for racial disparities they did not create. Wards Cove Packing Co. v. Atonio, 490 U.S. 642, 653 (1989). Without adequate safeguards at the prima facie stage, disparate-impact liability might cause race to be used and considered in a pervasive way and "would almost inexorably lead" governmental or private entities to use "numerical quotas," and serious constitutional questions then could arise. *Id.* at 653.

The litigation at issue here provides an example. From the standpoint of determining advantage or disadvantage to racial minorities, it seems difficult to say as a general matter that a decision to build low-income housing in a blighted inner-city neighborhood instead of a suburb is discriminatory, or vice versa. If those sorts of judgments are subject to challenge without adequate safeguards, then there is a danger that potential defendants may adopt racial quotas—a circumstance that itself raises serious constitutional concerns.

Courts must therefore examine with care whether a plaintiff has made out a prima facie case of disparate impact and prompt resolution of these cases is important. A plaintiff who fails to allege facts at the pleading stage or produce statistical evidence demonstrating a causal connection cannot make out a prima facie case of disparate impact. For instance, a plaintiff challenging the decision of a private developer to construct a new building in one location rather than another will not easily be able to show this is a policy causing a disparate impact because such a one-time decision may not be a policy at all. It may also be difficult to establish causation because of the multiple factors that go into investment decisions about where to construct or renovate housing units. . . .

Were standards for proceeding with disparate-impact suits not to incorporate at least the safeguards discussed here, then disparate-impact liability might displace valid governmental and private priorities, rather than solely "remov[ing] . . . artificial, arbitrary, and unnecessary barriers." *Griggs,* 401 U.S. at 431. And that, in turn, would set our Nation back in its quest to reduce the salience of race in our social and economic system. . . .

The Court holds that disparate-impact claims are cognizable under the Fair Housing Act. . . .

III

In light of the longstanding judicial interpretation of the FHA to encompass disparate-impact claims and congressional reaffirmation of that result, residents and policymakers have come to rely on the availability of disparate-impact claims. . . .

. . . [S]ince the passage of the Fair Housing Act in 1968 and against the backdrop of disparate-impact liability in nearly every jurisdiction, many cities have become more diverse. . . . The Court acknowledges the Fair Housing Act's continuing role in moving the Nation toward a more integrated society.

The judgment of the Court of Appeals for the Fifth Circuit is affirmed, and the case is remanded for further proceedings consistent with this opinion.

[Justices Alito, Roberts, Scalia, and Thomas dissented. The dissenting opinions of Justices Thomas and Alito are omitted.]

Problem 13A

Consider a relatively small regional bank that seeks to become more profitable by developing a marketing strategy of serving a particular demographic of two-income households, composed of college educated professionals with annual household incomes of at least $100,000. This bank, the New Bank of Northern Virginia (NBNV), developed a clear set of marketing tools and products designed for the particular demographic that it identified as its target customer. The business approach is similar to that taken by many other businesses that target specific consumer demographics to sell goods and services such as automobiles, wines, hand-crafted beers, fashion designs, and vacation destinations. Careful study of consumer demographics and targeting of marketing efforts and product sales can be highly effective and produce greater profits.

Based on its marketing strategy NBNV, with headquarters in the northern Virginia suburbs of Washington, D.C., opens seven branch offices: four in various high-income D.C. suburbs of northern Virginia; two branches in Chevy Chase, Maryland; and one branch in the Georgetown area of Washington, D.C. The strategy of providing banking services and mortgage financing to this particular demographic has made NBNV profitable, and has made it one of the financially strongest local banking operations in its region. As a result of NBNV's success, many banks in the region shifted to a similar strategy and adjusted their services and their branch-banking operations to conform to the new strategy. This marketing strategy targets high-income earners who use a lot of profitable banking services and buy high-end housing products suitable for profitable mortgage lending operations. Some detractors of the NBNV business plan refer to its strategy as *greenlining*, alluding to the slang term for money and seeking to analogize the strategy to the illegal practice of redlining.

After operating for seven years under its new strategy, NBNV is sued for failure to provide services to lower-income customers to the same degree as it does to customers in its targeted demographic. In other words, the complaint is that, as a result of its marketing strategy, NBNV makes a disproportionate amount of mortgage financing and banking services available to people of higher income and with a college education than is proportionate to the overall population of the broader Washington, D.C., regional area. As one consumer put it in a television news interview, "NBNV is *cherry picking* the best customers in the broader D.C. area and leaving a lot of people without a choice, simply because we don't fit their marketing image." A spokesperson for NBNV stated, "We are a business and we have a marketing plan just like any other business. We follow a business plan designed to keep us profitable and to make sure we stay in business while providing services to all people within our market." The spokesperson went on to say, "We don't turn away any creditworthy people, we just market to a particular demographic. What people are observing is our success in reaching our target market."

Federal law requires that all banks submit statistical reports describing their operations. Bank regulators report that NBNV's most recent report discloses the following customer base of people served: 50 percent white, 40 percent Asian, 5 percent African American, 3 percent Hispanic, and 2 percent other or not identified. Regulators report that this demographic profile is not representative of the population diversity in the greater Washington, D.C., area, and they confirm that NBNV does not make mortgage loans available in the vast number of communities that make up the D.C. metropolitan area. In D.C. itself, NBNV makes home loans only in the Georgetown area. Regulators also report that there are multiple neighborhoods and communities in the greater D.C. area with African American and Hispanic populations that meet the NBNV demographic target, but NBNV does not currently have branch banks in these communities.

(a) Discuss the potential issues involved in this situation. Focus on the competing tensions at play between NBNV acting as a business and the concerns of residents who live in communities with limited access to banking services that are ignored by NBNV because the general population of these communities does not comport with NBNV's target demographics.

(b) What are the arguments you might make for NBNV's position, for customers complaining of difficulty getting access to banking services, and from the perspective of society in general?

(c) Does it make a difference if more and more banks in the D.C. area adopt the same strategy as NBNV? At what point might it make a difference: 25 percent of banks, 35 percent of banks, 50 percent of banks, or 75 percent of banks?

(d) Should knowing how NBNV decides on where to locate branch banks make a difference to your analysis? Is branch location simply part of the business decision that is best determined by the business itself?

(e) Does it make a difference that NBNV's strategy is implemented through the physical location of branch-banking buildings, but more and more Americans use online banking services, including online mortgage loan services?

(f) What difference, if any, if NBNV has 5 percent of the market, 30 percent of the market, or 75 percent of the market?

A. THE SINGLE-FAMILY HOME

Probably the most highly desired type of home in America is the single-family detached house. This is a mainstay of the home ownership market. The typical single-family detached home is placed on a lot with buffer space between it, the road, and neighboring houses.

One of the significant changes in the single-family detached housing market is the rise of the Planned Unit Development (PUD) and other planned communities. Presently, a great deal of newly constructed housing is built in planned communities. Most such developments are carefully controlled by restrictions placed on the entire property by the developer, who then divides it into lots for individual housing units. The numerous restrictions go far beyond the typical general zoning requirements, covering a full array of relationships between the properties and owners in a community. In the traditional subdivision, the property restrictions are usually thought of as private matters and are placed against each lot within the subdivision for the benefit of all the lots. These private subdivision arrangements are governed by the general rules of basic property law related to covenants and servitudes. In contrast, the restrictions, plans, and map of a PUD or its equivalent usually go through a review and approval process conducted by the local government. The review is designed to make sure that the planned community meets the minimal standards for density, safety, and other areas of concern established by the local government. Usually the standards also provide for a process of homeowner participation in future decisions related to the property.

One of the key reasons for the growth and appeal of planned subdivisions and PUDs is that they allow a developer better to target a particular market for home sales. By establishing blanket restrictions affecting an entire community, these forms of individual housing can promote a certain "lifestyle" for each family within the development. The idea is that people no longer want to just buy a home, they want to buy a lifestyle. Thus, you can find PUDs with houses built around a golf course, a marina, or equestrian activities; some even have accommodations for private airplanes owned by each homeowner, with roadways and runways that interconnect.

In most planned communities with a significant number of restrictions, the developer creates a homeowners association (HOA) to implement and enforce the various rules and regulations. The HOA is typically organized as a nonprofit corporation. Every unit and every owner in the community is made a part of the HOA. Usually each unit is given one vote, and then the owners elect board members and officers to carry out the rules and mandates of the association. The HOA often enacts rules and regulations governing property use that supplement the recorded covenants and servitudes.

The HOA enforces the governing rules and can do so by bringing legal actions against violators. It can usually seek injunctive relief in court against potential and ongoing violations, and it can also take affirmative steps on its own. An injunction might be sought to prevent construction of an impermissible improvement on a lot, and affirmative action might be taken to hire someone to mow the lawn at a home where the yard has not been kept in proper order. The HOA also has the power to charge for actions taken and can place a lien against the property of a person who fails to pay. This lien can be foreclosed and thus is a powerful weapon for enforcement. In many respects, the HOA acts like a small city government. It polices the rules, reviews architectural plans, and collects fees that enable it to operate. Every unit is assessed a fee in the form of monthly or annual assessments or dues. Like a tax, these fees are almost always secured by a lien provided for in the recorded covenants.

Although many single-family detached homes are not in planned subdivisions or PUDs, clearly the trend in recent years is to place more and more restrictions on single-family housing.

REINER v. EHRLICH
Court of Special Appeals of Maryland, 2013
66 A.3d 1132

BERGER, Judge. This case arises out of a homeowners association's denial of a request to install a new roof on a home using materials not authorized by the bylaws of the association. Upon denial of the request, the homeowners, appellants Randall and Orna Reiner ("the Reiners"), filed a complaint in the Circuit Court for Montgomery County against the appellees, the homeowners association and sixteen individual homeowners in the community. . . . After holding a hearing, the circuit court dismissed the complaint as to the individual homeowners, and entered summary judgment in favor of the homeowners association. . . . This appeal followed. . . .

FACTUAL AND PROCEDURAL BACKGROUND

The Reiners own a house located in a community known as "Avenel." The Avenel community is comprised of over 900 homes in thirteen villages. The Reiners' home is located in the village of Player's Gate, where the Reiners have lived for 18 years.

The Avenel community is governed by a homeowners association ("the Association")[, which is] a Maryland corporation called "Avenel Community Association, Inc."...

The original roof of the Reiners' home was made of cedar shake material. In 2010, the Reiners submitted a request to the Association for approval to install an asphalt roof. The Association denied the Reiners' request on the basis that asphalt roofs were not permitted in the village of Player's Gate. The ... Reiners notified the Association — in writing — that they had signed a contract to install a new roof using asphalt shingles. The Association served the Reiners with a "cease and desist" notice, warning against the replacement of the Reiners' roof with asphalt shingles, or any other product not permitted by the bylaws of the Association.

... On October 7, 2011, the Reiners filed a complaint for declaratory judgment in the circuit court for Montgomery County ...

... The Reiners sought a declaratory judgment "with respect to use of roofing materials in the homes at Avenel," as well as declaratory relief regarding "any rules and standards" imposed and applied "throughout the Avenel community."...

Article XI of the Association's Declaration of Covenants, Conditions and Restrictions (hereinafter, the "Avenel–Declaration") provides in part:

> It shall be prohibited for any Owner or Vacant Lot Owner to undertake (1) any construction, which term shall include, in addition to the actual erection of a dwelling and its appurtenances, any staking, clearing, excavation, grading, or other site work, (ii) any landscaping, plantings or removal of plantings or removal of plants, trees or shrubs, or (iii) any modification, change or alteration of a Lot or Residential Unit, whether functional or decorative, except in strict compliance with this Article XI, and until the approval of either the New Construction Committee, Modifications Committee or Control Committee, as applicable, has been obtained.

Article XI of the Avenel–Declaration also contained provisions establishing a modification committee, which is responsible for considering requests for modifications, alteration, or additions to existing homes:

> Section 2. Modifications Committee. Subject to Section 3 below, the Modifications Committee ("MC") shall have exclusive jurisdiction over modifications, additions, or alterations made on or to existing Residential Units and the Lawn and Garden Areas appurtenant to such residential Units. The MC shall also be responsible for enforcing the Use Restrictions set forth in Article XII of this

Declaration. The MC shall consist of at least three (3) and no more than five (5) members, all of whom shall be appointed by the Board of Directors. The MC may promulgate and amend Modification Standards as well as Application and Review Procedures. Such modification Standards shall be in addition to, and not in lieu of, the Design and Development [Guidelines] established by the NCC [*i.e.,* the new construction Committee established by Section 3], which such design and Development Guidelines shall be followed by the MC. All reasonable costs incurred by the MC in reviewing and approving applications submitted to the MC shall be the responsibility of the applicant. Unless expressly waived by the MC, all applications for Review submitted to the MC shall be accompanied by a review fee of One Hundred Fifty Dollars ($150.00) or such other sum established by the MC.

The affidavit of the Association's general manager explained that these provisions prohibit owners from "altering or changing the roof style of their home without prior approval from the Association."

The Avenel–Declaration also contained a provision regarding roofing materials that may be used by homeowners. The provision, which was dated December 4, 2006 (the "2006 Roof Specifications"), indicated that asphalt roofs were expressly prohibited, subject to certain exceptions:

Asphalt roofs are expressly prohibited unless used by the builder as part of the original roof of your home or as part of the original roofs of other homes within your village, as outlined below.

The roofing materials listed as available options for homes in Player's Gate include the following:

Player's Gate: natural cedar shake or natural slate, synthetic cedar, synthetic slate

The 2006 Roof Specifications also referred to "different UL performance standards for fire, impact and wind" and listed materials that have been identified as "Class A fire rated roofs":

Just as roof shingles and slates are available in a variety of styles, colors, textures, and sizes, they are also offered with different UL performance standards for fire, impact and wind. These standards may be achieved, in part, by the underlayment material that is utilized in the installation of the product. Owners should consult with their roof contractor or manufacturer to obtain further information and details on this matter. Regardless of whether or not it has approved an alternative roof material or system, the Association does not make any representations as it relates to warranties, life-cycles, UL ratings or performance and safety standards, etc. Several roof materials and/or approved alternate roofs are identified by their manufacturers as Class A fire rated roofs. As noted, such rating may be achieved by the roof system installation method or may be achieved by the roof material itself. Among the various roofs approved by the Association, there are both Class A roof systems and Class A roof materials. Specific questions as to the type of rating and the manner in which such rating is achieved should be addressed to the roofing contractor or the manufacturer.

. . . .

DISCUSSION

. . . .

The general rule under Maryland law is that decisions made by a homeowners association's board of directors will not be disturbed unless there is a showing of fraud or bad faith. *See* Black v. Fox Hills North Cmty. Ass'n, 599 A.2d 1228 (Md. App. 1992). In *Black*, members of a homeowners association challenged the association's approval of a fence installed by other members of the community. The plaintiffs claimed that the fence was approved and installed in violation of the association's covenants and restrictions. We held that it did not matter whether the fence actually violated the association's declaration of covenants, because the enforcement of those rules was within the exclusive purview of the association. "Whether [the association] was right or wrong; the decision fell within the legitimate range of the association's discretion." *Id.* at 1231. We further explained: "Absent fraud or bad faith, the decision . . . was a business judgment with which a court will not interfere." *Id.* at 1231-32. "The 'business judgment' rule, therefore, precludes judicial review of a legitimate business decision of an organization, absent fraud or bad faith." *Id.* at 1231. Further, under the business judgment rule, "there is a presumption that directors of a corporation acted in good faith and in the best interest of the corporation." Danielewicz v. Arnold, 769 A.2d 274, 296 (Md. App. 2001). . . .

In sum, we hold that the business judgment rule applies because this case falls squarely within the purview of *Black*. Here, the Association rendered a decision denying the Reiners' roof request. The Reiners — much like the plaintiffs in *Black* — sued because they disagreed with the Association's decision. The Reiners did not allege any fraud or bad faith on the part of the Association. Under *Black*, "[t]he 'business judgment' rule, therefore, precludes judicial review" of that decision. Accordingly, the Association was entitled to summary judgment as a matter of law.[5] . . .

. . . Accordingly, we affirm the judgment of the Circuit Court for Montgomery County.

5. We also observe that, under *Black*, although the business judgment rule applies regardless of whether or not an association's decision was "correct," the Association's decision in this case comported with the Association's bylaws. The 2006 Roof Specifications prohibit asphalt roofs the in the Reiners' village, and instead identify four options available for use as roofing materials. The Association simply adhered to its bylaws in denying the Reiners' request to install an asphalt roof.

TURUDIC v. STEPHENS dba SUSAN ESTATES RESIDENTS' ASSOCIATION
Court of Appeals of Oregon, 2001
31 P.3d 465

HASELTON, Presiding Judge. . . . The principal issue on . . . appeal is whether the plaintiffs' keeping of two pet cougars on their property violated the covenants, conditions, and restrictions (CCRs) of a subdivision. . . .

The material facts are as follows: Plaintiffs Andy and Luisa Turudic are the owners of two American mountain lions,[1] more commonly known as cougars. In 1993, plaintiffs decided to move from Missouri to Oregon, in part because Oregon law, subject to certain statutory restrictions and local ordinances, permits the keeping of exotic animals such as cougars.

Plaintiffs purchased property in Susan Estates, a small subdivision in rural Yamhill County, in an area zoned "very low density, 5 acre minimum." There are no zoning restrictions on the type of animals that can be kept on a particular piece of property.

Before moving to Susan Estates, in researching the property, plaintiffs obtained [the set of CCRs] entitled "First Amendment to Declaration of Covenants and Restrictions" (amended CCRs), . . . adopted in 1987 as a comprehensive revision to the original CCRs. . . .

Plaintiffs began building their home in late spring 1994. Construction of the cougar holding pen, which meets or exceeds state standards for animal care and public safety[4] and has been approved by the Oregon Department of Fish and Wildlife, began in mid-September and was completed on October 13, 1994. Plaintiffs did not obtain the approval of the Susan Estates Homeowners' Association board before undertaking or completing either their home or the cougar pen project.

At 3:00 in the morning on October 19, 1994, plaintiffs, without notice to their neighbors, moved the cougars into the holding pen. Two days later plaintiffs first became aware of their neighbors' concerns about the cougars when a deputy sheriff contacted them in response to a neighbor's complaint.[5]

On November 8, 1994, a majority of the members of the Susan Estates homeowners' association met to discuss the cougar issue. Plaintiffs were not invited. At that meeting, the members agreed that the cougars were a

---

1. Mutchka, a female, is a South American variety; Pete Puma, a male, is a North American variety.

4. *See* ORS 609.325 (requiring that exotic animals be kept "under conditions of confinement or control that, given the nature of the animal, would be imposed by a reasonable and prudent keeper to avoid physical or financial risk to the public as a result of escape of the animal or otherwise"); OAR 603–011–0710 (detailing the design requirements for outdoor cages used to house exotic felines); OAR 635–044–0035 (requiring that any wildlife held in captivity be maintained in a manner that is sanitary, safe and not unhealthful for the animals).

5. The deputy sheriff confirmed that the pen met state wildlife requirements and did not pursue the matter further.

nuisance and should be removed from plaintiffs' property. They also resolved to disapprove any "cougar-cage outbuildings." Consequently, on November 30, 1994, counsel for the Association wrote to plaintiffs, expressing concerns both about the cougars and about plaintiffs' failure to seek Board approval for both their house and the cougar pen.

Plaintiffs responded by offering to build a secondary safety fence around the existing cougar pen, and by submitting house plans to the Board. Plaintiffs did not submit plans for the cougar pen. On February 22, 1995, a representative for the Association wrote to plaintiffs, stating that plaintiffs' house plans had been approved but that the cougar pen was rejected under the "nuisance provisions" of the CCRs:

> Plans for construction of current outbuildings or any future outbuildings for housing of cougars have not yet been submitted but construction has also been observed on-site. Such buildings are not approved and further, Association hereby directs such outbuildings to be removed immediately, and no further construction of cages for housing cougars or any other felid shall be constructed. This action is predicated on the basis of the nuisance provisions of Susan Estates Covenants and Restrictions.

. . . .

In March 1995, plaintiffs brought this action. Plaintiffs sought a declaratory judgment that neither the pen nor the cougars could be prohibited under the amended CCRs and that . . . the Association . . . acted unreasonably and capriciously in denying approval for the cougar pen. . . .

Defendants counterclaimed, alleging that the cougars were a nuisance under both the CCRs and common law. Defendants also filed two claims for injunctive relief—one requiring plaintiffs to remove the cougar pen because they had failed to obtain approval for the structure as required by the CCRs, and the other precluding plaintiffs from keeping cougars on their property. . . .

The trial court subsequently issued a detailed letter opinion [that made] three determinations that are central to this appeal. *First,* plaintiffs' maintenance of the cougars was not a nuisance under either the common law or the amended CCRs. *Second,* nevertheless, plaintiffs' maintenance of the cougars was not a permitted "residential use" under the CCRs. *Third,* construction of the cougar pen without the Board's prior approval violated the amended CCRs. Consequently, given its determination that the maintenance of the cougars was not a nuisance but that plaintiffs had otherwise violated the amended CCRs, the court entered a judgment rejecting plaintiffs' claims for declaratory relief and breach of contract, and rejecting defendants' nuisance-related counterclaims, but directing that both the cougars and the holding facility be removed from plaintiffs' property. . . .

. . . The amended CCRs, which all parties agree apply to plaintiffs' property, authorize the Board to regulate "the use . . . of the Property in such a manner as to preserve and enhance lot and structure values, farming, and to maintain the natural vegetation and topography." Amended CCRs, Art. IV, sec. 2. Limitations on "use" are set forth in Article V, section 1, which provides, in pertinent part:

> (b) *Use of the Property.* Property may be reasonably and normally used for agricultural farming, tree farming or residential use only.
>
> (c) *Nuisances.* No nuisance shall be permitted to exist or operate upon any Property so as to be detrimental to any other Property in the vicinity thereof or to its occupants. The decision of the Association as to what is a nuisance is presumptively correct. No normal or reasonable use of the Property, as described in subparagraph (b) above, shall be a nuisance.

Here, as noted, the trial court concluded that the cougars were not a nuisance under either the amended CCRs or common law. . . .

Defendants do not challenge those determinations on appeal. Thus, for purpose of this appeal, we necessarily assume that plaintiffs' keeping of the cougars is *not* a nuisance under either the common law or the CCRs.

Given that posture, the issue narrows to whether keeping the cougars is a permissible "residential use" within the meaning of Article V, subsection 1(b). In construing the "residential use" provision of the amended CCRs, we follow the methodology prescribed in Yogman v. Parrott, 937 P.2d 1019 (Or. 1997). Under *Yogman,* "[t]o interpret a contractual provision, including a restrictive covenant, the court follows three steps." First, the court must examine "the text of the disputed provision, in the context of the document as a whole. . . . If the provision is clear, the analysis ends." If, however, the provision, when so viewed, remains ambiguous, the court must look to "extrinsic evidence of the contracting parties' intent" to resolve the ambiguity. Finally, if that analysis is not dispositive, the court must look to relevant maxims of construction, including the maxim that restrictive covenants should be "construed most strictly against the covenant." *Id.* at 1021–22. . . .

"Residential," as commonly understood, means "of, relating to, or connected with residence or residences." *Webster's Third New Int'l Dictionary,* 1931 (unabridged ed 1993). "Residence," in turn, means "the place where one actually lives or has his home. . . ." *Id.* Thus, a "residential use" is one that involves activities generally associated with a personal dwelling.

Plaintiffs assert — and we agree — that keeping family pets is a "residential activity." *See* Aldridge v. Saxey, 409 P.2d 184 (Or. 1965) (concluding that covenant precluding the use of property for nonresidential purposes did not preclude the landowners from keeping 16 German Shepherds and 5 smaller dogs on their property). Plaintiffs further offered uncontradicted testimony that they keep and care for the cougars as pets and not for any commercial purpose, such as breeding or exhibiting the animals for pay. Andy Turudic described the role that the cougars play in plaintiffs' lives: "[They] are an integral part of our family life. We have a very strong bond with our animals. . . . They give me and my wife both immense pleasure." Thus, although the cougars may be more exotic than goldfish or hamsters, they are, nevertheless, indisputably family pets. Given that the cougars are family pets, and that their presence does not present a nuisance, the maintenance of the cougars constitutes a "residential use" within the meaning of the amended CCRs.

Defendants argue, however, that the amended CCRs permit only "reasonable" and "normal" residential uses — and assert that the keeping of cougars is neither. Defendants' argument fails for several reasons. First, as a textual matter, subsection 1(b) does not refer to "reasonable and normal . . . residential use." Rather, it states that the property may be "*reasonably* and *normally* used for [farming] or residential use only." (Emphasis added.) Thus, defendants' argument transforms adverbs into adjectives — a transformation that is particularly significant with respect to "normally" and "normal." It is one thing to say that property shall "normally" — *i.e.*, typically or usually — be used for farming and residential purposes. It is quite another to say that property can only be used for "normal" — *i.e.*, presumably ordinary or decidedly nonexotic — uses. Here, plaintiffs "normally" use their property for residential uses.

Second, to the extent that defendants claim contextual support for their "reasonable and normal" use argument, they point to the language of the nuisance provision, subsection 1(c). That reliance is, however, unavailing. Subsection 1(c) refers to "normal *or* reasonable" use — that is, it is phrased in the disjunctive, not defendants' putative conjunctive. Thus, any use described in subsection 1(b) that is *either* "reasonable" *or* "normal" is not a nuisance under subsection 1(c); a use that is not "normal," but is nevertheless "reasonable," must be permitted. . . .

Third, to the extent that the phrase "may be reasonably and normally used . . . for residential use only" remains ambiguous after resort to context, including subsection 1(c), the covenant is to be "construed most strictly against the covenant." *Yogman*, 937 P.2d at 1022. Here, that canon assumes special significance because of the conduct of the Association, which seeks to enforce the covenant. As noted, plaintiffs have undertaken considerable efforts to eliminate potential risks associated with keeping the cougars. Those efforts have been highly successful — so successful that the trial court found that any risk from the cougars did not rise to the level of a common–law nuisance: "[T]he potential for actual injury to a person is so remote that the fear of the neighbors cannot be said to be objectively reasonable."[14] Nevertheless, marginal risks remain — *e.g.*, the risk of a trespassing child thrusting his or her hand into the cage or of a stranger releasing

14. In addition, plaintiffs have had both cougars declawed and have had Mutchka, the female, spayed. Plaintiff took those measures to further reduce any risk posed by the cougars and to eliminate the chance that Mutchka might attract wild cougars when she is in estrus. Mutchka's spaying also eliminated any caterwauling, a loud, scream-like sound that female cougars make when they are in heat.

the cougars — and plaintiffs offered to undertake additional measures that would have eliminated even that potential. But the Association refuses to approve those reasonable measures. As the trial court explained:

> The principal danger of escape comes from human error. Mr. Turudic appears to be a responsible animal owner interested not only in the best interest of his animals, but also in the safety of his own family and neighbors. The likelihood of deliberate removal from the facility is very remote, at least not by Mr. or Mrs. Turudic. Likewise, the probability of an escape due to the negligence of the Turudics is remote, though possible. A procedure is followed in which the cougars are chained to the fence before the door is opened for entry. A double door or 'sally port' entry could be constructed which would not allow opening of the inner door until the outer door is secure. *Mr. Turudic indicated his interest in adding this, but ironically, it is clear that this addition to the cage would not gain approval of the Susan Estates board.*
>
> The holding facility would not protect a person from injury if the person stuck a hand or arm through the wire. While the danger would hopefully be recognized by an adult, a curious child might not. *Again, this potential problem could be addressed by construction of a secondary fence around the cage, but approval of the Susan Estates board would likely be required.* (Emphasis added.)

In effect, the Association contends that plaintiffs' maintenance of the cougars is not "reasonable" because of the Association's own refusal to approve reasonable safety measures. The self-serving circularity is patent. Such a construction of subsection 1(b) cannot be squared with the "construed most strictly against the covenant" canon.

We thus conclude that the keeping of the cougars in their holding pen is a permitted residential use under Article V, subsection 1(b) of the amended CCRs. That conclusion, however, necessarily depends on the premise that the cougars' holding pen lawfully exists, and will continue to exist, on plaintiffs' property. Consequently, we turn to the trial court's determination that the cougar pen must be removed from the property.

In requiring the removal of the cougar pen, the trial court reasoned that the amended CCRs required plaintiffs to seek advance approval of all structures, that plaintiffs had failed to seek approval for the cougar pen, and that the Association, pursuant to its approval authority, had denied approval for the cougar pen. Thus, the Association's denial of approval, and concomitantly its authority to do so, were central to the trial court's ruling.

We agree that, at least in the abstract, the amended CCRs give the Board the authority to either approve or disapprove construction of structures such as the cougar pen. In particular, the amended CCRs provide:

> No . . . building, fence or other structure shall be erected, placed or altered on any lot or parcel until the proposed building plans, plot plans showing the proposed location of such building or structures . . . have been approved in writing by the Board, its successors or assigns. Refusal or approval of plans or

location may be based by the Board upon any reason, including purely aesthetic conditions, which, in the sole discretion of the Board, shall be deemed sufficient. Amended CCRs, Art. V, sec. 1(e)(2).

. . . .

In its February 22, 1995, letter, the Board notified plaintiffs that structural approval for their cougar pen had been denied and that the cougar pen had to be removed. The letter further stated: "[N]o further construction of cages for housing cougars or any other felid shall be constructed. *This action is predicated on the basis of the nuisance provisions of the Susan Estates Covenants and Restrictions.*" (Emphasis added.) No alternative explanation was given, and the evidence at trial did not show any additional bases for the Board's decision to deny approval of the plans. For example, there was no evidence that the Board denied approval because the cougar pen violated any "aesthetic" or design requirements of the CCRs or because the cougars or their holding pen might adversely affect property values. Thus, the sole basis of the Board's denial of approval was its belief that maintenance of the cougars was a nuisance.

The trial court concluded that that denial was sufficient basis for enjoining plaintiffs to remove the cougar pen. We respectfully disagree for two related reasons. First, as the trial court explicitly concluded — and, again, defendants do not dispute on appeal — the cougars here are not a nuisance under the CCRs. Thus, while the Board may deny approval of a structure for any reasonable and not capricious reason, the sole basis for disapproval here was legally erroneous — and, indeed, objectively unreasonable: "[T]he fear of the neighbors cannot be said to be objectively reasonable." Denial on such a basis is unreasonable and capricious.

Second, in a related sense, the Board's disapproval was, in purpose and effect, a collateral preclusion of a lawful permitted use under the CCRs. That is, the Board's disapproval was not, actually, of the structure *qua* structure but of the structure's function. The disapproval of the holding pen here is analogous to a homeowners' association refusing to approve plans for a home that includes a billiard room because the association's members disapprove of billiards. Here, the keeping of pets, including exotic pets, in safe facilities is a permitted "residential use." Consequently, so long as the structure for holding such pets does not violate some other (*e.g.,* design-related) requirement of the CCRs, the preapproval process cannot be employed as a subterfuge to preclude that permitted use. Such a denial is unreasonable and capricious.

We thus conclude that the trial court erred in entering judgment for defendants on their second counterclaim for an injunction compelling the removal of the cougars' holding facility and on their third counterclaim for an injunction compelling the removal of the cougars themselves from plaintiffs' property. . . .

Problem 13B

Pinehaven Estates is a single-family PUD community that has covenants, conditions, and restrictions (CCRs) that regulate the architectural design, side and rear lot line setbacks, and the size and location of structures on all lots. The Pinehaven Homeowners Association also has adopted rules and regulations to control activities within the PUD. Pinehaven Estates is within the city limits of the City of Pinedale, whose local ordinances, including its zoning code, building code, and nuisance regulations, apply to all of its lots.

(a) Amy, the owner of one of the Pinehaven lots, has a home, completed three years ago, with a spacious backyard swimming pool. She hires a contractor, who begins to construct a cabana near one corner of the pool area. Her next-door neighbor, Brady, is concerned that the cabana is located only 12 feet from their common boundary line. Brady asks Amy whether she has obtained Association approval for the project. Amy replies that she hasn't. Brady reads his CCRs and believes that approval is necessary. He contacts Cindy, the President of the Association, but Cindy says that the Board has decided not to require the submission of plans for swimming pool improvements if they are constructed within the footprint of existing pool fencing. Does Brady have any recourse? What can be done if the Association refuses to take action?

(b) Suppose that Amy is constructing the cabana without a valid building permit issued by the City of Pinedale. Should Brady have the right to cause the Association or the City to enforce the building-permit regulation?

(c) Instead of the above facts, assume that the City has reviewed and approved Amy's plans for the cabana, but that the CCRs clearly require Association approval, which Amy has not obtained. Should Amy have the right to go forward, or should Brady (with or without the cooperation of the Association officers and board) have the right to stop the project?

(d) Two years ago Daryl bought a lot in Pinehaven Estates. At the time the CCRs permitted owners to enclose existing decks and to modify roofs by the addition of solar panels, without obtaining Association approval. In fact, when he purchased, Daryl was planning to add solar panels and to convert the back deck to a glass-enclosed aviary as soon as he could afford these improvements. Eighteen months after Daryl bought his lot, the members of the Association by majority vote amended the rules and regulations to require the Association's approval for the installation of solar panels and the construction of the aviary. This change was approved in accordance with the procedures outlined in the Association rules and regulations and consistent with the requirements of the covenants. Nine months after this change Daryl submitted plans for his new solar roof and aviary, but the Association rejected his plans. Daryl sues on the ground that he is bound only by the rules and regulations applicable at the time he bought the property. He asserts that he paid a considerable amount to purchase a home in this upscale development and should be governed by the rules known to him at the time of purchase. What do you think of the merits of Daryl's claim?

(e) What remedies do you believe are appropriate for violations of CCRs? Of the rules and regulations? If you were drafting remedies provisions for CCRs for a community like Pinehaven Estates, what express remedies would you include and why?

B. CONDOMINIUMS

A *condominium* is a single unit in a multiunit project together with an undivided interest in common areas and facilities of the project. The owner of a condominium generally has fee simple title to the unit and owns a percentage share of the common property as a tenant in common with her neighbors. Literally, the term condominium comes from the concept of *codominion*, which means that there are shared or overlapping spheres of power, control, or ownership.

Property held as a condominium is a form of ownership, and it is not any particular architectural style. The condominium form of housing ownership has become a major component of America's total housing stock. All states have statutes that govern the creation and operation of condominiums. Although most authorities believe a condominium may be created at common law, this has not proven workable due to a number of conceptual and procedural problems. The condominium statutes establish a specific set of ownership rights that are identified by reference to legal documents prepared in accordance with statutory requirements and filed with a government entity. Consequently, the first place to look when considering this form of property is at local state statutory law that enables the creation of this form of ownership. Once the state condominium statute is understood, case law must be consulted for purposes of interpretation and for examples of application in practice.

The primary legal document for a condominium project is the *Declaration of Condominium*, wherein a property owner declares the legally described property to be henceforth held in the condominium form. The declaration is filed in the local real property records so that all purchasers of condominiums will have actual or constructive notice of its contents. The declaration must spell out all the elements required to be addressed by the statutes and must clearly define by narrative reference, and usually by drawings, the identification of each ownership unit and all common property. The declaration must also address the rights and responsibilities of all unit owners regarding both the individual ownership property and the common property. Furthermore, the declaration establishes a *condominium unit owners association*, provides for rules and regulations to govern the orderly operation of the condominium, and authorizes assessments against each unit owner to pay for condominium expenses. With regard to assessments, the declaration usually provides rights and protections for lenders making mortgage loans to individual unit owners. In addition, there will usually be separate legal documents detailing the form and procedures governing the unit owners association.

The extent of the common property, usually called the *common elements*, is the distinguishing feature of the condominium form of ownership. A buyer's exclusive fee interest usually extends only to the interior space and surfaces of the unit. The common elements typically include the land, building systems, and project amenities. In a condominium development, there are likely to be both common elements and *limited common elements* associated with unit ownership. *Common elements* consist of all those portions of the condominium property that are not defined in the declaration as part of a unit. *Limited common elements* are those common elements defined in the declaration as being for the limited or exclusive use of a particular unit while not in themselves being part of the described unit. Examples include unit patios, balconies, window flower boxes, and parking spaces.

Some condominiums are set up so that the association is given a *right of first refusal* as to any unit that goes on the market for sale after the developer makes the initial sale (applies to the resale market). This right of first refusal gives the association some control over who can buy into the condominium. The right operates by giving the association the first option to purchase the unit on the same terms as are being extended to an arm's-length buyer who has executed an enforceable contract of purchase and sale.

In addition to the declaration of condominium, most condominiums are covered by a "blanket" set of rules and regulations enacted by the unit owners association. When a person challenges a condominium restriction, the standard of review applied by the court usually depends on the source of the restriction. The restrictions established in the declaration are given more deference than those passed by the association and its board. The items set forth in the declaration of condominium are generally considered to be equivalent to covenants running with the land, thus binding current and future owners unless they violate a statute, public policy, or a constitutionally protected right. Items passed by the association and its board are of lesser status and are subjected to a stricter standard of review. They are enforced so long as they (1) comply with the procedures established for their promulgation, and (2) reasonably relate to the promotion of the health, happiness, and welfare of unit owners (including aesthetic considerations).

ANDERSON v. COUNCIL OF UNIT OWNERS OF GABLES ON TUCKERMAN CONDOMINIUM
Court of Appeals of Maryland, 2008
948 A.2d 11

BATTAGLIA, Judge. In the present case, we are presented with the question of whether a condominium council of owners under the Maryland

Condominium Act is required to repair or replace property of an owner in an individual condominium unit after a casualty loss. We shall answer in the negative. . . .

The Gables on Tuckerman Condominium, located at 5800 Tuckerman Lane in Rockville, Maryland, was established by declaration, bylaws and plats recorded among the land records of Montgomery County in August of 1987. The Council of Owners of The Gables on Tuckerman ("Council of Gables") is the unincorporated association of all owners that was established by its Bylaws.[1]

Dianne Anderson owned a two-level town home in The Gables. At all times relevant, the Council of Gables carried a master condominium insurance policy on the property with a deductible of $10,000 per occurrence; Ms. Anderson was insured [for her interest in her individual unit] by a condominium owners "Condocover" policy issued by Erie Insurance Exchange ("Erie").

1. Article 8 of The Gables on Tuckerman Condominium's Bylaws states in part:

Section 3. *Duty to Maintain.* Except for maintenance requirements imposed upon the Council by the Declaration or these Bylaws, if any, the Unit Owner of each Unit shall, at his own expense, maintain the interior of his Unit and any and all equipment, appliances or fixtures situated within the Unit and its other appurtenances in good order, condition and repair and in a clean and sanitary condition, and shall do all redecorating, painting and the like which may at any time be necessary to maintain the good appearance of his Unit and such appurtenances. In addition to the foregoing, the Unit Owner of any Unit shall, at his own expense, maintain, repair and replace any plumbing fixtures, heating and air conditioning equipment, heat pumps and compressors, lighting fixtures, refrigerators, dishwashers, clothes washers and dryers, disposals, ranges, fireplace flues, and/or other equipment that may be in or appurtenant to his Unit. The Unit Owner shall also be responsible for routine maintenance, at his own expense, of the Limited Common Elements which he has a right to use and shall keep such limited common elements in good, clean and sanitary condition at all times. . . .
    Section 5. *Limitation of Liability.* The Council shall not be liable for any failure of water supply or other utilities or services to be obtained by the Council or paid for out of the Common Expenses, or for injury or damage to persons or property caused by the elements or by any Unit Owner or any other person, or resulting from electricity, water, snow, or ice which may leak or flow from any portion of the Common Elements or from any pipe, drain, conduit, appliance or equipment.

Section 1 of Article 13 of the Bylaws, entitled "Insurance," provides in part:

(a) . . . the Board of Directors, acting on behalf of the Council shall obtain and maintain, to the extent reasonably available, the following insurance, as a Condominium Master Insurance Policy the cost of which shall be an item of Common Expense: (1) Property insurance on the Common Elements and Units, exclusive of improvement and betterments installed in Units by Unit Owners, insuring against all risks of direct physical loss commonly insured against including fire and extended coverage perils. . . .
    (e) Any [master] insurance policy issued . . . does not prevent a Unit Owner from obtaining insurance for his own benefit. . . .
    (g) It is recommended by the Board of Directors that each Unit Owner obtain his own insurance policy on his Unit . . .

The Declaration of covenants and restrictions for The Gables on Tuckerman Condominium, Section 16 (A), states:

Maintenance, repair and replacement of the Unit shall be performed by the Unit Owner and such maintenance, repair and replacement shall not be an item of Common Expense subject to the lien for assessments created herein.

In July of 2004, the water heater on the upper level of Ms. Anderson's home began leaking and water flowed through the ceiling into the kitchen, "causing severe water damage to the carpet and walls of the unit," amounting to $6,358.23. No other condominium town home was affected, nor was any other part of the structure damaged. Ms. Anderson requested that the Council of Gables repair or provide proceeds to repair the damage. The Council of Gables declined, and subsequently, after Ms. Anderson paid the $250 deductible, Erie paid for the repairs.

Dianne Anderson, individually, and Erie filed a two count complaint in the Circuit Court for Montgomery County, seeking to recover $6,358.23, the amount expended to repair her home. . . . The court conducted a hearing on January 22, 2007, and thereafter . . . entered judgment in favor of the Council of Gables. Ms. Anderson and Erie appealed to the Court of Special Appeals on January 26, 2007. . . .

DISCUSSION

A condominium is "an estate in real property" that "typically involves an apartment building or other structure consisting of two or more separate apartments or units," i.e., "horizontal property" or multi-story "stacked units." *See* 1 Patrick J. Rohan & Melvin A. Reskin, *Condominium Law and Practice* §1.03[1][a] (2007). However, as the notion of a condominium has evolved, it has come to also refer to "[t]own houses," "offices," and even "stores" with the appropriate recorded declaration, bylaws and condominium plat. *Id.*

In Ridgely Condominium Ass'n v. Smyrnioudis, 681 A.2d 494, 495 (Md. 1996), we provided an overview of the condominium form of ownership, explicating that an owner has a "hybrid property interest":

> . . ."The term condominium may be defined generally as a system for providing separate ownership of individual units in multiple-unit developments. In addition to the interest acquired in a particular apartment, each unit owner also is a tenant in common in the underlying fee and in the spaces and building parts used in common by all the unit owners." 4B Richard R. Powell, *Powell on Real Property* ¶632.1[4] (1996).
>
> A condominium owner, therefore, holds a hybrid property interest consisting of an exclusive ownership of a particular unit or apartment and a tenancy in common with the other co-owners in the common elements.

. . . Discussing stacked-unit condominium regimes, Professor Richard R. Powell, in his treatise *Powell on Real Property*, defined the critical features of a condominium unit:

> One easy way to visualize a condominium unit is as a cube of air, the tangible boundaries of which are usually the finished side of the interior sheetrock, ceilings and floors. . . . [T]he condominium unit is generally seen by owners as the "inside" of their structure while the shell and "outside" of the building

is a common element. . . . A typical condominium unit consists of: the finished side of all interior walls, floors, partitions and ceilings; windows; kitchen cabinets and fixtures.

8 Richard R. Powell, *Powell on Real Property* §54A.01[2] (2000). . . .

The owner also possesses an undivided percentage interest, as a tenant in common, with the other owners, in the condominium's common elements, which,

> may include the land, foundations, columns, supports, walls, roofs, halls, lobbies, stairs, entrances, recreational areas, parking lots, gardens and installations for utilities. The common interest . . . represents the residual rights that the unit owners have in the property. The unit owners collectively own, as tenants in common, the entire condominium property, minus the airspaces consisting of the units. The rights to individual units are, in a sense, carved out of the tenancy in common.

1 *Condominium Law and Practice, supra* at §1.03[1][b]. Common elements can be further subdivided into limited common elements, which are allocated for the exclusive use of one or more, but fewer than all, owners, such as, for example, designated parking spaces, balconies, terraces or patios, as well as general common elements, such as grounds and roads. *Id.* . . .

We are called upon in this case to determine whether a condominium council of owners is required under the Maryland Condominium Act, Section 11-101 et. seq. of the Real Property Article, Maryland Code (1974, 2003 Repl. Vol.), to repair or replace what has commonly been thought of as property included in an individual condominium unit, after a casualty loss. Specifically, this case involves Section 11-114, which imposes the duty upon the council of owners to maintain insurance on the entire condominium property, "the *common elements* and *units,* exclusive of improvements and betterments installed in *units* by unit owners," and also only imposes the duty that "[a]ny portion of the *condominium* damaged or destroyed . . . be repaired or replaced promptly by the council of unit owners." . . .

[Plaintiffs] argue that Section 11-114 requires that the council of owners must provide insurance coverage for and be responsible for the repair and replacement of property in an individual condominium unit, after a casualty loss, and insist that Section 11-108.1 of the Act only requires that the owner perform ordinary maintenance, so that their "Condocover" insurance policies are irrelevant when a casualty loss is implicated. Essentially, [Plaintiffs] argue that ordinary maintenance, repair and replacement rests upon an owner under Section 11-108.1, while repair and replacement following a casualty loss are the obligation of the council of owners under Section 11-114 and must be covered by the master policy.

The Council, conversely, contend[s] that Section 11-108.1 of the Act is controlling and that the individual owners are responsible for maintenance, repair and replacement of the damaged contents of their own units. They also argue that [Plaintiffs'] reliance on the master policy, under Section 11-114, is misplaced because only the common elements and condominium structure are covered under the master policy.

When we examine the context of the entire Condominium Act, it becomes clear that the master insurance provision was intended to cover only damage sustained to the common elements or the structure of a condominium. Section 11-114 (c) of the Act defines "insured person" under the council of owners' master policy, providing in part:

> Insurance policies carried pursuant to subsection (a) of this section shall provide that:
>   (1) Each unit owner is an insured person under the policy with respect to liability arising out of his ownership of an undivided interest in the common elements or membership in the council of unit owners. . . .

Each owner is not an insured person with respect to his or her individual interest in his or her own property, but rather, is insured under the master policy only as to his or her collective undivided interest in the entire condominium property. Thus, the master policy is meant not to insure each owner's property or individual unit, but to protect the common interests of all owners as co-owners of the entire condominium.

Additionally, Section 11-108.1 of the Condominium Act dictates the responsibilities for maintenance, repair and replacement of common elements and units; it states:

> Except to the extent otherwise provided by the declaration or bylaws, the council of unit owners is responsible for maintenance, repair, and replacement of the common elements, and each unit owner is responsible for maintenance, repair, and replacement of his unit.

Section 11-108.1 of the Act thus recognizes the hybrid character of condominium ownership by differentiating between the treatment of common elements and the individual units, with the owner being responsible for damage to her or his "airspace.". . .

We conclude that the Maryland Condominium Act does not require the council of owners to repair or replace property of an owner in an individual condominium unit after a casualty loss. Thus, we affirm the judgments of the Circuit Court. . . .

Problem 13C

The Gulf Winds Condominium is a beach-front residential development consisting of 30 units in a three-story building, with amenities including a swimming pool and a poolside clubhouse. In August, tropical storm Jasmine hit the Gulf Winds and caused the following damage: (1) three balconies were ripped off the structure on the third-floor level, (2) the roof on the clubhouse collapsed, (3) ground floor units 101, 102, and 103 were flooded with four inches of water, causing damage to floor carpeting and to some furniture, and (4) flooding in units 101, 102, and 103 seeped into an electrical conduit, causing problems requiring replacement of a major electrical line that services these three units plus three additional units on the ground floor.

(a) Based on your general knowledge of the condominium form of ownership, who do you expect is liable for the loss for each type of damage? Who is responsible for arranging for repairs or replacement?

(b) To provide definitive answers to these questions, what documents would you want to obtain and review? Are there other facts you would seek to determine or other evidence you would seek to assemble?

(c) Assume that the Gulf Winds unit owners association carries a master policy of insurance that provides full coverage for the replacement cost of the clubhouse roof, and 75 percent of the owners vote not to repair the roof, but to demolish the clubhouse so that they can expand the pool or use the space for another purpose to be determined at a later date. Should the 25 percent of owners who want the clubhouse repaired be able to force rebuilding? Should the lenders holding mortgages on the units in the condominium be able to insist on rebuilding? If the clubhouse has to be rebuilt, must it be rebuilt to the same specifications as the old one, or can it be rebuilt in a lower-cost way, with the money saved used for another purpose, such as a "hurricane recovery party" with live music and an open bar?

(d) Assume that the association does not have insurance coverage on the balconies. Can the association or individual unit owners require that they be rebuilt? If so, who pays the costs?

C. COOPERATIVE HOUSING

Cooperative housing is another form of joint ownership in which a unit owner has exclusive use of a dwelling together with rights to shared or common areas. In a cooperative, title to all of the real estate is held by a nonprofit corporation, with each shareholder having the right to a dwelling unit pursuant to a long-term lease from the corporation. In some ways, a housing cooperative is similar to a condominium. For either form to work, project documents must clearly designate the ownership interests and use rights. A cooperative has a unit owners association and rules and restrictions much like those used in other forms of shared housing. Just as for condominiums, the cooperative unit owners are given voting rights and are assessed fees and charges based on allocations set forth in the organizing documentation. Like the condominium, the cooperative form of ownership can be applied to a variety of real estate activities, but it is almost always used in a multiunit housing building. Most cooperatives are located in urban areas, and although units in fashionable cooperative buildings can be very expensive, they also tend to be substantially cheaper (10 to 20 percent) than comparable units in condominium projects. In other words, the cooperative form of ownership is discounted relative to similar properties under alternative legal regimes.

The cooperative is distinguishable from the condominium and other forms of real property ownership in its use of a corporation as the vehicle for arranging joint ownership. In this regard, there are two legal approaches to the way in which an interest in a cooperative unit is categorized. In all cases, the purchase of a unit in a cooperative involves the acquisition of a stock certificate in the cooperative entity. This is treated as a personal property interest. Stock ownership carries a right to a lease for a particular unit in the cooperative. In many jurisdictions, the cooperative is, therefore, viewed as having both a personal property (stock certificate) and a real property (lease) component. In such a jurisdiction, each part of the transaction must comply with the appropriate rules related to either real property or personal property. In some jurisdictions, however, the cooperative form of ownership is considered to be a transaction involving the stock. The lease is considered to be ancillary, and, as a result, the entire interest is governed by the rules applicable to the stock as personal property.

The continuing viability of the cooperative housing market is driven mostly by a desire on the part of some homeowners to exercise a great deal of control over who will be their neighbors. Courts readily uphold express limitations on cooperative unit owners' transfers of ownership as long as those limits do not impose an unreasonable restraint on alienation, with *unreasonable* being understood within the unique context of the cooperative form of ownership.

Buying into a cooperative requires the approval of the cooperative board (sometimes called an *absolute right of approval*). This is a pure approval process with an "in" or "out" vote, unlike the condominium right of first refusal. The current owners are given a great deal of discretion with respect to whom they approve or do not approve to be fellow stockholders and unit owners. This is because the owners are all shareholders in a corporate entity that has the building as its primary asset, and the mortgage financing used to construct the building as its primary debt. Shareholders acquire rights to a lease of a unit in the building and share equal responsibility for the debts of the corporation. Thus, the cooperative owners do not just live in close proximity and share ownership of common elements, they are financially responsible for a shared debt. This factor has traditionally allowed cooperative boards to reject ownership applications without giving a reason for denial. When reasons are given for a denial, they have typically been upheld by the courts so long as the reason does not violate an antidiscrimination statute. Thus, a board cannot deny an applicant for the stated reason that the applicant is black, Jewish, Catholic, or Muslim. Discrimination based on race, ethnicity, or religious affiliation is illegal. However, a board can find a lot of sustainable reasons to turn down such applicants, even if it results in a building that is continually occupied only by white Protestants.

Some real-world examples of excluding people from housing cooperatives may help to demonstrate the strong demand for the right to discriminate with respect to future owners. Many people do not get approved. Some famous people who have been rejected by cooperatives are Cher, Barbara Streisand, Gloria Vanderbilt, and Richard Nixon. Gloria Vanderbilt was once rejected for the stated reason that the board was concerned about her financial ability to pay (the fact that the board did not like her male companion went unstated), and former President Nixon had the honor of being rejected by two different cooperatives in New York City. But you do not have to be famous to be considered undesirable for some cooperatives. You can be rejected for having poor taste in clothing or a pet that is not pleasing to the eye, for being overweight, or for having an occupation and a lifestyle that simply do not fit in well with the image of the cooperative. Lawyers are often unwelcome because they are assumed to be litigious. Political figures and movie stars are seen as attracting too much attention. Not surprisingly, minorities also seem to have difficulty getting approved by cooperative boards. The typical review process for approval to purchase involves a written application form with income disclosure information followed by a possible telephone interview and almost always a personal interview with board members. The board can disapprove an applicant at any point in the process.

40 WEST 67th STREET v. PULLMAN
Court of Appeals of New York, 2003
790 N.E.2d 1174

ROSENBLATT, Judge. In Matter of Levandusky v. One Fifth Ave. Apt. Corp., 553 N.E.2d 1317 (N.Y. 1990), we held that the business judgment rule is the proper standard of judicial review when evaluating decisions made by residential cooperative corporations. In the case before us, defendant [David Pullman] is a shareholder-tenant in the plaintiff cooperative building. The relationship between defendant and the cooperative, including the conditions under which a shareholder's tenancy may be terminated, is governed by the shareholder's lease agreement. The cooperative terminated defendant's tenancy in accordance with a provision in the lease that authorized it to do so based on a tenant's "objectionable" conduct.

Defendant has challenged the cooperative's action and asserts, in essence, that his tenancy may not be terminated by the court based on a review of the facts under the standard articulated in *Levandusky*. He argues that termination may rest only upon a court's independent evaluation of the reasonableness of the cooperative's action. We disagree. In reviewing the cooperative's actions, the business judgment standard governs, a cooperative's decision to terminate a tenancy in accordance with the terms of the parties' agreement.

I

Plaintiff cooperative owns the building located at 40 West 67th Street in Manhattan, which contains 38 apartments. In 1998, defendant bought into the cooperative and acquired 80 shares of stock appurtenant to his proprietary lease for apartment 7B.

Soon after moving in, defendant engaged in a course of behavior that, in the view of the cooperative, began as demanding, grew increasingly disruptive and ultimately became intolerable. After several points of friction between defendant and the cooperative, defendant started complaining about his elderly upstairs neighbors, a retired college professor and his wife who had occupied apartment 8B for over two decades. In a stream of vituperative letters to the cooperative — 16 letters in the month of October 1999 alone — he accused the couple of playing their television set and stereo at high volumes late into the night, and claimed they were running a loud and illegal bookbinding business in their apartment. Defendant further charged that the couple stored toxic chemicals in their apartment for use in their "dangerous and illegal" business. Upon investigation, the cooperative's Board determined that the couple did not possess a television set or stereo and that there was no evidence of a bookbinding business or any other commercial enterprise in their apartment.

Hostilities escalated, resulting in a physical altercation between defendant and the retired professor. Following the altercation, defendant distributed flyers to the cooperative residents in which he referred to the professor, by name, as a potential "psychopath in our midst" and accused him of cutting defendant's telephone lines. In another flyer, defendant described the professor's wife and the wife of the Board president as having close "intimate personal relations." Defendant also claimed that the previous occupants of his apartment revealed that the upstairs couple have "historically made excessive noise." The former occupants, however, submitted an affidavit that denied making any complaints about noise from the upstairs apartment and proclaimed that defendant's assertions to the contrary were "completely false."

Furthermore, defendant made alterations to his apartment without Board approval, had construction work performed on the weekend in violation of house rules, and would not respond to Board requests to correct these conditions or to allow a mutual inspection of his apartment and the upstairs apartment belonging to the elderly couple. Finally, defendant commenced four lawsuits against the upstairs couple, the president of the cooperative and the cooperative management, and tried to commence three more.

In reaction to defendant's behavior, the cooperative called a special meeting pursuant to article III (First) (f) of the lease agreement, which provides for termination of the tenancy if the cooperative by a two-thirds vote determines that "because of objectionable conduct on the part of the Lessee, the tenancy of the Lessee is undesirable."[3] The cooperative informed the shareholders that the purpose of the meeting was to determine whether defendant "engaged in repeated actions inimical to cooperative living and objectionable to the Corporation and its stockholders that make his continued tenancy undesirable."

Timely notice of the meeting was sent to all shareholders in the cooperative, including defendant. At the ensuing meeting, held in June 2000, owners of more than 75 percent of the outstanding shares in the cooperative were present. Defendant chose not attend. By a vote of 2,048 shares to 0, the shareholders in attendance passed a resolution declaring defendant's conduct "objectionable" and directing the Board to terminate his proprietary lease and cancel his shares. The resolution contained the findings upon which the shareholders concluded that defendant's behavior was inimical to cooperative living. Pursuant to the resolution, the Board sent defendant a notice of termination requiring him to vacate his apartment by August 31, 2000. Ignoring the notice, defendant remained in the apartment, prompting the cooperative to bring this suit for possession and ejectment, a declaratory judgment cancelling defendant's stock, and a money judgment for use and occupancy, along with attorneys' fees and costs.

Supreme Court denied the cooperative's motion for summary judgment and dismissed its cause of action that premised ejectment solely on the shareholders' vote and the notice of termination. The court declined to apply the business judgment rule to sustain the shareholders' vote and the Board's issuance of the notice of termination. Instead, the court . . . held that to terminate a tenancy, a cooperative must prove its claim of objectionable conduct by competent evidence to the satisfaction of the court.

Disagreeing with Supreme Court, a divided Appellate Division granted the cooperative summary judgment on its causes of action for ejectment and the cancellation of defendant's stock. . . . We agree with the Appellate Division majority that the business judgment rule applies and therefore affirm.

II. THE *LEVANDUSKY* BUSINESS JUDGMENT RULE

The heart of this dispute is the parties' disagreement over the proper standard of review to be applied when a cooperative exercises its agreed-

---

3. The full provision authorizes termination "if at any time the Lessor shall determine, upon the affirmative vote of the holders of record of at least two-thirds of that part of its capital stock which is then owned by Lessees under proprietary leases then in force, at a meeting of such stockholders duly called to take action on the subject, that because of objectionable conduct on the part of the Lessee, or of a person dwelling in or visiting the apartment, the tenancy of the Lessee is undesirable."

upon right to terminate a tenancy based on a shareholder-tenant's objectionable conduct. In the agreement establishing the rights and duties of the parties, the cooperative reserved to itself the authority to determine whether a member's conduct was objectionable and to terminate the tenancy on that basis. . . .

Levandusky established a standard of review analogous to the corporate business judgment rule for a shareholder-tenant challenge to a decision of a residential cooperative corporation. The business judgment rule is a common-law doctrine by which courts exercise restraint and defer to good faith decisions made by boards of directors in business settings . . . In *Levandusky,* the cooperative board issued a stop work order for a shareholder-tenant's renovations that violated the proprietary lease. The shareholder-tenant brought [an action] to set aside the stop work order. The Court upheld the Board's action, and concluded that the business judgment rule "best balances the individual and collective interests at stake" in the residential cooperative setting. *Levandusky,* 553 N.E.2d at 1321.

In the context of cooperative dwellings, the business judgment rule provides that a court should defer to a cooperative board's determination "[s]o long as the board acts for the purposes of the cooperative, within the scope of its authority and in good faith," *id.* at 1322. In adopting this rule, we recognized that a cooperative board's broad powers could lead to abuse through arbitrary or malicious decisionmaking, unlawful discrimination or the like. However, we also aimed to avoid impairing "the purposes for which the residential community and its governing structure were formed: protection of the interest of the entire community of residents in an environment managed by the board for the common benefit," *id.* at 1321. The Court concluded that the business judgment rule best balances these competing interests and also noted that the limited judicial review afforded by the rule protects the cooperative's decisions against "undue court involvement and judicial second-guessing," *id.* at 1322. . . .

[T]he procedural vehicle driving this case is Real Prop. Actions & Proceedings (RPAPL) §711(1), which requires "competent evidence" to show that a tenant is objectionable. Thus, in this context, the competent evidence that is the basis for the shareholder vote will be reviewed under the business judgment rule, which means courts will normally defer to that vote and the shareholders' stated findings as competent evidence that the tenant is indeed objectionable under the statute. . . .

Despite this deferential standard, there are instances when courts should undertake review of board decisions. To trigger further judicial scrutiny, an aggrieved shareholder-tenant must make a showing that the board acted (1) outside the scope of its authority, (2) in a way that did not legitimately further the corporate purpose or (3) in bad faith.

III

A. THE COOPERATIVE'S SCOPE OF AUTHORITY

Pursuant to its bylaws, the cooperative was authorized (through its Board) to adopt a form of proprietary lease to be used for all share-holder-tenants. Based on this authorization, defendant and other members of the cooperative voluntarily entered into lease agreements containing the termination provision before us. The cooperative does not contend that it has the power to terminate the lease absent the termination provision. Indeed, it recognizes, correctly, that if there were no such provision, termination could proceed only pursuant to RPAPL §711 (1).

The cooperative unfailingly followed the procedures contained in the lease when acting to terminate defendant's tenancy. In accordance with the bylaws, the Board called a special meeting, and notified all shareholder-tenants of its time, place and purpose. Defendant thus had notice and the opportunity to be heard. In accordance with the agreement, the cooperative acted on a supermajority vote after properly fashioning the issue and the question to be addressed by resolution. The resolution specified the basis for the action, setting forth a list of specific findings as to defendant's objectionable behavior. By not appearing or presenting evidence personally or by counsel, defendant failed to challenge the findings and has not otherwise satisfied us that the Board has in any way acted ultra vires. In all, defendant has failed to demonstrate that the cooperative acted outside the scope of its authority in terminating the tenancy.

B. FURTHERING THE CORPORATE PURPOSE

Levandusky also recognizes that the business judgment rule prohibits judicial inquiry into Board actions that, presupposing good faith, are taken in legitimate furtherance of corporate purposes. Specifically, there must be a legitimate relationship between the Board's action and the welfare of the cooperative. Here, by the unanimous vote of everyone present at the meeting, the cooperative resoundingly expressed its collective will, directing the Board to terminate defendant's tenancy after finding that his behavior was more than its shareholders could bear. The Board was under a fiduciary duty to further the collective interests of the cooperative. By terminating the tenancy, the Board's action thus bore an obvious and legitimate relation to the cooperative's avowed ends.

C. GOOD FAITH, IN THE EXERCISE OF HONEST JUDGMENT

Finally, defendant has not shown the slightest indication of any bad faith, arbitrariness, favoritism, discrimination or malice on the cooperative's part, and the record reveals none. . . .

Levandusky cautions that the broad powers of cooperative governance carry the potential for abuse when a board singles out a person for harmful

treatment or engages in unlawful discrimination, vendetta, arbitrary decisionmaking or favoritism. We reaffirm that admonition and stress that those
types of abuses are incompatible with good faith and the exercise of honest
judgment. . . .

The very concept of cooperative living entails a voluntary, shared
control over rules, maintenance and the composition of the community.
Indeed, as we observed in *Levandusky*, a shareholder-tenant voluntarily
agrees to submit to the authority of a cooperative board, and consequently
the board "may significantly restrict the bundle of rights a property owner
normally enjoys." 553 N.E.2d at 1320. . . .

Order affirmed, with costs.

Problem 13D

Dorothy May intends to purchase a unit in a wonderful new building in
her city. It has everything she is looking for, including security and service
personnel. She is contracting to buy unit 26 for $350,000. The building is a
cooperative. Dorothy comes to your law office to discuss representation in her
transaction. At your initial meeting, Dorothy explains that she knows a little
about real estate because her sister used to be a part-time salesperson about
ten years ago. Dorothy tells you that she knows there are three important types
of deeds used in conveyancing of real property: the general warranty deed, the
special warranty deed, and the quitclaim deed. What she wants to know from
you is your advice on which deed would give her, as buyer, the best protection
in her transaction. What would you tell her?

Problem 13E

You are an associate in a law firm that represents a number of shared
housing developments. In this capacity, your firm provides legal counsel to a
number of cooperative boards. You have been assigned by the partner in
charge to be responsible for the Ocean Breeze Cooperative. In that capacity,
you are visited by Dr. Sue Westminster, the president of the board. She comes
to you with a problem. A fellow doctor named Bill Wu is seeking to be
approved to buy into the Ocean Breeze. Sue tells you it is a sticky and very
confidential problem because Dr. Wu is Chinese and she does not think he
will fit in. Sue says, "The Ocean Breeze is very comfortable because the 20
units in the building are occupied by people who are very similar . . . share the
same values . . . you know, go to the same church and have a common ances-
tral history to be proud of. Some members of the cooperative have voiced
strong objection to letting in any Chinese . . . but it's not personal and it certainly is not just because he is Chinese . . . these members would feel the same
about Hispanics, blacks, and even Sicilians."

Having said this, Sue wants to know how she can best state a reason for denying Dr. Wu's application while being sure to avoid any personal liability as well as any liability for the cooperative. She says that she knows this sort of thing is done all the time, and she just wants you to make sure she proceeds in a way that will be legally defensible. She also states, "I am certain that you are quite a clever young lawyer or else your partner would never have assigned us to you. . . . Several of our cooperative members, myself included, do a lot of private investing and pay large amounts in legal fees to your firm every year. And, by the way, did you know that Debbie, one of your partners in the litigation department, is one of our cooperative members?" With that, Dr. Westminster departs your office, leaving instructions that you communicate with her by 10:00 A.M. the next morning concerning the necessary wording for the rejection letter to Dr. Wu.

In this situation, what do you think your legal and ethical obligations should be to the client, the firm, the bar, and the courts? How will you resolve this, and what practical dynamics will have to be confronted? How can you best deal with these conflicts and with your own personal ethical obligation and duty?

Problem 13F

Dan and Roxann, a middle-aged couple with two adult children, plan to sell their single-family home and replace it with a smaller housing unit where they will live. They have looked at many units in high-rise buildings in the city center and have identified several that they like. One issue is that some of the units are described as condominium units, and others as cooperative apartments. Dan and Roxann are a little confused about the differences between the two. As you are their lawyer and they have asked you to represent them in the sale of their home and in the purchase of a new home, they ask you to explain the difference.

Draft a letter to Dan and Roxann explaining the essential differences between condominium and a cooperative housing ownership. Also let them know about the differences they might experience in the approval process and the documentation they are likely to receive for both forms of housing. Advise them on some of the positive and potentially negative aspects of each type of ownership to help them make an informed decision.

D. TIME-SHARE HOUSING

Time-share housing takes the condominium concept one step further by dividing a unit's air space into blocks of time. The purchaser of a time-share gets the right to occupy a unit for a designated period of time (usually one or two weeks) each year. Most time-share properties are marketed as vacation alternatives. These units are offered as a way to own your vacation home instead of paying for a hotel room or renting a suite. You can thereby enjoy the benefits of equity appreciation, assuming that the value of the property does in fact increase over time.

Time-shares are not a major part of the housing market, but when taken together with the other types of properties discussed in this chapter they help to illustrate some of the many approaches available for structuring real estate development, ownership, and use. Legally, time-shares are like condominium units in that they involve use rights to a unit together with shared or common elements and expenses. The developer has several choices for structuring a time-share project. Each structure gives the buyer a different legal interest or "bundle of rights." The most basic choice is whether the buyer will have a real property interest or a personal property interest.

There are two ways the buyer can get a fee simple interest. The seller may convey undivided interests in the fee to all the buyers of time-share units as tenants in common, with a recorded instrument setting forth their rights to possess their designated intervals. Alternatively, the seller can convey a separate and distinct "interval estate" that includes as part of its definition the agreed-upon time parameters. Either type of fee interest is transferable by deed. In many time-share developments, the buyer doesn't get a fee interest. The buyer may receive the right to use the unit for a recurring annual period for a fixed term such as 30 or 40 years. Then the developer or some other entity retains the reversion in fee. At the end of the fixed period, all the time-share interests terminate. The buyer's interest may be characterized as either a lease or a contractual license. If it is a license, then it constitutes personal property and not an interest in real estate.

Another approach is to form a recreation or resort club, selling memberships in a club entity that entitle you to specific use privileges. The use privileges can be to a specific unit or to a designated class of units during your time interval. Some arrangements involve buying points in the entity, and the more points you buy the more use options you get. The particular structure of the ownership interest must be detailed in the documents creating the time-share property, and these documents must be carefully reviewed in order to establish the proper steps for transfer and the rights and limitations of ownership. As with other forms of communal ownership interests, there will be rules and regulations as well as some sort of owners association or management group. There will also be fees and assessments against owners to pay the expenses of upkeep on the property.

Almost all time-share properties include the option to participate in an exchange program that allows unit buyers to swap their use rights with people in other distant locations so that they need not always go to the same place on their vacation. This exchange feature probably accounts for the fact that the majority of unit owners in most time-shares live within a few hours' driving time from the location of the time-share property.

O'CONNOR v. RESORT CUSTOM BUILDERS, INC.
Supreme Court of Michigan, 1999
591 N.W.2d 216

PER CURIAM. A developer sought to sell interval ownership interests in a home located in a subdivision restricted to private residences. The circuit court enjoined the sales, but the Court of Appeals reversed. We reverse the judgment of the Court of Appeals and reinstate the judgment of the circuit court.

The Shanty Creek resort is a large development in Antrim County. Spread across many of its acres are golf courses, downhill and cross-country skiing areas, tennis courts, swimming pools, homes, condominiums, a hotel and convention center, and other recreational facilities. The residential portions of Shanty Creek include a number of separate areas for homes and condominiums. One of these is the Valley View subdivision, consisting of fifty-six lots in the northern part of the resort.

Development of Valley View is governed by a "declaration of restrictions" executed in November 1968 and amended in May 1970. Among the restrictions are the following:

> *Use of Property.* No lot shall be used except for residential purposes. No building shall be erected, altered, placed or permitted to remain on any lot other than for the purpose of one single dwelling not to exceed two stories in height. . . .
>   *Character of Buildings.* (a) No building shall be erected on any lot except a single, private dwelling of one, one-and-a-half or two stories, or a multi-level dwelling not exceeding two stories in height, and to be occupied by not more than one (1) family, for residence purposes only, and a private garage. . . .
>   *Enforcement of Restrictions.* If any person shall violate or attempt to violate any of the covenants or restrictions herein contained, it shall be lawful for any other person or persons owning any lot or building site in said subdivision to prosecute any proceeding at law or in equity against such person or persons, either to prevent them from so doing or to recover damages or other dues for such violation.

The restrictions are silent with regard to "interval ownership" or "time-sharing" arrangements, under which a person owns an occupancy right for a defined period each year.

Resort Custom Builders, Inc., constructed a home on Lot 7 of the Valley View subdivision. After its initial attempt to sell the home outright failed, Resort Custom Builders decided to market "interval ownership" shares. In a detailed January 27, 1994 document entitled "Declaration of Covenants: Conditions and Restrictions for Interval Ownership," Resort Custom Builders established the rights and responsibilities of those who would participate in the venture. Basically, a purchaser would buy occupancy rights in one or more week-long "intervals," along with a corresponding undivided interest in the property. Resort Custom Builders intended to sell occupancy rights for forty-eight weeks of the year, with four weeks reserved for maintenance. As is typical in time-sharing arrangements, interval owners could place their occupancy rights in commercial pools that facilitate trades with those who have occupancy rights in homes at other resorts.

Interval ownership in condominiums exists in other portions of Shanty Creek, but it is explicitly authorized by the documents governing development. Shanty Creek, however, also facilitates daily and weekly rentals of homes in Valley View and other residential areas. Some homeowners in Valley View rent their homes for use by other persons using this procedure. At least one home in Valley View is jointly owned by friends, and, as one would expect, many of the homes are jointly owned by married persons.

In March 1994, several Valley View property owners and the Shanty Creek Lodge Association sued to enjoin Resort Custom Builders from selling interval ownership interests. Plaintiffs claimed that interval ownership violated the use and character restrictions applicable to the property. The following month, Resort Custom Builders sold two one-week shares to Fred and Janet Ruppert, who financed the purchase with a mortgage to Franklin Bank, N.A. . . .

With regard to multiple ownership of a single residence, the trial court declined to "wade into the abstract question of how many owners it would take to become a violation of Valley View restrictions. . . ." Citing testimony that daily and weekly rental of private homes had not been extensive, the court likewise found it unnecessary to decide whether renting a house for a substantial portion of the year would violate the restrictions of the subdivision. Accordingly, the trial court declared the January 27, 1994 covenants, conditions, and restrictions for interval ownership null and void. In a declaratory judgment and permanent injunction, the court set aside the interval ownership document, as well as the Ruppert's' purchase and the accompanying mortgage. . . .

The Court of Appeals reversed. It explained that the law favors the free use of property, and held that interval ownership was not incompatible with "residential purposes":

> Restrictive covenants are construed strictly against those claiming the right to enforce them, and all doubts are resolved in favor of the free use of property. . . . The focus must be on the activity involved and how it parallels the ordinary and common meaning of use for residential purposes.
>
> We construe the covenant in favor of defendants and hold that based on the evidence presented, while interval ownership may be a business use, we find no reason to believe that nonresidential use associated with interval ownership will be obtrusive and detrimental to the property value of neighbors.

The plaintiffs have applied to this Court for leave to appeal.

This Court has never considered whether a residential-purposes restriction bars interval ownership or timesharing. . . .

In Wood v. Blancke, 8 N.W.2d 67 (Mich. 1943), a dispute arose in a subdivision permitting "one single residence" on each lot, and restricting use to "residence purposes only." Several residents sued to prevent a fellow property owner from maintaining a sizable flock of racing pigeons at his home.

Examining the situation in *Wood*, this Court emphasized that "all doubts are resolved in favor of the free use of property." *Id.* at 69. This principle is fundamental, and elsewhere we have refused to infer restrictions that are not expressly provided in the controlling documents. Margolis v. Wilson Oil Corp., 70 N.W.2d811, 812 (Mich. 1955).

"Restrictive covenants in deeds are construed strictly against grantors and those claiming the right to enforce them, and all doubts are resolved in favor of the free use of property." *Wood, supra*, at 69. . . .

As indicated, this Court has not decided a case involving interval ownership. Appellate courts of other jurisdictions have decided cases that bear some similarity, but these decisions are neither recent nor on all fours with the present case. We thus turn to our statement in *Wood* "that the usual, ordinary and incidental use of property as a place of abode does not violate the covenant restricting such use to 'residential purposes only,' but that an unusual and extraordinary use may constitute a violation," and our accompanying caution that "each case must be determined on its own facts." *Id.* at 69. . . .

Proceeding on that basis, we return to the trial court's analysis. We conclude that its reasoning is sound, and adopt it as our own:

> What's a residential purpose is the question. Well, a residence most narrowly defined can be a place which would be one place where a person lives as their permanent home, and by that standard people could have only one residence, or the summer cottage could not be a residence, the summer home at Shanty Creek could not be a residence if the principal residence, the place where they permanently reside, their domicile is in some other location, but I think residential purposes for these uses is a little broader than that. It is a place where someone lives, and has a permanent presence, if you will, as a resident, whether they are physically there or not. Their belongings are there. They store their golf clubs, their ski equipment, the old radio, whatever they want. It is another residence for them, and it has a permanence to it, and a continuity of presence, if you will, that makes it a residence.

The trial court then correctly determined that interval ownership did not constitute a residential purpose under the circumstances of this case:

> I don't think that's true of weekly—of timeshare units on a weekly basis of the kind, at least, of the kind being discussed here, . . . The people who occupy it, or who have these weekly interests in this property, they have the right to occupy it for one week each year, but they don't have any rights, any occupancy right, other than that one week. They don't have the right to come whenever they want to, for example, or to leave belongings there because the next resident, who is a one-fiftieth or one forty-eighth co-owner has a right to occupy the place, too, and the weekly owner has no right to be at the residence at anytime other than

during their one week that they have purchased. That is not a residence. That is too temporary. There is no permanence to the presence, either psychologically or physically at that location, and so I deem that the division of the home into one-week timeshare intervals as not being for residential purposes as that term is used in these building and use restrictions. . . .

For these reasons, we reverse the judgment of the Court of Appeals and reinstate the judgment of the circuit court.

Problem 13G

Seaside View is a timeshare development located in Big State. It consists of 50 individual residential units in a multifloor building. Seaside View is organized as a membership timeshare in which individuals purchase membership points and then can use their points to reserve use of a unit in the development for a week at a time. Points are sold in units of 10 with 10 points costing $1,000, such that 100 points cost $10,000. The more points one has, the more choices one has in reserving use of a unit. For example, 150 points might be enough for a one-week stay in a one-bedroom unit during peak season, but it might be good for a three-bedroom unit with a balcony during the off season. Similarly, 300 points might be good for two weeks during peak season or three weeks during off season.

A Big State statute provides: "No person shall sell or market an interest in real property in this State unless licensed for such purpose under the laws of this State. Acting in violation of this law shall result in a fine and be treated as a misdemeanor offense under the penal code of Big State."

Sally is a real estate broker in adjoining Small State, and she has clients who have expressed an interest in buying into the Seaside View timeshare development. Sally is aware of the statute in Big State that regulates who can sell and market real property, but she goes ahead and decides to work with the developer to sell timeshare memberships in Seaside View out of her office in Small State. Sally is properly licensed to sell and market real property in Small State, but is not licensed in Big State. Should Sally be liable for penalties in Big State?

E. HOUSING ACCESSIBILITY

Housing products must comply with regulations respecting accessibility to persons with disabilities. The Americans with Disabilities Act and related legislation has prompted transactional lawyers to become more familiar with issues of accessibility in real estate development. Although only 1 percent of the population of the United States uses a wheelchair, approximately

18-20 percent of American families have a family member with mobility impairment. In addition, our population is aging dramatically, and as people age they experience higher levels of mobility impairment. The estimation is that sometime shortly after 2020 between 20 and 25 percent of the population of the United States will consist of people age 60 or older. These numbers and trends indicate an increasing need to think about real estate development in terms of providing for the needs of all our citizens, and to account for the ability of people to age easily and safely in place. As we contemplate our role as real estate lawyers, we must be certain to understand the legal requirements, regulations, and goals of inclusive design and accessible development.

In general, the main sources of regulation related to disability include: Architectural Barriers Act (ABA), 42 U.S.C. §§4151-4157; Section 504 of the Rehabilitation Act (RHA) of 1973, 29 U.S.C. §794; Fair Housing Act (FHA), 42 U.S.C. §§3601-3619; and the Americans with Disabilities Act (ADA), 42 U.S.C. §§12101-12213. Collectively, these Acts outlaw discrimination against people with disability and they provide accessibility requirements for property development. Some of the regulations apply only to projects receiving federal funding, some apply to private property development, and some apply to government activities such as planning and zoning. In the area of land regulation, public planning and zoning restrictions would typically be subject to challenge under Title II of the ADA, whereas private land regulations (*e.g.*, homeowner association rules, covenants and restrictions running with the land) are typically challenged under the FHA. The two cases below provide an introduction to the application of disability law in a private real estate setting. For more information on this subject *see* Robin Paul Malloy, *Land Use Law and Disability: Planning and Zoning For Accessible Communities* (2015).

UNITED STATES v. EDWARD ROSE & SONS
United States Court of Appeals, Sixth Circuit, 2004
384 F.3d 258

SILER, Circuit Judge. This housing discrimination case turns on what doors must be accessible to the handicapped. At issue are two sets of apartment complexes, designed with an inaccessible front door, but an accessible back patio door. The district court granted the U.S. Justice Department ("government") a preliminary injunction halting the construction and occupancy of the buildings. The main defendant, the builder and owner, Edward Rose & Sons ("Rose"), appeals, arguing that court erred (1) by misconstruing the requirements of the Fair Housing Act, 42 U.S.C. §3601 *et seq.* ("FHA"), and (2) by incorrectly weighing the relative preliminary injunction interests and harms. We affirm the district court's grant of the preliminary injunction.

I. FACTUAL AND PROCEDURAL BACKGROUND

Defendant Rose constructed and owns the nineteen apartment buildings, located in Michigan and Ohio, at issue. These buildings are at various stages of construction, but all have the same basic design. The ground floor apartments at issue have two exterior entrances — a front door and rear patio door. The front door is closer to the parking lot, but is handicapped inaccessible because it can only be reached by descending stairs. At the bottom of the stairs is a landing shared by two front doors leading into two different apartments. The rear patio entrance is accessible, but is located farther from the parking lot.

The government alleged that the apartments violated the disability portions of the FHA. The district court granted a preliminary injunction, adopting the government's position that the front door was the "primary entrance" used by the public and guests, and as such, it was a "public" or "common area" that the FHA mandates be accessible. *See* 42 U.S.C. §3604(f)(3)(C)(i). In reaching this conclusion, the court relied on the Housing and Urban Development ("HUD") regulations, guidelines, and design manual. The preliminary injunction halts construction on the "covered dwellings" and restrains the defendants from occupying "covered dwellings" not yet leased. In this case, "covered dwellings" means simply the ground floor. *See* 42 U.S.C. §3604(f)(7) (stating if building has no elevator, only the ground floor is a covered dwelling subject to the FHA). Rose appeals. . . .

III. ANALYSIS

. . . .

The government asserts that because the landing at the bottom of the stairs is a "common area,"§3604(f)(3)(C)(i) mandates that the landing must be accessible. The landing in front of the entrances is not accessible because it can only be reached by the stairs. The government argues that this entrance is the "primary" door because it is in the front and closest to the parking lot. As such, it is the entrance most visitors will use, and thus the space or landing in front of the door is a public or common area. Additionally, the stair landing is shared by two entrances to two different apartment units, and thus a common area used by two tenants. . . .

We find that, in this particular case, the stair landing in front of the entrance is a common area that the statute mandates be accessible. The fact that two apartment units share the stair landing makes the space a common area. The plain meaning of "common use" unambiguously covers the entrance under dispute. At the time of the statute's enactment, dictionaries generally defined "common" as belonging to or shared by two or more individuals. *See The Oxford English Dictionary* 565 (J.A. Simpson & E.S.C. Weiner, eds., Clarendon Press 2d ed. 1989) (defining common as "belonging equally to more than one" and "possessed or shared alike by both or all."). . . .

Our ruling is narrow; we simply hold in this case that because the two apartments share the stair landing, the stair landing qualifies as a "common area" that must be accessible. We express no opinion on what the FHA would require if the stairs only led to one apartment unit entrance. . . .

In sum, we find that the stair landing qualifies as a "common area" that the FHA mandates be accessible. Thus, the government's likelihood of success on the merits is strong. . . .

Affirmed.

FAIR HOUSING BOARD v. WINDSOR PLAZA CONDOMINIUM ASSOCIATION
Supreme Court of Virginia, 2014
768 S.E.2d 79

GOODWYN, Judge. In these consolidated appeals, we consider various issues arising under the Virginia Fair Housing Law, Code §36–96.1 et seq. (VFHL), and the Federal Fair Housing Amendments Act of 1988, 42 U.S.C. §3601 et seq. (FHAA).

BACKGROUND

On March 4, 2009, Michael Fishel (Fishel) filed complaints with the Virginia Fair Housing Board (FHB) and the United States Department of Housing and Urban Development (HUD), alleging that Windsor Plaza Condominium Association (Windsor Plaza) had discriminated against him in violation of the VFHL and the FHAA. HUD transferred Fishel's complaint to the FHB.

On May 28, 2010, the FHB, after an investigation, determined that reasonable cause existed to believe that Windsor Plaza had engaged in a "discriminatory housing practice . . . in violation of . . . Code §36–96.3(B)(ii)." Pursuant to Code §36–96.14, the FHB referred the charge to the Attorney General on June 1, 2010.

On June 30, 2010, the Office of the Attorney General, on behalf of the Commonwealth, filed a complaint against Windsor Plaza in the Circuit Court of Arlington County. The complaint alleged that Windsor Plaza had violated Code §36–96.3(B)(ii) by failing "to make reasonable accommodations in rules, practices, policies, or services [that were] necessary to afford [Fishel] equal opportunity to use and enjoy [his] dwelling." . . .

FACTS

Windsor Plaza Condominium is located in Arlington County and is comprised of two condominium buildings, each with underground parking garages. When the condominium was first built, parking spaces in these garages were general common elements. The site plan for the buildings notes four parking spaces for use by disabled persons. Those parking spaces were designated as "HC" on the site plan.

In 1995, the developer of Windsor Plaza Condominium executed an "Amendment to Condominium Instruments" document. The amendment allowed the developer to assign the previously general common element parking spaces as limited common element parking spaces. Pursuant to the amendment, the developer deeded every parking space in the condominium's underground garages, including the four parking spaces designated for use by disabled persons (hereinafter "disabled parking spaces"), to individual unit owners "as a limited common element for the exclusive use of the unit owner of such condominium unit."

Fishel suffers from "severe osteoarthritis" and must use a wheelchair. In July 2007, [Fishel and his wife Eleanor (collectively "the Fishels")] purchased a condominium unit in the Taylor Street Building of Windsor Plaza Condominium. The Fishels received a "resale package," which they reviewed carefully for two days before purchasing their unit. In the resale package, a diagram of the parking garages showed four disabled parking spaces. The documents in the resale package also indicated that garage parking spaces at the condominium were limited common elements and that the developer had already assigned all of the parking spaces to individual unit owners.

Before buying their condominium unit, the Fishels visited the site and looked at the unit and underground parking garage. The Fishels saw the parking space that would be purchased with their condominium. They testified at trial that they knew the space was not a disabled parking space and that "[it] wasn't going to meet [their] needs." The Fishels did not inquire about the availability of disabled parking spaces in the garage before purchasing their condominium unit.

Soon after purchasing their condominium unit, the Fishels contacted Joseph Tilton (Tilton), Windsor Plaza's building manager, and informed him that Fishel was unable to park his van in their parking space. Tilton advised the Fishels to park in one of the disabled parking spaces, which they did "a couple times," but the Fishels were soon informed that they could not park in that space because it belonged to another condominium unit owner.

On July 30, 2007, the Fishels emailed Tilton, asking for "a larger parking space" in a better location. Windsor Plaza's Board of Directors (the Board) considered their request at a board meeting, and Tilton relayed the Board's response to the Fishels by email on August 23, 2007:

> The Board of Directors reviewed your request for a larger parking space at last night's meeting. As all existing garage spaces are individually owned by unit owners, assigning a different parking space to your residence is beyond the authority of the Board. This does not preclude you from advertising your

interest in trading parking spaces with another owner. If you would like to draft a flyer announcing your need for a larger space, we would be happy to post copies on both bulletin boards. Such a notice may facilitate an exchange of spaces, either as a casual agreement or as a permanent reassignment, based on the preferences of all parties involved.

Please contact us should you have any further concerns.

The Fishels responded to Tilton's August 23, 2007 email and asserted Fishel's "right . . . to park in a handicapped-designated space," but they indicated that they were reluctant to "go this route." The Fishels' email concluded, "Please ask the Board to review this issue again in an expedited manner. We need a parking space that we can actually use."

The next email from Tilton, dated September 12, 2007, related that the Board had met again and that "[a] copy of your request is being sent to the Condominium's counsel so he may instruct us in how to best accommodate your needs."

During the following months, the Fishels inquired periodically about the status of their request. On May 7, 2008, Windsor Plaza's attorney, Raymond Diaz (Diaz), informed the Fishels by letter that Windsor Plaza could not force any of the individual parking space owners to trade with them. Diaz asserted that "it has proven impossible for the Association to persuade the owner of the larger space to conclude an arrangement permitting you the use of the larger garage parking space."

In the same letter, Diaz offered to help the Fishels secure approval from the county to reserve a parking space on the street outside their condominium building. The Fishels rejected this proposal because in order to park on the street, Fishel would have to exit his car into traffic. Moreover, the curb was too steep, and the nearest entrance door was not handicap-accessible.

Diaz wrote another letter dated August 10, 2009, informing the Fishels that the owners of one of the disabled parking spaces were willing to enter into a licensing agreement that would allow the Fishels to use the disabled parking space. The Fishels did not accept this offer because, in the proposed agreement, the parking space owners reserved a right to reclaim the disabled parking space if they sold their condominium or if at some point they had a tenant who needed the disabled parking space.

On March 4, 2009, the Fishels filed complaints with the FHB and HUD. Thereafter, an investigator from the FHB visited the condominium building. Fishel testified that while he was in the garage with the investigator, Tilton walked by, and Fishel raised with Tilton the idea of converting a bicycle storage space, located in the garage, into an accessible parking space. Tilton expressed concern that doing so would be too expensive. Fishel testified that he offered to pay for the "disabled logo and everything." The circuit court found that Fishel did not present any evidence that this option was ever presented to the Board or its counsel.

ANALYSIS

. . . .

MODIFICATIONS AND ACCOMMODATIONS UNDER CODE §§36–96.3(B)(I) AND (II)

In support of its claim that Windsor Plaza discriminated against Fishel by failing to make reasonable accommodations in rules, practices, policies or services that were necessary to afford him equal opportunity to use and enjoy his dwelling, the Commonwealth presented evidence that the Fishels mentioned to Tilton that there was a common element bicycle storage area in the parking garage that was large enough to be converted into a parking space for Fishel. The circuit court ruled that such request constituted a reasonable modification request rather than a request for a reasonable accommodation.

The Commonwealth asserts that the circuit court erred in ruling that the request for the creation of the disabled parking space was not a request for an accommodation under Code §36–96.3(B)(ii). According to the Commonwealth, parking is a service, and Fishel sought an accommodation in the "rules, practices, and policies involving the provision of that service." The Commonwealth claims that modifications involve "structural changes" while accommodations involve "cosmetic changes" and that converting the bicycle space into a disabled parking space for Fishel would require only cosmetic changes. The Commonwealth further argues that Windsor Plaza's Policy Resolution No. 7 explicitly authorizes the Board to convert a common elements area, such as the bicycle space, into a limited common element parking space to accommodate the needs of a disabled person. Hence, because the Fishels' request to convert the bicycle space into an accessible parking space required cosmetic changes and an alteration in Windsor Plaza's parking policy, the Commonwealth concludes that its evidence supported a reasonable accommodation claim under Code §36–96.3(B)(ii).

According to Windsor Plaza, parking is not a service at the condominium because all parking spaces are limited common elements and are assigned to individual unit owners. Windsor Plaza argues that the circuit court correctly determined that the Commonwealth's evidence concerning the possible conversion of the bicycle space supported a cause of action for a reasonable modification because a "modification" is made to "premises," while an "accommodation" is made to "rules, policies, practices, or services."

Whether the Commonwealth's evidence supported a cause of action for failure to provide a reasonable accommodation under Code §36–96.3(B)(ii) requires statutory interpretation of the VFHL . . . .

The VFHL protects disabled persons from "unlawful discriminatory housing practices." *See* Code §36–96.3(A) (describing actions that qualify as "discriminatory housing practices"). Code §36–96.3(A)(9) provides,

It shall be an unlawful discriminatory housing practice for any person . . . [t]o discriminate against any person in the terms, conditions, or privileges of sale or rental of a dwelling, or in the provision of services or facilities in connection therewith because of a handicap of . . . that person.

"Discrimination" is defined several ways in the VFHL. Relevant to this appeal, Code §36–96.3(B)(i) states that "discrimination includes . . . a refusal to permit, at the expense of the handicapped person, reasonable modifications of existing premises occupied or to be occupied by any person if such modifications may be necessary to afford such person full enjoyment of the premises." Code §36–96.3(B)(ii) provides that discrimination also includes "a refusal to make reasonable accommodations in rules, practices, policies, or services when such accommodations may be necessary to afford such person equal opportunity to use and enjoy a dwelling."

The Commonwealth only asserts a violation of Code §36–96.3(B)(ii). It insists that parking is a service and that the Fishels requested a reasonable accommodation in that service when they requested that Windsor Plaza convert the bicycle space into an accessible parking space for them. However, the plain meaning of the word "service" does not encompass the underground garage parking scheme at Windsor Plaza Condominium.

"Service" is "[l]abor performed in the interest or under the direction of others; specif[ically], the performance of some useful act or series of acts for the benefit of another, usu[ally] for a fee." *Black's Law Dictionary* 1576 (10th ed. 2014). At the condominium, parking spaces have been assigned to individual unit owners as property rights appurtenant to their condominium units. These assigned parking spaces are limited common elements, which are "reserved for the exclusive use" of individual unit owners. Code §55–79.41. Because parking spaces are forms of real property at the condominium, they are not acts or labor performed to benefit the unit owners, and thus parking is not a service under Code §36–96.3(B)(ii). . . .

We conclude the ruling of the circuit court is faithful to the plain language of Code §§36–96.3(B)(i) and (ii). There was no evidence at trial concerning what would be involved in changing the bicycle storage space into a parking space. However, the Commonwealth acknowledges that converting the bicycle space into an accessible parking space for Fishel would require physical alterations, although slight, to the premises. Consequently, the circuit court did not err in determining that the Commonwealth's evidence concerning the conversion of the bicycle space into an accessible parking space supported a cause of action under Code §36–96.3(B)(i) for a reasonable modification rather than a cause of action under Code §36–96.3(B)(ii) for a reasonable accommodation.

SUFFICIENCY OF THE EVIDENCE: REASONABLE ACCOMMODATION CLAIM

The Commonwealth contends that it presented sufficient evidence of a violation of Code §36–96.3(B)(ii) to survive Windsor Plaza's motion to strike the evidence. The Commonwealth asserts that the parties stipulated at trial that Fishel is disabled and that it is necessary for him to have an accessible parking space. According to the Commonwealth, the evidence showed that Fishel asked for a larger parking space in a different location. The Commonwealth claims that in response Windsor Plaza proposed "two flawed solutions" and "ignored" Fishel's reasonable request to convert the bicycle storage space into an accessible parking space. It adds that even if all four disabled spaces were being used by disabled people, Windsor Plaza would nevertheless be required under the VFHL to consider converting the bicycle space into an accessible parking space for the Fishels. The Commonwealth argues that the Fishels' request for an accessible parking space is reasonable because Windsor Plaza is required by law to provide disabled parking spaces.

By contrast, Windsor Plaza maintains that the evidence showed that it offered the Fishels a reasonable accommodation but that they rejected the offer. According to evidence at trial, Windsor Plaza negotiated a licensing agreement in which the owners of a disabled parking space would allow the Fishels to use their space. Windsor Plaza insists that it is not obligated to provide a permanent accommodation.

To assert a reasonable accommodation claim under the VFHL, the plaintiff bears the burden to prove by a preponderance of the evidence that the requested accommodation is reasonable and necessary to give a disabled person the equal opportunity to use and enjoy housing. *See* Scoggins v. Lee's Crossing Homeowners Ass'n, 718 F.3d 262, 272 (4th Cir. 2013) (stating the elements of a reasonable accommodation claim under the FHAA). In the proceedings below, the parties agreed that Fishel is disabled and needs an accessible parking space in order to have an equal opportunity to enjoy his condominium unit, but they disagreed as to whether the Fishels requested a reasonable accommodation. . . .

The Fourth Circuit has recognized several factors a court can use to determine whether an accommodation is reasonable:

> In determining whether the reasonableness requirement has been met, a court may consider as factors the extent to which the accommodation would undermine the legitimate purposes and effects of existing zoning regulations and the benefits that the accommodation would provide to the handicapped. It may also consider whether alternatives exist to accomplish the benefits more efficiently. And in measuring the effects of an accommodation, the court may look not only to its functional and administrative aspects, but also to its costs.

Bryant Woods Inn, Inc. v. Howard Cnty., 124 F.3d 597, 604 (4th Cir. 1997) (analyzing whether a request for an exception to zoning regulations was reasonable). An accommodation is not reasonable if it poses "undue financial and administrative burdens or changes, adjustments, or modifications to existing programs that would be substantial, or that would constitute fundamental alterations in the nature of the program.". . .

The Fishels asked for a larger parking space in a different location. However, Virginia's Condominium Act permits the reassignment of limited common elements, such as the parking spaces at issue, only with the consent of all property owners affected by the reassignment. *See* Code §55.79.57(A). We hold that requesting, as an accommodation, the reassignment of limited common element parking spaces belonging to private individuals is unreasonable because Windsor Plaza has no authority to confiscate property belonging to one unit owner and to reassign that property to another. *See* Groner v. Golden Gate Gardens Apartments, 250 F.3d 1039, 1046 (6th Cir. 2001) ("As a matter of law, the [neighbor's] rights did not have to be sacrificed on the altar of reasonable accommodation.")

The Commonwealth also argues that its evidence showed that Windsor Plaza failed to provide the Fishels with a reasonable accommodation by refusing to convert the bicycle storage space into an accessible parking space. However, as stated previously, converting the bicycle space is a modification "of existing premises," not an accommodation "in rules, practices, policies, or services." Therefore, the Commonwealth's evidence concerning the bicycle space did not prove a request for a reasonable accommodation.

The Commonwealth's only evidence of an accommodation request refused by Windsor Plaza was that of reassigning one of the limited common element parking spaces to the Fishels. Because Windsor Plaza does not have the authority to reassign disabled parking spaces that are limited common elements without the consent of the owner of the parking space, this accommodation request was not reasonable, and we hold that the Commonwealth failed to satisfy its burden of proving that Windsor Plaza failed to provide a reasonable accommodation. Consequently, the circuit court did not err in granting Windsor Plaza's motion to strike the Commonwealth's evidence. . . .

CONTINUING VIOLATIONS

Finally, the Fishels claim that the circuit court erred in determining that Windsor Plaza's alleged violations of Code §36–96.3(A)(8) and (9) and 42 U.S.C. §3604(f)(1) and (2) were not continuing violations. They maintain that Windsor Plaza continues to discriminate against them in the sale of their condominium unit as well as continues to make housing unavailable by "operat[ing] a condominium premises that does not provide the accessible garage parking spaces required by [law]." Because Windsor Plaza continues to operate a condominium that lacks handicap-accessible parking while benefitting from the payment of the Fishels' condominium fees, the Fishels argue that "the statute of limitations does not bar [their] claims" because Windsor Plaza's latest discriminatory act falls within the statute of limitations period.

Windsor Plaza responds that the violations alleged by the Fishels are continuing effects, not continuing violations. Windsor Plaza contends that its alleged violations are the continuing effects of the developer's assignment of disabled parking spaces to individual unit owners and cannot extend the statute of limitations. . . .

The continuing violation doctrine is one in "which acts occurring outside the statute of limitations may be considered when there is a 'fixed and continuing practice' of unlawful acts both before and during the limitations period." Scoggins v. Lee's Crossing Homeowners Ass'n, 718 F.3d 262, 271 (4th Cir. 2013). One federal district court has explained the difference in continuing violations and continuing effects of past violations: "[A] continuing violation is occasioned by continual unlawful acts, not continual ill effects from an original violation." Moseke v. Miller & Smith, Inc., 202 F. Supp. 2d 492, 495 (E.D. Va. 2002).

In Moseke, the court concluded that the inaccessible features of three condominium complexes were "more akin to a continuing effect rather than a continuing violation under the FHA[A]." Id. at 507. Because the plaintiffs alleged design and construction claims under the FHAA and VFHL, the court reasoned that the last discriminatory act occurred when the defendants completed construction of the complexes. The court was not swayed by the plaintiff's argument that the violation was ongoing because the condominiums continued to operate without disabled parking spaces.

In this case, the circuit court correctly determined that the Fishels did not allege continuing violations of Code §§36–96.3(A)(8) and (9) and 42 U.S.C. §§3604(f)(1) and (2). The violations alleged by the Fishels—allowing disabled parking spaces to be assigned to residents as limited common elements without reserving a handicap-accessible parking space for the Fishels—occurred at one point in time. The Fishels' not being able to use a disabled parking space is a continuing effect of having assigned all the handicap-accessible parking spaces to other owners before the Fishels bought their condominium. Thus, the circuit court did not err in determining that the alleged discriminatory acts by Windsor Plaza are not continuing in nature but continuing in effect. Therefore, the circuit court did not err in sustaining Windsor Plaza's plea in bar to the Fishels' claims under Code §§36–96.3(A)(8) and 9 and 42 U.S.C. §§3604(f)(1) and (2). . . .

CONCLUSION

[The Supreme Court of Virginia affirmed the circuit court decision in favor of Windsor Plaza.]

14

Possession and Use of Mortgaged Property

By the fourteenth century, the English mortgage had assumed a settled form that has endured as part of the common law. The mortgagor conveyed title to the lender, with the lender holding a freehold estate. The lender, holding the historic relic called *seisin*, got all the incidents of title, the most important being the right to immediate possession. The borrower's only property right in the land was a future interest—title returned to the borrower upon timely repayment of the debt.

At first, the lender's estate and the borrower's right of redemption were cast in the form of a defeasible conveyance. The limitation or condition was that the mortgagor pay the debt by the specified due date, often called *law day*. If payment was timely made, the mortgagor then had the right to resume possession immediately. If not, then the mortgage terms provided for the mortgagee to keep title to the land. An alternate form was also used in English mortgage practice and, over time, became more popular than the defeasible conveyance. Lenders, in an effort to gain more control over the termination of their rights in the land, bargained for fee simple absolute title, making a promise to reconvey to the mortgagor in the event he timely paid the debt. Under this device, payment or tender of payment by the mortgagor would not automatically strip the mortgagee of his right to possession. Instead, it required the affirmative act of the lender in executing a conveyance back to the borrower.

This regime, grounded on freedom of contract between lender and borrower, allocated virtually all of the transactional risk to the borrower. Naturally, hardship sometimes resulted. In equity, the Chancellor began to intervene to protect deserving mortgagors from the harshness of the common law. Time was not of the essence in equity, despite the parties' agreement, because the lender could be made whole by payment of the debt with accrued interest. The debtor's right to pay late, as recognized by the Chancellor, became known as the *equity of redemption*. Over time, the muscle of equity became routine, thereby expanding equity's jurisdiction over mortgages as the common-law courts' jurisdiction shrank. Early in the seventeenth century, all mortgagors who had failed to pay their debt by law day, when they pled a present willingness and ability to pay, merited an equity of redemption, regardless of the reasons for nonpayment.

As a corollary to the newly found equity of redemption, the Chancellor refused to permit waivers, striking down devices that were said to "clog" the mortgagor's redemption right. As the Chancellor realized, lenders, then as today, generally control loan terms and loan documents. Thus, if borrowers could waive their redemption rights, lenders would routinely extract such waivers. The rule against clogging the equity of redemption developed in a series of cases involving lenders' crafty drafting attempts. It applied to all clauses set forth in the mortgage or in contemporaneous agreements that sought to nullify or restrict the borrower's right. For example, a side agreement in which the mortgagor agreed not to assert redemption rights later than one month after default in payment of the debt was an invalid clog.

During the pivotal seventeenth century, when equity transformed English mortgage law, the parties' allocation of possessory rights also changed. At the beginning of the century, the norm was still possession by the mortgagee from the time of the mortgage conveyance, but by the 1660s mortgagor possession until default had become the general practice.

The invention of the equity of redemption put mortgagees in a tenuous and uncertain position. The pendulum had swung, with a pro-mortgagor regime replacing the earlier pro-mortgagee regime. After default by the mortgagor, even if the mortgagee was in possession of the mortgaged land, the mortgagee was subject to the risk that at some point in the future, the mortgagor would file a bill in equity asserting his equity of redemption. To eliminate this title risk, mortgagees sought redress in equity. In the cases developing the equity of redemption, borrowers were plaintiffs. During the seventeenth century lenders became plaintiffs, filing bills alleging a mortgage default and asking for a decree ordering the borrower to pay by a fixed date or be forever barred from exercising the equity of redemption. The Chancellor responded favorably, setting a fixed date that he determined to be reasonable under the facts and circumstances. Such an action became known as *foreclosure*. It foreclosed, or barred, the mortgagor's redemption right. The procedure did not involve a sale of the land; if the mortgagor failed to redeem by the judicially set date, the mortgagee's title became absolute, at which point the mortgagee could elect to keep the land or sell it. Today, this type of decree is known as *strict foreclosure*. Presently in the United States only a few jurisdictions use strict foreclosure on a widespread basis. Instead, modern foreclosure procedure requires a public sale of the land, with the sales proceeds applied to the debt.

Modern United States mortgage law has as its mainstays the borrower's equity of redemption and the lender's right to foreclose on the property, relying heavily on traditional English mortgage law. There is not, however, unanimity as to the nature of the mortgagee's property rights in the land prior to foreclosure. In the United States, there are presently three different theories. A number of states, most of them in the East, cling to the English common-law tradition, holding that the mortgage instrument conveys fee title to the mortgagee.

A majority of states reject the title theory and hold that the mortgagee prior to foreclosure has only a *lien*. Under this approach, the mortgagor keeps legal and equitable title to the estate after signing the mortgage, and the mortgagee's property rights are limited to the right to foreclose after default. Essentially, the lender has a future interest that enables it to sell the property at foreclosure.

For many issues of mortgage law, it often does not matter what mortgage theory the state follows. It is principally important in analyzing the right of the mortgagee to obtain possession prior to the completion of foreclosure. The title theory dictates a baseline rule that the mortgagee has the right to possession, even prior to default. However, by contract the parties can change the principle that the right to possession follows legal title.

Several states—Ohio and Pennsylvania are prime examples—follow what is called an *intermediate theory* or *hybrid theory* of mortgages. These states split the difference between the title theory and lien theory, holding that the mortgagor retains title unless and until he defaults, and upon default the mortgagee automatically gets title. Compared to the title theory, the intermediate theory has the virtue of explaining why the mortgagor has the right to possession after signing the mortgage. Compared to the lien theory, the intermediate theory is pro-creditor in that it validates the position of a mortgagee who claims the right to take possession of the property upon a default prior to foreclosure. This may be significant because in many states foreclosure is not speedy; it may take months from the commencement of foreclosure to its completion.

In principle, the three mortgage theories should affect, in addition to analysis of possession, the allocation of other rights and duties between mortgagor and mortgagee and with respect to third parties. Whichever one has title should have all the incidents of title. At traditional English common law, courts followed the logic of the title theory rigorously, parceling out rights such as inheritance and marital property based on the conception that the mortgagee has title and the mortgagor has a mere personal right of redemption. In the United States, however, courts have cared much less for doctrinal neatness. In all title-theory states, the mortgagor is generally treated as the substantial owner of the property both with respect to rights (such as the right to sell, the right to develop, the right to recover for injury to property) and with respect to duties (such as the duty to pay real estate taxes and the duty to maintain the property in accordance with laws and in a reasonably safe condition).

There are, however, several areas besides possession in which the state's mortgage theory matters. First, much commercial property that is mortgaged produces income in the form of rents paid by tenants to the borrower-landlords. Loan documentation typically includes the borrower-landlord's collateral assignment of rents to the mortgagee, either as a provision of the mortgage or as a separate assignment instrument. In a title-theory state or intermediate-theory state, such an assignment may be unnecessary, because a mortgagee who is entitled to possession is automatically entitled to a security interest in the rents. Rents and profits are considered to be an incident of possession. Thus, the underlying title theory may protect a lender who, due to accident or some other reason, fails to obtain an express assignment of rents. Lien-theory states that follow the logic of their theory, refusing to let the parties contract around the theory, should refuse to recognize the efficacy of an assignment of rents prior to foreclosure. In essence, the lender receives the fruits of possession if he can collect rents before completing foreclosure. However, almost all lien-theory states give some effect to rent assignments, although typically they are more stingy than title-theory states. Commonly, in lien-theory states the mortgagee who holds an express assignment is often said to have only an "inchoate lien" on rents, which requires that the mortgagee take specific steps to collect rents. Usually this means the mortgagee must obtain actual or constructive possession of the property by bringing a foreclosure action, obtaining a court-appointed receiver, or some similar legal proceeding. In contrast, title-theory states, where the mortgagee already has title to the property, require less for the mortgagee to collect rents. Typically, it suffices to send a simple notice to the tenant requesting that future rents be paid directly to the mortgagee.

Second, in some title-theory states, a mortgagee who has not taken possession is personally liable on covenants made by the mortgagor that run with the land due to privity of estate. The most important application of this principle is in cases holding that when a commercial tenant mortgages its leasehold, the leasehold mortgagee becomes liable to the landlord for rent and other covenants.

Third, environmental liabilities of owners of contaminated land may extend to mortgagees who have title by virtue of the title theory of mortgages. Most of the concern has centered on the Comprehensive Environmental Response, Compensation, and Liability Act (CERCLA), also known as *Superfund*, 42 U.S.C. §§9601-9675. Under CERCLA, owners and operators of properties containing hazardous waste have statutory liability for the costs of cleanup. CERCLA, however, contains an exemption for a "lender that, without participating in the management of a . . . facility, holds indicia of ownership primarily to protect the security interest [in the] facility." *Id.* §9601(20)(E)(i). This exemption was apparently designed to protect title-theory lenders who hold "indicia of ownership," provided they refrain from participating in management decisions, and lenders who acquire ownership or possession as a result of foreclosure. CERCLA is not the only environmental law that raises issues concerning the treatment of mortgage lenders who hold title. Potential lender liability exists under other federal and state environmental statutes, many of which lack express provisions governing lender liability.

A. POSSESSION BY MORTGAGOR: DOCTRINE OF WASTE

Whenever real property is owned by more than one person, there is the potential for the doctrine of *waste* to come into play. The basic principle is that the owner who is in possession owes the other owners the duty not to damage or destroy the property. This duty not to commit waste applies to cotenants. The doctrine of waste also applies to protect the owners of future interests, such as reversions and remainders that will or may become possessory after a life estate expires. Moreover, a tenant under a lease arrangement owes the landlord the duty not to commit acts of waste, whether the property is commercial, residential, or unimproved.

From your beginning course in property, you may recall that the modern law of waste seeks to achieve a balance between the rights of the possessor and the rights of the other owners. The basic goal is to preserve the economic value of the property for the nonpossessing owners. Thus, a life tenant ordinarily cannot remove a house or cut valuable timber, and a cotenant cannot begin mining operations without reaching agreement with the other owners. Yet the possessor is entitled to make reasonable use of the property, and often reasonable use requires the making of some changes to the property.

In mortgage law, the doctrine of waste plays the same role of adjusting and shaping the legal relationships of multiple owners as it does in other contexts. Whether the mortgagee's interest is conceptualized as title or a lien, it is important to recognize that it is property, and therefore whenever land is mortgaged it is subject to multiple ownership by the mortgagor and mortgagee together. We can think of the mortgagee's property right as a type of future interest. If the mortgagor fails to repay the debt or perform his other obligations, the mortgagee has the right to look to the security—in other words, to obtain the property to satisfy the default. The law of waste performs the vital role of protecting the economic value of the mortgagee's right to security. Therefore, not only are there acts the mortgagor must refrain from doing, such as tearing down a valuable building, but the law of waste also imposes affirmative duties on the mortgagor. The labels *voluntary waste* and *permissive waste* often used by courts reflect this dual nature of waste.

Sometimes the extent of a mortgagor's liability for waste depends on a determination of whether the loss in value to the property results from *good faith* or *bad faith* waste. In some states, such as California, the distinction between good faith and bad faith waste becomes highly important because a mortgagor is liable for bad faith waste as an exception to the state's general policy of protecting borrowers from deficiency judgments in a foreclosure setting (in other words, borrowers are not personally liable to the lender when the property sells at a foreclosure sale for a price that is less than the outstanding mortgage amount; this often happens when the borrower is said to be "underwater"). Foreclosure is discussed in detail in Chapter 17.

FAIT v. NEW FAZE DEVELOPMENT, INC.
Court of Appeal of California, Third District, 2012
143 Cal. Rptr. 3d 382

ROBIE, Acting Presiding Justice. The owner of a parcel of real property with a building on it demolishes the building to make way for new development. Unfortunately, the owner is unable to complete the development and ends up defaulting on a purchase money promissory note secured by a deed of trust on the property. The holder of the note and deed of trust exercises the power of sale under the deed of trust and buys the property back at a foreclosure sale for less than the amount due under the note. The noteholder then sues the former owner and others for waste and impairment of security based on their demolition of the building, seeking as damages the loss of value in the property that resulted from the destruction of the building. Is such an action barred by the antideficiency statutes under the reasoning of Cornelison v. Kornbluth, 542 P.2d 981 (Cal. 1975)?

The answer to that question is "no." . . . The impairment of security that results from the destruction of a building is actionable waste, notwithstanding the antideficiency statutes, unless the destruction itself was somehow caused by the economic pressures of a depressed market. . . .

Defendant Allen Warren is the sole owner and director of defendant New Faze Development, Inc., a company Warren set up to carry out "[t]he functional development responsibilities for a variety of entities." Defendant New Faze Holdings is also wholly owned by Warren. New Faze Holdings "was set up to own and house property prior to going into construction."

Defendant Wendy S. Saunders was employed by New Faze Development from April 2006 through December 2007 as its director of project development. Defendant Jay Rivinius was employed by New Faze Development as its director of construction.

In February 2005, New Faze Holdings and another company, Soul First Properties, LLC (jointly, the "purchasers"), purchased from the Harrison Holland Fait and Barbara Fait 1990 Trust (the "1990 Trust") the real estate located at 2005 and 2007 Del Paso Boulevard for $525,000. The purchasers made a downpayment of $52,500 and executed a $472,500 promissory note to the 1990 Trust secured by a deed of trust on the property.

At the time of the sale in February 2005, there was a building on the property that housed two tenants: a church and a small social services agency. A new roof had been installed on the building in January 1999, and a new ceiling with new light fixtures had been installed in the space rented by the church in the summer of 2003. At the time of sale the building had fully functioning electrical and plumbing systems, the doors and windows were working and intact, and the building was free of graffiti.

The purchasers bought the property with the intent to redevelop it into a mixed-use development including retail, residential, garage, office, and restaurant services. The redevelopment plans required demolition of the existing building and, thus, eviction of the existing tenants, which was accomplished in the fall of 2005. The demolition occurred a year later in October 2006. Warren was the one who decided to demolish the building. As project manager, Saunders ordered the demolition. Rivinius signed an agreement to hold the city harmless from liability for the demolition.

In April 2007, the 1990 Trust transferred its interest in the note and deed of trust to Donna Fait and the Glenn Fait 2005 Trust (the "Faits").

Ultimately, the purchasers defaulted on their payments under the promissory note and failed to pay taxes and insurance on the property. As a result, the Faits initiated nonjudicial foreclosure proceedings under the deed of trust. In May 2009, the Faits bought the property at a public foreclosure sale for $14,097. At the time of the sale, there were more than $7,000 in property taxes owed on the property.

In July 2009, the Faits brought this action against the purchasers, New Faze Development, Warren, Saunders, and Rivinius (among others) for bad faith waste . . . . The cause of action for bad faith waste alleged that the purchasers and Warren committed waste by demolishing the building and failing to pay taxes on the property . . . .

In August 2010, New Faze Holdings, New Faze Development, Warren, Saunders, and Rivinius moved for summary judgment . . . .

The gist of their argument on the claim of "bad faith" waste was that they did not intend to harm the property, and they did not act maliciously or recklessly by demolishing the building because the demolition was "based on a good faith belief that the Property could be developed into a legitimate mixed use commercial project." . . .

In opposing the motion, the Faits argued they could prevail on the claim of "bad faith" waste because defendants acted "intentionally" in demolishing the building. In their view, "when waste was not committed solely or primarily as a result of the economic pressures of a market depression, the lender can recover" for "bad faith" waste. . . .

Relying on *Cornelison*, the trial court concluded that "[t]he issue of bad faith waste . . . hinges on whether defendants' conduct in demolishing the building was reckless, intentional despoilment, or malicious." Because defendants had shown that the building demolition was based on a good faith belief that the property could be developed, and they made substantial efforts to get the development project underway, the court concluded there was an "absence of recklessness and intent to despoil at the time of the demolition." Accordingly, the "bad faith" waste cause of action could not be maintained based on the demolition. Because the court found that New Faze Holdings's failure to pay the property taxes *could* qualify as "bad faith" waste, the court denied summary adjudication as to New Faze Holdings on the "bad faith" claim, but the court granted the motion as to the other four defendants. . . .

"Bad Faith" Waste

The Faits contend the trial court erred in granting summary judgment because, among other things, there are triable issues of fact as to whether "bad faith" waste was committed. . . .

As we will explain, the trial court erred in determining that the cause of action for "bad faith" waste based on the demolition of the building could not be maintained here because of an "absence of recklessness and intent to despoil at the time of the demolition." Under *Cornelison,* any waste that is not committed solely or primarily as a result of the economic pressures of a market depression qualifies as "bad faith" waste. *Cornelison, supra* at 990-91. Thus, it does not strictly matter whether those who demolished the building on the property did so based on a good faith belief that the property could be developed, or that they made substantial efforts to get the development project underway. As long as the demolition did not occur solely or primarily as a result of the economic pressures of a market depression, they can be liable for what the Supreme Court in *Cornelison* labeled "bad faith" waste. . . .

[The *Cornelison* court explained:]

It will be recalled that damages in an action for waste are measured by the amount of injury to the security caused by the mortgagor's acts, that is by the substantial harm which "impair[s] the value of the property subject to the lien so as to render it an inadequate security for the mortgage debt." . . .

[We] hold that [Cal. Civ. Proc. §580b, which protects purchasers from deficiency claims brought by sellers] should . . . not apply in the . . . instance of "bad faith" waste. We further hold that it is within the province of the trier of fact to determine on a case by case basis to what, if any, extent the impairment of the mortgagee's security has been caused . . . by the general decline of real property values and to what, if any, extent . . . by the bad faith acts of the mortgagor, such determination, in either instance, being subject to review under the established rule of appellate review. *Cornelison, supra* at 990-91. . . .

[In the case before us] defendants argued that *Cornelison* "defined 'bad faith waste' as 'reckless,' 'intentional,' or 'malicious' conduct," and they argued there was no such conduct here because "[t]he building demolition was based on a good faith belief that the Property could be developed." The trial court accepted this argument. We do not. . . .

Among those circumstances in which the devaluation of security is not the result of economic pressures of a depression are the "reckless, intentional, and at times even malicious despoilers of property" the Supreme Court mentioned in *Cornelison. Id.* at 991. But we do not understand the *Cornelison* decision to conclude that *only* such "despoilers of property" can be liable for "bad faith" waste. Rather "bad faith" waste occurs *whenever* the owner's impairment of the value of the security is not caused by the economic pressures of a market depression, whether the owner acts recklessly, intentionally, maliciously, or with some other mental state.

Applying that understanding of *Cornelison* here, we conclude the Faits are correct in arguing that triable facts exist as to whether "bad faith" waste was committed in this case. For purposes of determining liability for waste, it is not dispositive that defendants demolished the building as part of their effort to develop the property and thus (presumably) to add value to it. Indeed, defendants may have had the best of intentions, but that fact alone does not entitle them to escape liability for waste. The pertinent question is whether the demolition of the building, which is what the Faits claim impaired the value of the property as security for the note, was caused by the economic pressures of a market depression. Here, that is for the trier of fact to decide. . . .

The judgment is reversed, and the case is remanded to the trial court with directions to vacate its order granting the motion for summary judgment by New Faze Development, Warren, Saunders, and Rivinius and to enter a new order denying that motion. . . . The Faits shall recover their costs on appeal.

Problem 14A

Three years ago Serena bought a single-family home for $300,000 and financed it with a mortgage loan for $270,000 from Big Bank. The home was seven years old when she purchased it, and it included a backyard in-ground swimming pool. Serena almost never used the pool, and she disliked pool maintenance chores. Last April, without notifying Big Bank or getting its approval, she paid a contractor $8,000 for what's called a partial demolition and removal of the swimming pool (sometimes called "filling in the pool"). The contractor removed the tops of the pool walls, punched holes in the lower portions of the walls for drainage, and added fill dirt to bury the materials that remained. Serena previously obtained a quote for full demolition and removal (with all materials removed), but rejected that quote ($14,000) because it was more than she was willing to pay. Full removal is necessary if a building is planned on or near the former pool site. Serena is not planning to extend her house. The former pool site, though near the house, is now covered by grass and flowerbeds. Big Bank learns what Serena has done.

(a) Does Big Bank have a cause of action against Serena? If so, what should be its remedy?

(b) What result if (1) Serena's mortgage provides that "the mortgagor shall keep the property in reasonable repair and commit no waste thereon" or, alternatively, if (2) Serena's mortgage says nothing about repairs, replacements, or waste?

(c) Serena stops making her monthly mortgage payments to Big Bank. The bank declares a default, initiates nonjudicial foreclosure proceedings, and purchases the home at the public foreclosure sale. Big Bank bids $245,000, which is $20,000 less that the total amount of debt then owed by Serena. Big

Bank sues Serena personally for this deficiency. What result and why? Does it matter if the house is located in California, subject to the law described in Fait v. New Faze Development, Inc.?

B. POSSESSION BY MORTGAGEE

Mortgagee in possession is a term applied to a lender that takes physical control of a debtor's property prior to foreclosure. Generally, the reason the lender takes possession of mortgaged property is to preserve and protect its asset value. Such a lender is not considered to be the owner of the property simply as a result of taking possession, even in a state that follows the title theory or intermediate theory of mortgage law. For this reason, the mortgagee in possession has a special duty to the mortgagor to act prudently in taking care of the property, and must make a full accounting of rents and profits derived from the property.

WOODVIEW CONDOMINIUM ASSOCIATION v. SHANAHAN
Superior Court of New Jersey, Appellate Division, 2007
917 A.2d 790

PARRILLO, J.A.D. At issue in this appeal is whether a mortgagee in possession is liable for delinquent condominium common charges, which had accrued against the property's legal owner, for services furnished during the mortgagee's possession and control of the premises. We hold the mortgagee in possession is personally liable even though he is not the legal owner and therefore affirm the Law Division's ruling to that effect. However, we vacate the judgment entered and remand for a proper determination of the amount due.

The Woodview Condominium complex is a thirty-four unit housing development in Millville. Pursuant to a master deed and by-laws, the complex is governed by plaintiff Woodview Condominium Association, Inc. (Association), which is "responsible for the administration and management of the condominium and condominium property, including but not limited to the conduct of all activities of common interest to the unit owners." N.J.S.A. 46:8B-12. Among other things, the Association is charged with the duty to care for and maintain the common elements at the complex, in which the owners of the units have an undivided interest. N.J.S.A. 46:8B-3h. To fund this effort, the Association, pursuant to the master deed and by-laws, assesses and collects fees on a monthly basis to cover each unit owner's pro-rata share of common expenses, since the individual units are not separately metered for the water and utilities they consume. Common expenses are those "expenses for which the unit owners are proportionately liable" and include: "(i) all expenses of administration, maintenance, repair and replacement of the common elements; (ii) expenses agreed upon as common by all unit owners; and (iii) expenses declared common by provisions of [the Condominium Act] or by the master deed or by the bylaws." N.J.S.A. 46:8B-3e. As to the latter, the master deed includes "utility charges" among the common expenses for which unit owners must pay their proportionate share.

In April 1997, defendant Kevin Shanahan acquired title to two of the units at the Woodview complex. During his ownership, defendant defaulted on his obligation to pay the monthly condominium assessments, which he cured when sued by plaintiff. On January 11, 2000, defendant conveyed title to the two units to Tomas Pratts, Jr. who, in exchange, executed a one-year purchase money mortgage in the amount of $33,000 payable to defendant. One year later, on January 29, 2001, plaintiff filed an assessment lien on each property, totaling $3,192.50, apparently owing to Pratts' failure to pay the monthly condominium fees. Nine months later, in September 2001, Pratts also defaulted on his mortgage with defendant and as a result, defendant assumed control of both units as a mortgagee in possession. Although it is unclear from the record precisely when this occurred, as early as June 17, 2002, Pratts and defendant entered into a management agreement for the units. Defendant also rented out each unit to third parties, one lease commencing on April 29, 2003, and the other sometime in April 2004. Although defendant satisfied the Association's assessment liens, he never paid the monthly condominium fees while in possession and control of the premises. On March 2, 2005, defendant instituted a mortgage foreclosure action against Pratts and thereafter successfully resisted the Association's motion to appoint a rent receiver to apply rents collected to its monthly assessment charges.

Consequently, on April 13, 2005, plaintiff sued defendant and Pratts for conversion and on a book account. [A] default judgment in the amount of $70,418.92 was entered against [Pratts]. . . .

[The trial court entered] judgment in the amount of $41,200.24 [against defendant].

On appeal, defendant reiterates the argument that a mortgagee in possession is not liable for monthly assessments accrued during the time of his possession or control, but if so, then the matter must be remanded for a hearing on the amount due.

It has long been the view that if a mortgagor defaults in the payment of mortgage debt, the mortgagee has the right to take possession of the mortgaged property, subject to the mortgagor's right of redemption. To be sure, legal title remains in the mortgagor and the mortgagee in possession does not obtain an unfettered interest akin to fee simple ownership. Nevertheless, upon taking possession of the property, the mortgagee in possession has the right to occupy the property as well as the right to lease the property to a third party, and to collect the rent and profits. In addition, the mortgagee in possession has standing to sue a third party for damage to the property.

Concomitant with the entitlement to profits and rent, mortgagees in possession assume the duties of a provident owner, which requires "management and preservation of the property." Essex Cleaning Contractors, Inc. v. Amato, A.2d 411, 412 317 (N.J. Super. Ct. App. Div. 1974); *see also* United Nat'l Bank v. Parish 750, A.2d 238, 241, 242 (N.J. Super. Ct. Ch. Div. 1999) (noting that "the mortgagee in possession is bound to the actions of a 'provident' or 'prudent' mortgagor" which contemplates a "grave responsibility for the management and preservation of the property"). This is because although the mortgagee is in possession, legal title remains in the mortgagor, who has the right to redeem the property, and title only passes to the mortgagee at the conclusion of the foreclosure process.

Thus, mortgagees in possession have long been held to "the duty of treating the property as a provident owner would treat it, . . . of using the same diligence to make it productive that a provident owner would use" and "to keep it in good ordinary repair." Shaeffer v. Chambers, 6 N.J. Eq. 548, 557 (Ch. 1847). Indeed, a mortgagee in possession is liable both for damages to the property while in possession and in tort for injuries arising from "his actionable fault in utilizing the property or . . . his failure to perform duties imposed by law upon the owner of the land." *Essex Cleaning, supra* at 412. (quoting Osborne, *Law of Mortgages* 283 (2d ed. 1970)). Furthermore, "[a] mortgagee in possession may also be subject to prosecution by local governmental authorities for the failure of the mortgaged property to conform to housing codes, health and safety ordinances and other similar regulations." *United Nat'l Bank, supra* at 242. And, mortgagees in possession have been required to "pay taxes as they accrue on the property." *Id.*

Significant for present purposes, "a mortgagee in possession may be liable for services rendered to him in connection with the property during his occupancy thereof on the basis of an express or implied contract." *Essex Cleaning, supra* at 412. There, a mortgagor defaulted on a note, and the mortgagee took possession of the three commercial buildings securing the note. Prior to default, the mortgagor had contracted with a janitorial service to clean the buildings, and upon taking possession after the default, the mortgagee authorized the janitorial service to continue cleaning the buildings. Thereafter, the mortgagee in possession failed to pay the janitorial company for the services it had rendered, and the janitorial company filed suit. *Ibid.* The trial court held that the mortgagee in possession was not liable for the janitorial services because legal title to the buildings remained with the mortgagor. We disagreed and quoted with approval from Osborne, *Law of Mortgages* 283 (2d ed. 1970) (emphasis supplied):

> When a mortgagee goes into possession questions as to his personal liability arising out of his relations with third parties arise. Since he is the person in possession of the premises he is personally liable in tort for injuries resulting either through his actionable fault in utilizing the property or by reason of his

failure to perform duties imposed by law upon the owner of the land. *Even more clearly he is liable for goods and services furnished to him during his occupancy.*

At issue here is defendant's non-payment of the pro-rata share of common expenses related to utilities, administration and maintenance supplied to him during the time he was in possession of the units. These resources are undeniably goods and services as contemplated by *Essex Cleaning.* Although, unlike the mortgagee in possession in *Essex Cleaning,* defendant did not expressly or directly contract for these services with the Association, such an agreement is manifested by other conduct sufficient to establish a contract either implied-in-fact or implied-in-law.

Equitable considerations also support this conclusion. Defendant fully accepted the services either rendered directly or funded by the Association to ensure the premises' habitability and was therefore unjustly enriched by collecting rents without contributing his pro-rata share to their costs. In our view, having enjoyed the benefit of these goods and services throughout his possession and control of the premises, and consistent with the rights and duties of mortgagees in possession generally, defendant suffers the burden of their cost. . . .

Lastly, defendant argues that in contrast to the Association's remedies against the legal owner, plaintiff's only recourse against a mortgagee in possession is that afforded by N.J.S.A. 46:8B-21, which gives plaintiff's assessment lien a super priority over defendant's mortgage limited to the amount of six months of unpaid usual and customary common charges. We disagree. The statutory provision addresses the issue of lien priority upon the foreclosure sale rather than liability for goods and services received either before or during the pendency of foreclosure proceedings. Nothing in N.J.S.A. 46:8B-21 suggests that the limited super priority is the Association's exclusive remedy for unpaid assessments accrued during the tenure of a mortgagee in possession, or restricts the Association's ability to further seek a money judgment against that defaulting party. Accordingly, N.J.S.A. 46:8B-21 is not a statutory bar to payment of common charges during the pendency of foreclosure proceedings.

For all these reasons, we concur in the trial court's ruling holding defendant liable for the outstanding condominium fee assessments accruing during his possession and control of the units. However, a question remains as to whether the judgment is correct in the amount rendered. Since the mortgagee is not entitled to rents or profits accrued before the date of taking possession, it follows, as a matter of course, that defendant is not liable for delinquent condominium fees accruing before he came into possession of the realty. Here, however, it appears from the record that the judgment entered against defendant does in fact include monthly assessments accrued before defendant actually took possession of the two units and for which, therefore, he is not responsible. . . . [W]e deem it appropriate to remand the matter for the limited purpose of determining the date on which defendant became a mortgagee in possession and then appropriately adjusting the amount of the judgment based on that determination. . . .

Remanded for proceedings consistent with this opinion. The judgment is affirmed in all other respects.

Problem 14B

Best Bank, your client, is a mortgagee that has just taken possession of an office building that has 40,000 square feet of space. Cook, the owner who defaulted, finished construction six months ago. Half the building is occupied by tenants, the other half is unrented. "For Rent" signs, put up by Cook, are in front of the building. Internet ads and newspaper ads run by Cook have expired, and Best cannot find any real estate broker's agreements, signed by Cook, covering the property. Best did find, however, two unpaid bills in the building manager's office: an electric bill for $2,458 for the month ending four days prior to Best's entry into possession, and an assessment for $4,100 payable to the flood control district in which the property is located.

(a) Does Best have a duty to try to rent the unoccupied space? What measures, if any, should Best take?

(b) Does Best have a duty to pay the electric bill and the flood control assessment?

C. RECEIVERS

When the borrower defaults, the mortgagee has several remedies it may pursue prior to foreclosure. As discussed earlier, the mortgagee may seek to take possession directly (becoming a mortgagee in possession). For rent-producing property, a second choice is to invoke an *assignment of rents* clause contained in the loan documents. A third possible remedy is to obtain a court-appointed receiver, who will take possession and operate the property. Generally, receivership is used for income-producing or commercial properties, but it may be useful for owner-occupied housing if waste is threatened and foreclosure is likely to proceed slowly. Receivership is available in all states as an incident to an action for foreclosure. Receivership is an equitable remedy, and this means that courts usually look at a number of factors to decide whether to appoint a receiver. The standards for appointments vary from state to state, sometimes because of state statutes. In some states, therefore, it is easier than in others to get a receiver appointed. Most courts require that the mortgagee prove not only a material default by the borrower but also that a receiver is necessary to prevent further injury to the mortgagee. Typical facts include waste or the threat of waste committed by the borrower, inadequate security compared to the amount of the debt, and the borrower's insolvency or weak financial position.

Mortgage instruments often have a receivership clause, which typically authorizes the mortgagee to obtain the appointment of a receiver if the borrower defaults. Judicial attitudes toward such clauses diverge. Some courts pay substantial deference to them on the basis of freedom of contract. Other courts ignore them, reasoning that the remedy of appointing a receiver is inherently equitable in nature, and thus contractual provisions usurp the judicial function and are unenforceable. Some courts appear to adopt a middle ground, looking at a number of factors to determine whether a receiver should be appointed and treating the presence of a contract provision as one factor that is material but not controlling.

The scope of the receiver's powers may vary, according to the terms of the judicial appointment. Often the receiver is granted broad managerial discretion, including the right to enter into new leases and contracts. The receiver collects rents and income, makes repairs, and pays expenses (including the receiver's fees established by the court). The receiver holds the net proceeds for the benefit of the parties; usually they are held until foreclosure and then applied to the debt, but the appointment can provide for periodic distribution to the mortgagee. Sometimes a receiver's role is more limited; for example, the receiver might only collect rents.

In 2015, the Uniform Law Commission (ULC) approved the Uniform Commercial Real Estate Receivership Act to provide a consistent set of rules for courts to apply to receiverships involving commercial real estate. The intent is to achieve greater predictability and uniformity for owners, lenders, and other persons doing business related to properties in receivership. The Act requires notice and an opportunity for a court hearing before appointment of a receiver, unless special circumstances make that impossible. The Act provides an alternative to foreclosure by allowing a receiver, with court approval, to sell the property free and clear of liens and redemption rights.

Problem 14C

Gary owns an office building that he bought two years ago for $800,000. He paid $80,000 in cash, giving the seller, Sam, a promissory note for $720,000, secured by a purchase-money mortgage on the property. For 20 months, Gary timely made monthly payments of principal and interest, but he failed to make the last two payments, which were due May 1st and June 1st. On June 20th, Sam accelerated the maturity of the debt and filed an action to foreclose his mortgage. It is now June 25th and Sam has filed a motion for the appointment of a receiver. The debt, including accrued interest, is now $700,000. Should the court grant Sam's motion if:

(a) The present fair market value of the property has risen in a strong market and is between $840,000 and $870,000?

(b) The property has declined in value due to a weak market for office space rentals and has a present fair market value between $690,000 and $720,000?

(c) The property has declined in value as a result of physical deterioration caused by Gary's failure to make needed repairs, and it has a present fair market value between $720,000 and $750,000?

(d) Should it matter, in any of the situations in (a) through (c), whether Gary is solvent or insolvent?

(e) Should it matter, in any of the situations in (a) through (c), whether the mortgage contains a receivership clause providing:

> In the event of any default under the promissory note secured hereby or under the terms of this mortgage, the holder of this mortgage, in any action to foreclose it, shall be entitled to the appointment of a receiver, without regard to waste, adequacy of the security, or solvency of the mortgagor.

(f) Should it matter, in any of the situations in (a) through (c), whether the mortgage contains an assignment of rents?

(g) Should it matter, in any of the situations in (a) through (c), whether the state follows the title theory, intermediate theory, or lien theory of mortgages?

15

Residential Mortgage Products

In Chapter 14, we sketched the history of mortgage law, concentrating on a few basic principles that govern the traditional as well as the contemporary relationships between mortgagor and mortgagee. With this as background, we now explore the current situation in residential mortgage law by putting it into the market context. Large, growing financial markets support mortgage lending activities, and the dynamics of these markets shape the opportunities and the risks of real estate acquisition and investing. First, we consider access to credit for persons who want to enter the market to get home mortgage loans. Second, we examine the basic mortgage products that are exchanged in the markets and thus are available to borrowers. Third, we present a simple framework for understanding the primary and secondary mortgage markets. Last, we discuss the complex regulatory environment for home mortgage lending, including reforms that followed the market meltdown that began in 2007.

A. ACCESS TO MORTGAGE MARKETS

Lenders ration access to mortgage loans by developing and applying *underwriting standards*. This raises issues of law and policy, because some applicants are able to get mortgages, others are not, and others who are evaluated as presenting higher-than-normal risk are offered less advantageous terms. Lenders' underwriting decisions are heavily influenced by federal laws and regulations. The Dodd-Frank Wall Street Reform and Consumer Protection Act (Dodd-Frank), Public Law 111-203, 124 Stat. 1376 (2010) (discussed in more detail in Part E of this chapter) gave the Consumer Federal Protection Bureau (CFPB) jurisdiction to regulate mortgage lending. These rules were promulgated in response to the financial crisis of the first decade of the twenty-first century. They are designed to reduce the riskiness of mortgage lending and to eliminate a number of undesirable practices that were associated with the causes of the financial collapse. Dodd-Frank and the CFPB's implementing regulations have many detailed provisions that determine access to mortgages. The most fundamental change from prior practice allows a lender to make a loan only to a borrower who has demonstrated a reasonable ability to repay that loan.

The Community Reinvestment Act 12 U.S.C. §2901 (CRA), enacted by Congress in 1977, encourages depository institutions to meet the credit needs of all members of the communities that they serve. Even with legislation such as the CRA, however, homeownership rates in the United States historically have varied by race, and access to mortgage credit is considered an important factor in the observed differences. The degree to which legitimate business and economic factors explain the difference is a question that continues to be contentious. The 2010 census disclosed the following homeownership rates by race: Asian, 59 percent; black, 45.4 percent; Hispanic, 47.5 percent; white, 74.4 percent. Lending institutions must make annual reports on their activities under the Home Mortgage Disclosure Act (HMDA) of 1975, 12 U.S.C. §§2801–2810. In addition, the Federal Financial Institutions Examination Council, an interagency body that promotes uniform reporting standards for financial institutions, periodically publishes reports based on the HMDA information.

To understand access issues, we must think of mortgage lending as a business. For lenders, extending credit is an investment opportunity. Whereas a homeowner looks at the mortgage as a necessary living expense, the lender looks at it as a financial investment. Lenders make financial capital available for real estate activities because they find such activities to be rewarding in terms of economic profit. Making a loan represents an investment of capital upon which a profitable return must be earned. A lender thinks of any particular loan as just one of many possible investment options for its money. In this sense, the lender is much like any one of us when we take our hard-earned savings and contemplate investment options such as depositing money into a savings account, a money market fund, or retirement account, or purchasing stocks and bonds. When we think about these options, we consider the risk and the return on how we invest our money. A lender views real estate funding in a similar way. A lender has control over large amounts of capital and must make decisions on how best to invest that money to get a good return within an acceptable range of risk.

Access to credit is important for anyone who seeks to purchase property. Institutional lenders follow underwriting standards to decide who can borrow money and how much they can get. The lender cares about two key factors: the *willingness* and the *ability* of the debtor to repay the loan. These two factors are different because a person may be able to pay back a loan and yet refuse to do so as a result of a dispute with the bank or with the seller of the property, or because property values have dropped dramatically and the debtor becomes unwilling to pay any more to protect the declining asset, or perhaps for some totally unrelated reason. Similarly, a person may be more than willing to repay a loan and yet be unable to as the result of losing a job or some other hardship.

A lender considers a borrower's income, savings, outstanding debts, net worth, credit history, and employment history (ideally two years or more of steady employment with the same employer). Some of the factors used in the evaluation are more objective than others. Generally speaking, the factors related to ability to pay are more objective than those related to willingness to pay. Central to the determination of ability to pay is an evaluation of the income and other outstanding debt obligations of the borrower. The CFPB regulations describe this determination as Ability to Repay (ATR). With respect to income, traditionally many lenders followed a 28 percent rule, indicating that a debtor should not qualify for a loan requiring monthly mortgage payments exceeding 28 percent of gross monthly income. In addition, lenders traditionally used a 36 percent rule, indicating that a debtor should not have *total* debt payments (mortgage payments plus all other debt obligations) exceeding 36 percent of gross income. Today, many loans follow a 31 and 43 percent debt-to-income ratio (DTI) rather than the traditional 28 and 36 percent rule. These numerical guidelines are widely followed, though some variation may be made for particular borrowers, for particular types of loans, or for high-cost housing markets. To the extent that a local variation from these norms is used to calculate ability to pay, it is likely that most lenders in the given area would employ the same variation. The advantage to a simple numerical test is that it is fairly easy to calculate and leaves little room for discretion.

In contrast to a simple test for ability to pay, a potentially more subjective inquiry is made to determine willingness to pay. Credit and employment history must be evaluated, and any past credit problems (*e.g.*, late payments, defaults, foreclosures, bankruptcy) or payment disputes with other parties must be cleared up to the satisfaction of the lender. In the past, some writers identified the subjective inquiry related to willingness to pay as one factor leading to the different success rates of borrowers based on race. The suggestion was that in many cases the success rate of loan applicants is relatively even across races when the applicants' files and ability to pay numbers are of equal merit. At the same time, when there are issues of work history or potential credit problems that take additional time to evaluate, the evidence has indicated that loan officers have been generally more likely to work on clearing up these potential problems with respect to white applicants than black applicants. This can lead to a racial bias in observed success rates for mortgage financing. The reason is thought to be that loan officers, working on commissions, are more likely to assume that white applicants have a mistake in their file or that their credit issues are minor and will be easy to clear up with little effort. Today much of this potential for bias is constrained by having a *credit score* system, which rates borrowers on a 900-

point scale. The point scale system includes points related to both ability and willingness to pay and thus seeks to quantify the decision-making process for the loan officer, thereby dramatically reducing the opportunity for subjective bias in the decision-making process.

A person's credit score is sometimes referred to as her FICO score, in reference to Fair Isaac Corporation, which came up with the score process. Scores in the system range from 300 to 900 points, and the higher a person's score the better. Higher scores mean that the person is a better credit risk and will qualify for a lower-cost loan. In general, a score of 660 or better is acceptable for normal pricing. Scores over 700 get better loan pricing, and scores below 660 get greater scrutiny. Scores below 620 are considered high risk and usually require paying higher rates. Higher-risk borrowers, below a 620 score, may not qualify for a mortgage loan.

The requirements for self-employed borrowers are similar but there may be more paperwork and more scrutiny, particularly as to stated income. Generally, a lender will look for at least two years of self-employment history. A lender will generally want to see tax returns, profit and loss statements, a balance sheet of financial credits and debits, and other documentation to substantiate the credit status of a self-employed person or small business owner.

B. TYPES OF MORTGAGES AND PRICING

A number of mortgage products are commonly offered in the residential market. The important point to remember with respect to any of these products is that the lender views the mortgage (no matter what its form) as an investment, and thus any arrangement that increases risk, delays payment, or reduces interest below market rates will have to provide a way for the lender to recapture the seemingly forgone value in another way or form. In other words, there is "no such thing as a free lunch," as the saying goes, and your job is to understand how the "lunch" is being paid for. You need to know the various mortgage forms and the tradeoffs that they present to the people using them.

Before looking at specific types of mortgages, we will first consider three related topics: the concept of *points*; the *annual percentage rate* (APR), and the matter of *mortgage insurance*.

1. Points and Annual Percentage Rate

Institutional lenders that make home mortgage loans usually require the borrower to pay upfront fees called *points*. Instead of the term *points*, in the formal paperwork lenders typically identify these fees using more official names such as "loan processing fee," "loan discount," or "loan origination fee," but they all mean the same thing. Points are charged in addition to the interest on the loan and any other specific charges for such things as an application fee, credit check, survey, or title examination. Sometimes points are used to pay a commission to the loan officer who originates a loan. One point is equal to 1 percent of the loan amount. A point is also referred to as 100 *basis points*. Thus, 1 point charged for a $100,000 loan is $1,000, and if instead the lender charged 50 basis points, that would be the same as $1/2$ point or $500.

The borrower must pay the specified points before the loan is funded, so lenders collect them at or before the loan closing. They may be paid in one of two ways. Most commonly, the lender discounts the points by subtracting them from the face amount of the loan and disbursing funds equal to the difference. Alternatively, some lenders require that the borrower use out-of-pocket cash to pay the points. Only in the rare instance when the lender requires the borrower to pay points on a certain date before the loan closing does it matter how they are collected. The attorney or closing officer, however, should confirm how the points are to be assessed so that she can advise the borrower how much cash she must bring to the closing.

Instead of charging points, lenders and mortgage brokers often make an equivalent return by increasing the stated interest rate to produce a *yield spread premium*. This means that the loan has a market value that is greater than the stated amount of principal. For example, instead of lending $100,000 at 5 percent and charging one point, the lender will make the loan at 5.2 percent and no points and will sell the loan for 101 percent of its face value (a 1 percent premium).

The *APR*, or *annual percentage rate*, is a calculation of the cost of a loan using a federal formula set forth in the Real Estate Settlement Procedures Act (RESPA), 12 U.S.C. §§2601-2617, enacted in 1974. All the points and other expenses the lender requires the borrower to pay are treated as if they were interest, and the lender must add them to the stated interest to compute the "real" rate of interest or cost of the loan. Under RESPA, prior to closing, the lender must disclose to the borrower the APR, in addition to the quoted rate of interest that will appear in the promissory note. A primary purpose of the federal regulation is to foster competition by getting all lenders to use the same method and report the APR using the same format. Thus, borrowers receive standardized information about the cost of possible loans so that they can comparison shop.

2. *Mortgage Insurance*

Mortgage insurance protects a residential lender against risk of loss in the event a borrower defaults and the property is sold through foreclosure for a price less than the outstanding debt. Mortgage insurance should not be confused with title insurance or casualty insurance, nor should it be confused with "mortgage insurance" that pays off your loan balance if you die. The death benefit form of mortgage insurance is typically offered by a loan officer when making the loan or by an independent salesperson who obtains the borrower's name and address from the mortgage instrument when it is recorded after the loan closing. This type of mortgage insurance is really a form of term life insurance, and loan officers and other salespeople frequently receive commissions for selling it to borrowers.

Generally, lenders will require mortgage insurance for any loan that exceeds 80 percent of the appraised value of the property. Mortgage insurance is designed to protect the lender from a decline in property value. It is also a way of hedging against the inaccuracy of property appraisals when loans are made for a large percentage of their estimated value. For loans that are less than 80 percent of the appraised value of the property, lenders do not normally require mortgage insurance. The 20 percent or greater equity cushion is typically considered sufficient for purposes of protecting a lender from most reasonably predictable declines in a property's value.

There are two major forms of mortgage insurance that a real estate attorney is likely to encounter. The first is mortgage insurance offered by the public sector, including FHA (Federal Housing Administration) and VA (Department of Veterans Affairs) insurance. The FHA insures loans made to homebuyers for reasonably priced homes; there are purchase price caps for eligibility related to median home prices in an area. The FHA has specific underwriting guidelines that must be followed to qualify for its insurance program. Assuming the guidelines are followed, borrowers are generally allowed to take out a loan for as much as 95 percent of the purchase price. There are also some special government programs and variations that allow a borrower to borrow as much as 98 percent of the purchase price. The borrower pays the cost of FHA mortgage insurance at closing as a one-time fee. If the mortgage is paid off in the first several years, the borrower can usually get a predetermined percentage of the prepaid insurance fee refunded. FHA insurance is 100 percent insurance. This means that it covers the lender for the full amount of the loan. The VA plan is similar, with the program enabling veterans to obtain 100 percent financing, backed by a VA guaranty that the lender will be fully paid in the event of foreclosure. Both the FHA and VA plans enable home purchases with higher loan-to-value ratios than are generally available for conventional loans, which means that particularly high risks are covered by these plans.

The second type of insurance is *private mortgage insurance* (PMI), which lenders require for conventional loans that exceed 80 percent of the appraised value of the property. The borrower generally pays for PMI on a monthly basis at a set premium, which is added to the monthly sum for principal, interest, and escrow charges for items such as real estate taxes and casualty insurance. PMI reduces the risk to the lender and facilitates making mortgage loans available with down payments of much less than 20 percent.

Once the outstanding mortgage debt on the property falls below 80 percent of the appraised value (equity now exceeds 20 percent), the borrower has the right to have the PMI discontinued, thereby reducing the amount of the monthly check sent to the lender. PMI does not provide 100 percent insurance coverage for the lender. Typically, PMI will cover 20 to 25 percent of the value of the property. Thus, if a property should for some reason drop in value by 40 percent, the insurer covers only part of the loss, with the lender absorbing the excess. It is usually the lender's obligation first to bring legal action against a defaulting borrower and to pursue other remedies for the collection of unpaid loan amounts. After taking these measures, the lender may make a claim on the insurance for any shortfall. In some situations, however, the lender may be able to assign the matter to the insurer at various points in the process after a default. In such a situation, the insurer would take on more of the risk and cost of dealing with the borrower and the property. The specific rights and obligations of lender and insurer are contained in the insurance documents.

The ultimate consequence and value of mortgage insurance are that it expands the pool of potential homebuyers by reducing the need for substantial savings to be used as a down payment.

Problem 15A

Betty is contracting to purchase a new home. She contacts the loan officer at her local bank to inquire about a mortgage loan. Betty explains that she wants to purchase a home at a contract price of $400,000. She also explains that she will have some expenses when she hires a lawyer to help her and when she contracts for a survey. The bank officer also points out that she will have the cost of a credit check and a number of other expenses as a part of obtaining and closing on the proposed loan. The loan officer makes a good faith estimate of the total costs associated with the mortgage loan, including the information provided by Betty, to be about $4,500.

(a) Betty indicates that she is fine with the cost of the loan and asks the bank officer if she can borrow $404,500. Should the bank officer approve a loan for the full amount?

(b) The bank officer informs Betty that she will be charged 2 points on her loan. If Betty borrows $400,000, how much will the points be in dollars? If, instead, she borrows $300,000, how much will the points be in dollars?

(c) The bank officer tells Betty that he can get her a loan at 6 percent interest, but when Betty gets a disclosure form identifying the cost of her loan, it indicates that her interest APR on the loan is 6.5 percent. Betty contacts you to ask what her real interest rate is for this mortgage loan. Explain.

(d) As Betty reviews the loan closing documents, she notices that she is being charged a certain amount of money for something identified as PMI. Explain to Betty what she is paying for and why.

(e) Betty hires a lawyer to handle her loan closing and the closing of the purchase contract. She is paying her lawyer $1,500 for this service. Betty notices that the cost of her loan closing also includes a charge identified as "fee for Bank's Attorney $1,100." Betty asks you why she is being charged for the bank's lawyer, and she wonders if this is unethical. Can you explain the charge and answer the ethics question?

3. Fixed Rate Mortgage

Since the 1930s, the fixed rate mortgage (FRM) has served as the benchmark for housing finance. Still very popular today, the FRM offers a fixed rate of interest on the borrowed money that never changes over the life of the loan. Most FRMs are for a term of 30 years, but shorter-term FRMs, sometimes referred to as "quick pay" mortgages, are commonly offered for 15-year terms. Whichever loan term is used, all monthly payments are equal in amount, and each payment consists of two parts, an interest charge for the prior month and an amount applied to reduce the principal. This is called *amortization*, meaning the borrower is paying money according to a schedule to reduce the loan balance. The FRM is said to be "self-amortizing" because if the loan goes to full term, the last monthly payment will reduce the loan amount to exactly zero. Interest is "front-end loaded" in the sense that the early payments are virtually all interest with very little allocated to the reduction of principal. Each month slightly less interest is paid, with a tiny increase in principal repayment. Near the end of the loan term, most of the monthly payment goes to reduce principal rather than to pay interest. For example, consider a $200,000 fixed rate loan at 7 percent interest. On a 30-year term, the payment on such a loan will be $1,330.60 every month for the full term of the mortgage. For the first monthly payment, $1,166.67 is interest and the remaining $163.93 is principal. For the second payment, $1,165.71 is interest and $164.89 is principal. For the 360th and final payment of the 30-year term, $7.72 is interest and $1,322.88 is principal. The graph in Figure 15-1 shows the amortization of this 30-year loan.

Although this process may seem complicated, lenders use standard amortization formulas that they must make available to the borrower. Traditionally, they used amortization tables from books, but now computer software generates amortization schedules based on the original loan amount, the rate, and the length of the term. The reason that lenders front-end load a loan is simple; each month they want to be sure they collect all the interest they earn on the outstanding balance, and since the balance is large at first and gradually declines, they must take more interest out of the earlier payments. Borrowers may be dismayed that their early payments do so little to reduce their debt, but there is one upside. During the early years, the borrower gets a larger interest deduction for income tax purposes, with this tax benefit diminishing as the loan term progresses. Because of the time

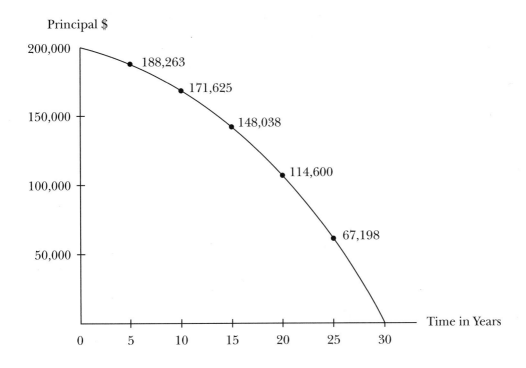

Figure 15-1
Example: Standard Amortization of 30-Year Loan

value of money, the deductions are worth more to the borrower in the early years than if they were deferred.

The borrower's selection of the length of the term involves tradeoffs. Of course, the shorter the loan term, the larger the monthly payment for the same amount borrowed. However, the shorter the term, the less the total interest paid, because the borrower has not used the lender's money for as long a period of time. The difference in total cost is dramatic. Returning to our $200,000 FRM at 7 percent, in addition to paying back the original $200,000 borrowed, the borrower will also pay $279,018 in interest over the life of the loan. In contrast, consider the cost of the same loan on a 15-year term. The monthly payment would be $1,798 and it would take 15 years to fully amortize the loan. In addition to paying back the original principal amount of the loan, the borrower will pay a total of $123,579 in interest. The 30-year term mortgage ends up costing much more than twice that of the 15-year loan. Whether the borrower qualifies for the 15-year loan typically depends on her ability to pay the additional $467 per month under the lending guidelines of 28 percent and 36 percent discussed in the first part of this chapter. If a borrower can afford the higher monthly payment and wants to pay off more quickly, the 15-year mortgage can save her over $155,000. From the lender's point of view, both loans are designed to be equally profitable. The reason for offering choices is to expand the market for loans by appealing to the investment and payment desires of different potential customers.

4. Adjustable Rate Mortgage

Adjustable rate mortgages (ARMs) are mortgages in which the interest rate changes during the term of the loan. ARMs are most popular when market interest rates are considered to be relatively high. Borrowers take ARMs during such time periods because they hope that rates will go down soon and that they will enjoy a future drop in the interest charged on the loan. If FRMs are priced very low, many people will take the opportunity to lock in to a lifetime of stable payments at what they hope will prove to be a desirably low interest rate. ARMs, in contrast, appeal to borrowers because they start with a lower interest rate than comparable FRMs. This can make them more afford-able at the outset, because the debtor's income requirements can be measured against the ARM's initial lower monthly mortgage payments. Consequently, some people use the ARM as a way to get into a property and worry about the problem of upward rate adjustments later. Lenders, however, should give some thought to a debtor's future ability to pay, because they do not want to be stuck foreclosing on the property in a year or two when the debtor is unable to pay a greatly increased mortgage bill. To evaluate any particular ARM, there are three main components to consider: the index, the adjustment period, and the caps.

Index. The *index* is the reference source used for making interest rate adjustments throughout the life of the loan. The interest rate on the outstanding principal balance will float or adjust on a regular basis in response to upward and downward movements in the index. The index must be clearly understood and expressed in the promissory note and in other loan documents. Examples of typical indexes for ARMs are: (1) the weighted average cost of funds to lending institutions as published by the federal government, (2) the Federal Housing Authority's average national mortgage rate determined from its field office reports, (3) the quoted rates for a specific category of U.S. Treasury Bills, and (4) the London Interbank Offered Rate (Libor). It is interesting that some U.S. home mortgage lenders desire the Libor rate, which as its name implies relates to European financial markets as quoted in London. Some lenders like to link part of their loan portfolio to Libor rates because they feel it gives them a bit of a hedge against what is happening in American financial markets.

For many ARMs, the adjusted interest rate includes a spread added to the current index rate. Thus, the loan documents may specify that the interest rate will be the rate for one-year U.S. Treasury Bills plus 3 percent, or the Libor rate plus 2.75 percent. Not all lenders use the same spread, and it is critical for the borrower to focus on the spread as much as the index itself. Also, the initial rate for an ARM is a fixed quote given by the lender, and it does not depend on what the index plus spread happens to be at or before loan closing. To market ARMs, most lenders quote an attractive, low interest rate that in effect functions as a "teaser" designed to lure borrowers. In other words, were the index plus spread used at closing, the initial rate might be 1¹/₂ or 2 percent higher.

Adjustment Period. In addition to selecting the index, the parties must agree on the frequency of the adjustments. Each time they refer to the index to change the mortgage interest rate, they will also need to change prospectively the borrower's monthly payments. At each change, a new amortization is made, taking account of the present principal balance, the new rate, and how many years of the term still remain.

Caps. Most ARMs have "caps" that limit how much the interest rate can move at an adjustment period. A typical cap might provide that the interest rate adjustment at the end of any adjustment period (assume 12 months) shall not exceed 2 percent in either direction no matter what happens to the index. There may also be a lifetime cap that sets the maximum limit for an interest rate adjustment during the life of the loan.

Convertibles. In the residential mortgage market, a hybrid mortgage called a *convertible* is sometimes used. This loan starts out as an ARM, but at a stated date in the future, usually after several years, it converts to a FRM at the then-prevailing FRM interest rate. Sometimes the conversion provision operates automatically, but often the borrower has the option to decide whether to invoke the conversion. The convertible mortgage can be a good choice if interest rates are high at the time the buyer takes out a home loan but rates are expected to drop in the next few years. With this conversion option, a borrower can take advantage of a drop in interest rates without all the costs associated with refinancing an existing loan. This, however, presumes that the fixed rate will be favorable at the time the conversion takes place.

BERGHAUS v. U.S. BANK
Court of Appeals of Kentucky, 2012
360 S.W.3d 779

COMBS, Judge. . . .

On December 19, 2003, [Rachel] Berghaus, a subprime borrower, signed a note for a residential mortgage loan. Decision One Mortgage Co., LLC (a subprime mortgage lender and, at that time, subsidiary of HSBC Finance Corporation) was the loan originator. The loan was one commonly identified as a 2/28 hybrid ARM (adjustable rate mortgage) since it contained both fixed and adjustable rate features. Berghaus borrowed $68,000.

According to the terms of the note, her first twenty-four monthly mortgage payments were based on a fixed rate of 7.49 percent. The amount of the remaining mortgage payments was to be adjusted every six months. The adjustments were subject to defined caps and a floor and were tied to a widely used variable index (the London Interbank Offered Rate— "LIBOR"), plus a "margin" of 7.24 percent (set by the lender). Pursuant to the note, the first rate change could not result in an interest rate exceeding 10.49 percent. And, regardless of the LIBOR index, Berghaus's interest rate would never change by more than one percentage point from the rate that she had been paying for the preceding six months. In no event was her interest rate ever to exceed 13.49 percent. Finally, the interest rate would never fall below the initial rate charged by the lender.

In addition to the note and various other closing documents, Berghaus signed a federal Truth-in-Lending disclosure statement. To secure repayment of the loan, Berghaus mortgaged her home at 51 16th Street in Newport, Kentucky.

Berghaus was advised in writing that the lender might transfer the note and mortgage. On March 1, 2004, Berghaus's note and mortgage were assigned to U.S. Bank in its capacity as trustee for the registered holders of Home Equity Asset Trust 2004-2, Home Equity Pass-Through Certificates, Series 2004-2.

In accordance with federal regulations, Berghaus was advised in writing and in advance of each of the periodic rate increases. By July 2007, Berghaus's interest rate had risen to 12.625 percent, and she could no longer afford the mortgage payments on her home.

On February 25, 2009, U.S. Bank, in its capacity as trustee, filed a foreclosure action against Berghaus. The bank alleged that Berghaus had defaulted on her obligations under the terms of the note and mortgage.

Berghaus answered the bank's complaint and denied the default. . . . Berghaus asserted a counterclaim alleging: (1) that Decision One Mortgage (the loan originator) had violated numerous provisions of the federal Truth-in-Lending Act ("TILA"), 15 U.S.C. §1601 *et seq.*; and (2) that Decision One Mortgage had "engaged in predatory lending practices and a bait and switch fraud" scheme to induce her to sign the loan documents. Based upon her assertions, Berghaus demanded statutory and punitive damages, costs, and attorney fees. She also sought release of the lien and dismissal of the foreclosure action.[2]

U.S. Bank filed a timely motion to dismiss for failure to state a claim upon which relief could be granted. On April 27, 2009, the bank filed a memorandum in support of its motion to dismiss Berghaus's counterclaims. It contended that Berghaus's TILA claims were time-barred. In the alternative, it argued that Berghaus was not entitled to relief since the bank as *an assignee*—and not the original lender subject to TILA's disclosure

---

2. Berghaus eventually disclaimed any right to rescission.

requirements — "enjoyed safe-harbor" under TILA's provisions. U.S. Bank contended that the fraud claims also must fail since Berghaus admitted that she had fully understood and consented to the loan documents at the time that she was asked to sign them.

On December 15, 2009, after hearing extensive oral arguments and after having reviewed the mortgage, note, adjustable rate rider, floor rate rider, and disclosure statement, the trial court granted the bank's motion to dismiss Berghaus's counterclaim. The court granted the motion to dismiss on the basis that U.S. Bank (again as assignee rather than the loan originator) was entitled to the protection of TILA's safe-harbor provisions. . . . This appeal followed.

The issue of safe harbor is a troubling one — both as to equity and the public policy of protecting borrowers that was supposed to be the *raison d'être* of truth in lending. We have discussed in detail whether an assignee of a loan has a duty — either direct or implied — to investigate loan application documents underlying the loans transferred to it, to discover any defects or omissions for which the assignor might have been responsible.

. . . There is no duty to investigate. An assignee under these circumstances enjoys safe harbor just as a *bona fide* purchaser for value (BFP) protected in other commercial transactions. However, while a BFP cannot claim that protection unless he is equitably entitled to do so, such is not the result in cases like the one before us now. U.S. Bank as an assignee is wholly entitled to claim safe harbor under the pertinent provisions. Berghaus has suffered a wrong for which the current state of the law lamentably provides neither remedy nor safeguard. . . .

Berghaus argues that the trial court erred by granting summary judgment in favor of the bank with respect to her counterclaims. She argues first that the court failed to fully consider her allegations that Decision One Mortgage had violated provisions of TILA by failing to disclose prior to closing the potential for an enormous increase in the interest rate on her loan and the existence of a rate floor. She contends that these omissions should have been apparent to U.S. Bank as the successor to Decision One Mortgage.

Congress enacted the Truth in Lending Act in 1968 in order to "assure a meaningful disclosure of credit terms so that the consumer will be able to compare more readily the various credit terms available to him and avoid the uninformed use of credit . . ." 15 U.S.C. §1601(a). The Act and its implementing regulation — drafted by the Federal Reserve Board of Governors and commonly known as "Regulation Z" (12 C.F.R. §226.1 *et seq.*)[3] — require *creditors* to disclose "clearly and conspicuously" (in writing and in a form that the borrower may keep) specific information pertaining to credit transactions. *See* 15 U.S.C. §§1632(a), 1635(a); 12 C.F.R. §§226.17, 226.18. If a

---

3. On July 21, 2011, TILA's general rulemaking authority was transferred to the Consumer Financial Protection Bureau pursuant to the Dodd-Frank Wall Street Reform and Consumer Protection Act. *See generally* Dodd-Frank Wall Street Reform and Protection Act, Pub. L. No. 111-203, 124 Stat. 1376 (2010).

creditor fails to make the required disclosures, the Act provides for a private right of action for statutory damages. 15 U.S.C. §1640(a)(1). In addition to damages, the borrower may also be entitled to collect costs and attorney's fees. 15 U.S.C. §1640(a)(3). Under certain limited circumstances, the borrower may even rescind the loan agreement or assert a right of set-off. *See* Beach v. Ocwen Federal Bank, 523 U.S. 410 (1998).

Berghaus was required by the Act's provisions to file her claims "within one year from the date of the occurrence of the violation . . ." 15 U.S.C. §1640(e). Where an alleged TILA violation is based upon insufficient disclosure, the limitation period generally begins as of the date of consummation of the transaction. Berghaus's loan agreement was consummated on December 19, 2003. She filed her counterclaim against U.S. Bank on April 1, 2009. Berghaus has not identified any facts that would serve to extend the ordinary limitations period in this case. Consequently, her claim for money damages, costs, and attorney fees is time-barred. U.S. Bank was clearly entitled to summary judgment with respect to this claim.

Her second contention is that the trial court erred in its determining that U.S. Bank could not be found liable for the common-law fraud allegedly perpetrated by Decision One prior to closing and by concluding that the bank was entitled to summary judgment with respect to this claim as well.

In her brief, Berghaus explains that although she originally applied for a 7.5 percent fixed-rate loan, Decision One fraudulently offered her the 2/28 hybrid ARM loan at closing. The trial court concluded that Berghaus's fraud claim was directly undermined by her own representations since she indicated that she understood before closing that her loan had a variable-rate provision and that it was not the traditional fixed-rate loan for which she had hoped to qualify.

However, Berghaus has not explained how U.S. Bank could be found liable for fraud. She has not alleged that U.S. Bank was involved in her loan transaction in any way. U.S. Bank acts as trustee for Home Equity Asset Trust 2004-2, which is the mortgage-backed securities trust pool that includes Berghaus's loan. Decision One originated Berghaus's loan in December 2003; the trust acquired the mortgage in March 2004. There is no indication whatsoever that U.S. Bank was directly involved with her transaction. Additionally, there is no suggestion that U.S. Bank acquired the note in any manner inconsistent with the exercise of good faith and due diligence. Thus, the trial court did not err by concluding that there was no genuine issue as to any material fact and that U.S. Bank was entitled to judgment as a matter of law as to this claim. . . .

Finally, Berghaus contends that the trial court erred by granting the bank's motion for summary judgment (based upon her default) and an order of sale.

While TILA claims asserted against a lender or assignee must be brought within one year of the violation, a consumer may raise violations of the Act as a defense to a debt-collection action even after the expiration of the period. 15 U.S.C. §1640(e). If a borrower asserts claims defensively, the TILA one-year statute of limitations does not apply. On appeal, we must determine whether the trial court erred by deciding that Berghaus's defense against U.S. Bank's action against her was unavailing.

Most important in our analysis of this issue is the fact that TILA's specific disclosure requirements apply *only to the initial lender* and not to a party to whom the creditor's rights are later assigned. The Act specifically provides that the "creditor," who has the duty to disclose, is limited to the person or entity "to whom the debt arising from the consumer credit transaction is initially payable on the face of the evidence of indebtedness. . . ." 15 U.S.C. §1602(g).

Under the provisions of the Act, a lender's assignee is ordinarily entitled to safe harbor and may be subject to liability only under a very narrow set of circumstances. The assignee can be held liable only for violations of the Act that are "apparent on the face of the disclosure statement . . ." 15 U.S.C. §1641(a), (e)(1)(A). A violation is apparent on the face of the disclosure statement only where "the disclosure can be determined to be incomplete or inaccurate by a comparison among the disclosure statement, any itemization of the amount financed, the note, or any other disclosure of disbursement" or if "the disclosure statement does not use the terms or format required to be used . . ." 15 U.S.C. §1641(e)(2)(A)-(B).

Berghaus does not contend that Decision One's disclosure statement failed to use the required terms or format. However, she does contend that Decision One violated TILA's disclosure requirements and that these violations were apparent on the face of the disclosure statement that was provided for inspection to its assignee, U.S. Bank. She contends that neither the potential for an enormous rate increase nor the existence of a rate floor was properly disclosed before the transaction was consummated. We disagree with this assertion.

Before Congress enacted the Mortgage Disclosure Improvement Act of 2008 (the MDIA), TILA, as implemented by Regulation Z, required creditors to disclose specific information relevant to a closed-end credit transaction. Creditors were routinely required to disclose with particularity: the identity of the creditor; the annual percentage rate (commonly referred to as "APR," a term of art that adds into the interest costs of a home loan various other charges, including the costs of private mortgage insurance and bank processing fees); the amount financed; the finance charge; the sum total of all payments; the number, amount, and due dates or period of payments scheduled to repay the total of payments; the nature of any late charges; notice that a security interest will be retained in the property purchased as part of the transaction; notice that credit life, accident, health or loss of income insurance is not required in connection with the loan; and the creditor's policy on loan assumption. 12 C.F.R. §226.18.

Special disclosures were triggered with respect to a loan on a borrower's primary residence. If the APR might increase in a transaction that was secured by the borrower's *principal dwelling* (with a term of more than one year), additional disclosures were required — namely, (1) the fact that the transaction contained a variable-rate feature and (2) a statement that specific variable-rate disclosures had been provided to the borrower at an earlier date. 12 C.F.R. §226.19(b). Additionally, the APR had to reflect a composite annual percentage rate that was based on the *initial* rate for as long as it was charged. For the remainder of the term, the APR had to reflect the rate that would have been applied using the index or formula in effect at the time of consummation. Some time in advance of the closing date,[5] disclosures had to be made explaining exactly how the interest rate and payment would be adjusted in connection with variable-rate transactions secured by the borrower's principal dwelling. *See* 12 C.F.R. §§226.19(b), 226.20(c). Finally, where the loan was secured by the borrower's residence, the creditor had to give the borrower good-faith estimates of the disclosures no later than 3 days after the lender's receipt of the credit application. 15 U.S.C. §1638(b)(1), (b)(2)(A).

The disclosure statement that Berghaus signed at closing was based upon a model form approved by the Federal Reserve Board. It indicated that Berghaus's lender was Decision One Mortgage and that her loan's APR was 8.6409 percent. It provided the total finance charge — the dollar amount that she could be expected to pay for the credit — and the total amount financed. It also provided the sum of these figures — the sum total of all her projected payments. The statement advised that the loan had a variable-rate feature and included a schedule of payments based on the initial interest rate (24 payments) and a subsequent interest rate increase (336 payments) based upon the LIBOR index as of the date of closing. As scheduled, the payments fully amortized the amount owed and complied with required payment disclosures. The disclosure also properly reflected Berghaus's acknowledgement that she had been provided the required variable-rate disclosures at an earlier date. The disclosure clearly advised Berghaus that a security interest in her home would be retained by the lender and that a subsequent purchaser of the property could not assume the remainder of the mortgage on its original terms. It provided relevant information with respect to the types of insurance that were and were not required by the loan, and it described the nature of the late charges that could be assessed on overdue payments. Finally, the disclosure indicated that the loan agreement included a prepayment penalty. Neither party disputes the contents or authenticity of the disclosure statement.

The existence of the loan's interest-rate floor and variable-rate feature were fully disclosed to Berghaus prior to consummation, and the disclosure statement appears on its face to comply with the TILA requirements as they existed before enactment of the MDIA. However, Berghaus suggests in her

---

5. Specifically, "at the time an application form is provided or before the consumer pays a non-refundable fee, whichever is earlier . . ." 12 C.F.R. §226.19(b).

brief that the information provided to her in the disclosure statement did not conform to information that was originally given to her by way of a good-faith estimate provided by Decision One. That alleged discrepancy would not have been apparent on the face of the disclosure statement. In order to become aware of the alleged discrepancy, U.S. Bank would have had to undertake an investigation of facts beyond what Congress required of assignees. Accordingly, U.S. Bank could bear no liability for this alleged violation, and Berghaus cannot assert it as a viable defense. The trial court did not err in so concluding. . . .

To summarize, we affirm the trial court's summary judgment in favor of U.S. Bank with respect to Berghaus's counterclaims. . . .

5. *No-Point Mortgage and Buy-Down Mortgage*

The no-point mortgage and the buy-down mortgage work in similar ways. Each of them can be offered with just about any form of mortgage. With the no-point mortgage, the borrower gets the loan at the stated interest rate without being charged any points at the closing. The buy-down loan involves an offer to provide financing at a below-market rate of interest. The central concept for both vehicles is that the borrower is offered a choice, but the choice is not free; the choice presented merely rearranges the manner in which the lender receives its profit.

As a marketing gimmick, the tradeoff between points and the mortgage interest rate can be effective. Some borrowers will lack cash and will choose a higher rate of interest rather than pay points. Others will be told that under the 28 percent and 36 percent rules they do not qualify for a loan at a particular rate, but if they have cash to pay points they can qualify for and obtain a loan with a lower rate of interest and a lower monthly payment. Those more fortunate borrowers who have both sufficient savings to pay lots of points and enough income to choose the option of a no-point mortgage will not all attach the same utility to the choices. Some borrowers will want to pay points with cash and then enjoy the prospect of a lower monthly payment. Other borrowers will not want to take money out of savings, and they will accept the higher monthly payments as they go along. Some borrowers in this group may also be seeking to borrow the maximum amount permitted, perhaps at a 95 percent loan-to-value ratio, and paying points at closing would in effect reduce the amount of money that they are really borrowing.

In selecting a tradeoff between interest rate and points, the borrower's expectations about how long she will own the property is an important consideration. A no-point or very low point mortgage benefits people who sell within a short period of time, such as four or five years. This is because of the way the mortgage is structured. The lender's calculation of the tradeoff between points and the interest rate is not based on the mortgage going to full term, but is based on a much shorter payback time. For a mortgage that bears several points, it takes about four to five years for the borrower to recover the value of the points in the form of lower monthly payments. With a no-point mortgage that stays in place beyond four or five years, the higher monthly payments will soon surpass the value of the points that were saved. Consequently, a no-point mortgage with a higher interest rate is often cheaper for a buyer who expects to be in the home for only a couple of years. Conversely, for a buyer expecting to stay longer than five years, it is generally cheaper to pay points and get a lower interest rate.

The buy-down mortgage requires that a fee be paid to a lender in exchange for offering a mortgage loan at a below-market rate of interest. Like the no-point mortgage, it reflects a tradeoff of interest rate and upfront payments. This fee can consist of a high number of points charged for a specific loan interest rate, or it can be packaged in a less visible way. The basic idea, however, is that this loan is called a buy-down mortgage precisely because a price has to be paid to obtain (buy) the lower rate of interest.

6. Balloon Mortgage

The balloon mortgage features regular monthly payments but has a much larger final payment due at the end of the term. Typically, the lender uses a long-term amortization schedule to calculate monthly payments but specifies a maturity date that is much sooner. The balloon loan, therefore, is not self-amortizing. The borrower has promised to make a big cash payment at the specified maturity date, which is called the *balloon payment*. This mortgage got its name from the image of someone blowing up a balloon. If the borrower cannot come up with the cash to make the payment, arrange for new financing, or sell the property, the entire transaction might "explode" against the borrower, who could lose the property through foreclosure.

Balloon mortgages are used for several reasons. Sometimes they are used as *bridge loans* for borrowers who want short-term financing pending the funding of a long-term loan. In the residential setting, bridge loans are commonly used to finance a home purchase when the borrower is trying to sell her old home but has not yet succeeded. As a buyer, she may not qualify for a standard mortgage loan while she still has the outstanding debt on the old home. As a way of getting the new home now, such a buyer might seek a short-term bridge loan to cover her for six months or a year pending the sale and payoff of the loan on the first house.

Second, the balloon loan is popular when current market interest rates are very high. The borrower gets this short-term mortgage in the hope that the market will dramatically drop by the time the balloon payment comes due. Third, home sellers who agree to help finance their buyers frequently offer balloon mortgages. This often happens when market interest rates are high and sellers are finding it hard to sell their homes. In such a setting, the seller usually does not want to wait 20 or 30 years to be paid in full. The parties agree to a balloon loan so the buyer can get into the house, with everyone hoping that the market will change before the term expires.

7. Other Mortgages

In addition to the mortgages already mentioned, there are several others that one might encounter. Under a *level payment adjustable rate mortgage* (LPARM), the interest rate is adjusted throughout the life of the loan but the monthly payment remains the same. It is a loan in which the borrower wants the stability of a known monthly payment, and the lender wants to shift the risk of rising interest rates to the borrower. As to the adjustment features of this mortgage, one must consider the same components discussed earlier for all ARMs. The difference with the LPARM is that, because of the commitment to level payments, the loan cannot be neatly amortized to zero over a fixed term of years. Instead, one of two things must happen: either the loan term is lengthened or shortened, or a balloon payment will be due at maturity. To the extent that the loan is not self-amortizing and the underlying debt increases, this is a loan with *negative amortization.*

The *shared appreciation mortgage* (SAM) is one in which a lender gives a borrower a favorable interest rate on a loan in exchange for a percentage interest in the equity appreciation of the property. A lender might, for example, take a 30 percent interest in the equity appreciation of the property, to be determined by appraisal and payable at some fixed point in time, such as at the earlier of when the mortgage is repaid or 10 years. A lender would make such a deal only if it expects property values to rise. If the equity payment is due when the borrower sells, then it can be subtracted from the seller's cash proceeds. If the amount is due when no sale has taken place, then the borrower must either come up with cash or refinance the equity component. The obvious difficulty with a SAM is that the borrower and the lender may disagree about the fair market value of the home. Thus, there has to be a clearly described process for fixing the value. There is also a potential problem when an owner makes improvements to the property after the loan is made. Will it be possible, for instance, to separate out the equity appreciation in the original property value as opposed to the appreciation attributable to the later improvements? From a tax perspective, will the amount paid as an equity appreciation fee be treated as interest? If so, when and how might it be deductible? Finally, is the lender a joint owner of the property for purposes of any contract, tort, or environmental liability that might arise in the future? One can readily see that although the SAM offers a borrower a way to get a mortgage at a below-market rate by giving the lender the promise of future money, it does raise many potential points of conflict between borrower and lender.

The *reverse annuity mortgage* (RAM) is a mortgage marketed to senior citizens who own their homes as a major source of wealth subject to little or no mortgage debt. For this group of elderly people, the RAM is designed as a way to provide a supplement to their retirement income while allowing them to remain in their homes. The concept behind the RAM is to pay the home-owner the value of her home over time with monthly annuity payments. The RAM reverses the typical mortgage structure. Instead of a borrower making monthly payments to the lender until the loan is paid in full, the RAM has the lender make payments to the debtor until the limit of a pre-established credit line is reached. The credit line is typically around 75 to 80 percent of the equity value of the home. The annuity may be either for the remainder of the borrower's lifetime or for a fixed term, such as 15 years. If a lifetime annuity is used, the size of the monthly payment to the homeowner is based on actuarial tables of life expectancy. The lender expects to be paid in full at the end of the process, which for a lifetime annuity occurs at the owner's death or, if sooner, the sale of the property by the owner. If a fixed term annuity is used, obvious problems arise when the owner lives long beyond the specified period. At that point, she will no longer get the annuity pay-ments that she grew accustomed to, and the lender will have its investment return delayed, and thus diminished, unless the loan documents call for payment of the debt at a stated time even if the debtor is still alive.

There are the *growing equity mortgage* (GEM) and the *graduated payment mortgage* (GPM), both of which work in a similar manner. Each offers an affordable monthly payment during the first few years but then makes up for this by dramatically increasing the monthly payments by steps in succeed-ing years in accordance with a prescribed formula (not an index). The idea behind these mortgages is that a person with the expectation of a rapidly rising income can get into a home now and make up the difference later as her income rises. Under the GEM there is also a pitch for "forced savings" as one's bigger monthly payments in succeeding years result in a quicker mortgage payoff, consequently enhancing the owner's equity value in the home.

There are also variations in loans known as *stretch mortgages.* These loans basically couple an adjustable interest rate with *an adjustable term* that can be stretched to extend payment for *a longer number of years* than the original term. In this way, the borrower deals with the same payments of a constant amount but can have adjustments made to the number of payments that will be required to pay off the loan. For some borrowers with fixed or limited income potential, this is a better alternative for getting a cheap loan than an adjustable rate mortgage, where monthly payments may go up dramatically from year to year.

The *price level adjusted mortgage* (PLAM) is generally more often talked about in textbooks than used in real life. The basic concept of the PLAM is that it seeks to adjust the value of the outstanding debt to account for infla-tion. Advocates of the PLAM focus on the fact that lenders fear that when they lend money today, inflation may make it less valuable when paid back. If, for example, I borrow $100 from you today and pay you back at the end of the year when there has been 10 percent inflation, I am really paying back the equivalent of only $90. The problem becomes worse in countries where annual inflation rates of 50 percent, 100 percent, or more are not without precedent. To avoid the risk of losing their profit as well as their principal, under these circumstances lenders will charge very high interest rates, which may make borrowing unaffordable to most people. The PLAM seeks to remove the risk of inflation from the setting of mortgage rates so that interest rates will reflect the actual cost of money, which is generally estimated to be as low as 3 percent.

The *interest-only mortgage.* As the name implies, this mortgage requires the borrower to pay interest only each month during the term of the loan. At the end of the term, or when the property is sold and the mortgage paid off, the borrower must pay back the entire principal plus any accumulated negative amortization that may be applicable under the terms of the mortgage. Some residential variations allow for interest only payments for a stated number of years; such as for 3 to 10 years. At the end of the interest only term, monthly payments increase substantially to cover full payments of interest and principal, and to make up for the early years of no repayment of principal. This can be a popular mortgage option in very high-cost areas with expected high rates of future equity appreciation. The borrower gets the property with a monthly payment within her reach and hopes that equity appreciation will be significant enough to generate a return at the end of the loan.

Piggyback mortgage loans are an alternative used in a few situations to get around PMI (private mortgage insurance). The piggyback loan involves making an 80 percent mortgage loan available to a borrower who really needs to borrow more than that amount to get in the home. The 80 percent loan is made not requiring PMI, and simultaneously a home equity loan is funded for an additional amount needed by the borrower: 10-20 percent. The piggyback mortgage can furnish 100 percent financing even though it is made to look as if the borrower made a 20 percent down payment. Such loans are coming under regulatory scrutiny, and they may be re-characterized as impermissible "loan splitting" arrangements if used to avoid required disclosures for certain "high cost" loans or if used to obscure the actual cost of credit to the consumer.

Problem 15B

Bill is a retired postal worker living on a fixed income in New York City. He has been a renter all of his life and now plans to retire to Arizona and buy a small house. Bill inquires at the bank about getting a mortgage loan to finance the purchase of a home that he found. The loan officer informs Bill that they have a number of loan options available. The loan officer indicates a number of the choices and asks Bill which of these he might prefer. Bill turns to you for some guidance. Can you explain to Bill some of the possible benefits and detriments for each of the following loans?

(a) A 5-year balloon mortgage at zero points, with interest-only payments for the entire 5-year term

(b) A level payment adjustable rate mortgage at 2 percent interest for a 30-year term

(c) A reverse annuity mortgage

(d) A 20-year fixed rate mortgage at 5 percent or a 20-year adjustable rate mortgage starting at 4 percent with no caps

(e) Bill is also presented with some tradeoffs and does not understand what the bank is doing. The bank offers a 20-year fixed rate mortgage at 6 percent and no points, at 5½ percent and 1 point, and at 5 percent and 1.25 points. Bill is unsure of what he is being asked to consider and how it is that the same loan can be made at all these different interest rates. Can you help him to understand?

C. MORTGAGE FINANCING AND THE CONTRACT OF PURCHASE

The contract of purchase must anticipate the prospect that the buyer will seek to obtain mortgage financing. It is of critical importance that the contract provide a structure for the financing by specifying who will take what steps to obtain financing and detailing the parties' obligations and rights throughout the process. Figure 15-2 depicts the standard residential home purchase transaction, with both seller and buyer having mortgage obligations with lenders.

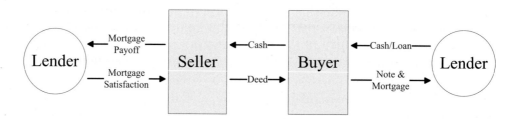

Figure 15-2
The Standard Sales Transaction with Mortgage Financing

In the standard transaction, the seller contracts to sell and convey the property to the buyer by some form of *deed*, and buyer agrees to pay a purchase price. Typically, the buyer does not have enough funds to pay "all cash," so the buyer makes a *down payment* and borrows the rest from a lender. In return, the borrower executes a *promissory note* in favor of the lender promising to repay the loan amount and a *mortgage* granting the lender a lien on the property. In a typical transaction, the seller has an outstanding loan against the property dating from the seller's earlier purchase or refinancing.

The seller takes the cash proceeds at the closing of the contract and uses these funds to pay off its lender on its outstanding loan balance. In return, the seller's lender will acknowledge payment of seller's obligation and execute a *satisfaction of mortgage* to relinquish its lien. If the price exceeds the loan pay-off amount, the excess is cash paid to the seller.

WALSH v. CATALANO
Supreme Court of New York, Appellate Division, Second Department, 2015
12 N.Y.S.3d 226

PER CURIAM. The plaintiffs [Emily Walsh and Jonathan Marks] entered into a contract to purchase real property from the defendant Linda Catalano (hereinafter the seller), pursuant to which the plaintiffs made a down payment of $45,500. The plaintiffs' obligations under the contract were contingent upon the issuance of a commitment from an institutional lender. The contract of sale provided that in the event that a commitment could not be obtained, the plaintiffs were entitled to the return of the down payment.

The plaintiffs subsequently received two separate commitments from an institutional lender, but these commitments were contingent upon a satisfactory appraisal of the subject real property. Before the conditions of these commitments could be satisfied, Hurricane Sandy struck the area and caused damage to the subject property. The institutional lender subsequently denied the plaintiffs' application for a mortgage loan based upon a post-storm appraisal that showed that the value of the property was not sufficient to secure the proposed loan amount.

The plaintiffs commenced this action to recover their down payment. They moved for summary judgment on the complaint, arguing that they were entitled to the return of the down payment since they never received a firm commitment from an institutional lender. They also argued that [the Uniform Vendor Purchaser Risk Act] required the seller to return the down payment to them, since that statute provides, in relevant part, that "if all or a material part" of the subject real property "is destroyed without fault of the purchaser . . . the vendor cannot enforce the contract, and the purchaser is entitled to recover any portion of the price that he [or she] has paid." General Obligations Law §5-1311(1)(a)(1). The Supreme Court denied the plaintiffs' motion. We reverse.

"For more than a century it has been well settled in this State that a vendee who defaults on a real estate contract without lawful excuse, cannot recover the down payment." Maxton Bldrs. v. Lo Galbo, 502 N.E.2d 184, 186 (1986). Where, however, the obligations of a purchaser under a contract of sale are contingent upon the issuance of a firm financing commitment by a lender, a purchaser may be entitled to recover the down payment if he or she was unable to secure a firm commitment in accordance with the terms of the contract.

Here, the contract of sale was conditioned upon the issuance of a written commitment from an institutional lender. The contract of sale expressly provided that "a commitment conditioned on the Institutional Lender's approval of an appraisal shall not be deemed a 'Commitment' hereunder until an appraisal is approved." Accordingly, the plaintiffs established their prima facie entitlement to judgment as a matter of law by demonstrating that they were unable to secure a firm commitment in accordance with the contract of sale, and that they were entitled to the return of their down payment pursuant to the terms of the contract. In addition, the plaintiffs demonstrated, prima facie, that they were entitled to a return of their down payment by virtue of General Obligations Law §5-1311, since a "material part" of the property was destroyed by Hurricane Sandy before legal title or possession of the property could be transferred. . . .

Accordingly, the Supreme Court should have granted the plaintiffs' motion for summary judgment on the complaint.

MALUS v. HAGER
Superior Court of New Jersey, Appellate Division, 1998
712 A.2d 238, cert. denied, 719 A.2d 642

WEFING, Judge. Defendants Kenneth and Jean Hager appeal from the trial court's grant of summary judgment in favor of plaintiffs Richard and Rosemarie Malus. We reverse.

The parties executed a contract dated March 3, 1996 under which plaintiffs agreed to purchase the Hagers' home in Tinton Falls, New Jersey for $140,000. Their contract contained a clause for attorney review; both parties were represented by counsel. Plaintiffs paid a deposit of $7,000, held in the trust account of Hagers' attorney. Paragraph C (iii) of the contract reads in pertinent part:

IF PERFORMANCE BY BUYER IS CONTINGENT UPON OBTAINING A MORTGAGE. The Buyer agrees to apply immediately for a mortgage loan. . . . The amount of the mortgage loan required by the Buyer is $133,000 and will be what is commonly known as the (Conventional) 30 year direct reduction plan with interest at no more than PREV percent[prevailing rate]. . . . IF THE BUYER FAILS TO OBTAIN SUCH MORTGAGE COMMITMENT OR FAILS TO WAIVE THIS CONTINGENCY BEFORE 45 Days after attny Review (DATE), THE BUYER OR SELLER MAY VOID THIS CONTRACT BY NOTIFYING THE OTHER PARTY WITHIN TEN (10) CALENDAR DAYS OF THE EXPIRATION OF THE AFOREMENTIONED DATE. . . . IF THE BUYER OR THE SELLER DOES NOT SO NOTIFY THE OTHER PARTY WITHIN THIS SPECIFIED TIME PERIOD, THE BUYER AND SELLER WAIVE THEIR RIGHTS UNDER THIS SECTION TO VOID THE CONTRACT.

Paragraph 25 of the contract provides in pertinent part:

FAILURE OF BUYER OR SELLER TO SETTLE:

In the event the Seller willfully fails to Close in accordance with this Contract, the Buyer may commence any legal or equitable action to which the Buyer may be entitled. In the event the Buyer fails to Close in accordance with this Contract, the payments made on account, at the Seller's option, shall be paid to the Seller as liquidated damages, or the Seller may commence any legal or equitable action to which the Seller is entitled, applying to such action the monies paid by the Buyer on account of the purchase price. Liquidated damages means the Seller will keep the money paid on account and not commence any legal action for the Buyer's failure to Close. . . .

Plaintiffs applied for a mortgage loan in accordance with paragraph C(iii) and, within the forty-five day period, obtained a commitment from Chase Manhattan bank for a mortgage loan.

The closing was scheduled to take place on July 15, 1996. On July 11, 1996, plaintiff Richard Malus was terminated, not for cause, from his employment. On July 12, 1996, defendants, unaware of this development and expecting the closing to take place on July 15, moved out of the home at Tinton Falls and placed certain of their belongings in storage until they were able to complete their own relocation.

Under the terms of Chase Manhattan's mortgage commitment, it retained the right to cancel the commitment letter "[i]f prior to funding, your financial condition or employment status adversely changes. . . ." In light of Mr. Malus's loss of employment, Chase exercised its rights under that reservation and declined to fund the mortgage.

Mr. and Mrs. Malus sought return of their $7,000 deposit. When Mr. and Mrs. Hager declined, this lawsuit resulted.

The trial court granted summary judgment to the plaintiffs on the basis of Northeast Custom Homes, Inc. v. Howell, 553 A.2d 387 (N.J. Super. Ct. Law Div. 1988). Plaintiff in that case was a custom builder and it prepared a contract defendants executed on January 24, 1987 for the purchase of a home then under construction for $857,486. Defendants were not informed of a right to have the contract reviewed by an attorney but were, after the contract was executed, referred to an attorney to assist in preparation for the closing. Defendants gave a deposit of $85,748. The contract stated it was "contingent upon buyer obtaining a conventional mortgage . . . within 45 days. . . ." Defendants obtained a timely mortgage commitment but Mr. Howell was terminated from his job approximately two weeks after the commitment was issued. His employer had advanced the deposit money and demanded its repayment. The lender then withdrew its commitment, based upon the change in his employment status. Northeast later sold the property for $835,000, a loss slightly in excess of $20,000. The parties commenced litigation over entitlement to the $85,748 deposit the Howells had previously made. The trial court in that case concluded that the Howells were entitled to the return of the deposit. In doing so, it construed "the mortgage contingency clause to mean that not only the mortgage commitment but also the availability at closing of the mortgage proceeds together constitute the condition precedent to the purchasers' obligation to perform." *Id.* at 391.

We disagree with that construction for its result is to place the parties in an intolerable state of limbo until the closing is finally consummated. Contracts such as these set firm deadlines for the occurrence of specified events in order that the parties are able to plan and to act with confidence that after a certain point there is an enforceable agreement. Confusion and uncertainty can only result from extending, as a matter of law, the mortgage contingency clause to the date of closing.

... We note that in this case, although the Hagers were later able to resell their home at the same contract price, that closing did not occur until approximately four months after the initial, scheduled date. The Hagers were responsible for the mortgage, taxes and maintenance on the premises in the interim and also incurred additional moving and storage fees.

If the parties wish to provide in their contract for an eventuality such as this, they are free to do so. We decline, however, to impose the risk of an otherwise firm deal unravelling upon an unknowing and blameless seller, leaving him with no ability to recoup his increased expenses.

We are satisfied that the matter is controlled by Paragraph 25 of the parties' contract. The Maluses having failed to close on this transaction, the Hagers were entitled to retain the deposit.

The judgment of June 4, 1997 is reversed and the matter is remanded for entry of judgment in favor of defendants.

D. PRIMARY AND SECONDARY MORTGAGE MARKETS

Now that we have a good idea of the types of products and some of the key terminology related to mortgages, it is time to explore the mortgage markets that function within the broader financial marketplace. In this section, we first discuss the primary mortgage market and then move on to the secondary mortgage market. The basic idea is that the primary market involves *loan originations* (homebuyers borrow money from lenders) whereas the secondary market involves *securitization* (lenders subsequently sell loans to investors).

1. Primary Mortgage Market

The *primary mortgage market* comprises four general segments or sectors: (1) saving by households and others, (2) lending by organizations and institutions, (3) borrowing by households and others, and (4) selling mortgages and notes through the secondary market. In this section, we focus on the relationship among these segments, particularly the first three segments, which constitute the primary mortgage market. The primary mortgage market is the market for originating loans with individual borrowers. A more complete discussion of segment four, the secondary mortgage market, is taken up in the next section of this chapter. Understanding the basic market relationships is essential to a real estate and mortgage law practice. Figure 15-3 illustrates the relationships among these market segments and also refers to alternative capital markets, which are explained in the following text.

In Figure 15-3, the intermediaries are the financial institutions and lenders that make funds available for real estate activities. These intermediaries generally include banks, savings and loans, mortgage companies, insurance companies, and pension funds. Each of these intermediaries takes in assets from savers. Banks and financial institutions use deposit accounts, certificates of deposit, and other investment vehicles to attract savings and investment assets. Having attracted these assets, the intermediaries look for ways to profit from their holding of the resources, and one way they do this is by making loans to real estate borrowers. These loans are seen as investments because they will be paid back with an interest return. Thus, the intermediary is a market facilitator who takes in large sums of money that are then used for lending purposes. This is an important and cost-effective way of putting savers and borrowers together.

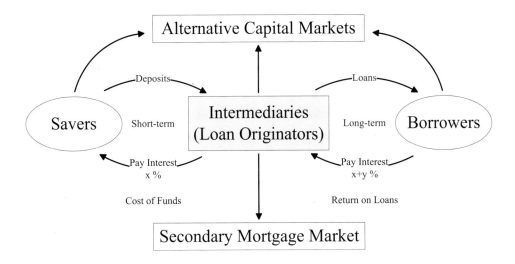

Figure 15-3
Primary Mortgage Market

Savers are looking at a variety of ways in which they can save money and earn a return on their investment. They may consider deposits to checking, savings, or money market accounts. They may look at certificates of deposit, commercial paper, time instruments, stocks, bonds, whole life insurance, or special retirement accounts. In each instance, the saver is considering the return that will be provided for saving in a particular investment form. Some forms of saving will be more risky than others, such as the difference between an insured bank deposit account and a stock investment in a start-up technology company. The saver will compare risk and return between these options and make a selection knowing that the greatest returns are likely to be found in the riskiest investments.

The main point here, however, is that savings fluctuate over the short run, and the ability to attract savers rests on a need continually to offer competitive returns to the people who invest. Cost of funds to intermediaries, therefore, are short-term market–sensitive.

Borrowers in our diagram include property buyers, including homebuyers and real estate developers. Although there are many other types of borrowing in our economy, we are concerned with borrowing directed at real estate activities.

Unlike savings, the lending side of our diagram is usually a long-term activity. For example, people deposit and spend their paychecks weekly or monthly, but they borrow for 3 to 5 years to purchase an automobile or for 15 to 30 years when they borrow to buy a home. This means that with respect to real estate activities, the intermediaries have a time horizon imbalance, because their cost of funds is affected by short-term swings in the market, while their returns are structured to long-term obligations. The lending side of the equation for a lender involves not only risk of default by the borrower, but also long-term uncertainty about inflation and money markets. Pegging the interest rate on a long-term fixed rate loan can be difficult, and if the lender sets the rate too low at the outset, it may end up losing a lot of money.

2. Secondary Mortgage Market

The *secondary mortgage market* developed because lenders look at mortgage financing as investments. Collectively, the promissory note and mortgage represent two different things. The note represents a right in the lender to collect payments over time (cash flow), and the mortgage represents a right in the lender to take the property if the borrower fails to pay the note. The secondary mortgage market focuses less on the mortgage aspects of the transaction and more on the cash flow represented by the note. When multiple notes that represent numerous cash flows are bundled together, they support the issuance of an investment instrument resting upon the projected cash flow. These investment instruments are mortgage-related *collateralized debt obligations* (CDOs) (also known as mortgage-backed securities) and are issued and sold to investors. If this is done properly, the investor in a security simply evaluates the security instrument without having to look into the underlying real estate transactions in which the individual mortgage loans were originated. In practice, investors rely on companies that specialize in rating securities to signal the risk associated with an investment. Thus, a ratings company might give a very low-risk CDO a rating of AAA, indicating that the investment is very secure. A medium-risk CDO might earn a rating of A or BBB, indicating its higher risk. A high-risk CDO (perhaps based on a lot of subprime mortgages) might not be rated at all or be given a very low rating. Based on the rating assigned to a security offering, investors are able to price the CDO relative to the perceived risk. A higher-risk CDO would be expected, for example, to provide the potential for a greater rate of return than a low-risk CDO would.

A problem in the financial collapse that began in 2007 was that the rating agencies were not doing a proper job of investigating the information behind the various CDOs that were being issued, and thus not providing high-quality information to potential investors. In addition, rating agencies were being paid to rate the CDOs by the people issuing the CDOs, and better ratings (low-risk ratings) resulted in higher payments to the agencies by the issuers of the CDOs. Consequently, there was an incentive not to look too closely at the information behind the CDO. The failure of good information and the mistaken belief that the value of the underlying real estate would continue to rise and support riskier credit resulted in a lot of poor and mispriced investments. When information became more transparent and real estate prices fell, the value of the CDOs dropped, and credit became less available. The declining ability to obtain credit slowed down further house sales, and this resulted in an economic slowdown. As the economy weakened and housing values dropped, more and more people realized that they were upside-down on their mortgages, and they either were unable to continue payments or simply decided not to continue payments on mortgages that exceeded the value of their homes. This compounded the economic problem by putting more houses on the market, via foreclosure sales, and reducing demand. Prices continued to drop, and credit remained tight.

The secondary mortgage market was originally developed as a vehicle for reducing lender risk while enhancing liquidity. The secondary mortgage market created an easy way in which lenders could diversify their investment portfolios by making it easy for a New York lender to buy California mortgages or securities backed by such mortgages, and for the California lender to act likewise in buying loans from east coast lenders. In today's marketplace, lenders do this in a rather indirect way by purchasing CDOs backed by mortgages originated in different parts of the country. In this way lenders become better able to smooth out their profit expectation by creating investment "baskets" with "eggs" gathered from many different markets. It facilitates commercial activity by moving money resources to the markets that need it most.

The use of CDOs in the form of mortgage-backed and mortgage-related securities also makes a lender's portfolio more liquid because these securities are in a form that can be readily sold and resold in an open market. Liquidity is facilitated by bundling large pools of mortgages together and then "slicing" the cash flow represented by those bundles into investment opportunities of varying risk. This process is identified as creating *investment tranches*. The various tranches, or slices, are a method of sorting risk associated with the individual loans in the pool. Different tranches support investment opportunities (securities) bearing different degrees of risk. Investors can then invest in a high-risk or low-risk element of the pool by investing in a security issued against a certain tranche. The different risks would be priced accordingly, and thus create more investment opportunities, capable of satisfying varied investment preferences in the market. In the typical situation a secondary market intermediary would buy pools of mortgages and bundle them into CDOs. The CDOs are issued in tranches of low risk, medium risk, and high risk. As cash flow comes in on the underlying mortgages, it is paid first with respect to the low-risk tranche, then to the medium-risk tranche, and finally to the high-risk tranche. To the extent that mortgage payments dry up (people default and do not pay), cash flow is diminished, and the reduction in cash flow is first attributed to the highest-risk tranche. Thus, the high-risk tranche is the first tranche to experience losses in the event of reduced cash flow, and the low-risk tranche is the last one to get reduced as class flow diminishes from such events as defaults.

A second consequence of the secondary mortgage market has been added uniformity of mortgage forms and law among the various states. The need to standardize mortgages for ease of investment opportunity has simplified the practice of residential real estate law and in some ways has helped make the real estate market move in the direction of other commercial markets. The reduced complexity opens the door to more transactions at lower costs and creates ownership and investment opportunities for an expanding number of individuals and groups. It also reduces the need for special expertise in residential real estate and mortgage law, facilitating the shift of work away from lawyers to nonlawyers.

The third consequence of the secondary mortgage market is that it has changed the structure of lending activity. Most lenders now sell the majority of their loans to investors in the secondary mortgage market. This, in turn, has several implications. First, the lenders must view their secondary mortgage market investors as their key customer base. Thus, they must make their mortgage terms and options respond to what investors would like to buy rather than to the needs or desires of particular local home loan applicants.

This change in the structure of the lending practice has had a great impact on how lenders make their profits. Rather than holding loans and profiting by collecting interest based on the loan terms, lenders have increasingly concentrated on upfront fee-generating activities. Now, many lenders think in terms of processing loan applications and loan originations for a fee.

They pocket the fee and sell the loan using the incoming funds from the sale as the source of additional capital for further lending. In this way the lending business becomes a highly service-oriented process in which profit is made on churning paper and money between borrowers and secondary market investors. In short, the lenders have positioned themselves out of being the end investor in the loan and instead now make substantial money by being intermediaries to a market that was virtually nonexistent prior to 1970.

In Figure 15-4 we see that the primary market is connected to the secondary market. The primary market intermediaries generally sell or deliver mortgages to the secondary mortgage market intermediaries. Typically, a primary market originator sells the mortgages for cash, which it then uses to originate additional loans (making fee income on the new loans). The secondary market intermediaries transform the mortgage pools into bundles of CDOs. These CDOs are "sliced" into tranches and sold to investors as explained above. Investor cash works its way back through the system so that the secondary intermediaries both make a profit and have cash to acquire more mortgages from the primary market originators.

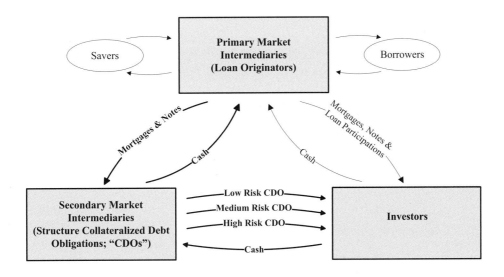

Figure 15-4
Secondary Mortgage Market

The diagram also indicates that general investors may buy securities, CDOs, whole loans, or loan participations either directly from originators or through the secondary market institutions. Nothing prevents an originating institution from selling to investors directly from its portfolio. Sale of whole loans and loan participations may be more significant in the commercial context than in the residential one, but it is important to see all of these activities in connection with the relationships among primary mortgage markets, secondary mortgage markets, and capital markets more generally.

The financial interrelationship between the primary and secondary market expands the pool of funds available for real estate activity. This expands the supply of available funds at every price point, simultaneously reducing the cost of borrowing. (This is a basic principle of economics: when the supply increases and all other variables are held constant, the price of the good or service declines.) Additionally, the interrelationship between these two markets has changed the nature of residential mortgage lending. Prior to the development of the secondary market (with substantial government involvement), lenders made long-term loans and held them as an investment in their loan portfolios. Today lenders originate loans to earn fees and points and generally sell them immediately to investors in order to obtain more funds for further lending. Profitability thus depends upon originating loans in large volumes and generating a lot of fees rather than on simply lending and holding loans for a long-term return.

In the secondary market, the prices paid by investors for mortgages are highly sensitive to market conditions and may fluctuate weekly or even daily. Mortgages are generally sold at a discount from "par," with par meaning full face value on the loan. The discount rate is established by the participants in the secondary mortgage market as sellers and investors make exchanges. If a mortgage is to be purchased at par, rather than at a discount, the buyer will generally charge a fee. Thus, a loan can be sold at less than face value (at a discount) or, in the alternative, at par with a fee paid to the buyer. For example, a large investor might purchase mortgages at par provided a $1/2$ percent fee is paid against the face value of the loans, or it might purchase the mortgages at a $1/2$ percent discount from par.

The discount rates used in the secondary market are related to the borrower's payment of "points," which are fees collected by lenders in the primary mortgage market to cover a number of their expenses and to generate profit. Points were discussed in more detail in section B(1) of this chapter. When a lender quotes the points or fees to prospective borrowers, it takes into account the present discount rates and fees for selling mortgages at par in the secondary market. Thus, if it anticipates selling to the investor at par with a $1/2$ percent fee, it adds this charge to its quote: the borrower in effect pays the secondary mortgage market fee, and the lender makes a profit by serving as intermediary.

In addition to the risk of mortgage default, which reduces the flow of cash supporting a mortgage-backed security, risk of loss can result from a dramatic fall in market interest rates. The price paid by the investor for a mortgage related security is based on the expected stream of income that will be generated by the flow of monthly mortgage payments. To calculate the return, it is necessary to estimate the life of the loans in the pool or, in other words, to predict how long the mortgages will remain outstanding. If interest rates drop dramatically, as they did in the early 1990s to 20-year lows, many people will pay off their higher-rate mortgages by refinancing at the current lower rates. This rush to make early payoffs means that mortgages get paid off quicker than expected, and investors in mortgage-related securities may find that the income stream supporting their investment is far less than originally expected. In a similar way, a major recession that puts many borrowers into default may jeopardize the expected income stream supporting a mortgage-related security.

The massive growth of the secondary mortgage market led to development of the *Mortgage Electronic Registration System* (MERS). MERS is a company created by the mortgage banking industry to facilitate the record keeping on mortgage operations. It operates an electronic mortgage registry that keeps track of the servicing rights and beneficial ownership interests in mortgage loans. With the buying and selling of mortgages in the primary and secondary markets, and with various parties undertaking the servicing and warehousing of mortgages, MERS makes record keeping easier and more efficient. A reason for using MERS is that one would otherwise have to do multiple recordings in the public records and take other steps to keep track of loans being bought and sold numerous times in the mortgage markets. MERS simplifies the process for the parties involved and maintains a database that electronically keeps track of the various interests in a given loan. Various courts have questioned the legal status of MERS in the context of conducting a foreclosure, and this has seemingly reduced the future significance of MERS, although MERS is still operating.

Another risk of the secondary mortgage market is that the economic reality of the underlying mortgage loans may be misstated. When the underlying real estate transactions are unsound, the induced market for securities based on the underlying cash flows will also be unsound. The mortgage market collapse that began in 2007 demonstrated this connection. The collapse illustrated the need to properly evaluate the underlying real estate transactions, as well as the mortgage-related securities issued against the underlying credit obligations. The collapse also reminded people of the need to assess risk properly when valuing and pricing these assets.

The secondary mortgage market continues to play an important and necessary role in real estate transactions, even as recent experience indicates the need for reform and continued vigilance to ensure the authenticity and economic reality of the underlying transactions. In response to the financial troubles that began in 2007, Dodd-Frank and the CFPB have initiated many reforms in lending practices and mortgage terms.

E. GOVERNMENT REGULATION AND MARKET REFORM

This section discusses the basic regulatory environment that governs the financing of home purchases, subprime lending markets, and the market collapse that began in 2007. The government extensively regulates private market real estate transactions. Thus, a lawyer cannot handle all aspects of the standard transaction by contract negotiation and drafting based on knowledge of the common law. Earlier in this chapter we mentioned Dodd-Frank and RESPA (the Real Estate Settlement Procedures Act). Several other key federal regulatory acts are also of broad applicability. These include: the Truth in Lending Act (TILA), the Home Ownership and Equity Protection Act (HOEPA), the Fair Housing Act (FHA), and the Equal Credit Opportunity Act (ECOA). Other regulatory requirements must be considered in various transactional settings. Staying current is not easy, because regulations frequently change over time. State regulations, as illustrated by the *United Companies Lending Corporation* case later in this section, also have important consequences.

The TILA, 15 U.S.C. §§1601-1677, discussed earlier in this chapter in the *Berghaus* case, requires disclosure of information with respect to loan financing, such as the APR and the cost of credit. The regulations implementing TILA are known as *Regulation Z*, 12 C.F.R. part 226. If the costs are not properly disclosed, there are penalties, including the right of the borrower to rescind within three years. TILA also applies to a practice known as *loan splitting*. The practice of loan splitting involves a situation in which a borrower expects to get one loan but the lender sets up the financing as two loans, splitting the total loan amount between the two loans and making one loan junior to the other. In such a situation, full disclosure requires that the borrower be given a clear understanding of the full costs of both loans, as if they were one. The key is to focus on whether the borrower expected to receive one or more loans. The disclosure requirement seeks to protect the consumer from added costs and fees that are more difficult to evaluate for multiple loans than for a single loan.

The HOEPA, 15 U.S.C. §§1602 and 1639, applies to nonpurchase-money loans secured by a primary residence. The Act defines certain *high-cost* loans with reference to thresholds established for fees and APR and requires certain disclosures be made with respect to these high-cost provisions. Its purpose is to protect consumers from unfair, deceptive, and predatory practices. HOEPA loans have certain restrictions on their terms and provisions. Penalties for violations include rescission during a three-year statutory period and other remedies, as in the case of a violation of TILA.

The FHA, enacted as Title VIII of the Civil Rights Act of 1968, 42 U.S.C. §§3601–3631, prohibits discrimination in the sale, rental, and financing of housing. The Department of Housing and Urban Development plays a major role in administering the FHA.

The ECOA, 15 U.S.C. §§1691–1691f, is enforced by the Consumer Protection Financial Bureau and prohibits credit discrimination on the basis of race, color, national origin, sex, marital status, or age or because one receives public assistance.

During the years preceding the financial crisis that began in 2007, many lenders significantly relaxed their underwriting standards, knowingly making riskier loans to less creditworthy borrowers. Such higher-risk loans, known as *subprime loans*, generally have higher fees, rates, or other costs in order to compensate lenders for the higher risk. The market differentiated these loans from *prime loans*. Customers with strong credit scores and low risk characteristics are able to get prime loans, bearing the best loan terms, in the prime mortgage market.

Subprime loans made it easier for potential borrowers to qualify for loans. This kept the housing markets active and, in most cases, kept housing prices strong. The prevalence of subprime lending during the 1990s and the first part of the 2000s led to continual increases in the rate of U.S. home ownership. The market for subprime loans was driven by several underlying assumptions: (1) a belief that subprime risk could be readily reduced or eliminated by secondary mortgage market activities that pooled millions of individual mortgages into bundles of diversified risk obligations, (2) a belief in the continuous ability of property values to appreciate as demand for housing continued to rise and supplies of land remained scarce (thus ensuring that the underlying collateral for the mortgage loans would cover any loses from default), and (3) a belief in the desirability of creating homeownership opportunities for a continuously expanding base of Americans.

Subprime loans take various forms, but generally fall into a couple of standard patterns. One main type of subprime loan is the *Alt-A mortgage* (short for Alternative-A paper; a prime loan is called *A paper*), made to borrowers who almost qualify for prime loans or whose loans lack full documentation. We address a few of the typical types of subprime mortgage loans. The *interest-only mortgage* loan, mentioned earlier in the discussion of mortgage products, delays repayment of principal and thus arranges for small payments in the early years, the idea being that borrowers could then refinance at a later date and take advantage of the equity appreciation in the property to swing a better deal on a refinance. Thus, the borrower could defer covering the real cost of the mortgage until a later date, when the appreciated value of the home would make it possible to refinance on better terms. This allows them to take advantage of rising real estate values, but when real estate values dropped (rather than continuing to appreciate), these loans left borrowers *underwater*, owing more on their home loans than their homes were worth. By the year 2005 it was estimated that this type of subprime loan accounted for 25 percent of the market.

The *option or negative amortization adjustable rate mortgage* worked on a similar set of expectations. This loan offered an adjustable rate mortgage set at a below-market rate such that payments would not cover the actual amortization of the loan. In this arrangement the debt on the loan continued to grow, but if a borrower believed that the property would continue to appreciate at a faster rate than the rising debt, it could be presented as a profitable investment.

The *piggyback loan*, also mentioned earlier in the discussion of mortgage products, was also popular as a way to qualify a borrower who had little or no money for a down payment. In this arrangement a loan was made for the down payment, and then, based on the fiction of the borrower having provided a down payment (from the first loan), a second mortgage would be funded to effectively provide 100 percent financing. This allowed borrowers with weak credit to qualify for loans that they would not otherwise be able to secure. In similar ways, a variety of adjustable rate mortgages, negative amortization, buy-down mortgages, and stretch mortgages were used to make loans to subprime borrowers. In all of these subprime mortgage arrangements it is important to understand that lowering the down payment, the initial interest rate, and monthly payment amounts at the start of the loan made it easier to qualify a borrower for a loan. This is because loan qualifications were based on ability to pay the initial payments on the mortgage without regard to the ability to pay at a later date, when the mortgage payments might be adjusted upward.

To the extent that borrowers had incomplete information, or intentional misinformation, subprime loans often presented the easiest way for people with below-standard credit ratings to obtain a mortgage. Similarly, to the extent that people believed that housing prices would continue to rise at a strong rate, they felt that the rising equity value of the home would more than offset the cost of subprime debt. While this might have seemed reasonable when based on an expectation of continually rising property values, it proved disastrous when the housing market collapsed.

The dramatic increase in the availability of subprime mortgage financing played a significant role in the financial crisis. A lot has been written, perhaps with a sense of "20/20" hindsight vision, with respect to the potential reasons for the shift in risk assessment with respect to borrowers with below-standard credit scores, but the bottom line is simply that the subprime loans being made were of lower quality and much higher risk than people anticipated, and were thus overvalued, or stated differently; they were mispriced relative to the actual risk of the underlying loan. As market conditions began to change, and people began to realize that the quality of many mortgage loans (and the secondary mortgage market securities issued against them) were riskier than previously thought, demand dropped and the bubble burst. In the wake of the bursting of the bubble, property values were adjusted downward, and many people were in the situation of having outstanding mortgage debts that exceeded the value of their home; they were said to be *upside-down* or *underwater*. Problems only became worse as many of the outstanding mortgages had adjustment provisions that raised interest rates and payments over time. The result included massive defaults on home mortgages, dramatically increased foreclosure rates in many parts of the country, major declines in property values and in the liquidity of real property assets, and a significant decline in overall consumer wealth in the United States (the home being many consumers' single largest wealth asset).

As more and more people experienced difficulty paying their mortgages, the *short sale* became more frequent as a way of trying to avoid foreclosure. A short sale is one in which the seller obtains permission from her lender to sell the property for less than the amount owed on the mortgage. The short sale is subject to lender approval, and the idea behind it is that the lender may take less of a loss on the mortgage loan by agreeing to the sale than by going through a foreclosure and suffering an even greater loss at a foreclosure sale.

As part of Dodd-Frank, in 2010 Congress passed the Mortgage Reform and Anti-Predatory Lending Act, 15 U.S.C. §1639, to address some of the perceived issues that lead to the collapse of mortgage markets beginning in 2007. Dodd-Frank called for the creation of a new government agency, the Consumer Financial Protection Bureau (CFPB). The CFPB, housed within the Federal Reserve System, began operation in 2011. It has regulatory authority over consumer financial products and services. Its jurisdiction includes banks, credit unions, home mortgage lenders, mortgage brokers and originators, mortgage loan servicers, providers of real estate settlement services, credit card issuers, financial advisors, and debt collectors. The CFPB has broad statutory authority to prescribe rules and issue orders and guidance. In exercising its rulemaking authority, the CFPB must consider the benefits and costs of rules on regulated businesses and consumers.

Many consumer protection functions previously handled by other federal agencies were transferred to the CFPB. The Federal Trade Commission (FTC) retained its authority to enforce TILA. When the CFPB and another agency both have statutory authority to issue consumer protection regulations, the CFPB's authority takes precedence — it has exclusive authority to prescribe rules. The Dodd-Frank Act also instructs courts to afford deference to the CFPB's interpretation of federal consumer financial protection laws, as if the CFPB were the only agency authorized to enforce such laws.

The CFPB has assumed the FTC's traditional role in defining "unfair" and "deceptive" trade practices in the context of home mortgage lending. Dodd-Frank adds to this the authority of the CFPB to prohibit "abusive" practices, although at this point in time it is not clear how much this may add to the "unfair" and "deceptive" prongs.

The CFPB, as required by Dodd-Frank, has developed new and simplified disclosure forms to be given to borrowers, replacing the separate disclosures previously required under RESPA and TILA.

Dodd-Frank regulates the way mortgages are sold. It requires lenders to retain a continuing economic interest in the loans they make so that they do not simply engage in passing off the full economic risk to later parties; the idea being that if they must retain some part of the economic risk of extending credit, they will use more care in assessing the credit worthiness of the borrower and of the transaction. Dodd-Frank also imposes substantial new requirements on the large mortgage servicing industry, imposing fiduciary-like obligations on the firms that receive and process borrowers' loan payments.

This part of Dodd-Frank addresses weaknesses in the operation and regulation of the primary and secondary mortgage markets. Decades earlier the Garn-St. Germain Act Depository Institutions Act of 1982, 12 U.S.C. §1464, tackled an earlier crisis in the mortgage markets. That Act, responding to the perceived needs at the time, gave us adjustable rate mortgages (prior to this Act all residential home mortgages were highly regulated fixed rate mortgages) and a variety of other regulatory changes that opened up the flexibility of primary market institutions so that they could function more like "free market" enterprises. Recent developments indicate that use of adjustable rate mortgages, and too much flexibility in structuring permitted loan operations, may have gone too far, and contributed to the perceived need for Dodd-Frank.

Dodd-Frank, responding to two of the perceived causes of housing boom and collapse, initiated reforms on real estate appraisal practices and mortgage lending standards. The Act mandated appraisal independence standards by adding a new provision to TILA. Section 129E covers appraisals used in consumer credit transactions secured by the consumer's principal dwelling. Appraisals used to support lenders' underwriting decisions must be based on an appraiser's independent professional judgment, free of influence or pressure that might be exerted by parties to the transaction.

Dodd-Frank requires lenders to take steps to ensure that borrowers have a reasonable ability to repay the loans that are extended to them (this means that lenders need to return to more traditional standards of judging willingness and ability to pay than those used in the years leading up to the collapse). Every lender must make "a reasonable and good faith determination based on verified and documented information that [the borrower] has a reasonable ability to repay the loan." 15 U.S.C. §1639c(a)(1). The Act at the same time creates a safe harbor for a "qualified mortgage" (QM), which must be fully self-amortizing, may not allow the borrower to defer any payments, and cannot have a term exceeding 30 years. Thus, a QM cannot have negative amortization or interest-only payments. QMs also have restrictions on points and fees (for example, no more than 3 percent of the loan amount for loans of $100,000 or more). A QM must be based on full documentation of the borrower's income and debts. A prepayment penalty is not allowed for an adjustable rate loan; one is generally allowed for a fixed-rate loan, provided that the penalty cannot extend beyond the first three years of the loan term and the lender must have offered the borrower an alternative loan with no penalty. A CFPB regulation imposes a debt-to-income ratio: the borrower's monthly payment must not exceed 43 percent of her income.

A home lender who violates the "reasonable ability to repay" standard is subject to substantial statutory damages, including attorneys' fees, augmented by the risk that borrowers will pursue their claims in class-action litigation. Lenders are still allowed to make non-qualified mortgages, subject to the ability-to-pay standard and other limitations imposed by the Dodd-Frank Act and CFPB regulations; for example, no prepayment penalties are allowed for non-qualified loans, a lender may not require single-premium credit insurance, and arbitration clauses are not allowed. But due to the lack of the safe harbor, lenders making non-qualified loans incur substantial risk. Moreover, Fannie Mae and Freddie Mac will not purchase non-qualified mortgage loans for securitization on the secondary mortgage markets. As a result, since Dodd-Frank was passed home mortgage lenders have generally made only QMs. Very few borrowers have obtained non-qualified loans.

UNITED COMPANIES LENDING CORPORATION v. SARGEANT
United States District Court, Massachusetts, 1998
20 F. Supp. 2d 192

YOUNG, District Judge. This case comes before the Court as a case stated. That is, the parties have stipulated to all material facts and it remains for this Court to review the record, draw such inferences as are reasonable and, applying the governing law, enter such judgment as may be appropriate. . . .

I. BACKGROUND

United Companies Lending Corporation ("United") makes, sells, and services refinancing, first lien residential mortgage loans which are used primarily for debt consolidation, home improvement, or major household purchases. United is licensed to do business in Massachusetts as a mortgage lender. United operates in the subprime market making loans to consumers who have a higher credit risk than borrowers in the prime market.

Subprime loans are more costly to the lender to originate, sell, and service than traditional "A credit" loans. In the subprime market, the lenders evaluate the credit-worthiness of a borrower "by establishing various risk classifications with associated pricing parameters." Joint Statement of Undisputed Facts ("Joint Stmt.") ¶3. There is no standard set of credit risk assessment criteria as exists in the prime market. The subprime market typically takes into consideration a potential borrower's (1) credit history; (2) the household debt-to-income ratio if the loan is approved; and (3) the combined loan-to-value ratio for home equity loan and other mortgage debt on the property. "Standards vary, however, within the subprime market, and different lenders may assign different weights for each of these factors, for a given credit grade. (One firm's 'B' loans may look like another firm's 'C' loans.)" Joint Stmt. ¶4.

Subprime loans have higher securitization costs associated with the sale of these loans on the private secondary market compared to loans in the prime market because they are "non-conforming" loans. United loans are also sold "with recourse" in the event of a default by the borrower. As a result of these terms, the risk to the lender on a subprime loan is substantially higher than on a prime loan. "Due to the higher risks and costs associated with subprime loans, the total cost of such loans to the borrower — as reflected in the Annual Percentage Rate ("APR") — is generally higher than the cost of loans by traditional lenders such as banks. Such costs typically include interest, origination fees or 'points' and other fees associated with the closing of the loan." Joint Stmt. ¶9.

Daisy Sargeant ("Sargeant") is the owner of a New England triple-decker in Dorchester, Massachusetts. She resides on the second floor and rents out the first floor and third floor apartments for $600 per month each. Desiring to make improvements to the interior and the exterior of the house, she responded to an advertisement in the Boston Herald regarding the availability of loans. She contacted the toll-free number in the advertisement and received a mortgage application. The advertisement was placed by a California-based mortgage broker, John P. McIntyre ("McIntyre"). McIntyre referred Sargeant's name to David Richard ("Richard"), a United mortgage loan originator located at the Warwick, Rhode Island office. Richard contacted Sargeant. Richard is the United agent with whom Sargeant dealt in obtaining the mortgage loan at issue.

On August 9, 1995, Sargeant completed the loan application and executed disclosure documents related to the loan. Sargeant was classified as a "C" borrower by United. On August 23, 1995, United approved Sargeant's loan. . . .

[On September 29] Sargeant . . . obtained a loan from United for $134,700. The mortgage had an adjustable interest rate with an initial rate of interest of 10.99 percent. The loan provided that the rate could be adjusted upward one percent every six months with a maximum interest rate of 16.99 percent. The initial annual percentage rate charged on the mortgage was 13.556 percent. . . . According to the settlement statement, Sargeant was assessed a brokerage fee payable to United in the sum of $13,461.40. United claims that this entry is incorrect and that the $13,461.40 was paid to United as an origination fee or "points." Sargeant was also charged a broker's fee in the amount of $4,150 made payable to McIntyre. Her total closing costs and fees equaled $23,029.87. Her initial mortgage payments were $1,281. Her previous mortgage payments were $956 per month.

Sargeant fell behind in the repayment of her loan and United initiated foreclosure proceedings against her. Sargeant then filed a consumer complaint with the Consumer Protection and Antitrust Division of the Massachusetts Attorney General's Office. . . .

II. DISCUSSION

Pursuant to his authority under the Massachusetts General Laws, the Attorney General has the authority to make rules and regulations interpreting what acts or practices by mortgage lenders and brokers are unfair or deceptive and, therefore, illegal under Mass. Gen. Laws ch. 93A, §2(a). *See* Mass. Gen. Laws ch. 93A, §2(c). "Such rules and regulations shall not be inconsistent with the rules, regulations and decisions of the Federal Trade Commission and the federal courts interpreting the provisions of 15 U.S.C. 45(a)(1)." *Id.* . . .

. . . Regulation 8.06(6) ("the Regulation"), which became effective August 1, 1992, states that:

> It is an unfair or deceptive practice for a mortgage broker or lender to procure or negotiate for a borrower a mortgage loan with rates or terms which *significantly deviate from industry-wide standards or which are otherwise unconscionable.* (emphasis added).

This is the regulation that United challenges in this case.

A. CONSISTENCY WITH LEGISLATIVE INTENT

. . . .

The Regulation, consistent with the Attorney General's rule-making authority, provides a basis for interpreting whether the charging of points is an unfair or deceptive practice. . . .

The fact that the charging of points is permissible where there is disclosure, without requiring the direct correlation between the amount charged and the services rendered, does not imply that such points may be charged without limit or that the charging of certain points does not constitute an unfair act. The Attorney General's regulations may proscribe even good faith business practices that could be unfair or deceptive. . . .

B. CONSISTENCY WITH APPLICABLE FEDERAL LAW

. . . .

In this case, the consumer injury at issue is a monetary harm. The Attorney General's Regulation attempts to prevent the charging of excessive origination fees or points in residential mortgage loan transactions which increase the debt obligation of the consumer and the potential for default. United argues that a limitation on the permissible origination fee or points charged would cause United either to charge a higher interest rate, thus increasing the cost of the loan to the consumer, or to withdraw from the Massachusetts mortgage market altogether, with the consequence that consumers like Sargeant could not obtain the loans and necessary credit to "get back on their feet." United argues that this cost outweighs the benefits of the Regulation and that the Regulation is thus inconsistent with the applicable Federal law. This Court disagrees.

Evidence in the record indicates that in 1995, the period when the loan transaction took place, the majority of subprime lenders did not charge ten points on loans but rather charged five points or less. . . . Although points may be necessary to raise the loan yield in order to obtain a return that is competitive with other types of loans, a two-fold increase above the average points charged by subprime market lenders is not necessary to achieve this objective, especially when the mortgage loan is an adjustable rate mortgage as opposed to a fixed mortgage.

United avers that market forces will ensure fairness in mortgage broker and lending practices . . . .

The economic circumstances surrounding the enactment of the Regulation establish the fallacy of this argument. With the abandonment of the inner-city neighborhoods by mainstream lending institutions during the 1970s and 1980s, the deregulation of the banking industry, the appreciation of real estate values in Massachusetts, and the rise of secondary mortgage market, the groundwork was laid for the lending practices that fueled the home improvement and second mortgage lending scams of the 1980s and early 1990s. . . . The new credit device was not without flaws, as the increase in home equity financing was paralleled by an increase in foreclosures. Julia Patterson Forrester, *Mortgaging the American Dream: A Critical Evaluation of the Federal Government's Promotion of Home Equity Financing*, 69 Tul. L. Rev. 373, 381-82 & n.38 (1994). Some of these foreclosures were precipitated by the unscrupulous behavior of unregulated mortgage brokers and lenders who engaged in predatory lending practices that included offering high-rate and high-fee loans to borrowers who lacked access to mainstream banks because of redlining practices, had marginal credit histories, and had limited financial sophistication. . . .

Redlining and reverse redlining[5] by banks, savings and loans, finance companies, and second mortgage companies impede the self-correcting elements of the market, rendering it unable to prevent consumer injury. This market failure prevents the borrower from taking action reasonably to avoid the financial pitfalls created by predatory lending. Mortgage lending practices in Massachusetts during the eighties and early nineties represented an instance of market failure. Government intervention to address this failing was appropriate. . . .

. . . As the consumer injury caused by reverse redlining and predatory lending is substantial, is not outweighed by countervailing benefits, and is not reasonably avoidable by the borrower, a determination that such

---

5. Redlining is the practice of denying the extension of credit to specific geographic areas due to the income, race, or ethnicity of its residents. The term was derived from the actual practice of drawing a red line around certain areas in which credit would be denied. Reverse redlining is the practice of extending credit on unfair terms to those same communities. *See* S. Rep. No. 103-169, at 21 (1993), reprinted in 1994 U.S.C.C.A.N. 1881, 1905; *see also* Reverse Redlining: Problems in Home Equity Lending Before the Senate Committee on Banking, Housing, and Urban Affairs, 103rd Cong. 243-471 (1993).

conduct is unfair is consistent with the rules, regulations, and interpretations of the Federal Trade Commission. . . .

This Court concludes that the Regulation is not inconsistent with the pronouncement of the Federal Trade Commission or federal courts' construing of 15 U.S.C. §45(a)(1). . . .

CONCLUSION

1. For the reasons stated herein, this Court declares that the Regulation is valid and enforceable.

2. The origination fee charged by United constituted an unfair and deceptive trade practice as the points charged substantially deviated from industry-wide practice in Massachusetts. Therefore, Sargeant is entitled to actual damages of $13,461.40 plus interest. McIntyre was not entitled to a brokerage fee as he failed to provide Sargeant with the requisite disclosure. Such failure to disclose constitutes an unfair and deceptive trade practice in violation of Mass. Gen. Laws ch. 93A, §2(a) and a violation of the disclosure requirements of Mass. Gen. Laws ch. 183, §63. Therefore, Sargeant is entitled to actual damages of $4,150 plus interest. Sargeant is also entitled to reasonable attorney's fees in prosecuting to her Chapter 93A claims. . . .

Problem 15C

Your bank client comes to you for advice. The client is concerned about a potential lawsuit that it has heard people talking about in the community. The bank officer has heard that the bank may be sued on behalf of low-income borrowers because it tends to make few loans to borrowers who want to buy low-cost housing. The banker explains that it costs as much for the bank to make a small loan as it does to make a big loan. The labor time, overhead, and expense is basically the same on all loans. At the same time, the bank earns money by charging fees and points and this income is much more profitable on the big loans. As a result, the bank tries to make big loans and avoid small ones. The bank also pays its loan officers a percentage commission on all loan applications that get approved for funding. Since the loan officers work on commission, they prefer the opportunity for originating big loans. The result is that less than 2 percent of the loans originated by the bank are for a dollar amount less than $200,000.

Your client seeks advice on the potential problems that might be raised by this situation. The client also wants to know if it will be appropriate to make more low-cost housing loans, provided that the bank can charge the borrower a higher interest rate or more fees, so as to enhance the profitability of the small loans. The client explains that while small loans produce an accounting profit, they really do not produce an economic profit unless the bank can charge these borrowers more for a loan.

CONSUMER FINANCIAL PROTECTION BUREAU v. GORDON
United States Court of Appeals, Ninth Circuit, 2016
819 F.3d 1179

Owens, Circuit Judge. Appellant Chance Gordon appeals from the district court's order of summary judgment in favor of the Consumer Financial Protection Bureau (CFPB) on its enforcement action for violations of the Consumer Financial Protection Act and Regulation O. We affirm in part, and vacate and remand in part, for reconsideration of the monetary judgment in accordance with this opinion.

I. BACKGROUND

Gordon, a licensed California attorney, was the sole owner and officer of the Gordon Law Firm (collectively Gordon), and provided home loan modification services. Due to changes in the law that prohibited charging upfront for these services, Gordon created the "Pre-Litigation Monetary Claims Program" (Program). In the Program, Gordon, for a flat fee, would prepare certain legal "products" advertised to help purchasers in their disputes with the lenders that owned their mortgages.

Gordon also created an attorney-client "pro bono" legal agreement, where he promised to provide certain legal services free of charge, including negotiating with the lenders to modify mortgages. Clients could receive these "pro bono" services only if they paid for the Program. Previously, Gordon charged clients for these same legal services.

To attract clients, Gordon hired Abraham Pessar to perform marketing and advertising services. Pessar sent direct mail marketing pieces to financially distressed homeowners. In early 2010, Pessar and his team began sending out a mailer titled "Notice of HUD Rights," which bore a Washington, D.C. return address to which neither Gordon nor Pessar had any personal or business connection. The mailer stated that it was provided "[c]ourtesy of the Qualification Intake Department," and that the recipient could have the right to participate in a repayment program that could prevent future foreclosure proceedings.

In June 2011, Pessar and his team created a new mailer labeled "Program: Making Homes Affordable," which closely resembled the federal government's "Making Home Affordable Program" (though the mailer disclaimed any affiliation with the government). Pessar's team also used websites and telephone calls to solicit consumers. Pessar claimed that Gordon reviewed and approved all marketing materials, while Gordon disputed his involvement and control over the mailers, websites, and telephone calls. . . .

In July 2012, the CFPB filed a civil enforcement action against Gordon, alleging that he violated two sections of the Consumer Financial Protection Act (CFPA) (12 U.S.C. §§5531, 5536) through unfair and deceptive practices — namely, suggesting that consumers would likely receive mortgage relief and that his operation was affiliated with the government. It also alleged that Gordon violated Regulation O (12 C.F.R. §§1015.1–11) by (i) receiving up-front payments for mortgage relief services before consumers entered into loan modification agreements with their lenders, (ii) failing to make the proper disclosures while communicating with consumers, (iii) advising consumers not to communicate with their lenders, and (iv) misrepresenting material aspects of his services. As relief, the CFPB sought a permanent injunction to prevent future violations, restitution, and disgorgement of compensation. The CFPB also filed an ex parte application for a temporary restraining order that would (a) prohibit Gordon from operating his business, (b) appoint a receiver, and (c) freeze his assets. The district court issued the TRO and later a preliminary injunction.

After receiving cross-motions for summary judgment, the district court in June 2013 ruled in the CFPB's favor. It concluded that Gordon violated the CFPA in numerous ways, including by representing that the Program would benefit his clients (it actually left them in a far worse position), and that his business was somehow affiliated with the government (it was not). It held that Gordon violated Regulation O for the reasons that the CFPB alleged. It also ordered $11,403,338.63 in disgorgement and restitution against Gordon and the Gordon entities, jointly and severally. This represents the amount that Gordon and Pessar collected from consumers from January 2010 through July 2012. . . .

III. ANALYSIS

. . . .

C. MERITS OF ACTION AGAINST GORDON

Gordon alleges that the district court erred in granting summary judgment in favor of the CFPB on its claims that he violated (1) 12 U.S.C. §§5531 and 5536 of the CFPA by engaging in deceptive advertising (counts one through three) and (2) Regulation O (counts four through seven).

a. Counts One through Three: Violations of the CFPA, 12 U.S.C. §§5531, 5536

Section 5536(a)(1)(B) states that "[i]t shall be unlawful for (1) any covered person or service provider . . . (B) to engage in any unfair, deceptive, or abusive act or practice." *See also id.* §5531(a) (stating that the CFPB may take action to "prevent a covered person or service provider from committing or engaging in an unfair, deceptive, or abusive practice under Federal law"). A "covered person" is "any person that engages in offering or providing a consumer financial product or service." *Id.* §5481(6)(A). Loan modification and foreclosure prevention services constitute "consumer financial product[s] or service[s]" under the statute. *Id.* §5481(5), (15)(A)(viii)(II).

The district court concluded that Gordon falsely represented that (1) consumers would obtain mortgage loan modifications that would substantially reduce mortgage payments or interest rates, (2) he would conduct forensic audits that would substantially reduce mortgage payments, and (3) he was affiliated with, endorsed by, or approved by the United States government. Gordon challenges these determinations on several grounds, all of which are unavailing.

First, Gordon argues that the district court erred in concluding at the summary judgment phase that his marketing materials deceptively suggested an affiliation with the United States government. An act or practice is deceptive if: (1) "there is a representation, omission, or practice that," (2) "is likely to mislead consumers acting reasonably under the circumstances," and (3) "the representation, omission, or practice is material." FTC v. Pantron I Corp., 33 F.3d 1088, 1095 (9th Cir. 1994).[7]

Gordon . . . asserts that the mailings were not deceptive. . . . Here, there can be no dispute that the net impression was deceptive. The mailer bore the Equal Opportunity Housing logo, stated that it was a "Notice of HUD Rights," and that it was provided courtesy of the "Qualification Intake Department." The CFPB submitted evidence that consumers were, in fact, deceived. Eventually, as Pessar testified, he stopped using the "Notice of HUD Rights" mailer, as callers were complaining because they thought they were getting in touch with a government agency. The only evidence Gordon submits in response are his "bald assertions" that the mailer was not deceptive, which is not sufficient to create a triable issue of fact.

Second, Gordon argues that, even if the marketing materials were deceptive, he cannot be held responsible because Pessar and his company were in charge of marketing, and Gordon had no control over the materials. An individual may be liable for corporate violations if "(1) he participated directly in the deceptive acts or had the authority to control them and (2) he had knowledge of the misrepresentations, was recklessly indifferent to the truth or falsity of the misrepresentation, or was aware of a high probability of fraud along with an intentional avoidance of the truth." FTC v. Stefanchik, 559 F.3d 924, 931 (9th Cir. 2009).[8]

There is no dispute of material fact that Gordon is liable under this test, as he had control over the marketing materials and knowledge of their contents. The CFPB submitted a declaration from Pessar stating that "Gordon had final decision-making authority for all marketing used by the

7. The term "deceptive act or practice" has an established meaning in the context of the Federal Trade Commission Act, 15 U.S.C. §45(a), and Congress used very similar phrasing in §5536(a)(1)(B). Compare §5536(a)(1)(B) (prohibiting "any unfair, deceptive, or abusive act or practice"), with 15 U.S.C. §45(a) (prohibiting "unfair or deceptive acts or practices"). Accordingly, we adopt that meaning here. See United States v. Novak, 476 F.3d 1041, 1051 (9th Cir. 2007) ("[C]ourts generally interpret similar language in different statutes in a like manner when the two statutes address a similar subject matter."). Moreover, the parties both apply cases interpreting §45(a) to inform their analysis of §5536(a)(1)(B).

8. We adopt the test for holding an individual liable for a corporation's actions used under the FTC Act. See supra n. 7. Neither party objects to the district court's use of this test, and both apply it in their briefing to this court.

operation." According to Pessar's testimony, "Gordon reviewed the scripts and any marketing material used by the operation, and he edited and modified those items." The CFPB also submitted a business plan for Pessar's and Gordon's loan modification venture that stated that "Mr. Gordon will assure that all advertising is legal.". . .

Third, Gordon argues the agreements that his clients eventually signed, which accurately described the services he would perform, corrected any deceptive practices in which Gordon or Pessar might have engaged. These written agreements, however, do not absolve Gordon of liability. A later corrective written agreement does not eliminate a defendant's liability for making deceptive claims in the first instance. . . .

b. Counts Four through Seven: Violations of Regulation O

In counts four through seven, the CFPB alleged that Gordon violated Regulation O by (1) receiving up-front payments for mortgage assistance relief services, (2) not making required disclosures, (3) informing consumers not to contact lenders, and (4) misrepresenting material aspects of his services. Regulation O contains several provisions that apply only to "mortgage assistance relief service provider[s]." 12 C.F.R. §§1015.3–1015.5. A "mortgage assistance relief service provider" is any person that provides "any service, plan, or program, offered or provided to the consumer in exchange for consideration, that is represented, expressly or by implication, to assist or attempt to assist the consumer with," among other things, obtaining a loan modification or preventing foreclosure. *Id.* §1015.2.

Gordon's only defense on these counts is that he was not a "mortgage assistance relief service provider" under the meaning of Regulation O because he did not provide the mortgage relief services at issue "in exchange for consideration." Instead, he argues, he charged fees exclusively for "custom legal products," and the loan modification services were provided free of charge, as part of a "pro bono program." This obvious attempt to evade the requirements of Regulation O fails. It is undisputed that Gordon's "pro bono" services were in reality in exchange for consideration, because consumers were eligible for the "pro bono" modification services only if they signed up for and paid the fees for the legal products. . . .

Because there is no dispute as to a material fact regarding Gordon's liability, the CFPB is entitled to summary judgment on all counts.

D. REMEDIES

Under the CFPA, the CFPB may seek various forms of relief in an enforcement action, including a permanent or temporary injunction, restitution, and disgorgement. 12 U.S.C. §§5564(a), 5565. Gordon argues that the district court abused its discretion when it (1) imposed an equitable monetary judgment against him in the amount of $11,403,338.63 and (2) granted CFPB's request for injunctive relief, which prohibits Gordon from providing any mortgage assistance relief product or service for a period of three years.

a. Monetary Judgment

As stated above, the district court entered a $11,403,338.63 judgment against Gordon for disgorgement and restitution. Disgorgement is a remedy in which a court orders a wrongdoer to turn over all profits obtained by violating the law. *See* SEC v. JT Wallenbrock & Assocs., 440 F.3d 1109, 1113 (9th Cir. 2006). A district court has "broad equity powers to order" disgorgement, and its "disgorgement calculation requires only a reasonable approximation of profits causally connected to the violation." *Id.* at 1113–14. . . .

Here, the CFPB demonstrated that Gordon, Pessar, and their respective entities collected $11,403,338.63 from consumers from January 2010 through July 2012. The burden then shifted to Gordon to demonstrate that the defendants' unjust gains were less than that amount. In most of his objections to the judgment, Gordon fails to meet this burden.

First, Gordon argues that the district court should not have included fees paid by "satisfied" consumers. There is no precedent for this proposition. *See Gill*, 265 F.3d at 958 (rejecting a defendant's claim that fees paid by consumers who have benefitted from the services should be excluded from restitution because there was "no authority" for such an argument). Moreover, even if there were, Gordon fails to point to any evidence regarding which or how many consumers were "satisfied" with their services, and therefore fails to meet his burden. . . .

Lastly, Gordon challenges the time period, January 2010 through July 2012, which the district court used to calculate the monetary judgment. While his argument is unclear, Gordon appears to argue that it was improper for the district court to include the time period prior to the effectiveness of Regulation O. *See* 12 C.F.R. §§1015.1–11. It also appears that the relevant provisions of the CFPA were not in effect for the entire time period. *See* Dodd–Frank Reform and Consumer Protection Act, Pub. L. No. 111–203, 124 Stat. 1376 (2010).

While retroactivity of legislation and regulations is not per se unlawful, we have a presumption against retroactivity that generally requires "that the legal effect of conduct . . . ordinarily be assessed under the law that existed when the conduct took place." Landgraf v. USI Film Prods., 511 U.S. 244, 265 (1994) (applying the presumption against retroactivity to statutes). . . . We vacate and remand for the district court to consider whether it is appropriate to include in its judgment against Gordon money that Gordon earned in the time period prior to the enactment or effectiveness of Regulation O and the relevant portions of the CFPA.

b. Injunctive Relief

"[T]he decision whether to grant or deny injunctive relief rests within the equitable discretion of the district courts." eBay Inc. v. MercExchange, LLC, 547 U.S. 388, 394, (2006). Gordon argues that the district court abused its discretion in ordering injunctive relief because it was not clear that Gordon's "wrongs [were] ongoing or likely to recur." FTC v. Evans Prods. Co., 775 F.2d 1084, 1087 (9th Cir. 1985) ("As a general rule, past wrongs are not enough for the grant of an injunction")....

... [T]he district court specifically found that Gordon presented an ongoing risk to consumers. This was not an abuse of discretion. The record reflects that Gordon was continually willing to evade and complicate the investigatory process in ways that undermined his "sincere assurances" against future violations. During the investigation, Gordon threatened the CFPB and California State Bar investigators with "lawlessness" and "anarchy." Many similarly colorful and vaguely threatening emails followed. The district court did not abuse its discretion in concluding that Gordon presented a risk of future harm if he immediately returned to working with distressed homeowners without limitation.

Additionally, the record reflects that the district court carefully considered the scope of the injunction and tailored it to match the risk of harm it identified and minimize the impact on Gordon's legal business. The district court concluded that the first proposed injunction was too broad, as it contained provisions that would "unduly limit Gordon's ability to engage in lawful employment" with restrictions that lacked "any corresponding benefit to consumers." It required the parties to meet and confer to compose a narrower injunction. Due to its reasonable finding of future harm and its efforts to narrowly tailor the injunction, there is no basis for holding that the district court abused its discretion. ...

IKUTA, Circuit Judge, dissenting: [All three judges in this panel decision agreed with Gordon that President Obama's appointment of Richard Cordray as Director of CFPB violated the constitution's appointment clause. In a lengthy opinion, Judge Ikuta dissented from the majority's conclusion that the Bureau nevertheless had standing under Article III to bring this enforcement action.]

16
Mortgage Obligations

The purpose of any mortgage is to secure the payment or performance of some obligation owed to the mortgagee. Usually, the obligation is a debt and, although there is no legal requirement that the debt be reflected by a writing, there almost always is a writing. When the parties have gone to the trouble of signing a mortgage, it would be remarkable if they neglected to commit the debtor's promise to pay to a written form. Most often the debt is evidenced by a promissory note, which is an instrument separate and apart from the mortgage. Two federal entities, the Federal National Mortgage Association (Fannie Mae or FNMA) and the Federal Home Loan Mortgage Corporation (Freddie Mac or FHLMC), both of which are active in the secondary mortgage market, have promulgated mortgage instruments which have uniform clauses, for use in all 50 states. The FNMA/FHLMC instruments, including their promissory note forms, are very widely used in residential lending.

A. PAYMENT OF THE DEBT

1. Usury

Usury laws limit the amount of interest a lender may charge on a loan. They generally apply to mortgage loans to the same extent as they do unsecured loans and loans secured by assets other than real property. Most usury laws are state laws, set forth either in state constitutions or in statutes. Traditional usury laws impose simple, fixed limits. A number of states have general ceilings of 10 percent or 12 percent per annum that apply to certain categories of loans. State usury laws vary considerably with respect to the maximum legal rate; the types of lenders, borrowers, and loan transactions that are covered; and the penalties imposed on lenders for usury violations. Sometimes state laws provide exemptions or different treatment for loans made to a corporate borrower as opposed to an individual borrower.

Most usury violations involve loan transactions that are more complex than the standard mortgage loan in which the parties simply execute a fixed interest rate loan that directly, on its face, exceeds the stated legal maximum. For example, loans with variable or adjustable interest rates often present usury problems. If an adjustment makes the interest rate exceed the maximum for a certain time period, some courts look at the entire loan term, spreading the interest over that period to see whether there is a violation. Other courts, however, hold that variable interest may not be spread over the term of the entire loan. There is a usury violation if, for any period, the lender bargains for too much interest. Lenders who are aware of the usury risks of variable rate loans are able to solve the problem by structuring the loan properly. The loan documents may add a "cap" to the interest rate clause, providing that notwithstanding the prime rate, the interest payable on the loan would never exceed 12 percent per annum. This would protect a lender even in a jurisdiction that rejects the spreading principle.

How interest is compounded on a loan may also raise usury problems. The maximum usury rates are generally interpreted as "simple interest" with interest compounded annually. Thus, with a 10 percent limit, a $10,000 loan outstanding for one year cannot yield any more than "simple interest" of $1,000. If the lender compounds interest more frequently, there is usury even though the stated interest rate is only 10 percent. For example, if interest is compounded monthly on the $10,000 loan, the total interest due at the end of one year will be $1047.12. Similarly, interest is usually paid in arrears, after it is earned, and if the loan documents provide for the borrower to prepay some amount of interest in advance, this may trigger a usury violation.

Hidden interest is another area where lenders sometimes get into trouble with the usury laws. Lenders often charge borrowers fees and amounts that are not denominated as interest, but legally they may constitute interest if they are paid for the use of the loan money. For example, points paid by the borrower to get the loan are generally considered interest, whether they are described as loan origination fees, processing fees, or discount points. This type of disguised interest is spread over the term of the loan to determine whether its use violates the usury laws. Borrower payments for other items, such as loan application fees or the lender's attorneys' fees, may or may not constitute hidden interest.

Lenders need to take great care not to violate state usury laws, because the penalties are often severe. At a minimum, the lender forfeits the interest that is in excess of the maximum rate permitted by the usury statute. This remedy does not have a great deal of bite in it, as the loan is simply recast to allow the lender to receive the maximum amount he could have bargained for lawfully. In many states, though, harsher penalties apply to discourage usury. The lender may have to pay statutory damages that are double or triple the amount of excess interest. In some states, no interest may be collected on the loan, leaving the lender with only the right to receive the loan principal;

in a few states, such as New York, the lender also loses his right to continue to collect principal.

When property is sold, often the buyer gets financing from the seller rather than from a third-party lender. Such instances of purchase-money financing may raise questions of usury when the seller bargains for a high price for the credit he extends. In most states a purchase-money loan is not subject to the usury laws and is thus legal per se. An exemption commonly called the *time-price* or *credit-sale doctrine* immunizes the seller's purchase-money financing from attack based on usury, regardless of how much the buyer pays. The explanation given by courts is that the parties' agreement about how and when the purchase price is to be paid does not involve a loan under the usury statute. The purchase and sale transaction is not separable into two distinct components of cash price and financing terms. The seller can quote a cash price and a credit price, and the difference between the two is not considered interest for purposes of usury. The difference, known as the *time-price differential,* can be anything the parties agree to. Moreover, in most states that apply the time-price doctrine, it doesn't matter how the parties refer to price and interest in their transaction.

The topic of usury, traditionally the domain of the states, is now a blend of state and federal law. To protect the national markets for home mortgage lending, Congress intervened by passing the Depository Institutions Deregulation and Monetary Control Act of 1980, 12 U.S.C. §1735f-7. The Act preempts state interest-rate limits on almost all loans secured by first liens on residential real property. Preemption means that there is no maximum rate that the lender may charge; the Act does not specify a federal usury limit.

Congress, not wanting to intrude unduly on state autonomy, gave the states the power to override preemption by passing superseding legislation. To do so, a state had to adopt a law prior to April 1, 1983, explicitly stating that the state did not want the federal Act to apply. Most states did not override federal preemption, but during the three-year window 15 states and Puerto Rico chose to reinstate their own usury laws. Most of these states with overriding legislation presently set no usury limit on first-lien residential loans, but they have preserved their authority to regulate by future enactment if they so choose.

RON KING CORP. v. R. & R. MOHRING ENTERPRISES, INC.
Supreme Court of New York, Nassau County, 2011
2011 N.Y. Misc. Lexis 4642

SHER, DENISE, Justice. . . .

. . . [D]efendant R. & R. Mohring Enterprises, Inc. ("Enterprises") entered into an agreement with the plaintiff [Ron King Corp.] on July 27, 2010, to wit; a Mortgage Note whereby defendant Enterprises promised to pay to the order of the loan holder the principal sum of $850,000 with interest thereon at a rate per annum of 18.00% and a default rate of interest of 24.00%. The loan was payable in full at maturity on August 1, 2011. The Mortgage Note was personally guaranteed by defendant Mohring. For the purpose of securing payment for the Mortgage Note, defendants Enterprises and Mohring, as mortgagors, executed, acknowledged and delivered to plaintiff, as mortgagee, a certain first priority Mortgage whereby defendants Enterprises and Mohring mortgaged to plaintiff certain real property known as 22 Bayville Avenue, Bayville, New York, 11709. . . . Pursuant to the Mortgage Note and the Mortgage, defendants Enterprises and Mohring were obligated to pay plaintiff monthly mortgage payments of principal and interest commencing on September 1, 2010, and thereafter on the first day of each month thereafter through and including the maturity date, August 1, 2011.

The Verified Complaint further alleges that defendants Enterprises and Mohring defaulted under the terms of the Mortgage Note and the Mortgage by failing and omitting to pay plaintiff payments due on October 1, 2010, and each and every month thereafter. Since defendants Enterprises and Mohring's defaults, no payments upon the obligations of said defendants have been made in accordance with the Mortgage Note and the Mortgage. On April 28, 2011, plaintiff elected to declare immediately due and payable the entire unpaid principal balance, together with interest due thereon and all other sums and amounts due and owing of said defendants to plaintiff. . . .

When a mortgagee produces the mortgage and unpaid note, together with evidence of the mortgagor's default, the mortgagee demonstrates its entitlement to a judgment of foreclosure as a matter of law, thereby shifting the burden to the mortgagor to assert and demonstrate, by competent and admissible evidence, any defense that could properly raise questions of fact to his or her default.

In the instant matter, plaintiff has produced the Mortgage and the unpaid Mortgage Note together with evidence of the mortgagors' default and therefore demonstrated its entitlement to a judgment of foreclosure as a matter of law.

The burden now shifts to defendant Mohring to assert and demonstrate, by competent and admissible evidence, any defense that could properly raise a question of fact to his default. In opposition to plaintiff's motion, defendant Mohring argues,

> The underlying mortgage note, dated July 27, 2010, which was made due and payable on August 1, 2011, provides for interest at the rate of 24.000%, upon borrowers's default. In addition to that stated interest rate, the defendant/ borrower also paid to the plaintiff/lender two points (2%) on the principal sum of the loan, ($850,000). Taken together (i.e. the stated interest rate of 24% and the two points (2%)) the subject loan becomes usurious, as a matter of law. . . . Where a lender attempts to collect interest which exceeds 25%, the obligation becomes void, ab initio, as criminally usurious. . . . In the instant case, the effective interest rate on the subject loan exceeds the criminally usury

rate of 25% per annum. It is well-settled that 'points' are considered interest on monies advanced, and are thus part of the calculation in determining what the actual, or effective, rate of interest is on a loan. In summary, it is respectfully submitted that the subject obligation should be declared criminally usurious; and, further, that the mortgage note should be declared void, plaintiff enjoined from prosecuting this action, and the note ordered surrendered and cancelled. . . .

In reply, plaintiff argues that "it remains noteworthy to mention that the mortgage being foreclosed is a *commercial mortgage loan* made by a sophisticated corporate borrower encumbering a vacant parcel of real property. . . ." . . .

Plaintiff further argues that defendant's Opposition is predicated on the "baseless and unfounded" allegation that the loan that is the subject of the instant foreclosure action is usurious. Plaintiff asserts that the defense of civil usury is not generally available to corporations and it is well established that the criminal usury statutes do not apply to defaulted obligations.

Plaintiff contends that "for the purposes of determining whether the Loan is usurious, the rate of interest on the Loan is calculated by adding 18% (the note rate) plus 2% (the fee paid at closing), for a total of 20% per annum. This sum being less than the criminal rate of 25%, the loan is therefore not usurious. Defendants attempt to confuse the court by adding loan origination fee to the default rate of interest, a rate that defendant was clearly able to avoid being charged had defendant honored its obligations under the note and mortgage."

The provision in an agreement to pay, after maturity, interest at a higher rate than permitted by the usury laws does not render a contract usurious if made in good faith and without intent to evade the usury laws. The debtor can avoid the higher interest rate by meeting his obligations under the mortgage. The defense of usury does not apply where terms of the mortgage and note impose a rate of interest in excess of the statutory maximum only after default or maturity. *See* Miller Planning Corp. v. Wells, 678 N.Y.S.2d 340 (App. Div. 2d Dept. 1998).

Accordingly, defendant Mohring's usury argument in Opposition to plaintiff's motion is without merit and he thereby failed to meet his burden to assert and demonstrate, by competent and admissible evidence, any defense that could properly raise a question of fact to his default. Therefore, plaintiff's motion . . . , for an order granting it summary judgment . . . is hereby granted. . . .

Problem 16A

Natalie, a real estate developer, is negotiating to buy from Rufus a block of land downtown, where she plans to build a luxury high-rise condominium community. The seller is holding out for a high price. Natalie is in need of obtaining as much financing as possible for this project. During negotiations, she asks if Rufus is willing to defer payment of part of the purchase price. At one point, Rufus mentions that he may be interested in taking one of the condominium units, on one of the building's highest floors, if he can get a great price. They reach and sign an agreement. The seller named in the contract of sale is the Rufus Family Trust, a family trust that has owned the land for the past eight years. At closing in accordance with the contract, Natalie pays the trust $200,000 and executes a promissory note to Rufus personally (not to the trust) secured by a mortgage on the land. The note bears interest at 10 percent per annum and is payable in full in four years. In addition, Rufus personally gets an option to buy a three-bedroom unit on the forty-second floor for $480,000. Natalie estimates that the condominium project will be completed and ready for occupancy 24 months after closing. Shortly after closing, she develops a project budget and a marketing prospectus, which shows pre-completion discounted selling prices. The unit set aside for Rufus's option is shown at $580,000. When Rufus sees the prospectus, he is quite pleased, as it confirms that he is getting a great deal—his option price is $100,000 below market value. A state usury statute requires that the interest rate on loans not exceed 12 percent per annum. Is this transaction usurious?

2. Late Payment

Lenders of course want their borrowers to pay their installment payments on time. To encourage prompt payment and penalize tardiness, many lenders include loan provisions that impose extra costs on borrowers who pay late. Most residential mortgage loans expressly provide for a late charge if the borrower fails to pay an installment after a specified grace period. There are several different ways late payments may be calculated. The most common type of late charge assessed today is a percentage of the unpaid installment; for example, for a default in making a $500 payment that is due every month, a $30 fee (which is 6 percent of the payment) might be imposed. Other variations lenders have employed include: (1) setting a fixed charge for all borrowers, such as $25, based on administrative expenses such as sending out late notices; (2) assessing a higher interest rate on the unpaid installment after default; and (3) assessing a higher interest rate on the entire principal balance after default. Borrowers have sometimes challenged the legality of various late-charge provisions, claiming that they amount to an unlawful penalty. Courts have generally analyzed late charges under the law of liquidated damages, which permits parties to contract for the payment of a fixed amount to be paid upon a breach, provided that actual damages are difficult or impracticable to calculate and the liquidated sum is a reasonable estimate of actual harm. The leading case in this area is Garrett v. Coast & Southern Federal Savings & Loan Ass'n, 511 P.2d 1197 (Cal. 1973), a class action that invalidated the following late charge provision (type (3) above):

The undersigned further agrees that in the event that payment of either principal or interest on this note becomes in default, the holder may, without notice, charge additional interest at the rate of two (2%) per cent per annum on the unpaid principal balance of this note from the date unpaid interest started to accrue until the close of the business day upon which payment curing the default is received.

The court observed:

We are compelled to conclude that a charge for the late payment of a loan installment which is measured against the unpaid balance of the loan must be deemed to be punitive in character. It is an attempt to coerce timely payment by a forfeiture which is not reasonably calculated to merely compensate the injured lender. We conclude, accordingly, that because the parties failed to make a reasonable endeavor to estimate a fair compensation for a loss which would be sustained on the default of an installment payment, the provision for late charges is void.

The court, however, was careful to note that the principal vice was the lack of proportionality between the late charge and the amount of the unpaid installment. To guide lenders in their drafting of other clauses, it stated that a late charge should be upheld "where it is established that the measure of actual damages would be a comparatively small amount and that it would be economically impracticable in each instance of a default to require a lender to prove to the satisfaction of the borrower the actual damages by accounting procedures."

For residential loans but not commercial loans, state and federal regulations commonly apply to regulate late charges. To protect borrowers from lenders who might try to assess high charges, many states have statutes that regulate late charges for residential mortgages. E.g., Cal. Civ. Code §2954.4 (late payment charge limited to greater of $5 or 6 percent of late installment; 10-day grace period); N.Y. Real Prop. Law §254-b (charge limited to 2 percent of late installment; 15-day grace period); Wis. Stat. Ann. §138.052(6) (charge limited to 5 percent of late installment; 15-day grace period).

At the federal level, residential mortgage lenders are subject to various regulations concerning late charges. Fannie Mae, for conventional mortgages (not federally insured or guaranteed), requires after 15 days a late charge equal to 4 percent of the late installment or such lesser amount permitted by state law. Freddie Mac authorizes but does not require a 5 percent late charge after 15 days. Mortgage loans insured by the Federal Housing Administration (FHA) and the Department of Veterans Affairs (VA) bear late charges of 4 percent of the unpaid installment after 15 days. 24 C.F.R. §203.25; 38 C.F.R. §36.4212(d). The U.S. Department of the Treasury authorizes federal savings associations to impose late charges on residential borrowers. The federal regulations generally preempt incon-sistent state laws. 12 C.F.R. §545.2. The regulation does not set a maximum charge, but it resembles some state statutes in its combination of disclosure principles and other substantive rules.

Problem 16B

You represent a lender who is planning to make a commercial loan on a small shopping center, payable in monthly installments at 8.75 percent per annum. Your client wants to charge a higher interest rate after material default by the borrower. The promissory note form that your client has used for other transactions reads:

> Should Payor default in the payment of any installment of principal or interest, such installment shall bear interest at the rate of 12 percent per annum from the date unpaid interest started to accrue until the close of the business day upon which payment curing the default is received. The entire principal balance shall bear interest at the last hereinabove stated rate after maturity, whether by acceleration or in due course.

Your client wants your advice with respect to this clause. What changes, if any, do you recommend? Your client also wants to know whether it's per-missible to charge a late fee in addition to raising the interest rate after default.

3. Prepayment

Prepayment means the borrower pays part or all of the principal before the due date specified in the promissory note. Prepayment may take place for an installment note or for a note with a single maturity date on which all of the principal plus accrued interest is due at one time. Prepayment may be total or partial. With total prepayment, the borrower pays the entire loan balance, with accrued interest, to the date of prepayment. The promissory note, being totally satisfied, is cancelled, and the lender releases the mortgage. Partial prepayment means the borrower pays some but not all of the principal before it matures. This commonly happens for installment notes, when the borrower elects to pay one or more installments before they are due.

Prepayment may be voluntary, when the borrower decides to make a payment before the time specified in the note. Alternatively, prepayment may be compelled by the lender and thus involuntary from the borrower's point of view. This might happen if the borrower defaults and the lender has the right to *accelerate* the maturity of the date or if the borrower sells the property and the mortgage contains a "due-on-sale" clause.

The economic effect of prepayment depends on the interest rate provisions of the promissory note and how they compare to market rates of interest at the time of prepayment. Almost always, when the borrower desires to prepay the note, totally or partially, the reason is because the interest rate is too high (from the borrower's viewpoint). Prepayment is attractive to the borrower because interest ceases to accrue on the prepaid principal; the borrower will not have to pay the interest on the loan that the lender would have continued to earn.

Notice that the borrower and the lender have diametrically opposed positions with respect to any potential prepayment, just as they do with respect to the setting of the interest rate generally. If the interest rate is high compared to the prevailing market, the borrower wants to prepay, and the lender wants to continue to receive its bargained-for rate (no prepayment). If the interest rate is low, the borrower does not want to prepay, and the lender would be delighted if for some reason the borrower decided to prepay or if the lender were able to cause the borrower to pay early (for example, if the lender were able to accelerate the maturity).

When may the borrower prepay a loan? This depends on the terms of the promissory note. Many notes have an express provision on the subject, either permitting prepayment at the borrower's option or restricting prepayment. Restrictions often consist of a complete prohibition on prepayment or the imposition of a charge to be paid by the borrower if the borrower prepays. Typically, the charge is called a *prepayment penalty* or a *prepayment premium* (the latter being the better word choice since it avoids the term "penalty") and is calculated as a percentage of the amount of principal being prepaid or as advance interest on the prepayment for a certain number of months. Sometimes the prepayment clause prohibits or restricts partial prepayment but permits total prepayment, the rationale being that partial prepayments create extra administrative expense for the lender because the lender must recalculate amortization for the remainder of the loan term.

LOPRESTI v. WELLS FARGO BANK, N.A.
Superior Court of New Jersey, Appellate Division, 2014
88 A.3d 944

PARRILLO, P.J.A.D. The underlying action was instituted by plaintiffs Salvatore and Margaret Lopresti against defendant Wells Fargo Bank, N.A., successor to Wachovia Bank, N.A. and First Union National Bank (Wells Fargo), alleging the Bank wrongly collected a prepayment penalty on a commercial loan to their business, Body Max, Inc. (Body Max), which plaintiffs personally guaranteed and secured by a mortgage on their primary residence. On defendant's motion for summary judgment, the trial judge dismissed plaintiffs' complaint, finding that the proscription against such a charge in the New Jersey Prepayment Law, N.J.S.A. 46:10B-1 to -11.1, does not apply to commercial transactions like the one involved here. Plaintiffs appeal and argue, alternatively, that if the fee is allowed, it is excessive.

The facts are not in dispute. On March 1, 2002, Body Max executed and delivered a Promissory Note to defendant's predecessor, First Union, as evidence of a $550,000 loan. The terms of this note included an interest rate of 6.75% and required Body Max to make "consecutive monthly payments of principal and interest in the amount of $4,898.00 commencing on April 1, 2002 and continuing on the same day of each month thereafter until fully paid." The total principal and interest accrued on the loan was "due and payable on March 1, 2007." In addition, this original note contained a prepayment provision setting a fee of 1% in the event Body Max paid the loan prior to the termination date:

> PREPAYMENT COMPENSATION. Principal may be prepaid in whole or in part at any time; *provided, however,* if principal is paid before it is due under this Note, whether voluntary, mandatory, upon acceleration or otherwise, such prepayment shall include a fee equal to 1% of the amount prepaid.
>
> Any prepayment in whole or in part shall include accrued interest and all other sums then due under any of the Loan Documents. No partial prepayment shall affect the obligation of Borrower to make any payment of principal or interest due under this Note on the due dates specified.

This note was executed by Salvatore Lopresti (Lopresti) in his capacity as President of Body Max.

In order to secure payment of its obligations under the original note, Body Max executed a Mortgage and Absolute Assignment of Leases dated March 1, 2002 to First Union. This mortgage covered Body Max's principal place of business, a gymnasium located on Delsea Drive in Washington Township. This document was also executed by Lopresti as President of Body Max.

Additionally, on March 1, 2002, Lopresti executed and delivered to First Union an Unconditional Guaranty to provide assurance that Body Max would fulfill its obligations under the original note. To secure payment and performance of the guaranty, plaintiffs executed and delivered a Mortgage and Absolute Assignment Agreement of Leases to First Union, covering the premises where their primary residence was located, also in Washington Township.

Pursuant to the loan transaction of March 1, 2002, First Union advanced the full $550,000 loan proceeds to Body Max. Body Max then transferred the funds to TD Bank in order to pay off a prior loan borrowed by Body Max. Plaintiffs did not personally receive any of the loan proceeds.

Thereafter, on December 20, 2005, Body Max modified the terms of its original note with Wachovia Bank, First Union's successor and Wells Fargo's immediate predecessor .... The terms of the modified note included an interest rate of 7.25% and called for "consecutive monthly payments of principal and interest in the amount of $4,228.19 commencing on

January 20, 2006, and continuing on the same day of each month thereafter until fully paid." All of the principal and interest on this modified note were "due and payable on December 20, 2020."...

The December 20, 2005 modified note also contained a prepayment provision, structured to compensate Wachovia for an early payoff of the loan, in the event market interest rates had fallen. The provision states:

COMPENSATION UPON PREPAYMENT OR ACCELERATION.

In addition to principal, interest and any other amounts due under this Note, Borrower shall on demand pay to Bank any "Breakage Fee" due hereunder for any voluntary or mandatory prepayment or acceleration, in whole or in part, of principal of this Note occurring prior to the date such principal would, but for that prepayment or acceleration, have become due. For any date of prepayment or acceleration ("Break Date"), a Breakage Fee shall be due if the rate under "A" below exceeds the rate under "B" below and shall be determined as follows:

Breakage Fee = the sum of the products of ((A–B) x C) for each installment of principal being prepaid, where:

> A = A rate equal to the sum of (i) the bond equivalent yield (bid side) of the U.S. Treasury security with a maturity closest to the Maturity Date as reported by The Wall Street Journal (or other published source) on the funding date of this Note, plus (ii) $1/2\%$.
> B = A rate equal to the bond equivalent yield (bid side) of the U.S. Treasury security with a maturity closest to the Maturity Date as reported by The Wall Street Journal (or other published source) on the Break Date.
> C = The principal installment amount being prepaid times (the number of days remaining until the scheduled due date for such installment divided by 360).

"Maturity Date" is the date on which the final payment of principal of this Note would, but for any prepayment or acceleration, have become due.

Breakage Fees are payable as liquidated damages, are a reasonable preestimate of the losses, costs and expenses Bank would incur in the event of any prepayment or acceleration of this Note, are not a penalty, will not require claim for, or proof of, actual damages, and Bank's determination thereof shall be conclusive and binding in the absence of manifest error.

Any prepayment in whole or in part shall include accrued interest and all other sums then due under any of the Loan Documents. No partial prepayment shall affect Borrower's obligation to make any payment of principal or interest due under this Note on the date specified in the Repayment Terms paragraph of this Note until this Note has been paid in full.

On May 19, 2010, Body Max attempted to refinance the original 2002 loan, as modified by the 2005 loan, in order to obtain a lower interest rate and to reduce the prepayment fees on the loan. However, about two months later, Wachovia declined Body Max's request due to the company's "negative equity positions and losses."

Subsequently, Body Max was able to obtain refinancing from TD Bank Commercial Lending (TD Bank) and requested a payoff amount from Wachovia for the balance of the loan. On July 21, 2010, Wachovia provided Body Max with a payoff of all amounts due on the loan. TD Bank then transferred the total payoff amount of $416,838.78 directly to Wells Fargo, which included $368,383.99 of principal, $148.38 of accrued interest and $48,306.41 in prepayment fees. A Settlement Statement was executed by TD Bank and Body Max evidencing the total amount of the loan owed to Wells Fargo, including the prepayment fee, that was advanced by TD Bank on behalf of Body Max.

According to Wells Fargo, plaintiffs did not issue any personal checks from any of their personal accounts to pay the principal loan or the $48,306.41 prepayment fee due to the Bank. Rather, as noted, the prepayment fees were paid by TD Bank directly to Wells Fargo out of the proceeds of its loan to Body Max . . . .

Pursuant to N.J.S.A. 46:10B-2, "[p]repayment of a mortgage loan may be made by or on behalf of a mortgagor at any time without penalty." Consequently, "[a]ny holder of a mortgage loan . . . who shall knowingly demand and receive prepayment fees . . . shall be liable to the mortgagor for the return of the whole amount of the prepayment fees so received, plus interest . . . ." N.J.S.A. 46:10B-5.

Thus, the Prepayment Law prohibits the charging of a prepayment fee on a "mortgage loan," which is defined as "a loan secured by an interest in real property consisting of land upon which is erected or to be erected, in whole or in part *with the proceeds of such loan,* a structure containing . . . dwelling units . . . ." N.J.S.A. 46:10B-1(a) (emphasis added). Moreover, a "mortgagor" is defined as "any person *other than a corporation* liable for the payment of a mortgage loan, and the owner of the real property which secures the payment of a mortgage loan[.]" N.J.S.A. 46:10B-1(b) (emphasis added).

The Prepayment Law applies to individual consumers, not commercial mortgagors . . . . [W]e have upheld the use of prepayment fees negotiated on commercial loans between sophisticated parties. *See e.g.,* Westmark Commercial Mortg. Fund IV v. Teenform Assocs., L.P., 827 A.2d 1154 (N.J. Super. Ct. App. Div. 2003) (holding that the prepayment premium on a commercial loan was permissible where the debtor freely entered into the contract, the terms of the contract were clear and unambiguous, and the parties were experienced and sophisticated) . . . .

In holding that the prepayment fee in *Westmark, supra,* was enforceable, we relied, in part, on the Restatement (Third) of Property: Mortgages §6.2 (1997). *Id.* at 1161. Specifically, the Restatement notes that "if the borrower fully understood and had the opportunity to bargain over the clause, either with the assistance of counsel or by virtue of the borrower's own experience and expertise, the clause will ordinarily be enforced." Restatement (Third), *supra*, §6.2 comment c. In addition, we reasoned that "to deem the [prepayment] clause unenforceable[ ] . . . would be providing defendants with a better contract than they were able to negotiate for themselves. . . ." *Id.*

Here, it is undisputed that the subject matter of plaintiffs' complaint involves a commercial loan to a business, and the loan proceeds were used for business, and not personal, much less residential home, purposes. Plaintiffs offer no proof to the contrary.

Nevertheless, plaintiffs argue that they fall within the Prepayment Law's definition of "mortgagor" because they are "any person other than a corporation" and they were liable for payment of the loan in the event Body Max defaulted. Specifically, they point to the guaranty executed as part of the initial promissory note, which provided their residential property as collateral security in the event Body Max defaulted on the loan. Plaintiffs' statutory interpretation is simply wrong.

On March 1, 2002, Body Max executed and delivered a Promissory Note to First Union as evidence of a $550,000 loan. Significantly, the borrower under the promissory note was not plaintiffs but their business, Body Max. In fact, the 2002 and 2005 loan documents that contained the prepayment provisions explicitly designate Body Max as the borrower.

Just as significant, the full amount of the loan was advanced to Body Max under the original note. In other words, Wells Fargo transferred the loan proceeds directly to Body Max's corporate account, not to plaintiffs' personal accounts, and the proceeds were not used in connection with plaintiffs' real property. Also, to secure the amounts advanced under the original note, Body Max executed and delivered a mortgage on the commercial property where the corporation conducts business.

Even more fatal to plaintiffs' position, the mortgage referred to in their complaint, although it covers their residence, does not secure a personal loan, since, as noted, the loan proceeds were not used in connection with plaintiffs' real property. Rather, the mortgage secures plaintiffs' personal guarantee of the obligations of their business, Body Max, under the Wells Fargo commercial loan. As such, because the loan proceeds from the bank were not used in connection with plaintiffs' real property, their residential mortgage is not a "mortgage loan" within the definition of N.J.S.A. 46:10B-1(a), and therefore Wells Fargo is not the "holder of a mortgage loan" subject to the protections against prepayment fees in the Prepayment Law.

In fact, neither plaintiffs' guarantee nor the mortgage on their residence provide for a prepayment fee, and plaintiffs did not pay the prepayment fee in this matter. Rather, the prepayment fee is expressly provided for in the note executed by Body Max and naming Body Max as the borrower. Pursuant to that contractual provision, it was Body Max that was charged the prepayment fee, and Body Max that paid all accounts owed to Wells Fargo, including the prepayment fee, when Body Max refinanced the loan with TD Bank.

To reiterate then, Body Max was the actual borrower and "mortgagor" under the Wells Fargo loan. The 2002 initial loan and the 2005 loan modification were both executed by Body Max and required the corporation to fulfill the loan obligations, including the prepayment fee. And to that end, Body Max fulfilled its obligations to Wells Fargo, including payment of the contractual prepayment fee, through its refinanced loan with TD Bank. And because of Body Max's corporate status, Wells Fargo, as holder of the mortgage loan, was exempted from the Prepayment Law's proscription against charging such a fee. N.J.S.A. 46:10B-1(b). Thus, we concur with the motion judge's holding that the Prepayment Law is inapplicable to the instant transaction.

We are therefore left with plaintiffs' alternative contention that the prepayment fee in the 2005 modified loan was excessive. Specifically, plaintiffs argue that the modified prepayment provision, which increased the 1% fee to over 13%, was unreasonable, and that the $48,306.41 prepayment charge amounted to an unlawful penalty or stipulated damage clause.

Defendant maintains that the "breakage fee" formula used to calculate the prepayment charge was structured to do nothing more than compensate the Bank for the investment value lost in the event Body Max paid the loan off early at a time when interest rates had fallen. Specifically, Wells Fargo contends that if the interest rates at the time of refinancing were higher than the interest rates when Body Max received funding for the loan, there would have been no prepayment fee. Thus, Wells Fargo asserts that the formula was not an arbitrary penalty, but rather a mechanism to protect its investment. We agree.

In asserting that the prepayment charge was unreasonable, plaintiffs rely exclusively on MetLife Capital Financial Corporation v. Washington Avenue Associates L.P., 732 A.2d 493 (N.J. 1998), which addressed the reasonableness of a 5% late fee on a commercial loan. At the outset, the Court determined that "liquidated damages provisions in a commercial contract between sophisticated parties are presumptively reasonable and the party challenging the clause bears the burden of proving its unreasonableness." Id. at 499. The Court found that the reasonableness of a stipulated damages provision requires a review of the totality of the circumstances. Id. After considering several factors regarding this late fee, including (1) the normal industry standard; (2) the use of the fee to compensate the lender for administrative costs; (3) the fact that the "loan involved an arms-length, fully negotiated transaction between two sophisticated commercial parties, each represented by counsel[,]"; and (4) the absence of fraud, duress or unconscionability on the part of the lender, the Court concluded that the borrower was unable to overcome the presumptive reasonableness of the fee. Id. at 500-02.

Here, too, plaintiffs have not overcome the presumptive reasonableness of the prepayment fee. As the trial court noted, the loan transaction involved sophisticated parties, who freely negotiated the terms of the loan, and the prepayment provision was "clearly spelled out" in the 2005 loan modification. In addition, as Wells Fargo asserts, the "breakage fee" was not an arbitrary penalty, but rather a carefully constructed formula used to protect the Bank's loan investment in the event interest rates dropped prior to the termination date. The formula sought to protect Wells Fargo's investment by accounting for the market interest rates at the time of prepayment in comparison to the interest rates at the time the loan was first advanced.[3] According to this formula, if the interest rates at the time Body Max prematurely paid the loan were higher than when it first received the loan, then there would have been no prepayment fee. Thus, the totality of the circumstances concerning the prepayment provision, including the sophistication of the parties involved, the use of the fee to compensate Wells Fargo, and considering that the formula used to calculate the breakage fee was "clearly spelled out," demonstrate that the charge was neither excessive nor unreasonable.

Finally, having found no violation by defendant of the Prepayment Law, and therefore no unlawful conduct or unconscionable commercial practice, plaintiffs simply have not established a viable, valid claim under the Consumer Fraud Act. Therefore, the dismissal of this count of plaintiffs' complaint was also proper.

Affirmed.

Problem 16C

Donna owns and runs a gymnastics studio. She wants to borrow $120,000 to use to buy additional gymnastics equipment and for other purposes that should help her business grow. She has substantial equity in the home where she lives. She goes to a bank where she applies for a home equity line of credit loan (see Chapter 15 for a review of this type of loan). The bank gives Donna a term sheet that states a floating rate of interest (1.2 percent above the bank's prime rate). It also includes a prepayment fee of 20 percent of the principal being prepaid at any time, and it prohibits partial prepayments — only a prepayment in full is allowed.

(a) Why do you think the bank included this prepayment provision? What is its purpose? Whom does it benefit?

(b) Assuming it is possible for Donna to get a quote from this bank or from another lender for a mortgage loan with no prepayment fee, what effect would its omission have on the pricing of the transaction? How do prepayment fees affect risk and return?

---

3. For each monthly installment payment due on the loan, the breakage fee was calculated as the difference between the yield on Treasuries with the same maturity as the loan, as of the date the loan was originally funded, and the yield on Treasuries as of the date the loan was prepaid. The result is a measure of the difference in the investment value of funds on the date of the loan and the date of the prepayment. This figure was then multiplied by the amount of each principal installment being prepaid times the number of days remaining until the scheduled due date for such installment divided by 360.

(c) If Donna accepts the bank's term sheet and the loan is subject to New Jersey law as described in Lopresti v. Wells Fargo Bank, would the prepayment provision be enforceable?

B. NONDEBT OBLIGATIONS

The vast majority of mortgages granted in the United States secure payment of debts. A common legal definition of the term *debt* is an obligation to pay a fixed amount of money. Most, but not all, debts secured by mortgages arise from loan transactions. Recall that some courts, in the context of usury under the time-price doctrine, do not consider credit extended by the seller to be a loan. A mortgage may also be granted to secure a debt that is not founded on agreement. For example, *A* sues his neighbor *B* for nuisance and obtains a judgment for damages, which *B* cannot immediately satisfy. *B* grants *A* a mortgage on his property to secure the judgment debt, payable in accordance with an accompanying promissory note, in exchange for *A*'s agreement to forbear from other efforts to collect the debt.

In most mortgage debt transactions, the mortgagor, in addition to promising to pay the debt, makes other promises. For example, the mortgagor covenants to pay real property taxes, to insure the improvements, not to commit waste, and not to sell or transfer the mortgaged property without the mortgagee's consent. In a construction mortgage, the mortgagor promises to complete the building being financed by the lender. These obligations are not themselves debts, as they are either nonmonetary or are not fixed in amount, but they are collateral to the debt held by the mortgagee. They are designed to preserve the value of the mortgagee's security while the debt remains unpaid. Once the debt is paid, these nondebt obligations vanish.

Occasionally mortgages are granted to secure obligations other than debts. When there is no debt owed either by the mortgagor or a third party but there is another secured obligation, such a mortgage may be valid. A simple rule might be to permit such a mortgage in all cases, provided that the underlying obligation is valid — that is, legally enforceable under contract law principles and other relevant rules. However, most courts require that the obligation have an ascertainable monetary value.

PAWTUCKET INSTITUTION FOR SAVINGS v. GAGNON
Supreme Court of Rhode Island, 1984
475 A.2d 1028

WEISBERGER, Justice. This is a civil action in interpleader brought by Pawtucket Institution for Savings (Pawtucket) to determine which creditors of R. & R. Construction Company (R. & R.) are entitled to the surplus remaining in Pawtucket's possession subsequent to a foreclosure sale of property belonging to R. & R. The decision of the trial justice awarded the entire surplus to the second mortgagee, appellee Lawrence E. Gagnon (Gagnon). The appellant, F. D. McKendall Lumber Company (McKendall), the third mortgagee, now appeals from the judgment of the Superior Court and contends that the second mortgage was invalid, therefore entitling it to the surplus. . . .

Pawtucket was the holder of a first mortgage on property located on Sweet Avenue in Pawtucket, Rhode Island dated January 24, 1966 of which R. & R. was the mortgagor. Upon default by R. & R., Pawtucket foreclosed on said property. At the public auction held on October 26, 1967, Gagnon, the second mortgagee of record, purchased the real estate for the sum of $81,000. After payment of the balance due on its note and expenses, Pawtucket deposited the surplus sum of $10,153.95 in the registry of the Superior Court. A complaint for interpleader joining as defendants the junior mortgagees, attaching creditors, mechanics lienors, and the United States as holder of a tax lien, was then filed by Pawtucket for the court's determination in respect to distribution of the surplus proceeds derived from the sale.

. . . Gagnon . . . entered into a written contract with R. & R. which provided that R. & R. would build a nine-unit apartment house at 155 Sweet Avenue, Pawtucket, Rhode Island, upon the agreement that Gagnon pay $82,000 for the building upon completion. Pursuant to the contract, Gagnon advanced the sum of $25,000 to R. & R. Subsequently, R. & R. executed and delivered a mortgage deed on the property to Gagnon to secure R. & R.'s obligations under the contract. The mortgage was recorded on September 7, 1966. It is undisputed that R. & R. did not complete the construction of the apartment building.

. . . McKendall . . . held a mortgage on the Sweet Avenue property in the face amount of $28,000, of which a remaining $16,236.40 was then due. The mortgage was recorded after Gagnon's mortgage on January 12, 1967. McKendall contends that Gagnon's mortgage, although prior in time of recording, is invalid and void in that it is not predicated upon any promissory note; it lacks consideration; was given to secure an obligation not legally enforceable by mortgage; and its terms are uncertain, vague, and fail to set forth clearly the obligation of R. & R., which is purportedly secured by the giving of said mortgage. Upon the trial justice's holding that the second mortgage to Gagnon was valid and enforceable, judgment was entered for Gagnon for the balance of funds held in the court registry. The issue presented before us is whether the obligation described in the Gagnon mortgage is capable of reduction to a definitely ascertainable amount so as to render the mortgage valid.

In the case at bar, the mortgage deed to Gagnon states: "This mortgage is given for the specific purpose of securing performance of a construction agreement between the mortgagor [R. & R.] and the mortgagee [Gagnon] relating to the erection of an apartment house on the within described premises, which, according to the terms of said agreement, are to be sold and conveyed by the mortgagor to the mortgagee upon completion of construction." Further, the deed purports "to secure the payment of TEN (10.00) DOLLARS and other valuable considerations with interest . . . as provided in a certain negotiable promissory note of even date herewith."

A mortgage is defined as "security for the performance of an act by some person." Osborne, *Handbook on the Law of Mortgages* §102 at 156 (2d ed. 1970). The Supreme Court of the United States long ago, speaking through Chief Justice Marshall, recognized that mortgagees were not precluded from successfully claiming under their mortgage because of a variance between the obligation described and the truly existing obligation so long as such obligation was actual and fair. Shirras v. Caig, 11 U.S. (7 Cranch) 34, 51 (1812).

This court has previously recognized that a legal mortgage is an executed conveyance requiring the same consideration as any other executed transfer of property. However, there must be an underlying obligation which the mortgage secures. Turner v. Domestic Investment & Loan Corp., 375 A.2d 956, 959 (R.I. 1977). . . . In the case at bar the mortgage deed . . . secures the performance of the obligations arising under the construction agreement referred to in the mortgage document.

According to the majority view the amount of the debt need not be stated precisely provided there exists sufficient description to make identification reasonably possible. "[T]he claim must be described and defined with such accuracy as to make identification reasonably possible and certain. . . . [I]n all jurisdictions the mortgage will operate as security for only those obligations which are covered by the agreement of the parties and identified by it." *Osborne*, §108 at 170. The construction agreement is identified in the mortgage, and thus the mortgage operates as security for this obligation. There exists a sufficient description of the debt to render identification reasonably possible. At the point of foreclosure, the mortgage secured Gagnon for $25,000 in payments made under the contract to R. & R. together with R. & R.'s obligation to complete the building. Therefore, we conclude that the amount secured by the mortgage is reasonably ascertainable and hence sufficient in form and content to constitute a valid mortgage.

The functional purpose of a mortgage is to serve as security for an obligation which is usually set forth in an instrument separate from the mortgage deed and customarily merely referred to by recitals in the mortgage. This practice underlies the rule that in the event of any discrepancy between the terms of the mortgage and those contained in the separate instrument of indebtedness in respect to any material element of the secured claim (e.g., amount, maturity, etc.), the mortgage recital must yield. *Osborne*, §108 at 171. In the instant action, there exists a conflict between the statements in the mortgage deed and those in the obligation referred to in said deed. Thus, the recital concerning the existence of a promissory note set forth in the mortgage deed must give way to the terms of the construction agreement referred to in which no promissory note is mentioned.[1] The absence of the promissory note fails to negate the existence of the obligation between the parties set out in the construction agreement. A mortgage is valid without any note or bond, so long as it secures an existing debt. 2 Jones, *Law of Mortgages*, §436 at 558 (8th ed. 1928). Therefore, we hold that the validity of the mortgage is not affected by the absence of a promissory note.

With respect to the issue of whether Gagnon sustained his burden of proof with regard to his claim to the foreclosure surplus, it is our opinion that sufficient evidence was presented to support Gagnon's claim to the funds deposited in the registry. . . . Gagnon introduced into evidence an *ascertainable* itemization of expenses required to finish the apartment building as proof of the costs of completing the work. At the trial below, McKendall failed to object to such evidence or to introduce rebuttal evidence on the issue of costs; and therefore, such costs shall be deemed prima facie the amount Gagnon was entitled to recover. These costs far exceed the amount of the surplus proceeds of the mortgage sale deposited into the registry of the court. The trial justice found, after considering all of the evidence both documentary and oral: "[T]here is no question in the Court's mind that Gagnon more than amply proved his damages and his entitlement to the sums now in the Registry of the Court. Even after these sums are paid to him, Gagnon is still out of pocket many thousands of dollars." . . .

Therefore, for the reasons stated, McKendall's appeal is denied and dismissed, the judgment below is affirmed, and the papers in the case may be remanded to the Superior Court.

Problem 16D

Nancy and Otis own neighboring rural parcels with a common boundary of 500 feet. They both would like to have a line of eucalyptus trees planted on the boundary, for which they will split the cost. Both neighbors are busy and are not sure which one will be able to get around to the project first. Because they want a written agreement now, they sign a "Reciprocal Easement and Mortgage Agreement," wherein each agrees that if the other does the landscaping work, (s)he will reimburse the other for half the cost. Each neighbor also grants to the other a mortgage on his (her) parcel to secure that obligation to pay half of the landscaping project costs. Are these mortgages valid?

---

1. It is undisputed that there was no promissory note. The reference to such note is part of a standard-form deed from which the printed recitation of the existence of a promissory note was not stricken.

C. ASSUMPTIONS AND TAKING SUBJECT TO MORTGAGE OBLIGATIONS

Mortgaged real property is often bought and sold, and when it is, two things can happen to the debt secured by the mortgage. The first alternative is that the mortgagor might pay off the debt. This is necessary for the seller to convey marketable title. For a sale transaction, usually the seller uses part of the purchase price paid at closing to pay the debt in full, with the lender executing a release of mortgage.

The other option is for the sale to close with the existing debt remaining in place. In this event, the mortgage survives the transfer, provided it is properly recorded. If the mortgage is unrecorded, but the transferee does not qualify as a bona fide purchaser, the mortgage still survives the transfer. When the debt and the mortgage continue, there are three different ways the parties may handle the debt. First, the buyer may *assume* the mortgage debt, in which case the buyer promises the seller that the buyer will pay all of the debt in accordance with its terms. The buyer may also *take subject to* the mortgage debt. This means that the buyer does not promise to pay the debt but agrees that the mortgage is permitted as an exception to good title and that the seller is not responsible for paying the debt.

With a loan assumption, the buyer, having expressly promised to pay the debt, is personally liable if he fails to do so. In contrast, a buyer who takes subject to has no personal liability if he fails to pay the debt. This is a form of *nonrecourse* financing. The buyer who takes "subject to" usually pays the debt, because, if he doesn't pay, he risks losing the property to the mortgagee, who may choose to foreclose. His advantage, compared to the assuming buyer, is that he does not have the risk of a personal judgment for all or part of the loan balance.

When the mortgage debt survives the closing, the third possibility is that the mortgagor/seller is still required to pay it. The mortgage is an encumbrance to title, which is to be removed when the seller pays off the debt. Obviously, such a transaction poses risk for the buyer because of the possibility that the seller will default by not making timely payments. This type of arrangement is commonly coupled with a form of seller financing called a *wrap-around mortgage loan*. With a wrap-around loan, the buyer gives the seller a promissory note, secured by a second mortgage on the property, and the seller uses installment payments made by the buyer to pay the mortgagee under the prior loan. Wrap-around mortgages are discussed further in Chapter 19.

The Assumption Triangle: Grantor's and Grantee's Position. The assumption of a mortgage loan results in a set of rights and obligations involving three parties: the mortgagor-grantor, the assuming grantee, and the mortgagee. The grantee is primarily liable to pay the debt; this is the meaning of the assumption agreement between the grantor and the grantee. Although many laypersons think the grantor is out of the picture legally after a loan assumption closes, this is not so. The grantor remains personally liable as the maker of the promissory note until the loan is paid in full, unless the mortgagee releases the grantor from liability. After the transfer, the grantor's liability becomes *secondary*, because the grantee is *primarily* liable. The grantor thus is a surety with respect to the debt, and the principles of the law of suretyship generally apply to govern the relationship between the grantor and the grantee. For the grantor to be released from liability on the mortgage debt, he must obtain a written release from the mortgagee. The legal relationships among the three parties may be visualized as a triangle:

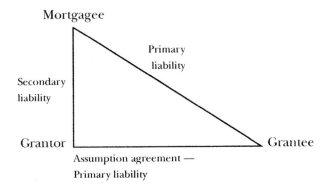

Figure 16-1
Assumption Liability Triangle

The Assumption Triangle: Mortgagee's Positions. In all states, the assuming grantee is personally liable to pay the debt to the mortgagee. In some cases of loan assumptions, an assumption agreement is entered into between the grantee and the mortgagee. Then the grantee's personal liability stems from straightforward enforcement of this agreement. But in many loan assumptions, there is no contract between the grantee and the mortgagee; indeed, often there is no contact whatsoever between them. Even so, the assuming grantee is personally liable to the mortgagee. Courts have employed two rationales, the first of which is that the mortgagee is considered a third-party beneficiary of the assumption agreement between the grantor and the grantee. The second rationale is that the mortgagee has derivative rights against the assuming grantee: by subrogation it steps into the grantor's shoes and enforces the grantee's promise to the grantor to assume the debt. Courts have often used suretyship principles to explain the basis for subrogation. The grantee is the principal obligor, the grantor is the surety, and the mortgagee is enforcing his right against the surety by taking the promise made by the grantee to the grantor-surety.

In some situations, if a mortgagee agrees with a later assuming mortgagor to material modifications of key terms and obligations of the loan, the original mortgagor is released from liability as a surety. In practice, if a lender wants to avoid the risk of losing the personal liability of the original mortgagor, it should include a provision in the mortgage documents that provides that no modification, extension, or adjustments made with the mortgagor or a later assuming party or successor in interest of the borrower shall release the original borrower from liability. At the same time, the original borrower should look for such a provision in the mortgage documentation when a transaction is being negotiated and seek an affirmative release from liability or an amendment, unless the borrower has no problem with potential future changes and loan modifications that may alter the underlying risk on the mortgage loan.

Problem 16E

Andy owns a single-family home on a one-acre lot and has a $200,000 mortgage against the property from when he acquired it three years earlier. The mortgage, in favor of Big Bank, is for a 20-year term, and is at a favorable rate of interest. On May 1, Andy conveys the property to Linda for $210,000. Linda acquires the property by paying Andy $10,000 cash and agreeing to make payments on the underlying mortgage.

(a) If Linda assumes the mortgage, but then stops making payments three months later, can Big Bank sue Andy and hold him personally liable? Can Big Bank sue Linda directly? If sued by Big Bank for the payments owed under the mortgage, can Andy sue Linda?

(b) Suppose that instead of assuming the mortgage Linda took title "subject to" the mortgage. Does this change any of your answers in part (a)?

(c) Suppose Big Bank recognizes that Linda is now making payments under the loan and that Andy has sold her the property. Linda is having financial difficulties because of the weak economy and negotiates with Big Bank to extend the term of the mortgage to 30 years, to increase the interest rate, and to adjust the amortization schedule by shifting to a level payment adjustable rate mortgage that permits negative amortization. Five years after making the adjustments to the mortgage with Big Bank, Linda defaults on the loan. Should Big Bank have the right to sue Andy?

SWANSON v. KRENIK
Supreme Court of Alaska, 1994
868 P.2d 297

MOORE, Chief Justice. This case presents a single legal issue regarding the rights between an original mortgagor/grantor and the first grantee of real property when the second grantee defaults. The superior court ruled that the original mortgagors, the Kreniks, were subsureties and therefore entitled to indemnification from the first grantee, Marie Swanson. On appeal, Swanson argues that she and the Kreniks became cosureties when the second grantees assumed the mortgage obligation. Swanson contends that, as a cosurety, she is entitled to contribution from the Kreniks for a proportionate share of the deficiency judgment resulting from the default.

We affirm.

I

... In 1977 Thomas Krenik and Leila Krenik executed a promissory note secured by a deed of trust on their property in favor of the Alaska Federal Savings and Loan Association of Juneau (Alaska Federal).

In 1981 the Kreniks conveyed the property to Keith Swanson and Marie Swanson, who assumed the Alaska Federal note and deed of trust. Alaska Federal consented to this assumption without releasing the Kreniks. The Swansons also executed a second deed of trust in favor of the Kreniks.

In August 1983, Marie Swanson[1] conveyed the property to Ray Rush and Howard Luther, Jr. With the consent of all parties, Rush and Luther assumed the Alaska Federal note and deed of trust as well as the second deed of trust. Rush and Luther executed a third deed of trust in favor of Swanson.

In 1986 Rush and Luther defaulted on the Alaska Federal obligation. In 1988 Alaska Federal filed suit against the Kreniks, Swanson, and Rush and Luther, seeking judicial foreclosure. Both Rush and Luther filed for bankruptcy in 1989. Swanson then filed a cross-claim against the Kreniks, alleging that she and the Kreniks were "joint co-debtors" and therefore jointly liable for any deficiency judgment. In turn, the Kreniks filed a cross-claim against Swanson, seeking entry of judgment against her based on the 1981 assumption agreement.

Superior Court Judge Brian Shortell granted Alaska Federal's motion for summary judgment in its foreclosure action on the first deed of trust. The court issued a decree of foreclosure and sale of real property and entered final judgment.

In the following months, both Swanson and the Kreniks moved for summary judgment on their respective cross-claims. Swanson argued that she and the Kreniks became cosureties when Rush and Luther assumed the mortgage debt. The Kreniks maintained that Swanson had no right of contribution from them and that Swanson had a duty to indemnify them for any amounts they were forced to pay Alaska Federal.[2] The court ruled in favor of the Kreniks.

After the foreclosure sale, the court issued a deficiency judgment to Alaska Federal against both Swanson and the Kreniks for a sum of $1,173,992. Swanson paid the judgment. This appeal followed. ...

---

1. Keith Swanson died in March 1983.
2. The Kreniks also sought summary judgment against Swanson based on the second deed of trust.

III

As both parties in this case recognize, when an original mortgagor transfers mortgaged land to a grantee who assumes the mortgage, the assuming grantee becomes the principal mortgage obligor and the mortgagor becomes a surety. Restatement of Security §83(c) and cmt. e (1941); *see also* First Interstate Bank v. Nelco Enters., 822 P.2d 1260, 1263 (Wash. Ct. App. 1992).

The parties agree that in 1981 the Swansons expressly assumed the Kreniks' mortgage obligation under the Alaska Federal note and deed of trust. The assumption agreement states in part that the Swansons "assume and agree to pay the [Kreniks'] indebtedness evidenced by the Note and Deed of Trust, and to perform all of the obligations provided therein." In 1981, therefore, the Swansons became the principal obligors on the debt. The Kreniks, who were not released from their obligation to Alaska Federal, became sureties. In the event of a default by the Swansons, Alaska Federal retained its right of recourse against both the Swansons and the Kreniks for any amount outstanding on the loan. If the Kreniks satisfied any amount due, their status as sureties would entitle them to indemnification from the Swansons. *See First Interstate Bank*, 822 P.2d at 1263 (if the surety discharges the mortgage debt, it is entitled to indemnification from the assuming grantee). Conversely, the Swansons would not be entitled to indemnification or contribution from the Kreniks for any deficiency satisfied by the Swansons.

Swanson's contention is that, upon Rush and Luther's assumption of the deed of trust in 1983, she and the Kreniks became cosureties. Her claim is based largely on Paragraph 10 of the 1983 Rush and Luther assumption agreement, which states (emphasis added):

> Rush and Luther, [the Kreniks] and Marie O. Swanson, whether principal, surety, grantor, endorser or other party hereto, *agree to be jointly and severally bound* . . . and expressly agree that the Note or any payment thereunder may be extended from time to time and consent to the acceptance of further security including other types of security all without in any way affecting the liability of said parties.

Swanson argues that this paragraph demonstrates the Kreniks' express consent to become joint debtors with her on the Alaska Federal deed of trust.

Swanson misinterprets this provision. Indeed, the fact that Paragraph 10 also binds Rush and Luther as jointly and severally liable with Swanson and the Kreniks would defeat Swanson's interpretation of the clause. We conclude that the language of Paragraph 10 establishes the Kreniks' agreement to be jointly and severally bound with all assuming grantees *as to the mortgagee,* Alaska Federal, in the case of a default on the loan. It does not, however, establish any relationship or hierarchy among the successive grantors regarding contribution or indemnity.

The relationship between Swanson and the Kreniks is clarified in Paragraph 13 of the 1983 Rush and Luther assumption agreement, which states (emphasis added):

> [The Kreniks] and Marie O. Swanson agree that their present liability under the Note and Deed of Trust *shall not be impaired, prejudiced or affected in any way whatsoever by this Agreement* or by sale or conveyance of said premises, or by the assumption by Rush and Luther of the Note and Deed of Trust or by any subsequent change in the terms, time, manner or method of payment of said indebtedness, or any part thereof contracted by [Alaska Federal] and Rush and Luther or the transferees of Rush and Luther, whether or not such changes or transfers have been consented to by [the Kreniks] and Marie O. Swanson.

The unambiguous terms of this provision indicate that the 1983 assumption agreement did not alter Swanson's obligations to the Kreniks under the previous assumption agreement. Accordingly, Swanson and the Kreniks did not become cosureties in 1983 as Swanson maintains. As between themselves, they remained principal obligor and surety, respectively. Therefore, with respect to Rush and Luther, who became the principal obligors, Swanson and the Kreniks became surety and subsurety, respectively. In this relationship, the Kreniks' liability on the deed of trust remains one step removed from that of Swanson, as it was under their original agreement. Therefore, Swanson is liable for the deficiency resulting from Rush and Luther's default on the deed of trust, and she is not entitled to contribution from the Kreniks. We find that, absent some express agreement to the contrary, a second grantee's purchase of property and assumption of a mortgage obligation does not modify the surety-principal obligor relationship created between the mortgagor and the first grantee in their previous transaction. . . .

Commentators have similarly observed that, where there is a series of conveyances accompanied by a chain of assumptions, "the liability for the mortgage debt is cast upon the grantees in the inverse order of assumption." Milton R. Friedman, *Discharge of Personal Liability on Mortgage Debts in New York*, 52 Yale L.J. 771, 774 n.13 (1943); *see also* Frederic P. Storke & Don W. Sears, *Transfer of Mortgaged Property*, 38 Cornell L.Q. 185, 198 (1953) (in an assumption chain, any grantee is a surety for subsequent grantees and a principal for earlier grantees). . . .

Lastly, we are unpersuaded by Swanson's argument that the equities of this case mandate a finding of cosuretyship. *See* Restatement of Security §146(c) (1941) ("A surety is a subsurety if he has so stipulated . . . except to the extent that his stipulation will inequitably increase the obligation of another surety."). In our view, the equities in the present situation fall on the side of the Kreniks. As original mortgagors, they had no real influence over their grantee's decision to convey the property to a second grantee, or over the selection of that grantee. They did not stand to directly benefit from the transfer. Their only real involvement in the transaction consisted of a reacknowledgement of their underlying obligation to Alaska Federal, so that the transfer could be accomplished. While it is unfortunate that Swanson is faced with a substantial obligation in this case, it would seem patently unfair to actually enlarge the Kreniks' original liability under the 1981 assumption agreement simply because Swanson transferred the property to a second grantee. . . .

The decision of the superior court is affirmed.

D. RESTRICTIONS ON TRANSFER BY MORTGAGOR

The general rule is that the mortgagor's interest in the property is freely alienable. This is true regardless of which theory of mortgage law (title, lien, or intermediate) the state follows (see Chapter 14). In a lien-theory state, the mortgagor who makes a conveyance transfers title; in a title-theory state, although the mortgagor cannot transfer "title," the mortgagor's equity of redemption, which amounts to "equitable title," is freely alienable.

This mortgage rule follows an underlying policy in favor of free transferability, which is basic to many areas of property law. In the mortgage context, the policy favoring free alienability is not so strong that it cannot be curtailed by the parties' contract. Certain restraints on alienation, voluntarily agreed to by mortgagor and mortgagee, are legally enforceable. The most common type of restraint is the *due-on-sale clause*, which provides that if the borrower sells the property without the lender's approval, the entire principal balance of the loan immediately becomes due and payable. Lenders developed the due-on-sale clause primarily to preserve their security by regulating ownership and occupancy of the mortgaged property. Later in the 1960s, lenders began using the clause to stop the financing of sales by loan assumption when interest rates were rising. Prior to 1982, state law governed the enforceability of due-on-sale clauses for both types of situations, except for loans made by federally chartered institutions that were subject to Federal Home Loan Bank Board regulations.

In 1982, Congress passed the Garn-St. Germain Depository Institutions Act, 12 U.S.C. §1701j-3, to preempt state laws that protected mortgagors from lender enforcement of due-on-sale clauses. The Garn-St. Germain Act in essence federalizes the automatic enforcement theory of due-on-sale clauses adopted by some states prior to the Act. In so doing, it resolved an intense economic, political, and legal debate that pitted borrowers and buyers against lenders. Under the Act, as a general rule, lenders may enforce due-on-sale clauses in accordance with their express terms. Passed in 1982, the Act responded to the same economic pressures associated with high inflation and rising interest rates that led to the 1980 federal preemption of state usury laws.

In principle, the Act is supposed to benefit not only lenders but also borrowers by making mortgage loan credit available at a lower cost and on a uniform, national basis. Residential lenders claimed that they would have to raise loan rates on new loans if they were unable to use due-on-sale clauses to retire unprofitable old loans. Most mortgagors move and repay mortgage loans long before the scheduled maturity of 30 years.

What is a due-on-sale clause for purposes of the legislation? The Act defines the term as "a contract provision which authorizes a lender, at its option, to declare due and payable sums secured by the lender's security instrument if all or any part of the property, or an interest therein, securing the real property loan is sold or transferred without the lender's prior written consent." *Id.* §1701j-3(a)(1).

In one respect, the Act protects residential borrowers by barring a lender's use of the due-on-sale clause for certain transfers, which are sometimes called "nonsubstantive transfers":

> (d) *Exemption of specified transfers or dispositions.* With respect to a real property loan secured by a lien on residential real property containing less than five dwelling units, including a lien on the stock allocated to a dwelling unit in a cooperative housing corporation, or on a residential manufactured home, a lender may not exercise its option pursuant to a due-on-sale clause upon—
>
> (1) the creation of a lien or other encumbrance subordinate to the lender's security instrument which does not relate to a transfer of rights of occupancy in the property;
>
> (2) the creation of a purchase money security interest for household appliances;
>
> (3) a transfer by devise, descent, or operation of law on the death of a joint tenant or tenant by the entirety;
>
> (4) the granting of a leasehold interest of three years or less not containing an option to purchase;
>
> (5) a transfer to a relative resulting from the death of a borrower;
>
> (6) a transfer where the spouse or children of the borrower become an owner of the property;
>
> (7) a transfer resulting from a decree of a dissolution of marriage, legal separation agreement, or from an incidental property settlement agreement, by which the spouse of the borrower becomes an owner of the property;
>
> (8) a transfer into an inter vivos trust in which the borrower is and remains a beneficiary and which does not relate to a transfer of rights of occupancy in the property; or
>
> (9) any other transfer or disposition described in regulations prescribed by the Federal Home Loan Bank Board.

12 U.S.C. §1701j-3(d). Prior to the Act, in many states the right of the lender to accelerate for transfers of these types was unclear. In some of the states that followed the automatic enforcement theory for due-on-sale clauses, it seems that acceleration would have been permitted. The Act preempts state law permitting such acceleration.

LEVINE v. FIRST NATIONAL BANK OF COMMERCE
Supreme Court of Louisiana, 2006
948 So. 2d 1051

WEIMER, Justice. After a homeowner and a national bank signed a mortgage which contained a due-on-sale clause, the homeowner transferred his property pursuant to a bond for deed which placed the transferees in immediate and exclusive possession and granted the transferees the right to demand specific performance and eventually acquire title. Claiming the bond for deed triggered the due-on-sale clause, the bank sued to foreclose. The homeowner responded with a suit for preliminary injunction and damages. Writs were granted in these consolidated cases, in part to determine whether, based on federal law, the bond for deed triggered the due-on-sale clause in the homeowner's mortgage absent the bank's approval of the transfer.

For the reasons that follow, we conclude the due-on-sale clause was triggered, which requires reversal of the judgment that was rendered in favor of the homeowner and against the bank for damages due to the seizure of the property. . . .

Dr. Jeffrey S. Levine completed his medical residency in gastroenterology and began practice in New Orleans, Louisiana. In anticipation of being married, Dr. Levine purchased a home at 2412 Mont Martre Avenue, Gretna, Louisiana, in 1996. In order to finance the purchase, Dr. Levine entered into a mortgage on the property with First National Bank of Commerce (Bank). Dr. Levine married on August 11, 1996.

Approximately a year later, the couple decided they wanted to locate to a less urban area, and Dr. Levine put his house on the market; they ultimately moved to Elizabeth City, North Carolina.

Shortly before he moved to Elizabeth City, Dr. Levine met Richard and Sandra Carrara, who wanted to purchase the Gretna property. Because Richard had recently retired and begun self-employment as a consultant for oil companies, the Carraras were ineligible for a conventional mortgage to purchase the property. On the advice of the agent selling the house, Dr. Levine and the Carraras entered into a Louisiana bond for deed on August 1, 1997, without notice to the Bank.

Under the terms of the bond for deed, the Carraras would make 84 monthly payments to Escrow–Serv, Inc., a bond-for-deed escrow agency. Escrow–Serv, Inc. would retain a $20.00 fee and forward the remainder of the monthly payment to Colonial Mortgage Company, the mortgage-servicing agency for the Bank, in satisfaction of the monthly installment specified in Dr. Levine's mortgage. At the conclusion of the seven-year term of the bond for deed, the Carraras were to pay off the remaining balance under the Bank's mortgage, and Dr. Levine would transfer title to the property to the Carraras. . . .

In August of 1997, Colonial Mortgage reported to the Bank that an entity other than Dr. Levine was making the mortgage payments. A Bank officer wrote to Colonial Mortgage and instructed that company not to accept any further payments from Escrow–Serv, Inc. On September 8, 1997, Colonial Mortgage wrote to Dr. Levine and advised him the Bank considered his entry into the bond for deed to be a violation of the due-on-sale clause of the Bank's mortgage. . . .

[After the Bank filed an action to foreclose and Dr. Levine filed an action for damages,] the Carraras filed a separate suit against Dr. Levine, alleging they were owed damages as a result of Dr. Levine's breach of the warranty of peaceable possession of the property. This suit was consolidated in the trial court with Dr. Levine's suit against the Bank. Dr. Levine answered the Carraras' demand, denying liability to the Carraras and further asserting a third party claim against the Bank for indemnification if he should be cast in judgment.

In October 2003, the consolidated matters proceeded to a jury trial. The jury found the Bank's actions in foreclosing on Dr. Levine's property to be the sole cause-in-fact of his damages, and awarded Dr. Levine a total of $300,000 for humiliation, embarrassment, and mental anguish. The jury also found the Bank's actions constituted unfair trade practices. Following the jury verdict, Dr. Levine filed a request for statutory attorney's fees . . . .

. . . In a separate judgment, the trial court rendered judgment against Dr. Levine and in favor of Richard and Sandra Carrara in the amount of $35,000 each, in addition to the attorney's fees incurred. In this judgment, the Bank was ordered to indemnify Dr. Levine for the amounts for which he was cast in judgment.

Following post-trial motions, which were denied, the Bank appealed from both judgments. . . .

DISCUSSION

The Bank's foreclosure was grounded on the proposition that Dr. Levine breached the terms of the mortgage agreement by transferring an interest in the secured property pursuant to a bond-for-deed contract. Two assertions form the crux of the Bank's argument in defense of Dr. Levine's demand for damages: 1) that a sale of the entirety of the property subject to the mortgage is not necessary to trigger the due-on-sale clause in the mortgage under Louisiana law; and 2) that Louisiana's substantive law interpreting the effect of a bond for deed is subject to certain preemptive provisions of federal law dealing with the application of the due-on-sale clause. We agree with the Bank's assertions. . . .

INTERESTS TRANSFERRED

It is undisputed that the mortgage instrument which contains the agreement between the Bank and Dr. Levine is identified as a "Louisiana–Single Family–FNMA/FHLMC Uniform Instrument," form 3019 1/91, Amended

5/91. Clause 17 of the document executed by the Bank and Dr. Levine reads in pertinent part:

> *Transfer of the Property or a Beneficial Interest in Borrower.* If all or any part of the Property or any interest in it is sold or transferred (or if a beneficial interest is sold or transferred and Borrower is not a natural person) without Lender's prior written consent, Lender may, at its option, require immediate payment in full of all sums secured by this Security Instrument. However, this option shall not be exercised by Lender if exercise is prohibited by federal law as of the date of this Security Instrument. [Emphasis supplied.]

Clearly, in the above clause, the creditor's right to accelerate the debt and demand payment in full of the outstanding obligation is not restricted to the sale of the entire property subject to the mortgage. Instead, the creditor's rights apply in the case of transactions in which (1) "any part" of the mortgaged property, or (2) "any interest" in the property, or (3) a "beneficial interest" in the borrower when the borrower is not a natural person is (a) sold or (b) transferred. . . .

Under the terms of the bond for deed executed by Dr. Levine and the Carraras, the Carraras obtained "the immediate right of exclusive possession of the herein described Property." The "contract is binding and heritable upon the heirs and assigns of all parties." Further, pursuant to Louisiana law, this bond for deed, which is "a contract to sell real property," conveyed to the Carraras the right to demand specific performance, i.e., the transfer of title by Dr. Levine upon the conclusion of the seven-year term of their bond-for-deed contract. Although the Levine/Carraras bond for deed did not convey full ownership, it did convey rights in the subject property, i.e., the right of immediate and exclusive possession coupled with the right to demand specific performance.[8] Thus, in the words of the due-on-sale clause previously quoted, the Levine/Carraras bond for deed "transferred" an "interest" in the property.

We conclude the Bank's first assertion — that a sale of the entirety of the mortgaged property was not necessary to trigger the due-on-sale clause in the mortgage under Louisiana law — is an accurate statement of the law.

FEDERAL LAW PREEMPTS LOUISIANA LAW

The Bank's next assertion is that Louisiana's substantive law interpreting the effect of a bond for deed on the due-on-sale clause in the mortgage is

---

8. Even a leasehold interest with a term greater than three years, according to 12 C.F.R. §591.2(b), constitutes a transfer of an interest in the property. If a lease for a term greater than three years, which allows possession of the property but not a right to acquire full ownership of the property, triggers a due-on-sale clause, then, a fortiori, a possessory interest such as the Carraras acquired in the bond for deed at issue here, coupled with their right to obtain full ownership, constitutes a transfer of an interest in the property which triggers the due-on-sale clause.

preempted by applicable provisions of federal law dealing with due-on-sale clauses. . . .

According to the unrefuted testimony of Joyce Schenewerk, former corporate counsel for the Bank, the Office of the Comptroller of the Currency (OCC) is the primary regulator of all national banks and has the authority to regulate all bank activities. Multi-state operations increase the importance of a national banking law framework. If a national regulatory framework were absent, banks would be subject to the laws of each state and municipal jurisdiction in which they operate, creating a patchwork of rules that would hamper the banking industry's day-to-day operation. . . .

Dr. Levine responds to the Bank's reliance on federal preemption by arguing that any preemption of due-on-sale clauses does not reach foreclosure proceedings, which remain subject to state regulations. Plaintiff quotes, "[T]he States have created diverse networks of judicially and legislatively crafted rules governing the foreclosure process, to achieve what each of them considers the proper balance between the needs of lenders and borrowers." BFP v. Resolution Trust Corporation, 511 U.S. 531, 541–542 (1994). Throughout this litigation, both Dr. Levine and the Carraras have maintained that state remedies are not preempted because of the inherent unfairness of a lending institution foreclosing on a "performing" loan, i.e., a loan that was never in default because the payments specified in the mortgage continued to be paid by the transferees in the bond for deed. In brief to this court, Dr. Levine avers:

> Neither Dr. Levine nor the Carraras ever (i) missed or failed to pay on time a payment on the Bank Mortgage, (ii) failed to keep insurance on the property, or (iii) failed to maintain the House. Never before had the Bank foreclosed on a performing loan where the sole reason for foreclosure was the entry of the mortgagor into a bond-for-deed agreement. Never before had the Bank even discovered that a mortgagor had entered into a bond-for-deed agreement without some outside agency informing them of that occurrence.

On the surface plaintiffs' argument casts the Bank's actions in an unappealing light, but the argument ignores the need for a uniform enforcement of due-on-sale clauses available to national banks in the various states. Unlike the situation involving bankruptcy regulations, the situation here involving federal laws relating to due-on-sale clauses demonstrates an innate need for uniform enforcement. Schenewerk explained at trial the Bank's use of Clause 17 in the Bank's mortgage document, a uniform provision contained in a nationally-standardized agreement, and why such provisions are required and enforceable under federal law:

> [E]very mortgage that's signed in the United States that is sold into the secondary market — when your mortgage is sold to either an investor or Ginnie Mae or Fannie Mae, one of the government agencies — those mortgages

have the best interest rates and the best payment terms. But the reason is the federal government subsidizes that program and keeps it going. And the way to keep it going in a national economy is to have one mortgage, even though we have fifty (50) states. And all fifty (50) states are different. No[] two (2) of them are the same. So, the way this works is everybody knows when they look at this mortgage, it says "Fannie Mae/Freddie Mac Uniform Instrument" on the bottom. It can be sold nationally. It can be packaged with mortgages from Alaska and people will know what it says and what it means. So, there are these twenty (20) uniform provisions that are the same everywhere. Everybody has got to pay taxes and keep insurance. . . . [T]hese mortgages make it possible for every homeowner in this country to afford a home, to buy a home, and to make payments for thirty (30) years. So, that's why it is a uniform document. And it's dictated, not by the lenders, but by Fannie Mae and Freddie Mac, the federal government.

. . . .

According to some authors, home buyers also benefit from the efficient operation of the secondary mortgage market, which requires uniform enforcement of due-on-sale clauses. Residential mortgages are routinely packaged by the lender (called a "mortgage banker") and sold to a secondary market "securitizer"—frequently Fannie Mae or Freddie Mac—or to other financial institutions for loans that do not qualify for sale to those entities.[14] . . .

While a due-on-sale clause would seem to be repugnant to one's right to transfer one's property to whomever he or she wished, this right is limited because of the detrimental impact on others, especially in the secondary mortgage market. As articulated in the codal provisions and regulations previously cited, Congress has clearly adopted a policy to limit one's right to transfer one's property that is encumbered by a mortgage with a due-on-sale clause, so as to make mortgages more readily transferable in the secondary mortgage market. While this policy can be debated in the halls of Congress, it is our obligation to apply laws as written and to respect Congress's intent regarding policy decisions. Placing a limit on one's ability to transfer one's property encumbered by a mortgage containing a due-on-sale clause, in theory, serves a greater good by fostering the secondary market and, in the long run, making home loans more affordable for everyone. Thus, preemption by federal law is necessary to preclude attempts by various states to limit enforcement of due-on-sale clauses by depriving lenders of the flexibility of accelerating the loans solely at the lenders' option. *See* Clause 17, *supra*: "Lender may, at its option, require immediate payment in full of all sums secured by this Security Instrument."

14. For discussion of the development and importance of the secondary mortgage market, see Robin Paul Malloy, *The Secondary Mortgage Market: A Catalyst for Change in Real Estate Transactions*, 39 Sw. L. Rev. 991 (1986).

CONCLUSION

We have concluded that the Bank cannot be liable to Dr. Levine for damages because damages for wrongful seizure are allowed only after an illegal seizure. The Bank's seizure of Dr. Levine's property was not illegal because the Bank accelerated its loan pursuant to Clause 17, the due-on-sale clause in its mortgage agreement. The due-on-sale clause was triggered when, via the bond for deed, Dr. Levine transferred an interest in the property, such as exclusive possession and the right to specific performance of the transfer of title. . . .

Thus, we reverse the judgment in favor of Dr. Levine and against the Bank, and we dismiss Dr. Levine's suit for damages with prejudice.

The Carraras filed for certiorari urging this court to reverse the judgment of the court of appeal which dismissed their claim against Dr. Levine. We granted certiorari in order to have the entire case before us. However, in light of our decision regarding Dr. Levine's claims against the Bank, we see no reason to disturb the results reached by the court of appeal on the Carraras' claim. Accordingly, we recall the writ grant in Number 06–C–0439.

KIMBALL, Justice, concurring. While I agree the due-on-sale clause was triggered under Louisiana law, I believe such a finding precludes a determination that federal law preempts Louisiana law in this case. As noted by the majority, the doctrine of preemption provides any state law that conflicts with federal law has no effect. Under the facts of the instant case, no conflict exists. . . .

FRENCH v. BMO HARRIS BANK, N.A.
United States District Court, Northern District of Illinois, 2012
2012 WL 1533310

ST. EVE, Judge. Appellant Thomas R. French ("French") appeals the March 9, 2012 order of the United States Bankruptcy Court for the Northern District of Illinois that granted the motion of Appellee BMO Harris Bank, N.A. ("Harris Bank") for relief from the automatic stay. For the following reasons, the Court vacates the order of the bankruptcy court, and remands this case for further proceedings consistent with this Order.

BACKGROUND

On or about October 31, 2003, Ann K. Sobotta executed a mortgage in the amount of $160,000 in favor of Harris Trust and Savings Bank, successor in interest to Appellee Harris Bank, that was secured by certain real estate at 34901 North Hiawatha Trail, McHenry, Illinois, 60051 (the "Property"). The mortgage contained a "due on sale" clause, which provides that:

> If all or any part of the Property or any Interest in the Property is sold or transferred . . . without Lender's prior written consent, Lender may require immediate payment in full of all sums secured by this Security Instrument. However, this option shall not be exercised by Lender if such exercise is prohibited by Applicable Law.

In or about July of 2009, Sobotta defaulted on her regular mortgage payments by failing to make required payments of principal and interest. Harris Bank thereafter filed a foreclosure action against the Property in the Circuit Court of Lake County on February 5, 2010. On or about June 16, 2010, following Sobotta's death, the Property was conveyed to French pursuant to an Independent Executor's Deed.

On January 13, 2012, during the pendency of the state foreclosure action, French filed a voluntarily petition (the "Petition") for relief in the United States Bankruptcy Court for the Northern District of Illinois under Chapter 13 of the United States Bankruptcy Code, 11 U.S.C. §§1301 *et seq.* Schedule A of the Petition lists the Property, valued at $190,000, as French's only real asset. Schedule D of the Petition identifies Harris Bank as a creditor of French that holds a secured interest in the Property in the amount of $135,000. In his Chapter 13 Plan, filed in the bankruptcy court, French proposes that the bankruptcy trustee make arrearage payments of $1,296 per month to "Harris Mortgage" for an estimated total payment of $50,000.

As an immediate consequence of French's bankruptcy filing, French "received the protection of an automatic stay" pursuant to Section 362(a) of the Bankruptcy Code. . . .

. . . [T]he bankruptcy court granted the motion [of Harris Bank for relief from the automatic stay.] . . .

DISCUSSION

French appeals the bankruptcy court's order lifting the automatic stay as to Harris Bank with respect to the Property. The bankruptcy court modified the automatic stay based solely on its conclusion that Section 1322(b)(2) of the Bankruptcy Code barred French from proposing a Chapter 13 plan that treats the mortgage that Harris Bank holds. *See* 11 U.S.C. §§1301, *et seq.*

Under Chapter 13 of the Bankruptcy Code, "individual debtors may obtain adjustment of their indebtedness through a flexible repayment plan approved by a bankruptcy court." Nobelman v. Am. Sav. Bank, 508 U.S. 324 (1993). Section 1322(b) enumerates the appropriate contents of a Chapter 13 plan, and provides, in relevant part, that the plan "may modify the rights of holders of secured claims, *other than a claim secured only by a security interest in real property that is the debtor's principal residence. . . .*" 11 U.S.C. §1322(b) (emphasis added).

The first step in determining whether a plan violates Section 1322(b)(2) is to identify the rights of the secured creditor at issue. . . .

Here, the bankruptcy court properly looked to the underlying mortgage instrument to ascertain Harris Bank's rights. The court identified one such right, namely Harris Bank's right under the "due on sale" clause to "deal only with the borrower to whom it made the original loan." The court observed that "due on sale clauses are . . . valid" in Illinois, and that "French's attempt to use his chapter 13 case to substitute himself as the borrower modified" Harris Bank's right under that clause "in violation of section 1322(b)(2)." Because French could not treat the mortgage in his Chapter 13 plan, the bankruptcy court reasoned, it was appropriate to lift the automatic stay to permit Harris Bank to foreclose on the Property.

On appeal, the parties dispute whether the bankruptcy court erred in holding that Section 1322(b)(2) prohibits a debtor, like French, who is not the original mortgagor, from treating a defaulted home mortgage in a Chapter 13 bankruptcy plan, where the mortgage contains a "due on sale" clause. Courts have apparently come down on both sides of this question. *Compare* In re Tewell, 355 B.R. 674, 680 (Bankr. N.D. Ill. 2006) (granting motion to modify automatic stay because debtor could not treat mortgage) *with* In re Flores, 345 B.R. 615, 617 (Bankr. N.D. Ill. 2006) (denying motion to modify automatic stay because debtor could treat mortgage). The Court, however, need not tackle that question because the "due on sale" clause at issue may not be enforceable under the circumstances of this case.

Although "due on sale" clauses are generally enforceable as a matter of Illinois law, federal law limits the validity of such clauses in certain circumstances. *See* Garn-St. Germain Depository Institutions Act of 1982 (the "Garn-St. Germain Act" or "Act") 12 U.S.C. §1701j-3. Under the Garn-St. Germain Act and its implementing regulations, a mortgage lender, among other restrictions, "shall not exercise its option pursuant to a due-on-sale clause upon . . . [a] transfer to a relative resulting from the death of the borrower." 12 C.F.R. §591.5(b)(1)(v)(A) (implementing 12 U.S.C. §1701j-3(d)(5)).

This restriction on the enforceability of due-on-sale clauses "creates a federal right" of the transferee, *see* Dupuis v. Yorkville Fed. Sav. & Loan Ass'n, 589 F. Supp. 820 (S.D.N.Y. 1984), and governs the "due-on-sale practices of . . . lenders . . . , in preemption of and without regard to any limitations imposed by state law on either their inclusion or exercise . . . ." 12 C.F.R. §591.5(a).

As applied to this case, French asserts (and Harris Bank does not dispute) that he is the nephew of the original borrower, Sobotta, his aunt. It is undisputed that French "obtained the [P]roperty" "from the estate of one Ann K. Sobotta," whose estate conveyed the Property to French following Sobotta's death in February of 2010. If French is the nephew of Sobotta, as he claims, then the Garn-St. Germain Act appears to preclude Harris Bank from "exercis[ing] its option pursuant to [the] due-on-sale clause" because French obtained title through "[a] transfer to a relative resulting from the death of the borrower." 12 C.F.R. §591.5(b)(1)(v)(A) (implementing 12 U.S.C. §1701j–3(d)(5)); *see also* In re Allen, 300 B.R. 105, 117 (Bankr. D.D.C. 2003) (observing that many courts have "permitted cure and reinstatement" where the mortgagee "was barred by 12 U.S.C. §1701j-3(d)(5) or (6) from accelerating the mortgage debt based on the transfer as the transfer was to a relative resulting from the death of the mortgagor or was to the mortgagor's child") (collecting cases).

If the Garn-St. Germain Act preempts any right that Harris Bank may otherwise have had under the "due on sale" clause as to French, then permitting French to treat the mortgage would not appear to modify Harris Bank's rights under that clause, in violation of §1322(b)(2). Plaintiff belatedly raised this argument in a sur-reply below, so the issue was never properly presented to the bankruptcy court for decision. Given the existence of this federal statute, and the important policies at stake, the Court vacates the bankruptcy court's order lifting the automatic stay, and remands this action to the bankruptcy court to consider, in the first instance, whether, and if so how, the Garn-St. Germain Act affects French's ability to treat the mortgage in his Chapter 13 plan. . . .

Problem 16F

Jane Homeseller wants to sell her house to John Homebuyer for $310,000. Her loan from Third Savings, which she took out when she bought the house 3 years ago, bears interest at 3.8 percent, has a present balance of $250,000, and is amortized over 30 years. Current residential interest rates for 30-year fixed rate loans are around 6 percent. John has an excellent credit rating; in fact, his salary is higher than Jane's. Jane and John agree that as part of the purchase price John will assume Jane's loan. Because the mortgage has a standard due-on-sale clause, they ask Third Savings to consent to the sale. Third Savings refuses to consent unless John agrees to an increase in the interest rate to 5.25 percent and also agrees to pay an assumption fee of $1,200. Does Third Savings have a right to impose these conditions? What if it required a rate increase to 6 percent? To 7 percent?

E. DEFAULT CLAUSES

Default and alleged default constitute the prime battleground of lenders and borrowers. From the lender's point of view, a loan that is in material default is a problem going to the essence of its expectations. At the outset of the transaction, the lender considered credit risk, evaluating the borrower's ability to pay and his evident willingness to pay.

When a loan default issue arises, it's important to realize that stress levels on both sides are very often high. And, when the borrower's default appears serious, the lender has to decide what measures to take and when.

In a mortgage loan with standard documentation, the promissory note and the mortgage are the places where *default* is defined. In more complex loans, other documents may also apply. The mortgage may refer to other documents, such as a loan agreement or an assignment of leases, to specify other events of default. The first step in analyzing a default scenario is straightforward. Has a default occurred and can the lender prove it? This depends primarily on the parties' express agreement. (Why primarily? Why not absolutely?) Analysis of every dispute about default must begin with a very careful reading of the documents. Sometimes the answer is clear, but other times the parties' language must be interpreted in light of the events that have transpired.

Problem 16G

Here are three clauses taken from a uniform Security Instrument promulgated jointly by two federal entities, the Federal National Mortgage Association (FNMA) and the Federal Home Loan Mortgage Corporation (FHLMC):

6. *Occupancy.* Borrower shall occupy, establish, and use the Property as Borrower's principal residence within 60 days after the execution of this Security Instrument and shall continue to occupy the Property as Borrower's principal residence for at least one year after the date of occupancy, unless Lender otherwise agrees in writing, which consent shall not be unreasonably withheld, or unless extenuating circumstances exist which are beyond Borrower's control.

7. *Preservation, Maintenance and Protection of the Property; Inspections.* Borrower shall not destroy, damage or impair the Property, allow the Property to deteriorate or commit waste on the Property. Whether or not Borrower is residing in the Property, Borrower shall maintain the Property in order to prevent the Property from deteriorating or decreasing in value due to its condition. Unless it is determined pursuant to Section 5 that repair or restoration is not economically feasible, Borrower shall promptly repair the Property if damaged to avoid further deterioration or damage. If insurance or condemnation proceeds are paid in connection with damage to, or the taking of, the Property, Borrower shall be responsible for repairing or restoring the Property only if Lender has released proceeds for such purposes. Lender may disburse proceeds for the repairs and restoration in a single payment or in a series of progress payments as the work is completed. If the insurance or condemnation proceeds are not sufficient to repair or restore the Property, Borrower is not relieved of Borrower's obligation for the completion of such repair or restoration.

Lender or its agent may make reasonable entries upon and inspections of the Property. If it has reasonable cause, Lender may inspect the interior of the improvements on the Property. Lender shall give Borrower notice at the time of or prior to such an interior inspection specifying such reasonable cause . . . .

9. *Protection of Lender's Interest in the Property and Rights Under this Security Instrument.* If (a) Borrower fails to perform the covenants and agreements contained in this Security Instrument, (b) there is a legal proceeding that might significantly affect Lender's interest in the Property and/or rights under this Security Instrument (such as a proceeding in bankruptcy, probate, for condemnation or forfeiture, for enforcement of a lien which may attain priority over this Security Instrument or to enforce laws or regulations), or (c) Borrower has abandoned the Property, then Lender may do and pay for whatever is reasonable or appropriate to protect Lender's interest in the Property and rights under this Security Instrument, including protecting and/or assessing the value of the Property, and securing and/or repairing the Property. Lender's actions can include, but are not limited to: (a) paying any sums secured by a lien which has priority over this Security Instrument; (b) appearing in court; and (c) paying reasonable attorneys' fees to protect its interest in the Property and/or rights under this Security Instrument, including its secured position in a bankruptcy proceeding. Securing the Property includes, but is not limited to, entering the Property to make repairs, change locks, replace or board up doors and windows, drain water from pipes, eliminate building or other code violations or dangerous conditions, and have utilities turned on or off. Although Lender may take action under this Section 9, Lender does not have to do so and is not under any duty or obligation to do so. It is agreed that Lender incurs no liability for not taking any or all actions authorized under this Section 9.

Any amounts disbursed by Lender under this Section 9 shall become additional debt of Borrower secured by this Security Instrument. These amounts shall bear interest at the Note rate from the date of disbursement and shall be payable, with such interest, upon notice from Lender to Borrower requesting payment.

Which of the following events constitutes a default? Does Lender have to take any action first to make the action an act of default? Which of the following events do you expect may be especially difficult for the lender to prove in court? For now, ignore various affirmative defenses and claims that the borrower may make to the effect that the parties' language should not be applied literally, as it is written.

(a) Borrower moved into the house the day the loan closed. Borrower has worked for General Computer Company for five years. One week before loan closing, she applied for a promotion in the company, which she just learned about. It would be a big step up and would require moving to the West Coast. Four months after loan closing, Borrower gets good news: "I got the promotion!" She promptly moves and rents the house, signing a one-year lease.

(b) Borrower, a *Home Improvement* kind of guy, added a solarium to the house. So far, only one major mistake has surfaced. The zoning administrator discovered that the solarium encroaches by four feet on the side setback line and is threatening to sue Borrower unless he removes the encroachment promptly. Mr. Home Improvement, tired of work, refuses, thinking this is no big deal.

(c) Borrower, an arsonist, burns his house to the ground.

(d) Husband and wife are Borrower, and husband has just gotten arrested for selling illegal drugs on the property. The federal government has brought a complaint seeking civil forfeiture of the property. Does it matter whether another provision of the security instrument contains Borrower's express promise not to use the property for illegal purposes? Would it make a difference if only wife was Borrower, but the government nevertheless brought a forfeiture action?

(e) Borrower just received a certified copy of a complaint, naming him as defendant. His neighbor, who owns the house in back of Borrower's, is asserting ownership by adverse possession of a 15-foot strip of Borrower's lot.

F. ACCELERATION

Acceleration is the process by which the lender, after default by the borrower, makes the entire debt due and payable. The due date for future installment payments or a balloon payment is moved up or "accelerated." In a sense, acceleration is the flip side of prepayment. When a borrower prepays, he is deciding that the debt should be paid now rather than in the future in accordance with the schedule of payments agreed to by the parties. When a lender accelerates, he is deciding that — because of the event of default — the debt should be paid in full now.

From the lender's perspective, acceleration is a key step in the foreclosure process. The lender's goal in foreclosure is to sell the mortgaged property and use the sales proceeds to repay the entire debt or as much of the debt as it can. Although it is possible in most jurisdictions to foreclose on an installment loan without acceleration, it is messy and usually not a good idea.

It is important to realize that virtually all loan documents explicitly address the issue of acceleration. Typically, the acceleration clause is contained in the promissory note. Acceleration or some aspect of acceleration is sometimes covered in the mortgage instrument as well. What happens if the loan documents lack an acceleration clause? Might the lender accelerate the debt on the theory of anticipatory repudiation? The traditional answer, applied by almost all courts, is that maturity of future installments cannot be accelerated. The mortgagee pays dearly for the error; it must either attempt to collect the installments as they fall due or wait until final maturity of the debt.

There are two basic types of acceleration clauses. One provides that the entire debt shall be due and payable if a specified event happens, such as a certain type of default. The parties' language is such that acceleration happens automatically if the event occurs. No action by the lender is necessary. Automatic acceleration clauses are not commonly used today. In the past they were employed fairly often, but now most acceleration clauses give the lender the option to accelerate maturity of the debt. The lender has the choice; it may declare an acceleration, insisting that the borrower pay the debt in full, or it may forbear. If the basis of the lender's right to accelerate is a default by the borrower in paying one or more installments of money to the lender, rather than accelerate the lender may decide to try to collect just the arrears. Most lenders believe the optional acceleration clause is preferable to an automatic acceleration provision because it gives the lender more flexibility and control.

Much litigation between lenders and borrowers focuses on issues of acceleration. Borrowers frequently challenge a lender's claim of acceleration on procedural as well as substantive grounds. Procedural challenges focus on the process followed by the lender. If the documents have an optional acceleration clause, the lender must take some affirmative action that demonstrates its intent to accelerate. Otherwise, the loan is unaccelerated, a point of highly practical significance. Prior to the moment of acceleration, the borrower has the right to cure the default and, if he does so, the lender cannot accelerate.

What affirmative act of the lender qualifies legally to accelerate the loan? There is no simple answer. A single act may suffice, or several steps may be required, such as notice to the borrower of intent to accelerate followed by an act evidencing acceleration. In some cases, a lender may validly accelerate a loan with no notice to the borrower whatsoever. Different states have different requirements, some judicial, others statutory. Many but not all states have enacted statutes that protect mortgagors, either by requiring notice prior to acceleration or by permitting the mortgagor to pay arrearages after acceleration, thereby reinstating the installment loan. Some statutes protect only residential mortgagors, but other statutes protect all mortgagors. Some federally chartered institutions are subject to federal regulations that deal with acceleration. Moreover, acceleration clauses often specify what steps the lender may take to accelerate, and in many but not all circumstances the courts defer to the parties' agreement as to the procedural steps for acceleration. In many promissory notes, the borrower waives the right to receive notices and demands of various types. Though such waivers are generally effective, courts tend to scrutinize them carefully. They often say that a waiver must specifically identify the rights that are being surrendered. If the waiver is worded generally or is ambiguous, it is likely to be construed against the lender, in favor of the borrower.

Substantive challenges to acceleration focus on whether the lender had a legally sufficient reason to insist on acceleration. Can the lender prove the alleged default? Even if the lender follows all the proper procedural steps, if it had no substantive right to accelerate, obviously it loses. Often the dispute is more complex than the basically straightforward question of whether an event of default occurred. The borrower may have defaulted, but general legal principles such as waiver or estoppel may bar the lender from accelerating. The most frequent fact pattern that invokes waiver or estoppel involves the lender's acceptance of a number of late payments. This conduct may send a message that late payments are permissible and may be tendered in the future without the borrower fearing repercussions. In effect, the lender is estopped by his conduct from claiming that time is of the essence. The lender cannot just accelerate when the borrower, yet again, tenders the money late. To make timely payment of the essence again, the lender must notify the borrower that from now on payments must be made on time or else he will exercise his option to accelerate the loan.

In addition to using waiver and estoppel to protect borrowers, most courts, at least in some class of cases, will safeguard borrowers from the harsh consequences of acceleration by evaluating how serious the default happens to be. If the court perceives great hardship to a borrower, especially when the default appears inadvertent and there is little risk to the lender if the loan remains unaccelerated, the court is likely to deny the lender's acceleration demand. Judicial explanations are often along one or more of the following lines: the default is technical, not material or substantial; the event has not impaired the lender's security; or general principles of equity permit the court to intervene to protect the borrower from a penalty or a forfeiture.

Problem 16H

(a) Lender lends $100,000 to Borrower, repayable in equal monthly installments of $800 per month for 30 years. One year later, when the loan balance is $98,600, Borrower defaults by failing to make the monthly payments due on April 1 and May 1. On May 14, Borrower mails a check for $1,600 to Lender. On May 16, the check arrives in Lender's mailbox as part of the morning delivery. That afternoon, Lender's loan officer, unaware of Borrower's check, declares acceleration and posts a letter to Borrower informing Borrower of that unhappy fact. Is the loan validly accelerated?

(b) Assume the same transaction, except Borrower mails the check by putting a properly addressed, stamped envelope into a U.S. Post Office mailbox on the morning of May 16. It is delivered to Lender the afternoon of May 18, two days after Lender's loan officer declared acceleration. Is the loan validly accelerated if (i) Lender promptly returns Borrower's check to Borrower, or (ii) Lender cashes Borrower's check, giving Borrower a credit for the amount of the check against the entire loan balance?

17

Foreclosure

Foreclosure is the process, after default, by which the lender gets value from the collateral to repay part or all of the debt. In many states, the process consists of litigation and is called *judicial foreclosure*. In others, foreclosure is usually done privately, outside the courts, by the mortgagee or by a third party such as a trustee under a deed of trust. This process is called *power of sale foreclosure* or nonjudicial foreclosure. In both basic types, the property is sold, with the sales proceeds applied to repay the debt. Foreclosure, regardless of the process used, is the sine qua non of secured financing. If law did not provide a foreclosure process, every creditor would be a general unsecured creditor. Creditors could still reach the debtor's assets upon default, but doing so would require a proceeding under the standard judicial machinery for collection of judgments. This would involve bringing an action on the debt, reducing it to a monetary judgment, and then reaching the desired property by making use of local procedures for attachment liens, judgment liens, levies, and execution sales.

There are some other advantages for lenders, in addition to the possibility of foreclosure, stemming from standard mortgage clauses, many of which we have discussed in prior chapters. For example, the borrower's promise to pay taxes on the property, not to commit waste, and not to sell the property without the lender's consent (the due-on-sale clause) all provide some protection to the lender, even if the lender does not or cannot foreclose. The main reason, however, why the mortgage reduces risk is that if the borrower defaults by failing to pay the debt or by breaking other promises, the lender has the option to do more than bring an action for breach of promise or an action on the unpaid installments or the accelerated debt. The lender also has the option to foreclose.

When thinking about foreclosure, one critical distinction to keep in mind is the difference between an action on the debt and a foreclosure action. The typical mortgage arrangement involves a promissory note and a mortgage document. The promissory note is a personal promise to repay the loan. Usually the note is a negotiable instrument under Article 3 of the Uniform Commercial Code. An action to enforce the instrument is a personal action brought against the borrower. The mortgage document gives the lender a preferred claim against a specific property that the borrower puts up as collateral for the loan. The foreclosure action is how the lender enforces its claim to the collateral. The distinction between the note and the mortgage has an impact on choice of laws. A mortgage must be governed and foreclosed in accordance with the law of the state where the property is located. On the other hand, the parties may include a choice-of-law provision in the note, which may select a different state.

Foreclosure or an action on the debt are the mortgage lender's two basic options when the mortgagor is not voluntarily paying the debt. Sometimes the mortgage lender wants to pursue both options. It is not necessarily an either-or choice. Why might the mortgagee want a judgment on the debt, even though she is foreclosing? If the value of the property is less than the debt and the mortgagee realizes this, she expects that foreclosure will result in a *deficiency*. The lender is generally able to pursue the borrower for a deficiency because the borrower has made a personal promise to pay the loan back in full in accordance with the terms of the promissory note. Thus, the borrower is personally liable for the full repayment when the collateral does not fully cover the outstanding debt. When this happens, along with foreclosure the mortgagee wants a judgment equal to the shortfall — this is called a *deficiency judgment*. If there is any prospect that the judgment may be collectible, the deficiency judgment is worth having.

Today, in the United States generally, the mortgagee has the option of suing on the debt, foreclosing on the property, or doing both. If both are sought, they may be pursued simultaneously or consecutively. Unless there are statutory or contractual restrictions, the mortgagee is not required to sue on the debt and foreclose at the same point in time (some jurisdictions do require that the mortgagee sue on the debt and foreclose at the same time; this is referred to as the *single-action* or *one-action*, rule). With a judicial foreclosure action, if the mortgagee anticipates a deficiency, a single action can seek both a foreclosure decree and a deficiency judgment against the borrower. The foreclosure action is considered to be an action in equity, with the action on the debt considered to be at law, but this combination is permissible given the modern procedural unification of law and equity.

The opposite of a deficiency resulting from foreclosure is a *surplus*. When the mortgaged property is worth much more than the unpaid debt, there is surplus value that belongs to the property owner, the mortgagor. If the auction sale at foreclosure is at a price that exceeds the debt, including the expenses of foreclosure, there are surplus proceeds. These proceeds are paid to the mortgagor, provided there are no third parties who have asserted claims against the mortgagor in the foreclosure action. If there are third parties with valid claims, such as junior lienors or tenants whose leases are terminated, they are compensated out of the surplus. Even in this circumstance, however, the surplus is used for the mortgagor's benefit, as it extinguishes the mortgagor's debts owed to third parties.

A. TYPES OF FORECLOSURE

There is no single way for a mortgagee to foreclose on the mortgaged property. State law determines what foreclosure processes are available, and they vary substantially. All states have foreclosure statutes that define and govern foreclosure proceedings, which must be consulted. In addition, the parties' contract, as reflected in the mortgage instrument, often affects how the lender may foreclose. Most mortgages have a foreclosure clause, which covers such matters as notices to be given to the borrower prior to foreclosure, time periods that must expire before the lender takes certain steps to foreclose, and where and when a foreclosure sale may take place. Although foreclosure rules and procedures vary markedly from state to state, there are common elements. These common elements are best understood by focusing on the three basic types of foreclosure presently used in the United States: strict foreclosure, judicial foreclosure with public sale of the property, and power of sale foreclosure (also called nonjudicial foreclosure).

1. Strict Foreclosure

English foreclosure is called "strict foreclosure." This is our American term for it; to the English it was just "foreclosure" with no ominous-sounding adjective. See Chapter 14 for a brief description of the historical steps in mortgage law leading up to strict foreclosure. Depending on your point of view (lender or borrower), the term "strict foreclosure" sounds either delightful or awful. The basic idea is that the Court of Chancery, at the instance of the mortgagee, "foreclosed" (barred) the mortgagor's equity of redemption by setting a final payment date. The judicial date was strictly enforced; hence "strict" foreclosure. If the mortgagor failed to pay by the judicially set date, the ballgame was over. With strict foreclosure, the mortgagee could just keep the property. After foreclosure, she could sell it, but she wasn't required to do so. If the mortgaged property was worth more than the debt, the mortgagee had no duty to account to the mortgagor for the surplus value. Today, England largely uses power of sale foreclosure, rather than historic strict foreclosure.

In the United States today, strict foreclosure is not in widespread use. Early on in our history, most communities came to believe that strict foreclosure was too harsh when the mortgagor had substantial equity in the property. Although in principle the court could alleviate harshness by setting a long time for final payment when the property was worth much more than the debt — for example, many months — judges usually did not do this, and often they did not even obtain evidence of property value.

2. Judicial Foreclosure

In judicial foreclosure, the mortgagee brings an action asking the court to issue an order calling for a sale of the mortgaged property. It resembles strict foreclosure in that both procedures are actions brought before a trial court, with a judge setting a date by which the mortgagor must pay or else lose the property. In both cases, the mortgagor loses her equity of redemption if she does not pay by the judicial deadline. The difference is what happens when the deadline arrives — that is, *how* the mortgagor loses the property. With strict foreclosure, the mortgagee just keeps the property, and if the mortgagee does not yet have possession, she is entitled to possession. With judicial foreclosure, a court-supervised public sale of the property occurs. Traditionally and still today, in many communities this is by public auction, outside on the courthouse steps. Usually a public officer such as the sheriff conducts the auction sale.

Judicial foreclosure developed in the United States to safeguard mortgagors from losses stemming from strict foreclosures. Judicial foreclosure is thought to be superior because the "market" decides how much the mortgaged property is worth. In principle, this protects the mortgagor with a large equity in the property because public bidding at the foreclosure sale is thought to provide the best opportunity for a sale that will yield a foreclosure surplus — the best chance that the price paid by the high bidder will exceed the mortgage debt. This assumption is based on the belief that an auction creates a market and that the price bid at an auction, therefore, reflects the fair market value of the property. From this perspective, it is assumed that the defaulting borrower has her best chance of getting a fair and full price for the property, which should present her best opportunity for receiving a foreclosure surplus. It should be noted that this "market" assumption is held in law even in situations where few or perhaps only one bidder is present at the foreclosure sale.

The procedural details of judicial foreclosure depend on state law, with a number of local differences, but there are some common key elements that revolve around the identification of which persons' rights are to be adjudicated. The lender, with her attorney's help, must decide whom to sue. A foreclosure decree binds parties who are defendants with proper service of process. Thus, nonparties are generally not bound by the foreclosure decree or the foreclosure sale, and this is important if nonparties have property rights in the foreclosed-upon property.

To answer the question of whom the lender should include as defendants in the foreclosure action, we need to consider the status of title to the mortgaged property that should pass to the foreclosure purchaser. The central goal of foreclosure is to give the purchaser *the same title the mortgagor had at the moment the mortgage was granted*. This is the lender's prime objective with respect to title. How is this accomplished? Foreclosure has to terminate not only the mortgagor's equity of redemption but also all junior interests. All rights in the mortgaged property, other than the mortgage itself, are either prior to or junior to the mortgage. The foreclosure terminates the mortgage that is being foreclosed. Prior interests are not terminated or affected by the foreclosure; that, in essence, is what it means to be prior. Junior interests are supposed to be cut off. Junior interests may consist of the full range of rights in real property that are recognized in our legal system — for example, leases, easements, covenants, junior mortgages, and judgment liens.

In terms of foreclosure procedure, the present owner of the property and all persons who hold junior interests are *necessary parties*. They are necessary in the sense that they have to be joined as defendants to accomplish the goal of transferring title to the buyer in the condition it was in when the mortgage was granted.

Another key element in foreclosure practice is identification of *proper parties*. A proper party is a person who has rights or duties with respect to the property or the debt but who is not a necessary party — the central title goal can be accomplished without making the proper party a defendant. This person is a "proper" party in the sense that it is useful to ascertain or define her rights or duties as part of the foreclosure proceeding. Joinder may be desirable, but it is not essential as with a necessary party. The significance of labeling a person as a "proper party" is that she can be joined without her consent. The proper party can be forced in as an additional defendant. Proper parties include holders of prior interests in the property and persons who are liable on the debt but who do not presently have an ownership interest in the mortgaged property. Thus, if the foreclosing mortgagee plans to seek a deficiency judgment, a guarantor or surety for that debt is a proper party in the foreclosure action. This includes a person treated as a surety because of having previously transferred the property to someone who either assumed or took subject to the mortgage (see Chapter 16).

ENGLISH v. BANKERS TRUST COMPANY OF CALIFORNIA, N.A.
District Court of Appeal of Florida, Fourth District, 2005
895 So. 2d 1120

STONE, Judge. We affirm a summary judgment of foreclosure in favor of Bankers Trust. The trial court properly allowed Bankers Trust to join [Shana] English in a re-foreclosure of a mortgage where it failed to join the true owner of the property, an indispensable party, in the first foreclosure.

There are no disputed issues of material fact. Bankers Trust first attempted to foreclose, in a separate case, in early 2002. It named only English, the original owner and mortgagor, as a defendant. That foreclosure resulted in a final judgment setting the debt at $73,839.75, and setting a foreclosure sale. Bankers Trust purchased the property at the foreclosure sale. Immediately thereafter, Bankers Trust learned of English's conveyance to Lesa Investments, and it brought a *de novo* foreclosure action naming both English and Lesa Investments. Another party, Van Zamft, was also added.

English does not deny the default in payment. Instead, she answers that, because there had been a prior foreclosure action and sale, she could not be joined in the re-foreclosure.

The trial court correctly concluded that the first action was void. Significantly, this is not a re-foreclosure to extinguish a junior lienor. Rather, this second action is an initial foreclosure as to the fee simple owner. Because Lesa Investments, the undisputed owner, was not a party to the first suit, the initial foreclosure judgment could not result in a valid sale, as the owner of the fee simple title was an indispensable party. Community Fed. Svgs. and Loan Ass'n v. Wright, 452 So. 2d 638, 640 (Fla. 4th DCA 1984).

If the initial sale were not void, then there would be merit in English's claim that res judicata precludes this second action as to a deficiency judgment. The first foreclosure sale, however, is void for failure to join the fee simple owner. . . .

We note that, more than a century ago, the Florida Supreme Court recognized that "a foreclosure proceeding resulting in a final decree and a sale of the mortgaged property, without the holder of the legal title being before the court will have no effect to transfer his title to the purchaser at said sale." Jordan v. Sayre, So. 329, 330 (Fla. 1888). If the foreclosure proceeding has no effect to transfer title because the legal title holder has not been joined, it is simply another way of saying that the foreclosure proceeding is void.

Although English may have a point in arguing that it is redundant to name her in the re-foreclosure of the property, there is no authority to support her position that joining her in the second foreclosure is precluded. Rather, it is reasonable to conclude that if the first foreclosure sale was invalid, because the legal title holder was not a party, then a second foreclosure action is necessary to enforce the mortgagee's rights.

It also follows that English's claim that the doctrine of merger precludes Bankers Trust from seeking a deficiency judgment must fail. If the first foreclosure sale and all related proceedings cannot stand, then the deficiency judgment awarded to Bankers Trust was also void.

With respect to the amount due from English, however, any such deficiency, including pre-judgment interest, is due only until the time of the original foreclosure proceeding. In White v. Mid-State Federal Savings & Loan Ass'n, 530 So. 2d 959 (Fla. 5th DCA 1988), the court held that where the senior mortgagee becomes the owner of the foreclosed property but re-foreclosure is necessary, it is error to continue to award interest, real property taxes, insurance premiums, and expenses for the period following the first foreclosure. . . .

Therefore, we reverse as to the amount of deficiency and remand for further proceedings. In all other respects, we affirm.

Problem 17A

Mary, the owner of a home in the Surfside subdivision, defaulted on her loan to Big Bank, which at the time had an outstanding balance of $100,000. Big Bank sued Mary to foreclose on the mortgage, properly joining all the necessary parties as defendants. At the foreclosure sale Jason purchased the property for $120,000. Assume that the full amount owed to Big Bank was $105,000, consisting of the outstanding balance, fees, interests, penalties, and costs. The title report done for the foreclosure revealed the following property interests in order of priority:

1. Utility easement granted to Bigtown Lighting and Power Co.
2. A driveway easement granted to an adjoining property owner.
3. Mortgage loan to First Bank. Balance due is presently $50,000.
4. Big Bank's mortgage. bal. $106,000
5. Lien held by Surfside homeowners' association for past-due monthly fees and assessments in the total amount of $10,000.
6. Lease from Mary to Betty for 12 months, calling for monthly rent of $2,000. On the date of the foreclosure sale, 4 months remained in the lease term.

(a) In this situation, who is a necessary party? a proper party?

(b) When Jason buys the property at the sale, does he take title free and clear of all these identified interests? If not, which survive, and why?

(c) At the foreclosure sale Jason paid $120,000; how should the officer in charge of the foreclosure distribute the proceeds of the sale? What if Jason's winning bid at the foreclosure sale had only been $108,000; or $95,000?

(d) Assume that when Mary defaulted on her mortgage with Big Bank, First Bank was notified of the default and decided that this was an event of default under its mortgage. First Bank had a *cross default* provision in its mortgage that made it an event of default for the borrower (Mary) to default on any obligation it owed to any party. First Bank decides to foreclose against Mary. Who is a necessary party and who is a proper party in the foreclosure by First Bank? Assume that the First Bank debt with all expenses totals $50,000 at the time of foreclosure. If Jason is the successful bidder at the First Bank foreclosure, with the same purchase price of $120,000 as in the previous situation, how should this amount be distributed?

3. Power of Sale Foreclosure

Foreclosure by power of sale, also called *nonjudicial foreclosure,* is in widespread use in a number of states. This type of foreclosure allows lenders to foreclose by selling the property without court involvement. All the steps in the foreclosure process, including the sale, are handled either by the lender or by a third party, such as the trustee under a deed of trust. The availability and validity of nonjudicial foreclosure depend on both the parties' agreement and the state foreclosure statutes. In any given transaction, nonjudicial foreclosure can be employed only if the mortgage instrument authorizes the procedure by granting a power of sale to the lender or to a third party such as a trustee. However, since mortgagees by and large control the drafting of loan documents, in states where nonjudicial foreclosure is common the proper clauses are virtually always included in the mortgage document.

State statutes govern nonjudicial foreclosure by specifying notice provisions, sales procedures, and other formalities the lender or her agent must observe. Such statutes, which the parties cannot contract around, are designed to protect mortgagors from the risks stemming from the fact that no disinterested third party such as a judge is supervising the foreclosure process. The lawyer who handles or facilitates a nonjudicial foreclosure must realize that the statutory requirements are not mere formalities. Punctilious observance is mandatory. A deviation from statutory requirements generally means that the foreclosure sale, even after completion, is subject to attack and invalidation. Any slipup means the lender or the foreclosure purchaser incurs great risk that after completion of foreclosure, the mortgagor or a third party with an interest in the property will challenge the sale.

The goal of nonjudicial foreclosure is the same as judicial foreclosure: to sell the property and apply the net sales proceeds to the debt. The goal with respect to title is also the same: to transfer to the foreclosure buyer the title in the condition it was in when the mortgage was granted. The reason for the nonjudicial alternative is to save the lender the time and expense of going to court. Judicial foreclosure, for example, usually provides safeguards to the mortgagor and to third parties, such as the buyer at foreclosure and the owners of junior interests. Such parties generally have less protection, both procedural and substantive, in the private, nonjudicial, context. Junior interest holders are entitled to notice of a judicial foreclosure, for instance (they are necessary parties and if omitted are not bound by the foreclosure), but in many nonjudicial foreclosure states, they are not entitled to notice of the foreclosure unless they have obtained such a right by contracting with the mortgagee.

Compared to judicial foreclosure, power of sale foreclosure is cheap and fast, which is why many states have it. In principle, the savings should benefit not only lenders, who incur lower foreclosure costs, but also borrowers. Losses from loans should be less if lenders can force a foreclosure sale without incurring court costs and waiting months for completion of judicial proceedings. This means less risk to the lender, and in a competitive market this reduced risk should also reduce the lender's price. A borrower who agrees to grant the lender a power of sale should in return pay a lower interest rate or bargain for other economically advantageous terms.

Foreclosure, as indicated earlier, is the province of the states, and there is substantial variation in local laws and procedures. During the past few decades, the federal government has chosen to intervene in several areas of real estate finance to supply uniform national practices and legal rules. In prior chapters, we discuss creation of the secondary mortgage market and preemption of usury laws and due-on-sale limitations. Federal intervention has also begun, on a limited basis, in the area of foreclosure. In 1981, Congress passed the Multifamily Mortgage Foreclosure Act, 12 U.S.C. §§3701-3717, to authorize nonjudicial foreclosure of mortgages on multi-family properties held by the Department of Housing and Urban Development (HUD). In 1994, the Single Family Mortgage Foreclosure Act, 12 U.S.C. §§3751-3768, extended the scheme to HUD's single-family mortgages. The acts provide for HUD to appoint a foreclosure commissioner to conduct the sale. Procedural rules, including notice requirements to borrowers and other interested parties, are supplied. The acts preempt state limits on the collection of deficiency judgments. The federal objective is to reduce the time and expense incurred by HUD when it uses state judicial foreclosure procedures, thus saving government resources by cutting the losses incurred due to mortgage default.

Problem 17B

Jack, an attorney named as trustee under a deed of trust, conducts a foreclosure sale. At the time, the debt is $105,000. Assume that all proper notices have been given, but the following happens at the sale:

(a) The first Tuesday of the month is the only day of the month that foreclosure sales may occur. An ice storm Monday night closes many roads in and leading to the city. Many local businesses are closed, but Jack lives very close to the courthouse. Jack and a lender's representative appear at the courthouse, and Jack conducts the sale with an audience of one, selling the property to the lender for $90,000.

(b) Jack's watch is fast. The sale is advertised for 10:00 A.M., but he starts the sale at 9:52. The sale takes approximately two minutes, and he and the sole bidder, the lender, are gone at 9:59. How do we know this? Assume (i) the borrower, with a prospective bidder, shows up at 10:02 ("would have been there on time, but parking's awful") and is surprised to find no action. Or (ii) as part of a plan to detect and suppress crime, the city has installed surveillance cameras on the courthouse facade and the borrower obtained a copy of the videotape, which shows Jack jumped the gun. The borrower has no evidence of prospective bidders who planned to show up at 10:00.

(c) Jack's watch is slow, plus parking is awful. He and the lender's rep show up at 10:16 and hold the sale.

(d) Assume that the state statute governing power of sale foreclosures provides that the sale must be made between the hours of 10:00 A.M. and 4:00 P.M. on the first Tuesday of the month. The statute further requires that written notice of the date, time, and place of sale must be posted and sent by certified mail to the debtor. What do you think the notice should say with respect to the time of sale?

B. FORECLOSURE SALE PRICES

A primary objective of foreclosure is to try to make the mortgage lender whole with respect to the debt obligation owed by the mortgagor. The owner of the obligation, whether the loan originator or a purchaser through the secondary mortgage market, considers its loans as financial investments. In other words, it looks for a financial return on the loan and does not anticipate having to own the property in the event of a default by the mortgagor. Consequently, foreclosure typically comes down to an action in which the lender hopes to recover all that it is owed on the debt by having a foreclosure sale in which a price will be bid for the property that adequately covers the outstanding debt amount. Should the price more than cover this amount, there will be a surplus to distribute to other claimants with an interest, including the debtor. Thus, the foreclosure sale and the adequacy of the price received for the property become critical to the foreclosure process. If, instead of a surplus, the price is below the amount of the outstanding debt, there will be a deficiency. The question then arises as to the fairness of allowing the foreclosing lender to sue the defaulting borrower for the deficiency in order to satisfy the full amount of the debt beyond the amount that could be recovered based solely on the foreclosure sale price.

In most states a combination of common-law rules and statutes attempt to balance the rights and liabilities of mortgagor and lender with respect to the property value as compared to the amount of the debt. Many states have statutes, often dating from the Great Depression of the 1930s, that either prohibit mortgage lenders from obtaining deficiency judgments or impose other limitations. The statutes vary widely. Sometimes they apply only to particular types of transactions for which the borrower is thought to need or deserve protection — for example, home loans or farm loans. In addition, the statutory restriction may depend on the type of foreclosure process; the mortgagee may be barred from obtaining a deficiency judgment if she forecloses by power of sale rather than judicially. If she desires a deficiency judgment, judicial foreclosure, which presumably offers the borrower greater procedural and substantive safeguards, is required. In some states, such as California, a seller of real property who takes back a purchase-money mortgage cannot obtain a deficiency judgment.

Another approach is *fair value legislation*, which, instead of an outright ban on deficiency judgments, permits such a judgment only to the extent the debt exceeds the "fair value" of the foreclosed property. Fair-value laws are an indirect attempt to solve the problem of inadequate prices paid at foreclosure sales. A low price is still permitted, but it is not used to calculate the deficiency.

Antideficiency judgment acts that simply bar any deficiency judgment for a class of mortgage loans raise market concerns. Consider how they affect the market risk of owning real property. When a statute applies, it transfers the risk of market declines in real estate values from borrowers to lenders. For policy reasons, borrower waivers of statutory protection are generally invalid, so the law insists that the lender bear at least part of the risk. Why should lenders be forced to assume this risk? Do lenders have better information about market values and trends than borrowers? Is the concept of antideficiency judgment acts consistent with general notions of what it means to be the "owner" of land, by which the owner has the potential benefit of appreciation along with the risk of falling value?

California and a handful of other states have enacted a *one-action rule*, which limits the mortgagee to a single action that must include foreclosure and may include, if appropriate, a deficiency judgment. The one-action rule serves several purposes. First, there is an efficiency rationale in protecting the mortgagor from having to defend multiple actions that arise out of the same lending transaction. Additionally, this limit of one action helps to conserve judicial resources. The rule compels the mortgagee to satisfy the debt out of the mortgaged property first, before chasing other assets owned by the mortgagor. The mortgagee cannot bring a personal action on the debt; the mortgagee must first exhaust the security the parties agreed to for the debt before making other collection attempts.

Foreclosure terminates the mortgagor's equity of redemption. This is the point of the foreclosure process. Up until the moment of the foreclosure sale, the equity of redemption means the mortgagor has the right to pay the debt and obtain a release of the mortgage. Depending on state law, the borrower may have an additional right called the right of *statutory redemption* that comes into play *after* the foreclosure sale. In a majority of states there are statutes creating post-foreclosure redemption rights under certain circumstances. Historically, statutory redemption dates back to the nineteenth century when, during economic depressions when land values were falling, legislatures provided for redemption for a fixed period after execution sales of real estate. The statutes were primarily directed at protecting landowners from judgment liens, but often courts interpreted the statutes to protect owners from mortgage foreclosure sales as well. Legislatures frequently amended the legislation; for example, it was common to lengthen the redemption period during hard times and shorten it during business recoveries. The statutory details vary widely from state to state, and thus a lawyer who represents lender, borrower, or foreclosure purchaser must carefully study the relevant statutory framework. The primary principles are sketched here.

Existence of right to redeem. In some states, statutory redemption is available after both judicial and power of sale foreclosures. In others, it is available after one but not the other foreclosure process. Tennessee, for example, authorizes statutory redemption following judicial foreclosure but not foreclosure by power of sale. Obviously, this makes power of sale foreclosure even more popular among lenders in Tennessee. In a few states, a mortgagor is permitted to waive the right of statutory redemption, but in most states waivers are not permitted.

Time period. The statutes set a fixed time period after foreclosure for exercise of the right to redeem. Presently, the period ranges from a few months to 18 months. Sometimes the period varies according to the type of the mortgaged real estate. For example, longer redemption periods may be allowed for owner-occupied housing and farmland, and shorter periods may be available for abandoned property.

Redemption price. In almost all states, the redemption price is the foreclosure sales price plus interest and foreclosure costs. In most states, a statutory rate of interest is specified (often 8 or 10 percent), but in some states the redemption price bears interest at the rate specified in the mortgage debt instrument. A few states, instead of basing redemption on the foreclosure purchase price, require the redemptioner to pay the mortgage debt plus interest. Missouri follows this approach generally, and Alabama does so, but only if the mortgagee is the purchaser at foreclosure. When there is a deficiency at foreclosure, this rule allows the purchaser to collect the amount of deficiency from the redemptioner.

Right to possession. In most states, the mortgagor has the right to possession during the statutory period. In effect, the foreclosure purchaser has bought a future interest—actually, a contingent future interest, given the possibility that redemption will occur. In a few states, the mortgagor must post bond to retain property, as a protection against waste. In a few states, the purchaser at the foreclosure sale is entitled to immediate possession, and if the redemption right is exercised, then possession reverts to the redemptioner.

Who can redeem. In some states, the redemption right is granted only to the mortgagor; in others, junior lienors are also entitled to statutory redemption. If a junior lienor redeems, in most states she gets title to the land — specifically, the same title the foreclosure purchaser had — just like a redeeming mortgagor. This contrasts with the junior lienor's right to redeem prior to foreclosure. There, the junior's redemption right is not to obtain title to the mortgaged property, but to pay the senior debt, thereby acquiring that debt by subrogation.

Effect of redemption on liens. Generally, the *mortgagor's* redemption revives preforeclosure liens other than the lien foreclosed upon, the policy being not to let the mortgagor's default and foreclosure destroy the liens she created. (In other words, a junior lienholder who did not get paid from the proceeds of foreclosure is able to revive her lien.)

Compliance with statutory requirements. Many courts have ruled that substantial compliance with procedural requirements for redemption is sufficient. Minor flaws in following requirements will not disqualify mortgagors and lienors who act to redeem. Redemption statutes are liberally construed to protect mortgagors and lienors.

FIRST BANK v. FISCHER & FRICHTEL, INC.
Supreme Court of Missouri, 2012
364 S.W.3d 216

LAURA DENVIR STITH, Judge. This case involves the question of whether the amount of the deficiency owed by Fischer & Frichtel Inc., a sophisticated commercial debtor, after a foreclosure sale of its property should be measured by the difference between the amount of the unpaid debt and the amount obtained at the foreclosure sale or, instead, by the difference between the amount of the unpaid debt and the fair market value of the property at the time of the foreclosure sale. The trial court submitted an instruction directing the jury to award the difference between the amount of the debt and the property's fair market value but then granted First Bank's motion for a new trial in light of its showing that Missouri case law instead requires the deficiency to be determined by the difference between the debt and the amount received at the foreclosure sale. Fischer & Frichtel appeals.

As discussed below, Missouri common law requires the deficiency to be measured by the amount received at the foreclosure sale, but if the sale price, alone or in combination with other factors, is so inadequate as to raise an inference of fraud, then the foreclosure sale can be voided. Missouri does not permit questions about the adequacy of the foreclosure price also to be raised in the deficiency action. Fischer & Frichtel argues that Missouri's traditional approach leads to unfairness where the debtor is unable to obtain alternative financing in time to submit a bid at the foreclosure sale and the lender is the only bidder. It says this concern has caused other jurisdictions to reject the traditional use of the foreclosure price to measure the deficiency and instead measure it by the fair market value of the property.

Each jurisdiction cited by Fischer & Frichtel that has changed from basing the deficiency on the foreclosure price to basing it on the property's fair market value made that change by statute. Further, the public policy rationales that Fischer & Frichtel offers as the basis to do so do not apply to a sophisticated commercial entity such as itself, which claims neither that it had inadequate notice to obtain alternative financing nor that the foreclosure sale itself had badges of fraud. The trial court's grant of a new trial to First Bank is affirmed, and the case is remanded.

FACTUAL AND PROCEDURAL BACKGROUND

First Bank is a privately owned company that provides both retail and commercial banking services to its clients. Fischer & Frichtel is a real-estate developer with more than sixty years of experience in the industry. From 2005 to the beginning of 2008, Fischer & Frichtel had hundreds of millions of dollars in revenue and earned tens of millions of dollars in profit. Among its business deals in June 2000 was the purchase of 21 lots in Franklin County for a residential development.

To finance the acquisition, Fischer & Frichtel borrowed $2.576 million from First Bank, in favor of which it executed a deed of trust pledging the lots as collateral for the loan. From 2000 to 2005, Fischer & Frichtel sold 12 of the 21 lots to homebuyers. Each time a lot was sold, Fischer & Frichtel made a principal payment of $126,000 to First Bank, which then released that lot from the deed of trust. Beginning in 2005, the housing market began to decline, and Fischer & Frichtel was unable to sell any of the nine remaining lots in this particular development.

Although the original maturity date on the loan from First Bank to Fischer & Frichtel was July 1, 2003, First Bank extended the maturity date six times. The final mutually agreed maturity date on the loan was September 1, 2008. In April 2008, First Bank and Fischer & Frichtel began to negotiate another extension of the maturity date, but due to the increased risk caused by the declining real estate market, First Bank sought a higher interest rate, a renewal fee, an increase in the amount of principal Fischer & Frichtel would pay on the loan each time it sold a lot, and either a $283,000 cash payment on the principal or a personal guaranty from John Fischer, the owner of Fischer & Frichtel. Fischer & Frichtel believed the new terms were too onerous, and the parties could not agree to an extension.

When the loan matured on September 1, 2008, Fischer & Frichtel was contractually obligated to pay First Bank the remaining principal on the loan, $1,133,875. Fischer & Frichtel chose instead to default on the loan, and First Bank foreclosed on the nine lots remaining unsold that were subject to the deed of trust. The foreclosure sale was held in December 2008, and First Bank acquired the nine unsold lots after making the sole bid of $466,000. Fischer & Frichtel did not bid and does not claim that the foreclosure sale was not properly noticed or conducted.

In November 2008, just prior to the foreclosure sale, First Bank filed suit against Fischer & Frichtel seeking to recover the unpaid principal and interest on the loan. At the trial in January 2010, Fischer & Frichtel presented expert testimony from an appraiser that, although First Bank paid only $466,000, the fair market value of the nine lots at the time of the foreclosure was nearly double that, $918,000. It also showed that internal First Bank documents valued the property at $1.134 million at the time of the default in September 2008. A First Bank employee testified that the bank determined the amount to bid in foreclosure by estimating that, in the declining real estate market, the value of the property to the bank was only $675,000, which should be discounted to $466,000 because First Bank needed to sell the property in bulk, not as individual lots, and the depressed real-estate market made finding a buyer extremely difficult.

At the close of trial, over First Bank's objection, the court instructed the jury that "[i]f you find in favor of [First Bank], then you must award [First Bank] the balance due [First Bank] on the [loan] on the date of maturity, less the fair market value of the property at the time of the foreclosure sale, plus interest." Accordingly, the jury found that the fair market value of the lots was $918,000, the value testified to by Fischer & Frichtel's expert, and that Fischer & Frichtel therefore owed First Bank $215,875 (the difference between the amount of unpaid principal on the loan and the fair market value of the property at the time of the foreclosure sale) plus $37,500 in interest. . . .

THE FORECLOSURE SALE PRICE IS THE MEASURE OF A DEFICIENCY

There are two general approaches to reviewing claims that the amount received for a property at a foreclosure sale is insufficient.

One approach is to allow the foreclosure sale price to be used in determining the deficiency only if the debtor does not challenge the adequacy of the foreclosure sale price in the deficiency action. If there is such a challenge, states that use this approach rely on a variety of standards, usually set by statute, for determining whether to reject the foreclosure sale price in favor of fair market value as a measure of the deficiency, ranging from whether there is a difference between the two prices,[2] to whether the foreclosure sale price is substantially lower than the fair market value,[3] to whether the foreclosure sale price is so much lower than the fair market value that it shocks the conscience.[4]

Fischer & Frichtel argues that Missouri should adopt the most liberal of these standards — that recommended by section 8.4 of the Restatement (Third) of Property, Mortgages (1997) — and always allow debtors to pay

2. *See, e.g.,* Utah Code Ann. §57-1-32 ("The court may not render [a deficiency] judgment for more than the amount by which . . . the indebtedness . . . exceeds the fair market value of the property as of the date of the sale"); Wis. Stat. Ann. §846.165 (no "judgment for deficiency [shall be] rendered, until the court is satisfied that the fair market value of the premises has been credited on the mortgage").

3. Mich. Comp. Laws Ann. §600.3280 (showing that "the amount bid was substantially less than its true value . . . shall constitute a defense to [a deficiency] action and shall defeat the deficiency judgment against [the debtor] either in whole or in part"); Tenn. Code Ann. §35-5-118 (in order to use the fair market value as the measure of a deficiency, the debtor must show the "property sold for an amount materially less than the fair market value of [the] property at the time of the foreclosure sale").

4. R.K. Cooper Const. Co. v. Fulton, 216 So. 2d 11, 13 (Fla. 1968) ("A shockingly inadequate sale price in the foreclosure proceeding can be asserted as an equitable defense and the trial judge has the discretion and duty to inquire into the reasonable and fair market value of the property sold").

only the difference between the debt and the fair market value of the property at the time of the foreclosure if the debtor challenges the foreclosure price.[5]

Missouri and many of the other states in which the method of measuring deficiencies is governed by the common law traditionally have followed a different approach, however. These states require a debtor to pay as a deficiency the full difference between the debt and the foreclosure sale price. They do not permit a debtor to attack the sufficiency of the foreclosure sale price *as part of the deficiency proceeding* even if the debtor believes that the foreclosure sale price was inadequate.

This does not mean Missouri does not give a debtor a mechanism for attacking an inadequate foreclosure sale price. Rather, a debtor who believes that the foreclosure sale price was inadequate can bring an action to void the *foreclosure sale* itself. Roberts v. Murray, 232 S.W.2d 540, 546 (Mo. 1950).... Since *Roberts*, the standard for voiding a foreclosure sale has been reaffirmed by numerous Missouri court decisions.

Fischer & Frichtel does not claim that this is not the current state of Missouri law, nor does it offer any reason why it failed to follow this approach and file an action attacking the validity of the foreclosure sale due to the inadequacy of the foreclosure sale price. Instead it argues that Missouri's standard for setting aside a foreclosure sale is so high that a debtor cannot realistically hope to meet it.

Missouri permits the debtor to void a properly noticed and carried out foreclosure sale only by showing that "the inadequacy ... [of the sale price is] so gross that it shocks the conscience ... and is in itself evidence of fraud." Cockrell v. Taylor, 145 S.W.2d 416, 422 (Mo. 1940). This is the predominant standard used by courts in determining whether to void the foreclosure sale, but what is sufficient to "shock the conscience" of a court seems to vary greatly. Some states, such as Oregon and Wisconsin, have found sale prices of more than half the fair market value sufficient to shock the conscience and set aside the sale, while others uphold sales for less than 40 percent of the fair market value. Missouri's standard for proving that a foreclosure sale "shocks the conscience" is among the strictest in the country; more than one Missouri case has refused to set aside a sale that was only 20 to

---

5. The Restatement (Third) of Property states in relevant part on this point:

§8.4 Foreclosure: Action For A Deficiency

(a) If the foreclosure sale price is less than the unpaid balance of the mortgage obligation, an action may be brought to recover a deficiency judgment against any person who is personally liable on the mortgage obligation in accordance with the provisions of this section.

(b) Subject to Subsections (c) and (d) of this section, the deficiency judgment is for the amount by which the mortgage obligation exceeds the foreclosure sale price.

(c) Any person against whom such a recovery is sought may request in the proceeding in which the action for a deficiency is pending a determination of the fair market value of the real estate as of the date of the foreclosure sale.

(d) If it is determined that the fair market value is greater than the foreclosure sale price, the persons against whom recovery of the deficiency is sought are entitled to an offset against the deficiency in the amount by which the fair market value, less the amount of any liens on the real estate that were not extinguished by the foreclosure, exceeds the sale price.

30 percent of the fair market value because of Missouri's historical practice of requiring an inference of fraud in addition to a sale price that "shocks the conscience." *Id.*

Fischer & Frichtel argues that this standard for setting aside a foreclosure sale is so high that it is only an illusory remedy for an unfairly low sale price and that because the foreclosure process inherently produces artificially low sale prices, it almost inevitably leads to windfalls for lenders. Fischer & Frichtel suggests that the foreclosure process is unfair in part because cash must be offered for the property by the bidder. This is a problem for the ordinary bidder, particularly a homeowner or small business owner, because the statutory minimum time period between notice of foreclosure and the actual sale is often less than a month, an insufficient amount of time to allow potential bidders to secure financing.

Fischer & Frichtel notes that the lender does not have this financing problem, as it does not have to pay with cash, but instead simply may deduct the purchase price from the amount of principal the borrower owes. Because realistically the lender often will be the sole bidder, it can buy the foreclosed property for far less than market value, sell the property at a profit and then collect a deficiency from the borrower based on the below-market value it paid for the property.[9] The lender receives both the benefit of buying the property for less than fair market value and also of only having to reduce the deficiency it is entitled to by the below fair market price paid at the foreclosure sale.

First Bank offers factual and policy rebuttals to many of these arguments.[10] The policy debate presented by the parties may explain why so many states have chosen to deal with this issue by statute, rather than by the common law, as still is the case in Missouri.

---

9. For example, assume that a lender loans the borrower $100,000; the borrower, having paid none of the principal, defaults; and the lender forecloses. The property is appraised at $130,000. Nevertheless, the lender is the only bidder at the sale and buys the property for $60,000. The lender can seek a deficiency against the borrower and will recover $40,000, the difference between the sale price at foreclosure and the amount of principal left on the loan. The lender then can sell the house for its appraised value of $130,000 and will gain $170,000 from foreclosing on a loan of only $100,000.

10. First Bank suggests that this Court should continue to follow the foreclosure sale price approach because changing to the fair market value approach will increase lending costs by shifting all the risk in the foreclosure process onto the lender. Under the fair market value approach, regardless of what happens to the market, the borrower knows it will owe a deficiency based solely on the fair market value at the time of the foreclosure sale. By contrast, if the lender buys the property, which Fischer & Frichtel agrees usually is the case, it holds all the risk, so that if property prices decline and the lender cannot sell the property for the fair market value at foreclosure, it incurs a loss. Furthermore, under the fair market value approach, the lender may feel forced to buy property likely to bring in less than the market price because it knows that it only will receive a deficiency for the fair market value of the property, regardless of how little it recovers in the foreclosure sale. First Bank also argues that the fair market value approach will increase costs by forcing lenders to determine the fair market value of every property they foreclose and by causing litigation over the true "fair market value" of the property.

Even more importantly here, however, nearly all of the problems that Fischer & Frichtel alleges concern *not the fairness of the deficiency determination itself but the fairness of the foreclosure sale price* due to lack of sufficient notice to obtain alternative financing or other bidders. . . .

It may be that Fischer & Frichtel advocates an alternative approach because it did not file a timely challenge to the foreclosure sale and could not have met the traditional standard for setting aside a foreclosure sale had it done so.[11] Or perhaps it is that the policy reasons raised by Fischer & Frichtel for lowering the burden required to show inadequacy of the foreclosure sale price principally apply to individuals and small businesses that have no realistic ability to bid themselves, not to a sophisticated business entity such as Fischer & Frichtel, which has not shown or alleged that it did not have adequate notice of the foreclosure sale, that the sale was not fairly conducted or that it did not have the financial means to offer an alternative bid. So far as the record shows, Fischer & Frichtel simply made a strategic choice not to bid, not to attack the amount received as inadequate under the traditional standard for setting aside a foreclosure sale and not to ask this Court to adopt a less onerous standard.[12] Fischer & Frichtel's suggested alternative would make those decisions irrelevant.

Moreover, Fischer & Frichtel has not identified any jurisdiction that has rejected the foreclosure sale price approach in favor of the fair market value approach based on the common law. All of the cited states that follow the fair market value approach either have always done so or have made the change to that approach based on statute.

While the fact that this matter is not addressed by statute does allow this Court greater discretion than otherwise would be the case, "[u]nder the doctrine of stare decisis, a decision of this Court should not be lightly overruled, particularly where . . . the opinion has remained unchanged for many years." Sw. Bell Yellow Pages, Inc. v. Dir. of Revenue, 94 S.W.3d 388, 390 (Mo. 2002).

Here, the public policy reasons that form the basis of Fischer & Frichtel's argument for modification of the more than century-old practice of using the foreclosure sale price have no application to a sophisticated debtor such as it. New York Store Mercantile Co. v. Thurmond, 85 S.W. 333, 336 (Mo. 1905). While the foreclosure sale price was barely more than 50 percent of the fair market value later determined by the jury, the lender gave cogent reasons for its lower bid due to the depressed real estate market and the bulk nature of the sale, as of trial the lender had not been able to sell the property, and Fischer & Frichtel has not argued it could not have purchased the

11. A review of the record shows that the foreclosure sale price of $466,000 was more than half the $918,000 fair market value the property determined by the jury, and no other indicia of fraud or misconduct are shown. These facts would not support voiding the foreclosure sale under current Missouri law. Judah v. Pitts, 62 S.W.2d 715, 720 (Mo. 1933).

12. This may have been a wise strategic decision, as First Bank marketed the property for $675,000, the amount at which First Bank valued it before discounting it because of the need to sell it in bulk, and, as of the trial, had not received a single bid.

property at the foreclosure sale (or indeed thereafter while the property was still on the market for $675,000, a good deal less than Fischer & Frichtel says is its fair market value).

This is not a case, therefore, in which to consider a modification of the standard for setting aside a foreclosure sale solely due to inadequacy of price or whether a change should be made in the manner of determining a deficiency where the foreclosure price is less than the fair market value.

For the reasons stated, the judgment of the trial court awarding a new trial is affirmed.

RICHARD B. TEITELMAN, Chief Justice, dissenting. I respectfully dissent. The purpose of a damage award is to make the injured party whole without creating a windfall. Accordingly, in nearly every context in which a party sustains damage to or the loss of a property or business interest, Missouri law measures damages by reference to fair market value. Yet in the foreclosure context, Missouri law ignores the fair market value of the foreclosed property and, instead, measures the lender's damages with reference to the foreclosure sale price. Rather than making the injured party whole, this anomaly in the law of damages, in many cases, will require the defaulting party to subsidize a substantial windfall to the lender. Aside from the fact that this anomaly long has been a part of Missouri law, there is no other compelling reason for continued adherence to a measure of damages that too often enriches one party at the expense of another. Consequently, I would hold that damages in a deficiency action should be measured by reference to the fair market value of the foreclosed property. . . .

I would reverse the judgment sustaining First Bank's motion for a new trial and order the trial court to enter judgment consistent with the jury's finding that the fair market value of the foreclosed property was $918,000 and that Fischer & Fritchtel therefore owed First Bank a deficiency of $215,875.

Problem 17C

During the boom years of Metropolis, apartment developers went crazy. Beginning three years ago, the rental market chilled considerably as a result of a combination of overbuilding and a weak economy. An apartment complex with 100 units, finished $2^{1}/_{2}$ years ago at a cost of $2.3 million, has an occupancy rate of 52 percent. Lender, holding a $2.1 million debt, purchased it at a foreclosure sale for $1 million. Lender now seeks a deficiency judgment. Should Lender recover, and, if so, how much, if the evidence shows:

(a) During the past year, seven other recently built Metropolis apartment complexes were sold at foreclosure, with the foreclosure prices ranging between 50 percent and 68 percent of construction cost.

(b) During the past year, nine recently built Metropolis apartment complexes were sold in voluntary sales that ranged between 78 percent and 93 percent of construction cost.

(c) Appraisers and economists basically agree that in two to three years, the rental market will absorb the oversupply of Metropolis apartment complexes, with average occupancy rates rising to the normal range of 92 to 98 percent, causing the market value of recently built, well-run, well-maintained complexes to eclipse their construction cost.

(d) In the above situations, does it matter whether the state has a fair value statute, an antideficiency judgment statute, or statutory redemption rights?

C. RESIDENTIAL FORECLOSURE ABUSES AND REFORMS

The collapse of the U.S. housing markets that began in 2007 led to a surge in the volume of residential foreclosures. Approximately 4 million families lost their homes to foreclosure between 2007 and early 2012. Millions more are presently in the foreclosure pipeline; one expert estimated that between 7.4 and 9.3 million more borrowers will lose their homes to foreclosure or a substitute between 2012 and 2018. Of those at risk for foreclosure, many are *underwater*; that is, they owe more on their mortgage loan than their home is worth. As of late 2012, more than 28 percent of homeowners with mortgage debt—over 14 million homes—were underwater.

Foreclosure is the final step documenting a tremendous loss in personal wealth. Homeowners have lost more than $7 trillion in home equity (home value in excess of mortgage debt), which represents more than half of the home equity that existed in early 2006. Wealth at the national level, in addition to the household level, was compromised. The foreclosure crisis, following the collapse of the housing finance securitization market, resulted in massive institutional losses as well as personal loss. Two of the most significant intermediaries in the residential housing market, the Federal National Mortgage Association (FNMA or Fannie Mae) and the Federal Home Loan Mortgage Corporation (FHLMC or Freddie Mac), lost incredible amounts, and the losses had to be covered by an enormous federal bailout funded by U.S. taxpayers.

The financial implications of the mortgage market collapse and of the dramatic rise in mortgage defaults have resulted in more than economic consequences. The effect of the significant rise in residential foreclosures ripples far beyond the realm of economics. The social consequences to foreclosed-upon families are severe. They are compelled to depart from their home and, usually, the neighborhood where they have chosen to live. Most are unable readily to re-enter the market for owner-occupied housing. They seek rental housing, or attempt to live with relatives or friends, seek subsidized housing arrangements, or become homeless.

The social consequences are not confined to the individuals who are forced to vacate their homes. Dwelling units that have gone through foreclosure or are threatened by foreclosure are much more likely to be abandoned than other residential properties. As foreclosure rates increase, so does the probability that affected units will remain vacant. There are two reasons for this. First, due to the flood of foreclosure proceedings, especially in states that require judicial foreclosure, the average foreclosure takes much longer than before, in some cases as long as two to four years. For many properties, this results in a longer period of vacancy between the departure of the mortgagor and the next occupant or a longer period of time in which the defaulting borrower lives payment-free in the property while awaiting the end of the foreclosure process. In either case, there is no one with an incentive to maintain the property during this time. Second, since the housing bubble began to collapse in 2007, the market for residential sales has remained weak. This means that even when lenders are able to complete foreclosure expeditiously, in many markets there is little opportunity for lenders to sell the foreclosed properties to buyers who will take occupancy or who will readily lease the properties to tenants. Foreclosed properties that remain vacant have negative impacts on neighborhoods and the surrounding communities. Neighboring property values are reduced by 0.9 percent to 1.1 percent by each foreclosure, the reduction being partially attributable to empty properties. Neighborhood crime increases by 6 percent to 7 percent. Vacancies and the associated problems of lack of repair and maintenance create public health risks, including infestations by vermin such as mosquitoes and other insects. There are fiscal impacts on local governments, who find that property taxes on vacant properties often become delinquent; yet the governments are faced with added expenses to provide essential services to blighted neighborhoods, such as police and fire protection.

The high volume of foreclosures in recent years revealed a number of flaws in foreclosure processes, some having to do with fairness to homeowners and others having to do with inefficiencies that impact not only homeowners, but also lenders and the broader communities.

Even in good times, foreclosure in many states was a lengthy process, but the post-2006 avalanche of foreclosure proceedings has made the situation much worse. The national average at the end of 2011 was 348 days to complete foreclosure. The longest averages were in New York, New Jersey, and Florida—1019, 964, and 806 days, respectively. Texas had the shortest foreclosure timeline at 90 days. Although, in general, foreclosure delay can be thought to benefit defaulting borrowers and harm lenders, evidence demonstrates that in many communities lenders have intentionally stalled the process. Lenders who are able to foreclose and gain title to residential units due to mortgagor default elect to hold off, believing that taking ownership of properties they cannot sell is not in their best interest. They have concluded that they would not be able to resell the properties due to the extremely weak market, and that they did not want to undertake responsibilities for maintenance and expenses during a lengthy period after the foreclosure. The very long foreclosure timelines result in inefficiency and added costs for the parties; in addition, there are negative effects on the communities when homes in the foreclosure pipeline become unoccupied.

One set of issues, which has given rise to much litigation, concerns who may commence foreclosure and based upon what evidence. For judicial foreclosure, the issue is what the complaint must allege and what underlying evidence the plaintiff must possess or present to the court. For nonjudicial foreclosure, the parallel issue is what documentation the lender or trustee must assemble and prepare. One issue is production of the original promissory note, signed by the borrower, which many lenders and loan servicers have had difficulty locating, primarily as a result of multiple transactions within the secondary market. Many lenders and servicers have solved this problem by signing *lost note affidavits*, which raise problems both of legality and, on occasion, of veracity. Other procedural issues include the need to prove default by the homeowner and the sending of proper notices to the owner prior to foreclosure.

Another issue involves whether the foreclosing party must be the *mortgagee of record*. Due to the nature of the secondary mortgage market, originating lenders frequently sell their loans. Traditionally, the selling lender endorsed and delivered the promissory note to the buyer, and executed and recorded an assignment of the mortgage in the local land records. This practice has changed. Many recent mortgages have named the *Mortgage Electronic Registration System* (MERS) as the mortgagee. MERS acts as a nominee of the originating lender, and when the mortgage is sold in the secondary market, MERS continues as the mortgagee of record. In many cases, homeowners have challenged foreclosures based on the involvement of MERS. They have generally failed, although in many states it appears that the foreclosure must be brought in the name of the real owner of the debt and cannot be brought by MERS as nominee.

Modern residential loans sold on the secondary market result in ownership being held by an investor or another entity, with a loan servicing company hired to "service" the loan by collecting and accounting for the monthly mortgage payments and handling other administrative tasks with respect to the loan, the property, and the borrowers. Mortgage servicers were ill equipped to handle the huge increases in loan defaults and foreclosures that took place after the collapse of the housing market, although the servicer agreements generally obligated the servicer to provide those additional services. Servicers lacked sufficient numbers of staff, their staff members were poorly trained, and servicers did not have economic incentives to perform default-related and foreclosure-related services competently. Servicers, through action and inaction, committed many different abuses.

One problem area relates to *short sales*, in which an owner contracts to sell her home for a price that is less than the outstanding balance on the mortgage loan (that is, the sales proceeds are "short" of the amount needed to repay the loan). When the owner is underwater, a short sale is the only type of sale available to the owner (unless the owner can find a fool who will pay substantially above market value). For a short sale to go through, the lender or its servicer must approve the transaction, by agreeing to release its mortgage in exchange for less than the loan balance. Although federal programs were created to encourage lenders to approve short sales in meritorious cases, lenders and servicers frequently delayed examining and approving paperwork for months. This often resulted in the buyer losing patience and walking away from the deal. That, in turn, often led to the seller abandoning her home or to a decision by the lender to foreclose when there no longer was a potential buyer.

Another frequent abuse is the practice of so-called *robo-signing*, in which an employee of the servicer or lender signs an affidavit without any review of the underlying loan documents (in other words, as if the affidavit is signed by a robot). Reports indicate that single employees signed thousands of affidavits each month, spending less than a minute on any one loan file. In other types of robo-signing, the affiant was fictitious (a fake name and a fake title), or the affiant purported to be an executive officer, but a low-level employee actually prepared and signed the document. The problem in each variety is falsehood; the affidavit states under oath that the affiant has personal knowledge of the facts stated therein. Yet the affiant, even if a real person, failed to verify information.

The federal government and 49 state attorneys general brought litigation against the five largest mortgage servicers. In 2012 the litigation culminated in a national consent settlement, with the servicers agreeing (i) to pay more than $20 billion to homeowners for various types of relief, (ii) to pay $5 billion to the federal and state governments, and (iii) to implement new standards for loan servicing and for foreclosure practices. The settlement requires that servicers send a uniform 14-day pre-foreclosure notice to borrowers in all states, setting forth the grounds for foreclosure, facts related to the loan account, and an indication as to how the borrower may obtain further information, including the name of the current investor who owns the loan. The servicer is obligated to offer loss mitigation alternatives to foreclosure, including loan modifications and short sales. Loss mitigation efforts are a condition precedent to commencing foreclosure. Servicers must offer a loan modification when the modification results in positive net present value to the investor, compared to proceeding with foreclosure, and other investor requirements are met. Although the settlement does not apply to all loan servicers, but only to the five largest, many of its terms are expected to be reflected in servicer standards to be issued by the federal Consumer Financial Protection Bureau.

Although stories about lender and servicer misbehavior are rampant, some people are concerned about borrower behavior. The problem of *strategic default* emerges when homeowners who have the ability to pay their mortgage loan decide to walk away from their properties, because they perceive that their property is "under water." Often they can obtain less expensive housing elsewhere. Similarly, some borrowers, during the boom leading up to the collapse, simply took on mortgages that were clearly beyond their means in an effort to make huge returns on their investments, or to live in a style well beyond what they could realistically afford. Others thought residential housing prices would just continue to rise indefinitely and used the availability of easy financing to acquire and "flip" properties for a profit. Consequently, there is blame enough to go around for everyone in the housing boom and its ultimate collapse.

ZERVAS v. WELLS FARGO BANK, N.A.
District Court of Appeal of Florida, Second District, 2012
93 So. 3d 453

WHATLEY, Judge. Anastasios and Dina Zervas appeal a final judgment of foreclosure entered in favor of Wells Fargo Bank, N.A., as trustee for the MLMI Trust Series 2005–FM1. We reverse because Wells Fargo did not establish that no answer which the Zervases might file could present a genuine issue of fact.

On October 6, 2009, Wells Fargo filed a mortgage foreclosure complaint against the Zervases when they stopped making their monthly mortgage payments in June 2009. Seeking additional time to obtain a mortgage loan modification, on November 9, 2009, the Zervases filed a motion to stay time for filing an answer to the complaint. Thereafter, on December 21, 2009, Wells Fargo filed a motion for final summary judgment . . . .

[O]n August 2, 2010, the trial court held a hearing on Wells Fargo's motion for final summary judgment and on that same day entered an order granting the motion. . . . On August 12, 2010, the Zervases filed a motion to set aside judgment and notice of filing proposed answer and affirmative defenses. The Zervases alleged several affirmative defenses, including the allegation that Wells Fargo failed to satisfy the condition precedent in paragraph twenty-two of the mortgage, which specifically required Wells Fargo to provide the Zervases with notice of the alleged default and a reasonable opportunity to cure.

We conclude that this case was not at issue when summary judgment was entered. The Zervases had not filed an answer and a default had not been entered against them. . . .

Most mortgages on the market contain an acceleration clause which is a condition precedent to filing a complaint for foreclosure. The clause in this case, like others this court has observed, is located in paragraph twenty-two of the mortgage and provides as follows:

Lender shall give notice to Borrower prior to acceleration following Borrower's breach of any covenant or agreement in this Security Instrument (but not prior to acceleration under Section 18 unless Applicable Law provides otherwise). The notice shall specify: (a) the default; (b) the action required to cure the default; (c) a date, not less than 30 days from the date the notice is given to Borrower, by which the default must be cured; and (d) that failure to cure the default on or before the date specified in the notice may result in acceleration of the sums secured by this Security Instrument, fore-closure by judicial proceeding and sale of the Property. The notice shall further inform Borrower of the right to reinstate after acceleration and the right to assert in the foreclosure proceeding the non-existence of a default or any other defense of Borrower to acceleration and foreclosure. . . .

Although Wells Fargo made the general allegation in its complaint that "[a]ll conditions precedent to the filing of this action have been met by Plaintiff," there is no evidence in the record that Wells Fargo complied with paragraph twenty-two. . . . Wells Fargo did not establish that the record would have no genuine issue of material fact where it did not address the notice of acceleration in the motion for summary judgment or accompany-ing affidavits.

We also note that the mortgage and note attached to the complaint show the lender to be Fremont Investment and Loan. On April 1, 2010, approximately six months after the complaint was filed, Wells Fargo filed a lost note affidavit, which alleged that the note was lost by its attorney sometime after the attorney received it on November 2, 2009. In their motion to dismiss, the Zervases alleged, among other grounds, that Wells Fargo did not have standing to bring the foreclosure complaint because it did not have a written assignment of the loan. Then on July 26, 2010, seven days before the hearing on the motion for summary judgment, Wells Fargo filed the note as a supplemental exhibit to its complaint. The note contains an endorsement in blank, but there is no evidence in the record establishing that the endorsement in blank was made to Wells Fargo prior to the filing of the foreclosure complaint. *See* Feltus v. U.S. Bank Nat'l Ass'n, 80 So. 3d 375, 377 n.2 (Fla. 2d DCA 2012) (holding that bank was required "to prove the endorsement in blank was effectuated before the lawsuit was filed").

We reverse the final judgment of foreclosure and remand for further proceedings.

PASILLAS v. HSBC BANK USA
Supreme Court of Nevada, 2011
255 P.3d 1281

HARDESTY, Justice. In this appeal, we consider issues arising out of Neva-da's Foreclosure Mediation Program and address whether a lender commits sanctionable offenses when it does not produce documents and does not have someone present at the mediation with the authority to modify the loan, as set forth in the applicable statute, NRS 107.086, and the Foreclosure Mediation Rules (FMRs).

Because NRS 107.086 and the FMRs expressly require that certain documents be produced during foreclosure mediation and that someone with authority to modify the loan must be present or accessible during the mediation, we conclude that a party's failure to comply with these requirements is an offense subject to sanctions by the district court. In such an event, the district court shall not direct the program administrator to certify the mediation to allow the foreclosure process to proceed until the parties have fully complied with the statute and rules governing foreclosure mediation.

Here, because respondents HSBC Bank USA, Power Default Services, and American Home Mortgage Servicing, Inc. (AHMSI), did not bring the required documents to the mediation and did not have access to someone authorized to modify the loan during the mediation, we conclude that the district court erred in denying appellants Emiliano and Yvette Pasillas's petition for judicial review. Therefore, we reverse the district court's order and remand this matter to the district court so that the court may determine sanctions.

FACTS AND PROCEDURAL HISTORY

The Pasillases purchased a home in Reno in 2006 with a loan from American Brokers Conduit. The note and deed of trust were allegedly assigned to HSBC.[1] Near the end of 2009, Power Default Services became a substitute trustee, removing HSBC from that role. Allegedly, the servicer for the Pasillases' loan is AHMSI.[2]

When the Pasillases defaulted on their mortgage and received a notice of election to sell, they elected to mediate pursuant to the Foreclosure Mediation Program provided for in NRS 107.086. Two separate mediations occurred, one on February 18, 2010, and one on March 8, 2010, but neither mediation resulted in a resolution.

While a representative of AHMSI was available by phone at both mediations, it is unclear whether HSBC was present or represented by counsel. There is some disagreement between the parties regarding who the respondents' attorneys represented at the mediations and at the hearing on the petition for judicial review. . . .

After both mediations were completed, the mediator filed a statement indicating that (1) "[t]he parties participated but were unable to agree to a loan modification or make other arrangements," (2) "[t]he beneficiary or his representative failed to participate in good faith," and (3) "[t]he beneficiary failed to bring to the mediation each document required."

---

1. The Pasillases claim that HSBC failed to provide a valid assignment; the one it provided during the mediation was signed by American Brokers Conduit but did not state who the assignee was.

2. The parties do not argue and we do not reach the question of whether AHMSI is a valid agent for HSBC or the real party in interest, or the "person entitled to enforce" the promissory note in this case.

The mediator also filed an addendum to his statement, wherein he stated that two pages of the mortgage note were missing, that the assignment purportedly assigning the mortgage note and deed of trust to HSBC was incomplete, that instead of an appraisal HSBC provided a broker's price opinion,[4] and that respondents stated they would need additional investor approval before agreeing to a loan modification. The mediator concluded that he would not recommend that the administrator issue a certificate authorizing further foreclosure proceedings because HSBC "failed to participate in [the] mediation in good faith as evidenced by its failure to produce required documents and information initially, or subsequently to cure its failures." The Pasillases subsequently filed a petition for judicial review in the district court. In the petition, the Pasillases requested sanctions in the form of a modification of their mortgage and attorney fees.

The district court conducted a short hearing [and] entered an order finding that "Respondent[s][have] met the burden to show cause why sanctions should not lie," and directed the Foreclosure Mediation Program administrator to issue a certification authorizing the foreclosure to proceed. The Pasillases appealed.

DISCUSSION

In resolving this appeal, we must determine whether the district court abused its discretion when it refused to enter sanctions against respondents for failing to satisfy express statutory requirements and allowed respondents to continue with the foreclosure process. We begin our discussion with a brief background of the Foreclosure Mediation Program.

THE FORECLOSURE MEDIATION PROGRAM

The Nevada Legislature enacted the Foreclosure Mediation Program in 2009 in response to the increasing number of foreclosures in this state. The program requires that a trustee seeking to foreclose on an owner-occupied residence provide an election-of-mediation form along with the notice of default and election to sell. NRS 107.086(2)(a)(3). If the homeowner elects to mediate, both the homeowner and the deed of trust beneficiary must attend, must mediate in good faith, provide certain enumerated documents,[5] and, if the beneficiary attends through a representative, that person must have

---

4. We note that while FMR 11(7)(b) currently allows for a broker's price opinion in lieu of an appraisal, the rules applicable to this matter called for an appraisal without mention of a broker's price opinion.

5. With regard to the documents required, NRS 107.086(4) provides that "[t]he beneficiary of the deed of trust shall bring to the mediation the original or a certified copy of the deed of trust, the mortgage note[,] and each assignment of the deed of trust or mortgage note." The FMRs echo this documentation requirement nearly word for word. FMR 5(7)(a). FMR 7(2) also provides that "[t]he beneficiary of the deed of trust or its representatives shall produce an appraisal . . . and shall prepare an estimate of the 'short sale' value of the residence."

authority to modify the loan or have "access at all times during the mediation to a person with such authority." NRS 107.086(4), (5); FMR 5(7)(a). After the conclusion of the mediation, the mediator must file a mediator's statement with the program administrator, indicating whether all parties complied with the statute and rules governing the program. If the beneficiary does not (1) attend the mediation; (2) mediate in good faith; (3) provide the required documents; or (4) if attending through a representative, have a person present with authority to modify the loan or access to such a person, the mediator is required to "submit . . . a petition and recommendation concerning the imposition of sanctions."[6] NRS 107.086(5). The homeowner may then file a petition for judicial review with the district court,[7] and the court "may issue an order imposing such sanctions against the beneficiary of the deed of trust or the representative as the court determines appropriate." *See* FMR 5(7)(f). But if the district court finds that the parties met the four program requirements, it will direct the program administrator to certify the mediation, allowing the foreclosure process to proceed.

RESPONDENTS FAILED TO MEET THE MEDIATION PROGRAM'S STATUTORY REQUIREMENTS

The Pasillases argue that respondents failed to meet the program's requirements — the document requirement because respondents failed to bring a complete mortgage note and failed to provide assignments of the note and deed of trust, and the loan modification authority requirement because they failed to have someone present at the mediation with the authority to modify the loan. We agree. . . .

Both NRS 107.086 and the FMRs use the word "shall" or "must" when listing the actions required of parties to a foreclosure mediation. Use of the word "shall" in both the statutory language and the FMRs indicates a duty on the part of the beneficiary, and . . . as it is used here, "must" is a synonym of "shall." We conclude that NRS 107.086(4) and (5) and FMR 5(7)(a) clearly and unambiguously mandate that the beneficiary of the deed of trust or its representative (1) attend the mediation, (2) mediate in good faith, (3) provide the required documents, and (4) have a person present with authority to modify the loan or access to such a person.

Here, the mediator's statement and his addendum to that statement, which were provided to the district court in the Pasillases' petition for judicial review, clearly set out respondents' failure to bring the required documents to the mediation and to have someone present with authority to modify the loan. Additionally, respondents do not dispute that they failed to bring all the

---

6. If the homeowner fails to attend the mediation, the administrator will certify that no mediation is required. NRS 107.086(6).

7. Generally, if the parties fail to reach an agreement and neither party files a petition for judicial review, the program administrator will certify the mediation, which allows the foreclosure process to proceed. NRS 107.086(3), (6), (7).

required documents to the mediation.[9] Although respondents argue on appeal that their counsel at the mediation "had the requisite authority and/or access to a person with the authority to modify the loan," they do not controvert the mediator's statement that their counsel claimed at the mediation that additional investor approval was needed in order to modify the loan. The record before the district court demonstrates that respondents failed to meet the statutory requirements. Nonetheless, respondents argue that the district court's conclusion that sanctions were unwarranted did not constitute an abuse of discretion because, despite the failures noted above, they mediated to resolve the foreclosure in good faith. We disagree.

The Supreme Judicial Court of Massachusetts recently reached the same conclusion regarding the production of assignments to mortgage notes and deeds of trust, albeit in a slightly different context. In U.S. Bank National Ass'n v. Ibanez, 941 N.E.2d 40 (Mass. 2011), two separate banks foreclosed on the mortgages of two homeowners whose properties the banks then bought at the foreclosure sales. *Id.* at 44. The banks later filed complaints in the lower court seeking a declaration that they had clear title to the properties. *Id.* Because the banks failed to show an interest in the mortgages at the time of the foreclosure sales, the sales were invalid, and the lower court entered judgment against the banks. *Id.* at 45. On appeal, the court determined that, similar to this case, the banks were not the original mortgagees and, therefore, they had to show that the mortgages were properly assigned to them in writings signed by the grantors before they could notice the sales and foreclosures of the properties. *Id.* at 51. In an attempt to prove that they had the authority to foreclose on the properties, the banks provided contracts purporting to assign to them bundles of mortgages; however, the attachments that identified what mortgages were being assigned were not included in the documents provided. *Id.* at 52. The court concluded that the banks demonstrated no authority to foreclose on the properties because they did not have the assignments. *Id.* at 53 ("We have long held that a conveyance of real property, such as a mortgage, that does not name the assignee conveys nothing and is void; we do not regard an assignment of land in blank as giving legal title in land to the bearer of the assignment."). The court additionally stated that "[a] plaintiff that cannot make this modest showing cannot justly proclaim that it was unfairly denied a declaration of clear title." *Id.* at 52. We agree with the rationale that valid assignments are needed when a beneficiary of a deed of trust seeks to foreclose on a property. . . .

In this case, despite the mediator's opinion that respondents did not participate in the mediation in good faith based on their failure to comply with the FMRs, the district court did not impose sanctions and instead

---

9. At oral argument, respondents' counsel argued that an assignment for the mortgage note was provided, but the name of the assignee was missing. We determine that an assignment provided without the name of the assignee is defective for the purposes of the Foreclosure Mediation Program because it does not identify the relevant parties.

entered a Letter of Certification that allowed respondents to proceed with the foreclosure process on the Pasillases' property. The district court essentially ignored the fact that respondents failed to bring "to the mediation each document required" and did "not have the authority or access to a person with the authority" to modify the loan, failures which we determine constitute sanctionable offenses. Thus, the district court's order directing the program administrator to enter a letter of certification and its failure to consider sanctions w[ere] an abuse of discretion because respondents clearly violated NRS 107.086 and the FMRs. This abuse requires us to remand the case for the district court to consider appropriate sanctions.

The nature of the sanctions imposed on the beneficiary or its representative is within the discretion of the district court. We have previously listed factors to aid district courts when considering sanctions as punishment for litigation abuses. See Young v. Johnny Ribeiro Building, 787 P.2d 777, 780 (Nev. 1990). However, we conclude that other factors, more specific to the foreclosure mediation context, apply when a district court is considering sanctions in such a case. When determining the sanctions to be imposed in a case brought pursuant to NRS 107.086 and the FMRs, district courts should consider the following nonexhaustive list of factors: whether the violations were intentional, the amount of prejudice to the nonviolating party, and the violating party's willingness to mitigate any harm by continuing meaningful negotiation.

Because, in this case, the foreclosing party's failure to bring the required documents to the mediation and to have someone present at the mediation with the authority to modify the loan were sanctionable offenses under the Foreclosure Mediation Program, the district court abused its discretion when it denied the Pasillases' petition for judicial review and ordered the program administrator to enter a letter of certification authorizing the foreclosure process to proceed. Therefore, we reverse the district court's order and remand this matter to the district court with instructions to determine the appropriate sanctions for respondents' violations of the statutory and rule-based requirements.

Problem 17D

Karin obtained a $260,000 mortgage loan to buy a condominium from First Bank, which immediately sold the loan in the secondary mortgage market. The loan is presently owned by XYZ Trust and is serviced by Best Servicing Co. Six months ago Karin stopped making monthly payments. After Best Servicing Co. sent Karin two notices of default and received no response, Best commenced foreclosure proceedings. Best has asked you for advice with respect to the following questions.

(a) Best cannot find the original promissory note signed by Karin. What should it do? Do we need to prepare a lost note affidavit? If so, what investigation should be taken first, who should sign the affidavit, and what should it say?

(b) Shortly after Best commenced foreclosure proceedings, Karin contacted Best to ask whether she could have her loan modified to reduce the monthly payments. How does this affect the pending foreclosure? How should Best respond?

D. EQUITABLE SUBROGATION

JOONDEPH v. HICKS
Supreme Court of Colorado, 2010
235 P.3d 303

EID, Justice. We granted certiorari to review the court of appeals' denial of equitable subrogation in a dispute over the priorities of various liens. Hicks v. Joondeph, 205 P.3d 432 (Colo. App. 2008). The respondent, Donald P. Hicks ("Hicks"), brought an action to determine his lien's priority and to foreclose the lien. The trial court granted summary judgment in favor of the petitioners, Shirley S. and Brian C. Joondeph ("the Joondephs") and CitiMortgage, Inc. ("CitiMortgage"), based on the doctrine of derivative equitable subrogation. Equitable subrogation is a doctrine under which a court may substitute a new lienholder into the priority position of a former lienholder when the new lienholder meets certain prerequisites. Derivative equitable subrogation, as recognized by the trial court, would allow a person who had been equitably subrogated to then convey his or her senior priority to new lienholders through a warranty deed. The court of appeals reversed, finding no basis in our law for applying derivative equitable subrogation in the form requested by the petitioners. It also found that the petitioners did not themselves qualify for equitable subrogation.

We now affirm the court of appeals. We hold that, because the petitioners had actual knowledge of the Hicks lien and were not operating under the mistaken assumption that they would obtain a senior priority position, the doctrine of equitable subrogation is inapplicable. We also decline to recognize the doctrine of derivative equitable subrogation as inconsistent with the "narrow confines" of our equitable subrogation doctrine. Hicks v. Londre, 125 P.3d 452, 458 (Colo. 2005) ("*Hicks*").

I.

The dispute before us involves residential property located in Englewood, Colorado ("the Property"). In September 2001, Hicks obtained a judgment in the amount of $413,773 against Robert Grubbs ("Grubbs"). Hicks recorded his judgment in Arapahoe County in October 2001 [thus creating a statutory judgment lien]. Three deeds of trust already encumbered the Property, putting Hicks in fourth priority position. First priority position was held by Washington Mutual Bank, NA ("WaMu").

In January 2002, Grubbs sold the Property to Kent and Jennifer Londre ("the Londres") for $1,510,000. The Londres provided part of the purchase price and obtained financing for the remainder from Chase Manhattan Mortgage Corporation ("Chase"). At the closing, the WaMu lien was paid in part and released, and the second and third priority liens encumbering the Property were released without payment. Despite a title search, the Londres and Chase did not discover Hicks' lien, which was not released at closing.

In June 2002, Hicks brought an action to foreclose his lien. The Londres and Chase countered by seeking to be equitably subrogated to the position that WaMu had held. In December 2005, this court held that, under the specific circumstances of their case, the Londres and Chase would be permitted to step into the first priority position once held by WaMu. The Hicks lien was thus left in junior position.

Three months before the *Hicks* opinion was released, in September 2005, the Londres sold the Property to the Joondephs for $1,900,000. The Joondephs supplied part of the purchase price and obtained financing for the balance from Affiliated Financing Group, Inc., who subsequently assigned its note and deed of trust to CitiMortgage. The new loan had different terms, including a different loan amount and maturity date, than those of the WaMu loan. The Hicks lien was disclosed on multiple occasions, and the Joondephs' title insurance policy included an endorsement protecting against any loss caused by the enforcement of Hicks' judgment. The warranty deed from the Londres explicitly excepted Hicks' judgment and enforcement action from its warranties of title.

Hicks filed the action underlying the present appeal in March 2006, seeking to obtain a declaratory judgment clarifying priority and to foreclose his lien. . . . In February 2007, the trial court granted summary judgment in favor of the petitioners. The trial court reasoned that, since the Londres and Chase had obtained senior priority status through equitable subrogation, the petitioners were entitled to senior priority as well because the warranty deed conveyed all interests of the prior owners, including their subrogation rights. Thus, the trial court concluded, the petitioners should be derivatively subrogated to the senior priority position once held by WaMu, then by the Londres and Chase. . . .

II.

Colorado's Recording Act sets out a "race-notice" system that protects buyers who record their liens without notice of prior unrecorded conveyances or liens. *See* §38-35-109(1), C.R.S. (2009). . . .

Under the Recording Act, once a senior lien is released, "junior lienholders just move up the line in priority." *Hicks*, 125 P.3d at 456. Under limited circumstances, however, the doctrine of equitable subrogation may create "a narrow exception" to the general rule of priority established by the Recording Act. *Id.* at 454. Equitable subrogation allows "the substitution of another person in the place of a [lienholder], so that the person in whose favor it is exercised succeeds to the rights of the" lienholder. Cotter Corp. v. Am. Empire Surplus Lines Ins. Co., 90 P.3d 814, 833 (Colo. 2004). Subrogation operates by treating the new lien as "a revival and assignment of the discharged obligation and security, rather than [as] a substitution of a new obligation in place of another." Land Title Ins. Corp. v. Ameriquest Mortgage Co., 207 P.3d 141, 145 (Colo. 2009). As an "assignee," a subrogee "stands in the shoes of" his subrogor and has all the rights of the former lienholder to whom he has been subrogated. Farmers Acceptance Corp. v. DeLozier, 496 P.2d 1016, 1018 (Colo. 1972). In essence, equitable subrogation allows a party who would normally fall in line behind another lienholder to instead assume a predecessor's higher priority position.

In *Hicks*, we set forth a comprehensive framework for determining whether equitable subrogation can be invoked to permit another party to step into the shoes of an original lienholder as subrogee. First, the following five prerequisites must be met:

> (1) the subrogee made the payment to protect his or her own interest, (2) the subrogee did not act as a volunteer, (3) the subrogee was not primarily liable for the debt paid, (4) the subrogee paid off the entire encumbrance, and (5) subrogation would not work any injustice to the rights of the junior lienholder.

125 P.3d at 456. These factors must be "invoked only within the overall context of equity and the specific facts of each case." *Id.* at 457. Thus, even when the five prerequisites are satisfied, we must "look to whether the party seeking subrogation acted with knowledge, negligence, or a degree of sophistication such that application of the doctrine would be inequitable." *Id.* at 457–58. . . .

A.

It is undisputed that the petitioners here had actual knowledge of the Hicks lien. The question in this case is whether their actual knowledge precludes them from invoking the doctrine of equitable subrogation. We believe it does. . . .

. . . [T]he lien in this case was disclosed to the petitioners on multiple occasions. In fact, the Joondephs' title insurance policy included an endorsement protecting against any loss caused by Hicks' claim, and the warranty deed from the Londres explicitly excepted Hicks' judgment and enforcement action from its warranties of title. . . . Given the circumstances, the petitioners had no basis on which to form a reasonable belief that they were entitled to first priority. . . .

This is not to say that actual knowledge precludes equitable subrogation in every case. We have recognized that equitable subordination is appropriate where, despite having actual knowledge, "the payor was induced by some mistake of fact to satisfy the senior deed . . . of trust." *Land Title Ins. Corp.*, 207 P.3d at 145. . . . Here . . . the petitioners were not operating under a mistaken belief that they would take priority position by virtue of some action taken by Hicks; in fact, they were fully aware of the Hicks lien and its priority position. Therefore, we find that equitable subrogation does not permit them to assume priority status.

B.

The petitioners also ask us to extend *Hicks* and recognize the doctrine of derivative equitable subrogation. In effect, derivative equitable subrogation would allow a subrogee to convey his senior priority through a warranty deed to a buyer regardless of whether junior lienholders had released their lien, whether junior lienholders had contractually agreed to remain subordinate, or whether the buyer could itself meet the requirements for equitable subrogation. We decline to expand our doctrine of equitable subrogation in this fashion.

No case in Colorado has recognized a doctrine of derivative equitable subrogation. Indeed, our recognition of the primary doctrine of equitable subrogation has been decidedly narrow in scope. . . . Expansion of the doctrine to include derivative claims — that is, to parties who were not involved in the initial transaction but who claim the equitable position of parties who were involved — would run afoul of the narrow view of equitable subrogation we have taken in this state. . . .

III.

We hold that, because the petitioners had actual knowledge of the Hicks lien and were not operating under the mistaken assumption that they would obtain a senior priority position, the doctrine of equitable subrogation is inapplicable. We also decline to recognize the doctrine of derivative equitable subrogation. We therefore affirm the court of appeals.

Problem 17E

In 2012, Able Insurance Co. refinanced a permanent loan on a small shopping center, lending $1,200,000 to Douglas Dowdy. The prior loan, made in 2007 for $1,000,000, had a balance due of $900,000 at the time of Able's refinancing. The refinancing involved payment of the old note in full, with a release of the 2007 deed of trust, and the execution and recording of Able's loan documents. In 2013, Douglas defaulted and Able foreclosed. Able hired Tom, a lawyer, to handle the power of sale foreclosure. Tom searched title and missed a mortgage for $100,000 from Douglas Dowdy to Easy Bank, which was made and recorded in 2010. Tom proceeded with the foreclosure, and at the sale Able purchased the property for $950,000.

(a) Does Easy Bank still have a mortgage, and if so, what is its priority if

1. Tom missed the mortgage because he did not do a careful title search?

2. Tom missed the mortgage because it was incorrectly indexed under the name "Dowd, Douglas"?

3. Tom missed the mortgage because it was incorrectly indexed under the name "Gowdy, Douglas"?

(b) As between Able and Tom, if legal action is required against Easy Bank to clear title, who should bear this expense? If Tom had discovered the Easy Bank mortgage prior to conducting the foreclosure sale, what should he have done?

E. DEED IN LIEU OF FORECLOSURE

When, after default, a mortgage loan is in trouble, foreclosure is often unattractive to both the lender and the borrower. The borrower may concede the lender's allegation of material default and realize that she does not have a meritorious defense. Perhaps the borrower defaulted because of a loss in income or other financial setbacks so that she can no longer afford to own the property with the present amount of debt on it. Thus, she has no realistic chance of reinstating the loan or refinancing.

With a situation like this, it may be mutually advantageous to both parties for the borrower to transfer ownership to the lender. Such a transfer is documented by what is called a *deed in lieu of foreclosure*. The lender gets title right away and can keep or sell the property however it wishes — for example, by listing it with a broker — without following public foreclosure sale procedures. In exchange for the transfer, the borrower receives satisfaction of all or part of the debt. The borrower is relieved of responsibility for the property and avoids being the target of foreclosure, a process that for some borrowers is an emotional strain and an embarrassment, as well as a potential financial hurt. If the borrower is concerned about a potential deficiency judgment, agreeing to give a deed in lieu of foreclosure may avoid or reduce that risk because the borrower will not have extra liability for foreclosure costs. Essentially, the deed in lieu of foreclosure transaction is a negotiated sale of the property to the lender, where the lender pays the purchase price by cancellation of debt. The biggest risk to the borrower is underpricing the property. If the borrower has substantial equity, the transaction may be unwise, even though the lender cancels the entire debt. It replicates a decree in strict foreclosure, where the lender has no duty to account to the borrower for surplus value.

The transaction also poses significant risks to the lender. First, after consummation of the transaction, the mortgagor may try to set aside the deed in lieu of foreclosure, claiming that the deed clogs her equity of redemption. Had the lender taken a deed to the property from the mortgagor contemporaneously with the grant of the mortgage, such a deed would be clearly invalid under the clogging principle.

Second, some courts are willing to scrutinize a deed in lieu of foreclosure transaction on grounds of inadequacy of consideration or unconscionability. The fairness of the exchange may be called into question because of the extreme disparity of bargaining position, with a lender pressing hard to persuade a borrower in dire straits to capitulate.

Finally, the lender who contemplates acceptance of a deed in lieu of foreclosure has to consider the risks that third parties may have rights. There are two basic problems here. First of all, the lender has a title concern, because a deed in lieu of foreclosure, unlike a properly conducted foreclosure, will not cut off junior interests that are subsequent to the mortgage. In addition to the title risk, there are other third-party risks if the mortgagor is or might be insolvent. Of course, given the default and the need to foreclose, insolvency is not at all unlikely. If the mortgagor files for bankruptcy or is pushed into bankruptcy within 90 days after the deed in lieu of foreclosure is given, the transfer may be set aside as a preference. Apart from bankruptcy, under the state law of fraudulent conveyances, there is the risk that other creditors of the mortgagor may attack the deed on the basis that it was given for less than market value.

In 2015, the Uniform Law Commission (ULC) approved the Uniform Home Mortgage Foreclosure Procedures Act in response to many problems concerning abuses that surfaced after the collapse of the U.S. residential market that began in 2008. The Act functions as an overlay to existing foreclosure laws in both judicial foreclosure and nonjudicial foreclosure states. The Act provides a statutory version of a deed in lieu of foreclosure, called a "negotiated transfer." This device enables a lender to secure title without going through a formal foreclosure procedure when the homeowner agrees to the proposed transfer. A negotiated transfer may result in compensation to the homeowner (often called a "cash for keys" agreement), and at a minimum the owner obtains full satisfaction of the mortgage debt. The lender must provide notice to any junior creditors with recorded interests in the property. Their rights are cut off by the negotiated transfer unless they file an objection to the negotiated transfer. A junior creditor who objects has a statutory redemption right—the junior may tender the amount of the debt due to the lender seeking the negotiated transfer, and then step into that lender's place.

GMAC MORTGAGE, LLC v. DYER
Court of Appeals of Indiana, 2012
965 N.E.2d 762

VAIDIK, Judge. Ronald Glenn Dyer had an FHA-insured loan that he defaulted on. Dyer and GMAC Mortgage, LLC, attended a settlement conference at which they agreed to proceed with a deed in lieu of foreclosure. After the settlement conference, GMAC drafted a written agreement. The agreement included a provision using language required by the U.S. Department of Housing and Urban Development (HUD) that neither GMAC nor HUD would pursue a deficiency judgment against Dyer. Dyer, however, was not happy with this provision because he did not think that it gave him enough protection. Accordingly, he refused to sign the agreement. Instead, Dyer wanted the agreement to provide that he was released from all personal liability. The trial court agreed with Dyer and ordered GMAC to rewrite the agreement. Because under federal law and HUD regulations deeds in lieu of foreclosure release the borrower from any obligation under the mortgage, the standard language used by GMAC was sufficient to release Dyer from all personal liability. We therefore reverse the trial court.

FACTS AND PROCEDURAL HISTORY

On November 14, 2008, Dyer and his now-deceased wife Ella Faye Dyer executed a note in the principal amount of $74,277.00 with Lend America for their Greene County, Indiana, home. The loan was an FHA-insured loan subject to federal statutes and HUD regulations. To secure payment of the note, Dyer and his wife executed a mortgage. The mortgage was eventually assigned to GMAC. Dyer later defaulted under the terms of the note and mortgage.

On January 19, 2010, GMAC filed a Complaint on Note and to Foreclose Mortgage. Dyer filed an answer and counterclaim, and GMAC filed an answer to Dyer's counterclaim. In addition, GMAC informed Dyer of his right to participate in a settlement conference, which is now required by Indiana law. . . .

At the settlement conference, the parties decided to proceed with a deed in lieu of foreclosure. . . .

On December 30, 2010, GMAC sent Dyer a deed in lieu of foreclosure agreement to sign and return. The agreement provided, in pertinent part:

> 10. Provided all terms and conditions of this Agreement are met and this transaction concluded, GMAC Mortgage, LLC, agrees that neither it nor the U.S. Department of Housing and Urban Development [will] pursue a deficiency judgment from the Mortgagor.

GMAC gave Dyer a January 10, 2011, deadline. Because Dyer did not believe that paragraph 10 released him from personal liability nor complied with HUD regulations, he never signed and returned the agreement. . . .

The trial court granted Dyer's motion [and ordered] the Plaintiff [to] include in the Deed in Lieu Agreement the following additional language:

> Upon execution and delivery by Mortgagor to GMAC Mortgage, LLC of the documents referenced herein, the Mortgagor is released from all personal liability in connection with the Note and Mortgage.

. . . .

DISCUSSION AND DECISION

. . . .

The facts are not in dispute. Importantly, the record shows that Dyer and GMAC agree upon several things. First, Dyer and GMAC agree that they decided to proceed with a deed in lieu of foreclosure at the settlement conference. *See* Appellant's Reply Br. p. 5 ("The record before the trial court is clear; the parties attended a settlement conference and agreed to allow a deed in lieu of foreclosure on the property."); Appellee's Br. p. 8 ("The parties agreed to resolve this foreclosure by the FHA loss mitigation option known as deed in lieu of foreclosure . . . ."). Second, both parties agree that a deficiency judgment cannot be sought against Dyer. Third, both parties agree that Dyer may not be held personally liable for any deficiency. Finally, both parties agree that the deed in lieu of foreclosure agreement must comply with federal law and HUD regulations. Their point of contention is the exact language that must be included in the deed in lieu of foreclosure agreement and whether the language used accomplishes their joint purpose of ensuring that Dyer is not held personally liable for any deficiency. Accordingly, we must determine whether GMAC's deed in lieu of foreclosure agreement precludes personal liability of Dyer under federal law and HUD regulations. The trial court agreed with Dyer, but we agree with GMAC. . . .

According to HUD, "The Deed–in–Lieu of Foreclosure allows a mortgagor in default, who does not qualify for any other HUD Loss Mitigation option, to sign the house back over to the mortgage company. Ref: Mortgagee Letters 2000–05 and 2002–13." U.S. Department of Housing and Urban Development, Deed–in–Lieu of Foreclosure Option, http://portal.hud.gov/fha/sf/svc/faqdilfact.pdf. The specific requirements include an "[a]cknowledgment that mortgagor(s) who complies with all of the requirements of the Agreement shall not be pursued for deficiency judgments." *Id.* . . .

HUD regulations are clear: a deed in lieu of foreclosure releases the borrower from all obligations under the mortgage and the deed in lieu of foreclosure written agreement must contain an acknowledgement that the borrower shall not be pursued for deficiency judgments. GMAC's proposed agreement contains the precise language required by HUD. . . .

Nevertheless, Dyer relies on a single federal district court opinion from 1999, Ingram v. Cuomo, 51 F. Supp. 2d 667 (M.D. N.C. 1999), as support that the "shall not be pursued for deficiency judgments" language is not protective enough because HUD may be able to intercept any future tax refund due to Dyer, even without a deficiency judgment, pursuant to the Deficit Reduction Act of 1984. We first note that Ingram came before Mortgagee Letter 00–05. Moreover, *Ingram* does not apply to the facts in this case. In *Ingram*, the borrower defaulted on her FHA-insured loan, the home was sold at a loss, and HUD sent the borrower notice that it intended to intercept any tax refund due to her in order to satisfy the balance owed. In this case, however, Dyer and GMAC avoided foreclosure by agreeing to proceed with a deed in lieu of foreclosure. This type of agreement clearly provides that the borrower cannot be pursued for deficiency judgments. Accordingly, *Ingram* does not impact the language that must be included in a deed in lieu of foreclosure agreement. . . .

Reversed and remanded.

ROBB, Chief Judge, concurring in part, dissenting in part. I concur in the majority's determination that a deed in lieu of foreclosure releases a borrower from any obligation under a mortgage pursuant to federal law and HUD regulations. However, I respectfully dissent from the majority's resolution of the case.

The majority laid out several facts that are not in dispute. Both parties agree they decided to pursue a deed in lieu of foreclosure after attending a settlement conference, a deficiency judgment cannot be sought against Dyer, Dyer cannot be held personally liable, and the deed in lieu of foreclosure must comply with federal law and HUD regulations. At issue is Dyer's request to have a provision in the deed in lieu of foreclosure agreement stating he is released from personal liability. GMAC contends the provision it included in its draft of the agreement stating neither GMAC nor HUD will pursue a deficiency judgment from Dyer is sufficient.

Although I find no reason to disagree with the majority that a deed in lieu of foreclosure releases a borrower from liability as a matter of law,[8] what would be the harm in including Dyer's requested provision? If a deed in lieu of foreclosure does in fact release a mortgagor from personal liability and if everyone agrees Dyer should be released from personal liability, the

---

8. It is worth noting, however, that GMAC chose to litigate against Dyer's requested provision rather than merely agreeing to its addition to the agreement. While GMAC certainly had the right to respond to Dyer's request for declaratory judgment and argue its drafted agreement was sufficient, this route would almost certainly be less cost-effective. If GMAC truly intends to not hold Dyer personally liable in any manner, this extra cost would serve no purpose.

requested provision would only clarify this reality. HUD regulations do not prohibit parties adding language in addition to what is required, and Dyer is not attempting to remove a provision required by HUD. For these reasons, I would affirm the trial court's grant of summary judgment requiring a revision of the agreement to include Dyer's requested provision. In all other respects, I concur with the majority.

18

Mortgage Substitutes

As we have seen in prior chapters, mortgage law contains significant protections for borrowers, many of which apply based on the parties' status regardless of their agreement in fact. For example, the mortgagor may not waive his equity of redemption when he enters into a loan transaction — this constitutes an impermissible *"clogging" of the equity of redemption.* And if the lender seeks to foreclose because of a default by the mortgagor, the lender must comply with statutory foreclosure procedures designed to protect both the mortgagor and holders of junior interests. The terms of the parties' loan documents are not permitted to override the anticlogging and foreclosure rules that seek to give the mortgagor sufficient time to save his rights in the property.

In essence, this means that the parties' status as mortgagor and mortgagee overrides their contract in fact in a number of respects. In particular, a mortgagee cannot bargain for greater rights with respect to the land that secures the debt than the basic rights stemming from the mortgage itself. "Once a mortgage, always a mortgage," courts have said. A prime example is the rule barring a mortgagee from taking, by collateral agreement, title to the land. If, along with a mortgage, a mortgagor signs and delivers a deed conveying the property to the mortgagee, authorizing the mortgagee to record the deed upon default, the deed is a nullity. The mortgagee hopes that this will avoid the need for costly and time-consuming foreclosure if the mortgagor defaults, but courts invariably dismiss such deeds as unlawful attempts to clog the mortgagor's equity of redemption.

A closely related concept comes into play when the parties, instead of trying to modify mortgage law or create their own mortgage law, try to avoid mortgage law altogether. For various reasons, people have often sought this outcome. A borrower may want to hide the fact that he needs money or is taking on debt. A lender may think mortgage law protects mortgagors too much. This party may prefer a substitute arrangement, and the other party who wants or needs credit may agree. Thus, parties will seek to avoid mortgage law by refraining from the use of standard mortgage loan documents like promissory notes, mortgages, and deeds of trust. Instead, they may structure their transaction in some other way. As a starting point, it is important to realize that for centuries courts, both in England and the United States, have tried to understand the motivations of lenders who seek to escape mortgage law in order to gain legal advantages over borrowers. Courts have looked to substance over form, consistently ruling that if the parties' transaction basically is a loan, with real property as security if the borrower fails to repay, then mortgage law applies, regardless of how the parties label or characterize their deal. This is a *disguised mortgage*; at the lender's insistence, the parties have disguised their mortgage as something else, but the court has sharp eyesight. The label *equitable mortgage* is also used in this context, meaning that the transaction is not a formal, legal mortgage, but it is a function of equity jurisprudence to intervene and impose a duty on the holder of legal title to recognize an equity held by the grantor.

This chapter considers the principles that apply to a range of alternative arrangements involving land and deferred payments. These arrangements are referred to as *mortgage substitutes* because they perform economic functions similar to those of standard mortgage transactions. The label "mortgage substitute" does not mean that mortgage law must apply to the transaction — sometimes it does, and sometimes it does not. Deciding when it will and when it should is complex, requiring the decision maker to weigh a number of variables concerning the parties' bargaining process, circumstances, and documents.

A. SALES AND DISGUISED MORTGAGES

The classic case of the disguised mortgage is the loan that masquerades as a straight-out sale, using a warranty deed to convey title to the buyer (lender). The deed is just a regular deed, the type commonly used in all sales transactions. It is called *absolute* because, unlike a mortgage, it says nothing at all about the grantor ever getting the property back or the grantee relinquishing his rights if the debt is paid. The lender orally promises to reconvey to the borrower if the borrower timely repays the debt. As long ago as 1470, English courts ruled that such transactions were really mortgages. Distinguishing sales from mortgages is not always easy, and many courts have struggled with this problem. Typically, it is the grantor under a warranty deed who claims the transaction really is a mortgage loan. The grantee's (lender's) payment (loan) is taken in exchange for the original conveyance, with the grantor (borrower) tendering repayment at a later date in exchange for a reconveyance of title. In the typical dispute, the grantee resists this argument and seeks to quiet title in itself. From the cases addressing this problem, no single test has emerged. Rather, courts have looked at many factors to decide whether the deed used by the parties was a mortgage. In disputes of this sort, a key distinction to keep in mind is the difference between parol evidence and written evidence. If the grantor can produce written evidence of the debt or that he has a right to reacquire title, this strengthens his case. Many disputes revolve primarily around the interpretation of writings. For example, there may be an absolute deed and a promissory note, signed by the grantor and payable to the grantee. The primary issue will be how those two writings relate to each other: Are they independent transactions? Is the debt represented by the note outstanding, or has it been paid? Is the note secured or unsecured? Was the note cancelled in exchange for conveyance of title to the property?

In some disputes there is no written evidence of a debt, a mortgage, or a right of the grantor to reacquire the conveyed real estate. Such written proof, however, is not essential. Parol testimony is admissible, in spite of the statute of frauds. One justification is that the testimony "explains" rather than "contradicts" the deed. Alternatively, we may say the claim is essentially for reformation of the deed. Under a reformation action, a court can change an instrument based on parol testimony indicating that the parties made a mistake. Historically, in English law the rule permitting parol testimony that an absolute conveyance was intended to be defeasible predated the Statute of Frauds of 1677, and courts did not think the statute was intended to alter this long-established rule. Regardless of the rationale, it should be acknowledged that there is tension between the use of parol evidence to "impeach" an absolute deed and the policies underlying the statute of frauds. For this reason, many courts have tried to put such evidence on a leash. The burden of proof is on the party claiming that the deed is a mortgage. Moreover, it is often said that there is a presumption that an absolute deed is bona fide. To overcome this presumption, the proponent must prove a mortgage by clear and convincing evidence, a standard that is higher than a preponderance of the evidence.

JOHNSON v. WASHINGTON
United States Court of Appeals, Fourth Circuit, 2009
559 F.3d 238

WILKINSON, Circuit Judge. Marion and Vivian Johnson appeal the district court's grant of summary judgment on their claim that defendants violated various consumer protection laws when purchasing the Johnsons' home. The Johnsons argue that the purported sale of their home actually created an equitable mortgage under Virginia common law, thereby obligating defendants to comply with federal and state lending laws . . . . Because we find that the transaction was an absolute sale that did not give rise to any debt between the parties, we conclude that it did not create an equitable mortgage. We likewise find no merit in the Johnsons' claim of fraud. We therefore affirm the judgment of the district court.

. . . In December 1995, Marion and Vivian Johnson paid approximately $130,000 to purchase a home in Norfolk, Virginia. In 2002 or 2003, they refinanced their mortgage with NovaStar Mortgage, Inc. ("NovaStar"). In 2005, they fell two months behind in their mortgage payments and sought to refinance again. By this time, plaintiffs claim the home had appreciated to $260,000, with the Johnsons holding about $100,600 in equity in the home and the remaining $159,400 representing the outstanding balance on the NovaStar mortgage. In hopes of refinancing, Mr. and Mrs. Johnson contacted Warren Robinson, a mortgage broker and the president of D & D Home Loans Corporation, who told them it would be difficult to refinance because of their poor credit history and previous bankruptcy filings.

In May 2005, Robinson referred the Johnsons to Jason Washington, a private investor. When Washington met with the Johnsons, he presented them with an "Offer to Purchase Real Estate" that stated that Washington would purchase the home for $212,800. The couple signed this document without reading it. They then met with Washington on June 30, 2005, for a real estate closing, at which they signed a HUD-1 Settlement Statement and a deed conveying title to Washington.

To finance his purchase of the house, Washington took out two mortgages from Finance American, which were secured by deeds of trust on the property. Of the $212,800 total sales price, Washington used $166,600.05 to pay off the Johnsons' NovaStar mortgage. He gave the Johnsons a check for $44,410.56, which was listed as the "Amount to Seller" in the HUD-1 Settlement Statement.

One week later, Washington and Mr. and Mrs. Johnson signed a Contract for Deed of Real Property ("Contract") that gave the Johnsons an option to repurchase the property within thirteen months for $249,079. This amount included an initial down payment of $36,279 and a final payment of $212,800. The Contract also provided that the Johnsons would remain at the home in return for making monthly payments of $1,896.64 for twelve months, with the first payment due on August 1, 2005. The Contract provided that the Johnsons would lose the option to repurchase after thirteen months, and that the Contract would become a lease agreement if their monthly payments were over five days late. Washington used most of the Johnsons' monthly payment amount to satisfy his payments on the Finance American mortgages. Mr. and Mrs. Johnson continued to live at the property and make monthly payments to Washington, but they stopped making payments in February or March 2006.

In March 2007, the Johnsons filed a twelve-count complaint against Robinson, Washington, and D & D Home Loans Corporation, alleging *inter alia* fraud, breach of contract, violations of the Truth in Lending Act, 15 U.S.C. §1601 *et seq.*, and predatory lending practices under the Virginia Mortgage Lender and Broker Act, Va. Code §6.1-422. . . . They also alleged that Robinson and Washington had misled them about the nature of the transaction by making statements such as "Washington does not want your house" and by telling them they could refinance again in twelve to thirteen months. . . .

The Johnsons raise claims under both the Truth in Lending Act ("TILA") and the Virginia Mortgage Lender and Broker Act ("MLBA"). The TILA is a federal statute that requires clear disclosure of terms in consumer credit transactions. 15 U.S.C. §1601 *et seq.* Its protections apply only to loans, not to sales. Similarly, the MLBA governs the practices of licensed lenders and brokers, but does not apply to real estate sales. Va. Code §6.1-422. Therefore, to show that defendants were required to comply with these laws, the Johnsons must show that their transaction in fact created a lending relationship.

Under Virginia law, a deed that is absolute on its face "is presumed absolute unless the party challenging the presumption can prove by clear, unequivocal and convincing evidence" that it is not. In re Seven Springs, Inc., 159 B.R. 752, 755 (Bankr. E.D. Va. 1993). "The existence of a debt is the test." Holladay v. Willis, 43 S.E. 616, 618 (Va. 1903). . . .

In assessing whether an equitable mortgage exists, courts ask two questions. First, they ask whether the parties enjoyed a borrower-lender relationship, signified by the presence of a debt secured by title to the property. . . .

The requirement of a debt between the parties is more than a formality. As the Supreme Court of Appeals of Virginia noted in *Holladay*, "[a] mortgage without a debt to support it is a legal solecism," and "neither the intention of the parties nor their express contract can change the essential nature of things." 43 S.E. at 618. This rule is especially important in the context of equitable mortgages. Because such mortgages are an exception to the general rule that parole evidence is inadmissible to contradict the terms of a contract, the proof necessary to sustain them "must be so convincing as to leave no doubt on the mind that a mortgage, and not an absolute conveyance, was intended." *Id.* at 617. . . .

In addition, absent some debt between the parties, the grantee (Washington) has no personal recourse against the grantor (the Johnsons) if the property later sells at a loss or the grantee cannot otherwise recover on his investment. As the court noted in *Holladay*, this lack of recourse clearly shows that the parties lacked a debtor-creditor relationship. *Id.* at 618. And because purchase and lease-back arrangements such as the Johnsons' are so common, allowing courts of equity to find equitable mortgages based on the testimony of one party alone — a party who later regrets the transaction — could potentially convert any number of real estate sales into equitable mortgages.

The Johnsons acknowledge that the court must find some debt between the parties. But they argue that the Contract's option to repurchase constituted such a debt, and that the consequence of not making the repurchase payments was the loss of their home. But Virginia law is clear: an option to repurchase is not an obligation to repurchase, and therefore does not constitute a debt between the parties. In *Holladay*, the defendant purchased the plaintiff's property. As part of the transaction, he also paid off a debt the plaintiff owed on the property. The parties later executed an option agreement that let the plaintiff repurchase the property within two years. *Holladay, id.* at 616-17. The Supreme Court of Appeals of Virginia ruled that there was no debt between the parties because the defendant's "payment of [the plaintiff's] indebtedness did not constitute a new debt." *Id.* at 618. Therefore, the transaction constituted a sale with an option to repurchase, not an equitable mortgage. . . .

In response, the Johnsons cite several cases for the proposition that an option to repurchase does constitute a debt between the parties. Snavely v. Pickle, 70 Va. 27 (1877); Tuggle v. Berkeley, 43 S.E. 199 (Va. 1903); Magee v. Key, 191 S.E. 520 (Va. 1937); Johnson v. Johnson, 33 S.E.2d 784 (Va. 1945). But these cases all involved a promise to repay a specific debt advanced by the grantee and secured by a deed to the property. In *Tuggle*, for example, a woman conveyed a lot and residence to her son-in-law in exchange for his payment of $600 of delinquent taxes on the property. 43 S.E. at 199-200. The deed stated that the son-in-law would reconvey the property to her if she repaid the $600 plus interest. *Id.* The Supreme Court of Appeals of Virginia found that the transaction involved an implied promise to repay the debt, and therefore created an equitable mortgage. . . .

Even if the Johnsons could show they owed some debt to Washington, we would still need to find equitable circumstances to conclude that the transaction created an equitable mortgage. In *Seven Springs*, 159 B.R. at 756, the court narrowed the list of relevant circumstances to four: "(1) intentions of the parties; (2) adequacy of consideration; (3) retention of possession by the grantor; and (4) satisfaction or survival of the debt." The Johnsons were not unsophisticated parties: both had college degrees and previously had completed at least two real estate closings and one refinance. In fact, they conceded that they had never read the documents or asked any questions about the transaction, which would have yielded information about the terms of the sale. Given that the Johnsons were on notice that they could not refinance again, and given the clear terms of the documents they signed, it is difficult to credit their argument that they merely intended to take out a loan from Washington.

Next, the Johnsons argue that finding an equitable mortgage is proper because Washington's purchase price of $212,800 was less than the home's claimed value of $260,000. But this difference is much less than the disparate values seen in cases finding an equitable mortgage. *See, e.g., Magee,* 191 S.E. at 522 (where the grantor received 58 percent of the property's market value). Nor do the Johnsons show that they could have received more for the house given market conditions and their need to sell quickly.

Indeed, the Johnsons benefited from the transaction in several respects: they owed nothing to NovaStar or to any other mortgage company, they could remain in the home, and they could walk away at the end of twelve months if they were no longer able or no longer wished to live there. . . . Given their circumstances, they likely received the best deal they could get. And to the extent they did face hardship—for example, in their inability to pay the final portion of the repurchase price — it arose not from the terms offered by Washington, but from the Johnsons' inability to attract financing. The Contract's terms did not present an impossible barrier to repurchasing. But the Johnsons' odds of obtaining the necessary financing would clearly depend on their creditworthiness. The Johnsons faced a difficult situation not because Washington offered them unattainable terms, but because, due to their poor credit history and previous bankruptcy filings, lenders would be unlikely to regard them as an acceptable credit risk. . . .

Finally, we reject the Johnsons' claim of fraud because the statements made by Washington and Robinson (*e.g.*, "We want to help you") were either accurate or were forward-looking statements of opinion. Even assuming that Robinson did mislead the Johnsons, which we do not suggest, the documents that they signed plainly stated the terms of the transaction and more than corrected any misleading oral statements. Plaintiffs cannot be heard to complain when they failed to read the relevant documents. We therefore affirm the judgment of the district court.

Problem 18A

In 2007, Karen and her husband Mark Piper acquired a 40-acre parcel of property and were attempting to develop it as a subdivision of residential lots named Crystal Springs. In 2009, the Pipers began having difficulty meeting a mortgage obligation to Western Life Insurance Co. on the property. In June, Western obtained a foreclosure judgment against the property for $200,000. Carol and Jim Strong, who were neighbors and parcel owners in the subdivision, expressed an interest in helping the Pipers maintain ownership in order to preserve the Pipers' development plan. Together the Pipers and Strongs tried to convince Western to reinstate the mortgage with the loaning of the Strongs' credit to the Pipers. Western, however, refused the proposed reinstatement.

To avoid the foreclosure sale, on October 1, 2009, the Pipers entered into an agreement with the Strongs whereby the Strongs paid the Pipers $200,000, the amount of the foreclosure judgment, which the Pipers turned over to Western to satisfy the judgment. In exchange for the payment, the Pipers executed a warranty deed on the property to the Strongs. In a separate agreement signed at the same time, the Strongs granted the Pipers a two-year option to repurchase the property. The documents were drafted by an attorney retained by the Strongs.

After a negotiated extension of one year, the option to repurchase expired in 2012. In 2013, the Pipers attempted to pay the Strongs the amount advanced, with interest, to regain possession of the property. The Strongs refused to accept payment or return the property. The Pipers filed suit, claiming the initial transaction was a mortgage, not a sale.

(a) Suppose the Pipers testify that despite what the documents indicate, they believe the money was a loan. The Strongs, on the other hand, testify there was no loan, merely an option for the Pipers to repurchase the land if they became financially able to do so. Based on this testimony and the preceding facts, should the trial court grant summary judgment? If so, for which party?

(b) Suppose appraisers testify at trial as to the property's fair market value. The Pipers' expert values the land at $340,000 as of October 1, 2009, and the Strongs' expert testifies: "The reasonable market value of the property on October 1, 2009, for a quick sale was $240,000 to $248,000." On cross-examination, the Pipers' expert concedes that her appraisal assumed a generous amount of time for marketing the property and that a quick sale, conducted under constraints like foreclosure sales, would in all probability not yield a price in excess of $250,000. Which side does this evidence on value favor? What if both sides agreed that the value on October 1 was $205,000? was $500,000? Is it relevant whether after October the property value remained stable, declined, or rose sharply?

(c) Does it matter what the Pipers and Strongs agreed to as the option price? Suppose (i) the option price was the same as the purchase price, $200,000, i.e., the Strongs would make no profit; (ii) the option price was $250,000 if the option was timely exercised at any time during the two-year period; (iii) the option price was equal to $200,000 plus interest at the rate of 14 percent per annum calculated from October 1, 2009, to the date of closing.

(d) You are the lawyer for the Pipers in this litigation. Do you have enough facts to persuasively argue that the transaction is an equitable mortgage? What other facts would you attempt to ascertain, and why might they be relevant?

(e) You are the lawyer for the Strongs in this litigation. What additional facts do you hope to discover? Suppose instead that you are the lawyer who handled drafting the deed and option agreement for the Strongs in 2009. What, if anything, could you have done differently to reduce the risk of an equitable mortgage challenge?

(f) Suppose that instead of the option agreement, along with the warranty deed on October 1, 2009, the Pipers and Strongs signed a purchase agreement, naming a price of $250,000, with both parties obligated to close on October 1, 2011. How does this change the arguments about whether the transaction is a sale or an equitable mortgage?

B. THE NEGATIVE PLEDGE

Recall that the basic point of a mortgage is that the lender knows that if the borrower fails to pay the debt, there is a specific asset set aside that the lender can reach. Through foreclosure, the lender can force a sale of the asset and apply the sales proceeds to the debt. This greatly reduces the risk of the loan to the lender. The lender has a property right in the asset — he has locked in his priority and has, for example, a first mortgage or a second mortgage. Perhaps there's another way for the lender to accomplish this objective. An unsecured loan is just about as good as a secured loan if the lender can be certain that, upon default, he can obtain a judgment lien and that his judgment lien will have first priority. How might the lender seek that certainty? This is the idea behind the *negative pledge* or *negative covenant*. The lender identifies a particular asset owned by the borrower, and the borrower promises not to convey or encumber that asset until the loan is repaid. This way, the lender is assured that if there's a default, the lender can obtain a first-priority judgment lien on the asset.

TAHOE NATIONAL BANK v. PHILLIPS
Supreme Court of California, 1971
480 P.2d 320

TOBRINER, Justice. Defendant Beulah F. Phillips appeals from a judgment of the El Dorado County Superior Court that holds that an instrument entitled, "Assignment of Rents and Agreement Not to Sell or Encumber Real Property" (hereinafter referred to as "the assignment") was intended to be an equitable mortgage, and decrees its foreclosure.

We conclude that this judgment must be reversed. Plaintiff bank, which occupied the more powerful bargaining position and deliberately chose to use a standardized form providing for the assignment of rents and a covenant against conveyances, cannot be permitted to transform this assignment into a mortgage contrary to the reasonable expectation of its borrower. On examining the terms and purpose of the assignment, we conclude that it is not reasonably susceptible of construction as a mortgage at the instance of the bank, and thus that the trial court erred in invoking extrinsic evidence offered by the bank to prove it to be a mortgage.

Defendant and three co-venturers embarked on a real estate development in the Lake Tahoe area. About April 20, 1965, the venturers not only needed further capital but also owed plaintiff sums due on overdrafts on their accounts. Plaintiff agreed to lend $34,000 to defendant, who transferred the funds to the venture's account. In return, defendant gave plaintiff a single-payment promissory note, payable on demand or on May 20, 1965. At the same time plaintiff executed and delivered to defendant an instrument entitled: "Assignment of Rents and Agreement Not to Sell or Encumber Real Property."[2] This document provided that as security for the loan

2. The assignment reads as follows:

ASSIGNMENT OF RENTS AND AGREEMENT NOT TO SELL OR ENCUMBER REAL PROPERTY In consideration and as security for a loan made or purchased by TAHOE NATIONAL BANK (hereinafter called "Bank") which loan is evidenced by a promissory note in favor of Beulah F. Phillips dated April 20, 1965, in the amount of Thirty Four Thousand and 00/100 ($34,000), the undersigned, and each of them, (hereinafter sometimes called "Borrower") hereby covenant and agree with Bank as follows: 1. The real property referred to herein is located in County of El Dorado, State of California, and is described as follows: "Lot 270, Tahoe Keys Unit No. 1, as said lot is shown on the Official Map of said Tahoe Keys Unit #1, filed in the office of the County Recorder of the County of El Dorado, State of California, on May 11, 1959, in Map Book C, Map No. 7." 2. Borrower hereby assigns to Bank all moneys due or to become due to Borrower as rental or otherwise for or on account of such real property, reserving unto Borrower the right to collect and retain any such moneys prior to Borrower's default under the terms of the loan described

defendant assigned to plaintiff all rent due from the realty described therein and agreed not to encumber or convey that property. The bank was authorized to record the instrument and did so on May 27, 1965.

The real property described in the document was not the venture's apartment development, but defendant's residence, which she owned one-half in fee and one-half as trustee under the testamentary trust of her deceased husband. This property was unencumbered as of April 20, 1965. On December 6 of that year defendant recorded a declaration of homestead on the property.

Mr. Ross, president of plaintiff bank, testified that the venturers first requested an unsecured loan but that he refused to issue the loan without security and requested collateral; that defendant then offered her residence as collateral and showed him an FHA appraisal at $34,400. The venturers required the money within two hours, and, for reasons which are not entirely clear,[3] Mr. Ross determined that the bank could not conveniently prepare a trust deed within that time limit; consequently he selected instead a form for an assignment of rents and agreement against conveyances. The document was prepared by his secretary and executed by the parties.

Mr. Ross acknowledged that his bank and other banks make unsecured loans upon agreements by the debtor to maintain unencumbered assets of sufficient value in the county. He denied, however, that his purpose in having defendant sign the document in issue was merely to insure that she would have unencumbered assets reachable by the bank; he maintained that he took the document "knowing it was in actuality a mortgage instrument against that house in lieu of a deed of trust."

Mrs. Phillips testified that she did not intend to sign or believe that she was signing any security interest "like a mortgage or deed of trust." She added that since she owned half her interest as trustee she believed that she lacked authority to execute a mortgage or trust deed on the property.

---

above; 3. Borrower will not create or permit any lien or encumbrance (other than those previously existing) to exist on said real property and will not transfer, sell, assign or in any manner dispose of said real property or any interest therein without the prior written consent of Bank; 4. Bank is hereby authorized and permitted to cause this instrument to be recorded at such time and in such places as Bank at its option may elect; 5. This agreement is expressly intended for the benefit and protection of Bank and all subsequent holders of the note described above. Borrower warrants and represents that Borrower owns the above-described real property. 6. This agreement shall remain in full force and effect until the loan described above shall have been paid in full or until twenty-one (21) years following the death of the last survivor of the undersigned, whichever first occurs. Dated: April 20, 1965 (s) Beulah F. Phillips.

3. Defendant's attorney inquired of Mr. Ross: "Wouldn't it have been just as easy to prepare a deed of trust on a form as an assignment of rents?" Mr. Ross answered: "No, it would not have been, simply because of the recording from the Tahoe Valley area into Placerville of the deed of trust with an amendment or new title policy showing our position if there had been a proper first deed of trust of record."

This answer of Mr. Ross is inconsistent with his assertion that the assignment was intended to be a mortgage on defendant's property. If the bank requires the protection of a title policy before executing a trust deed, and prompt recording of the trust deed, logically the bank should impose the same conditions on execution of an instrument intended to serve the purpose of a trust deed.

Plaintiff brought suit against the venture on various notes and over-drafts and, in its fifth cause of action, asked foreclosure of the assignment as an equitable mortgage. The court entered judgment against the venturers, jointly and severally, for $92,386 plus costs, interest, and attorney's fees. It further found that the assignment was an equitable mortgage securing $34,000 of the debt, and decreed its foreclosure. Mrs. Phillips alone appealed; her appeal challenges only that portion of the judgment finding the assignment to be an equitable mortgage and ordering foreclosure. . . .

Assignments similar to the present one are "used by many banks in conjunction with small, nominally unsecured loans such as home improvement loans." California Real Estate Secured Transactions §2.37 (Cont. Ed. Bar 1970) (hereinafter cited as "CEB").[6] They provide the lender with a measure of security, an assignment of rents and a contractual guarantee that property in which the debtor has an equity will remain unencumbered and unconveyed, and thus available for levy and execution should the creditor reduce his debt to judgment. Indeed, the plaintiff bank commonly makes loans upon the "security" of a promise by the debtor not to convey or hypothecate property, using for that purpose forms similar to that at issue here.

Thus we are not dealing with homemade security instruments in which the parties labor to produce a mortgage but fall short of the legal requirements and must be rescued by a court of equity. The form used was carefully drafted to produce a security interest with incidents differing from that of a mortgage.[8] As Justice Friedman pointed out in his dissenting opinion in the Court of Appeal [in this case]: "Here is a bank which prepared its own printed form, selected a particular one from its array of forms and handed it to the customer for signature. Doubtless the bank had printed forms of trust deed, perhaps even a few dusty, yellowed mortgages. Now the bank

Bank Form

6. A covenant against conveyances and encumbrances is sometimes referred to as a "negative pledge" agreement. See G. Osborne, Mortgages §§43-44 (1951); Coogan, Kripke, and Weiss, The Outer Fringes of Article 9: Subordination Agreements, Security Interests in Money and Deposits, Negative Pledge Clauses, and Participation Agreements, Harv. L. Rev. 229, 263-264 (1965). As summarized in the article by Coogan, Kripke, and Weiss: "The case law in this area is rather thin and in general dates from the depression. It indicates that a purely negative covenant creates no security interest in the property described." 79 Harv. L. Rev. at 264.

8. See CEB §2.37. Comment, 12 U.C.L.A. L. Rev. 954, 962, 964 (1965), discusses the purpose of assignments such as that employed in the present case:

[L]enders are willing in some instances to advance credit on the basis of a long pay-off period to a person who appears to have property which may be attached or secured in case the debtor becomes in financial difficulty. However, when the property is transferred, the credit picture immediately shifts and the lender wants to be in a position to accelerate maturity at once; he is no longer willing to take the risk over the long pay-off period — a risk he would gladly take if the property remained "locked with the debtor."

The comment adds:

Even though the Financial Code prohibits savings banks and trust companies from securing their loans by taking second liens, lending institutions have made real estate loans to homeowners using the negative pledge agreement when the property specified in the agreement was already encumbered by a prior mortgage or trust deed on the theory that no security interest was created by the negative pledge agreement.

claims that by the printed form it selected, it intended to create the legal effect of a form it did not select." We conclude that the plaintiff, having selected a form for "assignment of rents and agreement not to sell or encumber real property," is bound by the terms of that agreement.

We turn now to the language of the assignment. Its title gives no hint of a power of foreclosure. It contains no language of hypothecation, no provisions imposing a lien or creating a mortgage, no discussion of foreclosure. . . .

Plaintiff points out that the assignment specifies that it was given "as security for a loan," and that the word "security" may signify a right of foreclosure. *See* Civ. Code §2924; Coast Bank v. Minderhout, 392 P.2d 265, 266-67 (Cal. 1964). That phrase, however, appears in the preamble which, read as a whole, states that "as security for a loan . . . the undersigned . . . hereby covenant and agree with Bank as follows." The natural interpretation of this language is that it is the six covenants of the borrower that "secures" that loan; that the word "security" in the preamble does not create additional rights and duties not specified in the covenants.

Plaintiff further contends that the term "security," and the provisions of the assignment describing the real property and permitting recordation, render the assignment ambiguous, thus requiring extrinsic evidence to determine whether it places a lien on defendant's property. . . .

Since the alleged ambiguities appear in a standardized contract, drafted and selected by the bank, which occupies the superior bargaining position, those ambiguities must be interpreted against the bank. . . .

In the present case, we conclude that to permit a creditor to choose an allegedly ambiguous form of agreement, and then by extrinsic evidence seek to give it the effect of a different and unambiguous form, would be to disregard totally the rules respecting interpretation of adhesion contracts, and to create an extreme danger of over-reaching on the part of creditors with superior bargaining positions. The bank must bear the responsibility for the creation and use of the assignment it now claims is ambiguous; it is only "poetic justice," CEB §2.38, if such ambiguity is construed in favor of the borrower.[13] Legal alchemy cannot convert an assignment into an equitable mortgage, violating the customer's reasonable expectation and bestowing upon the bank the riches of an hypothecation of title.

We recognize that in Coast Bank v. Minderhout, *supra*, we ordered foreclosure as an equitable mortgage of an instrument similar to the assignment in the present case, but we do not consider that case controlling. The agreement in *Coast Bank* contained an acceleration clause and stated that the loan was intended to improve the property described in the agreement — both characteristics indicative of a mortgage and both absent in the present

---

13. Usually it will be the lender who chooses an ambiguous instrument, but Kogan v. Bergman, 53 Cal. Rptr. 371 (Ct. App. 1966), was that rare case in which the borrower drafted an ambiguous security device. The court gave the creditor an election to enforce the note as a secured or an unsecured note. *Id.* at 377.

assignment. Of greater significance is the differing context of *Coast Bank* and the present case. In *Coast Bank*, the borrower had breached a covenant prohibiting conveyance of the realty. Such a breach confronts the court with a difficult problem in fashioning a remedy. An award of damages would prove ineffective; "the maximum damages the bank could suffer from breach would be the amount of the debt, the same amount for which it could get a judgment on the note." CEB §2.38. Specific performance of the covenant against conveyances might create an invalid restraint against alienation. *See* Coast Bank v. Minderhout, *supra* at 268. . . .

In the present case defendant has performed all terms of the assignment,[14] with the result that defendant's interest in the realty, over the homestead exemption, is available to satisfy the bank's judgment on the note. If this security is not fully adequate, such is the result of the bank's choice of the governing instrument. . . .

Part 2 of the judgment against defendant Beulah Phillips is reversed.

SULLIVAN, Justice (dissenting). I dissent. . . .

In *Coast Bank* . . . this court unanimously held: "An agreement that particular property is security for a debt also gives rise to an equitable mortgage even though it does not constitute a legal mortgage." *Coast Bank*, *supra* at 266-67.

> Specific mention of a security interest is unnecessary if it otherwise appears that the parties intended to create such an interest. . . . [T]he question presented is not what meaning appears from the face of the instrument alone, but whether the pleaded meaning is one to which the instrument is reasonably susceptible. . . . The instrument restricts the rights of the Enrights [defendants] in dealing with their property for plaintiff's benefit; it describes itself as "For use with Property Improvement Loan," it specifically sets forth the property it covers, and it authorizes plaintiff to record it. These provisions afford some indication that the parties intended to create a security interest and are clearly sufficient to support the pleaded meaning.

Id. at 267.

Of the four factors mentioned by the court in *Coast Bank* as indicating that the parties intended the instrument to create a security interest, only the second is absent in the case now before us. In addition, the Assignment contains an assignment of rents, a provision typically found in deeds of trust. . . .

---

14. The declaration of homestead by defendant did not breach her covenant against encumbering or conveying the property. "A homestead right is not an estate in the land, but a mere privilege of exemption from execution of such estate as the holder occupies." Arighi v. Rule & Sons, Inc., 107 P.2d 970, 972 (Cal. Ct. App. 1940). . . . The filing of a declaration of homestead creates no rights in third persons, and does not diminish the title of the declarant; it cannot be encompassed within the definition of an encumbrance.

The attempt by the majority to distinguish *Coast Bank* on its facts is equally unpersuasive. They first observe that in *Coast Bank* the agreement provided for an acceleration of the note in the event of a breach of the agreement. While it is true that the agreement in *Coast Bank* contained an acceleration clause whereas the Assignment before us does not, the court in *Coast Bank* did not find the acceleration clause to be a significant, much less essential, circumstance in concluding that the agreement created a lien on real property. . . .

Finally, we are urged to distinguish *Coast Bank* on the basis that the defendant in that case breached the agreement by conveying the property. However, in the instant case, defendant has also breached the Assignment by declaring a homestead on her property. A declaration of homestead is neither a conveyance nor an encumbrance for other purposes, but it does exempt the property from execution or forced sale. . . .

Problem 18B

Woody owns a small "strip" shopping center worth $3 million, encumbered by a mortgage loan with a present balance of $2 million held by Last Life Insurance Co. Your client, Crest Investors, wants to loan Woody $400,000 to be repaid in four annual installments of principal of $100,000 each, with interest also paid annually. Crest is unwilling to make an unsecured loan to Woody, but Woody does not want to grant a second mortgage on the center. Crest is leaning toward the use of a negative pledge agreement and wants your advice. Is this a good idea? Can you assist Crest in structuring it properly? In particular, consider the following:

(a) Should Crest use all or part of the document signed in *Tahoe National Bank*, entitled "Assignment of Rents and Agreement Not to Sell or Encumber Real Property"? Do you recommend any additions or changes to that language?

(b) Crest has reliable written evidence that the balance due on the Last Life Mortgage loan does not exceed $2 million. Is there any need for you to study the Last Life mortgage instrument? Suppose the mortgage has a broadly worded due-on-sale clause.

(c) Should Crest record or not record the negative pledge agreement that you are drafting?

(d) Suppose litigation results over the negative pledge agreement that you are drafting. Who might be the plaintiff? Who might be the defendant or defendants? Will the court decide that the agreement is an equitable mortgage held by your client, Crest? Are you certain?

(e) Suppose that for some reason a court holds that the negative pledge agreement is not an equitable mortgage. Does this portend loss or disaster for Crest? Why or why not?

(f) How should this matter be resolved under California law, as that law is presented in the above case? Now suppose you are in a state, like most states, that has no relevant case law. Does this bear on your advice to the client about whether to use a negative pledge? Assuming the decision is made to use a negative pledge agreement, will you draft differently for a California transaction than you will for a transaction governed by another state with no reported case law? Imagine that the shopping center is located in California, but Woody is a Utah resident and Crest Investors is located in and does business only in Utah. Which state's law will apply to the negative pledge agreement? Do the parties have the ability to choose?

C. INSTALLMENT LAND CONTRACTS

An *installment land contract*, also known as a *contract for deed*, is one type of arrangement for buying land. It is an executory contract under which the purchase price is payable in installments, usually monthly or annually, with the seller obligated to transfer title by deed when final payment is made. The buyer takes possession of the real estate at the outset of the transaction when the contract is signed, thus getting the use and enjoyment of the land before he completes the payments. Installment land contracts are used primarily in consumer transactions. The land may be improved — for example, with a single-family house — or unimproved, in which case the purchaser typically takes possession and builds a house or adds other improvements. There are two markets where installment land contracts are often employed, one involving merchant sellers and one involving nonmerchant sellers. Developers of vacation or resort property sometimes sell lots pursuant to installment land contracts. Occasionally new vacation homes are sold the same way. For a vacant lot, often the purchaser plans to wait before arranging for the construction of a vacation home, and in the meantime the installment land contract lets the purchaser select his lot and start making payments without the need for a substantial down payment. Individuals who own used homes or vacant lots also sometimes sell using installment land contracts. These sellers, who are not merchants, are providing a form of financing for buyers who probably cannot qualify for a standard mortgage loan because they are not able to make a substantial down payment or they have weak credit ratings. For this reason, the land contract is sometimes called the "poor man's mortgage," the connotation typically not being pejorative but instead supportive of a device that expands the availability of credit.

Installment land contracts are rarely used for transfers of commercial property or for transfers of undeveloped land that is slated for commercial development. It is also rare to find a residential developer who sells completed homes by means of land contracts. Instead, buyers of new housing obtain standard mortgage financing.

The most important thing to remember about the installment land contract is that it is an executory contract, and therefore the entire set of contract rules and remedies generally will apply. The main difference is the parties' time horizon. For a normal executory contract, sometimes called a "marketing contract," the period between contract signing and closing will be weeks or months. This period is determined by how long it takes the parties to prepare for closing and includes chores such as searching title and arranging financing. For an installment land contract the parties have agreed to postpone closing for a number of years, with the buyer in possession in the meantime. It is still an executory contract, but the period during which it remains executory is a long time, not a short time. Because contract law generally applies, we should keep in mind all the usual contract principles. For example, the contract must satisfy the statute of frauds or fall within one of the recognized exceptions. Risk of loss is on the buyer if there is no contract provision governing the matter, provided the jurisdiction follows the majority view of equitable conversion. If either party to the installment land contract breaches, the other party's remedial choices normally include expectancy damages, rescission, and specific performance.

The installment land contract has special features that distinguish it from short-term marketing contracts, and that is why we study it separately in this chapter. It is a long-term contract, pursuant to which the purchaser takes possession and often improves the property. The purchaser gradually pays the entire purchase price over time, which is unlike the short-term contract that calls for just one relatively small deposit prior to closing. Because of the long-term nature of the installment land contract and the payment schedule, the contract buyer builds up substantial equity in the property, which may be forfeited to the seller if the buyer breaches. A large volume of cases address the seller's remedies when the buyer defaults, with modern law generally evolving to protect the buyer from incurring a substantial loss of value.

Besides issues surrounding seller's remedies, the second primary area that merits special attention concerns the rights and duties of third parties. Because land contracts remain in effect for many years, transfers often take place. Third parties deal with the seller or the purchaser, acquiring interests through voluntary transfers (for example, sales and mortgages) as well as involuntary transfers (for example, foreclosures, judgment liens, and bankruptcies). Such transfers raise issues not only between transferor and transferee, but also with respect to the other party to the land contract.

In thinking about how the law should handle remedies and transfers, we should bear in mind how the parties structured their deal. The basic concept behind the installment land contract is that the seller does not part with title until the entire purchase price is paid. There is great similarity in function between an installment land contract and a purchase-money mortgage transaction, whereby the buyer gets a deed at closing and gives a mortgage back to the seller. The distinction, in principle, is that after taking possession, the contract buyer has only contract rights, while the seller still has legal title, but the mortgagor buyer has legal title subject to the seller's mortgage.

Is this difference one of substance, or merely one of form?

PETERSEN v. HARTELL
Supreme Court of California, 1985
707 P.2d 232

REYNOSO, Justice. This appeal by plaintiff vendees who wilfully defaulted in making payments under an installment land sale contract requires us to reconsider such vendees' right to completion of performance. Though we upheld specific performance in MacFadden v. Walker, 488 P.2d 1353 (Cal. 1971), the trial court below concluded that the granting of such relief is only discretionary and dependent upon a weighing of the equities. Accordingly, it denied specific performance, adjudged that plaintiffs had no interest in the property, and awarded plaintiffs only restitution of the installments they had paid, with interest. . . .

I.

Defendant is administratrix of the estate of Juanita Gaspar who, upon the death of her first husband in 1946, succeeded to sole ownership of a 160-acre tract of unimproved land southeast of Fort Bragg in Mendocino County. In the late 1960's she entered into agreements with three of her grandchildren to sell small portions of the land at $1,500 per acre, with no down payment and monthly installments of $50 or less. The agreement now relied on by plaintiffs was embodied in a written contract, executed in November 1967, providing for the sale to granddaughter Kathy Petersen and her husband, Richard Petersen, of slightly more than six acres for a total purchase price of $9,162, payable at $50 per month. The buyers were given the right to pay the entire balance of the purchase price at any time. There was no provision making time of the essence or specifying remedies in the event of default.

Although the contract was drafted by Richard Petersen, who was then a recent law school graduate, the trial court found that no undue influence or overreaching was employed by either of the Petersens in the preparation or execution of the agreement. The price of $1,500 per acre was set by Mrs. Gaspar, who wished to give her grandchildren the opportunity to acquire small portions of her property. She was dependent, however, on income from the land contract payments, along with her social security benefits, to make ends meet.

The Petersens missed occasional payments in 1968, 1969, 1971, and 1972. Of the 65 payments due from November 1967 through March 1973, they made 58 payments totaling $2,900. In April 1973 the couple separated and their payments ceased. Kathy Petersen testified that about that time she spoke about the separation to her grandmother, who said it was important to take care of the children first and that she (the grandmother) would "get by."

In September 1975 Kathy Petersen sent Mrs. Gaspar a check for $250 as "back payments." Mrs. Gaspar's attorney then wrote the Petersens, stating that Mrs. Gaspar elected to terminate the contract. In February 1976 Mrs. Gaspar wrote to Kathy Petersen, returning the latter's check and explaining that she considered the contract broken. In September 1976 Richard Petersen wrote to the attorney requesting reinstatement of the contract and a statement of the amounts due, and enclosing a $250 money order, which the attorney promptly returned on instructions from Mrs. Gaspar.

In October 1976, Mrs. Gaspar died. Kathy Petersen then assigned all her interest under the contract to Carol Ranta as trustee for the two minor children of the Petersen marriage. Thus, the plaintiffs in the present action are Richard Petersen and the two children, who appear through Ranta as their guardian ad litem. . . .

II.

. . . The Petersens' monthly payments were erratic and delinquent almost from the beginning even though the seller made clear her need of the payments for her support. By April 1973 the Petersens had made only 58 out of the 65 payments then due, and their first attempt to reinstate the contract was not until 29 months later, when they tendered only $250 out of the $1,800 that was by then overdue and unpaid.

The issue, therefore, is whether plaintiffs, despite their wilful defaults in payments, now have an absolute right to a conveyance of the property in exchange for payment of the entire balance of the purchase price (together with interest and any other damages) in light of their substantial part performance and the seller's notice of election to terminate the contract on account of such defaults.

III.

. . . For at least a century in this state, a seller of land being sold under an installment contract who sues to quiet title because of the vendee's default in installment payments has been required to give the vendee a reasonable opportunity to complete performance. In Keller v. Lewis, 53 Cal. 113, 118 (1878), this court explained:

It is a *universal rule* in equity never to enforce either a penalty or forfeiture. 2 Story's Eq., 1319, and cases cited. On the contrary, equity frequently interposes to prevent the enforcement of a forfeiture at law. In the view of a Court of Equity, in cases like the present, the legal title is retained by the vendor as security for the balance of the purchase money, and if the vendor obtains his money and interest he gets all he expected when he entered into the contract. True, he is not bound to wait indefinitely after the failure of the purchaser to comply with the terms of his agreement. If the payments are not made when due, he may, if out of possession, bring his ejectment and recover the possession; but if he comes into *equity* for relief, his better remedy, in case of persistent default on the part of the vendee, is to institute proceedings to foreclose the right of the vendee to purchase; the decree usually giving the latter a definite time within which to perform. Hansborough v. Peck, 5 Wallace, 506.

Under the circumstances of this case, as presented by the pleadings and evidence, the decree of the District Court should have fixed a day within which the defendants should pay the balance due upon the contract, and costs, etc., or be forever foreclosed of all right or interest in the lands, or to a conveyance thereof.

In subsequent decisions this court has continued to uphold that procedure for giving the vendee an opportunity to complete performance as "in consonance with equity." Kornblum v. Arthurs, 97 P. 420, 421 (Cal. 1908); *accord*, Cross v. Mayo, 140 P. 283, 288 (Cal. 1914). There is no indication in those cases that the provision for a right of redemption in a decree that would otherwise foreclose the vendee's rights in the land was contingent on any showing of facts that would mitigate the wilfulness or seriousness of the vendee's default. To the contrary, in Kornblum v. Arthurs, this court approved a provision for redemption by a vendee whose suit for rescission was held barred by laches because he had purchased the lot in question on speculation, been granted an extension of time for an additional payment, and only then, after the real estate market had partially collapsed, sought rescission.

In those early cases, however, the vendee who failed to exercise the right to redeem by completing the payments forfeited payments already made, apparently without regard to whether the amounts paid exceeded the seller's damages. Cross v. Mayo, *supra*; Kornblum v. Arthurs, *supra*. Thereafter, this court decided that even a wilfully defaulting vendee may be entitled to restitution under section 3369, which provides that "[n]either specific nor preventive relief can be granted to enforce a penalty or forfeiture in any case." That section "precludes the court from quieting the vendor's title unless he refunds the excess of the part payments over the damage caused by the vendee's breach." Freedman v. The Rector, 230 P.2d 629, 632-33 (Cal. 1951). Such restitution is a matter of right for the wilfully defaulting vendee who proves that the payments made to the seller exceed the amount necessary to give the seller the benefit of his bargain . . . .

We think that as a matter both of stare decisis and of sound public policy, a vendee who has made substantial payments on a land installment sale contract or substantial improvements on the property, and whose defaults, albeit wilful, consist solely of failure to pay further amounts due, has an unconditional right to a reasonable opportunity to complete the purchase by paying the entire remaining balance plus damages before the seller is allowed to quiet title. We read *Keller* and its earlier progeny as so holding. As *Keller* itself observes, "the legal title is retained by the vendor as security for the balance of the purchase money, and if the vendor obtains his money and interest he gets all he expected when he entered the contract." 53 Cal. at 118. To that statement we add that the seller may be entitled to damages in addition to interest. Whatever the amounts due, their payment in full makes the seller whole regardless of the nature of the vendee's defaults in payments . . . .

Finally, we think that to retain specific performance under MacFadden v. Walker, *supra*, as the utmost remedy available in a suit initiated by a wilfully defaulting vendee unduly burdens courts and litigants with time-consuming and expensive legal proceedings. The present case is illustrative. To settle a dispute over land sold for a total price of only $9,162 required two days of nonjury trial in which eight witnesses (only two of whom were parties) testified to circumstances bearing on whether the vendees' defaults were sufficiently egregious to bar them from specific performance under *MacFadden*. Yet, as already explained, if defendant seller had sued to quiet title, plaintiffs would have been entitled as a matter of right to a conveyance of title in exchange for payment of the balance of the purchase price with interest and damages . . . . The [Petersens'] complaint . . . , rather than being designated as one for specific performance, is more appropriately referred to as one to redeem the vendee's interest in real property.

Accordingly, we conclude that plaintiffs are entitled to a conveyance of title to the property in exchange for payment of the entire remaining balance due under the contract together with interest and any consequential damages as determined by the court. Should plaintiffs fail to make such payments within a reasonable time fixed by the court, the adjudication that plaintiffs have no further interest in the property should become effective only upon defendant's payment of the sums due to plaintiffs as restitution . . . .

The judgment is reversed.

Bird, Chief Justice, concurring and dissenting. I agree with the majority that an unconditional right of redemption exists for most wilfully defaulting vendees under security device installment land sale contracts.

However, there is no reason to deny the right of redemption to vendees whose payments prior to default amount to less than "a substantial part of the purchase price." This court has under certain circumstances treated substantial partial payment as a prerequisite to relief from forfeiture. However, the substantial partial payment requirement has been applied only where the relief granted to the defaulting vendee was not redemption but *reinstatement* of the contract upon payment of delinquent amounts . . . .

The predominant use of installment land sale contracts has been to finance the purchase of housing by low income families and individuals unable to qualify for conventional mortgage financing or government loan guarantee programs. *See* Note, *Reforming the Vendor's Remedies for Breach of Installment Land Sale Contracts*, 47 So. Cal. L. Rev. 191, 193-198 (1973).

Providing installment contract vendees the same protections that are afforded to mortgagors would eliminate some abusive practices of vendors, who have exploited the lack of legal sophistication and limited capacity to litigate of their low-income clients. *See id.* at 197 n.36, 205-06, 211. Most important, defaulting vendees would be able to avoid the loss of their homes by paying only the delinquent amounts.[4] Under the majority's holding, a wilfully defaulting vendee may avoid this fate only by paying the outstanding balance in full. This is an unjustifiably harsh burden to place on the low-income and middle-income families and individuals who will be most affected.

MOSK, Justice, dissenting. I dissent.

The majority misread precedent and rely on questionable "policy" to reach a result that flouts what is undeniably equitable. Our long history of cases holds that when a vendee in an installment land sale contract wilfully defaults, it is in the trial court's discretion to weigh the equities and discern whether redemption is warranted. The trial court reacted properly to the overwhelming evidence and exercised its discretion to deny specific performance to vendees who have been wilfully untrustworthy and derelict in the performance of contract duties.

The majority place principal focus on a line of cases beginning with Keller v. Lewis, 53 Cal. 113 (1878). There they find authority for their holding that a wilfully defaulting vendee has an unqualified right to the equity of redemption with respect to an installment land sale contract. However, a careful examination of the *Keller* line reveals that an absolute right was never contemplated. In each of the cases in the series the vendee was given a time in which to perform, but the temporal requirement was either at the behest of the vendor or was the result of the court's examination of the equities of the case . . . .

Reliance is placed on the policy against forfeitures. Freedman v. The Rector, 230 P.2d 629, 631 (1951). But two kinds of forfeitures are presented when a vendee party to an installment land sale contract defaults and title is quieted in the vendor: the loss of installments previously paid and the loss of the benefit of the bargain. The policy against forfeitures prevents a court from quieting title in the vendor unless he refunds to the vendee the excess of previously paid installments above his damages from the default. Freedman v. The Rector, *supra* at 632-33. However, there is no such application of

---

4. Before a vendee may reinstate the contract in this manner, however, he or she must also pay the vendor's reasonable costs and the trustee's or the attorney's fees. *See* Civ. Code, §2924c, subd. (a)(1). Thus, even if there were more than one wilful default, the vendor would be fully protected.

the policy against forfeitures to the loss of the benefit of the bargain. In fact, our cases have specifically held otherwise . . . .

As the majority readily admit, the equities in the case at bar weigh heavily against the vendees . . . .

As between the deliberately defaulting vendees and the elderly vendor who desperately needed the modest payments on the contract for her very survival, the equities clearly favor the latter. I am mystified at how the majority can conclude the ends of justice compel their callous result and rejection of the trial court's rational exercise of discretion. There being no reason to overturn our prior cases and ignore the policies clearly articulated therein, I would affirm the judgment denying the vendees specific performance.

LUCAS, J., concurs [with Justice Mosk's dissent].

Problem 18C

Happy Acres Mobile Home Park sells lots in its mobile home park to purchasers using installment land contracts. Lots, which are improved with utility hookups and asphalt driveways, cost $16,000. Five years ago, Polly signed an installment land contract, providing for the $16,000 price to be paid in monthly installments of $171.94 per month for 15 years. The monthly payment includes interest at 10 percent per annum. Polly paid all monthly installments on time for 59 consecutive months, until this summer (her payments made total $10,144.46). She failed to make the payments due June 1 and July 1, and on July 6, Happy Acres sent her a notice of termination, which stated that Happy Acres was terminating the contract due to her default and that she should vacate possession of the lot and move her mobile home during the next 25 days. The contract states:

> If Buyer defaults in paying one or more monthly installments to Seller, then Seller shall have the right to terminate this contract by written notice to Buyer, in which event Seller shall have the immediate right to re-enter and take possession of the premises. In the event Seller so terminates this contract, Seller shall be deemed relieved and discharged from any claims or obligations of any kind under this contract, and all payments made by Buyer shall be retained by Seller and shall be deemed rent for Buyer's use and occupancy of the premises up to the date of termination.

(a) Is Happy Acres' notice of termination valid? Does Happy Acres have the right to retain the payments it has received? Does it matter whether there is evidence of the rental value of the lot? Suppose that Happy Acres rents some of its unsold lots to tenants and that five years ago, when it sold to Polly, it charged $120 per month rent and it presently charges $160 per month rent.

(b) If a court denies Happy Acres the right to terminate the contract and retain all payments made to date, what alternative remedies should Happy Acres have?

(c) Should the parties' rights and remedies depend on the reason for Polly's default? For example, perhaps she lost her job or had unexpectedly high medical expenses; or alternatively she changed her lifestyle, deciding she preferred to spend her income on a new car and an expensive vacation and thus didn't have enough money left to continue paying Happy Acres.

(d) Polly bought her mobile home for $70,000 five years ago and it has a present fair market value of $50,000. It would cost $10,000 to move the mobile home to another site in the community. Should this affect the parties' rights and remedies? What if, instead of a mobile home, Polly had spent $100,000 for the construction of a prefabricated home placed on a slab foundation, and it wasn't economically feasible for the home to be moved?

(e) Suppose the facts show that Polly had not always paid on time until this summer, but she frequently made late payments in the past. About one-third of the time, she paid between the 5th and 25th of the month. Only twice did she pay later than the 25th. Once was 30 months ago, the other time 24 months ago. In both cases, Happy Acres phoned her on the first day of the following month and demanded payment, and both times she made a double payment on the next day for the last month and the current month. The contract does not provide for a late charge or penalty, and Happy Acres never tries to assess one. When Polly defaulted this time, Happy Acres called her on July 1, leaving an urgent message on her answering machine. Polly did not return the call prior to the July 6 notice of termination. How do these facts affect the analysis of the parties' rights?

19
Junior Mortgages

We have already discussed junior mortgages in a number of places in this book. In this chapter, we focus on the market for junior mortgages, the special position of the junior mortgagee, and her legal relationships with the owner-mortgagor and the senior lienholder.

Junior mortgages can be used to *leverage* a property owner's investment. Leverage is not a complicated economic concept. All it means is that the owner or developer is obtaining funds from lenders or investors to do a real estate project or to finance a completed project. These funds may be from debt financing (*e.g.*, mortgage financing) or from equity financing when the investor takes an interest in a capacity such as a partner, joint venturer, or shareholder in the project. In a "highly leveraged" deal, the developer is getting a lot of financing — debt or equity or both — and has little of her own money or capital invested or committed to the project. Leverage directly affects risk and return. The higher the leverage, the greater the potential return on the owner's out-of-pocket investment.

It is very common for real property owners who have an existing first mortgage, and who have equity in their property because its value exceeds the balance on the first mortgage, to decide they want to borrow additional funds. There are any number of reasons why they might want cash: their business may need capital for expansion or modernization; they may have debts to pay; they may need money for health care or to pay for their children's education; they may have the opportunity to purchase an investment that looks good to them; they might want to take a nice vacation. Although they might be able to get an unsecured loan for any of these purposes, they may find that lenders insist on collateral in the nature of a second lien on their property. Even if collateral is not required, in almost all cases the prospective borrowers will learn that the cost of the loan will be less if they agree to give security. As we have discussed before, this reduces the credit risk to the lender and enables the lender to offer a lower interest rate and more attractive terms than are possible for unsecured lending.

Be careful not to confuse the term "secondary financing" or "second mortgage" with the secondary mortgage market, which we studied in Chapter 15. These terms refer to completely different concepts. The secondary mortgage market involves the sale of primary mortgages from the originating lender to investors, and a very high percentage of those mortgages are first mortgages. It is true that second-lien residential mortgages (home improvement loans and home equity line-of-credit loans) are increasingly traded on the secondary mortgage market, but their priority has nothing to do with identifying the market in which they are traded. In contrast, the term *secondary financing* means there is already a first mortgage on the property, which has priority. It implies nothing about whether the lender might keep the loan or sell it to a new or "second" owner.

A junior mortgage is the primary type of secondary financing that is secured by property. A junior mortgage may be a second mortgage, third mortgage, or even fourth mortgage. In states where the principal security instrument is something other than a mortgage, the same ranking occurs, with the junior lenders generally using the same type of instrument as the first lenders. Thus, in California and Texas there are second and third deeds of trust, and in Georgia there are second and third security deeds. There is no legal or logical limit to how many mortgages may encumber a single piece of property, but for obvious practical reasons having to do with property value and transaction costs, one seldom encounters more than a handful of mortgages on one property in the real world. Note, however, that there can be many junior liens other than mortgages, and a troubled or delinquent property owner might incur a large number of mechanic's liens, judgment liens, and the like ranked against a single asset.

Other forms of secondary finance besides junior mortgages are used in real estate finance on occasion, but they are not common. For example, when a borrower owns rental property that is subject to a mortgage, a secondary lender may take a first assignment in one or more of the borrower's leases. Functionally in terms of risk, this is a second position because even though the lease is not part of the mortgagee's collateral, if that lease is junior to the mortgage, a properly conducted mortgage foreclosure will result in termination of that lease. Alternatively, when the borrower is an entity, a secondary lender may get a first lien on the ownership interests in the entity — for example, a pledge of corporate shares or a collateral assignment of partnership interests. Again, although the lender nominally has a first position, if the entity's only or principal asset of value is real estate subject to a first mortgage, the lender has the risk of being second in line. Another possibility is that the borrower will sign a negative pledge agreement covering the property that has equity. In each of the alternative types of secondary financing mentioned here, the secondary lender probably will have more risk than if she obtained a standard second mortgage. The main situation in which such an alternative might make sense for a particular deal is when there is an impediment to the owner's granting a second mortgage or to the lender's receiving a second mortgage. The first mortgage may prohibit second mortgages, or, if the lender is a financial institution, for regulatory reasons a second mortgage loan might be inappropriate or inadvisable.

In any case, it must be remembered that secondary financing is also an alternative to merely refinancing under a new first mortgage. That is, one might get a further advance under a first mortgage, roll the first mortgage over into a new larger first mortgage loan from the same lender, or simply pay off the first loan by borrowing from a new lender and taking on a larger debt. Generally, this route will not be taken if the current first loan has a favorable interest rate that would be upset on refinancing, or if no provision is made in the first mortgage for future advances. In addition, refinancing may have higher transaction costs than getting a second or junior loan, depending on the way in which a particular jurisdiction taxes mortgage lending and recording. Consequently, there may be sound business reasons for not simply replacing a current first loan with a new and bigger first loan.

In recent years, an increasing proportion of the market for homeowner second loans has consisted of home equity lines of credit. Home equity loans, secured by second mortgages, are amortized over a fixed term that is generally much shorter than the standard 30-year length of a first mortgage. Terms ranging from 5 to 15 years are typical, and homeowners on the average prepay home equity loans faster than first mortgage loans because the interest rates are higher. These secondary loans generally carry a higher rate of interest than a first mortgage because there is a greater risk that they will not get paid in full in the event of a mortgage foreclosure. This is because the earlier creditors will be paid first. A borrower who is approved for a home equity line of credit has the choice of how much actually to borrow, up to the maximum, at any time while the relationship continues.

Problem 19A

Amber plans to purchase some land and construct a small office building that she will lease out. Her estimated budget is $4 million with $500,000 for land acquisition and $3.5 million to construct improvements. The project will take one year to complete, through lease-up. The investment expectation is that the completed project will have a value of $4.5 million.

(a) Assume Amber invests her own cash and spends the entire amount at the outset, even though she would likely spend it over the course of construction. Upon completion, the property is worth $4.5 million. In this all-cash transaction, what is the rate of return on Amber's investment?

(b) Assume that Amber obtains a $3 million mortgage loan and provides $1 million of her own cash. Upon completion, the project is worth $4.5 million. Using the mortgage as leverage, what is the rate of return on Amber's cash investment?

(c) Assume the same facts as in (b), except that Amber also gets a $500,000 junior mortgage loan, thus reducing her contribution to $500,000. Upon completion, the project is worth $4.5 million. Now what is the rate of return on Amber's cash investment?

(d) Assume the same facts as in (c), except that Amber also gets a $400,000 third mortgage loan, thus reducing her contribution to $100,000. Upon completion, the project is worth $4.5 million. What is the rate of return on Amber's cash investment?

(e) As Amber increases her leverage in the project, what happens to the rate of return on her cash investment? What happens to the amount of equity that she has in the project? What happens to the risk of borrower default and foreclosure taken on by the lenders? What happens if the economy suffers a major downturn and the project is worth only $3 million upon completion? What risks can you identify for each of the lenders, and what steps might you take to reduce or shift those risks?

A. PROTECTING THE JUNIOR MORTGAGE

The primary risk to the junior mortgagee is that the senior debt holder will foreclose, and the proceeds of sale will be insufficient to cover the full junior debt. As we saw in Chapter 17, if the senior mortgagee forecloses properly and the junior fails to act, the junior loses all of her property rights in the property that serves as the collateral for her loan. Now she is an unsecured creditor and is in a terrible position. Because the mortgagor has suffered a foreclosure on the property, the prospect that the mortgagor will voluntarily pay the junior debt in the near future is very remote. She therefore must hope that the mortgagor owns other assets — in addition to the foreclosed-upon property — that she can proceed against to satisfy the debt. This great risk of foreclosure under the senior mortgage is the reason why junior mortgages cost more than first mortgages. Risk and price are related, and the junior lender must charge a higher interest rate or take other measures to increase its yield (for example, by collecting upfront fees) to take account of her risky position. Thus, when the market interest rate for a particular type of first mortgage is 10 percent, if there is sufficient equity in the property to justify secondary financing, the rate for a second mortgage might be 12 or 13 percent.

In addition to pricing its mortgage loans differently to account for greater risk, junior lenders typically take other steps to protect their loans. A few of these additional steps include verifying the outstanding loan amount of the senior loans and determining if the senior loans permit negative amortization or additional funding, inclusion of a cross-default provision in the junior mortgage so that any default on the senior loan is an automatic default on the junior loan, a right to notice of any default on the senior loan, and a right to cure a default by the borrower on the senior loan.

Often a senior and junior mortgage cover precisely the same real property, but it is not at all unusual for there to be differences in the land, improvements, fixtures, and other types of collateral that are covered by competing mortgages and security documents. When secured creditors have liens that attach to different assets but there is some overlap, disputes over priorities often arise. The most common problem arises when the senior creditor seeks to foreclose and she has more assets as collateral than the junior creditor. When this happens, courts often apply the doctrine of *marshalling of assets*. This is a rule of equity that ranks or arranges the multiple assets in order, requiring that the senior creditor first proceed against the asset that is not subject to a junior lien. Some courts have applied marshalling only if a single debtor has created both debts. Thus, under this view, marshalling would not apply if a purchaser who assumes or takes subject to a mortgage granted by her seller later encumbers only part of the property covered by the first mortgage.

In re *MARTIN*
Supreme Court of Oklahoma, 1994
875 P.2d 417

SIMMS, Justice. This is a Certified Question of Law from the United States Bankruptcy Court for the Western District of Oklahoma based upon the following facts.

John R. Martin and Elsie B. Martin, debtors, filed a petition for relief under Chapter 13 of the United States Bankruptcy Code and subsequently converted the case to one under Chapter 12 of that code. Debtors own three parcels of property: (1) Lot 10, Block 10, Sights Acres Addition to the City of Clinton, Custer County, Oklahoma ("Homestead"); (2) Northwest Quarter of Section 36, Township 13 North, Range 18 W.I.M. ("Farm property"); and, (3) An undivided 100 acre mineral interest underlying the Northwest Quarter of Section 30, Township 12 North, Range 17 W.I.M. ("Minerals").

Debtors' bankruptcy schedules place the following values on the properties: (1) $53,250 on the homestead; (2) $45,600 on the farm property; and, $50,000 on the minerals. However, the secured creditor, Oklahoma Bank & Trust Company (Bank), disputes the values Debtors have placed on the properties, and a hearing on Bank's valuation motion is to be reset by the parties. Nevertheless, Debtors' indebtedness exceeds the value of the properties.

Debtors are indebted to the Small Business Administration ("SBA") in the amount of $44,057.65 with the debt secured by a first lien on the homestead and a second lien on the farm property. The indebtedness of Debtors of $40,510.26 to the State of Oklahoma/Commissioner of the Land Office ("CLO") is secured by a first lien on the farm property. Finally, Debtors are indebted to Bank in the amount of $151,346.94, and Bank is secured by a third lien on the farm property and first lien on the minerals.

Relying upon 42 O.S. 1991 §17 and 24 O.S. 1991 §4, Bank requested an order of marshalling of Debtors' assets. Bank urged the Bankruptcy Court to declare SBA's claim be satisfied out of the homestead property. With SBA's claim satisfied, Bank could then satisfy a part of its claim out of the excess value of the farm property after CLO's claim was satisfied. If the court excluded the homestead from marshalling, then CLO would have first priority to satisfy its claim against the farm property with SBA being entitled to the excess of that farm property. Bank's interest in including the homestead property in the marshalling of debtors' assets is quite clear.

Debtors objected to such marshalling, contending that Okla. Const. Art. XII, §2 and 31 O.S. 1991, §1, as well as public policy, prohibit Bank from compelling the satisfaction of SBA's claim from the homestead. Debtors further requested an order compelling the creditors to marshall their claims away from the homestead. The Chapter 12 Trustee aligned with Debtors in contending the homestead should be excluded from the marshalling of assets. . . .

Our inquiry must begin with the doctrine of marshalling of assets. This doctrine "rests upon the principle that a creditor having two funds to satisfy his debt may not, by his application of them to his demand, defeat another creditor, who may resort to only one of the funds." Meyer v. United States, 375 U.S. 233, 236 (1963). Thus, under marshalling, a senior lienholder must satisfy his claim by first resorting to property in which a junior lienholder has no interest. The doctrine is codified at 24 O.S. 1991, §4 which provides:

> Where a creditor is entitled to restore [sic, "resort"] to each of several funds for the satisfaction of his claim, and another person has an interest in or is entitled as a creditor to resort to some but not all of them, the latter may require the former to seek satisfaction from those funds to which the latter has no such claim, so far as it can be done without impairing the right of the former to complete satisfaction, and without doing injustice to third persons.

The Bank also cites 42 O.S. 1991, §17 in support of its claim for marshalling. Section 17 reads:

> Where one has a lien upon several things, and other persons have subordinate liens upon or interests in, some but not all of the same things, the person having the prior lien, if he can do so without the risk of loss to himself, or injustice to other persons, must resort to the property in the following order, on the demand of any party interested: 1. To the things upon which he has an exclusive lien; 2. To the things which are subject to the fewest subordinate liens; 3. In like manner inversely to the number of subordinate liens upon the same thing; and, 4. When several things are within one of the foregoing classes, and subject to the same number of liens, resort must be had, — (a) To the things which have not been transferred since the prior lien was created; (b) To the things which have been so transferred without a valuable consideration; and, (c) To the things which have been so transferred for a valuable consideration.

Thus, Oklahoma statutory law contains provisions designed and intended to allow for the marshalling of assets in situations such as the one at bar where there are multiple properties and multiple creditors. However, the doctrine of marshalling of assets is not without exceptions. When our state constitution was drafted, its writers had the foresight to include a provision exempting homestead property from forced sale. Okla. Const. Art. XII, §2. Section 2 provides:

> The homestead of the family shall be, and is hereby protected from forced sale for the payment of debts, except for the purchase money therefor or a part of such purchase money, the taxes due thereon, or for work and material used in constructing improvements thereon; nor shall the owner, if married, sell the homestead without the consent of his or her spouse, given in such manner as may be prescribed by law; Provided, Nothing in this article shall prohibit any person from mortgaging his homestead, the spouse, if any, joining therein; nor prevent the sale thereof on foreclosure to satisfy any such mortgage.

Although this provision does not specifically state that a homestead may not be marshalled against, its intent is clear. Homestead property is exempt from any forced sale except in those specifically enumerated cases such as for the purchase money of the homestead or for taxes due thereon. Conspicuously absent from the authorized exceptions to this constitutional provision are instances of marshalling. Those enumerated exceptions are the only claims which regard the creditor's rights to the property as equal to or exceeding the rights of the debtor.

In addition to the constitutional homestead exemption, statutory law contains a homestead exemption as well. . . .

The Oklahoma Legislature has made its intention quite clear in enacting this homestead exemption. The statutory homestead exemption, as well as the constitutional homestead exemption, prohibits homestead property from being forcibly sold for the payment of debts except under the specifically enumerated exceptions. Marshalling of assets is not one of those exceptions.

In addition, not only do the terms of the homestead exemption provisions make it clear that the homestead is excluded from marshalling, but the equitable nature of the doctrine of marshalling of assets also militates against allowing marshalling of homestead property. The doctrine was founded in equity and natural justice and is designed to promote fair dealing. . . .

In the majority of jurisdictions which have passed on the issue, it is held that the debtor has a right to compel the secured creditor to marshal away from the homestead. . . .

Debtors' protected equity in their homestead is superior to Bank's equity interest in marshalling. Application of the marshalling doctrine to allow Bank to force the sale of exempt property although it does not have a mortgage voluntarily given by Debtors or a claim for purchase money or taxes or improvements is in direct contravention of our constitution and statutes. The fact that this equitable doctrine has been codified by statute, 24 O.S. 1991, §4, *supra*, does not defeat or change its purpose. . . .

Thus, we join the majority of jurisdictions and adopt the exception holding that a debtor is entitled to exclude the homestead from marshalling of assets.

Question Answered.

HODGES, Chief Justice, with whom SUMMERS, Justice, joins, dissenting. . . .

As the majority recognizes, the purpose of [the two Oklahoma marshaling statutes] is to allow marshaling under the facts of this case. However, the majority suggests that these statutory provisions do not apply in this case because to do so would cause injustice to third persons, namely the debtor, which is prohibited by the provisions. This position is insupportable, especially where the debtor has voluntarily mortgaged the property and received purchase money. . . .

The majority also would find an exception implied in section 2 of article 12 of the Oklahoma Constitution and title 31 section 1 of the Oklahoma Statutes and an exception based on equity. I cannot agree that these two provisions on which the majority relies imply an exception and, even if an exception is implied, that such an implication should override explicit statutory mandates. Neither should equitable principles be applied to negate express legislative language. . . .

I would hold that the Oklahoma Constitution and the Oklahoma Statutes do not create or authorize an exception to the marshaling of assets when the debtor has voluntarily mortgaged the homestead property to secure payment of a debt and the Oklahoma marshaling statutes, Okla. Stat. tit. 42, §17 and tit. 24, §4 (1991), permit secured creditors to compel the marshaling of assets against homestead property which has been intentionally mortgaged.

Problem 19B

Gary and Jean own their home, valued at $600,000, and they wish to purchase a small camp on a nearby lake for $300,000. They refinanced their home mortgage, which had an existing balance of $200,000 debt on the home, to generate the $300,000 needed to acquire the camp property. The end result of the refinancing is that they borrowed $500,000 secured by a first mortgage on the two properties. One year later Gary and Jean purchased a $30,000 motor boat to use at the camp. When they purchased the boat they gave the Seacraft Boat Company $5,000 cash and signed a repayment agreement for the balance, secured by an Article 9 security interest in the boat and a second mortgage on the camp property. One year later, Gary and Jean encountered financial difficulties and defaulted on their loans. Gary and Jean's creditors foreclose. Property values have plummeted. At the time of the foreclosure sale, the home is worth $520,000, the camp is worth $200,000, and the boat is worth $10,000. Which assets may each creditor proceed against? Which creditor is likely to raise the doctrine of marshalling of assets, and with what result? How should the court, in a judicial foreclosure proceeding, handle the foreclosure and the distribution of proceeds?

B. MORTGAGE SUBORDINATION

A particular piece of real property is often subject to more than one lien, and whenever this is the case, it may become necessary to establish the priority of those liens. As a general principle, as we have seen earlier, priorities are ranked according to the idea of "first in time, first in right," subject to modification by state recording statutes. Sometimes specialized state statutes also affect priorities. For example, a mechanic's lien statute may give a worker or supplier of materials a special priority, and under Article 9 of the UCC the seller of a fixture who extends purchase-money credit is granted a prior status over some earlier mortgages or security interests.

When there are two or more mortgages on a property, it often happens that the general legal principles for priority are inappropriate or inadequate. The owner and the mortgagees may desire a different ranking than the general rules would produce based on the chronology of the parties' respective transactions. Even if there is no need to re-rank the priorities, there may be a need to make more definite the parties' respective rights and obligations with respect to certain matters. When either or both of these needs are present, the parties may use contract law to handle their concerns. The type of contract they sign may vary, but for real estate financings it is usually referred to as a *subordination agreement*. In contrast, for corporate finance and personal property financings, the arrangement is usually called an *intercreditor agreement*. The purpose of the agreement, whatever its name, is to establish or modify the relative rights of the creditors in their dealings with the borrower and the property that serves as collateral.

RANIER v. MOUNT STERLING NATIONAL BANK
Supreme Court of Kentucky, 1991
812 S.W.2d 154

SPAIN, Justice. This action arises out of the interpretation of a subordination agreement. In 1977, Phyllis Ranier loaned $200,000 to Algin and Doris Nolan and secured the promissory note with a first mortgage lien on their house and lot located in Montgomery County, Kentucky. In 1983, the Nolans applied for a home improvement loan with the Mount Sterling National Bank (Bank) to repair their home which was damaged by fire. Before approving the loan, the Bank required Mrs. Ranier to subordinate her lien on the Nolan property to the Bank's mortgage lien.

On February 28, 1983, Mrs. Ranier and the Bank executed a subordination agreement. The agreement, drafted by the Nolans' attorney, stated in pertinent part as follows:

> WHEREAS, Doris C. Nolan and Algin H. Nolan have entered into a loan agreement with the Mt. Sterling National Bank, Mt. Sterling, Kentucky, whereby they will borrow **the total sum of $125,000** from the Mt. Sterling National Bank, to be secured by a first real estate mortgage on the above described property in favor of the Mt. Sterling National Bank, and it is intended by the parties hereto that the above referenced real estate mortgage lien in favor of Thelma Phyllis Ranier . . . shall become a second and junior mortgage lien to the new first real estate mortgage lien in favor of Mt. Sterling National Bank. (Emphasis added.)

The Nolans then executed a six-month promissory note on March 8, 1983, in favor of the Bank in the amount of $125,000 and secured the note with a first mortgage lien on the Nolan property. The future advance clause of the mortgage stated that ". . . the total indebtedness at any one time outstanding shall not exceed the sum of . . . $125,000. . . ."

Without notice to Mrs. Ranier, the Bank, in July 1985, approved an additional loan to the Nolans in the amount of $75,000 to complete the repairs on their property. The Nolans signed a new promissory note in favor of the Bank in the amount of $200,000. The Nolans' original note in the amount of $125,000 was marked "renewed" by the Bank and returned to the Nolans. The note remained secured only to the extent of the Bank's first mortgage on the Nolan property. The record indicates that the note was renewed several times and a total sum of $95,269.04, including $17,182.82 in principal and $78,269.32 in interest, had been paid to the Bank. The Bank applied the principal and interest to the unsecured portion of the note.

The Nolans defaulted on their notes. A foreclosure action was instituted by the Bank and the Nolan property was sold by the Master Commissioner for $181,000. Both the Bank and Ranier moved for summary judgment on the issue of their respective priorities in the proceeds of the foreclosure sale. The trial court granted summary judgment in favor of the Bank on the issue of priority and awarded it the sum of $140,216.48, which included the original promissory note principal amount of $125,000, plus interest, court costs, and attorney's fees. Mrs. Ranier received the balance of $35,892.09.

Ranier appealed to the Court of Appeals which affirmed the decision of the trial court. . . .

The Court of Appeals held that . . . the terms of the subordination agreement governed the Bank's priority. The Court of Appeals and the trial court stated that the agreement did not contain any provision which prohibited the Bank from making additional loans to the Nolans nor any requirement that the payments made by the Nolans be applied to the original secured portion of the note.

We agree with the lower courts that the subordination agreement does not contain any provision which prohibited additional loans from the Bank to the Nolans, nor does it provide specifically that any payments received from the Nolans would be used first to reduce the original secured portion of the renewed promissory note. The Bank did not breach the subordination agreement when it renewed the note and approved an additional unsecured loan in the amount of $75,000 to complete the repairs on the Nolan residence. But we do believe that the Bank has breached its implied covenant of good faith and fair dealing when it failed to give notice to Mrs. Ranier of its subsequent loan to the Nolans and when it unilaterally applied the mortgage payments it received from the Nolans first to the unsecured portion of the new promissory note. . . .

Prior to the parties entering into the subordination agreement, Mrs. Ranier held a first mortgage position on the Nolan property. She was asked by the Bank and the Nolans to subordinate her advantageous security position in favor of the Bank so that the Bank would approve a $125,000 home improvement loan to the Nolans. Mrs. Ranier then acquiesced and entered into the subordination agreement in the good faith belief that her mortgage would be subordinated only to the extent of $125,000, on which the Nolans were making regular payments. The Bank then loaned the Nolans an additional $75,000. No notice was given to Mrs. Ranier, nor did she agree to further subordinate her mortgage to an additional $75,000. The renewed note in the amount of $200,000 was, in fact, two notes containing a $125,000 secured note and a $75,000 unsecured note. The Bank clearly benefited from the subordination agreement because it was able to obtain a first lien on the property and then it subverted the agreement by applying the payments it received from the Nolans, not to the $125,000 debt, but to the unsecured portion of the note. Mrs. Ranier has been relegated, to her detriment, to an inferior position in the proceeds of the foreclosure sale while the Bank has been allowed to collect on both its unsecured and secured notes, including interest, court costs, and attorney fees. We do not believe that the intent of Ranier when she entered into the agreement was to place her pre-existing first mortgage in the status of a second mortgage in perpetuity. Her intent clearly was that her mortgage be temporarily subordinated to the Bank's mortgage to the extent of $125,000. . . .

We recognize the rule that, as between the two of them, a creditor receiving payments from his debtor, without any direction as to their application, may apply them to any legal debt, secured or unsecured, which he holds against his debtor. Straub v. Chemical Bank, 608 S.W.2d 71 (Ky. App. 1980). But where a third-party creditor executes a subordination agreement in favor of said creditor, the latter has an implied duty under equitable principles to apply the payment it receives from the debtor in a manner which does not prejudice the third-party creditor's subordinated security interest. . . .

The decisions of the Court of Appeals and Montgomery Circuit Court are reversed and the matter is remanded to the trial court. The proceeds of the foreclosure sale shall be distributed in accordance with this decision.

WINTERSHEIMER, Justice, dissenting. I respectfully dissent from the majority opinion because I do not believe the subordination agreement requires the interpretation placed on it by the majority and the doctrine of equitable subrogation is not applicable. . . .

The subordination agreement does not make any provision about the application of payments. There is no reference to any preexisting indebtedness, nor a limitation on the total indebtedness. . . .

I believe the circuit judge and the Court of Appeals have correctly analyzed the language of the subordination agreement, and I would not disturb their decision.

Problem 19C

Dale and Rosemary sell 30 acres of farmland for $600,000 to Brian, who plans to use the land to develop a small shopping center project. In the sale, Dale and Rosemary agree to take and hold a purchase-money mortgage in the amount of $300,000. After closing on the deal with Dale and Rosemary, Brian secures a lender for his construction of the shopping center. Brian will borrow $4 million for the project. His lender, Big Bank, requires a first mortgage lien against the property. Brian goes to Dale and Rosemary and offers them $10,000, to be paid on completion of the shopping center, in exchange for their agreement to subordinate their purchase-money mortgage to Big Bank's construction mortgage. Brian presents Dale and Rosemary with a simple, "plain English" subordination form that provides:

> Dale and Rosemary, as the Mortgagees under a certain purchase-money mortgage recorded in book 2314 at page 778, public records of Green County, in the original principal amount of $300,000, do hereby agree to subordinate the lien of their mortgage to that of Big Bank as made to Brian or his successors, assigns, or any entity in which he is a principal, in the amount of $4 million.

The parties sign the form, and Brian begins construction. Brian finishes construction of the improvements but defaults on both mortgage loans because he is not able to lease the center to rent-paying tenants. He also failed to pay Dale and Rosemary the $10,000 promised in exchange for the subordination. Big Bank puts the project into foreclosure.

(a) In the foreclosure sale, the property sells for $3.5 million. Who gets the proceeds of the sale?

(b) During the course of construction Brian encountered a number of cost overruns. In order to complete the project, Big Bank had to lend Brian an extra $500,000 during construction. At the time of the foreclosure sale he owed Big Bank $4.5 million and Dale and Rosemary $300,000 on the purchase-money mortgage, plus the promised $10,000. The foreclosure sale brings in $4.1 million. How should the court distribute the proceeds?

(c) During the course of construction Dale and Rosemary extended an additional $50,000 of credit to Brian secured under a further advances clause in their purchase-money mortgage. At the time of the foreclosure sale, Brian owed Big Bank $4 million in principal plus $200,000 in accrued interest. Brian owed Dale and Rosemary $300,000 on the purchase-money mortgage plus the $50,000 advance plus the promised $10,000. How should the court distribute the proceeds?

C. WRAP-AROUND MORTGAGE

A wrap-around mortgage is a special type of junior mortgage in which the junior debt includes or "wraps" the senior debt. Both of the debts are installment obligations, and the borrower under the wrap-around mortgage pays the holder of the junior debt and mortgage, who in turn pays the holder of the senior debt. Typically, a wrap-around is used in one of two circumstances, either as a form of seller financing to enable a buyer to purchase a property or as a technique for refinancing a property. When parties use a wrap-around rather than ordinary junior financing, the most common reason is to preserve the economic value of an interest rate on the senior loan that is below the prevailing market rate at the time the wrap transaction is consummated. Tax planning is another reason why wraps are sometimes used for seller-financed deals. Income tax from the sale of property at a gain may be paid to the government over time, rather than all at once in the year of sale, if the seller chooses to use what is called the installment method of reporting gain. More favorable tax treatment is available to the seller if the deal is properly structured as a wrap-around rather than a straight sale in which the buyer assumes or takes subject to the seller's existing mortgage debt. The total amount of gain is the same either way, but there is more deferral of payment until later years.

Wrap-around transactions are complicated compared to ordinary mortgage loans, and this complexity adds risk not only for the wrap-around lender, but also for the wrap-around borrower. The wrap-around lender has continuing personal liability on the senior debt. The wrap-around borrower undertakes the risk that the wrap-around lender will default in the payment obligation on the wrapped senior debt. In effect, the borrower has selected the wrap-around lender as an agent or intermediary who is to be responsible for remitting the borrower's payment to the holder of the senior debt. One additional reason wrap transactions are generally riskier than standard financing techniques is legal uncertainty. Although parties have used wrap loans in the United States at least since the 1920s, they have not generated a large body of case law, and in most states there are no statutes that provide guidance on the parties' rights and obligations. In particular, matters such as the proper way to accelerate and foreclose a wrap obligation are often unsettled.

HOLLAND v. McCULLEN
District Court of Appeal of Florida, Second District, 2000
764 So. 2d 810

CAMPBELL, Acting Chief Judge. In this appeal from the entry of a partial summary judgment, appellants argue that genuine issues of material fact precluded the entry of summary judgment. We agree as to the civil theft count, and reverse the partial summary judgment as to that count. Otherwise, we affirm.

Appellants, [Michael] Holland and Van-Eng Properties (seller) held a parcel of residential real estate in Venice, Florida. At the time seller originally purchased the property, it assumed the mortgage of Raymond Dean, the original mortgagor. Under that first mortgage, seller, as the new mortgagor, was obligated to pay Midfirst Bank (Bank) all mortgage payments and to maintain hazard insurance on the property. Failure to do so would result in acceleration of the note.

When seller sold the real estate to appellees, Jerry and Catherine McCullen (buyers), in August 1994, buyers gave seller a purchase money second wraparound mortgage. Under the second mortgage, seller agreed to continue to make payments on the first mortgage, and buyers agreed to pay seller on the second mortgage. Buyers agreed under this second mortgage to comply with all terms and conditions of the first mortgage except for the payment of principal and interest [and hazard insurance and real estate taxes payable through the loan escrow account]. . . .

In November 1996, Bank informed seller that it had increased the amount of the monthly payment due Bank by $233.00, which represented the cost to Bank to insure the property. Bank had obtained insurance for the two-year period from January 5, 1996 through January 5, 1998. When seller tendered the January 1997 mortgage payment, Bank refused it, claiming that seller owed Bank the total cost of insuring the property for that two-year term. Bank also rejected seller's February and March 1997 payments.

Because seller did not tell buyers that Bank had refused seller's payments for January, February, and March 1997, buyers continued to make payments. They stopped in April 1997, when they received notice of the Bank's foreclosure action.

On April 2, 1997, Bank filed a complaint against buyers and seller to foreclose the first mortgage. Bank alleged that buyers defaulted by failing to pay the installment due November 1, 1996, and all subsequent payments. The failure to maintain insurance on the property had caused Bank to accelerate the note and declare it to be in default. Buyers filed a three-count crossclaim against seller, alleging breach of contract, requesting indemnification, and requesting damages for civil theft. The parties subsequently stipulated to the mortgage foreclosure, leaving only the crossclaim to be resolved. On October 21, 1999, the trial court approved the stipulation.

. . . The trial court entered partial summary judgment in favor of buyers on all three counts of the crossclaim.

. . . The first count, for breach of contract, alleged that seller had breached the contract by failing to make the agreed payments on the first mortgage, resulting in default. There were no genuine issues of material fact concerning this count because seller had stipulated to the mortgage foreclosure. By doing so, seller admitted that it had breached the first mortgage by defaulting on the payments. Although seller argues that it did not agree to the allegations contained in the foreclosure complaint, seller cannot have it both ways. It cannot agree to the foreclosure and then not admit to any of the foreclosure allegations.

Similarly, there were no genuine issues of material fact concerning buyers' right to indemnification. The second mortgage provided that in the event of default of the first mortgage due to failure to make payments or interest, seller would indemnify buyers against any loss, cost or expense, including reasonable attorney fees, at trial or on appeal. Because the stipulated mortgage foreclosure determined that the first mortgage was defaulted due to failure to pay, there was no genuine issue of material fact concerning the indemnification count.

However, we believe that there is a genuine issue of material fact on the civil theft count. In order to prove civil theft, the movant must prove by clear and convincing evidence that the defendant acted with intent. Section 812.014, Florida Statutes (1997), provides:

(1) A person commits theft if he or she knowingly obtains or uses, or endeavors to obtain or to use, the property of another with intent to, either temporarily or permanently: (a) Deprive the other person of a right to the property or a benefit from the property. (b) Appropriate the property to his or her own use or to the use of any person not entitled to the use of the property.

Because seller, in fact, tendered buyers' payment to Bank, and Bank rejected it, the issue of seller's intent to wrongfully deprive buyers of their money remains a genuine issue of material fact. In view of this evidence, it was error to determine on a motion for summary judgment that seller had the intent to deprive buyers of their money or to appropriate their money to its purposes. . . .

Affirmed in part; reversed in part.

Problem 19D

Beatrix owns a fourplex building in a trendy urban neighborhood. She rents all four dwellings to tenants. She has a mortgage loan held by Newtown Savings and Loan with a present balance of $350,000, payable in monthly installments of $5,113. These payments fully amortize the debt over the remaining term of 7 years. The interest rate is fixed at 6 percent per annum, and the mortgage contains a standard due-on-sale clause. Present market rates on loans of this type from financial institutions are in the range of 7.2 to 7.5 percent. Beatrix and Joakim agree that Joakim will buy her fourplex for $550,000. He has $50,000 for a down payment, and the parties agree that Beatrix will finance the remaining $150,000 that Joakim needs.

(a) One possibility is that Joakim will assume Beatrix's existing loan from Newtown, and Joakim will execute a $150,000 promissory note payable to Beatrix secured by an ordinary mortgage on the fourplex property. Which mortgage will have priority and why? After closing, who will make payments on the Newtown mortgage loan? Who will make payments on the new loan for $150,000?

(b) Assume that instead Beatrix and Joakim enter into a wrap-around transaction. Explain how this would work. What would be the amount of the wrapped debt? The wrap-around debt? After closing, who will make payments on the Newtown mortgage loan? After closing, who will make payments on the wrap-around debt? Who will be responsible for paying real estate taxes and hazard insurance premiums on the fourplex property?

(c) What are the advantages and disadvantages of the two approaches for financing described in (a) and (b) above? Which approach is better for Beatrix? for Joakim? for both parties?

20

Basic Commercial Real Estate

The commercial real estate market should not be thought of as completely different from the residential markets that we have already studied. In many ways, the commercial market is merely a more complex version of its residential counterpart. All of the same market context considerations discussed in this book apply in both situations. The number of parties involved in the commercial transaction is likely to be greater, the amount of money at risk is usually higher, and the underlying legal issues are generally more difficult to address. Even so, the methods of thinking about residential transactions are equally useful when thinking about commercial ones. A good understanding of the residential real estate transaction will help you comprehend the dynamics of the commercial exchange. Likewise, as we learn more about the commercial exchange, we are better able to comprehend and appreciate the potential complexity of what is sometimes referred to as a "simple" residential transaction.

A. SELECTING A DEVELOPMENT ENTITY

Commercial real estate transactions typically involve a number of matters related to entity selection. The development process is a risky undertaking and involves transactions among a number of parties. Consequently, the developer is confronted with the question of how best to organize for conducting the business at hand. Few, if any, developers are likely to proceed with a project in their individual capacity. Instead, the typical developer will look for a vehicle or a means of conducting business that will limit personal liability. In considering the limits to liability, a developer generally is concerned with two key matters. First, the developer wants to limit his personal liability. This means that, as an individual, the developer does not want to risk his home, savings, or personally held investments. Second, the developer wants to protect as many business and corporate assets as possible. This is important when the developer has other businesses or other real estate holdings that are not held in his personal name but are held in some recognized business form, such as by a corporation or by a limited partnership, in which the developer has control or a substantial pecuniary interest.

A developer typically selects the corporate, limited partnership, or limited liability company (LLC) form of doing business. These vehicles allow developers to limit their liability to the capitalization of the entity itself. The corporate form can be useful when there are only a couple of shareholders who will put up the investment equity to get the project going. They can each be shareholders and control the company while limiting their financial exposure if the deal proves to be unsuccessful. Another popular choice for developers is the limited partnership. Typically, the general partner of the limited partnership is the developer, and the limited partners are the investors. It is normal for the general partner in such an arrangement to also be a limited liability entity such as a corporation or a limited partnership. The limited partnership is therefore a nice vehicle for syndicating investment interests in the undertaking. The LLC provides certain tax benefits, but in general is structured like a partnership while providing the limited liability of a corporation. In most of these entities, the developer usually takes the responsibility for putting the deal together and managing its successful completion. For this the developer generally receives certain fees and financial interests, in addition to any other investment returns on the transaction.

If a developer is active in real estate markets, he is likely to create a new development entity for each new transaction in which he engages. By doing so, the developer protects his business assets and ensures that a default or bankruptcy on one particular project will not destroy other financially healthy activities of the overall enterprise. The developer must be careful to properly capitalize his development entity and to operate it as a separate company. If the entity is undercapitalized and not treated as a separate legal entity, the developer may become personally liable for the acts and omissions of the entity. This is the case, for example, when such circumstances give rise to "piercing the corporate veil" of an entity, thus exposing the principals to liability.

Problem 20A

Margaret and Tom form the Big Apple Corporation with the purpose of using this entity to engage in a particular real estate development project. The project involves the acquisition of land and the construction of a $75 million office building. Margaret and Tom have plenty of investment capital, but they select the corporate form because they saw a late-night television program that informed them of the way to avoid personal liability and make money by operating as a corporate entity. This seemed to make much more sense than undertaking the project in their individual capacities. In forming the corporation, Margaret and Tom each contributed $1,000 in cash. Then they went to a lender, First Bank, who loaned Big Apple $65 million secured by a mortgage on the office building project. Big Apple also borrowed about $5 million from a creditor, Gain Capital, evidenced by an unsecured promissory note. Margaret and Tom personally loaned the remaining $5 million to Big Apple, secured by a second mortgage on the project. After the project was completed, Big Apple had difficulty in leasing the office space because of the bad economic climate. Soon Big Apple defaulted on all its loans, and the mortgagees commenced foreclosure.

At the foreclosure, who should be paid in what order of priority? What might you do if you are the attorney for the unsecured creditor, Gain Capital, assuming the foreclosure value of the property is $69 million?

B. COMMERCIAL LENDING AND ARTICLE 9 OF THE UCC

A commercial real estate transaction involves financing issues that extend beyond the law of real property and of mortgages. A number of the issues that arise require an understanding of the Uniform Commercial Code (UCC). The UCC can apply to the use of a promissory note, which usually is an Article 3 negotiable instrument, and it can apply to methods of payment in a transaction that can be governed by Articles 3, 4, and 4A. In addition, Article 2 of the UCC, covering "goods," might apply when a sale of real property includes a transfer of appliances or other items of personal or movable property. Taking security for a loan can also raise UCC problems. In particular, some items of collateral cannot be secured by a real estate mortgage and require an Article 9 security interest. Similarly, Article 9 priority rules can come into play with respect to fixtures that can be secured under the law of the UCC and the law of real property mortgages.

In the commercial financing area we are especially concerned with the security given for the loan. We need to be sure that a lender has taken the correct steps to encumber the various property rights of the debtor that are offered as collateral for the loan. At the same time, the lender must take the appropriate steps to achieve *perfection* of its security interest in the collateral. Perfection is necessary to establish a lien priority as against other competing claimants, including the bankruptcy trustee if the debtor enters bankruptcy. Proper documentation and perfection are important in this process, to ensure that the lender has a right to proceed against the identified property in the event of default and also to protect its priority in situations in which multiple claims are asserted against the debtor's assets. Frequently the collateral does not have sufficient value to satisfy all of the claims. The documentation requirements and the perfection and priority rules differ between real property mortgage law and the law under the UCC.

Under both real property law and the UCC, this documentation involves getting and perfecting a security interest in the collateral. With respect to real property, the proper documentation centers around the real estate mortgage, and "perfection" involves recording the mortgage in the local public records so as to establish the priority of the lender's lien. Under the UCC, the security interest is covered by Article 9 and requires a security agreement, and perfection usually involves filing a financing statement in the appropriate state office or taking possession of the collateral. The method of perfection and the appropriate place to file under Article 9 vary depending on the type of collateral in question.

Generally speaking, mortgage law applies to collateral consisting of real property and to things that are fixtures according to state law. Article 9, which is also adopted as state law, generally applies to personal property as well as to fixtures. Consequently, a lender will have to think of securing its transaction by categorizing items of collateral into one of three primary types: real property to be governed by a mortgage, fixtures to be governed by both mortgage law and Article 9 of the UCC, and other personal property to be governed only by Article 9. Actually, a fourth category of property sometimes comes into play. Section 9-109 excludes from the scope of Article 9 some types of property that are neither real property nor fixtures. One example is the assignment of an interest in an insurance policy. Thus, a lender who looks to a fire insurance policy to protect its interest in an insured building must achieve its goal through a body of law that is neither real property law nor UCC law. State common law and state non-UCC statutory law will determine how the lender gets a collateral interest in the insurance policy. There are also hybrids, such as aircraft, ships, and some forms of intellectual property, which are partially within and partially outside the scope of Article 9. If, for example, a lender wants a developer to put up registered copyright as part of the collateral for a loan, a federal filing is necessary, because federal law preempts the Article 9 filing system.

Problem 20B

Betty owns a certain piece of real property with a four-story office building located on it. The office building is about five years old and is fully leased. Veronica agrees to buy the property from Betty for $3 million. Veronica and Betty structure the deal as a transfer of the land by warranty deed, with the building and all improvements transferred as personal property by bill of sale.

(a) Veronica has two lenders. She gets $500,000 from Big Bank, for which she signs a first mortgage on the land, and she gets $2.5 million from Commercial Credit Co., for which she signs an Article 9 security agreement. If all the parties agree to this arrangement, should they be allowed to divide and treat the property in this manner? What is the impact or binding nature of their arrangement on third parties? Do they need to do anything more to bind third parties, and if so, what would you recommend?

(b) Assume instead that Veronica buys the property from Betty and takes a transfer of everything by warranty deed. In this exchange, she borrows $500,000 from Big Bank and gives it a first mortgage lien on the property. She pays the other $2.5 million in cash. Six months after the deal, Veronica approaches Commercial Credit and offers to give it an Article 9 security interest in the entire building in exchange for an extension of a revolving line of credit not to exceed $2 million. In the event of a default on both loans and a foreclosure by Big Bank, should it be bound by the severance of the building from the land as attempted by Veronica and Commercial Credit?

(c) The previous parts of this problem focus on the land, the building, and the improvements as collateral. Are there other property rights that Veronica has or may acquire in connection with the office building that might serve as collateral? Which of those rights can be treated under the mortgage? Under an Article 9 security agreement? Under other types of documents? If there are multiple financing documents, perhaps involving multiple creditors, how might one coordinate the various roles played by the documents, so as to reduce and manage risk?

C. DRAGNET AND CROSS-COLLATERAL CLAUSES

FISCHER v. FIRST INTERNATIONAL BANK
Court of Appeal of California, Fourth District, 2003
1 Cal. Rptr. 3d 162

AARON, Justice. . . . Plaintiffs Karl and Pamela Fischer appeal from a summary judgment order and final judgment in favor of defendant First International Bank (FIB or the bank). . . .

The Fischers' appeal presents the following question: When a bank enters into a written loan agreement that specifies the collateral for two different loans, and does not state that the loans will be cross-collateralized against each other, may the bank subsequently enforce a broadly worded "dragnet" clause contained in the fine print of a standard form deed of trust securing one of the loans? On the particular facts of this case, we conclude that the trial court erred by granting summary judgment in defendants' favor on this issue. . . .

In 1989, Karl and Pamela Fischer purchased two contiguous commercial lots located at 2102 Main Street in Ramona, California, for $310,000. They took out a $707,000 construction loan from FIB and invested another $750,000 to construct a large family dining and recreation center on the property.

In 1998, the Fischers entered into negotiations with FIB for two additional loans: a takeout loan in the amount of $730,000 to pay off the existing construction loan (Loan #1) and an equipment loan in the amount of $325,000 (Loan #2). On September 14, 1998, FIB and the Fischers entered into a written agreement regarding the terms and conditions of the loans (the "September Agreement"). The agreement was drafted by FIB in the form of a letter to the Fischers signed by both a loan officer and a senior vice-president, to be countersigned by the Fischers. According to the loan officer, the September Agreement was intended to define the terms of the loans to the Fischers.

The September Agreement specified the identities of the borrowers, the dollar amounts of the loans, the purpose of each loan, the term of each loan, the interest rates, loan fees and packaging fees, the terms pertaining to prepayment and assumability, and the estimated closing costs. The September Agreement also included the following provision specifying the collateral for each of the two loans:

Collateral:
Loan #1: First deed of trust on commercial property located at 2102 Main Street, Ramona, CA
Loan #2: Second deed of trust on commercial property located at 2102 Main Street, Ramona, CA
Second deed of trust on single-family residence located at 14382 Blue Sage Road, Poway, CA

The agreement included express conditions pertaining to each of the loans. One of the conditions for Loan #2 was a "second deed of trust on the residential property located at 14382 Blue Sage Road, Poway, CA 92064." There was no such condition for Loan #1. . . .

The signed September Agreement contained no reference to cross-collateralization of the loans. According to the Fischers, they "specifically negotiated" the loan agreement so that their Blue Sage residence would not be collateral for Loan #1. This was one of their "main objectives" in negotiating the agreement.

On September 30, 1998, the Fischers went to the bank to sign final loan documents, including a deed of trust for their residence. They met with FIB Vice President Steve Pollett. The Fischers brought a copy of the September Agreement with them to this meeting. According to the Fischers, Pollett assured them that their home was collateral only for Loan #2, as stated in the September Agreement. The Fischers pointed out that the proposed deed of trust incorrectly stated that their home would be collateral for both loans. Pollett agreed that this was a mistake, and told the Fischers they did not have to sign the incorrect deed of trust because their home was not needed as collateral for Loan #1, but rather, only for Loan #2. The bank subsequently changed the deed of trust so that the definition of the word "note" referred only to the $325,000 loan for Loan #2.

According to Mr. Fischer, Pollett said that if the Fischers were to sell their Blue Sage residence, any equity from the sale would be used only to pay off the balance of Loan #2. . . .

The deed of trust signed by the Fischers for their Blue Sage residence stated in bold and capital letters that the deed was "GIVEN TO SECURE (1) PAYMENT OF THE INDEBTEDNESS AND (2) PERFORMANCE OF ANY AND ALL OBLIGATIONS OF TRUSTOR UNDER THE NOTE, THE RELATED DOCUMENTS, AND THIS DEED OF TRUST." On a separate page of definitions, the word "Note" was defined to mean "the Note dated September 30, 1998 in the principal amount of $325,000." The phrase "in the principal amount of $325,000" was inserted in larger print than the other definitions contained on the standard form. However, the word "Indebtedness" was broadly defined in the fine print as follows:

> The word "Indebtedness" means all principal and interest payable under the Note and any amounts expended or advanced by Lender to discharge obligations of Trustor or expenses incurred by Trustee or Lender to enforce obligations of Trustor under this Deed of Trust, together with interest on such amounts as provided in this Deed of Trust. In addition to the Note, the word "Indebtedness" includes all obligations, debts and liabilities, plus interest thereon, of Borrower to Lender, or any one or more of them, as well as all claims by Lender against Borrower, or any one or more of them, whether now existing or hereafter arising, whether related or unrelated to the purpose of the Note, whether voluntary or otherwise, whether due or not due, absolute or contingent, liquidated or unliquidated and whether Borrower may be liable individually or jointly with others, whether obligated as guarantor or otherwise, and whether recovery upon such Indebtedness may be or hereafter may become barred by any statute of limitations, and whether such Indebtedness may be or hereafter may become otherwise unenforceable.

The deed of trust also included a "Due on Sale" provision giving FIB the right to "declare immediately due and payable all sums secured by this Deed of Trust upon the sale or transfer, without the Lender's prior written consent, of all or any part" of the Blue Sage residence.

Finally, the deed of trust contained a provision stating: "This Deed of Trust, *together with any Related Documents*, constitutes the entire understanding and agreement of the parties as to the matters set forth in this Deed of Trust." (Italics added.) The phrase "Related Documents" was defined to "mean and include without limitation all promissory notes, credit agreements, loan agreements, environmental agreements, guaranties, security agreements, mortgages, deeds of trust, and all other instruments, agreements and documents, whether now or hereafter existing, executed in connection with the Indebtedness."

In 1999, the Fischers decided to sell their Blue Sage residence. . . . [T]he Fischers sold their home. After paying off Loan #2 through escrow, there was $125,000 left over from the sale.

. . . FIB demanded that any funds remaining from the sale of the residence be applied to Loan #1. . . .

According to the Fischers, they would not have sold their home if they had known that FIB was going to take the money that remained after the balance of Loan #2 was paid. The Fischers allege that they intended to use the proceeds from the sale of their home as working capital, and that without these funds, they were forced to sell their commercial property and business for below fair market value. . . .

The Fischers filed suit against FIB . . . alleging breach of contract, conversion and misappropriation of money, breach of fiduciary duty, fraud in the inducement, negligent misrepresentation, breach of the implied covenant of good faith and fair dealing, and false promise.

The trial court granted summary judgment in favor of [FIB]. . . .

The trial court found that the dragnet clause contained in the deed of trust defeated all of the Fischers' causes of action as a matter of law. Finding no ambiguity as to the parties' intent regarding collateralization of the loans, the court applied the literal language of the dragnet clause and concluded that the bank had a right to apply the proceeds from the sale of the Fischers' residence to both loans. We disagree with the trial court's conclusion and find that there are triable issues of fact regarding whether the parties mutually agreed to cross-collateralization of the loans.

A "dragnet" clause (also known as an "anaconda" clause) is a clause stating that a mortgage secures all the debts that the mortgagor may at any time owe to the mortgagee. . . .

Courts in different jurisdictions have adopted widely varying approaches to broadly worded dragnet clauses that purport to apply to all existing and future debts and obligations. *See generally* Annot., *Debts Included in Provision of Mortgage Purporting to Cover All Future and Existing Debts (Dragnet Clause)—Modern Status,* 3 A.L.R.4th 690 (1981). In many states, a dragnet clause will not be applied to other existing debts unless such debts are explicitly described in the security agreement. . . .

At the opposite extreme are courts that view the literal language of a generally worded dragnet clause as conclusive evidence of the intent of the parties that the clause encompass all other debts. *See, e.g.,* Hamlin v. Timberlake Grocery Co., 204 S.E.2d 442, 444-45 (Ga. Ct. App. 1974). . . .

In a number of jurisdictions, courts have adopted an approach somewhere between these two extremes. These courts examine a variety of factors to determine whether the parties intended the dragnet clause to apply to existing debts. . . . The factors these courts consider in assessing the intent of the parties include: (1) whether the dragnet clause is boilerplate; (2) whether the other debts are of the same kind as the primary debt; (3) whether the other loans are listed in the dragnet clause; and (4) whether the debt which the lender seeks to have included in the dragnet clause is otherwise fully secured.

California courts have taken an intermediate position with regard to the validity of dragnet clauses. . . .

Because a dragnet clause is one of the provisions "least likely" to be understood by a layperson reading the fine print of a deed of trust, California limits the enforcement of such a provision "to those transactions where objective evidence discloses the intention of the *debtor and the creditor* to enlarge the lien to include other obligations." 4 Miller & Starr, *California Real Estate* §10.12 (3d ed. 2000). The proponent of a dragnet clause bears the burden of establishing that the parties intended all existing or contemporaneous loans to be included within its scope. . . .

Applying these general principles, we do not find an objectively clear and unambiguous expression of mutual intent to cross-collateralize Loan #1 and Loan #2. Preliminarily, the presence of the dragnet provision would have been discernable to a borrower only by cross-referencing from the highlighted security provision to the fine print of a 177-word, two-part definition of the word "indebtedness" filled with legal jargon that would have been incomprehensible to the average layperson. The first part of the definition of "indebtedness" expressly referred only to the $325,000 note for Loan #2. Yet, the second part purported to make the deed act as security for all other "obligations, debts and liabilities" in language so sweeping that it encompassed even debts "barred by any statute of limitations" or "otherwise unenforceable." . . .

In contrast to the deed of trust, the September Agreement did not include a dragnet provision that would have permitted cross-collateralization of the two loans. Significantly, the agreement was not silent on the subject of collateral; it specifically identified the collateral for each of the two loans and expressly stated that the business would serve as collateral for both loans, but that the Blue Sage residence would serve as collateral for Loan #2 only. Cross-collateralization was not a condition of either of the loans according to the terms of the September Agreement.

As with any contract, the September Agreement must be construed according to the "ordinary and popular" meaning of its language. . . . Because the September Agreement specifically addressed the subject of collateral and did not mention cross-collateralization, we believe that any layperson reading its plain language would have understood it to mean exactly what it said: that the Blue Sage residence would serve as collateral for Loan #2, but not Loan #1. The clear terms of the September Agreement would have precluded the bank from using the residence as collateral for Loan #1. . . .

. . . [W]e therefore conclude that the conflicting provisions of the September Agreement and the deed of trust create a triable issue of fact regarding the true intentions of the parties. At a minimum, the loan agreement creates ambiguity as to whether the parties mutually intended to permit cross-collateralization. Parol evidence is admissible to resolve this ambiguity. . . .

. . . Accordingly, we must reverse the judgment in the bank's favor. . . .

D. LEASES AS FINANCING DEVICES

Two commonly used arrangements that are likely to appear in a complex commercial real estate transaction are the *ground lease* and the *sale and leaseback*. Each of these two arrangements has its own tax and entity selection implications. For our purposes, however, we will focus on the use of these arrangements as tools to facilitate financing of a transaction. The basic idea behind each arrangement is that the project to be developed or managed (a mall or an office building, for instance) will be constructed on or transferred to a leasehold estate. If the project is one to be constructed, the developer will typically become the tenant on a long-term ground lease. If it is a completed project that is being sold, it is generally the current owner or operator of the project that sells the fee interest and remains in possession with use of the property as a tenant under a long-term leaseback arrangement. See Figure 20-1.

Two common situations lead to the use of a ground lease. The first is when a developer identifies land for a suitable development project but the owner refuses to make an outright sale of the fee ownership. An owner may want to keep control of the ownership of property for many reasons, but if he refuses to sell the fee, a developer may still be able to negotiate a lease allowing the use of the property for a stated number of years.

The second situation involves the developer using the ground lease as a source of financing. Because the developer will acquire less than the full fee ownership of the property and will have to pay rent and be subject to lease restrictions on its use of the property, acquisition costs are lower than for an outright fee purchase.

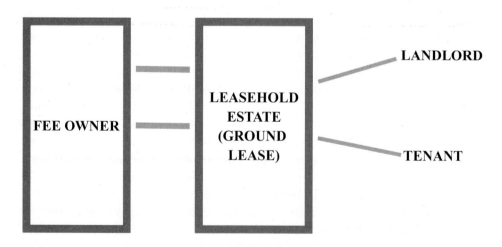

Figure 20-1
**Ground Lease: A Fee Simple Converted to a Fee Plus a Landlord
and Tenant Position on the Lease.**

The developer must make sure that the term of the ground lease is both long enough and stable enough in its duration to allow adequate amortization of the cost of any improvements to be constructed on the land. The terms of the lease will also have to be sufficient to provide an adequate return on investment to the developer. As a consequence, the fee owner and the developer will have to agree on terms under which both parties will share in the expected profit from the undertaking. For the developer to recoup investment costs on a major construction project, the lease will probably have to be long-term.

The ground lease must be made to fit correctly with other sources of financing. Probably construction lending will have to be secured by a mortgage that will have priority over the lease. This means that the fee owner under the lease must agree to subordinate the lease to any subsequently approved construction loan. If the lease is prior in time and is not subordinated, a default on the lease by the tenant developer could lead to a lease termination and the end of the tenant's leasehold interest. The construction mortgage would be unsecured, because the estate that secured it is no longer in existence. Because the fee owner will want the deal to be marketable, it will generally agree to a subordination provision in the ground lease. A condition of that subordination is likely to be that the fee owner approve of the terms and identity of the construction lender to which it will subordinate.

A great deal of commercial real estate is rental property. After entering into a ground lease, the developer as landlord will enter into subleases that allow tenants to occupy space in the contemplated improvements. Some of these subtenants are likely to obtain their own financing for purposes such as the purchase of tenant fixtures and improvements. Thus, there will be another layer of leases and potential creditors to deal with in the transaction. One of the issues to be addressed is the relationship between the fee owner and these subtenants. Generally, two documents are used to address this relationship. These documents relate to attornment and nondisturbance. The *attornment agreement* provides that all the subtenants must agree to attorn to or look to the lender if the lender should take over the project, primarily as the result of a default by the developer. The implication is that the subtenant cannot use the lender takeover as an excuse to change the terms of its lease with the developer. The *nondisturbance agreement* flows in the opposite direction, in that it obligates the lender to leave the subtenants undisturbed in their leases. Rents cannot be arbitrarily raised or terms changed simply because the lender takes over as the new landlord under a sublease. The nondisturbance agreement, as might be anticipated, is given by the lender only to key subtenant stores that are essential to making the property a success — in other words, the tenants that have market power. In contrast, all subtenants will be expected to enter into an attornment agreement.

The landlord generally views the ground lease as a passive investment. The landlord does not want an active role in ownership, even though it technically owns the land. As a result, the landlord usually sets up the ground lease as a *triple net lease,* which means that all the normal costs of ownership are placed on the tenant (developer). The costs of property taxes, insurance, and maintenance are all shifted from the fee owner to the tenant under such an arrangement.

To develop a basic understanding of the sale-leaseback transaction, consider a simple example. Giovanni owns and operates a commercial investment company. One of his business assets is the four-story building that serves as his business headquarters. For simplicity, assume that the building is worth $1 million and that it is debt-free. As a result of financial losses from investments in international stocks and derivative issues, Giovanni finds himself in need of additional operating capital. One thing that Giovanni could do in such a situation is go to a lender and ask to borrow money against the equity value of his building. He would get a cash infusion for his business and would execute a mortgage in favor of the lender. He would then pay back the lender under the terms of the promissory note and mortgage agreement. As an alternative to this, Giovanni might offer an investor the opportunity to purchase the building. The sale, however, would be part of a complementary arrangement whereby Giovanni agrees to lease the building back from the new owner. In this way, Giovanni would sell the building but still have its use, so that he can continue to operate his business. The result is similar to the mortgage loan transaction, in that Giovanni gets a cash infusion from the sale, keeps possession of the property, and makes monthly payments. In the sale and leaseback arrangement, the monthly payments are for rent rather than a mortgage payment, but the rent payment will come close to being the same as a comparable mortgage payment for a similar amount of cash amortized over a similar term. At the end of the leaseback period, Giovanni will generally have the right to buy back the building at some nominal amount. However, the sale and leaseback arrangement implies a different relationship between the lender/investor and Giovanni than does the mortgage transaction. With the sale and leaseback, the lender becomes the owner of the property and the landlord under a long-term lease. This means that lease law and the implications of ownership and of landlord and tenant relations apply between the parties. Default remedies and other legal rights and duties may differ in such a setting when compared to the lender and debtor relationship of a standard mortgage transaction. See Figure 20-2.

It is important to note that Giovanni could also have split his interest in the building and created two investment opportunities. He could have sold the fee simple land interest and leased back the use of the land on which the building sits, thus creating a ground lease, and he could also have sold the building separate and apart from the land, with its own leaseback arrangement. Sometimes by dividing a property into a variety of separate property

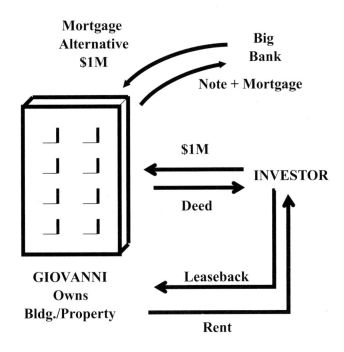

Figure 20-2
Sale and Leaseback

interests, you can enhance its value by making it possible to reach more types of investors who have different investment objectives and different amounts to invest. By properly structuring the sales and leases of the split estates in the property, it is possible that Giovanni can get more total cash than he would get by merely selling it as one complete unit (with or without a leaseback) or by mortgaging it out as collateral for a single loan.

No matter how the sale and leaseback is structured, it will tend to involve a long-term lease, and thus will be drafted with many of the same features and provisions as a ground lease. For income tax purposes, it is important that the lease make economic sense beyond merely being a disguised mortgage. This means that lease payments should not be exactly what mortgage payments would be if the deal were done as a loan instead of a sale and leaseback. It also means that the repurchase option for the tenant at the end of the lease should not be merely nominal. If the lease has independent economic merit, the buyer will get the tax benefits of ownership. If, however, the sale is merely a way of transferring tax benefits between the parties, it is likely to be ignored by the IRS. The analysis here is similar to that used under §1-203 of the UCC to determine whether a transaction structured as a lease of personal property or fixtures is really a lease or merely a disguised security interest. If it is really a security interest, the parties must comply with the relevant law despite the fact that they have labeled their transaction a lease exchange.

E. COMMERCIAL FINANCING

The financing of commercial real estate development consists of two broad categories of lending activity. The first category, construction lending, includes funding for basic land acquisition, infrastructure development, and construction of planned improvements on the property (sometimes collectively referred to as "ADC" funding when the construction loan covers all three functions of **A**cquisition, **D**evelopment, and **C**onstruction). The second category of lending, permanent lending, involves long-term financing for a project after construction is complete. Construction loans and permanent loans differ in their structure and in the role that they play in facilitating commercial real estate activity.

1. Construction Loans

Construction loans are typically short-term loans in the range of 6 to 24 months. Although construction loans are subject to the usual market risk factors that affect all real estate loans, they carry especially high risk. The construction loan is funded in the expectation of success for a project that has not even been built. At the outset, a typical commercial real estate project exists as a developer's idea and is represented by drawings, architectural plans, legal documentation, and marketing data. A construction lender may be asked to lend $5 million, $50 million, $200 million, or more for a project that does not yet exist. There are several important risks involved in such an undertaking. First, the developer may borrow the funds and never complete the project. Second, the developer may complete the project but do so in a way that fails to comply with the original plans and specifications, so that the completed project is substandard and has less value than anticipated by the lender. Finally, the project may be completed properly but turn out to have less appeal with consumers than originally anticipated, or market changes during the construction period may have lowered the desirability and value of the undertaking. In each of these situations, the construction lender is worried about the same things — namely, the value of the collateral for its loan and the likelihood of its being repaid.

In some respects, the lender's worst-case scenario is when the borrower defaults with the construction project partially finished. Imagine the trouble when a lender loans out millions of dollars for construction activity and ends up with an unfinished project that has a poorly constructed foundation and a substandard steel structure. It is conceivable that the property is less valuable in its current state than it was as vacant land. Despite the amount of money poured into such a project, the "improvements" may have to be substantially removed or redesigned to render the property useable or saleable. In other words, property may lose value at certain stages during construction, especially if work or materials going into the project prove to be substandard. In this and other situations, the construction lender is always concerned about getting the project completed in accordance with approved plans and specifications, and about having access to sufficient collateral in the event of a developer default.

The construction loan requires careful evaluation and close supervision. Because there is no finished product, no office building or shopping center to look at in evaluating the loan, a construction lender must have a staff of in-house experts capable of determining the viability of the developer's plans and specifications. The lender's staff must be able to review plans and specifications for construction and understand the marketing, economic, and accounting projections related to cost and profitability expectations. In essence, the construction lender must truly understand the details of the developer's "sales" pitch when he comes to seek funding for a particular project. In some ways, this expertise may help the developer, inasmuch as the lender takes a serious second look at the development proposal and may administer a healthy dose of reality to an overly enthusiastic entrepreneur. A construction lender must also be able to supervise the construction process throughout the term of the loan. Constant supervision is required to ensure that the money being extended is in fact being used for the approved purposes. This means that the construction lender has to keep track of construction progress and the rate and quality of production. It must be certain that dollars loaned are spent on the project in question rather than misdirected to some other location. It must also be able to determine that the money is being used to purchase and install materials of proper quality and in accordance with all approved plans and specifications as well as with all zoning, labor, and environmental regulations.

As a result of issues like those just discussed, construction loans are typically structured as recourse loans and are funded as *draw-downs* against the full loan amount. A *recourse loan* is one in which the borrower has personal liability on the promissory note in the event of a default. This is the standard case in a residential loan but is usually accomplished by indirect means in a commercial real estate transaction. A developer/borrower is usually some form of a limited liability entity such as a corporation or a limited partnership. The borrower, as such, will have only limited liability, even on a recourse loan. In such a case, the lender may want the ability to get at more than the limited assets of the development entity. It may seek additional financial guarantees from the developer entity or a related developer company. It is also likely to require *a personal guarantee* from the individual principal(s) who constitute the developer entity. The *loan guarantee* might be secured by a pledge of assets as further collateral for the loan to the development entity. In the event of a default, the construction lender could then foreclose on the real property, the construction materials, and the borrower entity assets, and also pursue any assets used to support the loan guarantees. This is a form of recourse loan in both the direct and indirect sense, because the loan documents themselves, including the note and mortgage, are typically of a recourse nature with the limited liability entity, and the additional and personal guarantees are executed as a side agreement between the parties so that the lender can reach assets beyond those used to capitalize the development vehicle. The lender thus receives the added benefit of recourse against the individual(s) behind the developer entity, but the developer is still allowed to act within a protective sphere of limited liability with respect to any other parties involved in the development project. Naturally, the use of a guarantee, as well as its scope, is highly negotiable and depends on a number of factors, such as the working relationship between borrower and lender and the market clout of each party.

In a *draw-down loan*, the full loan amount is not released to the borrower at the time of closing on the loan. While construction proceeds, the lender makes periodic disbursements, which are called *draw-downs*. This establishes a correlation between the money disbursed and the value of improvements added to the property, while also making it easier for the lender to supervise the developer's compliance with the loan. A draw-down schedule might indicate, for instance, that $500,000 will be released at closing for purposes of preparing the land and pouring the building foundation. When this is accomplished within the agreed time frame and in accordance with the loan conditions, the developer will be entitled to a second draw of $500,000 to be used for placing the first floor of the building, and a third draw for accomplishing yet another phase in the construction plan, and so on until completion. In this way, the lender limits its loss exposure at any given time and makes it easier to supervise the progress of construction. Generally, if a developer fails to meet any of a series of conditions precedent to a draw, the lender will be excused from making any further disbursements or advances under the loan. Such an event would also normally be considered an event of default and trigger an acceleration clause making the entire construction loan immediately due and payable.

Construction loans also must deal with another problem, which is that the developer will generally have little or no actual income during the time period of this short-term loan. The developer may be building an income-producing property like an office building, an apartment building, or a shopping center, yet while construction is going on little (if any) income will be generated by the building. Consequently, the construction lender must deal with the fact that payments are not likely during the construction process. Instead, the developer will borrow the interest expense as part of the loan. Construction loans typically expire at the time scheduled for completion of construction. At this time, the borrower will not have cash on hand to repay the loan. To handle this problem, the borrower usually arranges to repay the construction loan by obtaining a permanent loan on the property.

For similar reasons the loan is likely to set out *performance standards* requiring a certain percentage of units, or a set amount of space, to be sold or leased in advance of funding the loan, and as prerequisites to additional draw-downs on the loan.

Another popular way to handle financing of a commercial project involves combining construction loan financing with *mezzanine financing*. Sometimes this type of financing is referred to as mezzanine capital. The term alludes to the mezzanine level in a theater, which lies between the main floor and the balcony. The word *mezzanine* means "middle." In real estate financing, mezzanine capital fills the gap between the debt financing and the equity participation (equity contribution) made by the developer and other investors. In the construction phase, the debt financing is represented by the construction loan. In general, the developer may be expected to put up equity equal to about 10 percent of the project cost. The construction loan typically finances between 50 and 80 percent of the project cost. The difference between this amount and the project cost is sometimes financed by a mezzanine loan. The mezzanine financing is in the middle between the secured debt financing (secured by the construction mortgage and related documents) and the equity contribution, which is at risk. The mezzanine financing is in the middle in another sense, as well. The mezzanine financing is not fully secured, but it is also not fully exposed to the same risk as the equity contribution. Typically, mezzanine financing will be done as an extension of credit to the partners or equity holders of the borrower, with the lender taking a pledge of the parties' equity interests (including rights to a distribution of income). In the event of a default, the mezzanine debt is paid only after the senior secured debt, but prior to a return of any equity to the borrower and other investors. A mezzanine lender generally requires interest payments to be made on the borrowed funds plus something more. The "something more" is often an equity stake in the project, such as an option for the lender to convert some portion of the obligation into an equity interest, which can be valuable when a project is successful.

2. Permanent Loans

Permanent loans generally have a term that is anywhere between 10 and 30 years. Unlike the construction loan, therefore, the permanent loan is a long-term loan. As a long-term loan, the permanent loan embodies the risk related to a long time horizon. Compared to the construction loan, however, the risk factors are very different. To begin with, the project is completed by the time the permanent loan is made, so there is no need to supervise work production. The lender can look at a finished project and evaluate its construction quality, its income position, and its market viability. If the project involves tenants, the lender can review the number and quality of leases. Although a finished project being evaluated for a long-term loan raises issues of risk, the risk here is much different and much simpler to assess and control than the risk involved with actual development and construction.

Permanent loans require a different kind of supervision than do construction loans. At the completion of the project, all the people providing labor, materials, or services to the project should be fully paid. Thus, there should be little concern about unpaid bills and liens that could upset the priority of the permanent mortgage. A good title examination should be able to assess priority issues prior to any permanent funding. Supervision will be required, however, with respect to the operation of any income-producing property. The permanent loan will be paid back on a regular basis, usually monthly. These monthly payments are expected to be paid out of income revenue from the property. Therefore, the permanent lender may want to have access to continuing information about the financial well-being of the project, so that any early signs of a problem can be detected. In addition, it is not uncommon for a permanent lender to take a percentage interest in the cash flow from an income-producing property. This might involve a percentage of developer income over and above some set level. By sharing some of the revenue from a successful project, a developer may be able to lower its loan costs. This arrangement can provide a lender with extra revenue and profit from lending operations, but it also adds to the need to supervise the developer's accounting. For instance, how will the developer's expenses be figured, and what will count as income? Will percentages be based on net or gross amounts, and what accounting standards will apply?

Sometimes a permanent lender structures the loan as a *convertible mortgage*. This is different from the residential convertible loan discussed in Chapter 15, under which an adjustable interest rate becomes fixed. Here it means that the permanent lender is given a set or predetermined option for swapping part of the mortgage debt for a given percentage of equity in the project. Thus, debt is converted into equity, much like the situation when convertible shares in a corporation are exchanged for common stock. The convertible mortgage can be a good deal for the lender if the project turns out to be very successful. It is advantageous to the developer if it helps to entice a lender into making a favorable loan.

The permanent loan is based on a finished project that is relatively easy to evaluate and that has a predictable cash flow. As a consequence, the permanent loan will often be structured as a *nonrecourse* loan. This means that the developer will not typically have to make any personal guarantee on the loan. Instead, the lender will take the property with its income stream as the sole collateral for the loan.

3. Take-Out Arrangements and Three-Party Agreements

Given the very different focus and type of risk associated with each of the two key categories of loans, it is not surprising that lending institutions tend to specialize and develop particular expertise. Although statistics on market shares by institution shift over time in response to various regulatory and market factors, general observations can be made. The high-risk construction loan business is dominated by commercial banks, savings and loans, and other major primary financial market participants. These lenders are joined by a variety of other institutions when it comes to permanent financing. Very active in the long-term and less risky permanent loan business are major insurance companies, like Aetna and Prudential, as well as pension funds like those of the United Auto Workers, the Teamsters, and Teachers Annuity. For these institutions, permanent funding is a stable long-term source of income flow with relatively low risk. For a developer, these institutions control billions of dollars in assets that can be tapped to capitalize a variety of real estate projects.

The process by which the permanent lender steps in to pay off the construction loan and roll the debt over into a long-term permanent loan is referred to as the *take-out*. Literally speaking, the permanent lender takes the construction lender out of the deal by replacing the construction loan and mortgage with its own and by paying off the mortgage debt in a process that refinances the obligation under the terms of the permanent loan. For the take-out to work effectively in practice, both lenders must carefully coordinate their loan documentation and transactional expectations. The two lenders must coordinate the timing for completion of the building so that money will be available when it is needed. They must also agree on what qualifies as "completion" of the building, so that there will be no disagreement as to when and if permanent financing conditions have been met.

There are essentially three types of take-out arrangements that can be considered by a developer and a lender: *lock-in, stand-by*, and *open-ended*. The *lock-in take-out* is one in which the developer obtains a firm commitment from a permanent lender to take over the construction loan by paying off the construction lender and rolling the debt into a long-term mortgage obligation. It is considered a firm commitment because the permanent lender legally obligates itself to make the anticipated loan on the terms and conditions stated in the loan commitment. However, if a term or condition of the commitment is not complied with, the permanent lender can legally refuse to fund the loan. Failure to fund the take-out when the conditions of the commitment are met can result in an action for breach against the lender.

The *stand-by take-out* is a loan commitment that the developer hopes will not have to be used. The stand-by commits a permanent lender to be prepared to fund a take-out if called on to do so, and, like the lock-in, it sets out terms and conditions that have to be met prior to the lender's having to fund. The stand-by is unlike the lock-in in that the lock-in is expected to be used, whereas the stand-by is in place for use only if needed, but is generally not expected to be used. To better comprehend a stand-by, consider the typical context in which it is used. Sometimes a project is planned and organized at a time when mortgage interest rates are very high. The developer may still want to go forward, because a great deal of time and money may have been invested in preparing for construction. Perhaps a lot of work went into land acquisition or obtaining zoning approval, and the developer does not want to lose the opportunity to go forward. Also consider that the construction process may take 18 or 24 months, and the developer is expecting the market to change in its favor by the time construction is complete. To start the construction process and get a construction lender, the developer may agree to take loan terms from a permanent lender that it hopes it will not really have to live with for the long-term period after a take-out. Instead of getting a lock-in commitment with a permanent lender as a prerequisite to obtaining the construction loan, the developer may get a stand-by, which sets up a permanent loan take-out with an *option* to avoid it and seek an alternative source or deal for permanent financing in the event that interest rates drop. In the case of both the lock-in and the stand-by, the developer pays a substantial fee for getting a permanent lender to commit to funding a take-out, just as it must pay a similar fee to the construction lender for making the loan available. These fees are very similar in purpose to the fees and points paid by a homebuyer seeking a residential mortgage, as discussed earlier in this book.

The *open-ended take-out* is very different from the other two types. It basically means that there is no commitment for a permanent loan take-out of the construction loan. Instead, the developer and the construction lender proceed with the understanding that the take-out process remains open. The hope and expectation is that by the time it is needed, a source of long-term funding will be in place. If not, the construction lender may have to take over the project or reluctantly agree to roll its construction loan over into a longer-term loan until some other arrangement is made. The developer takes the risk that it may lose the project if it is unable to line up the permanent funding at a later date. An open-ended arrangement is used when the developer and construction lender feel that they can get a better deal by making successful progress on the project and lining up a permanent source of funding at a time when the value of the project is more readily assessable and when market conditions might be more favorable. A construction lender may also be less worried and willing to accept an open-ended arrangement when the developer is a very rich entity or when the proposed project has major tenants and user commitments in place even before construction commences. Such strong financial positions reduce the risk to the construction lender by increasing the probability of success for the project and reducing the risk that the developer will have insufficient assets in the event of a default.

A commercial real estate project involves a close working relationship between the developer, the construction lender, and the permanent lender. The developer is charged with conceiving the idea for a project, getting equity investors, and putting the deal together. The construction lender takes on the high-risk funding of construction and must have expertise with respect to building practices and short-term money management. The permanent lender takes out the construction loan by paying off the construction lender and then rolls the developer's debt over into a long-term mortgage. Although the relationship is easily depicted as linear, with the construction loan being first relative to the permanent loan, the general case is that the permanent loan has to be arranged first. The economic feasibility of a project depends heavily on the costs of the permanent loan, and for this reason developers usually have to fix their permanent financing costs at an early stage in the development process. Moreover, a construction lender is not likely to agree to do its part unless it knows that a take-out is in place. Each party must work with each of the others, and all three are interdependent.

The written agreement that binds together the developer, the construction lender, and the permanent lender is the *three-party agreement*, which is sometimes also referred to as the *buy-sell agreement*. The three-party agreement is designed to spell out the conditions under which the various parties undertake to work with each other. Its primary legal objective is twofold. First, it is designed to put each of the parties in privity with each of the others; second, it is designed to give each party a right of specific performance against each of the others. Having privity is important when each party will be relying on documents, representations, and warranties that are related. Establishing privity in the three-party agreement avoids potential legal problems later on by eliminating a common contract defense based on a claimant's not having privity. It also means that the lenders do not have to go through the developer to reach each other; they are able to sue each other directly as a result of being in privity with one another.

The provision for specific performance is also important. It means that all parties can demand specific performance from any one of the others. Thus, the developer can seek specific performance against each of its lenders, and each lender can seek to use the same remedy if the developer attempts to switch to another lender. Likewise, each of the lenders can seek this remedy against the other with respect to the take-out obligation. If the permanent lender unfairly refuses to fund the take-out, the construction lender and the developer might seek specific performance. Reciprocally, if the developer seeks a permanent loan from a different lender (one offering a better deal, for instance), the permanent lender can seek specific performance. A developer might try to do this if interest rates drop during the course of construction and it can get a better deal elsewhere. The permanent lender may, in other words, be entitled to do the take-out in accordance with the deal that everyone thought looked good and desirable prior to commencement of construction. It must be remembered that specific performance is an equitable remedy, and the ultimate ability to get an equitable remedy will turn on the discretion of the court. Nonetheless, it constitutes a powerful bargaining chip between the parties and helps bolster the evidence of expectation and reliance among the parties. This makes the case for equitable recovery stronger while also enhancing the remedies at law for damages.

In thinking about the typical commercial lending process, it is probably best to think in terms of a circular, rather than a linear, process. Because of the interconnected nature of commercial lending, the permanent loan is not simply a loan that comes after a construction loan. As we have been discussing, these two loans, though serving different functions, are dependent on each other. Consequently, we should think of the coordination of commercial loans as a circular and nine-step process. See Figure 20-3. Each later step depends on an earlier one, and each early step must be coordinated with expectations as to later steps. Thus, the process is one that is dynamic and integrated with documents related to multiple steps in the process having to be negotiated and drafted simultaneously. A commercial developer works through these steps in completing a given project and at the end of a project is ready to start the cycle all over again with a new project. (In reality many large developers will be in various stages of multiple projects at the same time.) The key steps in this process are: (1) a developer gets an idea for a project, lines up investors, and gets

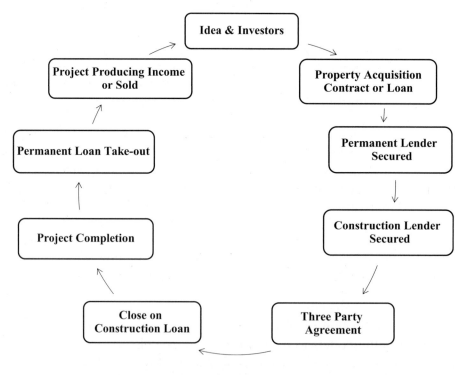

Figure 20-3
Commercial Lending Process

the process in motion; (2) there is a property acquisition contract or loan arrangement to acquire the land for the project; (3) a permanent lender is secured with a lock-in commitment; (4) a construction lender is secured with a construction loan commitment; (5) the three parties coordinate documents and execute a three-party agreement; (6) the developer closes on the construction loan and starts construction under a draw-down financing arrangement; (7) construction on the project is completed in accordance with the plans and specifications; (8) the permanent lender takes out the construction lender and closes on the long-term mortgage with the developer; and (9) the property is either sold off to other investors or begins producing income and enters into the property management phase. At this point, the process has come full circle and the developer starts over with step one on a new project.

Problem 20C

Fletcher, Inc., is a developer, and it enters into commitments with Big Bank for a construction loan and Insure U for permanent loan financing on a proposed $100 million apartment building complex. In planning the project, Fletcher has engaged the Suzan Bee Architectural Design Co. to prepare all the drawings and specifications for the project. It has also hired T&J Construction to act as the general contractor for the actual construction work. About halfway through the construction phase of the development, Fletcher runs into financial problems and finds that it is unable to complete the project. Big Bank takes over the project and seeks to complete the project, with the expectation that finishing it will enhance its value and that the take-out will still be possible.

(a) When Big Bank takes over the project from the defaulting developer, Suzan Bee refuses to let it use the plans and specifications. Big Bank needs the plans and specifications so that it can properly finish the construction. Suzan Bee claims that they are the work product of her firm, and the contract for use was with Fletcher and not Big Bank. Suzan Bee suggests that she might be able to turn over the plans if she gets a release from Fletcher and a professional fee increase of $30,000 for various items for which she claims she was originally underpaid in the deal with Fletcher. Big Bank wants to know whether Suzan Bee has a legitimate point and, if so, what Big Bank might have done to prevent such a problem when it structured its deal with Fletcher.

(b) When Big Bank takes over the project from the defaulting developer, it also hears from T&J Construction. T&J claims that other projects have opened up, and it is getting offers to work for more money elsewhere. Suddenly the construction market is taking off, probably as a result of falling interest rates and a good long-term outlook for low levels of inflation. T&J claims that market conditions have changed and that its deal was with Fletcher. Now that Big Bank is in the picture, a new deal has to be worked out, as T&J has no contractual obligation to work for Big Bank. T&J wants to increase the general contractor's fee on the deal by 15 percent. When Big Bank objects, T&J says it is a cost of doing business, and Big Bank can either seek the added expense as damages from Fletcher or build it into the end price of the project by adjusting rents. Big Bank wants to know whether T&J's position might be correct and, if so, what it should have done to prevent this type of price change from happening when it takes over a project from a defaulting borrower.

(c) In both of the preceding situations, what happens if Big Bank has to pay more to complete the project? Will it be able to make Insure U take out the construction loan at a new higher amount that reflects the added expenses? Should Insure U be able to walk away from the take-out obligation (even if the amount stays the same) on the assertion that its obligation runs only to Fletcher?

(d) Assume that the construction loan is to run for 18 months, with a take-out to occur between December 1 and December 30 of the following year. Fletcher does not default on the construction loan, but the project is not complete by December 30. Should Insure U be able to avoid the take-out obligation on the ground that the completion date was not met and that such a date was a condition precedent to funding under its loan documents and its loan commitment? Should it make a difference if the $100 million project is substantially complete; everything is done with the exception of some interior door and carpet installation estimated to cost $35,000? if the project is substantially complete except for work valued at $200,000? $500,000? $1 million? Should the reason for delay make a difference: a labor strike, bad weather, back-ordered supplies, etc.?

(e) Assume that the construction of the apartment building gets completed, and that Insure U does the take-out. Also assume that the building is in full operation, and that one year later the permanent loan is defaulted on and Insure U proceeds with a foreclosure to take over the project. Will Insure U's mortgage be sufficient as security for such things as rent deposits held by Fletcher, or for insurance rebates and apartment services contract discounts payable to Fletcher? Is a real estate mortgage a proper way to secure such collateral?

TEACHERS INSURANCE & ANNUITY ASSOCIATION v. ORMESA GEOTHERMAL
United States District Court, Southern District of New York, 1991
791 F. Supp. 401

KIMBA M. WOOD, District Judge. Teachers Insurance and Annuity Association of America ("TIAA" or "Teachers"), a New York corporation that is an institutional lender, brought this action against a prospective borrower alleging breach of a commitment letter agreement that "circled" a "blended" interest rate of 10.64 percent for a twenty-year loan of $25,000,000. After a sharp decline in interest rates rendered the agreement less advantageous to the borrower, the borrower took a negotiating stance allegedly designed to alter or scuttle the transaction, and finally refused to continue negotiating with TIAA, claiming that TIAA had "walked" from the deal. Plaintiff and defendant Ormesa each seek damages for breach of contract. . . .

I. LIABILITY

A. BACKGROUND AND ORIGINS OF THE TRANSACTION

Defendant Ormesa Geothermal ("Ormesa") is a general partnership formed under the laws of California to construct a geothermal power plant in the Imperial Valley of California (the "Project"). . . .

The financing arrangements for the Project were complex. The Project contemplated the placement of three types of debt financings and the contribution of equity funding. With respect to the debt, the Project needed approximately $50,000,000 of interim or "construction" financing (the "Construction Loan") for the period during which the Project would be constructed. It then needed approximately $50,000,000 of long-term financing (the "Long-term Loan") to replace the Construction Loan when construction was completed. The Construction Loan and the Long-term Loan were to be 90 percent guaranteed by the United States Department of Energy (the "DOE"). At the time TIAA was negotiating the transaction at issue in this litigation (the "Transaction") with Ormesa the Long-term Loan was to have been 90 percent guaranteed by the DOE, and the Loan was to have been made through the issuance of two sets of notes, with the unguaranteed notes at a higher rate of interest. In addition to the Construction Loan and the Long-term Loan, the Project also needed approximately $10,000,000 of subordinated financing (the "Subordinated Loan"), to be funded at the time the Construction Loan closed. It would also require the equity contribution of LFC (the "Equity Contribution") at the time of the closing of the Construction Loan.

The construction lender on the Project was Bankers Trust Company ("Bankers Trust"). . . . As a condition to closing its Construction Loan, Bankers Trust desired a "takeout" commitment by a long-term lender, to provide the Long-term Loan to repay and thus replace or "take out" the Construction Loan. The collateral for the Construction Loan would also secure the Long-term Loan after it replaced the Construction Loan. Therefore, documents with respect to the Long-term Loan were drafted and negotiated concurrently with those relating to the Construction Loan and the Subordinated Loan.

B. ORMESA'S SEARCH FOR LONG-TERM FINANCING; THE COMMITMENT AGREEMENT

In the fall of 1985, Ormesa retained E. F. Hutton as its agent for the purpose of obtaining the Long-term Loan for the Project. The E. F. Hutton employees with principal day-to-day responsibility for the Transaction were Vince Castellano, and, after Castellano's departure from E. F. Hutton in August 1986, Gerald Gminski. . . .

Among the prospective lenders contacted by Castellano were TIAA and John Hancock Mutual Life Insurance Company ("John Hancock"), an insurance company that invests, inter alia, in debt securities obtained in private placements. Because the Ormesa loan was highly complex, requiring negotiation with several entities including the DOE, and because it required fixing the interest rate far in advance of funding, only sophisticated institutional lenders were likely to (and did) show serious interest in the transaction. For these reasons, Ormesa had to increase the interest rate from that contained in its original offer in order to interest investors. In late January 1986, TIAA and John Hancock each expressed a willingness to provide 50 percent (or approximately $25,000,000) of the total of approximately $50,000,000 for the Long-term Loan. The interest rate for the Long-term Loan was to be a blended rate (*i.e.*, the weighted average of (1) the interest rate on the 90 percent portion of the total debt, which was guaranteed, and (2) the higher interest rate on the 10 percent portion, which was non-guaranteed) equal to the sum of (a) the yield, on a date to be determined, on a hypothetical 13-year United States Treasury Note, plus (b) 150 basis points. (A basis point is $1/100$ of a percent; thus, 150 basis points represents 1.50 percent.)

Ormesa offered the portion of the Long-term Loan that was to be guaranteed by the DOE (the "Guaranteed Notes") with "call protection," that is, an agreement that (1) the Guaranteed Notes could not be repaid prior to a certain time, and that (2) after that time, they could be repaid only with a premium intended to give a lender the benefit of its bargain over the term of the loan. This type of call protection is common in long-term lending to preserve for the lender the benefit of its bargain. Early in the negotiations, TIAA advised Ormesa that it wanted call protection not only for the Guaranteed Notes but also for the Non-guaranteed Notes, and Ormesa agreed to this.

Because TIAA and John Hancock were comfortable with complex transactions of this type, they found this transaction, on these terms, to be highly attractive.

On February 7, 1986, TIAA, John Hancock and Ormesa "circled" the transaction at a blended rate of 10.64 percent. When a financing is "circled," the parties orally agree that they will do the transaction on the specified terms, and the interest rate and certain other key economic terms are, by this oral agreement, fixed. It is the custom in the financial community that once the parties circle a deal, neither party tries to change the interest rate that has been agreed. . . .

On February 20, 1986, TIAA's Finance Committee approved the Long-term Loan and authorized TIAA to proceed with the Transaction. On February 26, 1986 John Hancock's Committee of Finance approved the Long-term Loan and authorized John Hancock to proceed with the Transaction. On February 24, 1986, TIAA sent a commitment agreement to Ormesa for signature, and on February 26, 1986, John Hancock did so. . . .

After John Hancock and Ormesa committed to the Long-term Loan, John Hancock committed itself to a "match funding," *i.e.*, it incurred "matched" obligations relying on the income it would receive pursuant to the Long-term Loan. As a result, John Hancock stood to suffer a substantial loss if its share of the Long-term Loan did not fund. Ormesa knew, no later than the end of June 1986, that John Hancock would suffer a substantial loss if John Hancock's share of the Long-term Loan did not fund.

Interest rates dropped precipitously between February 7, 1986, when the interest rate for this transaction was circled, and July 25, 1986. By July 25, the average of the levels of the 10-year and the 20-year Treasuries — the average used in fixing the original circled rate — dropped 197 basis points. Application of the lower rate would save Ormesa about $1,000,000 a year in interest. Ormesa was aware of this drop in interest rates, and its attempts to back out of the Transaction were motivated by the drop in interest rates. . . .

Ormesa decided that it was cheaper to defend and/or settle the litigation that Ormesa anticipated than to perform pursuant to the Commitment Agreement. This decision, and the actions Ormesa took to implement it, violated Ormesa's duty to negotiate in good faith. . . .

Call protection for the Long-term Lenders was an integral part of the Transaction; it was expressly provided for in the commitment agreements of both TIAA and John Hancock. . . .

. . . TIAA and John Hancock did not repudiate or withdraw from the Transaction, nor did they intend to do so. Indeed, they were trying to do exactly the opposite. The Transaction was an extraordinarily attractive one for them, at a level of 200 basis points above the then prevailing market, and John Hancock had match-funded the Transaction and would suffer a multi-million dollar out-of-pocket loss if it did not fund, as Ormesa was aware. TIAA and John Hancock were working to preserve the Transaction. . . .

DISCUSSION

Ormesa's primary legal contention is that the commitment letter did not bind the parties to complete the transaction because it did not contain all the material terms of the contemplated loan: Ormesa contends that a mutually satisfactory resolution of those to-be-agreed terms would be required in order to bind the parties to complete the transaction.

Ormesa contends that it was further contemplated that once all material terms were satisfactorily negotiated, TIAA and Ormesa would execute loan documents that themselves would be subject to certain conditions that would have to be satisfied before the loan would be made, and that these conditions were never satisfied. Ormesa contends that the only binding agreement in the TIAA commitment letter was that Ormesa would pay certain TIAA expenses. . . .

Here the Commitment Agreement expressly said it was a "binding agreement":

> If the foregoing properly sets forth your understanding of this transaction, please *evidence acceptance of the conditions* of this letter *by having it executed* below by duly authorized officers of Ormesa Geothermal *and by returning one executed counterpart* to TIAA. . . . *Upon receipt by TIAA of an accepted counterpart* of this letter, *our agreement* to purchase from you and your agreement to issue, sell and deliver to us, . . . the captioned securities, *shall become a binding agreement between us.* (Exh. P-1 at 2, emphasis added).

Although there were many open terms to be negotiated, all of the crucial economic terms of the loan were set forth in the Commitment Letter, including the amount and term of the loan, the interest rate, the repayment schedule, the portion of the loan to be guaranteed by the United States government, the security for the guaranteed senior secured notes, the period during which the loan would not be callable, and prepayment penalties applicable thereafter. The language of the agreement suggests that the Commitment Agreement was intended to be, and was, a binding agreement. . . .

The parties' actions in the context of the negotiations . . . also suggest that the Commitment Agreement was intended to be, and was, a binding agreement. . . .

The open terms . . . were terms that customarily are left for later negotiation once the critical terms such as loan amount, term, interest, description of any security and guaranty, and prepayment penalties have been agreed. . . .

. . . Teachers' partial performance is merely one act among many that suggests that the commitment was viewed as binding. . . . Teachers partially performed its contract with Ormesa by committing $25 million of its funds to the transaction; the court rejects Ormesa's contention that because Teachers did not physically segregate these funds, there was no commitment of the funds by Teachers. . . .

It is customary for borrowers and lenders in transactions similar to the one at issue here to accord binding force to preliminary agreements similar to the Commitment Agreement.

I conclude that the Commitment Agreement was a binding preliminary agreement that obligated the borrower and the lenders to seek to effectuate a final loan agreement upon the agreed terms by negotiating in good faith to resolve the other terms customarily found in such agreements.

Ormesa breached its duty to negotiate in good faith to resolve the issues left open by the Commitment Agreement. By, among other things, insisting upon a lowered interest rate, Ormesa attempted to change and undercut terms that had been agreed to in the Commitment letter. . . .

I. DAMAGES

Under New York law, a party injured by breach of contract should be placed in the same economic position as it would have been in had the contract been performed. Teachers Insurance & Annuity Assn v. Butler, 626 F. Supp. 1229, 1236 (S.D.N.Y. 1986). TIAA is thus entitled to damages equal to the discounted present value of the incremental interest income TIAA would be expected to lose as a result of the breach.[6] Specifically, the lost interest income is measured as the difference between (a) the interest income TIAA would have earned had the contract been performed, and (b) the interest income TIAA would be deemed to have earned by timely mitigating its damages — *i.e.*, by making an investment with similar characteristics at the time of the breach. . . .

Using the assumptions adopted in this decision, TIAA's damages are $4,094,530 for the whole loan on a blended basis. . . .

The foregoing shall constitute the court's findings of fact and conclusions of law. Judgment may be entered accordingly.

Problem 20D

(a) In the *TIAA* case there is discussion of the lenders wanting "call protection" in their loan arrangements with the borrower. What is call protection, and what is it intended to accomplish? Why does a lender want such protection, and why should a developer agree to it? Draft a call protection provision that you might offer for use in a transaction such as the one described in the *TIAA* case.

(b) In the *TIAA* case we are told that John Hancock "match-funded the transaction." What does this mean? Why is match-funding done?

4. Loan Participations

Lenders often partner with other financial institutions to provide funding for significant development projects. When they do this they are structuring a loan participation. The originating lender is generally referred to as the lead lender. Participating lenders are generally investors in the loan or financing part of the deal. Three key areas of concern with loan

---

6. The court rejects Ormesa's contention that the "payment of expenses" language in the Commitment Agreement limits TIAA to reimbursement of its expenses, rather than damages. The court finds that the "payment expenses" language has to do only with allocation of expenses to the borrower whether or not the loan closed, not with remedy for breach. *See* Walter E. Heller & Co. v. American Flyer Airline Corp., 459 F.2d 896, 900 (2d Cir. 1972). The court also finds that Ormesa failed to meet its burden of proving that TIAA failed to mitigate its damages. Ormesa claims that TIAA turned down loans at interest rates higher than that in the Commitment Agreement (10.64 percent), but does not indicate the nature, quality or risk of these investments, or the reason they did not eventuate. *See* Jenkins v. Etlinger, 432 N.E.2d 696, 698 (N.Y. 1982).

participations involve (1) the allocation of risk on the loan as between the lead lender and the loan participants, (2) the allocation of managerial and administrative duties, and (3) remedies for breach.

SUN AMERICAN BANK V. FAIRFIELD FINANCIAL SERVICES, INC.
United States District Court, Middle District of Georgia, 2010
690 F. Supp. 2d 1342

C. ASHLEY ROYAL, District Judge. Set against the backdrop of a nationwide real estate collapse, this case presents a dispute between two banks to determine which will bear the risk of loss in a failed beachfront condominium development in north Florida. In November 2006, Defendant Fairfield Financial Services, Inc., ("Fairfield") agreed to loan $21,840,000 ("the Construction Loan") to fund the construction of a 14-unit luxury condominium project near Jacksonville, Florida. The Borrower was Acquilus III, LLC, a company wholly owned by Florida developer Herbert Lee Underwood. Underwood was an established customer of Fairfield and was the primary guarantor of the Construction Loan. At the time Fairfield originated the Construction Loan, its portfolio of loans to Mr. Underwood included three loans for the purchase of raw land, totaling $12,412,500.

To reduce its overall risk exposure in the Underwood relationship, Fairfield sold participation interests in the Construction Loan to several banks. One of those participant banks was a predecessor in interest to Plaintiff Sun American Bank ("Sun American"). In a Participation Agreement with Fairfield dated February 27, 2007, Sun American's predecessor agreed to fund 16.056% of the Construction Loan, up to a maximum amount of $3,500,000. Sun American continued to fund its proportion of the monthly draws on the Construction Loan until April 9, 2008.

On April 21, 2008, Sun American learned for the first time that Fairfield had lowered the credit rating of the Construction Loan three times, between May 2007 and November 2007, because of the borrower's declining liquidity. On May 15, 2008, Sun American notified Fairfield that it considered Fairfield's failure to disclose the liquidity issues and the resulting credit rating changes to be a material default of the Participation Agreement and demanded that Fairfield repurchase the participation interest. Fairfield refused.

Sun American filed the present lawsuit on October 7, 2008, alleging breach of the disclosure requirements of the Participation Agreement and seeking to enforce the Agreement's repurchase clause. In response, Fairfield has filed a counterclaim, alleging that Sun American breached the Agreement by failing to contribute to draw payments after April 2008. Both parties have filed motions for summary judgment.

Upon review of those motions, . . . the Court finds that there are no genuine issues of material fact and that Sun American is entitled to judgment as a matter of law. . . .

I. FACTUAL BACKGROUND

The dispute in this case turns on the interpretation of the terms of the Participation Agreement, and the background facts of this case are essentially undisputed. Fairfield does not dispute that it changed its credit classification of the Construction Loan and its other Underwood loans three times in 2007. At the outset of the project, the Underwood relationship was classified as a level 4, or "acceptable" risk. Between May and November of 2007, the risk rating was changed three times, finally being rated a level 7, or "substandard" risk.

In May 2007, Fairfield reclassified the Loan from level "4" to level "5," meaning that the Construction Loan would be placed on the bank's watch list. In September 2007, the Construction Loan was again reclassified to level "6," meaning that it was a "special mention loan." In November 2007, Fairfield reclassified the Construction Loan a third time, to a level "7," signifying a potential loss of principal and interest. Sun American did not learn of these changes in the credit rating until April 2008.

Each time Fairfield changed the classification, the change reflected increased credit risk on the credit relationship due to concerns about Underwood's liquidity and ability to repay. Fairfield's concerns were based largely on information obtained in its administration of its three land loans to Underwood, information that was not available to Sun American. Sun American did not learn about Underwood's liquidity problems or the changes in the risk rating until April 2008, more than a year after these problems first became apparent to Fairfield. Fairfield contends that it had no obligation to disclose its risk rating changes or information arising from the administration of the land loans, in which Sun American was not a participant.

A. THE PARTICIPATION AGREEMENT

The obligations of Fairfield and its Participating Banks were governed by a Participation Agreement provided by Fairfield. . . . Several provisions in the Agreement outline the responsibilities and obligations of Fairfield, as the Originating Bank, and of Sun American, as a Participating Bank. Generally, the Originating Bank is obligated to oversee and administer the loan, while the Participating Banks are responsible to make their own independent credit evaluations.

In the context of the Originating Bank's duty to administer the Loan, the Agreement requires Fairfield to provide its Participating Banks with full disclosure of information related to the credit relationship. The Agreement's disclosure requirements are primarily set forth in Sections 4, 10, and 11. These three provisions, read together, reflect an intent that Fairfield be completely open in communication to its participants.

In Section 4, Fairfield commits to provide written notice to the Participating Banks of any changes in the status of its credit relationship with the Borrower. In its entirety Section 4 provides:

> 4. *Credit Condition of the Borrower(s); Access to Credit Information.* **It is understood and agreed that Participating Bank, and not Originating Bank, is responsible for making the ultimate credit decision through the Participating Bank's own review of information pertaining to the Loan.** Consequently, credit evaluation performed by Originating Bank must be independently verified and supplemented by Participating Bank's review of individual Borrower(s) information with respect to each Loan, sufficient for Participating Bank to make its own credit decision with respect to its purchase of a Participation Interest in the Loan and to monitor the loan on an ongoing basis. In the event Originating Bank decides to terminate its credit relationship with a Borrower, *or materially downgrades its relationship with a Borrower,* Originating Bank will promptly provide written notice of such determination to Participating Bank. (bold in original, italics added).

Much of the controversy in this case hinges on the definition of the term "downgrade," which is not otherwise defined in the Agreement.

Section 10 of the Agreement imposes additional disclosure requirements on Fairfield. In Section 10, Fairfield agrees to notify its participants of any "default" by the Borrower. Section 10 provides, in its entirety:

> 10. *Default by Borrower.* Originating Bank shall promptly, after Originating Bank's having knowledge thereof, inform Participating Bank of any circumstances (a "*default*") which in Originating Bank's reasonable judgment: (a) constitute a material default under the Loan Documents and of the salient facts known to Originating Bank concerning such default; or (b) could have a material, adverse [effect] on the Loan or the value of the Collateral securing the Loan. Originating Bank shall keep Participating Bank fully informed with respect to such circumstances and any actions taken by Originating Bank in connection therewith.

Section 10 specifically defines "default" to include not only actual default under the terms of the loan agreement, but also more broadly to include any circumstances that "could have a material, adverse effect on the Loan." Fairfield is expected to keep its participants "fully informed" of such circumstances. The disclosure provisions of Section 10 are very broad, reflecting an intent to require complete openness by the Originating Bank.

The Agreement's goal of complete openness and full disclosure is underscored in Section 11, which requires Fairfield to make its entire file available to the participants and to furnish participants with copies of all documents it receives. Section 11 provides:

11. *Files and Records.* Originating Bank shall keep and maintain at its offices, such files and records of matters pertaining to the Loan . . . as it would were the Loan made solely by Originating Bank. All such files and records shall be available for inspection by Participating Bank or its agent during normal business hours. Originating Bank shall furnish to Participating Bank copies of the Loan Documents and all other documents and information Originating Bank shall receive from time to time, whether pursuant to the Loan Documents or otherwise relative to the Loan or the Borrower(s).

Read as a whole, therefore, the Agreement reflects an intent to obligate the Originating Bank to keep its participants fully informed, essentially requiring Fairfield to provide the participants with as much information as Fairfield itself possesses. It does not in any way authorize Fairfield to withhold information pertinent to the Construction Loan.

The Agreement imposes duties on the Participating Banks as well. While Fairfield, as the Originating Bank, has the duty to keep its Participating Banks fully informed, the Participating Banks have a duty to exercise their own judgment and analysis of the Borrower's creditworthiness. In the Agreement, therefore, Sun American represents and warrants "that it has done its own due diligence in identifying Borrower(s) and loan purposes, as well as underwriting the Loan made to Borrower(s) under its own lending criteria." The Agreement assigns the Participating Bank the responsibility to monitor the loan on an ongoing basis and to do its own independent credit evaluation in addition to the evaluation performed by Fairfield. Thus, the Agreement stipulates that "credit evaluation performed by Originating Bank must be independently verified and supplemented by Participating Bank's review of individual Borrower(s) information." The Participating Bank "is responsible for making the ultimate credit decision through the Participating Bank's own review of information pertaining to the Loan."

In the event of a breach by the Originating Bank, the Agreement provides a repurchase remedy to the Participating Bank. This remedy permitted Sun American to demand that Fairfield buy back its participation interest upon notice of default and opportunity to cure. With regard to breach, Section 13 of the Agreement provides:

13. *Breach by Originating Bank.* Participating Bank shall, in addition to all other remedies available to it at law or in equity, have the unilateral right (but not the obligation) to sell to Originating Bank, regardless of regulatory or self-imposed lending limits of Originating Bank, its Participation Interest for an amount equal to the aggregate of all principal, interest, fees and other sums due with respect to its Participation Interest, if:

    a. Originating Bank shall fail to cure any default by Originating Bank under this Agreement within thirty (30) days after notice from Participating Bank specifying the default; . . .

Participating Bank shall have the right to maintain an action for specific performance against Originating Bank to enforce Participating Bank's rights under this Section 13.

In the event of breach, then, the Agreement's remedy provision allows Sun American to recover any principal it had previously advanced on the Construction Loan, along with accrued interest on that principal and other funds advanced in connection with the Loan.

B. FAIRFIELD'S CREDIT RATING SYSTEM

Fairfield, like most banks, maintained a credit rating system to classify its loans according to risk. Fairfield's rating system used a scale of 1 to 10, with level 1 signifying zero risk and level 10 signifying a total loss. At the time Fairfield approved the Loan for the Acquilus III project, the Loan was classified as a 4. Fairfield's Senior Vice President, Steven Stillman, explained that a level 4 credit "would be generally a middle market to small business, well-managed, [with an] established history, a history of profitability, but highly dependent upon bank credit." A level 4 credit rating reflects an "acceptable" level of risk, "nothing . . . that can't be managed." Stillman characterized the level 4 credit as "the bread and butter of the banking industry."

Each higher level of the rating system reflects a higher degree of risk to the bank. A level 5 classification, known as a "watch" rating, suggests "a slight weakness, but nothing that should result in any loss on the loan." A level 6 classification is known as a "special mention," indicating a higher degree of risk due to changes in market conditions or the borrower's status, but without an expectation of loss. At level 7, a loan is considered "substandard." A level 7 loan "has a very defined weakness that may or may not result in a loss." A loss may not be expected to any individual loan, but some losses will be expected among the bank's entire portfolio of seven-rated credits. A level 8 loan is classified as "doubtful," with some loss expected, and a level 9 loan is considered a loss. Level 10 reflects an actual charge-off of the loan.

Fairfield reconsidered its risk ratings for loans on at least an annual basis. It also reconsidered risk ratings whenever warranted by circumstances such as a change in market conditions or a change in the condition of the borrower. Changes in the terms of credit, such as the extension of new loans to the same borrower, might also trigger reevaluation of the rating. In cases where Fairfield had a number of loans related to one person or entity, as in the case of its loans to Mr. Underwood's businesses, Fairfield considered the entire group of loans to be a single credit relationship. Fairfield assigned its risk ratings to the relationship as a whole, rather than to the individual loans separately.

C. FAIRFIELD'S RELATIONSHIP WITH UNDERWOOD

Based largely on its previous relationship with Underwood, Fairfield considered the Acquilus III project to be a good credit risk at the outset of the condominium project. Underwood was an experienced real estate developer and an established customer of Fairfield with a "proven track history of being able to build projects of this magnitude." Underwood personally guaranteed the loan, as did his development company, Eagle Development, Inc. Prior to applying for the Acquilus III Construction Loan, Underwood had fully repaid three loans from Fairfield, including two construction loans in excess of four million dollars. Moreover, the project itself had the promise of success, as Mr. Underwood had already obtained purchase commitments and deposits on half of the planned units in the building.

At the time Fairfield originated the Construction Loan, Underwood also had a high net worth and substantial liquidity. . . .

At the time Fairfield originated the Construction Loan, Underwood's companies had three previous loans outstanding with Fairfield, all used for the purchase of raw land. These three loans are collectively referred to as "the land loans." Loan number 8100240, known as the "Acquilus III land loan," was a loan in the amount of $1,837,500 to pay for the purchase of the land on which the Acquilus III condominium project was to be built. Loan number 8100243, known as the "Acquilus Waterfront Harbour loan," was a loan in the amount of $6,075,000 to fund the purchase of a 5.62 acre site for another condominium project. Loan number 8100324, known as the "Acquilus IV loan," was a loan in the amount of $4,500,000 to pay for the purchase of yet another beachfront site. All three loans were secured by the property they were used to purchase. Underwood was to pay the interest accruing on these loans from his own funds, then repay the loans at maturity by refinance into a development or construction loan. Underwood also personally guaranteed each of the loans.

The Construction Loan, loan number 8100241, was "substantially different in its structure and source of repayment from the raw land loans." Fairfield agreed to loan Acquilus III $21,840,000 to finance the construction of the condominium building on the property purchased through the Acquilus III land loan. These loan funds would be disbursed in monthly draws to cover the expenses of construction. The Construction Loan included an interest reserve, so that each monthly draw included an amount to pay interest on the Loan from loan funds. The Loan was to be paid in full at maturity, upon completion of the construction, using funds obtained from sale of the condominiums or through refinance. Like the land loans, the Construction Loan was personally guaranteed by Underwood. Fairfield considered all four loans guaranteed by Underwood—the three land loans and the Construction Loan—to be a single relationship. Fairfield assigned its risk ratings to the relationship as a whole, not to each loan separately. . . .

Fairfield's extensive relationship with Underwood required it to seek participants to provide additional funding for the Acquilus III project. Banks routinely sell participations on loans, in order to comply with legal lending limits or to avoid becoming "overly concentrated with one customer or in one market or within one product type." Banking regulations limit exposure to any particular borrower to prevent negative impacts on a bank's financial conditions. In addition to the limits imposed by the regulation, Fairfield had its own internal hold limits, used to determine whether a loan had to be participated. For the Acquilus III Construction Loan, Fairfield sold participations in the amount of $15,252,500, limiting its exposure to $6,587,500. Fairfield also sold participations in the Acquilus IV loan and the Acquilus Waterfront Harbor loan.

Among the banks Fairfield solicited for participation in the Construction Loan was Sun American. . . .

D. PROBLEMS IN THE RELATIONSHIP

Despite the promising beginnings of the Acquilus III project, Fairfield began to experience problems in its relationship with the various Underwood enterprises even before Independent (the predecessor to Sun American) had closed on the Participation Agreement, as Underwood's liquidity problems made it more and more difficult to meet his obligations on his various loans. These liquidity problems soon led Underwood to become delinquent on his payments on the three land loans. Fairfield changed the credit rating of the relationship three times between May and November 2007, first from a 4 to 5, then from a 5 to a 6, and finally from a 6 to a 7. Fairfield never informed Sun American of the early liquidity problems, the developing delinquencies on the three land loans, or the negative changes in its credit ratings. . . .

The first hint of trouble in the relationship occurred in February 2007, just four months after Fairfield approved the Acquilus III Construction Loan and before the parties executed the Participation Agreement. By the time Independent signed the Agreement, the $852,919 interest reserve account at the Security Bank of Glynn County had dwindled to nothing. On February 8, 2007, Tim Finney, a credit analyst at Fairfield noted in an email that Underwood had taken approximately $180,000 from the account and had used it to pay expenses and payroll related to the Acquilus III and Acquilus Waterfront Harbor projects. This left slightly less than $60,000 in the account, a situation Finney described as "not good." A week later, the account was empty. On February 13, 2007, Margaret Clay notified Finney in an email that Underwood had cashed another check in the amount of $60,000, and that the Glynn County account now showed a negative balance of (-$129.03). . . . Despite the importance of the interest reserve account in the loan approval documents, Fairfield never informed Independent that the account had been cleaned out prior to the closing of the Participation Agreement.

Underwood's diminished liquidity led to the first reclassification of the risk rating in May 2007. . . .

As the spring of 2007 turned into summer, Underwood's liquidity problems began to be manifest in his credit relationship with Fairfield, as he began to fall behind on interest payments on the land loans. On June 21, 2007, Finney emailed Underwood personally to notify him that the three land loans were past due. . . .

As of July 10, Underwood still had not made the June payments for the Acquilus IV and Acquilus Waterfront Harbour loans. . . .

Correspondence from August 2007 indicates that Underwood was having difficulty paying his subcontractors on the Acquilus III project and was seeking to use funds from the Construction Loan to pay his interest on the land loans. . . .

Despite the apparent use of Construction Loan funds to pay interest costs and the use of escrow funds to pay construction costs, Underwood again fell behind on his payments on the land loans. . . .

As Underwood's liquidity declined and the three land loans fell further into delinquency, Fairfield proposed to remedy the situation by lending Underwood more money. As Stillman observed, Underwood was "asset rich and cash poor," and the new loan was seen as a way to convert one of his assets into a temporary cash source. . . .

This fourth land loan came to be known as the "Spoonbill Harbor" loan. Fairfield loaned Underwood $1,560,000, secured by a 3.25 acre tract appraised at $2.4 Million. The proceeds of this loan were to be used to pay off a first mortgage on the Spoonbill Harbor property itself, then to pay interest on the other three land loans. In this instance, the participants were notified. On October 5, 2007, Stacie Shearer emailed the Participating Banks to inform them that a new loan had been issued . . . . Shearer's email has no mention of Underwood's ongoing liquidity issues or of the delinquencies in payment on the land loans. . . .

Although the Participants were notified of the Spoonbill Harbor loan, there is no indication in the record that they were ever notified of the continuing delinquencies in the land loans, the increasing liquidity concerns, or the changes in the credit rating from a 4 in May to a 7 in November. . . .

Sun American interpreted the Spoonbill Harbor loan as a sign of trouble. On October 16, 2007, Sun American's chief credit officer, Robert Garrett, explained his concerns about the new loan in an email to Felipe Lozano, Sun American's relationship manager for the Construction Loan. . . .

In December, Sun America received another hint that all was not well with the Underwood relationship. On December 17, 2007, Jimmy Davis sent a memorandum to the participants to notify them that Fairfield was proposing an exchange of collateral. . . .

Aside from the single email informing participants of the Spoonbill Harbor loan in October 2007 and the memo regarding the substitution of collateral in December 2007, there is nothing in the record to indicate that

Sun American ever received notice of the problems Mr. Underwood was experiencing with his loan portfolio until April 2008. . . .

On April 21, 2008, Stillman organized a conference call with representatives of the participant banks. The purpose of the call was to introduce himself to the participants and tell them his thoughts about the loan. During the call he informed the participants that he considered the credit to be substandard. He also informed the participants that Acquilus III had failed to pay 2007 property taxes and did not have the resources to do so. Fairfield proposed using contingency funds from the construction budget to pay part of the tax bill and asked the banks to fund a "protective advance" to pay the rest. The announcement that Underwood was in a perilous financial condition and that Fairfield had rated the loan substandard several months earlier caught Sun American by surprise. . . . Shortly after the telephone conference, Sun American made the decision to withdraw from participation and cease contributing to draws.

Felipe Lozano sent a letter to Fairfield dated May 15, 2007, which notified Fairfield that Sun American considered it to be in material default of the Participation Agreement. Lozano's letter outlines five categories of default . . . [and] goes on to complain about Fairfield's "lack of transparency" in its dealings with participants. . . . As a result of these alleged defaults, Sun American ceased contributing to construction draws and demanded that Fairfield repurchase its participation interest "by no later than 05/19/08." Fairfield . . . responded on May 30, 2008, with a letter demanding that Sun American continue to participate in funding construction draws and threatening legal action against Sun American "and all those personally involved." Sun American sent a second notice of default and demand for repurchase in September, then filed this lawsuit in October.

II. FAIRFIELD'S BREACH OF CONTRACT

The undisputed facts set forth above demonstrate that Fairfield breached its obligations under the Participation Agreement to provide full information to the Participating Banks, including Sun American. Specifically, Fairfield breached Sections 4 and 10 of the contract. . . .

A. SECTION 4 — MATERIAL DOWNGRADES

The Court finds as a matter of law that Section 4 of the Participation Agreement required Fairfield to notify Sun American each time it decided to change the credit rating of the Construction Loan and the related land loans. These changes were material downgrades in Fairfield's credit relationship with the Borrower. . . .

The Participation Agreement assigns Fairfield primary responsibility for administering the Loan. In connection with this responsibility, Fairfield commits to provide notice to Participating Banks not only in the event of a material downgrade or the termination of a credit relationship, but upon knowledge of any circumstances that "could have a material, adverse effect on the Loan or value of the Collateral securing the Loan." Participation Agreement ¶10. . . .

Nothing in the Participation Agreement gives Fairfield the right to withhold information about the Loan from its participants. . . .

It is undisputed that Fairfield downgraded its credit evaluation of the Underwood relationship three times between May and November of 2007, but did not disclose these downgrades until April 2008. In doing so, Fairfield breached the explicit provisions of Section 4 of the Participation Agreement and the implicit requirement of full disclosure and open communication between the Originating Bank and the Participating Banks.

B. SECTION 10 — CIRCUMSTANCES OF DEFAULT

Fairfield not only withheld notice of its downgrades in the credit relationship; it also failed to keep Sun American informed of many of the facts that supported these downgrades. These facts related to important events in the relationship with Underwood that increased the risk of the Construction Loan. In withholding this information, Fairfield breached Section 10 of the Participation Agreement, which requires the Originating Bank to notify Participating Banks of "any circumstances . . . which in Originating Bank's reasonable judgment . . . could have a material, adverse [effect] on the Loan or the value of the Collateral securing the Loan." This breach was yet another violation of its duty to maintain open communication with its participants. . . .

Fairfield's failure to disclose information about Underwood's diminishing liquidity and his land loan delinquencies is inexcusable. It had superior knowledge about Underwood's position, but refused to share this knowledge with participants. As a result, the participants were deprived of an opportunity to make informed decisions about their own risks in the construction project. Meanwhile, Fairfield took steps to protect its own interests in the land loans. . . .

The liquidity problems that first became evident even before Sun American signed off on the Participation Agreement could and eventually did in fact have a material adverse effect on the Construction Loan. By the time Fairfield finally disclosed these problems, Underwood's guarantee was practically worthless. Fairfield had an obligation to disclose these problems promptly, and its failure to do so was a breach of the Participation Agreement.

III. REMEDIES

The undisputed evidence having shown that Fairfield breached its duty to provide full disclosure to Sun American under Section 4 and Section 10 of the Participation Agreement, the question turns to the remedy for the breach. The Participation Agreement, at Section 13, provides a specific remedy: repurchase of the participation interest. Section 13 provides

> **Breach by Originating Bank**: Participating Bank shall, in addition to all other remedies available to it at law or in equity, have the unilateral right (but not the obligation) to sell to Originating Bank, regardless of regulatory or self-imposed lending limits of Originating Bank, its Participation Interest for an amount equal to the aggregate of all principal, interest, fees and other sums due with respect to its Participation Interest, if:
>
>   a. Originating Bank shall fail to cure any default by Originating Bank under this Agreement within thirty (30) days after notice from Participating Bank specifying the default; . . .
>
> Participating Bank shall have the right to maintain an action for specific performance against Originating Bank to enforce Participating Bank's rights under this Section 13.

Section 13 provides Fairfield an opportunity to cure any breach. If it is unable or unwilling to cure the breach, Fairfield must repurchase the Participation Interest at the Participating Bank's demand. For the reasons set forth below, the Court finds that the repurchase clause in Section 13 is an enforceable remedy. The undisputed evidence shows that Sun American provided Fairfield with proper notice and that Fairfield failed and was unable to cure its breaches of Section 4 and Section 10. Because of these breaches, Fairfield was obligated to repurchase Sun American's interest. In failing to repurchase, Fairfield is now liable for its breach of Section 13. . . .

As Fairfield no doubt contemplated in drafting the Participation Agreement, the repurchase requirement of Section 13 is a suitable remedy for the breach of the Originating Bank's disclosure obligations. The purpose of the disclosure requirements is to give the Participating Banks a full opportunity to make informed decisions about the administration of the loan and to manage its own risks. Fairfield's failure to disclose made it the sole master of the risk, and the best remedy available is to make it bear the full burden and benefit of that risk. The repurchase clause, therefore, requires Fairfield to take full responsibility for the loan, after it has failed to give the Participating Banks a meaningful opportunity to participate. . . .

Whether repurchase is construed as liquidated damages or specific performance, it is a reasonable remedy for a serious breach with consequences that cannot be measured. . . .

Requiring Fairfield to repurchase the Participation Interest in this case is the most reasonable means of restoring the parties to the position they would have been in absent the breach. Precise legal damages would be impossible to calculate because such calculation would require speculation into what Sun American would have done with the information Fairfield was obligated to disclose. . . .

Where Fairfield deprived its participants of power to manage their own risk, the most appropriate remedy is to have Fairfield assume full responsibility for the risk. Only Fairfield had sufficient knowledge to make fully-informed decisions about the Acquilus III project. Fairfield used this knowledge to control management of the Construction Loan. By repurchasing Sun American's Participation Interest, Fairfield bears the costs or obtains the benefits of its own risk management and cannot externalize those costs or benefits on Sun American. The repurchase clause is not a penalty, therefore, but a reasonable attempt to address the probable loss that would occur in the event of inadequate disclosure. . . .

IV. CONCLUSION

Based on the undisputed evidence, interpreted in the light most favorable to Fairfield, the Court finds that Fairfield breached its disclosure obligations under Sections 4 and 10 of the Participation Agreement. The undisputed evidence further shows that Sun American gave Fairfield due notice of its breach and that Fairfield was unable to cure its breach within thirty days. Fairfield has since refused to repurchase the Participation Interest as required by Section 13. Accordingly, the Court finds that there are no genuine issues of material fact and that Sun American is entitled to judgment as a matter of law. The parties are hereby directed to confer and prepare a stipulation of damages consistent with the measure of damages defined above, to be submitted in writing with twenty days of the date of this order.

F. LAND ASSEMBLY AND PUBLIC-PRIVATE PARTNERSHIPS

Sometimes government entities and related boards or authorities coordinate the steps for planning, acquisition, development, and financing for major commercial real estate projects. The typical situation involves some type of industrial development or urban development agency, authorized by state statute to assist in economic development. The statutes define the range and scope of the authority of such entities. Development authorities often provide tax incentives, bond-related financing, and other strategic benefits to developers that either reduce costs (thus enhancing potential profits) or make land assembly easier. These public-sector entities assist private developers in facilitating the location of a major retail, entertainment, warehousing, or manufacturing facility in a given community. State law often empowers the authority with the right of eminent domain, which it uses in the land assembly stage of the project. The use of eminent domain for economic development takings has proven to be controversial. In property or another course some of you may have studied the case of Kelo v. City of

New London, 545 U.S. 469 (2004), holding that a Connecticut plan to condemn homes for the private development of an office park and marina did not violate the Public Use clause of the Fifth Amendment. After *Kelo* a number of states reformed their takings laws to curb uses of eminent domain by state entities that were perceived to be aggressive or unjustified, often by state legislation that required particular findings of "blight" or imposed other hurdles.

McLEMORE v. HYUNDAI MOTOR MANUFACTURING ALABAMA, LLC
Supreme Court of Alabama, 2008
7 So. 3d 318

STUART, Justice. [The Russells and the McLemore group] sued the Industrial Development Board of the City of Montgomery ("the IDB") and Hyundai Motor Manufacturing Alabama, LLC ("Hyundai"), alleging breach of contract. Specifically, they alleged that the IDB, on behalf of Hyundai, exercised options to purchase their real property but failed to pay them in accordance with the most-favored-nation clause in the option agreements the same price per acre that was paid to another landowner. The trial court entered summary judgments for the IDB and Hyundai. We affirm in part, reverse in part, and remand.

In September 2001, various officials of the State of Alabama, the City of Montgomery ("the City"), the Montgomery County Commission ("the County"), the Montgomery Area Chamber of Commerce, and the Montgomery Water Works Board began making preparations to secure options to purchase property in the Montgomery area to create an incentive package in the hope that they could persuade Hyundai to build an industrial plant in the Montgomery area for the purpose of manufacturing and assembling motor vehicles. This intent is evidenced by a signed letter to Hyundai from the City, the County, and the Industrial Development Board stating that they, "in partnership with the State," would commit to providing an industrial site to Hyundai at no cost. Although the funds to purchase the property were to be provided by the City and the County only, the option agreements on the property were acquired by the IDB, whose primary role in industrial projects is to "serve as the entity through which monies flow for the purchase of land for the ultimate use in industry."[1] B.M. Ahn, the Hyundai representative in charge of Hyundai's project to open a plant in the United States, testified during his deposition that one of the basic elements of an incentive package is "free land" offered to an automobile company as part of the incentive for the company to locate in a certain

---

1. The IDB explained in its brief to this Court that it is involved in the process "to comply with laws for tax breaks and incentives to the industry."

area. Ahn stated that Hyundai had no role in acquiring the options on the land.

The Russells owned approximately 328 acres of land in Montgomery County. In the fall of 2001, Reuben Thornton, the chairman of the IDB, entered into an option agreement on behalf of the IDB to purchase the Russells' property for an industrial project.[2] The agreement provided an option period of 120 days and stated:

> 3. If Purchaser elects to exercise this Option the purchase price for the Property shall be determined as follows:
>
> Seller and Purchaser shall each, at its own cost and expense, secure a current appraisal of the Property. The purchase price shall be the average of the two appraisals provided, however, in no event shall the purchase price be less than $4,500 per acre and further provided that the purchase price shall in no event be less than the price per acre paid to any other landowner included in the project planned for the Property. The acreage shall be determined by a good and accurate survey provided by Purchaser.[3] . . .

In February 2002, Thornton, on behalf of the IDB, entered into an option agreement with the McLemore group, who owned approximately 54 acres of land near the Russell property. The terms in the option agreement with the McLemore group are identical to the terms in the original option agreement between the Russells and the IDB.

The IDB also acquired four additional option agreements with land-owners near the property belonging to the Russells and the McLemore group. During the acquisition process, the IDB approached Joy Shelton about an option to purchase her property; however, she refused to enter into an option agreement. The IDB decided that the Shelton property was not necessary for the incentive package. By mid-March 2002, the IDB determined that it was not going to designate any additional funds, other than the funds already committed, to this particular project. The State and the IDB sent the incentive package, including the proposed project site, to Hyundai for consideration.

On March 28, 2002, Ahn contacted Todd Strange, then the director of the Alabama Development Office. He stated that Hyundai had not decided whether to locate the plant in Montgomery or in Kentucky but that additional property would need to be acquired for the rail access Hyundai required if Montgomery was to be selected as the site for the Hyundai plant. Ahn informed Strange that he would need an answer by noon of the next day as to whether the property could be acquired. Strange met with various State, City, and County officials to discuss Hyundai's request.

2. At Hyundai's request, the IDB did not reveal the identity of the potential industrial project.

3. The provision "the purchase price shall in no event be less than the price per acre paid to any other landowner included in the project planned for the Property" is known as a most-favored-nation clause or a price-escalation clause.

Recognizing that the City and the County would not provide additional funds to acquire more property and that the other option agreements contained most-favored-nation clauses, they decided to ask CSX Transportation, Inc., the rail company, to acquire the option to purchase the Shelton property. On March 29, 2002, Strange sent David Hemphill, an assistant vice president for CSX, the following letter via facsimile:

> Last evening, Thursday, March 28, 2002, at 6:05 p.m. Central Standard Time, I received a call from Mr. B.M. Ahn, President Hyundai Motor Company, U.S. from Seoul, Korea. He told me they were in the final stages of the decision and needed to make modifications to their Montgomery site layout because the CSX Railroad yard estimate had come in extremely high. In their (Hyundai's) redesign, he wanted to do parallel tracks running north and south on the eastern side of the property boundary. His engineers told him he would not have enough room unless [additional property was] obtained in the southeast corner of the quadrant. This property had been discussed a couple of months ago but we had been told as recently as two weeks ago that it would not be necessary. So accordingly, we did not pursue any options. . . .
>
> As I indicated to you last night, our option agreements have a 'most favored nation' clause where we agreed to pay no more for any one parcel than any of the other parcels. Accordingly, I assembled a working group of the local Chamber of Commerce executives, engineering expertise, Dave Echols[5] and myself. We decided the most appropriate course to follow would be to ask CSX to obtain a parcel for rail access to keep it outside the project agreement. As you know CSX's agreement with Hyundai is separate and this property in their view is for rail access only. . . .
>
> Dave, as you can appreciate there are a lot of details to be worked out, but the spirit and concept is for CSX to obtain the needed parcel for rail access and whatever the purchase price, CSX would be made whole in a manner we mutually agreed upon.

Also on March 29, 2002, Hemphill sent the following e-mail to Dave Echols:

> Regarding the [Shelton property] that will need to be purchased, you asked if CSX would be willing to buy this property for the State and Montgomery at approximately $8,000.00 an acre. There is no contract or option on the property currently and you estimate it will cost us approximately $750,000.00 which you are willing to refund to us in some fashion during the track construction phase. Randy Evans,[6] in principle agreed to this and I ask that you fax us a letter outlining exactly what you have in mind. The purpose of doing it this way rather than what you did in getting control of the other 1600 acres is to avoid paying the other landowners $8,000.00 an acre which would have a negative impact of $10,000,000.00 on the site cost. The railroad does not get good land

5. Echols was the project manager at the Alabama Development Office for the Hyundai project.
6. Evans is another CSX official involved in the Hyundai project.

values in a situation like this and so I think there will be upward pressure on that $8,000 number. Moreover, the other landowners will get wind of this ploy and may create negative community publicity. . . . In your letter to us we would ask that you indicate exactly how you intend to pay us during the track work construction.

Mayor Bobby Bright, mayor of the City of Montgomery and an ex officio member of the IDB, was selected as the main representative to meet with Shelton to acquire an assignable option agreement designating the City as the purchaser of the Shelton property. Before Bright agreed to meet with Shelton, he told Strange and other State officials that the City and the County would not provide any additional money toward the project. They assured him that the City and the County would not be asked or expected to contribute any funds toward the purchase of the Shelton property and that the option would be assigned to either CSX or the State. Randy George, president of the Montgomery Area Chamber of Commerce and secretary of the IDB, and Elaine McNair, a member of the Chamber of Commerce, went with Bright to meet with Shelton. Bright obtained an assignable option, designating the City, not the IDB, as the purchaser of the property; the purchase price of the property was $12,000 per acre. . . .

On April 1, 2002, Hyundai announced that it was going to build the plant in Montgomery. On April 15, 2002, the various State and local governmental entities involved, including the IDB, entered into a project agreement with Hyundai detailing the location and development of the plant ("the project agreement"). The project agreement, in section 3.1 of Article 3, stated that "the Montgomery IDB presently holds purchase options necessary to acquire fee simple title to each parcel of real estate comprising the Project Site." The project agreement further provided in section 3.4 that the IDB was to exercise each option and in section 3.6(a) that the IDB was then to transfer title of the property to Hyundai. Section 3.20 of the project agreement, entitled "CSX Agreement," provided separately for the acquisition of the Shelton property, stating:

> The State and Local Governments shall use their best efforts to cause CSX Transportation to enter into an agreement with [Hyundai] in form satisfactory to [Hyundai], which will provide for rail service for [Hyundai] on terms and conditions as favorable to [Hyundai] as those offered to other automobile manufacturers. In addition, the State and City shall use their best efforts to cause CSX Transportation to provide the incentives set forth in the letter from CSX Transportation dated December 17, 2001. The State represents and warrants that [Hyundai] will acquire fee simple title to [the Shelton property] for use in connection with construction of a rail switch yard by or before September 30, 2002. If and to the extent [Hyundai] makes any payment for the cost of acquiring such acreage, the State shall reimburse [Hyundai] for such costs by increasing by an equivalent amount the monies made available from the State in Training Equipment Fund pursuant to Article 4 by no later than the last

quarter of the calendar year 2003. The City agrees that it will zone such additional acreage the same as the Project Site. The Local Governments agree to abate taxes that are applicable to such additional acreage in the same manner and to the same extent as . . . abatement of taxes of the Project Site.

The IDB assigned the options on the property owned by the Russells and the McLemore group to the City and the County. On May 14, 2002, the City and the County purchased the property for $4,500 per acre. The City and the County then deeded the property to the IDB, which then deeded the property to Hyundai.

The City never exercised its option on the Shelton property. . . . On May 31, 2002, the day the option agreement on the Shelton property was to expire, CSX entered into a real-estate sales contract for the purchase of the property at $12,000 per acre. When Hyundai learned that CSX, and not the State, was to pay for the rail installation and that Hyundai would be expected to enter into a long-term contract with CSX, Hyundai decided to install the rail using its own funds. As a result of Hyundai's decision not to involve CSX in rail installation, CSX assigned the real-estate contract to Hyundai. According to the assignment contract, CSX assigned the contract to Hyundai on May 28, 2002, three days before the real-estate contract between CSX and Shelton was executed. On July 12, 2002, funds from the State of Alabama Incentives Finance Authority were transferred to Hyundai to pay for the Shelton property, and Hyundai purchased the property.

After all the land was acquired and deeded to Hyundai, Hyundai leased all the property, including the Shelton property, to the IDB so that the Alabama Department of Transportation ("ALDOT") could perform site preparation on the property.[8] Additionally, the IDB entered into a tax-abatement agreement with Hyundai so that Hyundai's property could receive the previously agreed upon abatement from ad valorem taxation and other tax incentives. The Shelton property was included in the tax-abatement agreement.

Subsequently, the Russells and the McLemore group each filed a breach-of-contract action against the IDB and Hyundai, alleging that the IDB and Hyundai had breached the most-favored-nation clause in the option agreements by not paying them $12,000 per acre for their property. According to the Russells and the McLemore group, the Shelton property was "included in the project agreement" and, consequently, they should have been paid, as Shelton was paid, $12,000 per acre for their property. The trial court . . . entered summary judgments for the IDB and Hyundai. The Russells and the McLemore group appealed. . . .

---

8. In order for ALDOT to perform site preparation, the property had to be owned by a governmental entity. Therefore, Hyundai leased the property to the IDB so that a governmental entity would have a possessory interest in the property, which would allow ALDOT to perform the site preparation.

ISSUES

. . . .

The Russells and the McLemore group contend that the trial court erred in entering a summary judgment for Hyundai because, they say, the IDB, the City, the County, and the State were acting as agents of Hyundai or were involved in a joint venture with Hyundai to acquire the land for the project site; therefore, they maintain, Hyundai is also liable for the alleged breach of the contract. . . .

The Russells and the McLemore group did not present substantial evidence indicating that the IDB, the City, the County, or the State were acting as Hyundai's express, implied, or apparent agent with regard to the acquisition of their property. The option agreements do not state that the IDB or Thornton, the chairman of the IDB, was acting as an agent of Hyundai; therefore, there is no evidence of express agency. Additionally, we find no evidence of implied agency. Nothing before us creates an inference that Hyundai participated in identifying the location of the property proposed for the project site, that it was involved in drafting the option agreements, that it met with the property owners, or that it was a party to the option agreements. Therefore, the Russells and the McLemore group did not present substantial evidence of express or implied agency. Likewise, the Russells and the McLemore group did not present substantial evidence of apparent agency. The evidence indicates that Hyundai was never involved in selecting the properties for acquisition, that it did not participate in any of the negotiations for the option agreements, and that no Hyundai representative was ever present or communicated with any property owner. Indeed, Thornton testified that the IDB's purpose in obtaining the option agreements was to "acquire land on behalf of the City and County" in order to "serve the City of Montgomery and promote industry." Thus, the evidence indicates that the IDB, the City, the County, and the State were not acting to acquire the properties as an agent or under the direction of Hyundai, but at their own direction and on their own initiative to entice Hyundai to build an automobile plant in Montgomery County.

The Russells and the McLemore group urge that evidence of an agency relationship is found in the project agreement. They direct this Court to a provision in the project agreement that required the IDB to exercise the option agreements, to unify the title of the property constituting the project site for transfer of the title of the property to Hyundai, to transfer title of the property to Hyundai, and to perform the site preparation for the property to Hyundai's specifications. Additionally, they point out that the option agreements were not exercised until after the project agreement was signed.

The project agreement, however, does not evidence an agency relationship. The option agreements were acquired before the IDB, the City, the County, and the State had a relationship with Hyundai. The testimony indicates that they were executed as part of the creation of an incentive package to encourage Hyundai to select the Montgomery area as the site for its automobile plant, and the project agreement is evidence of Hyundai's acceptance of the package. As Ahn testified, the reason for the project agreement and its requirements was to allow Hyundai to obtain control over the property. Moreover, nothing in the project agreement indicates that Hyundai selected the location for the project or that it was bound by the option agreements or the sales agreements for the property. Thus, the project agreement does not provide substantial evidence of the existence of an agency relationship. . . .

The Russells and the McLemore group contend, in the alternative, that Hyundai is liable for breach of contract because, they say, Hyundai was engaged in a joint venture with the IDB, the City, the County, and the State to acquire their property. According to the Russells and the McLemore group, they presented substantial evidence of the existence of a joint venture through the language in the project agreement indicating a sharing of efforts, property, skill, money, and knowledge to purchase and develop property for a manufacturing plant for a community of interest. . . .

> The elements of a joint venture have been held to be: a contribution by the parties of money, property, effort, knowledge, skill, or other assets to a common undertaking; a joint property interest in the subject matter of the venture and a right to mutual control or management of the enterprise; expectation of profits; a right to participate in the profits; and usually, a limitation of the objective to a single undertaking or ad hoc enterprise. While every element is not necessarily present in every case, it is generally agreed that in order to constitute a joint venture, there must be a community of interest and a right to joint control. Flowers v. Pope, 937 So. 2d 61, 66 (Ala. 2006).

The record does not contain substantial evidence to create a jury question with regard to the existence of a joint venture involving Hyundai. Nothing in the evidence supports a finding of a community of interest. Hyundai never had a joint ownership interest with any of the alleged joint venturers in the property of the Russells or the McLemore group upon the closings on the property. Additionally, Hyundai did not provide financing for the purchase of the property, and it had no risk or expenses with regard to the purchase. Thus, nothing supports a finding of a community of interest involving Hyundai with regard to the acquisition of the property to constitute the project site. *Cf. id.* at 68 (holding that there was no community of interest because the alleged joint venturers did not have an equal proprietary interest and only one of the alleged joint venturers bore the risks and paid the expenses).

Moreover, the record indicates that Hyundai did not have a right of control with regard to how the property was obtained. Nothing indicates that Hyundai controlled the actions of the IDB or other governmental entities with regard to the selection of the property for the project site, the negotiation of the option agreements on the property, or the drafting of the option agreements. Thus, substantial evidence of right of control by Hyundai is not presented in the record.

Although the evidence does tend to establish that a joint venture may have existed between the IDB, the City, the County, and the State for the purpose of enticing Hyundai to locate an automobile-manufacturing plant in Montgomery County, substantial evidence does not exist to create a jury question as to whether Hyundai was a participant in the joint venture. The evidence indicates that Hyundai merely evaluated Montgomery's incentive package, compared it to the incentive packages offered by other communities, and determined that Montgomery provided the best place to build its plant. . . .

Because substantial evidence of neither an agency relationship nor a joint venture is present in the record, the summary judgment for Hyundai is affirmed.

[The court held that it was a jury question as to whether an amendment to the Russells' option agreement waived the "most favored nation" clause.]

The Russells and the McLemore group contend that the trial court erred in entering a summary judgment for the IDB because, they say, there is a genuine issue of material fact as to the meaning and application of the most-favored-nation clause in the option agreements. The IDB argues that, pursuant to the doctrine of merger, the Russells' and the McLemore group's execution and the delivery of the deeds to their properties to the City and the County merged the option agreements into the deeds and discharged any additional debt owed for the properties; therefore, the IDB contends, their breach-of-contract claims are barred.

When an option is exercised, the agreement becomes a contract between the parties. . . .

> Under the doctrine of "merger," ordinarily, in the absence of fraud or mistake, when a contract to sell and convey real estate has been consummated by the execution and delivery of a deed, as in this case, the preliminary contract becomes functus officio, and the deed becomes a sole memorial of the agreement, and upon it the rights of the parties rest; but the doctrine may be inapplicable to cases in which stipulations of the preliminary contract, instead of becoming merged in the deed, are incorporated therein and thus survive to confer independent causes of action, and in such instances the intention of the parties is of paramount importance.

Eubanks v. Pine Plaza Joint Venture, 562 So. 2d 220, 221-22 (Ala. 1990).

. . . However, a deed does not have to set forth the amount of consideration. §35-4-34, Ala. Code 1975.

. . . .

If, however, there is no consideration expressed, . . . [a]nd . . . , if a deed mentions a consideration, and adds the words for other considerations, . . . proof may be received to show what those other considerations are.

In Gilliland v. Hawkins, 112 So. 454, 457 (Ala. 1927), this Court stated that

> the consideration clause of a deed is open to the influence of parol proof, except for two purposes: First it is not permissible for a party to the deed to prove a different consideration, if such change vary the legal effect of the instrument; and, second, the grantor in a deed, who acknowledges the receipt of payment of the consideration, will not be allowed, by disproving the fact, to establish a resulting trust in himself. Subject to the two restrictions stated, it has always been held that the consideration in a deed may always be inquired into, and any other or any additional consideration may be shown, if not inconsistent with that expressed in the deed.

Thus, the mere execution and delivery of a deed does not merge the consideration in the contract of sale into the deed. . . .

Here, the deeds in question provide that the consideration is "$10.00 and other valuable consideration." This recitation of consideration permits inquiry into like consideration for the sale of the properties, and the Russells' and the McLemore group's breach-of-contract claims are not barred by the doctrine of merger. . . .

Next, we must determine whether the language in the option agreements is ambiguous. According to the Russells and the McLemore group, the language in the most-favored-nation clause is ambiguous and a genuine issue of material fact exists for the jury as to whether the Shelton property was part of "the project planned for this Property" and, if the Shelton property is part of the project, whether, like Shelton, the Russells and the McLemore group should have been paid $12,000 per acre. . . .

The IDB argues that it cannot be held to have breached the option agreements because, it says, Hyundai decided to purchase the Shelton property with funds provided by the State at a price greater than $4,500 per acre. The IDB reminds this Court that the evidence establishes that it refused to have any involvement with the purchase of the Shelton property. It further argues that the evidence establishes that the IDB did not pay any landowner with which it executed an option agreement more than $4,500 per acre. It reasons that the only reasonable interpretation of the option agreements is that the most-favored-nation clause obligated the IDB to pay all landowners with which it executed an option agreement the same amount. It argues that the fact that another entity paid Shelton a greater amount does not establish that the IDB breached the option agreements with the landowners to whom it paid $4,500 per acre.

Additionally, the IDB argues that the option agreements are unambiguous with regard to which parcels of land were "included in the project planned for this Property." They disagree with the Russells and the

McLemore group that the Shelton property is part of the project and maintain that the project agreement defines the "project planned for this Property" as only the property as to which the IDB had obtained options to purchase.

We agree with the Russells and the McLemore group that the language in the option agreements is ambiguous, that it cannot be resolved by rules of contract construction, and that they presented substantial evidence creating a genuine issue of material fact for the jury as to the meaning and application of the most-favored-nation clause in the option agreements. . . . Because reasonable persons can differ on the meaning of the clause, *i.e.*, whether the language "price per acre paid to any other landowner included in the project" obligated the IDB to pay the Russells and the McLemore group $12,000 per acre and whether the Shelton property was included as part of the project site, the evidence presents questions for the jury to resolve, and the summary judgment for the IDB is reversed. . . .

Problem 20E

(a) In *McLemore*, what was the purpose behind the theories of agency and joint venture raised by the Russells and the McLemore group?

(b) In *McLemore*, much is made of the price term in the option agreements and the consideration clause in the deeds used at the closing of the option agreements, with the legal analysis centered on the doctrine of merger, ambiguity (or the lack thereof), and parol evidence. The standard recitation of consideration ("$10 and other valuable consideration") is boilerplate, designed to hide the true consideration but to signal that the grantee has in fact paid valuable consideration, but does the phrase create its own potential problems? With the benefit of hindsight, if you were representing the Russells and the McLemore group, would you have drafted the most-favored-nation clause or the consideration clause differently? What if you were representing IDB or the other entities involved in the property acquisition?

(c) In a transaction like the one in *McLemore*, what assurances might Hyundai want with respect to zoning, utilities, and other services so that it can operate its manufacturing and assembly facility? Identify some of the particular assurances that you might require as an attorney for Hyundai in such a transaction, and think about how you would use contract provisions, opinion letters, and other tools to obtain the assurances desired for your client.

(d) Assume in *McLemore* that Alabama law authorized the IDB or one of the local governments to condemn the properties owned by the Russells, the McLemore group, Shelton, and others within the project boundaries. Would that have changed the land assembly strategy? If so, how?

(e) Is the use of a development entity to fund private market enterprises good public policy? Consider that the subsidy to Hyundai in 2002 was $252 million to create 2,000 jobs. In 1993 Alabama put together a $258 million package of incentives to attract a Mercedes facility, and in 1999 it provided $158 million in benefits to Honda. Alabama is not alone in facilitating this type of activity. Many other states have attracted or retained businesses with similar deals. These types of projects are sometimes considered a positive form of public-private partnership for development. Are these types of projects a wise use of public funds? How do they impact future investment? How do they influence the dynamic of competition among states, as well as among private entities? Is this a winning strategy at the local, state, national, or global level?

Table of Cases

Index

Second mortgages. *See* Junior mortgages

Sections, Government Survey System, 234

Security interests
    commercial lending, 603–605
    executory contracts, 92–93
    interaction with real estate law, 603–605
    mortgages. *See* Mortgages
    perfection of, 337
    possession and use of mortgaged property, 416
    under Uniform Commercial Code Article 9, 92–93, 108, 337, 593

Seisin, covenant of, 223, 413

Selling broker, 29

Servitudes by implication, 292

Settlement. *See* Closing

Shared appreciation mortgages (SAMs), 447

Shelter rule, bona fide purchaser, 285–298

Short sales, 465, 542–543

Signature, electronic, 84–85

Single-family homes, 370–382
    Covenants, Conditions and Restrictions (CCRs), 371–382
    in planned communities. *See* Planned Unit Development (PUD)
    private subdivision arrangements, 370–371

Single Family Mortgage Foreclosure Act of 1994, 529

Slander of title, 179, 198–203

Social policy in real estate, 353

Sovereign immunity, 292

Special (or limited) warranty deeds, 220

Specific performance, 187, 188–193

Stand-by take-outs, 619–620

Statement of record, developer's, 135–136

Statute of Frauds
    compliance of real estate contracts with, 84–92
    disguised mortgages, 563
    electronic signatures, 84–85
    land descriptions, 233, 245, 247–249
    land installment contracts, 576
    letters of intent, 65
    memorandum of contract, 84, 247
    options, 65
    purchase agreement, 84

Statutory equity of redemption. *See* Equity of redemption

Stigma-related defects of property, 136–150

Strategic default, 543–544

Stretch mortgages, 448

Strict foreclosure, 414, 523–524

Subdivisions. *See* Planned Unit Development (PUD)

Subordination, 593–597
    agreements, 593
    ground leases, 611
    inter-creditor agreement, 593
    by oder of recording documents, 593

Subprime loans, 462–464

Subrogation, equitable, 551–555

Substitutes for mortgages. *See* Mortgage substitutes

Sunk costs, 11

Superfund, 416

Suretyship, law of, 499

Surplus, 52–523

Surveys and surveyors
    adjoining properties, relationship of property to, 240
    "as-built" survey, 241–242
    boundary survey, 241
        priority of conflicting title elements, 242
    as conditions, 107
    defined, 238
    discrepancies between possession and record deed, 240
    evidence used, 238–239
    existence of property, establishing, 239
    generally, 238–239
    physical improvements, location of, 240–241
    reasons for, 239–241
    sample evaluation of property line facts, 243–245, 246
    title survey, 241
    topographic survey, 241
    types of surveys, 241–242
    unrecorded easements and other facts not of record, 241
    water boundaries, 241

Take-out arrangements, 618–629
    defined, 619
    lock-in take-out, 619
    open-ended take-out, 620
    stand-by take-out, 619–620

Taxes
    developer entities and, 602
    income taxes
        mortgage interest deduction, 436–437
        wrap-around mortgages, 597
    property taxes, loan escrow, held in, 173

Telephone calls, as electronic communications, 85

Temporal risk, 13–15

Third parties
    abstractors' liability to, 302–303
    attorneys' duties to, 129–132
    deeds of lieu of foreclosure, effect on, 55
    drafting executory contracts, considered when, 106–107
    installment land contracts, 576–577
    warranties of condition of property, 150–155

Three-party agreements, 621–622
    buy-sell agreement, 621–622
    privity, 621
    specific performance, 621–622